Fish Phenology:
anabolic adaptiveness in teleosts

SYMPOSIA OF THE ZOOLOGICAL SOCIETY OF LONDON
NUMBER 44

Fish Phenology:
anabolic adaptiveness in teleosts

*(The Proceedings of a Symposium held at
The Zoological Society of London
on 6 and 7 April 1978)*

Edited by

P. J. MILLER

*Department of Zoology, The University,
Bristol, Avon, England*

Published for

THE ZOOLOGICAL SOCIETY OF LONDON

BY

ACADEMIC PRESS

1979

ACADEMIC PRESS INC. (LONDON) LTD
24/28 Oval Road, London NW1 7DX

United States Edition published by
ACADEMIC PRESS INC.
111 Fifth Avenue, New York, New York 1003

British Library Cataloguing in Publication Data

Fish phenology.—(Zoological Society of London.
Symposia; no. 44).
1. Teleostei—Ecology—Congresses
2. Fishes—Ecology—Congresses
3. Phenology—Congresses
I. Miller, Peter James   II. Series
597'.5'04543   QL614   79-40966

ISBN 0-12-613344-1

Printed in Great Britain by
J. W. ARROWSMITH LTD, BRISTOL BS3 2NT

Contributors

BAKER, B., *School of Biological Sciences, Bath University, Claverton Down, Bath, England* (p. 89)

ELLIOTT, J. M., *Freshwater Biological Association, Far Sawrey, Ambleside, Cumbria LA22 0LP, England* (p. 29)

GARROD, D. J., *MAFF Fisheries Laboratory, Lowestoft, Suffolk NR33 0HT, England* (p. 361)

GORDON, J. D. M., *Scottish Marine Biological Association, Dunstaffnage Marine Research Laboratory, P.O. Box 3, Oban, Argyll PA34 4AD, Scotland* (p. 327)

KNIGHTS, B. J., *MAFF Fisheries Laboratory, Lowestoft, Suffolk NR33 0HT, England* (p. 361)

LOWE-MCCONNELL, R. H., *Streatwick, Streat, nr. Hassocks, Sussex BN6 8RT, England* (p. 219)

MANN, R. H. K., *Freshwater Biological Association, River Laboratory, East Stoke, Wareham, Dorset BH20 6BB, England* (p. 161)

MILLER, P. J., *Department of Zoology, The University, Bristol BS8 1UG, Avon, England* (pp. 1, 263)

MILLS, C. A., *Freshwater Biological Association, River Laboratory, East Stoke, Wareham, Dorset BH20 6BB, England* (p. 161)

PAYNE, A. I., *Department of Biological Studies, Lanchester Polytechnic, Priory Street, Coventry CV1 5FB, England* (p. 383)

PURDOM, C. E., *MAFF Fisheries Laboratory, Lowestoft, Suffolk NR33 0HT, England* (p. 207)

SCHAFFER, W. M., *Department of Ecology and Evolutionary Biology, University of Arizona, Tucson, Arizona 85721, USA* (p. 307)

SCOTT, D. B. C., *Department of Zoology, The University, St. Andrews, Fife, Scotland* (p. 105)

SIMPSON, B. R. C., *Department of Zoology, The University, Bristol BS8 1UG, Avon, England* (p. 243)

URSIN, E., *The Danish Institute for Fishery and Marine Research, Charlottenlund Slot, DK-2920 Charlottenlund, Denmark* (p. 63)

WIGHAM, T., *University of Wales Institute of Science and Technology, Cardiff, Wales* (p. 89)

WOODHEAD, A. D., *Department of Biology, Brookhaven National Laboratory, Upton, Long Island, NY 11973, USA* (p. 179)

WOOTTON, R. J., *Department of Zoology, University College, Aberystwyth, Wales* (p. 133)

Organizer and Chairmen

ORGANIZER

P. J. MILLER, on behalf of The Zoological Society of London.

CHAIRMEN OF SESSIONS

BAGENAL, T. B., *Freshwater Biological Association, Far Sawrey, Ambleside, Cumbria LA22 0LP, England*

BARRINGTON, E. J. W., FRS, *2 St Margaret's Drive, Alderton, Tewkesbury, Glos. GL20 8NY, England*

GREENWOOD, P. H., *Department of Zoology, British Museum (Natural History), Cromwell Road, London SW7 5BD, England*

MARSHALL, N. B., FRS, *6 Park Lane, Saffron Walden, Essex, England*

Acknowledgements

The personal view of fish phenology introducing this Symposium stems from an early enthusiasm for tropical aquaria and native gobies, subsequent concern with fish growth and reproduction and, latterly, an increasing desire to define ultimately useful goals for academic pursuits. To all my colleagues in the present volume, I am most grateful for their skilful elaboration of the very diverse themes in the development of this wide-ranging subject. The opportunity for such collaboration was provided by the Zoological Society of London; here, my thanks are due to Dr H. G. Vevers for his encouragement of the project, and to Miss Unity McDonnell for her work on the organization of the meeting and resulting editorial tasks. For promoting interest in this important aspect of modern zoology, with its clear potential for benefit to mankind, I am indebted to all who participated in the actual event: contributors, chairmen and audience. Finally, I must thank Mrs J. Ablett for her careful preparation of indexes for this volume.

Contents

A Concept of Fish Phenology

P. J. MILLER

Energetics of Freshwater Teleosts

J. M. ELLIOTT

Principles of Growth in Fishes

E. URSIN

Endocrine Aspects of Metabolic Coordination in Teleosts

B. I. BAKER and T. WIGHAM

Environmental Timing and the Control of Reproduction in Teleost Fish

D. B. C. SCOTT

Energy Costs of Egg Production and Environmental Determinants of Fecundity in Teleost Fishes

R. J. WOOTTON

Demographic Aspects of Fish Fecundity

R. H. K. MANN and C. A. MILLS

Senescence in Fishes

A. D. WOODHEAD

Genetics of Growth and Reproduction in Teleosts

C. E. PURDOM

Ecological Aspects of Seasonality in Fishes of Tropical Waters

R. H. LOWE-McCONNELL

The Phenology of Annual Killifishes

B. R. C. SIMPSON

Adaptiveness and Implications of Small Size in Teleosts

P. J. MILLER

The Theory of Life-History Evolution and its Application to Atlantic Salmon

W. M. SCHAFFER

Life-style and Phenology in Deep-sea Anacanthine Teleosts

J. D. M. GORDON

Fish Stocks: Their Life-history Characteristics and Response to Exploitation

D. J. GARROD and B. J. KNIGHTS

Physiological and Ecological Factors in the Development of Fish Culture

A. I. PAYNE

Symp. zool. Soc. Lond. (1979) No. 44, 1–28

A Concept of Fish Phenology

P. J. MILLER

University of Bristol, Bristol, Avon, England

SYNOPSIS

Traditional usage and definition of the term "phenology" relate to the observation of seasonality in nature. A new, expanded idea of the subject, and etymology of the word itself, have prompted a revised application to the study of cyclical events in constructive metabolism (anabolism), here explored with reference to teleost fishes. Examples of circannual and circadian rhythms in teleost anabolism are noted, and the suggestion made that phenology will embrace all aspects of this metabolic division, as the essentially oscillatory progress of anabolism comes to be revealed. The nature and control of energy and material partitioning in the teleost "open system" are briefly discussed. A selective survey of such anabolic fields as maintenance, reproduction, storage and growth pays special attention to the nature of expenditure on reproductive effort, and to the seasonality of growth in certain gobioid fishes. The cyclical history of individual life, with the topic of senescence, leads into the idea of population phenology, concerning the changes with time in the overall anabolic achievement of a phyletic line. The great economic importance of these aspects of fish phenology is summarized in relation to fisheries and pisciculture. Finally, the unifying influence of fish phenology is emphasized.

Seasonal cycles in the natural world, and their correlation with solar and lunar periods, have been a subject of interest to mankind since prehistoric times (Hawkes, 1963; Smith, 1970). Calendars of annual events, such as the spawning of salmon, the migration of elvers or the visits of herring, have accumulated in the folk knowledge of cultures world-wide. With early understanding that human welfare depends on such cycles, measures to ensure their regular periodicity and amplitude have long involved attention to the supernatural (Fraser, 1922).

The scientific study of periodic phenomena in plants and animals was termed "Phänologie" by Fritsch (1858), following an idea of the Belgian botanist Morren (Hopp, 1974), and the name has since been anglicized to "phenology" (Murray, 1888). Having coined the original in a year-book of climatic and geodetic observations, Fritsch regarded phenology as a science linking meteorology, botany and zoology, and forming an aspect of physical geography in which a time dimension complemented spatial distribution. The essential data of phenology have thus come to be traditionally gathered and reviewed in conjunction with an annual record of climatic change (Preston, 1883; Ihne & Hoffmann, 1884), and phenology is often practised as a "field technique of agricultural meteorology" (Lieth, 1974; Wielgolaski, 1974), ostensibly perhaps with little usage in ichthyology or zoology as a whole. Williams (1949) employing phenology as "the scientific study of the seasons" noted that the current *Encyclopaedia Britannica* paid more attention to phrenology than to phenology, which was omitted then and which is still unspecified in the present (fifteenth) edition. Nevertheless, innumerable observations relevant to phenology do exist for fishes, even though the term has appeared only very rarely in the section on fish in the *Zoological Record*.

Modern lexicographers have defined phenology as "study of the times of recurring natural phenomena, especially in relation to climatic conditions" (Fowler & Fowler, 1964) and "the study of organisms in relation to climate" (Macdonald, 1972). However, a new importance for phenology has recently emerged with the need for predictive ecology to consider seasonality and its rhythmical consequences in ecosystem dynamics (Fretwell, 1972; Taylor, 1974). Renewed interest has in turn led to a rather more expansive and fertile definition. Quoted by Lieth (1974), the US/IBP Phenology Committee regarded phenology as "the study of the timing of recurring biological events, the causes of their timing with regard to biotic and abiotic forces, and the interrelation among phases of the same or different species". Further qualification noted that "the unit of study may vary from a single species (or variety, clone, etc.) to a complete ecosystem. The area involved may be small (for intensive studies on all phenophases of entire ecosystems) or very large (for interregional comparison of significant phenophases). The unit of time is usually the solar year with which the events to be studied are in phase. The events themselves may cover variable time spans, often much shorter than the solar year." After reading this definition, no one could doubt the importance of phenology as a direction for research, since its limits would seem to include virtually all ecology itself and, if "causes of timing" are explored, a considerable sector of physiology. It leads to the vast topics of periodicity in living systems and the influence of environment on life. The object of this paper is to form a more practicable idea of phenology by considering traditional use of the word, its etymology and the underlying similarities of the biological phenomena encompassed by the science. In this volume, different aspects are discussed with reference to teleost fishes, but the basic concept applies to all living organisms.

"Phenology" is obtained from the Greek root φαίν-(phain-), meaning, essentially, "showing", "appearing" or "becoming manifest" (Liddell & Scott, 1940).[a] The same root is employed in "phenotype", a category of organism defined by appearance, and "phenomenon", as something perceived. "Phenomenology" is a philosophical movement concerned with the description of phenomena as consciously experienced, without theories about their causal explanation. It is to be hoped that phenology, as well as recording natural phenomena, will aspire to understanding at least their immediate causes. Bearing in mind, therefore, that there are semantic and etymological grounds for associating phenology with both

---

[a] I am most grateful to Mr T. Wiedemann for his advice on this interpretation.

biological seasonality, or temporal fluctuation in life phenomena, and organismic manifestation, or increasing negentropy in a biological system, the science of phenology can be redefined as "the study of cyclical events in constructive metabolism (anabolism)". This definition agrees with much of the traditional coverage, except perhaps for such obviously catabolic phenomena as migration. Fishes, being largely mute, do not, fortunately, present the vocal isophenes so popularly mapped for song-birds. In present use, attention must be restricted to the more quantitative aspects of constructive metabolism, rather than to more qualitative topics of differentiation.

Constructive metabolism or anabolism represents a somewhat arbitrary division of the overall, highly integrated course of fish metabolism. In this paper, usage of these terms follows Hochachka (1969), who defined metabolism as "the totality of chemical processes that [a cell or organism] is capable of performing", anabolism as "synthetic processes that produce complex organic cellular components" and catabolism, the converse metabolic pathway, as involving "essentially degradative processes in which large organic molecules are broken down to simple cellular constituents with release of chemical free energy". According to individual preference, the term metabolism has been restricted to catabolic functions by several authors, while usage of anabolism may exclude complex molecules lost to the body as secretions or gonadal products. Here, all the latter are considered within anabolism, which thus includes, as well as the material of structure and storage, those products of biosyntheses within the fish, which are routinely discharged and later degraded outside the body, either for functional maintenance of the individual or genetic maintenance of the species.

The operation of metabolism supports the fish as an "open system" of energy transduction (von Bertalanffy, 1960), through which a flow of energy and materials is sustained by the intake of dietary macromolecules. Part of this input, brought by assimilative processes, of varying efficiency, into physiological use within the body, and augmented by products of internal breakdown, forms a substrate for the reactions of intermediary metabolism, which provide a pool of material and energized molecules for all final processes of metabolism (Hochachka, 1969). A portion of this is expended as catabolism, with the dissipation of energy for kinetic purposes of a chemical or mechanical nature within the organism, and in behavioural—again mechanical—response to external situations, to achieve survival, feeding and reproduction. The alternative employment for intermediary metabolites is towards biosynthesis or anabolism, whereby energy and material is held within the system, transiently or over longer periods, for maintaining structure and secretion, increasing body size and complexity, storing against future restrictions of input, maturing gametes and provisioning young.

These basic metabolic functions are common to all metazoans. In teleost fishes, metabolism operates a body of complex vertebrate structure, which, although still living in the primitive aquatic habitat of the chordates, represents the most advanced level in fish-like organization. Over the last one hundred million years, "teleosts have become fishmasters of the hydrosphere" (Marshall, 1965), with a present diversity of at least 18–20 000 species (Cohen, 1970). Estimates of numbers of individuals, and space available for these, have been attempted by Horn (1972). The present dominance of teleosts may be attributed to various modifications which have promoted metabolic efficiency and flexibility. Thus, structural changes in jaw skeleton and musculature have improved net return in feeding energetics, and greatly extended trophic opportunities to a wide range of animal and plant food (Alexander, 1967). Thanks to the reduced exoskeleton, hydrodynamic improvements in body proportions and appendages, and the transformation of a lung-like air-bladder into a hydrostatic organ, aquatic locomotion is achieved with more sparing use of energy. The teleost system also permits function and fitness over a very wide range in adult body size, from a few milligrams of *Schindleria* to a record 2235 kg of *Mola*, so that adaptation in growth patterns, especially towards smaller dimensions, has permitted the colonization of many different ecotopes (Miller, this volume p. 263). Temporary storage has become possible in virtually every organ of the body, even the skeleton (Phleger, Patton, Grimes & Lee, 1976). In development, the ability to produce very small, free-living postlarvae has permitted exploitation of more than one ecosystem during life history, with individual fecundities of considerable magnitude. There is, however, a necessary weakness in teleost physiology, resulting from metabolic heat loss in the countercurrent system of gill ventilation. Despite a high degree of homeostasis relative to many environmental variables, teleosts are still mostly obligate poikilotherms, with limited acclimatory possibilities often compensated by behavioural thermoregulation (Brett, 1971). Other teleost features have recently become disadvantageous for many species. With ample segmented musculature neatly arranged along the vertebral column, and impressive natural abundance of relatively small, lipid-stocked individuals, teleosts are tempting and vulnerable food organisms for increasingly skilful predation by mankind, being easily collected, and then conveniently filleted or reduced.

Having noted anabolic processes in the context of overall metabolism, and some basic features of the teleost open system, it becomes necessary to consider cyclicity in anabolism. According to Grebe (1962), everything in nature has rhythm and unending motion, and there is certainly increasing evidence that effective functioning of teleost metabolism depends on cyclical processes (Schwassmann, 1971; Thorpe, 1978). On a yearly scale, the major goals of anabolism—growth, deposition and reproduction— are obviously pursued by many species in a seasonal fashion correlated with hydrographic and biotic changes in a fluctuating environment. Such overt seasonality in anabolism must form a major area of fish phenology, and many examples are summarized by Shulman (1974). Apart from circannual cycles revealed by measurements of growth, gonad condition and depot materials, a corresponding seasonality has also been detected in the underlying mechanisms controlling synthesis or mobilization. These include seasonal changes in production of pituitary somatotrophic and gonadotrophic hormones (Swift & Pickford, 1965), thyrotrophic hormone (Singh, 1967), gonadal steroids (Billard & Breton, 1978), corticosteroids (Woodhead, 1975; Wingfield & Grimm, 1977) and thyroid activity (Swift, 1960). Evidence for annual fluctuation in localized syntheses of the teleost skin is shown by seasonal changes in glycine uptake of scale-pocket cells (Ottaway & Simkiss, 1977) and in alkaline phosphatase activity (Fouda & Miller, 1979).

However, modern studies have indicated a much finer temporal pattern of anabolic cyclicity, derived ultimately from the earth's rotation and juxtaposition rather than from its revolution. This is biorhythmicity of a circadian or circatidal nature. Such rhythms have been amply demonstrated in various behavioural and other catabolic functions studied in teleosts, and are typically entrained by photoperiod or tidal oscillation (Olla & Studholme, 1978; Gibson, 1978). These catabolic changes may be expected to impose effects of comparable periodicity on daily scope for anabolism within the same integrated metabolic system, perhaps by affecting food intake (Thorpe, 1977), growth efficiency (Brett, 1971; Craig, 1977a) or degree of muscular activity (Olla & Studholme, 1978). There is now, in fact, good evidence for circadian rhythms in various aspects of teleost anabolism (Baker & Wigham, this volume p. 89). For example, within the endocrine systems influencing growth, storage and maturation, daily cycles have been found in plasma levels of growth hormone and prolactin (Leatherland, McKeown & John, 1974; McKeown & Peter, 1976), and in pituitary gonadotrophin content (O'Connor, 1972; De Vlaming & Vodicnik, 1977). The timing of gonad maturation in a number of teleosts has also been shown to depend on a circadian rhythm in sensitivity to the inductive effects of light (Baggerman, 1972; Chan, 1976; Sundararaj & Vasal, 1976). Among anabolic end-products in teleosts, a daily fluctuation in hepatic lipogenesis is noted by Meier & Burns (1976), while, for somatic growth, a rhythm of similar period in glycine incorporation by scale-pocket cells is described by Ottaway & Simkiss (1977). Long-term running of a circadian growth cycle is suggested by the preservation of daily growth layers in teleost otoliths (Pannella, 1971). Experiments with the cichlid, *Tilapia mossambica* (Peters), suggest that formation of these daily marks requires entrainment of an internal clock by a 25-h light/dark regime (Taubert & Coble, 1977). A monthly and bimonthly pattern is also apparent in the growth history of otoliths studied (Pannella, 1974). Annual changes in otolith structure are often used for age-determination of individual fish when manifest in relation to marked circannual fluctuation in growth and reproduction (Blacker, 1974). Discovery of a circadian rhythm in otolith

deposition now holds great promise as suggesting a means for age
determination in young fishes or in species, especially many of the tropics,
which have not experienced seasonal growth checks or limited breeding
seasons (Brothers, Mathews & Lasker, 1976; Struhsaker & Uchiyama,
1976), a useful practical outcome from a somewhat academic field of fish
phenology.

Fluctuation, at a wide range of periodicity, would therefore seem to be
a normal part of the more conspicuous aspects of teleost anabolism. The
question arises as to whether all the component processes of constructive
metabolism within the cell operate in a cyclical manner and thus come
within the province of phenology as here defined. On theoretical
grounds, this may be expected from the assumption that fish metabolism
obeys certain oscillatory features of living systems summarized by von
Bertalanffy (1960) and Sollberger (1962). Those relevant here include,
notably, the property of acclimation, widely reported in fishes (Fry, 1971;
Hochachka & Somero, 1971), and tendencies for "undershoot" and
"overshoot" in response to perturbation, characteristic of a system
responsive to both an input variable and its derivatives (or other higher
order terms) (Hubbell, 1971; Calow, 1976). For short steps in anabolism,
disturbance of a circadian or ultradian frequency may be endogenous, or
of external origin, bearing directly or by repercussion from more sensitive
reactions. At present, it is debatable whether the persistent circadian
rhythms of teleost metabolism are basically controlled by some internal
timing pulse or by responsiveness to regular environmental variation,
including geophysical factors imperceptible to human consciousness
(Palmer, 1976). The study of endogenous rhythms in fish anabolism has
never excluded such subtle influences. The teleost otoliths, whose growth
pattern may show seasonal change under constant temperature and
salinity (Irie, 1960), might even qualify as suitable receptors for variation
in, say, electromagnetic fields, since a piezoelectric function has been
attributed to these structures (Morris & Kittleman, 1967). Alternatively,
one theory of internal timing does depend on a cyclical anabolic
phenomenon of intrinsic production, envisaged as transcription from
DNA "chronons" (Ehret & Trucco, 1967). From whatever causation,
cellular reactions and enzyme activity would seem to present a picture of
routine fluctuation, a variety of Waddington's "homeorhesis" noted by
Calow (1976). A basic adaptive value of this situation could lie in the
separation of incompatible processes (Atkinson, 1977). Since those directed towards anabolism and catabolism may form such opponents, it is
obvious that fish phenology must be pursued into the realm of molecular
biology.

Having traced the limits of fish phenology, the various divisions of
biosynthetic activity may now be examined. It should be remembered that
a living system as elaborate as the teleost embodies a high degree of
interactional complexity (Wimsatt, 1976) whose theoretical decomposition into subsystems should not mask the essential feature of

functional interdependence between branches of metabolism. However, for conceptual simplicity, it has proved possible to construct schemes of energy and material flow through the teleost body as partitional hierarchies in both anabolic and catabolic usage (Warren & Davis, 1967; Beamish, Niimi & Lett, 1975; Elliott, 1976b and this volume p. 29; Webb, 1978). The underlying biochemical reactions by which this partitioning is achieved are described by Atkinson (1977). Here, it should be noted that the direction, rate and duration of metabolic processes during individual life history are the outcome of interaction between genetic control systems and limitations, and a particular cellular environment, itself determined by other intrinsic factors and the effect of outside environment on the whole organism. This more or less cyclical and dynamic system of energy allocation from and to the pool of intermediary metabolites creates the gross phenology—the succession of "phenophases"—characterizing individuals and species. In this sequence, a specific pattern of temporal emphasis on one or another of the anabolic categories has emerged as a result of selection for optimal fitness in a particular ecotope (Taylor, Gourley, Lawrence & Kaplan, 1974; Calow, 1977).

Under given conditions, all teleosts have a certain minimum requirement of energy and material to meet essential work and repair for continued existence. The anabolism of structural maintenance, together with "basal" or "standard" metabolism, describing indispensable catabolism in the resting state, must head the line of resource priorities when food input is limiting. In the adult, when further anabolism occurs, practical observation suggests that gonad maturation, accumulation of stores and then somatic growth are undertaken in that order of priority. When food appears unlimited, all anabolic functions may be served, as during the marine phase in the life history of anadromous salmonids. Under pathological conditions, the queue may be jumped by "metabolic drain" into a large parasite, with reduced growth and delayed maturation as described by Pennycuick (1971) for sticklebacks. A basic aim of fish phenology must be to account for these patterns and sequences in anabolism, both in the commercial sense of budgeting and efficiency, and in the explanatory meaning of the verb. Questions of proximate causation relate to how mechanisms act within the fish to control onset and balance between the various phenophases of life, and to how these are affected by events in and around the fish. An early discussion of classical phenology in relation to combined effects of environmental variables is given by Shelford (1930). Examination of ultimate influences would concern the reasons why particular genetic traits for anabolic features should have evolved as those conferring maximum fitness in specific surroundings.

From cybernetic principles, it is possible to devise simple models of interrelationships between catabolism, growth and reproductive expenditure within a living organism (Hubbell, 1971; Calow, 1973). These systems depend on stabilizing negative feedback, an almost universal feature of energy regulation. At any one time, size attained and current growth rate are thus compared within the body against "desired size". A "desired growth rate" signal, then generated, together with current growth rate, serve as inputs to another comparator, from which a "growth rate error" indication is transmitted elsewhere for adjustment of absorption, catabolism and gonadal development in relation to growth. The latter is finally modified according to constraints set by the framework of the system. A more or less temporary "memory" of previous anabolic experience is accredited to a model of this kind. In fish, compensatory reduction in catabolism, when food intake decreases (Simpson, 1978), is believed to suggest interrelationships of this nature, as may gamete resorption under similar circumstances (Wootton, this volume p. 133). Such proposals for control systems are of great value in planning the operation of research into fish anabolism (Calow, 1977). However, locating the structural basis and isolating the substances likely to be involved in comparison and transfers is still at an early stage. For teleosts, most is known about the endocrine aspects of metabolic integration (Baker & Wigham, this volume p. 89). Thus, in reproduction, a core control sequence for gonad maturation can now be delineated, even to the stages of ovulation (Kuo & Nash, 1975; Jalabert, 1976; Hirose, 1976), while the susceptibility of this system to environmental cues, especially with respect to photoperiod, has been widely investigated (summarized by De Vlaming (1972), Htun-Han (1977) and Scott (this volume p. 105)). Although much has been learned about fish somatotrophic hormone, the mechanisms of control in somatic growth still afford scope for biochemical speculation derived from what has been suggested in mammalian physiology. Drawing from the stem-cell theory of Burch (1968), and from agents of mitotic control (Bullough, 1975), it is possible to envisage a tissue-specific system (chalones versus mesenchymal factors), with interaction between tissue-coding and mitotic-control factors for organismic control of cell turnover and build-up in relative and overall growth of body parts, all acting to influence the responsiveness of tissues to a general growth inducer. Somatotrophic hormone, or a derivative, would be the obvious agent for this latter role, probably in synergism with other substances among the many on record as influencing general body growth (Holley, 1975). Liberation of somatotrophic hormone is likely to be modulated by external influences and assimilatory intake affecting the hypothalamic–hypophysial axis of neuroendocrine control (Holmes & Ball, 1974). "Growth memory" would be an increasing discrepancy between stem-cell growth and coding factor levels from the various tissues. However, a stem-cell reference system has yet to be found in fishes. For mammals, lymphoid tissue as a possible location was favoured by Burwell (1963). Under present conditions of speculation, this hypothetical centre might be most appropriately imagined as next to the somewhat less nebulous master clock of vertebrate organization, which is supposed to lie in or near the suprachiasmatic nucleus of the mammalian hypothalamus (Palmer, 1976), but whose presence is still to be confirmed in fishes (Matty, 1978).

In coding a multiplicity of tissues, Burch's theory does find a vital use for the so-called redundant DNA present in the vertebrate genome. Perhaps the polyploidy, which is believed to have accompanied the origin of vertebrates (Ohno, 1970), is thus correlated with the greatly increased complexity of fish structure.

The anabolism of maintenance in fishes would seem to be largely directed towards surface care, preserving interfaces in a functional condition which often requires rapid biosyntheses of complex molecules and membrane structures. For example, the gut epithelium of goldfish, although more persistent than that of mammals, has a normal life of less than 20 days (Hyodo–Taguchi, 1968). Expenditure to replace desquamated epithelial cells and enzymes, sometimes even a peritrophic membrane (Rosenthal & Paffenhöfer, 1972), and the renewal of the skin mucus "cuticle", for use in locomotion, homeostasis and protection (Bullock & Roberts, 1975; Pickering & Macey, 1977), are aspects of maintenance anabolism difficult to quantify but nonetheless essential for overall survival. For practical reasons, losses from the gut lining are usually included in measures of unassimilated food. Estimates from unfed fish suggest that the amount lost is small (Elliott, 1976a), but must be greater if the normal activity of processing ingested food promotes both secretion and abrasion within the alimentary canal. A cyclical nature for all these processes could be inferred from the widespread circadian rhythms in feeding and locomotion followed by many teleosts. An extreme example of a markedly cyclical and highly adaptive maintenance process is shown by a defensive function of the body exterior in parrotfishes (Scaridae). In some Caribbean forms, preparation for sleep involves secretion of a diaphanous nightgown of mucus, which, when vacated the following morning, collapses into a substantial if unaesthetic lump of biosynthesis (Winn, 1955). The value of this habit is in survival rather than modesty. At night, the reef is scouted by moray-eels which eat more of those parrotfishes sleeping uncovered (Winn & Bardach, 1959). From experimental work (e.g. Brett, Shelbourn & Shoop, 1969; Elliott, 1976b), system maintenance must also show seasonal fluctuation relative to temperature and other variables, and this metabolic condition, with no growth gain, is a functional state experienced by many temperate and polar species for a goodly part of the year (Warren & Davis, 1967). In response to harsh sub-zero temperatures of winter, a circannual rhythm in content of macromolecular serum antifreeze may be another essential part of maintenance for teleosts of high latitudes (Duman & DeVries, 1975).

Before sexual maturity, somatic growth constructs a support system for the operation of forthcoming reproductive events, in a form able to survive, to gather material for gonad maturation and use, and to place the gametes in temporal and spatial situations optimal for survival of progeny. Maturation introduces reproduction as a potentially overriding anabolic commitment (Woodhead, this volume p. 179). To a faster or slower extent, this may even be inimical to system maintenance as the cause of "reproductive senescence" (Calow, 1977; Jones & Johnston, 1977), but frequently has a more obvious effect in seasonal growth cessation among many adult fishes (Iles, 1974). Genetic potential for growth after maturity must ultimately depend on the extent to which increased adult size enhances reproductive success (Taylor *et al.*, 1974), but proximal mechanisms for diverting resources into the gonads rather than into the somatic body can be artificially reversed by various means in pisciculture (Payne, this volume p. 383). Antagonism between gonado-trophic and somatotrophic hormones is suggested by the "anabolic" effects of sex steroids known to increase growth rate in a number of teleosts (e.g. Hirose & Hibiya, 1968a,b).

The magnitude and periodicity of energy and material expenditure on reproduction forms an enormous part of fish phenology; study of salmonids and clupeids, among other teleosts, has contributed much basic data for modern theorizing on the evolution of reproductive patterns in life history. The subject of reproductive phenology in fishes faces questions of developmental phasing (time of maturation in life-span), frequency (semelparity versus iteroparity), outlay (reproductive effort), bestowal (investment per offspring), timing (breeding seasonality relative to environment) and consequences (effect on viability of the reproducer). Every contributor to this symposium has considered at least one of these topics in detail, and here only some general discussion of the nature of reproductive effort will be made.

The process of reproduction in the adult fish requires an allocation of material and energy from that in transit or already stored within the body (Fig. 1). The proportion of physiologically useful resources devoted

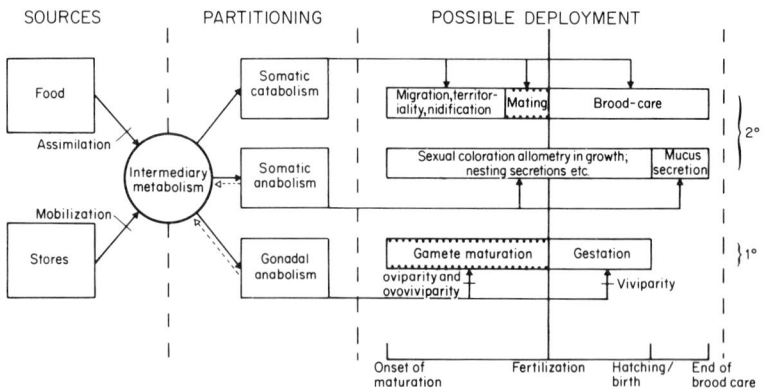

FIG. 1.   The sources, major partitioning and possible deployment of energy and material as reproductive effort in teleosts; essential requirements with horizontal edging; reclaim possibility indicated by broken lines; 1°, 2°, primary and secondary sectors.

to reproduction, subject to both proximate and ultimate controls, has been defined as "reproductive effort" (Williams, 1966). Within the energy budget of the fish, expenditure on reproduction may be divided into (1) a "primary" sector, involving prezygotic maturation biosyntheses and storage within the gametes, notably expressed in oocyte size and number, with postzygotic contributions in viviparous species and (2) a "secondary" sector, itself divisible into (a) the anabolism of secondary sexual characters, not only the material of more obvious sexual dimorphism, as shown in coloration and finnage, but even pheromones known to feature in teleost reproduction (Bardach & Todd, 1970), and, rarely, material for nest building or mucophagy by young (Balon, 1975) and (b) the catabolism of reproductive behaviour, expended, in varying proportions, on the activities of migration, territoriality, nidification, courtship, and, in oviparous species, brood-care. Of these, gonad maturation, and mating behaviour immediately prior to fertilization, are obviously reproductive necessities. The great variety of further elaboration in the deployment of reproductive effort by teleosts are summarized by Breder & Rosen (1966) and Balon (1975). Among extremes in secondary expenditure must be the anadromous behaviour of salmonids. The spawning migrations of female sockeye salmon entail loss of over 90% of body fats and 50–60% of total body protein (Idler & Clemens, 1959), admittedly without an in-built cost ceiling on reproductive effort. It is also important to remember that reproductive effort varies in kind between the sexes, most obviously in relation to yolk deposition in the eggs. Thus, in Windermere perch, gonadal energy loss at spawning, relative to yearly somatic loss, was found to be 87·1% in females but only 9·6% in males, which were believed to expend more in activity (Craig, 1977b). The disparity in expenditure on gametes is not reflected in greater longevity of male perch, since a higher maximum age is reached by females (Le Cren, 1958). Among teleosts in general, when the sexes differ in mortality rate, it is usually the males which have a shorter lifespan (Beverton & Holt, 1959). Perhaps the "risk" element of increased activity, with greater exposure to predation, contributes towards this phenomenon (Pianka, 1976).

  The magnitude of reproductive effort, in conjunction with other life-history features, has been discussed for many groups of animals and plants. Stearns (1976) has rightly noted that reproductive effort is a rate phenomenon, i.e. the rate at which resources, beyond those required for maintenance, are diverted into reproduction rather than somatic growth. Typically, the rate and direction of expenditure must be subject to cyclical fluctuation relative to the complex of parental biosyntheses and activity which always precedes, and sometimes follows, the act of gametic fusion. A complete description of reproductive effort must ideally comprise
    1. the identification of the various destinations for energy and material utilized to achieve the goal of reproduction,
    2. measurement of the frequency and amplitude of investment-rate cycles in these directions during reproductive life,

3. summation of expenditure in each sector, and for the function of reproduction as a whole, over the same period,

4. comparison of the temporal pattern of deployment and apportioning of resources between these sectors and

5. assessment of reproductive cost in relation to contemporary rate-cycles and levels of somatic growth and maintenance demands.

A complete account of such complexity has yet to be compiled for any teleost, and must pose some practical difficulties for exact measurement, especially in catabolism. However, a very convenient and widely used method for assessing what is probably the major component of reproductive effort in most fishes is by gonadosomatic index, an instantaneous ratio or percentage of ripe gonadal to somatic or total weight. The use of energy units in this type of comparison was believed by Tinkle & Hadley (1975) to be a more precise measure of reproductive effort, and would also allow for the higher calorific cost of building ovarian rather than somatic tissue (Jones & Johnston, 1977). It should be remembered that the relative magnitude of gonad development is still only an approximate indication of prezygotic primary reproductive anabolism. Especially in the female, non-gametogenic growth of the gonads is usually included, and, in viviparous forms, postzygotic commitment may not be separated. A better approach is to determine weight or calorific value of eggs produced in a spawning or over a given period, usually estimated from known weight of the egg and fecundity (Jones & Johnston, 1977), or by subtraction of smaller gonad weights from the largest observed in a season (Valiela, Wright, Teal & Volkmann, 1977). Values for the dry weight of eggs produced from a single annual spawning in herring and cod range from 3 to 8·6% of body weight (19–32% in energy content). At the opposite extreme of reproductivity anabolism, small epibenthic warm-water species may produce monthly, for several months, at least two-thirds of maternal dry weight (Miller, this volume p. 263). In species which spawn more than once in a breeding season, measurement of reproductive effort obviously requires an accurate idea of spawning frequency. For small and adaptable fishes, aquarium studies, albeit in more or less artificial surroundings, can supply information about spawning potential, and also permit investigation of proximate factors affecting number of broods (Kenmuir, 1973: Wootton, this volume p. 133; Miller, this volume p. 263). Otherwise, size-frequency distribution of oocytes in the mature ovary has long been used as an indicator of repeat-spawning (Qasim, 1956; Götting, 1961). However, when such is the case, only the ripe oocytes, and the next batch, at intermediate vitellogenesis, are normally distinguishable from the many smaller cells. This pattern, seen, for example, in the common goby, *Pomatoschistus microps* (Krøyer), while suggesting repeat-spawning, fails to reveal the capacity for producing as many as nine broods by some individuals (Miller, this volume p. 263). Recently, more discriminating measurement of oocytes in the shanny, *Blennius pholis* L., has revealed a polymodal distribution, which is believed to correspond with much more frequent spawning within the season than was formerly thought (Shackley & King, 1977). Results from this technique, which may be applicable to species unlikely to breed in captivity, still need confirmation against a detailed spawning history.

Closely tied with reproduction is the anabolism of storage within the fish system. Depot strategies in metazoans have been discussed by Calow & Jennings (1977), in relation to changing availability and predictability of food supply. As Pianka (1976) noted, hoarding of storage materials is a means of transferring ecosystem productivity foraged in one part of the year, or area of distribution, for expenditure at another time or place, when conditions exist for optimal reproductive success but not for support of reproductive anabolism or activities by direct feeding. In teleosts, depot substances, typically triglyceride lipids, may reach as high as 30% of body weight at the end of a feeding season. Phenology of storage is most familiarly associated with temperate or low arctic marine species in a markedly seasonal but fairly predictable ecosystem. A good example, in relation to feeding patterns and spawning, has been quantified by MacKinnon (1972) for the American plaice, *Hippoglossoides platessoides* (Fabricius), and the whole subject widely reviewed by Love (1970) and Shulman (1974). Biochemically, fishes have been termed "lipid-specialists" by Cowey & Sargent (1972) and, in utilizing a great variety of these energy-rich compounds, can sometimes store this commodity so well as to be combustible when dried. Thus, candle-smelt or eulachon, *Thaleichthys pacificus* (Richardson), were formerly used by the Nishka Indians of southern Alaska as torches before civilization brought them a less malodorous source of illumination (Swan, 1880).

Among the three accumulative categories of adult anabolism, only somatic growth represents a normally lasting addition to individual biomass, leading to a net gain in material more or less capable of further growth together with its extracellular products. Beneath the tangible surface, of course, the subject of cell kinetics and material turnover within the teleost body represents a largely unexplored field. The final magnitude attained by the fish—maximum size—and the temporal sequence of intermediate stages—the growth pattern—may be expected to have adaptive significance relative to survival, feeding and reproductive opportunities during individual lifespan in a particular ecotope (Schoener, 1971; Hespenheide, 1973; Miller, this volume p. 263). Much thought has been devoted to the formulation of these incremental patterns. The exercise is of more than theoretical interest, since the resulting expressions are of practical value for calculation of yield in exploited fish populations, both wild (Ricker, 1975) and captive (Sperber, From & Sparre, 1977). The modern approach, reviewed by Ursin (this volume p. 63), now has a biological rationale, rather than depending on equations from economics or even ballistics, and acknowledges the cyclical aspects of fish growth (Pitcher & MacDonald, 1973; Jones & Johnston,

1977; Ursin, this volume p. 63). An equally important area of research has been the study of environmental influences on fish growth, whose susceptibility is shown by widespread seasonality. A numerous and potentially variable range of factors are now believed to act on the intrinsic control of growth (Beamish *et al.*, 1975; Weatherley, 1976; Weatherley & Rogers, 1978), with the outcome forming a response domain in an increasingly multidimensional system (Alderdice, 1972). A comprehensive investigation into merely a few of the factors affecting growth in just one species of teleost must now anticipate a great expenditure of time and resources. Elliott (1976b) noted that a study of bioenergetics in the brown trout, *Salmo trutta* L., with effect on growth as a major objective, occupied about 21 man–woman years. Photoperiod and salinity are two other easily adjusted environmental features which are known to influence growth (Gross, Roelofs & Fromm, 1965; Payne, this volume p. 383). In both nature and domestication, other, more subtle, factors, such as scent (Yu & Perlmutter, 1970), sight (Wirtz, 1974) and proximity (Li & Brocksen, 1977) of fellow fishes must interact to exert a complex sociobiotic effect, quite apart from the possibility of more obvious resource limitations.

My interest in fish phenology originated partly from attempts to explain seasonal growth changes in small estuarine and inshore gobiid fishes, whose contrasting life histories are discussed later (Miller, this volume p. 263). Growth patterns for two species studied in Manx waters (Miller, 1961, 1963, 1965, 1975) are shown in Figs 2 and 3. Specific growth

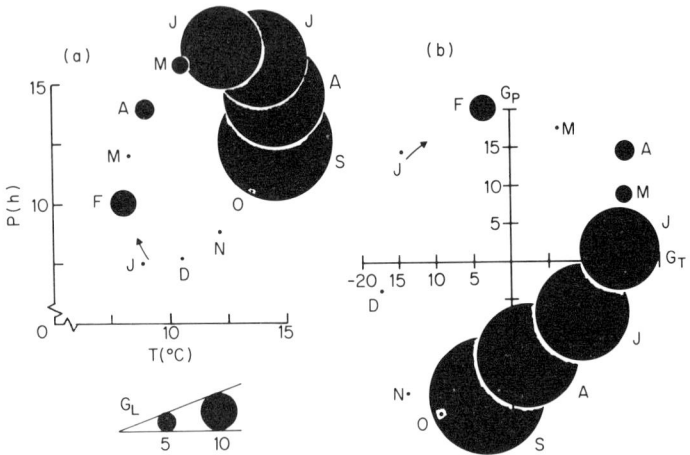

FIG. 2. Monthly specific growth rate (circles) of juvenile *Gobius paganellus*, at Poyll Brein, Isle of Man, for year (J–D) from January of first winter of life (as arrowed), in relation to sea temperature (T) and daylength (P): (a) monthly mean absolute values; (b) specific rates of change (G_T, G_P). Specific growth rate (G_L) is derived from monthly changes in mean standard length, and adjusted for standard length of 2·5 cm. From Miller (1961, 1963).

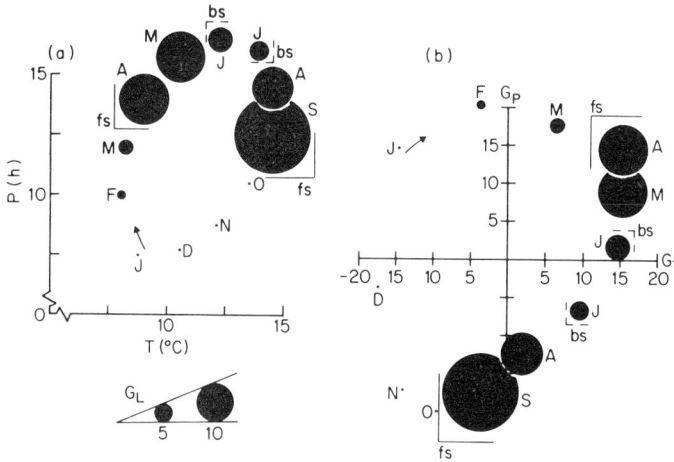

FIG. 3. Monthly specific growth rate (circles) of *Pomatoschistus microps*, in the Silver Burn estuary, Isle of Man, year (J–D) from January of first winter of life (as arrowed), in relation to sea temperature (T) and daylength (P): (a) monthly mean absolute values; (b) specific rates of change (G$_T$, G$_P$). Specific growth-rate (G$_L$) derives as Fig. 2; fs, feeding season; bs, peak spawning months (with highest proportion of ripe females). From Miller (1963, 1975 and unpublished).

rate (Medawar, 1945) is displayed against the annual cycle in absolute values of sea temperature and daylength, as well as that in rate and direction of change by these environmental variables. In the juvenile rock goby, *Gobius paganellus* L., a warm temperate species reaching a northern limit of distribution along the western British Isles, a clear relationship is apparent between growth rate and higher temperatures of summer, commencing at a time of maximum increase in temperature and ending abruptly as temperatures fall more rapidly in autumn. The growth period coincides with declining photoperiod. In common gobies, *Pomatoschistus microps*, of the same age, but already maturing after the first winter of life, growth begins in spring at temperatures much lower than those in autumn when this process stops. Reduction in growth rate during June and July would seem correlated with peak spawning frequency by individuals during a long breeding season. This growth check, accompanying reproduction in many other teleosts and discussed earlier, is here reflected in the formation of a summer scale annulus, outside an earlier spring annulus laid down on resumption of growth in April (Miller, 1975). In subsequent work, the relationship between lean dry somatic weight and body length, and between the former and similarly treated gonad stages, was determined, employing a gravimetric method for total lipid estimation (Folch, Lees & Sloane Stanley, 1956) and drying tissues at 105°C. Using this information in conjunction with known frequency of spawning, it has become possible to suggest that the average female *P. microps*, starting in April at standard length 2·7 cm, and spent at 3·65 cm at the end of July, might grow to 4·9 cm, if the material used in the eggs of an estimated six broods were to be diverted to somatic growth. In the laboratory, *P. microps* remaining immature under low photoperiod make much better growth than fish brought to earlier maturation at higher day length (Miller, 1973). Another species, the sand goby, *Pomatoschistus minutus* (Pallas), commences to breed somewhat earlier in the year than *P. microps*, with a unimodal adult growth cycle occurring only after the breeding season and consequently no second scale annulus produced (Healey, 1972b; Lee, 1974). The late autumn-winter cessation of growth in *P. microps* seems hardly a direct consequence of cold, since, in captivity, individuals will feed and grow moderately well at temperatures as low as the average for February (8·05°C) in the area studied, under both long and short day length. Examination of gut contents, using a modified "points" system, reveals that food intake in the wild is minimal during winter, as was also found by Healey (1972a). This biotic factor, rather than obvious physical ones, would thus seem to be responsible for absence of growth in *P. microps* over the winter months and may perhaps be attributed to reduced availability, or even food quality, of prey during these months (Healey, 1971). One enigma of phenology in *P. microps* is the late summer growth experienced by adults immediately after the breeding season and only a few months before most individuals of this short-lived species disappear in their second autumn (Miller, 1975). In discussion, Dr W. M. Schaffer suggested to me that ability to grow after a long and supposedly debilitating breeding season would have strong selective advantage by enhancing fecundity in the small proportion of individuals who do survive into the beginning of a second season. This idea would give adaptive significance to what might be interpreted as a vigorous systemic response to a growth rate "error" accumulated during the breeding check on growth.

For teleosts in general, individual existence, with a series of anabolic cycles, from which size and reproductive fitness are derived, may be viewed as a single cycle in development and decline of organization, exemplified most simply by the rise and fall of growth rate or the cycle of growth acceleration (Medawar, 1945). Before a physiological limit is reached, many fishes suffer ecological death (Bonner, 1965), most obviously by predation, and the reproductive phenology of a species is obviously closely tied to the mortality pattern likely to be experienced by individuals (Stearns, 1976, 1977). Later onset of senescence has been recorded in a number of teleosts, and this intrinsic erosion of maintenance capability with time would also seem a suitably anabolic theme for fish phenology (Woodhead, this volume p. 179).

The connection between senescence and growth stage, maturation and degree of reproductive effort is of general biological interest. A positive correlation between growth rate, lower asymptotic length, and mortality rate was found in teleosts by Beverton & Holt (1959), and Comfort (1961) determined experimentally that senescence appeared among female guppies when about three-quarters of limiting size had been reached. The impact of reproduction on longevity has been mentioned above. Castration of semelparous Pacific salmon greatly prolongs their life expectancy (Robertson, 1961), but, conversely, neotenic male parr do not suffer early death (Flain, 1971). It would seem that maturation-induced senescence requires the coincidence of appropriate phases in body and gonad growth. In some fish, parental death may be an inevitable consequence of other metabolic activities making greater contribution to fitness than immortality. However, in Pacific salmon, the selective value of hyperadrenocorticism might not only be as a means for unusually high energy release in the catabolism of spawning migration (Brett, 1972), but as a convenient inducer of death once breeding is complete. The consequence of death and decomposition of the adult population is enrichment of the freshwater ecosystems in which the succeeding generation feeds and grows before descent to the sea (Northcote, 1978). In conjunction with the precise homing instinct characterizing salmonids, post-reproductive death could be regarded as an altruistic adaptation transferring the high productivity of cold-temperate shelf seas to freshwater habitats, initially poorer but perhaps affording greater protection to offspring (Thompson, 1959). In a reverse direction, the migration of eels may serve to enrich the depths of the Sargasso Sea. For successful semelparity, both cases would meet the requirement of resource predictability for the next generation, in a quantity itself related to number of offspring likely to be produced.

The immediate object for phenological study must be the individual fish in its life history, but the phenology of an individual cannot be isolated from the anabolic patterns of others sharing common ancestry within a panmictic population. The rest of its own kind forms part of the selective environment against which fitness is tested. The panmictic population, regarded as a basic evolutionary unit (Ehrlich & Raven, 1969), can be envisaged as a section across the time dimension of a phyletic line of genealogical relationship in which individuals form transient components. The spatial distribution of this series in time has been compared to the reticulate structure of a fern stele (Taylor & Taylor, 1977). To find an animal simile for the phenological aspect of its biomass, the phyletic line may be likened to a very long rigid earthworm, whose terminal segments are in circular contraction and whose body has fixed with several waves of longitudinal contraction (Gray & Lissmann, 1938). At any one time section, the collective anabolic achievement will constitute a population biomass, or standing crop, which, in teleosts, may range between such extremes as the millions of tons of Pacific anchovy or Arctic cod to perhaps 100–200 g of Mexico spring desert pupfish, *Cyprinodon nevadensis* Eigenmann & Eigenmann, inhabiting a total species range of about 300 litres of relatively hot water (Brown, 1971). From inception as a distinct, interbreeding population, the biomass of a phyletic line, and its particulate distribution into numbers of individuals, should firstly expand

and then show more or less overt fluctuation with time, depending on environmental scope and genetic changes affecting reproductive rate within the line itself. Over the same time, spatial distribution may alter in relation to age, season and longer-term hydrographic changes. Such biomass changes will have a seasonal component, based on cycles in growth, storage, maturation and mortality rate among individuals (Weatherley, 1972). Fluctuations of longer, epochal periodicity have been much investigated, from the aspect of population numbers, in relation to exploitation of commercial species (Nikolskii, 1969; Popova, 1978). These cycles are the outcome of a complex interaction between density-dependent and density-independent factors of the whole environment, involving periodic phenomena, with, in turn, an effect on net reproduction at given population density, itself a function of age distribution and maturation patterns within the population (Ricker, 1954; Larkin, 1973; Cushing, 1975a, b; Cushing & Horwood, 1977; Backiel & Le Cren, 1978; Garrod & Knights, this volume p. 361). Not many populations display such regular periodicity in biomass as that depicted for Skenna River sockeye by Larkin & McDonald (1968) and, even there, the underlying age-composition of the spawning stock was found to vary below overall peaks. Nevertheless, biomass fluctuation would seem to be a normal feature of the temporal span of various fish species. This anabolic cycling, a measure of success in individual phenology, can be regarded as phyletic phenology, which, with population dynamics as a biomass phenomenon, constitutes a subject of great significance in world fisheries. Eventually, the anabolic history of the evolutionary line will terminate with extinction, as individual adaptiveness fails in a changing environment or with genetic subdivision of the originally homogeneous population. The recent fate of the northeastern Atlantic herring exemplifies the marked decline in biomass which might be expected when long established features of reproductive and somatic anabolism, attuned to fluctuation in the aquatic ecosystem, can no longer counter the intensity and selectivity of a relatively new mammalian predator from the land (Burd, 1974).

    Mention of populations and biomass suggests standing crops, productivity and yield, which, apart from general ecological relevance, indicate the practical justification for fish phenology. The ecological link between mankind and the teleosts is primarily a trophic one, the product of fish phenology being a suitable raw material for ours, either consumed directly or, with more waste, processed industrially to support other species utilized by man. There is an increasing need for this commodity but, in contrast to modern use of warm-blooded vertebrates, the bulk of fish eaten by man, or his domesticated animals, is still got by hunting, about 85% of the catch being obtained from the sea (Wilimovsky, 1976). Comparisons have been drawn between present-day pursuit of fish in the wild, and Palaeolithic exploitation of terrestrial faunas, but there are certain fundamental differences in the nature of these confrontations. As a result of scientific research over the last century, an enormous amount of knowledge has been gained about the phenology of teleost species subject to commercial fisheries. Such information, about growth cycles, reproduction, lifespan, etc. has all been translated into theories about population dynamics and productivity which have formed a basis for what has been termed "rational fishing" or optimal exploitation in keeping with stock conservation (Graham, 1943; Gulland, 1974; Garrod & Knights, this volume p. 361). Although the concept of maximum sustained yield might seem a highly desirable biological goal, conflicting interests of an economic or political nature make precise definition of a generally satisfactory level or "optimal yield" difficult to achieve (Larkin, 1977; Hilborn & Walters, 1977). Acceptance of a more dynamic set of fishing constraints (Walters & Hilborn, 1976) has been supported by catastrophe theory (Jones & Walters, 1976). Fisheries regulation of the future may perhaps be based on the induction, rather than deduction, of population phenology. Perversely, as science has developed to permit closer understanding of fish phenology and the response of stocks to exploitation, human techniques and patterns of predation have become more complex and mobile (Pope, 1973) but basic human nature remains that of a food-gathering primate, with delight at immediate abundance overcoming fear of ultimate scarcity.

Should application of fish phenology be towards cultivation rather than exploitation? The answer must be in compromise. In the hydrosphere, there is still a variety of fish biomass remaining to be harvested (Wilimovsky, 1976; Gordon, this volume p. 327), given that other aspects of human development can be controlled to preserve the overall aquatic environment and that economic difficulties of collection and sale can be overcome. The rise of the British "fish-and-chips" trade in the 19th century (Burgess, 1965) shows that human consumers can be persuaded to enjoy a wider trophic niche. It should also be remembered that, while the operation of fisheries encounters land-based problems, the essential anabolism of wild fishes costs nothing and is based on food of higher quality, and space of greater extent, than would be practicable to supply in captivity. Finally, unlike the ancient hunters, we do not yet compete for living space with our fish prey, although plans for aquatic ranching may be an ominous beginning.

The other direction of applied fish phenology is towards pisciculture, a form of animal husbandry which can be conducted at a relatively higher level of efficiency, in yield per investment, than that for other vertebrates maintained on land (Bardach, 1978). The anabolic interests of fish phenology are exactly those which have occupied improvers of domestic mammals and birds since the initial results of the Agricultural Revolution. To succeed, it is necessary to know how growth and reproductive patterns in selected species respond to the artificial conditions of domestication, and how to improve over natural yield by altering genetic constraints (Purdom, this volume p. 207), feeding the system (Payne, this volume p. 383), changing the environment (Brett, 1974) and selectively operating appropriate threshold switches (Holling, 1966) in the anabolic control mechanisms noted earlier. The subject has been reviewed by Anderson (1975), Bardach (1978) and Payne (this volume p. 383). Existing knowledge is now sufficient to increase production of fish by aquaculture enormously but, again, practical benefits depend on integrating yield with economic and social factors more complex than the technical problems (Shepherd, 1975).

Originally, Fritsch emphasized the unifying nature of phenology. In its present form, discussion of the subject has assembled a range of specialist views which might not otherwise be voiced in the same symposium. It is also worth noting that fish phenology unites a series of themes extending from the molecular biology of control systems to the highly topical one of augmenting world resources of human food. As such, it is attractive to both student and researcher in supplying a moral justification for gratifying their enthusiasm for fishes.

REFERENCES

Alderdice, D. F. (1972). Responses of marine poikilotherms to environmental factors acting in concert. In *Marine ecology* 1, *Environmental factors*, Pt 3: 1659–1722. Kinne, O. (ed.). London: John Wiley & Sons.

Alexander, R. McN. (1967). *Functional design in fishes*. London: Hutchison University Library.

Anderson, J. I. W. (1975). The aquacultural revolution. *Proc. R. Soc. Lond.* (B) **191**: 169–184.

Atkinson, D. E. (1977). *Cellular energy metabolism and its regulation*. New York: Academic Press.

Backiel, T. & Le Cren, E. D. (1978). Some density relationships for fish population parameters. In *Ecology of freshwater fish production*: 279–302. Gerking, S. D. (ed.). Oxford: Blackwell Scientific Publications.

Baggerman, B. (1972). Photoperiodic responses in the stickleback and their control by a daily rhythm of photosensitivity. *Gen. comp. Endocr.* Supp. 3: 466–476.

Balon, E. K. (1975). Reproductive guilds of fishes: a proposal and definition. *J. Fish. Res. Bd Can.* **32**: 821–864.

Bardach, J. E. (1978). The growing science of aquaculture. In *Ecology of freshwater fish production*: 424–446. Gerking, S. D. (ed.). Oxford: Blackwell Scientific Publications.

Bardach, J. E. & Todd, J. H. (1970). Chemical communication in fish. In *Communication by chemical signals*: 205–240. Johnston, J. W., Moulton, D. G. & Turk, A. (eds). New York: Appleton-Century-Crofts.

Beamish, F. W. H., Niimi, A. J. & Lett, P. F. K. P. (1975). Bioenergetics of teleost fishes: environmental influences. In *Comparative physiology-functional aspects of structural materials*: 187–209. Bolis, L., Maddrell, H. P. & Schmidt-Nielsen, K. (eds). Amsterdam: North Holland.

von Bertalanffy, L. (1960). Principles and theory of growth. In *Fundamental aspects of normal and malignant growth*: 137–259. Nowinski, W. W. (ed.). Amsterdam: Elsevier.

Beverton, R. J. H. & Holt, S. J. (1959). A review of the life spans and mortality rates of fish in nature, and their relation to growth and other physiological characteristics. *Ciba Fdn Colloq. Ageing* **5**: 142–180.
Billard, R. & Breton, B. (1978). Rhythms of reproduction in teleost fish. In *Rhythmic activity of fishes*: 31–53. Thorpe, J. E. (ed.). London & New York: Academic Press.
Blacker, R. W. (1974). Recent advances in otolith studies. In *Sea fisheries research*: 67–90. Harden Jones, F. R. (ed.). London: Elek Science.
Bonner, J. T. (1965). *Size and cycle, an essay on the structure of biology.* Princeton: University Press.
Breder, C. M. & Rosen, D. E. (1966). *Modes of reproduction in fishes.* New York: Natural History Press.
Brett, J. R. (1971). Energetic responses of salmon to temperature. A study of some thermal relations in the physiology and freshwater ecology of sockeye salmon (*Oncorhynchus nerka*). *Am. Zool.* **11**: 99–113.
Brett, J. R. (1972). The metabolic demand for oxygen in fish, particularly salmonids, and a comparison with other vertebrates. *Resp. Physiol.* **14**: 151–170.
Brett, J. R. (1974). Tank experiments on the culture of pan-size sockeye salmon (*Oncorhynchus nerka*) and pink salmon (*O. gorbuscha*) using environmental control. *Aquaculture* **4**: 341–352.
Brett, J. R., Shelbourn, J. E. & Shoop, C. T. (1969). Growth rate and body composition of fingerling sockeye salmon, *Oncorhynchus nerka*, in relation to temperature and ration size. *J. Fish. Res. Bd Can.* **26**: 2363–2394.
Brothers, E. B., Mathews, C. P. & Lasker, R. (1976). Daily growth increments in otoliths from larval and adult fishes. *Fish. Bull., U.S.* **74**: 1–8.
Brown, J. H. (1971). The desert pupfish. *Scient. Am.* **225**: 104–110.
Bullock, A. M. & Roberts, R. J. (1975). The dermatology of marine teleost fish. I. The normal integument. *Oceanogr. mar. Biol. Ann. Rev.* **13**: 383–411.
Bullough, W. S. (1975). Mitotic control in adult mammalian tissues. *Biol. Rev.* **50**: 99–127.
Burch, P. (1968). *An inquiry concerning growth, disease and ageing.* Edinburgh: Oliver & Boyd.
Burd, A. C. (1974). The north-east Atlantic herring and the failure of an industry. In *Sea fisheries research*: 167–191. Harden Jones, F. R. (ed.). London: Elek Science.
Burgess, G. H. O. (1965). *Developments in handling and processing fish.* London: Fishing News (Books) Ltd.
Burwell, R. G. (1963). The role of lymphoid tissue in morphostasis. *Lancet* **1963**: 69–74.
Calow, P. (1973). The relationship between fecundity, phenology, and longevity: a systems approach. *Am. Nat.* **107**: 559–574.
Calow, P. (1976). *Biological machines.* London: Arnold.
Calow, P. (1977). Ecology, evolution and energetics: a study in metabolic adaptation. *Adv. ecol. Res.* **10**: 1–62.
Calow, P. & Jennings, J. B. (1977). Optimal strategies for the metabolism of reserve materials in microbes and metazoa. *J. theoret. Biol.* **65**: 601–603.
Chan, K. K. S. (1976). A photosensitive daily rhythm in the female medaka, *Oryzias latipes.* Can. J. Zool. **54**: 852–856.
Cohen, D. M. (1970). How many recent fishes are there? *Proc. Calif. Acad. Sci.* **38**: 341–345.

Comfort, A. (1961). The expected rate of senescence and age-dependent mortality in fish. *Nature, Lond.* **191**: 822–823.

Cowey, C. B. & Sargent, J. R. (1972). Fish nutrition. *Adv. mar. Biol.* **10**: 383–492.

Craig, J. F. (1977a). Seasonal changes in the day and night activity of adult perch, *Perca fluviatilis* L. *J. Fish Biol.* **11**: 161–166.

Craig, J. F. (1977b). The body composition of adult perch, *Perca fluviatilis*, in Windermere, with reference to seasonal changes and reproduction. *J. Anim. Ecol.* **46**: 617–632.

Cushing, D. H. (1975a). The natural mortality of the plaice. *J. Cons. int. Explor. Mer* **36**: 150–157.

Cushing, D. H. (1975b). *Marine ecology and fisheries.* Cambridge: University Press.

Cushing, D. H. & Horwood, J. W. (1977). Development of a model of stock and recruitment. In *Fisheries mathematics*: 21–35. Steele, J. H. (ed.). London & New York: Academic Press.

De Vlaming, V. L. (1972). Environmental control of teleost reproductive cycles: a brief review. *J. Fish Biol.* **4**: 131–140.

De Vlaming, V. L. & Vodicnik, M. J. (1977). Diurnal variations in pituitary gonadotropin content and in gonadal response to exogenous gonadotropin and prolactin in *Notemigonus crysoleucas*. *J. Fish Biol.* **10**: 371–383.

Duman, J. G. & DeVries, A. L. (1975). The role of macromolecular antifreezes in cold water fishes. *Comp. Biochem. Physiol.* **52A**: 193–199.

Ehret, C. F. & Trucco, E. (1967). Molecular models for the circadian clock. *J. theoret. Biol.* **15**: 240–262.

Ehrlich, P. R. & Raven, P. H. (1969). Differentiation of populations. *Science, Wash.* **165**: 1228–1232,

Elliott, J. M. (1976a). Energy losses in the waste products of brown trout (*Salmo trutta* L.). *J. Anim. Ecol.* **45**: 561–580.

Elliott, J. M. (1976b). The energetics of feeding metabolism and growth of brown trout (*Salmo trutta* L.) in relation to body weight, water temperature and ration size. *J. Anim. Ecol.* **45**: 923–948.

Flain, M. (1971). Repeated spawning and survival of male quinnat salmon in New Zealand (note). *NZ. J. mar. freshw. Res.* **5**: 519–521.

Folch, J., Lees, M. & Sloane Stanley, G. H. (1956). A simple method for the isolation and purification of total lipids from animal tissues. *J. biol. Chem.* **226** (A): 497–509.

Fouda, M. M. & Miller, P. J. (1979). Alkaline phosphatase activity in the skin of the common goby, *Pomatoschistus microps* (Krøyer), in relation to cycles in scale and body growth. *J. Fish Biol.* (in press).

Fowler, H. W. & Fowler, F. G. (eds). (1964). *The concise Oxford dictionary of current English.* 5th edition. Oxford: Clarendon Press.

Fraser, J. G. (1922). *The golden bough.* Abridged edition. London: Macmillan.

Fretwell, S. D. (1972). *Populations in a seasonal environment.* Princeton: University Press.

Fritsch, K. (1858). Instruction für phänologische Beobachtungen. *Jb. K.K. Centr. Anst. Met. Erdm.* **5** (Anhang): 51–84.

Fry, F. E. J. (1971). The effect of environmental factors on the physiology of fish. *Fish physiol.* **6**: 1–98.

Gibson, R. N. (1978). Lunar and tidal rhythms in fish. In *Rhythmic activity of fishes*: 200–213. Thorpe, J. E. (ed.). London & New York: Academic Press.

Götting, K.-J. (1961). Beiträge zur Kenntnis der Grundlagen der Fortpflanzung und zur Fruchtbarkeitsbestimmung bei marinen Teleosteern. *Helgol. Wiss. Meeresunters.* **8**: 1–41.

Graham, M. (1943). *The fish gate.* London: Faber & Faber.

Gray, J. & Lissmann, H. W. (1938). Studies on animal locomotion. VII. Locomotory reflexes in the earthworm. *J. exp. Biol.* **15**: 506–517.

Grebe, J. J. (1962). Time: its breadth and depth in biological rhythms. *Ann. N.Y. Acad. Sci.* **98**: 1206–1210.

Gross, W. L., Roelofs, E. W. & Fromm, P. O. (1965). Influence of photoperiod on growth of green sunfish, *Lepomis cyanellus. J. Fish. Res. Bd Can.* **22**: 1379–1386.

Gulland, J. A. (1974). Fishery science, and the problems of management. In *Sea fisheries research*: 413–429. Harden Jones, F. R. (ed.). London: Elek Science.

Hawkes, J. (1963). *Man and the sun.* London: Cresset Press.

Healey, M. C. (1971). The distribution and abundance of sand gobies, *Gobius minutus*, in the Ythan estuary. *J. Zool., Lond.* **163**: 177–229.

Healey, M. C. (1972a). On the population ecology of the common goby in the Ythan estuary. *J. nat. Hist.* **6**: 133–145.

Healey, M. C. (1972b). Bioenergetics of a sand goby (*Gobius minutus*) population. *J. Fish. Res. Bd Can.* **29**: 187–194.

Hespenheide, H. A. (1973). Ecological inferences from morphological data. *A. Rev. Ecol. Syst.* **4**: 213–229.

Hilborn, R. & Walters, C. J. (1977). Differing goals of salmon management on the Skeena River. *J. Fish. Res. Bd Can.* **34**: 64–72.

Hirose, K. (1976). Endocrine control of ovulation in medaka (*Oryzias latipes*) and ayu (*Plecoglossus altivelis*). *J. Fish. Res. Bd Can.* **33**: 989–994.

Hirose, K. & Hibiya, T. (1968a). Physiological studies on growth-promoting effect of protein-anabolic steroids on fish—I: effects on goldfish. *Bull. Jap. Soc. scient. Fish.* **34**: 466–472.

Hirose, K. & Hibiya, T. (1968b). Physiological studies on growth-promoting effect of protein-anabolic steroids on fish–II: effects of 4-chlorotestosterone acetate on rainbow trout. *Bull. Jap. Soc. scient. Fish.* **34**: 473–481.

Hochachka, P. W. (1969). Intermediary metabolism in fishes. In *Fish physiology* 1: 351–389. Hoar, W. S. & Randall, D. J. (eds). New York & London: Academic Press.

Hochachka, P. W. & Somero, G. N. (1971). Biochemical adaptation to the environment. *Fish Physiol.* **6**: 99–156.

Holley, R. W. (1975). Control of growth of mammalian cells in cell culture. *Nature, Lond.* **258**: 487–490.

Holling, C. S. (1966). The strategy of building models of complex ecological systems. In *Systems analysis in ecology*: 195–214. Watt, K. C. F. (ed.). New York & London: Academic Press.

Holmes, R. L. & Ball, J. N. (1974). *The pituitary gland.* Cambridge: University Press.

Hopp, R. J. (1974). Plant phenology observation networks. In *Phenology and seasonality modeling*: 25–43. Lieth, H. (ed.). Berlin: Springer.

Horn, M. H. (1972). The amount of space available for marine and freshwater fishes. *Fish. Bull. US. natn. ocean. atmos. Admn* **70**: 1295–1297.

Htun-Han, M. (1977). The effects of photoperiod on reproduction in fishes—an annotated bibliography. *MAFF Div. Fish. Res. Libr. Inf. Leafl.* No. 6: 1–30.

Hubbell, S. P. (1971). Of sowbugs and systems: the ecological energetics of a terrestrial isopod. In *Systems analysis and simulation in ecology* 1: 269–323. Patten, B. C. (ed.). New York & London: Academic Press.

Hyodo-Taguchi, Y. (1968). Rate of development of intestinal damage in the goldfish after X-irradiation and mucosal cell kinetics at different temperatures. *Proc. Symp. Gastrointest Rad. Inj., Wash.*: 25–28.

Idler, D. R. & Clemens, W. A. (1959). The energy expenditures of Fraser River sockeye salmon during the spawning migration to Chilko and Stuart Lakes: 1–80. (Quoted in Brett, 1972.)

Ihne, E. & Hoffmann, D. (1884). *Beiträge zur Phänologie*. Giessen: the authors.

Iles, T. D. (1974). The tactics and strategy of growth in fishes. In *Sea fisheries research*: 331–345. Harden Jones, F. R. (ed.). London: Elek Science.

Irie, T. (1960). The growth of the fish otolith. *J. Fac. Fish. Anim. Husb. Hiroshima Univ.* 3: 203–229.

Jalabert, B. (1976). *In vitro* oocyte maturation and ovulation in rainbow trout (*Salmo gairdneri*), northern pike (*Esox lucius*), and goldfish (*Carassius auratus*). *J. Fish. Res. Bd Can.* 33: 974–988.

Jones, D. D. & Walters, C. J. (1976). Catastrophe theory and fisheries regulation *J. Fish. Res. Bd Can.* 33: 2829–2833.

Jones, R. & Johnston, C. (1977). Growth, reproduction and mortality in gadoid fish species. In *Fisheries mathematics*: 37–62. Steele, J. H. (ed.). London & New York: Academic Press.

Kenmuir, D. H. S. (1973). Observations on a breeding pair of *Tilapia rendalli rendalli* Boulenger 1896 in an experimental tank at Lake Kariba Fisheries Research Institute. *Hydrobiologica* 43: 365–370.

Kuo, C.-M. & Nash, C. E. (1975). Recent progress on the control of ovarian development and induced spawning of the grey mullet (*Mugil cephalus* L.). *Aquacult.* 5: 19–29.

Larkin, P. A. (1973). Some observations on models of stock and recruitment relationships for fishes. *Rapp. P.-v. Cons. perm. int. Explor. Mer* 164: 316–324.

Larkin, P. A. (1977). An epitaph for the concept of maximum sustained yield. *Trans. Am. Fish. Soc.* 106: 1–11.

Larkin, P. A. & McDonald, J. G. (1968). Factors in the population biology of the Skeena River. *J. Anim. Ecol.* 37: 229–258.

Le Cren, E. D. (1958). Observations on the growth of perch (*Perca fluviatilis* L.) over twenty-two years with special reference to the effects of temperature and changes in population density. *J. Anim. Ecol.* 27: 287–334.

Leatherland, J. F., McKeown, B. A. & John, T. M. (1974). Circadian rhythm of plasma prolactin, growth hormone, glucose and free fatty acid in juvenile kokanee salmon, *Oncorhynchus nerka. Comp. Biochem. Physiol.* 47A: 821–828.

Lee, S.-C. (1974). *Biology of the sand goby* Pomatoschistus minutus (*Pallas*) (*Teleostei: Gobioidei*) *in the Plymouth area*. Ph. D. Thesis: University of Bristol.

Li, H. W. & Brocksen, R. W. (1977). Approaches to the analysis of energetic costs of intraspecific competition for space by rainbow trout (*Salmo gairdneri*). *J. Fish Biol.* 11: 329–341.

Liddell, H. G. & Scott, R. (1940). *A Greek–English lexicon*. 9th edition, revised by H. Stuart Jones. Oxford: Clarendon Press.

Lieth, H. (1974). Purposes of a phenology book. In *Phenology and seasonality modeling*: 3–19. Lieth, H. (ed.). Berlin: Springer.

Love, R. M. (1970). *The chemical biology of fishes*. London & New York: Academic Press.

Macdonald, A. M. (ed.) (1972). *Chambers twentieth century dictionary*. Edinburgh: Chambers.
MacKinnon, J. C. (1972). Summer storage of energy and its use for winter metabolism and gonad maturation in American plaice (*Hippoglossoides platessoides*). *J. Fish. Res. Bd Can.* **29**: 1749–1759.
Marshall, N. B. (1965). *The life of fishes*. London: Weidenfeld & Nicolson.
Matty, A. J. (1978). Pineal and some pituitary hormone rhythms in fish. In *Rhythmic activity of fishes*: 21–30. Thorpe, J. E. (ed.). London & New York: Academic Press.
McKeown, B. A. & Peter, R. E. (1976). The effect of photoperiod and temperature on the release of prolactin from the pituitary gland of the goldfish, *Carassius auratus* L. *Can. J. Zool.* **54**: 1960–1968.
Medawar, P. B. (1945). Size, shape and age. In *Essays on growth and form presented to D'Arcy Wentworth Thompson*: 157–187. Le Gros Clark, W. C. & Medawar, P. B. (eds). Oxford: Clarendon Press.
Meier, A. H. & Burns, J. T. (1976). Circadian hormone rhythms in lipid regulation. *Am. Zool.* **16**: 649–659.
Miller, P. J. (1961). Age, growth, and reproduction of the rock goby, *Gobius paganellus* L., in the Isle of Man. *J. mar. biol. Ass. U.K.* **41**: 737–769.
Miller, P. J. (1963). *Studies on the biology and taxonomy of British gobioid fishes*. Ph.D. Thesis: Liverpool University.
Miller, P. J. (1965). The biology of the goby *Pomatoschistus microps*. *Rep. Challenger Soc.* **3**: 42–43.
Miller, P. J. (1973). Effects of photoperiod on growth in gobiid fish. *Proc. Challenger Soc.* **4**: 197–198.
Miller, P. J. (1975). Age-structure and life-span in the common goby, *Pomatoschistus microps*. *J. Zool., Lond.* **177**: 425–448.
Morris, R. W. & Kittleman, L. R. (1967). Piezoelectric property of otoliths. *Science, N.Y.* **158**: 368–370.
Murray, J. A. E. (1888). *A new English dictionary on historical principles; founded mainly on the material collected by the Philological Society*. 7(2). Oxford: Clarendon Press.
Nikolskii, G. V. (1969). *Theory of fish population dynamics as the biological background for rational exploitation and management of fishery resources*. Edinburgh: Oliver & Boyd.
Northcote, T. G. (1978). Migratory strategies and production in freshwater fishes. In *Ecology of freshwater fish production*: 326–359. Gerking, S. D. (ed.). Oxford: Blackwell Scientific Publications.
O'Connor, J. M. (1972). Pituitary gonadotropin release patterns in pre-spawning brook trout, *Salvelinus fontinalis*, rainbow trout, *Salmo gairdneri* and leopard frogs, *Rana pipiens*. *Comp. Biochem. Physiol.* **43A**: 739–746.
Ohno, S. (1970). *Evolution by gene duplication*. London: Allen & Unwin.
Olla, B. L. & Studholme, A. L. (1978). Comparative aspects of the activity rhythms of tautog, *Tautoga onitis*, bluefish, *Pomatomus saltatrix*, and Atlantic mackerel, *Scomber scombrus*, as related to their life habits. In *Rhythmic activity of fishes*: 131–151. Thorpe, J. E. (ed.). London & New York: Academic Press.
Ottaway, E. M. & Simkiss, K. (1977). "Instantaneous" growth rates of fish scales and their use in studies of fish populations. *J. Zool., Lond.* **181**: 407–419.
Palmer, J. D. (1976). *An introduction to biological rhythms*. New York & London: Academic Press.

Pannella, G. (1971). Fish otoliths: daily growth layers and periodical patterns. *Science, N.Y.* **173**: 1124–1126.

Pannella, G. (1974). Otolith growth patterns: an aid in age determination in temperate and tropical fishes. In *Ageing of fish*: 28–39. Bagenal, T. B. (ed.). Old Woking, Surrey: Gresham Press.

Pennycuick, L. (1971). Quantitative effects of three species of parasites on a population of three-spined sticklebacks, *Gasterosteus aculeatus. J. Zool., Lond.* **165**: 143–162.

Phleger, C. F., Patton, J., Grimes, P., & Lee, R. F. (1976). Fish-bone oil: percent total body lipid and carbon-14 uptake following feeding of 1-^{14}C-palmitic acid. *Mar. Biol.* **35**: 85–89.

Pianka, E. R. (1976). Natural selection of optimal reproductive tactics. *Am. Zool.* **16**: 775–784.

Pickering, A. D. & Macey, D. J. (1977). Structure, histochemistry and the effect of handling on the mucus cells of the epidermis of the char *Salvelinus alpinus* (L.). *J. Fish Biol.* **10**: 505–512.

Pitcher, T. J. & MacDonald, P. D. M. (1973). Two models for seasonal growth in fishes. *J. appl. Ecol.* **10**: 599–606.

Pope, J. G. (1973). An investigation into the effects of variable rates of the exploitation of fishery resources. In *The mathematical theory of the dynamics of biological populations*: 23–34. Bartlett, M. S. & Hiorns, R. W. (eds). London & New York: Academic Press.

Popova, O. A. (1978). The role of predaceous fish in ecosystems. In *Ecology of freshwater fish production*: 215–249. Gerking, S. D. (ed.). Oxford: Blackwell Scientific Publications.

Preston, T. A. (1883). Report on the phenological observations for the year 1882. *Nature, Lond.* **27**: 234.

Qasim, S. Z. (1956). Time and duration of the spawning season in some marine teleosts in relation to their distribution. *J. Cons. perm. int. Explor. Mer* **21**: 144–155.

Ricker, W. E. (1954). Stock and recruitment. *J. Fish. Res. Bd Can.* **11**: 599–623.

Ricker, W. E. (1975). Computation and interpretation of biological statistics of fish populations. *Bull. Fish. Res. Bd Can.* No. 191: 1–382.

Robertson, O. H. (1961). Prolongation of the life span of kokanee salmon (*Oncorhynchus nerka kennerlyi*) by castration before beginning of gonad development. *Proc. natn. Acad. Sci. U.S.A.* **47**: 609–621.

Rosenthal, H. & Paffenhöfer, G.-A. (1972). On the digestion rate and calorific content of food and feces in young gar fish. *Naturwissenschaften* **59**: 274–275.

Schoener, T. W. (1971). Theory of feeding strategies. *A. Rev. Ecol. Syst.* **2**: 369–404.

Schwassmann, H. O. (1971). Biological rhythms. *Fish Physiol.* **6**: 371–428.

Shackley, S. E. & King, P. E. (1977). The reproductive cycle and its control; frequency of spawning and fecundity in *Blennius pholis* L. *J. exp. mar. Biol. Ecol.* **30**: 73–83.

Shelford, V. E. (1930). Phenology and one of its modern descendants. *Q. Rev. Biol.* **5**: 207–216.

Shepherd, C. J. (1975). The economics of aquaculture—a review. *Oceanogr. mar. Biol. Ann. Rev.* **13**: 413–420.

Shulman, G. E. (1974). *Life cycles of fish.* New York: Wiley.

Simpson, T. H. (1978). An interpretation of some endocrine rhythms in fish. In *Rhythmic activity of fishes*: 55–68. Thorpe, J. E. (ed.). London & New York: Academic Press.

Singh, T. P. (1967). Influence of photoperiods on the seasonal fluctuations of TSH content of the pituitary in a freshwater catfish, *Mystus vittatus* (Bloch). *Experientia* **23**: 1016–1017.

Smith, A. (1970). *The seasons.* London: Weidenfeld & Nicholson.

Sollberger, A. (1962). General properties of biological rhythms. *Ann. NY. Acad. Sci.* **98**: 757–774.

Sperber, O., From, J. & Sparre, P. (1977). A method to estimate the growth rate of fishes, as a function of temperature and feeding level, applied to rainbow trout. *Medded. Danm. Fisk.-Havunders.* (N.S) **7**: 275–317.

Stearns, S. C. (1976). Life-history tactics: a review of the ideas. *Q. Rev. Biol.* **51**: 3–47.

Stearns, S. C. (1977). The evolution of life history traits: a critique of the theory and a review of the data. *A. Rev. Ecol. Syst.* **8**: 145–171.

Struhsaker, P. & Uchiyama, J. H. (1976). Age and growth of the nehu, *Stolephorus purpureus* (Pisces: Engraulidae), from the Hawaiian Islands as indicated by daily growth increments of sagittae. *Fishery Bull., U.S.* **74**: 9–17.

Sundararaj, B. I. & Vasal, S. (1976). Photoperiod and temperature control in the regulation of reproduction in the female catfish *Heteropneustes fossilis. J. Fish. Res. Bd Can.* **33**: 959–973.

Swan, J. G. (1880). The eulachon or candle-fish of the north west coast. *Proc. U.S. natn. Mus.* **3**: 257–264.

Swift, D. R. (1960). Cyclical activity of the thyroid gland of fish in relation to environmental changes. *Symp. zool. Soc. Lond.* No. 2: 17–27.

Swift, D. R. & Pickford, G. E. (1965). Seasonal variations in the hormone content of the pituitary gland of the perch, *Perca fluviatilis* L. *Gen. comp. Endocr.* **5**: 354–365.

Taubert, B. D. & Coble, D. W. (1977). Daily rings in otoliths of three species of *Lepomis* and *Tilapia mossambica. J. Fish. Res. Bd Can.* **34**: 332–340.

Taylor, F. G. (1974). Phenodynamics of production in a mesic deciduous forest. In *Phenology and seasonality modeling*: 237–254. Lieth, H. (ed.). Berlin: Springer.

Taylor, H. M., Gourley, R. S., Lawrence, C. E. & Kaplan, R. S. (1974). Natural selection of life history attributes: an analytical approach. *Theoret. pop. Biol.* **5**: 104–122.

Taylor, L. R. & Taylor, R. A. J. (1977). Aggregation, migration and population mechanics. *Nature, Lond.* **265**: 415–421.

Thompson, W. F. (1959). An approach to population dynamics of the Pacific red salmon. *Trans. Am. Fish. Soc.* **88**: 206–209.

Thorpe, J. E. (1977). Daily ration of adult perch, *Perca fluviatilis* L. during summer in Loch Leven, Scotland. *J. Fish Biol.* **11**: 55–68.

Thorpe, J. E. (ed.) (1978). *Rhythmic activity of fishes.* London & New York: Academic Press.

Tinkle, D. W. & Hadley, N. F. (1975). Lizard reproductive effort: caloric estimates and comments on its evolution. *Ecology* **56**: 427–434.

Valiela, I., Wright, J. E., Teal, J. M. & Volkmann, S. B. (1977). Growth, production and energy transformations in the salt-marsh killifish *Fundalus heteroclitus. Mar. Biol.* **40**: 135–144.

von Bertalanffy, L. (1960). Principles and theory of growth. In *Fundamental aspects of normal and malignant growth*: 137–259. Nowinski, W. W. (ed.). Amsterdam: Elsevier.

Walters, C. J. & Hilborn, R. (1976). Adaptive control of fishing systems. *J. Fish. Res. Bd Can.* **33**: 145–159.

Warren, C. E. & Davis, G. E. (1967). Laboratory studies on the feeding bioener-getics, and growth of fish. In *The biological basis of freshwater fish production*: 175–214. Gerking, S. D. (ed.). Oxford: Blackwell Scientific Publications.

Weatherley, A. H. (1972). *Growth and ecology of fish populations*. New York & London: Academic Press.

Weatherley, A. H. (1976). Factors affecting maximisation of fish growth. *J. Fish. Res. Bd Can.* **33**: 1046–1058.

Weatherley, A. H. & Rogers, S. C. (1978). Some aspects of age and growth. In *Ecology of freshwater fish production*: 52–74. Gerking, S. D. (ed.). Oxford: Blackwell Scientific Publications.

Webb, P. W. (1978). Partitioning of energy into metabolism and growth. In *Ecology of freshwater fish production*: 184–214. Gerking, S. D. (ed.). Oxford: Blackwell Scientific Publications.

Wielgolaski, F. E. (1974). Phenology in agriculture. In *Phenology and seasonality modeling*: 369–381. Lieth, H. (ed.). Berlin: Springer.

Wilimovsky, N. J. (1976). Obtaining protein from the oceans: opportunities and constraints. *Trans. N. Am. Wildl. nat. Res. Conf.* **41**: 58–78.

Williams, C. B. (1949). The biology of the seasons. *New Nat.* No. 5: 2–14.

Williams, G. C. (1966). *Adaptation and natural selection*. Princeton: Princeton University Press.

Wimsatt, W. C. (1976). Complexity and organization. In *Topics in the philosophy of biology*: 174–193. Grene, M. & Mendelsohn, E. (eds). Boston: Reidel.

Wingfield, J. C. & Grimm, A. S. (1977). Seasonal changes in plasma cortisol, testosterone and oestradiol-17β in the plaice, *Pleuronectes platessa* L. *Gen. comp. Endocr.* **31**: 1–11.

Winn, H. E. (1955). Formation of a mucous envelope at night by parrot fishes. *Zoologica, N.Y.* **40**: 145–147.

Winn, H. E. & Bardach, J. E. (1959). Differential food selection by moray eels and a possible role of the mucous envelope of parrot fishes in reduction of predation. *Ecology* **40**: 296–298.

Wirtz, P. (1974). The influence of the sight of a conspecific on the growth of *Blennius pholis* (Pisces Teleostei). *J. comp. Physiol.* **91**: 161–165.

Woodhead, A. D. (1975). Endocrine physiology of fish migration. *Oceanogr. mar. Biol. Ann. Rev.* **13**: 287–382.

Yu, M.-L. & Perlmutter, A. (1970). Growth inhibiting factors in the zebra fish, *Brachydanio rerio* and the blue gourami, *Trichogaster trichopterus*. *Growth* **34**: 153–175.

Symp. zool. Soc. Lond. (1979) No. 44, 29–61

Energetics of Freshwater Teleosts

J. M. ELLIOTT

Freshwater Biological Association, Windermere Laboratory, The Ferry House, Ambleside, Cumbria, England

SYNOPSIS

The energy budget of a fish can be divided into four components: energy intake, energy losses in faeces and excretory products, energy required for metabolism and the total change in the energy value of body materials (growth or loss in energy content). Quantitative work on these components is reviewed with special emphasis on freshwater teleosts. The problems of estimating the daily energy intake in the field are discussed and most methods are shown to be inadequate chiefly because they ignore the assumption of an exponential rate of gastric evacuation. Quantitative changes in the maximum, maintenance and optimal energy intakes are examined and it is concluded that energy intake should never be expressed as a percentage of fish weight. The various factors affecting the energy losses in the waste products are considered and it is shown that these losses should never be assumed to be a constant fraction of the daily energy intake. Estimates of metabolism from measurements of oxygen consumption and from the other components of the energy budget are shown to be comparable, but the weight exponent must not be assumed to be constant for different levels of metabolism. The various factors affecting growth and growth efficiency are discussed and the energy content per unit weight of fish is shown to vary markedly. Finally, some growth models are briefly examined and criticized.

INTRODUCTION

All animals must obtain their energy requirements from their food. Some constituents of the food are used for catabolism and anabolism (carbohydrates, fats, proteins) whilst others do not provide any energy but are essential (minerals, vitamins, water). As the latter constituents are not included in energy budgets, they may be forgotten, but it is important to remember in any study of bioenergetics that the absence of essential vitamins and minerals will lead to poor growth even though the energy intake is adequate for growth.

Kleiber (1961a) has described the history of bioenergetics from its early beginnings in the 18th century, and has also emphasized (Kleiber 1961b) the importance of the classic work of Brody (1945). The study of energy budgets for fish was pioneered by Ivlev (1939a,b,c, 1945, 1961) and grew rapidly after Winberg (1956, 1961, 1962) reviewed the literature and developed his "balanced equation". Although the work of Fry (e.g. 1947, 1957, 1971) has been chiefly on respiration of fish, it has had a profound influence on the study of energetics. The International Biological Programme (IBP) was responsible for an increased interest in

fish bioenergetics and the IBP book edited by Gerking (1967) contains
reviews of the literature, whilst the methodology is reviewed in the
companion volume edited by Ricker (1971). More recent reviews are
those of Phillips (1969, 1972), Hastings & Dickie (1972), Weatherley
(1972) and Beamish, Niimi & Lett (1975).

This paper is a selective review of work on the various components of
the energy budget, and is deliberately biased towards quantitative studies
in which the data have been analysed in detail. Most of the examples are
from my own work on brown trout, not only because I am familiar with
this work but also because it is one of the few attempts to describe the
major components of the energy budget in terms of equations developed
from the results of a large number of experiments. The final part of the
review considers some of the models used to describe the relationship
between growth and the amount of food consumed by the fish. Symbols
originally defined by Ricker (1971) are used throughout this review.
Energy units are given in calories but can be converted to absolute joules
($1 \, cal = 4 \cdot 184 \, J$) as recommended by the Royal Society (1972).

THE COMPONENTS OF THE ENERGY BUDGET

An energy budget for a given period of time is described by the basic
equation:

$$C = F + U + \Delta B + R \tag{1}$$

where

$$R = R_s + R_a + R_d$$

C is the total energy content of the food consumed by the fish, F is the
energy value of the faeces, U is the energy value of the excretory
products, ΔB is the total change in the energy value of body materials
(growth or loss in energy content) and includes any reproductive
products released by the fish, R is the total energy of metabolism and is
subdivided into three components: R_s is the energy equivalent to that
released in the course of metabolism in unfed and resting fish (standard
metabolism), R_a is the energy required for swimming and other activity,
R_d is the energy required for the processes of digestion, movement and
deposition of food materials (including specific dynamic action).

The relationships between these components are summarized in Fig.
1. Additional symbols in Fig. 1 are the proportions of the daily energy
intake lost in the faeces (P_F), lost in the excretory products (P_U), absorbed
by the fish (P_A) and available for growth and metabolism (P_P). The latter
component may also be called the physiologically useful energy (Winberg,
1956) or metabolizable energy (Beamish et al., 1975). The energy
requirements for absorption, digestion and transportation of food are
distinct from those for specific dynamic action (SDA) but experimentally

Daily energy intake
$C = F + U + \Delta B + R$

% loss in
faeces $(100P_F)$

Faeces
$F = CP_F$

% loss in
excretory products
$100\ P_u$

% efficiency
$100\ P_P$

Absorbed materials
$C - F = CP_A$

Excretory products
$U = CP_u$

% Gross eficiency
$100\ \Delta B/C$

Physiologically useful
energy
$C-F-U = CP_P$

Growth or loss
$\Delta B = C-F-U-R$
$= CP_P - R$

Metabolism
$R=C-F-U-\Delta B$
$=CP_P - \Delta B$
$=R_s + R_a + R_d$

Standard metabolism
$R_s = R-R_a-R_d$

Activity
$R_a =R-R_s-R_d$

Digestion, movement,
deposition of food
$R_d = R-R_s-R_a$

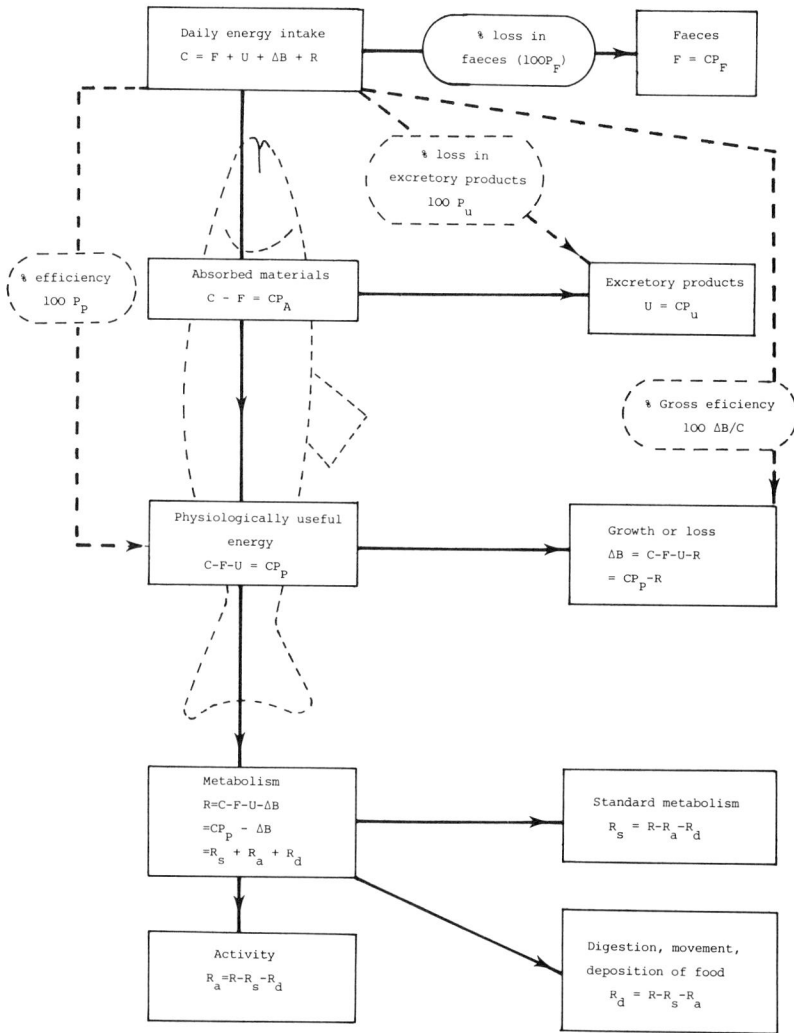

FIG. 1. Summary of the losses and uses of the daily energy intake of a trout. The boxes contain the major components of the energy budget and the ovals contain the percentage efficiencies of changes between these major components. Direct pathways are shown as solid lines whilst broken lines indicate pathways which include more than one component.

difficult to separate. Therefore the term "apparent specific dynamic action" can be used for all these energy requirements (Beamish, 1974) and its equivalent to R_d. Although the relationships given in Fig. 1 are in general agreement with the schemes proposed by other workers (e.g. Ivlev, 1939c; Winberg, 1956; Warren & Davis, 1967; Brett, 1970), the position of apparent SDA has been criticized by Niimi & Beamish (1974) who have suggested that it would be better placed between energy losses in the faeces and energy losses in the excretory products. Their argument is that absorbed amino acids must be deaminated or transaminated, chiefly in the liver, to provide compounds for storage or utilization whilst the liberated NH groups are either excreted or available for the synthesis of new amino acids. This disagreement cannot be resolved until more is known about the role of the component R_d in the energy budget.

Daily Energy Intake

Estimation in the field

The daily food consumption of a fish in a tank can be measured directly, but it is more difficult to measure food consumption in the field. Various indirect methods have been used or proposed, and these include the estimation of the total energy requirements of the fish, i.e. F, U, ΔB and R are estimated and their sum is assumed to be an estimate of C (e.g. Winberg, 1956; Mann, 1965, 1967; Healey, 1972; Morgan, 1974), the estimation of the nitrogen requirements from a nitrogen budget (e.g. Meien et al., 1937; Gerking, 1954, 1962; Shul'man, 1962; Karzinkin & Krivobok, 1964; Smith & Thorpe, 1976), and use of a known relationship between food consumption and growth rate (e.g. Allen, 1951; Horton, 1961; Warren et al., 1964; Paloheimo & Dickie, 1965, 1966a, b; Carline & Hall, 1973; Elliott, 1975c,d). Some of the models used in the latter relationship will be discussed later. As these indirect methods are only suitable for mean estimates over long periods of time, there are good practical reasons for direct estimates of the daily food consumption in the field, especially when information on diel changes in energy intake is required. Kevern (1966) and Kolehmainen (1974) used a radioisotope method to estimate food consumption in the field, but most workers have simply used the stomach contents of fish sampled at regular intervals of time throughout a 24-h period.

The rate at which food passes through the stomach will partially affect the quantity of food in the stomach, the appetite of the fish and the rates of food absorption and faecal losses. It is therefore important to estimate this rate. The reviews of Windell (1967) and Magnuson (1969) show that little attempt was made to fit mathematical models to the data in early studies. More recent work has shown that the rate of gastric evacuation is exponential in a number of species, including cod, *Gadus morhua* L., (Tyler, 1970); sockeye salmon, *Oncorhynchus nerka* Walbaum, (Brett & Higgs, 1970); brown trout, *Salmo trutta* L., (Elliott, 1972); perch, *Perca fluviatilis* L., (Griffiths, 1976; Thorpe, 1977) and bluegill, *Lepomis macrochirus* Raf., (El-Shamy, 1976), but not in largemouth bass, *Micropterus salmoides* Lacepède, (Beamish, 1972). As enzyme reactions are essentially exponential processes (Fábián, Molnár & Tölg, 1963; Jennings, 1965), it is not surprising that the rate is exponential. The exponential rate is apparently unaffected by fish size, meal size and frequency of feeding (Tyler, 1970; Brett & Higgs, 1970; Elliott, 1972), but is affected by long periods (>seven days) of food deprivation (Elliott, 1972; Griffiths, 1976), by the fat content of the food (Elliott, 1972), and especially by the water temperature (Fig. 2).

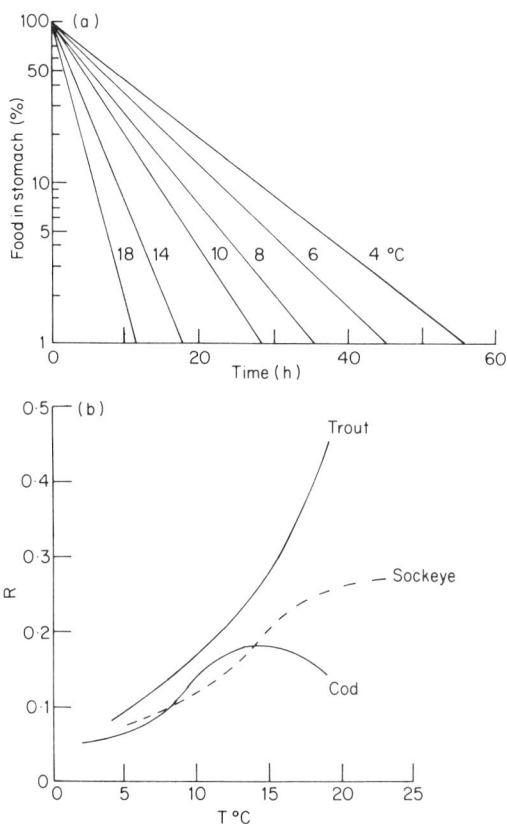

FIG. 2(a). The relationship between the percentage of a meal remaining in the stomach and time at different temperatures (note that ordinate is on log scale). (b) The relationship between the evacuation rate (R) and temperature ($T°C$) for three species of fish.

The relationship between evacuation rate and temperature usually follows an exponential curve (e.g. trout in Fig. 2b) or power law (e.g. sockeye in Fig. 2b) (Molnár & Tölg, 1962; Fábián et al., 1963; Molnár, Tamássy & Tölg, 1967; Brett & Higgs, 1970; Edwards, 1971; Elliott, 1972; Schneider, 1973; Maliyenko, 1975; Windell et al., 1976). Cod are exceptional (Fig. 2b) because they have an optimal (15°C) rather than a maximum temperature for gastric evacuation (Tyler, 1970). More general equations for trout estimate the rate and time for the gastric evacuation of different food organisms at temperatures between 3·8 and 19·1°C (Elliott, 1972). These equations have been applied not only to brown trout in the laboratory but also to brown and rainbow trout, *Salmo gairdneri* Rich., in a Pyrenean stream (Elliott, 1973). Similar equations are needed for other species so that realistic methods can be developed to estimate the daily food consumption and hence the daily energy intake of fish in the field.

Direct methods for estimating food consumption in the field were reviewed by Elliott & Persson (1978) who have shown that most of these methods ignore the assumption of an exponential rate of gastric evacuation. The popular method of Bajkov (1935) grossly underestimates the daily food consumption, and the more recent methods of Staples (1975a,b) and Thorpe (1977) also provide low values. Two new methods were proposed by Elliott & Persson (1978). Both methods assume that the evacuation rate is exponential, the first method assumes that the feeding rate is constant whilst the second assumes that this rate decreases with time within the period between sampling. The latter period should be about three hours so that nine samples are taken over a 24-h period. In the first model the amount of food consumed (C_t) increases linearly whilst the stomach contents (S_t) increase curvilinearly, but in the second model C_t increases to an asymptote whilst S_t increases to a maximum and then decreases to a final value that is much lower than the final value of S_t in the first model (Fig. 3).

The first method was found to be adequate for various sizes of trout feeding at different ration levels, even when feeding was restricted to only a small part of the period between sampling. It was inadequate, and the second method more appropriate, for large fish feeding close to the maximum or satiation level. As large fish will rarely be able to feed to satiation in the field, the simpler first method will be adequate for most situations and the energy intake (C_t) at the end of t hours is given by

$$C_t = \frac{(S_t - S_0\, e^{-Rt})Rt}{1 - e^{-Rt}} \qquad (2)$$

where S_0 and S_t are the stomach contents at the beginning and end of the period between sampling (0–t h) and R is the evacuation rate. A slightly simplified version of eqn (2) has recently been used to estimate the daily energy intake of perch in Windermere (Craig, 1978). Large fish may feed close to satiation when they are reared in enclosures and the second method may be more appropriate:

$$C_t = C_{\max} - (C_{\max} - S_0)\, e^{-bt} \qquad (3)$$

where $C_{\max}$ is the satiation amount and b is a constant that can be found

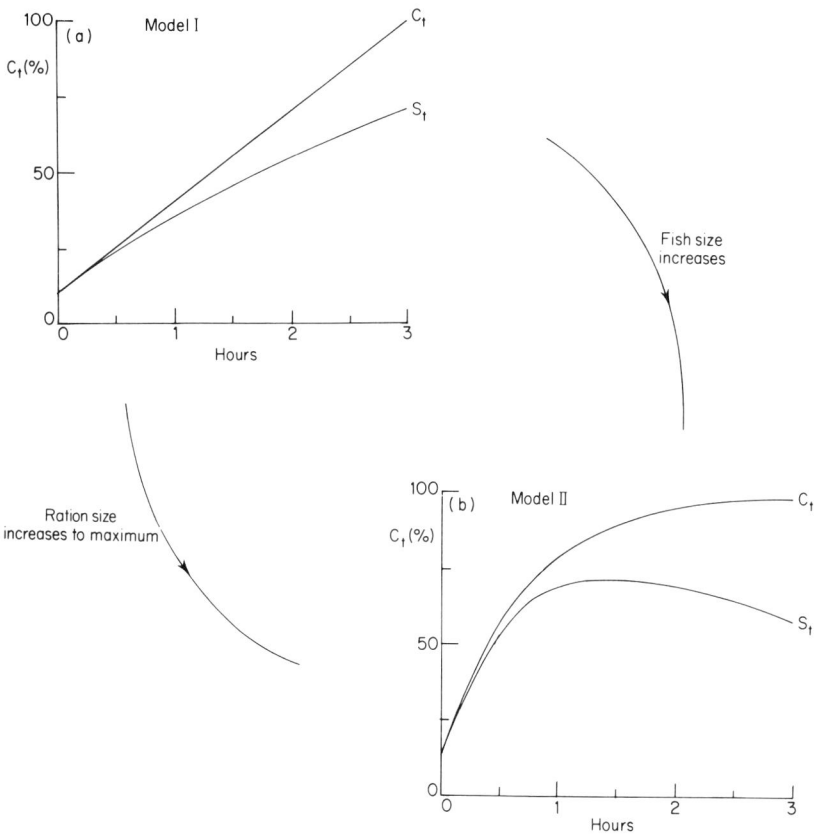

FIG. 3. Changes in the amounts of food consumed (C_t) and in stomach (S_t) over three hours: (a) according to the first model; (b) according to the second model.

from a complex equation describing the change in stomach content with time (see Elliott & Persson, 1978). With both methods, the daily energy intake is simply estimated by ΣC_t over 24 h. Although these two methods may not be applicable to all species of fish, they are based on realistic assumptions and are therefore an improvement on earlier methods. The adequacy of the new methods cannot be assessed until they have been tested on many species of freshwater fish with different patterns of feeding.

The problems of estimating the daily energy intake have been discussed in detail because this component is one of the weakest links in the calculation of energy budgets for fish in the field. Even when the energy intake is estimated indirectly from the sum of the other components of the energy budget or from growth models, a direct estimate should also be made so that the adequacy of the indirect method can be checked. The need for such a procedure is well illustrated by a study of energy budgets for the sand goby, *Pomatoschistus minutus* (Pallas), (Healey, 1972).

Maximum, maintenance and optimal energy intake

It is important to estimate levels of energy intake that produce known responses. The obvious lower limit is zero energy intake and the upper limit is the maximum energy intake in a day (C_{max}). The maintenance energy intake (C_{min}) maintains a fish without any change in its energy content ($\Delta B = 0$), and the total energy content of the fish decreases (ΔB negative) at an energy intake less than C_{min}. The range between C_{min} and C_{max} is the "scope for growth" or "anabolic scope", and is the range within which the total energy content of the fish increases (ΔB positive) (Warren & Davis, 1967; Elliott, 1976c; Brett, 1976a,b).

If the maximum energy intake in a meal (= satiation ration) and the number of meals in a day are known, then C_{max} can be calculated. Several workers have found that both fish weight and water temperature affect the satiation ration and hence C_{max} (e.g. Brett, Shelbourn & Shoop, 1969; Brett & Higgs, 1970; Brett, 1971; Niimi & Beamish, 1974; Elliott, 1975a,b; Staples, 1975b; Sperber, From & Sparre, 1977). There has been little attempt to develop general equations to describe the relationship between these variables but the following equation was suitable for brown trout (Elliott, 1975a,b,c)

$$Y = aW^{b_1} e^{b_2 T} \tag{4}$$

where Y is either the satiation ration (Q cal day^{-1}) or C_{max} cal day^{-1}, W g is the live weight of the trout, $T°C$ is the water temperature, and a, b_1 and b_2 are constants over certain temperature ranges (values given in Table I). This equation estimates the energy intake of trout of different weights at different temperatures (Fig. 4a–c). The satiation ration increases with temperature to a plateau between 13 and 18°C, then decreases rapidly. These changes also illustrate the effect of temperature on voluntary food intake or "appetite" in trout. The number of meals per day (N) is not significantly affected by fish weight but increases from one meal at about 4°C to three meals at about 18°C. The final estimates of C_{max} are applicable to trout in the weight range 5–300 g at temperatures between 4 and 22°C. There is a marked decrease in the daily intake above 18°C.

The weight exponent in eqn (4) varied between 0·753 and 0·767 for trout, depending upon the temperature range (Table I), but values as low as 0·547 (Staples, 1975b) and as high as 0·837 (Sperber *et al.*, 1977) have been recorded for other species. Several workers express the daily food consumption as a proportion of fish weight. As the weight exponent is usually less than one, this proportion will decrease as fish weight increases and comparisons cannot be made unless fish of similar weight are used. Therefore the daily energy intake should never be expressed as a proportion of fish weight.

Few workers have examined the time taken to satiate a fish in one meal, but rainbow trout were satiated in one hour at 10°C (Ishiwata, 1968) and sockeye salmon were satiated in one hour at 15°C, independent of size (Brett, 1971). In a detailed study of satiation time in brown trout (Elliott, 1975a,b), both fish weight and temperature affected the satiation time (t_{sat} min) and the relationship was well described by eqn (4) with $Y = t_{sat}$. The graphical presentation of the equation shows that a small trout of less than 10 g is satiated in less than 10 min whilst a large fish of 300 g has to feed continuously over 2 h before it is satiated (Fig. 4d). Therefore the probability of a small trout feeding to satiation in the field is high, but large trout will rarely be able to fulfill their appetite unless food is abundant. These differences in satiation time support the earlier conclusion that eqn (2) will usually be adequate for estimating energy intake because large fish will rarely feed to satiation in the field.

The maintenance energy intake (C_{main}) is also affected by the fish weight and the water temperature (e.g. Brett et al., 1969; Solomon & Brafield, 1972; Kelso, 1972; Niimi & Beamish, 1974; Sperber et al., 1977). In brown trout the relationship between the three variables was well described by eqn (4) with $Y = C_{main}$ (Elliott, 1975d, 1976c). The weight exponent varied between 0·716 and 0·737, and was therefore lower than the values for C_{max} (cf. values of b_1 in Table I). As both C_{max} and C_{main} can

TABLE I

Values of the constants a, b_1 *and* b_2 *in eqns (4) and (5)*

Component	Temperature ($T°C$)	a	$b_1 \pm 95\%$ C.L.	$b_2 \pm 95\%$ C.L.
C_{max}	3·8–6·6	2·902	0·762 ± 0·027	0·418 ± 0·035
	6·6–13·3	15·018	0·759 ± 0·023	0·171 ± 0·012
	13·3–17·8	26.433	0·767 ± 0·041	0·126 ± 0·031
	17·8–21·7	$3·241 \times 10^7$	0·753 ± 0·086	−0·662 ± 0·054
C_{opt}	3·8–6·8	2·902	0·762 ± 0·027	0·418 ± 0·035
	6·8–15·0	15·116	0·767 ± 0·046	0·138 ± 0·011
	15·0–19·5	753·852	0·767 ± 0·017	−0·118 ± 0·006
C_{main}	3·8–6·6	6·169	0·716 ± 0·107	0·224 ± 0·102
	6·6–19·5	12·031	0·737 ± 0·058	0·105 ± 0·016
P_F	3·8–20·4	0·212	−0·222 ± 0·0224	0·631 ± 0·0350
P_u	3·8–20·4	0·0259	0·580 ± 0·0110	−0·299 ± 0·0162
R_{max}	3·8–17·8	3·890	0·770 ± 0·0254	0·204 ± 0·00394
	17·8–19·5	$2·215 \times 10^7$	0·757 ± 0·0208	−0·663 ± 0·0175
	19·5–21·7	28·833	0·756 ± 0·0440	0·0325 ± 0·0288
R_{main}	3·8–7·1	3·802	0·723 ± 0·0998	0·245 ± 0·0811
	7·1–19·5	11·866	0·721 ± 0·0417	0·0915 ± 0·0112
R_s	3·8–7·1	4·126	0·734 ± 0·0257	0·192 ± 0·0125
	7·1–19·5	8·277	0·731 ± 0·0220	0·0938 ± 0·00407

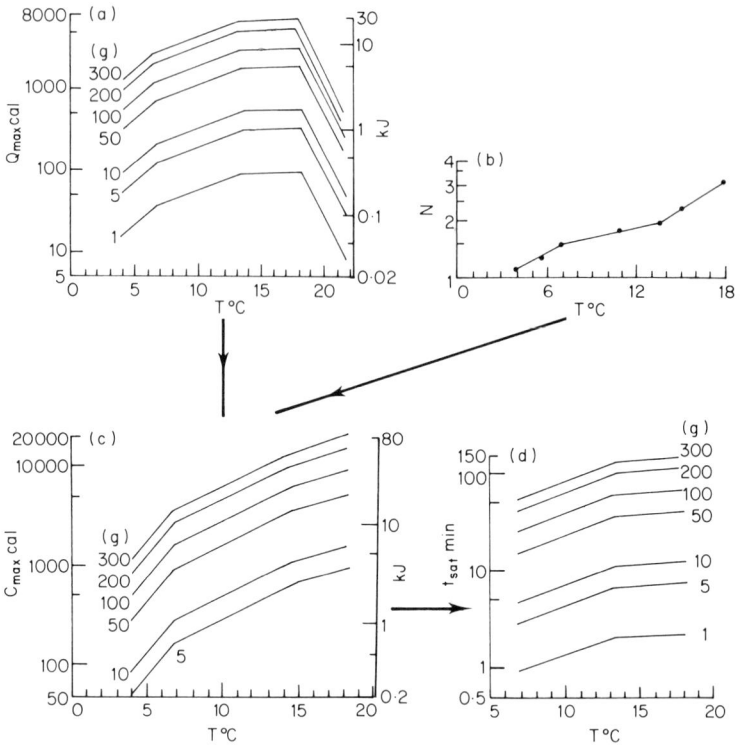

FIG. 4. The relationship between: (a) the maximum energy intake in a meal and water temperature for different live weights of trout; (b) the number of meals in a day and temperature; (c) the maximum energy intake in a day and temperature for different live weights of trout; (d) the satiation time and temperature for different live weights of trout.

be estimated for trout, the "scope for growth" (anabolic scope) can also be estimated for fish in the weight range 5–300 g and the temperature range 3·8–19·5°C. An example for a 50-g trout shows that the scope for growth increases with temperature up to about 18°C and then rapidly decreases to zero at 19·5°C (Fig. 5). A similar pattern has been found in sockeye salmon (Brett, 1976b).

The third level of energy intake that is of value is the optimal level (C_{opt}). This is the energy intake that produces the greatest increase in the energy content of the fish for the least energy intake, and is therefore the value at which gross efficiency ($\Delta B/C$) is maximal. Both fish weight and temperature also affect C_{opt} (Brett *et al.*, 1969; Huisman, 1976), and the relationship for brown trout was once again found to be well described by eqn (4) with $Y = C_{opt}$ (Elliott, 1975d, 1976c). Values of the weight exponent were very similar to those for C_{max} (Table I). The position of

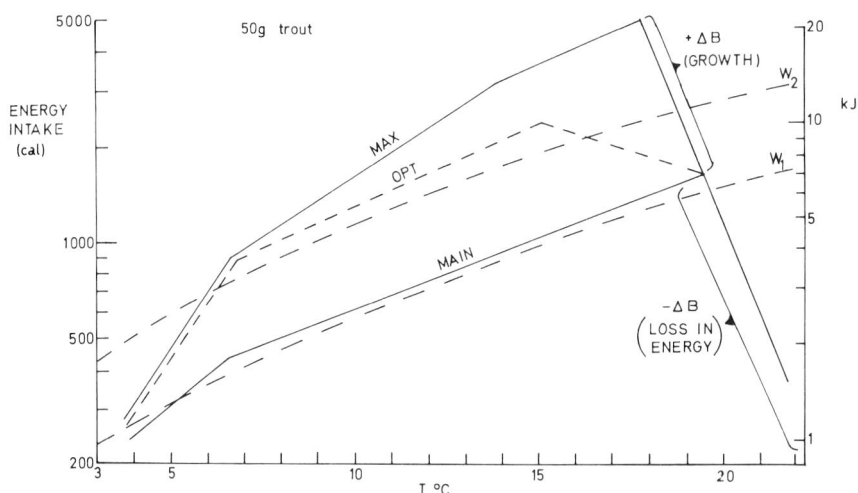

FIG. 5. Relationship between the maximum, optimal and maintenance energy intake (C cal day^{-1}) for trout of 50-g initial weight. Winberg's estimates of the daily energy intake required for resting metabolism (W_1 cal day^{-1}) and twice resting metabolism (W_2 cal day^{-1}) are also given.

C_{opt} within the scope for growth is shown in Fig. 5 and the importance of C_{opt} in relation to gross efficiency will be discussed later.

Although the general energetics equation of Winberg (1956) will be discussed later, it is useful to briefly compare Winberg's estimates of the daily energy intake required for resting metabolism (W_1) and twice resting metabolism (W_2). W_1 is very close to C_{main} in the temperature range 3·8–19·5°C and W_2 is close to C_{opt} in the range 6·5–16·5°C (Fig. 5).

This brief review has shown that it is important to know the maximum, maintenance and optimal daily energy intakes over a wide range of fish sizes and water temperatures. It is obviously preferable that the relationship between energy intake, fish size and temperature is expressed in terms of equations that can be used to estimate C_{max}, C_{main} and C_{opt} for other fish of the same species. Finally, the common practice of expressing energy intake as a proportion of fish weight should cease, because it is valid only in the rare case of a weight exponent of one and because it invalidates comparisons between fish of different sizes.

Energy Losses in the Waste Products

Winberg (1956) first proposed that about 15% of the daily energy intake is lost in the faeces and that 3–5% is lost in the excretory products. He therefore concluded that about 80% of the energy intake was available for growth and metabolism, and was therefore called the physiologically useful energy. This figure has been accepted uncritically by many workers in the construction of energy budgets. Few workers have measured the energy losses in the waste products for different fish sizes, ration sizes and water temperatures, and most studies on excretion in fish are actually on the composition of the urine and the problems of salt and water balance.

Energy losses in the faeces (F cal day^{-1}) include not only undigested food but also minute quantities of material secreted by the fish (e.g. mucus), or material sloughed from the gut wall, or even some nitrogenous waste products (e.g. amino acids, uric acid). Faecal losses in carnivorous fish vary from 2 to 31% of the energy intake (Gerking, 1955; Menzel, 1960; Davis & Warren, 1965; Pandian, 1967; Brocksen, Davis & Warren, 1968; Birkett, 1969; Iwata, 1970; Beamish, 1972; Edwards, Finlayson & Steele, 1972; Solomon & Brafield, 1972; Brocksen & Bugge, 1974; Elliott, 1976b). Some workers have also found that the percentage loss in the faeces increases as the ration level increases (Kinne, 1960; Pandian, 1967; Solomon & Brafield, 1972; Elliott, 1976b) and as the temperature decreases (Brocksen & Bugge, 1974; Elliott, 1976b). The size of the fish also affects the absolute losses in the faeces. When these losses were expressed as a proportion (P_F) of the daily energy intake of trout, the values were very similar for different weights of fish and the relationship between P_F, temperature ($T°C$) and ration size expressed as a proportion of the maximum energy intake (C/C_{max}) was given by (Elliott, 1976b)

$$P = aT^{b_1} e^{b_2(C/C_{max})} \tag{5}$$

where $P = P_F$ and a, b_1 and b_2 are constants whose values are given in Table I. P_F decreases as temperature increases and the level of energy intake decreases, and values vary from 31% of the energy intake for fish on maximum rations at 3°C to 11% for fish on the lowest rations at 22°C (Fig. 6a). Therefore Winberg's value of 15% would be too low for most combinations of ration size and temperature. It is also possible to estimate the proportion of the daily energy intake absorbed by the trout ($P_A = 1 - P_F$). The absorption efficiency increases with a decreasing level of energy intake and increasing temperature, but the temperature effect is less marked above about 15°C.

The chief excretory product in freshwater teleosts is ammonia which is excreted primarily from their gills and forms between 80 and 98% of the amino-derived nitrogen in the excretory products of feeding fish (Black, 1957; Kleerekoper & Mogensen, 1959; Brett, 1962; Forster & Goldstein, 1969; Brafield & Solomon, 1972; Brett & Zala, 1975; Elliott, 1976b; Guerin-Ancey, 1976). Urea is the other major excretory product and occasionally forms a high proportion of the total nitrogenous excreta, especially under hatchery conditions or in starving fish (Fromm, 1963; Burrows, 1964; Olson & Fromm, 1971; Brett & Zala, 1975). Other excretory products appearing in very small quantities in the urine are uric acid, creatine, creatinine, amines and amino acids.

METABOLISM AND GROWTH

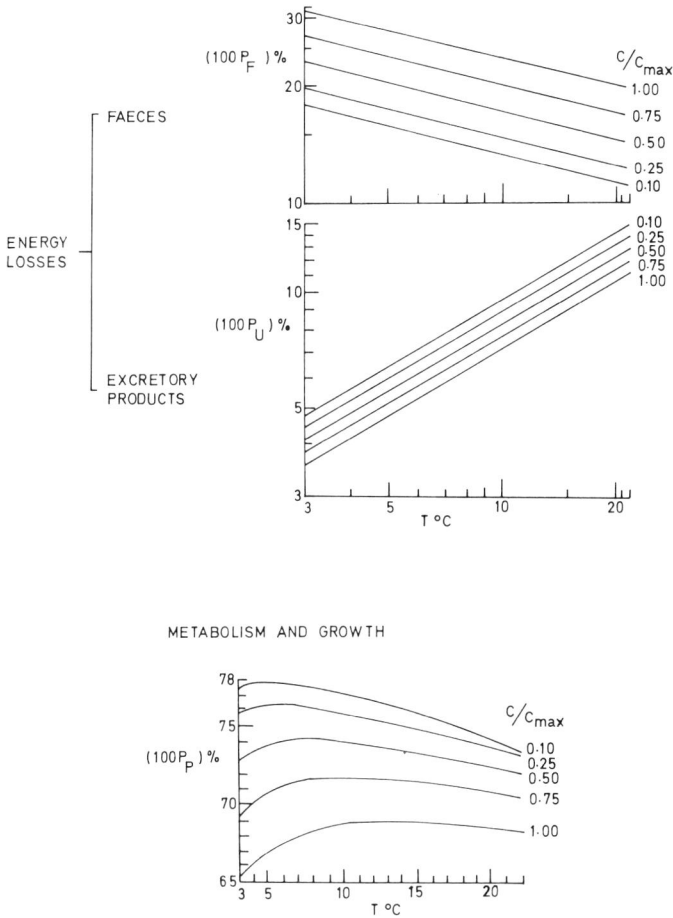

FIG. 6. The relationship between the proportion of the daily energy intake lost in the faeces and excretory products or available for metabolism and growth, and the water temperature at different levels of energy intake (C/C_{max}).

Winberg (1956) erroneously assumed that the energy value of the chief excretory product, ammonia, was negligible. The actual values are $5\cdot94$ cal mg^{-1} for ammonia-nitrogen and $5\cdot51$ cal mg^{-1} for urea-nitrogen (Elliott & Davison, 1975). Therefore the energy losses in the excretory products will be frequently higher than 3–5% of the daily energy intake, this being the range proposed by Winberg.

Energy losses in the excretory products (U cal day^{-1}) increase as both the fish size and the water temperature increase (Savitz, 1969; Elliott, 1976b; Guerin-Ancey, 1976), and are also affected by the ration size (Savitz, 1971; Elliott, 1976b). When these losses were expressed as a proportion (P_u) of the daily energy intake of trout, the values were very similar for different weights of fish and the relationship between P_u, temperature and ration size was well defined by eqn (5) where $P = P_u$ (values of the constants a, b_1 and b_2 are given in Table I). P_u increases as temperature increases and the level of energy intake decreases, and values vary from 3·6% of the energy intake for trout on maximum rations at 3°C to 15·1% for fish on the lowest rations at 22°C (Fig. 6b). Therefore Winberg's value of 3–5% is too low for most combinations of ration size and temperature. As P_F and P_u respond to temperature and level of energy intake in opposite ways, the proportion of the energy intake lost in both faeces and excretory products $(P_F + P_u)$ is less variable than its two components. The proportion of the daily energy intake available for growth and metabolism $(P_P = 1 - P_F - P_u)$ increases as ration size decreases, slightly increases with temperature at low temperatures and slightly decreases with temperature at high temperatures (Fig. 6c). Winberg's value of 0·8 for P_P is obviously too high for brown trout and a range of 0·70–0·75 is more appropriate for most combinations of temperature and ration size.

The composition of the food organisms also affected the energy losses in trout (Elliott, 1976b). As the ratio of fat to protein in the food decreased, P_F increased and P_u decreased. The physiological processes responsible for these variations are not well known but a high fat content reduces the rates of gastric evacuation (Elliott, 1972) and ammonia excretion (Atherton & Aitken, 1970). It is remarkable that these variations in P_F and P_u appeared to cancel each other out, so that the total losses in the waste products were similar with different foods and the value of P_P remained fairly constant at each ration level and temperature.

Energy Required for Metabolism

The total energy of metabolism $(R \text{ cal day}^{-1})$ can be measured directly from measurements of oxygen consumption or indirectly from the other components of the energy budget. Many workers have measured oxygen consumption and it is generally agreed that this is affected by many factors including fish size, water temperature and the activity level (see reviews of Beamish & Dickie, 1967; Fry, 1971; Brett, 1972; Weatherley, 1972). Few workers have attempted to measure metabolic rates directly in the field, but ultrasonic telemetry was recently used for this purpose (Priede & Tytler, 1977; Priede & Young, 1977). In their extensive review of the literature, Paloheimo & Dickie (1966a) concluded that the estimation of metabolism from food intake and growth studies is preferable to its estimation from oxygen consumption because the former can be recorded over extensive periods whereas the latter method is experimentally exacting, necessitates the confinement of fish in special apparatus and is usually limited to short periods of time. The most important difference between the two methods is that the fish are usually unfed in studies of oxygen consumption whereas the important variations in metabolic rate with different foods and ration sizes can be studied by the energy budget method. Beamish (1964a,b) has shown that there are formidable problems in obtaining reliable data on metabolism, especially standard metabolism, because of the complex relationship between metabolism and factors such as oxygen tension and the activity of the fish.

It is difficult to measure the lower and upper limits for metabolism and thus define the "scope for activity" or "scope for metabolism" (Brett, 1976b). The lower limit is usually called the standard metabolism (R_s) and is the energy equivalent to that released in the course of metabolism in unfed, resting fish. The upper limit is active metabolism (F_{max}) and is the maximum sustained rate of oxygen consumption under continuous forced activity. This rate was found to be equivalent to the metabolism of fish fed on maximum rations (Paloheimo & Dickie, 1966a), but this equality will clearly depend upon the maximum sustained swimming speed of the fish. It is also possible to estimate the maintenance metabolism (R_{main}) from the energy budget, and thus the range of metabolism within which growth occurs.

Most workers agree that the relationship between metabolism and fish weight is a power law (e.g. Fig. 7a,b). Values of the weight exponent are very similar in oxygen consumption experiments and feeding experiments, and usually lie between 0·7 and 0·9 with an extreme range of 0·5 to 1·0 (Winberg, 1956, 1961; Beamish, 1964a; Paloheimo & Dickie, 1966a; Fry, 1971; Kamler, 1976). The weight exponent may significantly decrease as the age of the fish increases (Kamler, 1976) or as the level of metabolism decreases (Brett & Glass, 1973; Elliott, 1976c; Staples & Nomura, 1976). Different relationships have been used to describe the effect of temperature on metabolism, and these vary in complexity from the empirical curve of Krogh (Ege & Krogh, 1914) to various multiple regression equations. In a study of brown trout (Elliott, 1976c), the relationship between metabolism, fish weight and water temperature was well described by eqn (4) with $Y = R_{max}$ or R_{main} or R_s. The weight exponents for R_{main} and R_s were much lower than those for R_{max} (cf. values of b_1 in Table I).

As both R_{max} and R_s can be estimated for trout that are not swimming against a strong current, the "scope for activity" can also be estimated in the weight range 5–300 g and the temperature range 3·8–19·5°C. An example for a 50-g trout shows that this scope increases from almost zero at 3·8°C to a maximum at about 18°C and then rapidly decreases to almost zero at 19·5°C (Fig. 7c). Similar changes with temperature have been found in other species, including rainbow trout (Dickson & Kramer, 1971) and sockeye salmon (Brett, 1976b). In trout R_{main} is slightly higher than R_s throughout the temperature range and also lies close to R_{max} at low temperatures (Fig. 7c). Winberg's estimate of the energy required for resting metabolism (W_R) lies between R_s and R_{main} within most of the temperature range 3·8–19·5°C.

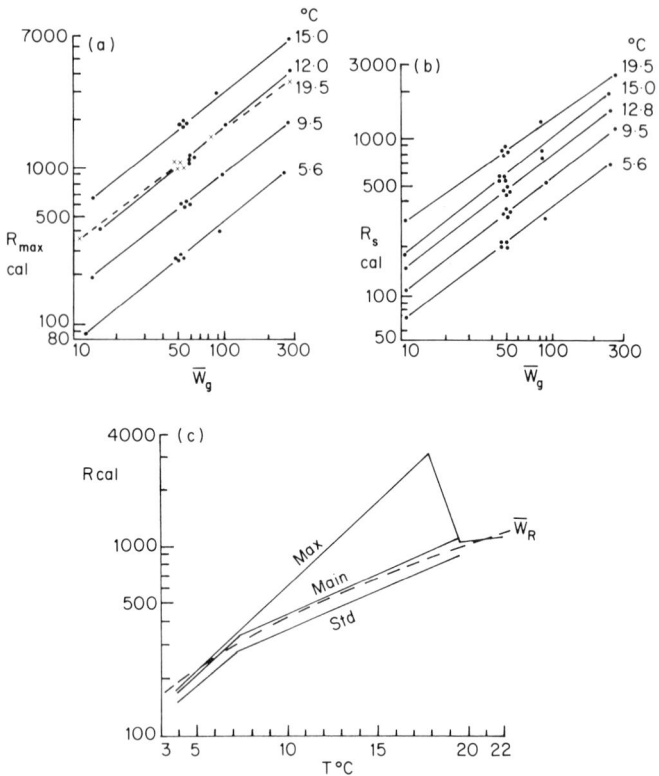

FIG. 7(a). Relationship between the energy required for metabolism (R_{max} cal day^{-1}) and the mean weight of the trout ($\bar{W}g$) at different temperatures (°C) (closed circles and crosses were used for 12·8 and 19·5°C respectively because the values for these temperatures were similar). (b) Relationship between the energy required for standard metabolism (R_s cal day^{-1}) and the mean weight of the trout ($\bar{W}g$) at different temperatures (°C). (c) Comparison between Winberg's estimates of the energy required for resting metabolism (W_R cal day^{-1}) and the energy required for standard, maintenance and maximum metabolism (all figures from Elliott, 1976c, reproduced by permission of the British Ecological Society).

When R_s is subtracted from the total metabolism (R), the remaining energy is required for the other components of metabolism, R_a and R_d. The energy required for swimming and other activity (R_a) includes the energy requirements for catching food, avoiding predators and migrating. Fish activity has proved difficult to measure and there is disagreement on the appropriate terms used to discuss activity (see review of Beamish & Dickie, 1967). The energetic costs of moderate levels of swimming activity are relatively low (Brett, 1964; Brett & Sutherland, 1965), and Warren & Davis (1967) thought it unlikely that swimming activity accounts for a large part of the total metabolism of growing fish. When fish are swimming long distances or against strong currents, the component R_a will obviously increase and may become the major component of metabolism. Webb (1975) has produced an excellent review of the hydrodynamics and energetics of fish propulsion. An interesting method was developed by Feldmeth & Jenkins (1973) who measured the frequency of the caudal-fin beat in undisturbed rainbow trout in a stream, and used a known relationship between this frequency and metabolic rate to estimate the energy expenditure of the swimming fish. Finally the study on rainbow trout by Li & Brocksen (1977) is notable because it is probably the only study in which an attempt was made to estimate the energetic costs of intra-specific competition for space.

The final component of metabolism is the energy required for the processes of digestion, movement and deposition of food materials (R_d). This component is also called "apparent specific dynamic action" (Beamish, 1974) and is often difficult to separate from R_a in feeding fish. When the swimming activity of the fish is low, most of the metabolic requirements within the scope for activity are probably due to R_d and this component increases markedly with increases in temperature and energy intake. Most of this increase in metabolic rate is probably due to the deamination of amino acids, chiefly in the liver, but the exact biochemistry of the process is unknown (Beamish et al., 1975). Apparent specific dynamic action has been measured in only two studies (Muir & Niimi, 1972; Beamish, 1974), and there is an urgent need for more information on this component.

This brief review has shown that estimates of metabolism from measurements of oxygen consumption and from the other components of the energy budget are comparable, and that there are good practical reasons why the latter method is often preferable to the former method. It has also shown that the weight exponent cannot be assumed to be constant for different levels of metabolism in the same species. Although there has been a great deal of work on certain aspects of metabolism in fish, very little is known about the combined effects of activity and energy intake on the components of metabolism.

Total Change in the Energy Content of a Fish

The change in the energy value of a fish (ΔB cal day^{-1}) can be positive or negative. When the daily energy intake is less than the maintenance level, the total energy content of the fish decreases. This decrease is more marked than the corresponding decrease in wet weight because the water content usually increases. Several workers have found that when fish are starved, there is an immediate decrease in fat content followed by a gradual decrease in protein content whilst the water content increases (e.g. Idler & Clemens, 1959; Phillips, Livingston & Poston, 1966; Brett et al., 1969; Niimi, 1972; Elliott, 1976a). When the energy intake is less than the maintenance level, the amount of protein catabolized depends upon the energy intake and the protein sparing effect, i.e. the utilization of carbohydrate and fat to meet the energy requirements of metabolism. This sparing effect has been demonstrated in fish reared in enclosures and fed on prepared diets with a high carbohydrate and fat content (Buhler & Halver, 1961; Tiemeier, Deyoe & Wearden, 1976; Halver, 1972).

When the daily energy intake is above the maintenance level, the total energy content of the fish increases. The "scope for growth" has already been discussed and the principles of growth in fishes are reviewed by Ursin (this volume p. 63). I will therefore consider only a few aspects of growth.

The extra energy available to the fish can be used for production of gonad or soma or both. Therefore, ΔB may be positive but a fish may not grow because all the surplus energy is being used for gonad production and eventually for the production of eggs or sperm. As the energy intake and growth rate of a fish increase, the proportion of the energy intake used for gonad production usually increases. This strategy is not shown by all fish and some species favour gonadial production at the expense of somatic production, whilst the reverse occurs in other species (Wootton, this volume p. 133 and Mann & Mills, this volume p. 161). Some species will therefore tend to be r-selected whilst others are K-selected, but most will probably lie within the $r–K$ continuum (see Southwood, 1976).

Many workers have measured growth in terms of wet weight and have found that the mean specific growth rate ($G_w\%$ day^{-1}) changes with several factors, including fish weight, water temperature and ration size (see reviews by Brown, 1957; Weatherley, 1972). An example for brown trout on maximum rations (from Elliott, 1975c) shows that G_w decreases markedly as the weight of the fish increases and that this effect is most marked at about 13°C which is the optimal temperature for growth of trout on maximum rations (Fig. 8). It is often assumed that there is only one optimal temperature for growth of each species and sometimes there is strong disagreement over this temperature value, e.g. the various values suggested for brown trout (Pentelow, 1939; Wingfield, 1940; Brown, 1946a,b,c; Swift, 1955, 1961). However, it is not generally realized that as the ration size decreases, the optimum temperature for growth also decreases. An example of these changes is shown in Fig. 9, with growth expressed in terms of energy units. The level of energy intake affects the temperature range over which the total energy content of the trout increases (ΔB positive) and the optimal temperature for the maximum ΔB, with values ranging from 16°C at an energy intake of about 4000 cal day^{-1} to about 4°C at only 250 cal day^{-1}. A similar relationship was found between G_w and temperature with ration size in mg dry weight, and the optimal temperature for growth decreased from about 13°C at the maximum ration to about 4°C at the minimum ration for growth (Elliott, 1975d). Brett et al. (1969) have found similar changes in young sockeye salmon. It is therefore important to define the ration size as well as the temperature at which maximum growth occurs. These relationships may affect the behaviour of the fish. If their energy intake is low, they can achieve maximum growth by moving into water of the appropriate optimal temperature. For example, trout of live weight close to 50 g will not grow ($\Delta B = 0$) on a daily energy intake of about 1000 cal at 14.5°C, but the growth will be about 350 cal day^{-1} for the same energy intake at 8°C (Fig. 9). Therefore trout may move into colder water when the food supply is reduced and such a response could explain the movements of brown trout in Eye Brook reservoir (Taylor, 1978).

The optimal energy intake (C_{opt}) has already been discussed and has been shown to be the energy intake at which gross efficiency ($K_G = \Delta B/C$) is maximal. Isopleths of K_G for trout of initial weight close to 50 g show that K_G exceeded 33% in a zone within 8–11°C, and then decreased with both increasing and decreasing temperature, energy intake and ΔB (Fig. 10a). When K_G was calculated in terms of wet weight, the general pattern of the isopleths was similar but the values of K_G were much lower than the equivalent values measured in terms of energy units (Fig. 10b). These differences were chiefly due to differences in the energy content of the trout and their food, and when K_G was maximal, the weight of food eaten by the trout was about five times the increase in the weight of the fish (100 $K_G = 20\%$) but the energy content of the food was only about three times the increase in the total energy content of the fish (100 $K_G = 33\%$). Brett et al. (1969) constructed similar isopleths for sockeye salmon and

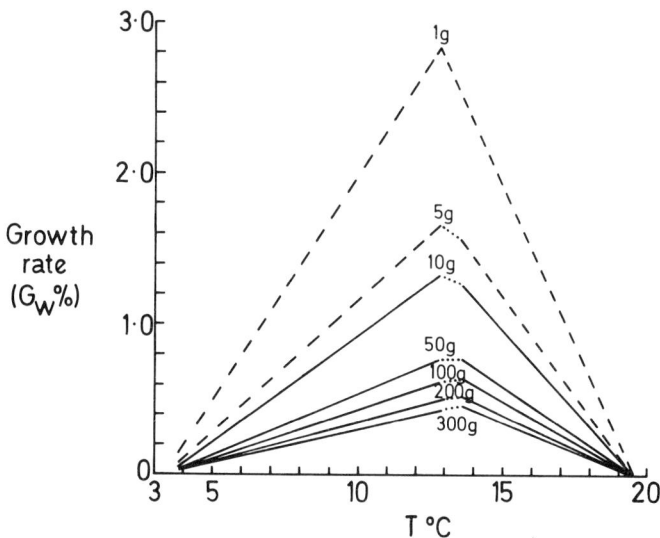

FIG. 8. Relationship between specific growth rate ($G_W\%$ day^{-1}) and water temperature (T°C) for different live weights of trout on maximum rations (from Elliott, 1975c, reproduced by permission of the British Ecological Society).

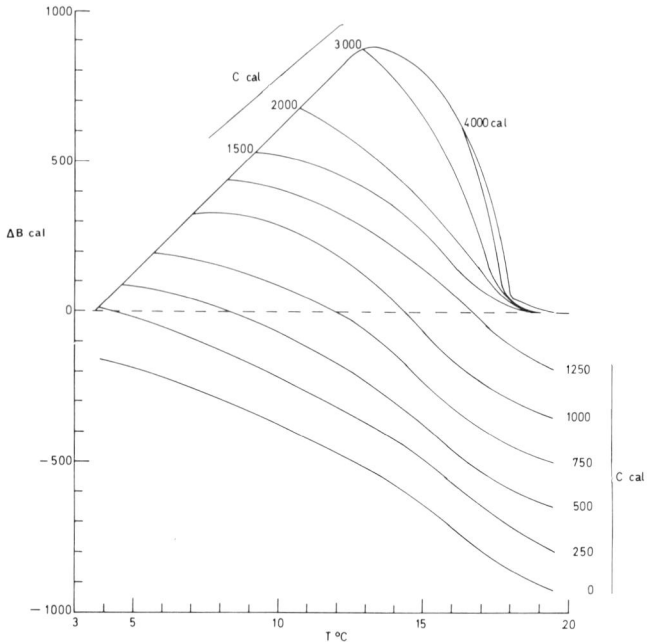

FIG. 9. Relationship between the mean change in energy content (ΔB cal day^{-1}) and temperature ($T°$C) at fixed levels of energy intake (C cal day^{-1}) for trout of initial weight close to 50 g (from Elliott, 1976c, reproduced by permission of the British Ecological Society).

found that K_G in terms of wet weight had a maximal value of 25% in a zone within 9–10°C. Isopleths of K_G have not been constructed for other species, but some values of K_G for several species are included in the review of Paloheimo & Dickie (1966b). It is surprising that some workers (e.g. Winberg, 1956) have suggested that K_G is unaffected by temperature. The isopleths for trout (Fig. 10) clearly show that both temperature and energy intake affect K_G and that the optimal temperature for maximal K_G can be well below the optimal temperature for growth on maximum energy intake.

Finally, it must be strongly emphasized that growth expressed in terms of an increase in weight cannot be converted into energy units simply by using a constant energy value. The energy content per unit weight of fish changes markedly with variations in the energy intake and energy requirements of the fish (e.g. Brett et al., 1969; Groves, 1970; Jezierska, 1974; Staples & Nomura, 1976; Kamler, 1976; Elliott, 1976a; Meakins, 1976; Craig, 1977; Grayton & Beamish, 1977). For example, the energy value of trout fed on rations ranging from zero to maximum in the temperature range 3·8–21·7°C varied from 5185 to 6133 cal g^{-1} for dry

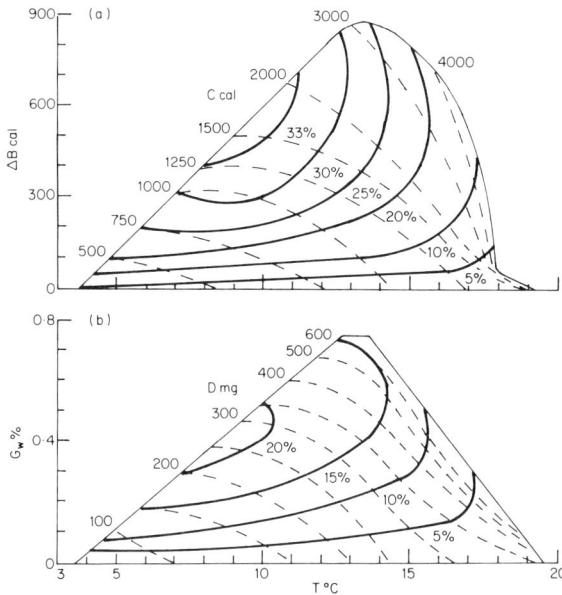

FIG. 10. (a) Gross efficiency measured in terms of energy values for trout of initial weight close to 50 g. Percentage efficiencies are drawn as isopleths over the curves relating ΔB to temperature at fixed levels of energy intake (from Elliott, 1976c). (b) Gross efficiency measured in terms of wet weight (from Elliott, 1975d) (both figures reproduced by permission of the British Ecological Society).

weight and 980 to 1711 cal g^{-1} for wet weight (Elliott, 1976a). Therefore growth models expressed in terms of energy units must make allowance for these variations in energy content.

GROWTH MODELS

Pütter (1920) was probably the first to propose a metabolic growth model by defining growth as the difference between anabolism and catabolism. He assumed that the weight exponents of anabolism and catabolism were $\frac{2}{3}$ and 1 respectively, and this assumption would be incorrect for most species of fish. The importance of this pioneer study is that it has led to other growth models, including the popular model of von Bertalanffy (1938, 1957) and its derivatives (e.g. Beverton & Holt, 1957). Von Bertalanffy's model is applied to growth in length or weight, and when it is fitted to annual size-for-age data, it often gives a correct estimate of fish size at one time per year. The original model ignores seasonal variations in growth but these variations are included in two modified versions (Pitcher & Macdonald, 1973). Ursin (1967) also developed a model for growth from the original concepts of Pütter. Although his model has a large number of parameters, it does include many aspects of growth and attempts to reconcile the divergent views of students of growth and students of the physiology of metabolism. Ursin's model has unfortunately not received the attention it deserves, possibly because some workers find it diffcult to understand (e.g. Weatherley, 1972). This model has been used in a study of rainbow trout (Sperber *et al.*, 1977) and is described in detail by Ursin (this volume p. 63).

A different model for growth in length or weight was developed chiefly from theoretical arguments by Parker & Larkin (1959), and was found by them and others (Cooper, 1961; Larkin & Ayyanger, 1961) to describe the growth of several species of fish. Elliott (1975c) developed a similar model from growth studies of trout fed on maximum rations. This similarity between growth models developed in two very different ways is both remarkable and encouraging, for it provides strong evidence that the model is a realistic one for the growth of salmonids. The effect of temperature is not included in the Parker–Larkin model but is included in Elliott's model thus

$$W_t = [(a + b_2 T) b_1 t + W_0^{b_1}]^{1/b_1} \qquad (6)$$

where W_0 and W_t are the initial and final live weights (g) respectively over t days at $T°C$, and a, b_1 and b_2 are parameters. This equation is a good model for describing the growth of both wild and hatchery-reared brown trout feeding at the maximum level on a variety of food organisms. Equation (6) was used to calculate growth curves at different mean annual temperatures (Fig. 11). The mean live weight of trout fry that were just starting to feed was found to be 0·09 g (range 0·07–0·12 g) and therefore this value was used for W_0. As these curves represent maximum growth rates, it would be remarkable if brown trout in fresh water ever attained these rates over four years. The values for 10°C are 0·09 g (age 0 years), 21·5 g (1 year), 138 g (2 years), 438 g (3 years), 1010 g (4 years). These weights are slightly higher than those attained in the best trout streams. Several factors will reduce the maximum growth rate and these include the loss of gonadial products (Le Cren, 1962), an increase in swimming activity during migrations and a reduction in the food supply.

The most popular energetics model for fish is the "basic equation" of Winberg (1956)

$$0·8C = R + \Delta B \qquad (7)$$

where the metabolic rate (R) is assumed to be twice resting metabolism and is estimated from an assumed relationship between oxygen consumption, body weight and temperature. This equation has been used in numerous studies on freshwater fish, including several species in the Thames river, England (Mann, 1965); predatory fish in the Vistula river, Poland (Backiel, 1971); brown and rainbow trout in a Pyrenean stream, France (Elliott, 1973) and perch in Windermere, England (Craig, 1978).

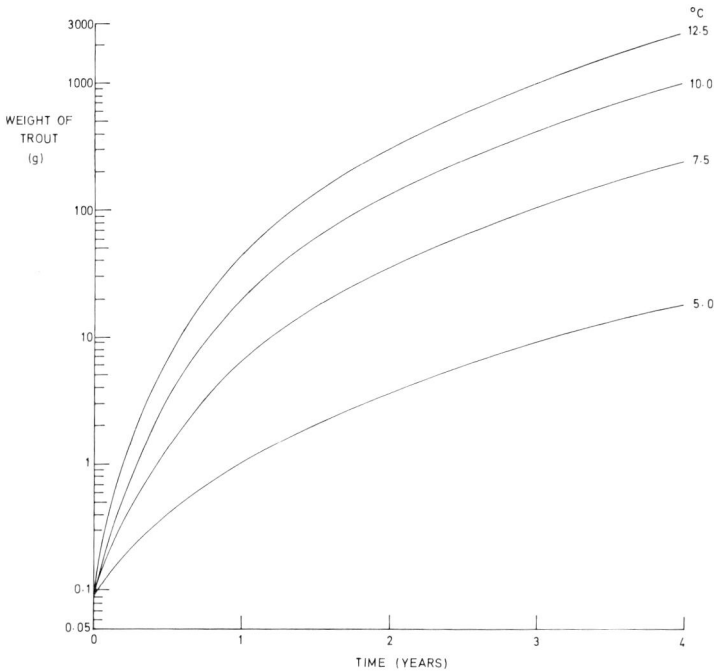

FIG. 11. Theoretical growth of trout at different mean annual temperatures.

The assumptions inherent in the basic equation were justified by Winberg and later by Mann (1965) and Paloheimo & Dickie (1966a). However, these assumptions can be criticized. It has already been shown that Winberg's value of $0·8\,C$ for the energy available for growth and metabolism is often wrong. He also assumed that the energy equivalent (Q_{ox}) for converting rate of oxygen consumption into energy units was $5\ \mathrm{cal\ ml^{-1}}$ oxygen consumed, but this value is too high for a carnivorous fish that utilizes ammonia as its chief excretory product and a value of $4·63\ \mathrm{cal\ ml^{-1}}$ is more appropriate (Elliott & Davison, 1975). The relationship between the level of metabolism and temperature is assumed to follow Krogh's curve, but this will rarely be true over a wide range of temperature. The energy values of the fish and their food are assumed to be the same, but this will rarely be true except for piscivorous species. Finally, there are problems in defining the levels of activity and energy intake for resting and twice resting metabolism. It has been shown in this review that Winberg's estimate of resting metabolism for salmonids lies between R_s and R_{main} for brown trout (Fig. 7c), and that his estimates of the daily energy intake required for resting and twice resting metabolism often lie close to C_{main} and C_{opt} respectively (Fig. 5). Although Winberg's equation can be justifiably criticized, it often works (!) and if the erroneous assumptions were corrected, it would provide a very useful model for the study of energetics in fish.

A "K-line" model was developed by Paloheimo & Dickie (1965, 1966a,b) who reanalysed the data of other workers and found that the logarithm of the gross efficiency (log K_G) decreased with increasing ration size (R). The K-line model therefore provides a relationship between growth and ration size, and was thought to be independent of fish size and temperature. Several workers have questioned the validity of the K-line model and suggested that it is restricted to a limited size range of fish fed at a relatively high ration level (Warren & Davis, 1967; Rafail, 1968; Brett *et al.*, 1969; Gerking, 1971; Elliott, 1975d; Brett & Shelbourn, 1975; Staples & Nomura, 1976; Huisman, 1976). Kerr (1971a,b) strongly criticized these conclusions and developed the model to predict the growth efficiency of fish in the field. However, it has been shown in this review that K_G is highest at the optimal ration and therefore the K-line model will be applicable only in the range between the optimal and maximum rations. As both rations vary with temperature and fish weight, there will be a corresponding variation in the range of ration sizes over which the K-line can be used. Therefore the K-line model is applicable only at high growth rates and high ration levels.

A different model was developed to describe the relationship between ration size and the growth rate of brown trout within the scope for growth (Elliott, 1975d), and the model was later modified to describe the relationship between the daily energy intake (C) and growth rate expressed as a percentage of the maximum growth rate ($P = 100 \, \Delta B / \Delta B_{max}$ where $\Delta B_{max} = P_P C_{max} - R_{max}$)

$$C = a_1 W^{b_1} \exp \left[b_2 P + (a_2 + b_3 P) T \right] \qquad (8)$$

where W g is the live weight of the fish, $T °C$ is the water temperature and a_1, a_2, b_1, b_2 and b_3 are parameters whose statistical estimates are given in Elliott (1976c). This equation appears to be a good model for trout feeding on a variety of food organisms in both the stream and the laboratory. When equations are available not only for the components of the energy budget (e.g. Table I) but also for the relationships between these components (e.g. eqn 8), models can be constructed to examine the relative changes in the major components. An example is given in Fig. 12 which also summarizes some of the relationships discussed in this review.

From this brief review of growth models, it is concluded that bioenergetic models of growth should be based on realistic assumptions. It must not be assumed that the energy values of the fish and their food are the same, or that the energy value of the fish is constant and interconvertible with weight, or that the energy losses in the waste products are a constant fraction of the energy intake, or that the weight exponent is constant and unaffected by variations in energy intake or metabolism. This list could be extended but the general point is that these assumptions have been made erroneously in many studies on the energetics of freshwater teleosts.

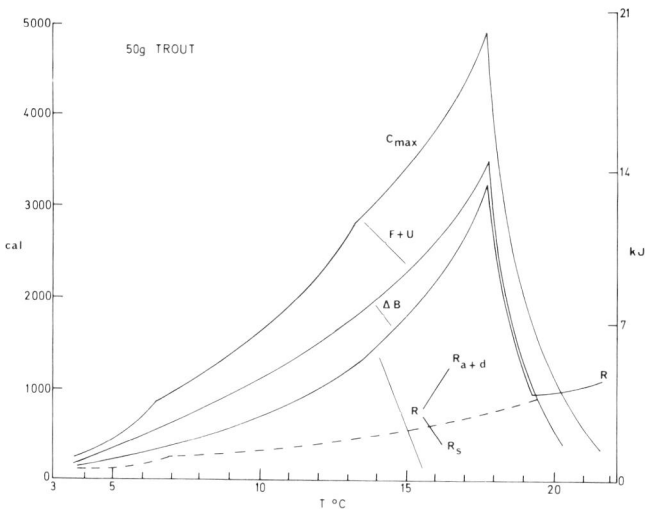

FIG. 12. Division of the major components of the energy budget for trout of 50-g live weight.

At the beginning of this review, I stressed the need for more accurate methods for the estimation of energy intake. There is a similar need for realistic models of the relationship between energy intake and growth, and these models must be applicable to fish in the field. In the last few years, there has been a welcome increase in work on the quantitative ecology of freshwater fish and a few workers summarize their results in equations that can be used for prediction. This work leads to the development of models that can be used for the scientific management of freshwater fisheries, and this should surely be one of the ultimate goals of freshwater ecologists.

ACKNOWLEDGEMENT

I wish to thank Mrs P. A. Tullett for all her help in the preparation of this paper.

REFERENCES

Allen, K. R. (1951). The Horokiwi Stream: a study of a trout population. *Fish. Bull. N.Z.* **10**: 1–238.
Atherton, W. D. & Aitken, A. (1970). Growth, nitrogen metabolism and fat metabolism in *Salmo gairdneri* Rich. *Comp. Biochem. Physiol.* **36**: 719–747.

Backiel, T. (1971). Production and food consumption of predatory fish in the Vistula River. *J. Fish. Biol.* **3**: 369–405.

Bajkov, A. D. (1935). How to estimate the daily food consumption of fish under natural conditions. *Trans. Am. Fish. Soc.* **65**: 288–289.

Beamish, F. W. H. (1964a). Respiration of fishes with special emphasis on standard oxygen consumption. II. Influence of weight and temperature on respiration of several species. *Can. J. Zool.* **42**: 177–188.

Beamish, F. W. H. (1964b). III. Influence of oxygen. *Can. J. Zool.* **42**: 355–366.

Beamish, F. W. H. (1972). Ration size and digestion in largemouth bass, *Micropterus salmoides* Lacepède. *Can. J. Zool.* **50**: 153–164.

Beamish, F. W. H. (1974). Apparent specific dynamic action of largemouth bass, *Micropterus salmoides*. *J. Fish. Res. Bd Can.* **31**: 1763–1769.

Beamish, F. W. H. & Dickie, L. M. (1967). Metabolism and biological production in fish. In *The biological basis of freshwater fish production*: 215–242. Gerking, S. D. (ed.). Oxford: Blackwells.

Beamish, F. W. H., Niimi, A. J. & Lett, P. F. K. P. (1975). Bioenergetics of teleost fishes: Environmental influences. In *Comparative physiology—functional aspects of structural materials*: 187–209. Bolis, L., Maddrell, H. P. & Schmidt-Neilsen, K. (eds). Amsterdam: North-Holland Publishing Co.

Beverton, R. J. H. & Holt, S. J. (1957). On the dynamics of exploited fish populations. *Fishery Invest., Lond.* (2) **19**: 1–533.

Birkett, L. (1969). The nitrogen balance in plaice, sole and perch. *J. exp. Biol.* **50**: 375–386.

Black, V. S. (1957). Excretion and osmoregulation. In *Physiology of fishes* **1**: 163–199. Brown, M. E. (ed.). New York & London: Academic Press.

Brafield, A. E. & Solomon, D. J. (1972). Oxy-calorific coefficients for animals respiring nitrogenous substrates. *Comp. Biochem. Physiol.* **43**A: 837–841.

Brett, J. R. (1962). Some considerations in the study of respiratory metabolism in fish, particularly salmon. *J. Fish. Res. Bd Can.* **19**: 1025–1038.

Brett, J. R. (1964). The respiratory metabolism and swimming performance of young sockeye salmon. *J. Fish. Res. Bd Can.* **21**: 1183–1226.

Brett, J. R. (1970). Fish—the energy cost of living. In *Marine aquaculture*: 37–52. McNeil, W. J. (ed.). Oregon, U.S.A.: Oregon State University Press.

Brett, J. R. (1971). Satiation time, appetite, and maximum food intake of sockeye salmon (*Oncorhynchus nerka*) *J. Fish. Res. Bd Can.* **28**: 409–415.

Brett, J. R. (1972). The metabolic demand for oxygen in fish, particularly salmonids, and a comparison with other vertebrates. *Respir. Physiol.* **14**: 151–170.

Brett, J. R. (1976a). Feeding metabolic rates of young sockeye salmon *Oncorhynchus nerka*, in relation to ration level and temperature. *Tech. Rep. Fish. mar. Serv. Can.* No. 675: 1–43.

Brett, J. R. (1976b). Scope for metabolism and growth of sockeye salmon, *Oncorhynchus nerka*, and some related energetics. *J. Fish. Res. Bd Can.* **33**: 307–313.

Brett, J. R. & Glass, N. R. (1973). Metabolic rates and critical swimming speeds of sockeye salmon (*Oncorhynchus nerka*) in relation to size and temperature. *J. Fish Res. Bd Can.* **30**: 379–387.

Brett, J. R. & Higgs, D. A. (1970). Effect of temperature on the rate of gastric digestion in fingerling sockeye salmon, *Oncorhynchus nerka*. *J. Fish. Res. Bd Can.* **27**: 1767–1779.

Brett, J. R. & Shelbourn, J. E. (1975). Growth rate of young sockeye salmon, *Oncorhynchus nerka*, in relation to fish size and ration level. *J. Fish. Res. Bd Can.* **32**: 2103–2110.

Brett, J. R., Shelbourn, J. E. & Shoop, C. T. (1969). Growth rate and body composition of fingerling sockeye salmon, *Oncorhynchus nerka*, in relation to temperature and ration size. *J. Fish. Res. Bd Can.* **26**: 2363–2394.

Brett, J. R. & Sutherland, D. B. (1965). Respiratory metabolism of pumpkinseed (*Lepomis gibbosus*) in relation to swimming speed. *J. Fish. Res. Bd Can.* **22**: 405–409.

Brett, J. R. & Zala, C. A. (1975). Daily pattern of nitrogen excretion and oxygen consumption of sockeye salmon (*Oncorhynchus nerka*) under controlled conditions. *J. Fish. Res. Bd Can.* **32**: 2479–2486.

Brocksen, R. W. & Bugge, J. P. (1974). Preliminary investigations on the influence of temperature on food assimilation by rainbow trout *Salmo gairdneri* Richardson. *J. Fish Biol.* **6**: 93–97.

Brocksen, R. W., Davis, G. E. & Warren, C. E. (1968). Competition, food consumption and production of sculpins and trout in laboratory stream communities. *J. Wildl. Mgmt* **32**: 51–75.

Brody, S. (1945). *Bioenergetics and growth.* New York: Reinhold.

Brown, M. E. (1946a). The growth of brown trout (*Salmo trutta* Linn.). I. Factors influencing the growth of trout fry. *J. exp. Biol.* **22**: 118–129.

Brown, M. E. (1946b). The growth of brown trout (*Salmo trutta* Linn.). II. The growth of two-year-old trout at a constant temperature of 11·5°C. *J. exp. Biol.* **22**: 130–144.

Brown, M. E. (1946c). The growth of brown trout (*Salmo trutta* Linn.). III. The effect of temperature on the growth of two-year-old trout. *J. exp. Biol.* **22**: 145–155.

Brown, M. E. (1957). *The physiology of fishes.* **1**. New York & London: Academic Press.

Buhler, D. R. & Halver, J. E. (1961). Nutrition of salmonid fishes. IX. Carbohydrate requirement of chinook salmon. *J. Nutr.* **74**: 307–318.

Burrows, R. E. (1964). Effects of accumulated excretory products on hatchery reared salmonids. *Res. Rep. U.S. Fish Wildl. Serv.* **66**: 1–12.

Carline, R. F. & Hall, J. D. (1973). Evaluation of a method for estimating food consumption rates of fish. *J. Fish. Res. Bd Can.* **30**: 623–629.

Cooper, E. L. (1961). Growth of wild and hatchery strains of brook trout. *Trans. Am. Fish. Soc.* **90**: 424–438.

Craig, J. F. (1977). The body composition of adult perch, *Perca fluviatilis* in Windermere, with reference to seasonal changes and reproduction. *J. Anim. Ecol.* **46**: 617–632.

Craig, J. F. (1978). A study of the food and feeding of perch, *Perca fluviatilis* L., in Windermere. *Freshwat. Biol.* **8**: 59–68.

Davis, G. E. & Warren, C. E. (1965). Trophic relations of a sculpin in laboratory stream communities. *J. Wildl. Mgmt* **29**: 846–871.

Dickson, I. W. & Kramer, R. H. (1971). Factors influencing scope for activity and active and standard metabolism of rainbow trout (*Salmo gairdneri*). *J. Fish. Res. Bd Can.* **28**: 587–596.

Edwards, D. J. (1971). Effect of temperature on the rate of passage of food through the alimentary canal of the plaice *Pleuronectes platessa* L. *J. Fish Biol.* **3**: 433–439.

Edwards, R. R. C., Finlayson, D. M. & Steele, J. H. (1972). An experimental study on the oxygen consumption, growth and metabolism of the cod (*Gadus morhua* L.) *J. exp. mar. Biol. Ecol.* **8**, 299–309.

Ege, R. & Krogh, A. (1914). On the relation between the temperature and the respiratory exchange in fishes. *Int. Rev. Hydrobiol.* **7**: 48–55.

Elliott, J. M. (1972). Rates of gastric evacuation in brown trout, *Salmo trutta* L. *Freshwat. Biol.* **2**: 1–18.

Elliott, J. M. (1973). The food of brown and rainbow trout (*Salmo trutta* and *S. gairdneri*) in relation to the abundance of drifting invertebrates in a mountain stream. *Oecologia* **12**: 329–347.

Elliott, J. M. (1975a). Weight of food and time required to satiate brown trout, *Salmo trutta* L. *Freshwat. Biol.* **5**: 51–64.

Elliott, J. M. (1975b). Number of meals in a day, maximum weight of food consumed in a day and maximum rate of feeding for brown trout, *Salmo trutta* L. *Freshwat. Biol.* **5**: 287–303.

Elliott, J. M. (1975c). The growth of brown trout (*Salmo trutta* L.) fed on maximum rations. *J. Anim. Ecol.* **44**: 805–821.

Elliott, J. M. (1975d). The growth rate of brown trout (*Salmo trutta* L.) fed on reduced rations. *J. Anim. Ecol.* **44**: 823–842.

Elliott, J. M. (1976a). Body composition of brown trout (*Salmo trutta* L.) in relation to temperature and ration size. *J. Anim. Ecol.* **45**: 273–289.

Elliott, J. M. (1976b). Energy losses in the waste products of brown trout (*Salmo trutta* L.). *J. Anim. Ecol.* **45**: 561–580.

Elliott, J. M. (1976c). The energetics of feeding, metabolism and growth of brown trout (*Salmo trutta* L.) in relation to body weight, water temperature and ration size. *J. Anim. Ecol.* **45**: 923–948.

Elliott, J. M. & Davison, W. (1975). Energy equivalents of oxygen consumption in animal energetics. *Oecologia* **19**: 195–201.

Elliott, J. M. & Persson, L. (1978). The estimation of daily rates of food consumption for fish. *J. Anim. Ecol.* **47**: 977–993.

El-Shamy, F. M. (1976). Analyses of gastric emptying in Bluegill (*Lepomis macrochirus*). *J. Fish. Res. Bd Can.* **33**: 1630–1633.

Fábián, Gy., Molnár, Gy. & Tölg, I. (1963). Comparative data and enzyme kinetic calculations on changes caused by temperature in the duration of gastric digestion of some predatory fishes. *Acta biol. hung.* **14**: 123–129.

Feldmeth, C. R. & Jenkins, T. M. (1973). An estimate of energy expenditure by rainbow trout (*Salmo gairdneri*) in a small mountain stream. *J. Fish. Res. Bd Can.* **30**: 1755–1759.

Forster, R. P. & Goldstein, L. (1969). Formation of excretory products. In *Fish physiology* **1**: 313–350. Hoar, W. S. & Randall, D. J. (eds). New York & London: Academic Press.

Fromm, P. O. (1963). Studies on renal and extra-renal excretion in a freshwater teleost, *Salmo gairdneri*. *Comp. Biochem. Physiol.* **10**: 121–128.

Fry, F. E. J. (1947). Effects of the environment on animal activity. *Univ. Toronto Stud. biol. Ser.* No. 55 [*Publ. Ontario Res. Lab.* No. 68]: 5–62.

Fry, F. E. J. (1957). The aquatic respiration of fish. In *The physiology of fishes* **1**: 1–63. Brown, M. E. (ed.). New York & London: Academic Press.

Fry, F. E. J. (1971). The effect of environmental factors on the physiology of fish. In *Fish physiology*: 1–98. Hoar, W. S. & Randall, D. J. (eds). New York: Academic Press.

Gerking, S. D. (1954). The food turnover of a bluegill population. *Ecology* **35**: 490–498.

Gerking, S. D. (1955). Influence of rate of feeding on body composition and protein metabolism of bluegill sunfish. *Physiol. Zoöl.* **28**: 267–282.

Gerking, S. D. (1962). Production and food utilization in a population of bluegill sunfish. *Ecol. Monogr.* **32**: 31–78.

Gerking, S. D. (ed.) (1967). *The biological basis of freshwater fish production.* Oxford: Blackwells.

Gerking, S. D. (1971). Influence of rate of feeding and body weight on protein metabolism of bluegill sunfish. *Physiol. Zoöl.* **44**: 9–19.

Grayton, B. D. & Beamish, F. W. H. (1977). Effects of feeding frequency on food intake, growth and body composition of Rainbow trout (*Salmo gairdneri*). *Aquaculture* **11**: 159–172.

Griffiths, W. E. (1976). Feeding and gastric evacuation in perch (*Perca fluviatilis* L.). *Mauri Ora* **4**: 19–34.

Groves, T. D. D. (1970). Body composition changes during growth in young Sockeye (*Oncorhynchus nerka*) in freshwater. *J. Fish. Res. Bd Can.* **27**: 929–942.

Guerin-Ancey, O. (1976). Experimental study of the nitrogen excretion of bass (*Dicentrarchus labrax*) during growth. I. Effects of temperature and weight on the excretion of ammonia and urea. *Aquaculture* **9**: 71–80.

Halver, J. E. (ed.) (1972). *Fish nutrition.* New York & London: Academic Press.

Hastings, W. H. & Dickie, L. M. (1972). Feed formation and evaluation. In *Fish nutrition*: 327–374. Halver, J. E. (ed.). New York & London: Academic Press.

Healey, M. C. (1972). Bioenergetics of a sand goby (*Gobius minutus*) population. *J. Fish. Res. Bd Can.* **29**: 187–194.

Horton, P. A. (1961). Bionomics of brown trout in a Dartmoor stream. *J. Anim. Ecol.* **30**: 311–338.

Huisman, E. A. (1976). Food conversion efficiencies at maintenance and production levels for carp, *Cyprinus carpio* L., and rainbow trout, *Salmo gairdneri* Richardson. *Aquaculture* **9**: 259–273.

Idler, D. R. & Clemens, W. A. (1959). The energy expenditure of Fraser River salmon during the spawning migration of Chilko and Stuart Lakes. *Prog. Rep. int. Pacif. Salm. Fish. Commn* 1959: 1–80.

Ishiwata, N. (1968). Ecological studies on the feeding of fishes IV. Satiation curve. *Bull. Jap. Soc. Sci. Fish.* **34**: 691–694.

Ivlev, V. S. (1939a). [The energy balance of the growing larva of *Silurus glanis*.] *Dokl. Akad. Nauk SSSR* **25**: 87–89. [In Russian.]

Ivlev, V. S. (1939b). [The effect of starvation on energy transformation during the growth of fish.] *Dokl. Akad. Nauk SSSR* **25**: 90–92. [In Russian.]

Ivlev, V. S. (1939c). [Energy balance in the carp.] *Zool. Zh.* **18**: 303–318. [In Russian.]

Ivlev, V. S. (1945). [The biological productivity of waters.] *Usp. sovrem. Biol.* **19**: 98–120. [In Russian.] (*Fish Res. Bd Can. Transl. Ser.* 394.)

Ivlev, V. S. (1961). *Experimental ecology of the feeding of fishes.* New Haven: Yale University Press.

Iwata, K. (1970). Relationship between food and growth in young crucian carps, *Carassius auratus cuvieri*, as determined by nitrogen balance. *Jap. J. Limnol.* **31**: 129–151.

Jennings, J. B. (1965). *Feeding, digestion and assimilation in animals.* London: Pergamon Press.

58   J. M. ELLIOTT

Jezierska, B. (1974). The effect of various type of food on the growth and chemical composition of the body of perch (*Perca fluviatilis*) in laboratory conditions. *Polskie Archwm Hydrobiol.* **21**: 467–479.

Kamler, E. (1976). Variability of respiration and body composition during early developmental stages of carp. *Polskie Archwm Hydrobiol.* **23**: 431–485.

Karzinkin, G. S. & Krivobok, M. N. (1964). Balance sheet experiments on nitrogen metabolism of fish. In *Techniques for the investigation of fish physiology*: 91–105. Office of Technical Services, Washington, No. 64–11001.

Kelso, J. R. M. (1972). Conversion, maintenance and assimilation for Walleye, *Stizostedion vitreum vitreum*, as affected by size, diet and temperature. *J. Fish. Res. Bd Can.* **29**: 1181–1192.

Kerr, S. R. (1971a). Analysis of laboratory experiments on growth efficiency of fishes. *J. Fish. Res. Bd Can.* **28**: 801–808.

Kerr, S. R. (1971b). Prediction of fish growth efficiency in nature. *J. Fish. Res. Bd Can.* **28**: 809–814.

Kevern, N. R. (1966). Feeding rate of carp estimated by a radioisotopic method. *Trans. Am. Fish. Soc.* **95**: 363–371.

Kinne, O. (1960). Growth, food intake and food conversion in a euryplastic fish exposed to different temperatures and salinities. *Physiol. Zoöl.* **33**: 288–317.

Kleerekoper, H. & Mogensen, J. A. (1959). The chemical composition of scent of freshwater fish with special reference to amines and amino acids. *Z. vergl. Physiol.* **42**: 492–500.

Kleiber, M. (1961a). *The fire of life, an introduction to animal energetics.* New York: John Wiley & Sons.

Kleiber, M. (1961b). Metabolic rate and food utilization as a function of body size. Brody Memorial Lecture I. *Res. Bull. Mo agric. Exp. Stn* No. 767: 1–42.

Kolehmainen, S. E. (1974). Daily feeding rates of Bluegill (*Lepomis macrochirus*) determined by a refined radioisotope method. *J. Fish. Res. Bd Can.* **31**: 67–74.

Larkin, P. Z. & Ayyanger, K. V. (1961). Applications of the Parker equation to growth of aquatic organisms. *Proc. Alask. Sci. Conf.* **11**: 103–124.

Le Cren, E. D. (1962). The efficiency of reproduction and recruitment in freshwater fish. In *The exploitation of natural animal populations*: 286–296. Le Cren, E. D. & Holdgate, M. W. (eds). Oxford: Blackwells.

Li, H. W. & Brocksen, R. W. (1977). Approaches to the analysis of energetic costs of intraspecific competition for space by rainbow trout (*Salmo gairdneri*). *J. Fish Biol.* **11**: 329–341.

Magnuson, J. J. (1969). Digestion and food consumption by skipjack tuna (*Katsuwonus pelamis*). *Trans. Am. Fish. Soc.* **98**: 379–392.

Maliyenko, A. V. (1975). Rate of passage of food through the alimentary canal in juveniles of some fish species from the Kremenchung reservoir. *Hydrobiol. J.* **11**: 65–68.

Mann, K. H. (1965). Energy transformation by a population of fish in the River Thames. *J. Anim. Ecol.* **34**: 253–275.

Mann, K. H. (1967). The cropping of the food supply. In *The biological basis of freshwater fish production*: 243–257. Gerking, S. D. (ed.). Oxford: Blackwells.

Meakins, R. H. (1976). Variations in the energy content of freshwater fish. *J. Fish Biol.* **8**: 221–224.

Meien, V. A., Karzinkin, G. S., Ivlev, V. S., Lipin, A. N. & Sheina, M. P. (1937). [Utilization by two-year-old carp of the natural food supplies of a pond.] *Zool. Zh.* **16**: 209–223. [In Russian.]

Menzel, D. W. (1960). Utilization of food by the Bermuda reef fish, *Epinephelus guttatus*. *J. Cons. perm. int. Explor. Mer* **25**: 216–222.

Molnár, G., Tamássy, E. & Tölg, I. (1967). The gastric digestion of living, predatory fish. In *The biological basis of freshwater fish production*: 135–149. Gerking, S. D. (ed.). Oxford: Blackwell Scientific Pubications.

Molnár, G. & Tölg, I. (1962). Relation between water temperature and gastric digestion of largemouth bass (*Micropterus salmoides* Lacepède). *J. Fish. Res. Bd Can.* **19**: 1005–1012.

Morgan, R. I. G. (1974). The energy requirements of trout and perch populations in Loch Leven, Kinross. *Proc. R. Soc. Edinb.* (B) **74**: 333–345.

Muir, B. S. & Niimi, A. J. (1972). Oxygen consumption of the euryhaline fish, (*Kuhlia sandvicensis*), with reference to salinity, swimming and food consumption. *J. Fish. Res. Bd Can.* **29**: 67–77.

Niimi, A. J. (1972). Changes in the proximate body composition of large-mouth bass (*Micropterus salmoides*) with starvation. *Can. J. Zool.* **50**: 815–819.

Niimi, A. J. & Beamish, F. W. H. (1974). Bioenergetics and growth of largemouth bass (*Micropterus salmoides*) in relation to body weight and temperature. *Can. J. Zool.* **52**: 447–456.

Olson, K. R. & Fromm, P. O. (1971). Excretion of urea by two teleosts exposed to different concentrations of ambient ammonia. *Comp. Biochem. Physiol.* **40**A: 999–1007.

Paloheimo, J. E. & Dickie, L. M. (1965). Food and growth of fishes. I. A growth curve derived from experimental data. *J. Fish. Res. Bd Can.* **22**: 521–542.

Paloheimo, J. E. & Dickie, L. M. (1966a). Food and growth of fishes. II. Effects of food and temperature on the relation between metabolism and body weight. *J. Fish. Res. Bd Can.* **23**: 869–908.

Paloheimo, J. E. & Dickie, L. M. (1966b). Food and growth of fishes. III. Relations among food, body size and growth efficiency. *J. Fish. Res. Bd Can.* **23**: 1209–1248.

Pandian, T. J. (1967). Transformation of food in the fish *Megalops cyprinoides* I. Influence of quality of food. *Mar. Biol.* **1**: 60–64.

Parker, R. R. & Larkin, P. A. (1959). A concept of growth in fishes. *J. Fish. Res. Bd Can.* **16**: 721–745.

Pentelow, F. T. K. (1939). The relation between growth and food consumption in the brown trout (*Salmo trutta*). *J. exp. Biol.* **16**: 446–473.

Phillips, A. M. (1969). Nutrition, digestion and energy utilization. In *Fish physiology* **1**: 391–432. Hoar, W. S. & Randall, D. J. (eds). New York & London: Academic Press.

Phillips, A. M. (1972). Calorie and energy requirement. In *Fish nutrition*: 1–28. Halver, J. E. (ed.). New York & London: Academic Press.

Phillips, A. M., Livingston, D. L. & Poston, H. A. (1966). Use of calorie sources by brook trout. *Progve Fish-Cult.* **28**: 67–72.

Pitcher, T. J. & MacDonald, P. D. M. (1973). Two models for seasonal growth in fishes. *J. appl. Ecol.* **10**: 599–606.

Priede, I. G. & Tytler, P. (1977). Heart rate as a measure of metabolic rate in teleost fishes; *Salmo gairdneri*, *Salmo trutta* and *Gadus morhua*. *J. Fish Biol.* **10**: 231–242.

Priede, I. G. & Young, A. H. (1977). The ultrasonic telemetry of cardiac rhythms of wild brown trout (*Salmo trutta* L.) as an indicator of bioenergetics and behaviour. *J. Fish Biol.* **10**: 299–318.

Pütter, A. (1920). Studien über physiologische Ahnlichkeit. VI. Wachstumsähnlichkeiten. *Pflügers Arch. Ges. Physiol.* **180**: 298–340.

Rafail, S. Z. (1968). A statistical analysis of ration and growth relationship of plaice (*Pleuronectes platessa*). *J. Fish. Res. Bd Can.* **25**: 717–732.

Ricker, W. E. (ed.) (1971). *Methods for assessment of fish production in fresh waters.* (2nd edn). [IBP Handbook No. 3.] Oxford: Blackwell.

Royal Society (1972). *Metric units, conversion factors and nomenclature in nutritional and food sciences.* London: Royal Society.

Savitz, J. (1969). Effects of temperature and body weight on endogenous nitrogen excretion in the bluegill sunfish (*Lepomis macrochirus*). *J. Fish. Res. Bd Can.* **26**: 1813–1821.

Savitz, J. (1971). Nitrogen excretion and protein consumption of the bluegill sunfish (*Lepomis macrochirus*). *J. Fish. Res. Bd Can.* **28**: 449–451.

Schneider, J. C. (1973). Rate of food digestion by yellow perch (*Perca flavescens*) in relation to size of perch, size and type of food, and temperature. *Fish. Res. Rep. Mich. Dep. nat. Resour., Fish. Div.* No. 1803: 1–20.

Shul'man, G. E. (1962). [Nitrogen balance and food consumption of the Azov Anchovy, *Engraulis encrasicholus maeoticus* Pusanov.] *Dokl. Akad. Nauk SSSR* **147**: 724–726. [In Russian.] (Published in translation by the National Science Foundation, 1963.)

Smith, M. A. K. & Thorpe, A. (1976). Nitrogen metabolism and trophic input in relation to growth in freshwater and saltwater *Salmo gairdneri. Biol. Bull. mar. biol. Lab. Woods Hole* **150**: 139–151.

Solomon, D. J. & Brafield, A. E. (1972). The energetics of feeding, metabolism and growth of perch (*Perca fluviatilis* L.) *J. Anim. Ecol.* **41**: 699–718.

Southwood, T. R. E. (1976). Bionomic strategies and population parameters. In *Theoretical ecology*: 26–48. May, R. M. (ed.). Oxford: Blackwells.

Sperber, O., From, J. & Sparre, P. (1977). A method to estimate the growth rate of fishes as a function of temperature and feeding level applied to rainbow trout. *Meddr Danm. Fisk.-og Havunders.* NS **7**: 275–317.

Staples, D. J. (1975a). Production biology of the upland bully *Philypnodon breviceps* Stokell in a small New Zealand lake. I. Life history, food, feeding and activity rhythms. *J. Fish Biol.* **7**: 1–24.

Staples, D. J. (1975b). Production biology of the upland bully *Philypnodon breviceps* Stokell in a small New Zealand lake. III. Production, food consumption and efficiency of food utilization. *J. Fish Biol.* **7**: 47–69.

Staples, D. J. & Nomura, M. (1976). Influence of body size and food ration on the energy budget of rainbow trout *Salmo gairdneri* Richardson. *J. Fish Biol.* **9**: 29–43.

Swift, D. R. (1955). Seasonal variations in the growth rate, thyroid gland activity and food reserves of brown trout (*Salmo trutta* Linn.). *J. exp. Biol.* **32**: 751–764.

Swift, D. R. (1961). The annual growth-rate cycle in brown trout (*Salmo trutta* Linn.) and its cause. *J. exp. Biol.* **38**: 595–604.

Taylor, A. H. (1978). An analysis of the trout fishing at Eye Brook—a eutrophic reservoir. *J. Anim. Ecol.* **47**: 407–423.

Thorpe, J. E. (1977). Daily ration of adult perch, *Perca fluviatilis* L. during summer in Loch Leven, Scotland. *J. Fish Biol.* **11**: 55–68.

Tiemeier, O. W., Deyoe, C. W. & Wearden, S. (1965). Effects of growth of fingerling channel catfish of diets containing two energy and two protein levels. *Trans. Kans. Acad. Sci.* **68**: 180–186.

Tyler, A. V. (1970). Rates of gastric emptying in young cod. *J. Fish. Res. Bd Can.* **27**: 1177–1189.

Ursin, E. (1967). A mathematical model of some aspects of fish growth, respiration and mortality. *J. Fish. Res. Bd Can.* **24**: 2355–2453.

von Bertalanffy, L. (1938). A quantitative theory of organic growth. *Hum. Biol.* **10**: 181–213.

von Bertalanffy, L. (1957). Quantitative laws in metabolism and growth. *Q. Rev. Biol.* **32**: 217–231.

Warren, C. E. & Davis, G. E. (1967). Laboratory studies on the feeding, bioenergetics and growth of fish. In *The biological basis of freshwater fish production*: 175–214. Gerking, S. D. (ed.). Oxford: Blackwell.

Warren, C. E., Wales, J. H., Davis, G. E. & Doudoroff, P. (1964). Trout production in an experimental stream enriched with sucrose. *J. Wildl. Mgmt* **28**: 617–660.

Weatherley, A. H. (1972). *Growth and ecology of fish populations*. London & New York: Academic Press.

Webb, P. W. (1975). Hydrodynamics and energetics of fish propulsion. *Bull. Fish. Res. Bd Can.* No. 190; 1–158.

Winberg, G. G. (1956). [*Rate of metabolism and food requirements of fishes.*] Minsk: Belorussian State University. (*Fish. Res. Bd Can. Transl. Ser.* No. 194: 1–253.)

Winberg, G. G. (1961). [New information on metabolic rate in fishes.] *Vop. Ikhtiol.* **1**: 157–165. (*J. Fish. Res. Bd Can., Transl. Ser.* No. 362.)

Winberg, G. G. (1962). [The energy principle in studying food associations and the productivity of ecological systems.] *Zool. Zh.* **41**: 1618–1630. (*J. Fish. Res. Bd Can., Transl. Ser.* No. 433.)

Windell, J. T. (1967). Rates of digestion in fishes. In *The biological basis of freshwater fish production*: 151–173. Gerking, S. D. (ed.). Oxford: Blackwell.

Windell, J. T., Kitchell, J. F. *et al.* (1976). Temperature and rate of gastric evacuation by rainbow trout. *Salmo gairdneri. Trans. Am. Fish. Soc.* **105**: 712–717.

Wingfield, C. A. (1940). Effect of certain environmental factors on growth of brown trout. *J. exp. Biol.* **17**: 435–448.

Symp. zool. Soc. Lond. (1979) No. 44, 63–87

Principles of Growth in Fishes

E. URSIN

Danish Institute for Fishery and Marine Research,
Charlottenlund Slot, Charlottenlund, Denmark

SYNOPSIS

Growth of a fish can be conceived as primarily a problem of internal control at the cellular level or at the organ level. It can also be conceived as primarily a problem of interaction with the environment. The metabolic growth model, developed step by step since 1920, is such a model and has found wide application in ecology and farming. This paper focuses on this model.

The model accounts for the storing of energy or matter (ingestion, digestion, assimilation) on one side and for the liberation or discard of energy or matter as measured by oxygen consumption and spawning losses on the other side. Anabolic as well as catabolic processes are described as functions of temperature. The problem of search for food, itself an extensive subject, is skirted to be dealt with elsewhere.

The importance of the literature on respiration as a function of body size as a source of information of the shape of growth curves is emphasized and examples of the computation of growth curves are given.

The metabolic growth model is described both in everyday language and in mathematical terms. Certain subjects, however, are touched on in only one of these presentations.

INTRODUCTION

As a starting point for a growth model, the truism can be taken for instance, that what remains in the body equals what comes in minus what goes out. What remains we call growth. A truism, however, has no information. To build a model or to develop a hypothesis (which is the same thing) is to introduce information into a truism. The first step could be to say "the mass coming in" instead of "what comes in". The acceleration of gravity is conveniently introduced in the next step because we usually measure the weight of a fish rather than its mass. This is most simply done by keeping it constant thereby replacing mass by weight. Another convenient and perhaps not very restrictive assumption is that the specific gravity is constant and equals one. Then we can speak of weight or volume as we like. Such assumptions are often made tacitly and perhaps even unconsciously so that it is difficult to find out on which assumptions a growth hypothesis is based. Body size, whichever way it is measured, must be a concept of the hypothesis because no realistic growth model of reasonably wide application can neglect the influence of the size of the animal upon the growth processes. The truism introduced in the first lines of this paper is likely to lead to a growth model of the metabolic type stressing the fate of food items. Growth, however, has many aspects. There are growth phenomena at the cellular and at the organ level. One model may be of biochemical nature and stress the importance of the rate of molecular interactions, another may be biophysical and centred on the rate of transport of molecules in the body. If a living organism functions with optimum economy—as it probably does after a long period of evolution—then any reasonably wide aspect of its functions probably can be used to deduce a hypothesis of growth.

If there are several ways to describe growth and if, for instance, growth in weight follows an asymmetrical sigmoid curve then mathematically different formulations may be arrived at, these having only one thing in common, namely, that by a suitable choice of parameter values they describe body weight as an asymmetrical sigmoid function of time. Their importance as analytical models of growth is determined by the information contained in the parameters. A growth model can of course be entirely empirical. For instance, it has been observed in decapod crustaceans that the logarithm of the relative increase in length between moults and the logarithm of the duration of the intermoult period are both linearly related to carapace length. Dividing the first expression by the second one gives the rate of growth in length (Hartnoll, 1978). The parameters of the common metabolic growth model (Pütter, 1920: von Bertalanffy, 1934; Brody, 1945; Winberg, 1956; Beverton & Holt, 1957; Warren & Davis, 1967; Jones & Johnston, 1977) contain explicit or implicit information on oxygen consumption as a function of food consumed. The cell differentiation model (Weiss & Kavanau, 1957) has different implications, namely on the reproductive ability of cells as a function of cell differentiation, but leads to a hypothesis (the Gompertz equation) fitting growth curves of fishes as do several other hypotheses. The negative feedback model of Weiss & Kavanau (1957) and Rashevsky (1960) considers certain molecular reactions promoting and inhibiting growth. It is assumed that each organ secretes into the blood a specific substance inhibiting the growth of that organ, but not of any other. It is produced by every cell in the organ. If one organ happens to have grown too big the concentration of the growth-inhibiting substance produced by this organ increases and its growth slows down until the rest of the body is "big enough" at which time the concentration is down to normal. In its simplest form this hypothesis leads to a logistic growth curve—a symmetrical sigmoid—but can be elaborated (Weiss & Kavanau, 1957) by incorporating elements of the cell differentiation model to a complicated expression giving a sigmoid with no restrictions on the inflection point.

Which of the above mentioned models is to be preferred depends on their field of application and on the accuracy with which they describe observations of growth. They are fractions of the pattern of the living organism having a small area of overlap where they describe body size as a function of time. The mathematical formulation may differ or it may be exactly the same. In the latter case, however, the physiological interpretation of the parameters differs from one model to another. The cell differentiation model and the negative feedback model are "introvert" models with obvious applications to problems of medicine and pharmacology. The metabolic model is "extrovert" in the sense that it involves the environment through food consumption and therefore is of particular interest to students of ecology in general and fisheries management and aquaculture in particular.

This is the only model considered below. It is described first in English and then in mathematical language. This may seem an excessive use of space, but each of these languages has its advantages. Most biologists read English fluently whereas few read mathematical expressions with ease. The mathematical language is superior in the precision achieved in the description of logical flow. In everyday language the definition of many words is so vague that it is easily overlooked that the same word is used differently in separate sentences. Precisely this characteristic, however, makes the everyday language fit for expressing vague ideas, not yet ripe for a rigorous formulation. There are therefore sections in the English text which are not repeated in the mathematical section.

THE METABOLIC GROWTH MODEL

This account is to a large extent based on papers by Ursin (1967) and Andersen & Ursin (1977). Specific references to these papers which would be numerous are usually avoided in order to promote fluency of reading. The incorporation of spawning follows to a large extent Jones & Johnston (1977). The search for food, and ingestion as a function of food concentration, are subjects not covered by this paper. They are discussed by Warren & Davis (1967), Andersen & Ursin (1977) and Ursin (in press).

The Food Budget

Here I consider the disposition of a food item in the fish body. The way it is used depends on its chemical composition. Parts of it are useless, as for instance the calcareous deposits of an echinoderm. Other parts will be used more or less efficiently depending on the composition of the food. Fish can use fat in their metabolism, but are assumed to metabolize protein at the same time. Surplus food may be stored as fat in the connective tissue in a process which is not growth proper as we are used to understand it because other tissues do not grow correspondingly. This phenomenon can probably be dealt with by distinguishing between indispensable matter and expendable matter in each cell, but it is premature to discuss it in detail. We are therefore at present forced to assume that the fish eats a balanced diet with the same energy contents as the fish itself. Bivalve shells, etc., are vomited or passed with the faeces, but are disregarded even though, by their mere bulk, they may prevent the fish from eating as much as it otherwise could. These limitations to the realism of the model should be remembered. When a food item as defined under these restrictions is ingested and digested, part of it is absorbed through the gut wall into the blood. The rest passes with the faeces. Winberg (1956) suggested that 80% is assimilated. This still seems good enough as an overall average although notably higher percentages are sometimes found (Beamish, 1972). The figure may change with temperature and with the rate of feeding, but available information is too scanty and too contradictory to be generalized.

The assimilated part of the food covers several needs. One fraction provides energy for the treatment of the food (the feeding catabolism, or apparent specific dynamic action of Beamish (1974)): catching and swallowing food items, producing digestive enzymes, active transport through membranes, building small molecules (amino acids, etc.) into big molecules (proteins, DNA, lipoids, etc.) and deaminating proteins stored as fat. The waste is disposed of in the urine and by diffusion through the gills and skin. Digestive enzymes must to some extent pass with the faeces, but the energy lost in this way is not known. Not even the total metabolic loss due to feeding is well known. Forty percent of the assimilated food may be a good guess (Sperber, From & Sparre, 1977) but also lower values have been estimated (Elliott, 1976; see pp. 80–83). Adopting the value of 40% and with 80% assimilated as suggested above we find this kind of loss to be 32% of the ingested food. Another fraction of the assimilated food covers such metabolic needs as are not connected with feeding. When the fish is not eating, this quantity can be measured as weight loss if the chemical composition of the body does not change. It can therefore be called the fasting catabolism. It seems to vary by at least a factor of six from the most sluggish to the most active species (pp. 79–80). In young brown trout, *Salmo trutta* L., fed to satiation (Elliott, 1976; see pp. 80–83), it amounted to 27% of the energy contents of the ingested food, and to 34% of the absorbed food. We can also consider only the food available for growth, reproduction and other metabolic needs after feeding catabolism, as defined above, is accounted for. The percentage then increases to 47%. Fasting catabolism amounted to 61% of total catabolism. The food necessary to maintain the fish's weight is often called the maintenance requirements. These cover (1) some food not assimilated and passed with the faeces plus enough food to cover (2) the feeding catabolism necessary to supply a net production amounting to (3) the fasting catabolism. Thus if the indispensable requirements of a fish are 1 g day^{-1}, then—with the assumptions made above—1 g is 60% of what the fish must assimilate and this again is 80% of what it has to eat. It must eat $1/0·6/0·8 = 2·08 \text{ g day}^{-1}$ in order to keep its weight constant when its fasting catabolism is 1 g day^{-1}.

In mature fish, gonad production claims its share of the food. It seems that the more the fish eats and the faster it grows the higher the fraction of assimilated food spent on gonad production, as found by Raitt (1968) in Norway pout, *Trisopterus esmarki* (Nilsson), a small gadoid fish. Generalizations, however, cannot be made at present. Gonad weight usually is negligible in immature fish and also in mature fish a short time after spawning. Females spawning annually build up a gonad weighing 10–40% of the body weight. These losses influence the growth curve and even the mortality rate according to Jones & Johnston (1977). If a female eats three times its body weight between two consecutive spawnings then the direct spawning losses amount to 3–13% of total food or 4–17% of assimilated food. The cost of building the gonad instead of ordinary body tissue is not known, but may be higher because there probably are periods when the gonad grows so fast that matter must be transferred from other parts of the body, depriving the cells of their content of expendable matter. Jones & Johnston (1977) found food conversion efficiencies for whiting, *Merlangius merlangus* L., of 0·30 for growth and 0·23 for reproduction but, because of the approximate nature of the calculation, did not consider the difference significant. Fecundity, which is the number of eggs spawned per female during the spawning season, is usually proportional to the body weight after subtraction of a certain initial weight. Often, the fraction spawned referred to above is not well known even when fecundity is. Rarely does the same paper state the calorific content of the fish body and of the eggs and also the number of eggs. Information on egg size and numbers does not suffice because eggs usually absorb water at spawning time. Gonad size is not sufficient either because some fishes spawn over a period of time and there may be rapid egg growth shortly before spawning. Jones & Johnston (1977) calculated from various sources the energy content of eggs in herring, *Clupea harengus* L., cod, *Gadus morhua* L., and whiting and found spawning losses of 16–28% of the total energy content of the fish. These figures have to be adjusted if the production cost of one calorie of egg substance is different than that of one calorie of somatic tissue. The male gonad often weighs less than the female gonad. This does not necessarily imply smaller spawning losses in males because sperm, consisting almost exclusively of DNA, RNA and lipoids, is likely to be the most expensive substance in the fish body. The spawning losses therefore may appear partly in the maintenance metabolism in the period when sperm is produced. Measurements of sperm production in fishes are not known to me, but de Wilde & Berghuis (1978) collected eggs and sperm from a tellinid clam and measured the calorific values. For both sexes they found spawning losses of about 25% of the soft parts of the animal.

    Assimilated food not already disposed of as described above is built into the fish's tissues as growth proper. A fish larva may increase its weight by a factor of 1000 or more in the first three months of life (Jones, 1973) and may grow 25% day^{-1} in the first days (Ishibashi, 1974). Old fish grow very little if at all when yearly data for weight-at-age are considered, but there may be alternating periods of growth and weight loss in the course of the year. The efficiency of food conversion (growth proper plus gonad production, divided by food ingested) cannot, with the figures used above, exceed 48% because 20% was assumed undigested and 32% lost in feeding catabolism. It must be below 48% because fasting catabolism is never zero. In practice, an efficiency of 50% has been observed occasionally in young rainbow trout, *Salmo gairdneri* Richardson, whereas the average figure (at suitable temperature and feeding) was 38% (Sperber *et al.*, 1977). The net efficiency (growth proper plus gonad production, divided by food absorbed) similarly cannot exceed 60% with the figures used above and must be lower. Daan (1973) found for North Sea cod in their second year that 37% of the ingested food was converted into growth proper and none into gonad production. For cod in their tenth year the figures were 3% for growth proper and 11% for gonad production.

The Dependence of Growth upon Body Size

The curve of growth in weight of a fish usually looks approximately as in Fig. 1A although the figure actually represents the average growth of a population (North Sea herring). Using weight-at-age data at yearly intervals, and smoothing, an apparently asymptotic sigmoid curve is obtained as indicated in Fig. 1. The growth rate, Fig. 1B, shows large seasonal fluctuations particularly in mature fish. Note the almost vertical drops of the curve at three years of age, four years, etc., when the gonadal products are lost. In mature herring of both sexes, they account for abut 20% of the fish's weight. The smoothed growth rate, as read from the smooth curve of Fig. 1A, has a maximum at the inflection point of the sigmoid. The relative, or specific, growth rate (Fig. 1C) is high in very young fish and except for seasonal variation decreases through the lifetime of the fish. Fish larvae can probably have specific growth rates of 10 month^{-1} but these early stages are not covered by the herring data in Fig. 1. Curves of growth in length resemble a curve of "growth" of the cube root of body weight (Fig. 1D) except that—because of the vertebral column—length does not decrease appreciably when the fish loses weight. This is illustrated in Fig. 2A. The fish loses condition (gets thinner), as often described by the "condition factor" (Fig. 2B), which is the fish's volume expressed as a percentage of the cube whose side is the length of the fish. The curve of growth in length is often found to have no inflection point when seasonal variation is disregarded. The first part of the curve, however, is not well known. There may be an inflection in the early part of the curve but at a much younger stage than the inflection on the curve of growth in weight.

It was realized a long time ago (Pütter, 1920; Beverton & Holt, 1957) that curves of the desired shape can be obtained on the assumptions (1) that processes of feeding and growth ("anabolic processes") are proportional to the surface of the gut through which the food enters the body and (2) that processes of decomposition ("catabolic processes") are proportional to the weight of the fish because they take place all over the body. The argument is too simple because it overlooks the fact that oxygen required for catabolic processes must enter the body through a surface, predominantly the surface of the gills, but also through the skin in general. If the various stages of the growing fish are similar bodies, then anabolic and catabolic processes alike should be proportional with body weight to the power of two-thirds and with the square of body length. If the organs of the fish change shape in simple and regular ways the rate of processes may be proportional to constant powers (other than two-thirds) of body weight. The gill surface usually increases with a power between two-thirds and one. This is in accordance with numerous observations on respiration as a function of body weight (Brody, 1945; Zeuthen, 1947; Hemmingsen, 1960) indicating a power of about 0·75.

If the same power holds for anabolic processes, growth would be unlimited if not checked by spawning losses. Unfortunately, there is little information on the size dependence of anabolic processes in fishes except for salmonids (Parker & Larkin, 1959; Elliott, 1976; Sperber *et al.*, 1977). These suffer high spawning losses, even to the extent of killing the fish, and their anabolism is proportional to a power of body weight as high as that of catabolism or even higher. Spawning losses consist of the direct loss in shedding gonadal products, and of catabolic losses due to extra activity (e.g. migration) connected with spawning. The latter are difficult to measure and unsatisfactorily known. In most other fish families, the direct spawning losses seem to be smaller than in salmonids and do not alone account for the observed reduction of the growth rate in old, mature fish. Either the total spawning losses are greater than known at present or else anabolic processes are proportional to a lower power of body weight than catabolic processes. There is scattered evidence (Parker & Larkin, 1959; Fonds, 1975) that anabolic processes even in non-salmonids can be proportional to a high power (0·75–0·80) of body weight. It is not clear how this can be made consistent with the information on spawning losses (p. 67). It seems as if immature fish would grow too slowly or adults grow too big. However, there is also evidence to the effect that a growth curve based on a low power of weight for anabolic processes and on fairly small spawning losses is incorrect for the larval stages. The calculated specific growth rate is extremely high in the first days, but decreases rapidly. Observations (Laurence, 1977) on pleuronectid larvae fed to satiation show a steady increase of about 10% day^{-1} until metamorphosis. Such stability might be achieved also in the model by letting the anabolic power of body weight change at the first time when organs change shape rapidly. The data necessary for such an amendment are not yet available.

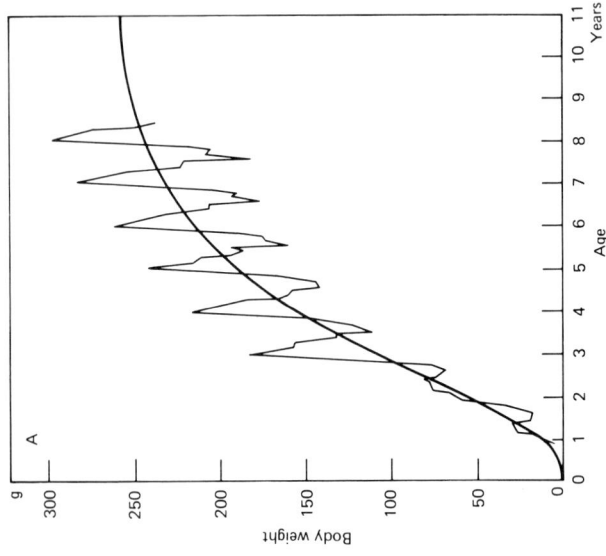

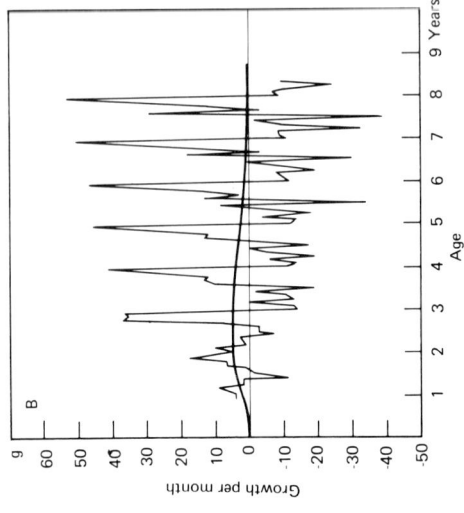

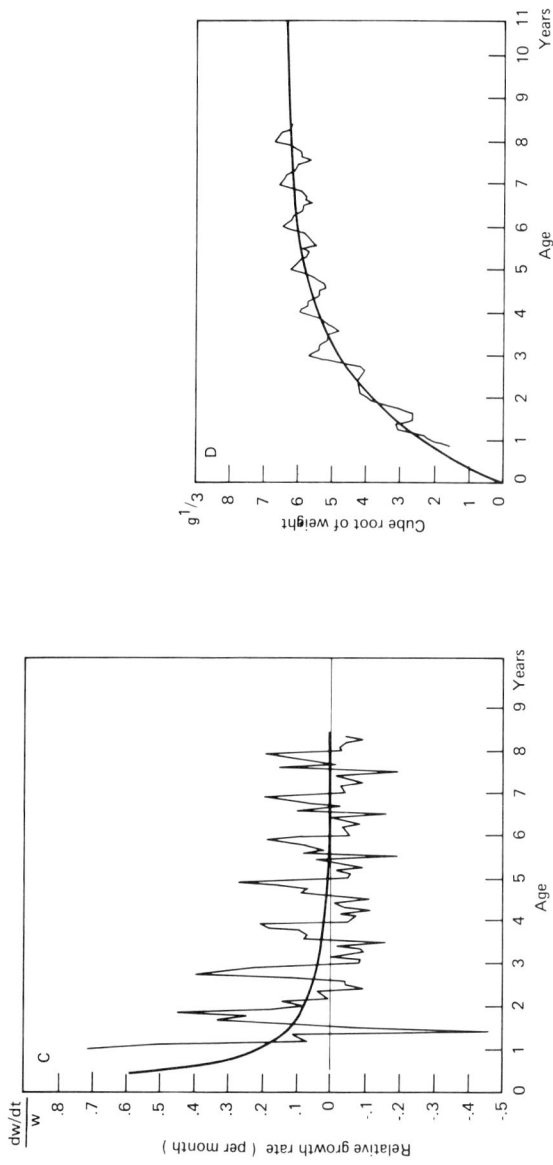

FIG. 1. Growth in weight of North Sea herring, *Clupea harengus*, (summer and autumn spawners) with seasonal variation due to spawning and to variation in growth rate. The smooth curves are calculated from $w(t) = 262[1 - \exp(-0.46t)]^3$, probably the simplest expression producing the shape of a growth curve. In (D) the smooth curve resembles a curve of growth in length (various sources; K. Popp Madsen, pers. comm.).

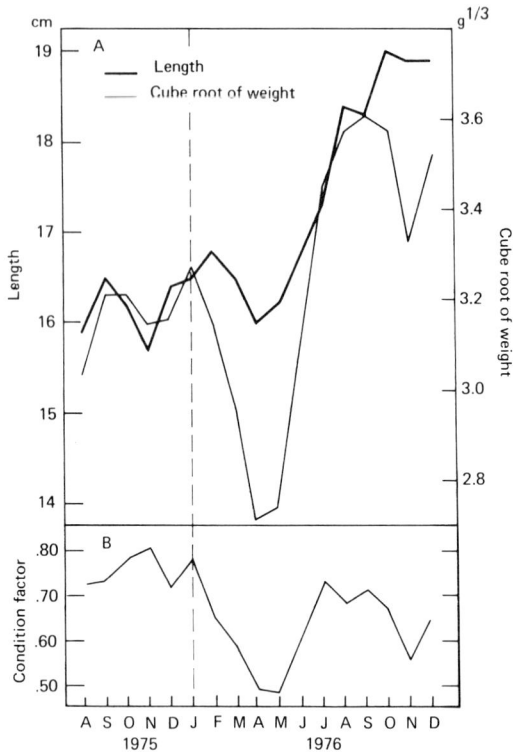

FIG. 2. Length and the cube root of body weight in Norway pout (*Trisopterus esmarki*) hatched in 1974 (NW North Sea; N. Lundgaard, pers. comm). Weight decreases considerably in winter. Length does not because of the vertebral column. The ensuing variation of the condition factor is shown.

The Influence of Temperature

Processes of growth and decomposition are temperature dependent like most other chemical processes. Simple chemical processes are often exponential functions of temperature as sometimes expressed by the quantity Q_{10}, which is the factor by which the rate of a chemical process increases when the temperature increases by 10°C. One often finds $Q_{10} \approx 2$. Growth and metabolism are mostly enzymic processes behaving approximately as described by the Michaelis–Menten equation which contains two rate constants. Both of these may be assumed to be functions of temperature, but not necessarily the same function. It has been found already by Ege & Krogh (1914) that respiration (i.e. decomposition) is almost but not quite an exponential function of temperature with $Q_{10} \approx 2$. The deviation from an exponential relationship can be described as the effect of an underlying Michaelis–Menten type process (Ursin, 1967).

Growth processes as a function of temperature are difficult to investigate independently of the catabolic processes. An approximate picture of the relationship is obtained when studying the growth rate of very young fish because in these the specific growth rate (growth in unit time divided by body weight) is very large as compared to the specific fasting catabolism. Such observations of growth usually have a distinct maximum and steep downward slope at high temperatures. Most fishes seem to live mainly on the left leg (Fig. 3, top) of the curve, but some (e.g. the guppy, *Poecilia reticulata* Peters) seem to live at temperatures symmetrical about the maximum (Ursin, 1963). Catabolic processes (Fig. 3, middle) cover only a small part of the left leg of the temperature-modified Michaelis–Menten curve. They increase until at some temperature the fish becomes moribund. The growth curve (Fig. 3, bottom) has a distinct maximum. If the fish of Fig. 3 had lived permanently at 30°C, as guppies can, it would never have reached the weight of 100 mg which it actually did.

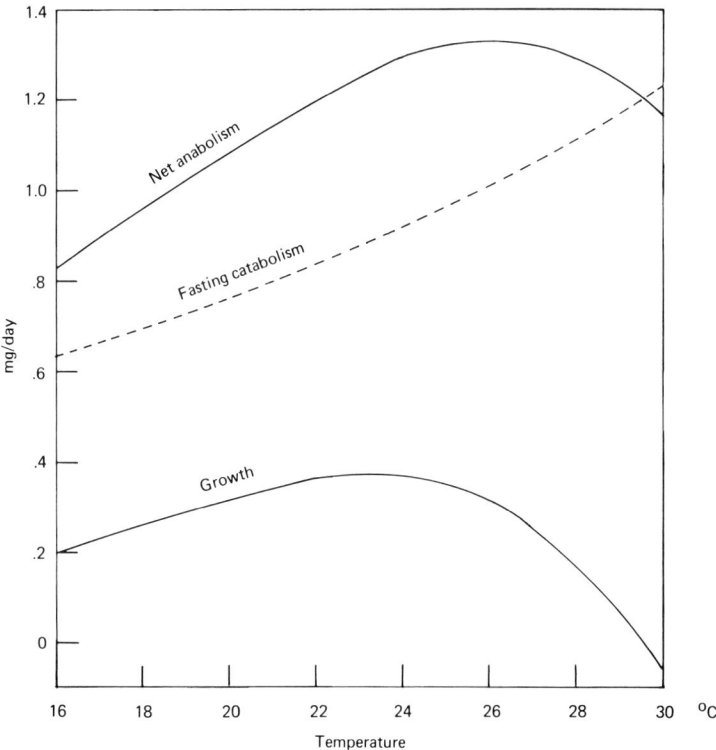

FIG. 3. Growth of a male guppy, *Poecilia reticulata*, weighing 100 mg, at a range of temperatures. Net anabolism is assimilation minus metabolism caused by feeding. Fasting catabolism is the metabolism required for processes independent of feeding. Growth is the difference. From Ursin (1967), redrawn.

Curves describing fish growth as a function of salinity (Gibson & Hirst, 1955; Kinne, 1963) also seem to have a maximum, but the underlying physiological mechanisms remain obscure.

The Influence of Oxygen

Because respiration is a prerequisite to growth as described above it can be assumed that growth depends on oxygen concentration in the same way as respiration does, but observations are not available. Oxygen uptake as a function of oxygen concentration can be described in terms of the permeability of cell membranes and diffusion (Rashevsky, 1960). The rate of respiration of many fishes is in practice independent of oxygen contents at levels above two-thirds saturation. Fishes like the brook trout, *Salvelinus fontinalis* Mitchill, which normally live in over-saturated water, may require almost saturated water for their respiration to be virtually unhampered (Job, 1955).

A FORMULATION IN MATHEMATICAL TERMS

The description below is deterministic. For a closely related stochastic growth model, see Sperber *et al.* (1977). Begin with the truism referred to on p. 63:

$$\text{GROWTH} = \text{IN} - \text{OUT}$$

and use units of g body weight (wet). Assume constant energy content, for instance 1 kcal g^{-1}. Consider initially the time before first spawning and the periods between successive spawnings.

Food Consumption and Assimilation

The term IN is determined by food consumption and by the efficiency of food conversion. Using infinitesimal notation we can express the rate of food consumption as

$$dR/dt = fhw^m, \tag{1}$$

where R is food consumed; w, body weight; f, feeding level ($0 \leqslant f \leqslant 1$); t, time and h, coefficient of food consumption. In aquaculture, f can be made an independent variable. In nature, it is a function of food concentration. The coefficient h can be expanded as a function of temperature, τ, measured in degrees centigrade (Ursin, 1963, 1967)

$$h(\tau) = \frac{1}{a_0 \exp(p_0\tau) + a_1 \exp(-p_1\tau)} \simeq \frac{h_m}{\cosh p_h(\tau - \tau_m)}. \tag{2}$$

The first expression of equation (2) is derived from the Michaelis–Menten expression for the rate of enzymic processes and the Arrhenius equation for the temperature dependence of simple chemical processes. The second expression of equation (2) is a symmetrical approximation where h_m is the maximum value of h, attained at temperature τ_m.

The fraction β of the ingested food is absorbed. Sperber *et al.* (1977) describe β as a decreasing function of the feeding level in the following way

$$\beta = \beta_0(1 - Af),$$

with

$$0 \leqslant A < 1 \qquad (3)$$

whereas other authors (Ursin, 1967; Elliott, 1976) use expressions involving exponentials. Winberg (1956) puts β constant. We have

$$\text{faeces} = (1 - \beta)\, dR/dt = (1 - \beta_0(1 - Af))fhw^m \qquad (4)$$

which does not concern the IN–OUT equation because the part of the food ending up as faeces never enters the fish body proper. The absorbed food is

$$\text{IN} = \beta\, dR/dt = \beta_0(1 - Af)fhw^m. \qquad (5)$$

Metabolic Losses

OUT has two terms: losses due to feeding and assimilation activities (feeding catabolism) and losses due to processes independent of feeding (fasting catabolism). Feeding catabolism amounts to the fraction α of the assimilated food. Fasting catabolism is assumed proportional to the oxygen-absorbing surfaces

$$\text{Feeding catabolism} = \alpha\beta\, dR/dt. \qquad (6)$$

$$\text{Fasting catabolism} = kw^n. \qquad (7)$$

$$\text{OUT} = \alpha\beta\, dR/dt + kw^n = \alpha\beta fhw^m + kw^n. \qquad (8)$$

Sperber *et al.* (1977) discuss the possibility that α is a function of the feeding level.

Like h, k can be expanded as a function of temperature as

$$k(\tau) = \frac{1}{a_2 \exp(p_2\tau) + a_3 \exp(p_3\tau)} \approx k_0 \exp(p_k\tau) \qquad (9)$$

which is "Krogh's respiration curve" (Ege & Krogh, 1914). The simpler expression is a fair approximation only within temperature intervals of 10 or 15°C.

Growth

The original expression, GROWTH = IN − OUT, can now be replaced by

$$dw/dt = (1-\alpha)\beta \, dR/dt - kw^n$$
$$= (1-\alpha)\beta_0(1-Af)fhw^m - kw^n \tag{10}$$
$$= Hw^m - kw^n;$$

$$H = (1-\alpha)\beta_0(1-Af)fh \tag{11}$$

which for constant H can be solved analytically when one of the conditions $m = n$, $m = 1$ or $n = 1$ is fulfilled. Putting $dw/dt = 0$ gives

$$w = W_\infty = \left(\frac{H}{k}\right)^{1/(n-m)} \tag{12}$$

W_∞ is an asymptote for $n > m$ and H constant. The curve then has an inflection at

$$w = W_I = W_\infty = \left(\frac{m}{n}\right)^{1/(n-m)} \tag{13}$$

Putting $m = \frac{2}{3}$ and $n = 1$ in the growth equation takes us back to Pütter (1920) with an expression easily integrated (Beverton & Holt, 1957) as

$$w(t) = W_\infty\{1 - \exp\left[-(t - t_0)k/3\right]\}^3, \tag{14}$$

with $W_\infty = (H/k)^3$ and with t_0 chosen such that $w(t_0) = 0$. The value $n - m = \frac{1}{3}$ tends to overemphasize the fasting catabolism to an extent corresponding to spawning losses. The expression therefore often gives a good representation of the growth of an adult fish and is widely used by fishery biologists who are often interested in annual growth rates disregarding the seasonal variation (see Fig. 1A and D). Growth in weight is easily transformed into growth in length on the assumption that $w = ql^3$, where l is body length and q a constant. For fishes of ordinary shape we find $q \simeq 0\cdot01$. Thus

$$dl/dt = El^{3m-2} - Kl^{3n-2}; \tag{15}$$

$$E = \frac{H}{3q^{1-m}}; \tag{16}$$

$$K = \frac{k}{3q^{1-n}} \tag{17}$$

which for $m = \frac{2}{3}$ and $n = 1$ reduces to

$$dl/dt = E - Kl; \tag{18}$$
$$E = \frac{H}{3q^{1/3}}; \tag{19}$$

$$K = k/3. \tag{20}$$

This is easily integrated as

$$l(t) = L_\infty\{1 - \exp\left[-(t - t_0)K\right]\}, \qquad \text{where } L_\infty = E/K. \qquad (21)$$

The quantity $100q$ is often called the condition factor. Generalizing, we write

$$w = ql^3 = (\hat{q}l^{b-3})l^3 = \hat{q}l^b. \qquad (22)$$

Assuming that the expression for dw/dt remains the same we get

$$l(t) = L_\infty\{1 - \exp\left[-(t - t_0)K\right]\}^{3/b}, \qquad \text{where } L_\infty = [H/(k\hat{q}^{1/3})]^{3/b}. \ (23)$$

It is sometimes desirable to define the feeding rate and metabolism necessary for the fish to just maintain its weight, the so-called maintenance ration and maintenance metabolism. The weight loss of a fasting fish (the fasting catabolism) is kw^n. Assuming a constant fraction assimilated we find the maintenance ration by putting

$$kw^n = Hw^m = (1 - \alpha)\beta(dR/dt)_{\text{maint}} \qquad (24)$$

from which

$$(dR/dt)_{\text{maint}} = \frac{k}{(1 - \alpha)\beta}w^n. \qquad (25)$$

Multiplying by β gives the maintenance rate of assimilation

$$\text{IN}_{\text{maint}} = \frac{k}{1 - \alpha}w^n \qquad (26)$$

which of course equals the maintenance metabolic rate

$$\text{OUT}_{\text{maint}} = \alpha\beta(dR/dt)_{\text{maint}} + kw^n = \frac{k}{1 - \alpha}w^n. \qquad (27)$$

Growth Modified by Spawning

Assuming spawning to be momentaneous, the growth curve is produced by integrating first until the age of first maturity. Body weight is then reduced by a fraction π simulating the loss of gonadal products, and the integration procedure is resumed with a starting weight of $(1 - \pi)w_{\text{before}}$ where w_{before} is the weight immediately before spawning. This is repeated at each consecutive spawning. An alternative is to retain (almost) the differentiability of the entire growth curve by assuming spawning normally distributed about a certain date. A Gauss expression is introduced as an extra term in the growth equation

$$dw/dt = Hw^m - kw^n - \varphi(I, \sigma, t)\pi(I)w, \qquad (28)$$

where

$$\varphi(I, \sigma, t) = \frac{1}{\sigma\sqrt{2 \times 3 \cdot 1416}} \exp\left[-\frac{1}{2}\left(\frac{t - I}{\sigma}\right)^2\right].$$

Assuming annual spawning periods, I is the age in integral years counted so that the age is zero in the first one-half year, one in the following year, etc. The fraction spawned is $\pi(I)$ which is zero until six months before the first spawning when it takes on a constant, positive value.

The growth models of this paper are supposed to describe the growth of an individual fish. In practice, they are often used, and apparently to a good approximation, to describe the growth of a year-class of fish represented by their average body size. Because individual specimens attain maturity at different ages $\pi(I)$ can be multiplied by the fraction of the population which is mature at age I.

Oxygen Consumption

It was found above that the metabolic rate which is also the rate of excretion measured in units of biomass equivalents can be described as

$$OUT = \alpha\beta fhw^m + kw^n. \tag{29}$$

Note that in the present model excretion stands for metabolic losses measured by the biomass lost. In this context it is immaterial whether combustion is complete or not. In models accounting for energy rather than biomass the word excretion often means unmetabolized wastes in urine, etc. A conversion factor ω is needed to find the oxygen consumption. It varies with the fat content of the fish because the combustion of fat requires much oxygen. Accordingly, ω values from $0\cdot23$ in flatfish to $0\cdot64$ in fat herring have been calculated. With O denoting the oxygen consumption, we write

$$dO/dt = \omega(\alpha\beta fhw^m + kw^n) \simeq aw^\gamma \tag{30}$$

and realize that for $m \neq n$ the shape of the oxygen consumption curve depends on the feeding level f. For f equal to zero we have the oxygen consumption of the fasting fish, $dO/dt = \omega kw^n$ with $\gamma = n$.

Comparing the respiration of species of different size is a different topic because h is a function of species size. Confining ourselves to the case $m < n$ this can be demonstrated by defining somewhat arbitrarily the "species size" $\hat{w}$ as the size W_I at the inflection point of the growth curve for maximum feeding level, $f = 1$. We have

$$\hat{w} = \left(\frac{m}{n} \frac{(1-\alpha)\beta h}{k}\right)^{1/(n-m)} \tag{31}$$

from which

$$h = \frac{n}{m} \frac{k}{(1-\alpha)\beta} \hat{w}^{n-m}. \tag{32}$$

Assume for the moment that n is a universal constant and consider a large number of species living each at its own characteristic activity level as described by its k value. We can then assume an average value $\hat{k}$ and after substitution for h obtain an expression for the oxygen consumption of a fish fed to satiation as a function of species size

$$\mathrm{d}O/\mathrm{d}t = \omega\left(\frac{n}{m}\,\frac{\alpha}{1-\alpha}+1\right)\hat{k}\hat{w}^{n} = a\hat{w}^{\gamma} \tag{33}$$

indicating, that the exponent γ estimated from respiration experiments (Zeuthen, 1947; Hemmingsen, 1960) is the n of the growth equation. With $n \simeq 0 \cdot 75$ it seems to apply to most taxonomic groups of animals.

Estimates of Fasting Catabolism

The coefficient k of fasting catabolism determines to a large extent the shape of a growth curve. Most authors discussing the value of k in general terms use the Pütter formulation of the catabolic term of the growth equation: kw, introducing a bias because $n = 1$ is an overestimate. Using for the moment κ to designate the "true" value of k, we have

$$kw^{n} = (\kappa w^{n-1})w. \tag{34}$$

On estimating k from growth curves by the standard methods of fishery biologists (Beverton & Holt, 1957), we estimate the quantity κw^{n-1} as if it were a constant where w takes on some kind of mean value of the body weights of the fish used in the estimation. Large values of k are therefore usually found for small species and small values for big species. We shall here seek estimates of k devoid of this bias.

Hemmingsen (1960) recalculated available observations of oxygen consumption to kcal spent h^{-1} at 20°C. Assuming that one gram wet weight of an "average" animal represents 1 kcal we can read from his Fig. 2 the rate of weight loss of a poikilotherm weighing 1 g as $\mathrm{d}w/\mathrm{d}t = -0 \cdot 631$ mg $h^{-1} = -5 \cdot 53$ g year^{-1}. Observations of standard metabolism were used with preference by Hemmingsen, but few authors cared about the feeding level of the animal. Standard metabolism corresponds to a lower level of activity than $\hat{k}$ which is determined from animals behaving normally. On the other hand, Saunders (1963), working on cod weighing a few hundred grams, found that respiration continued to decrease in the first week after a substantial meal. This seems a longer time than most authors kept their animals fasting before respiration experiments. Using equation (33), we therefore probably can put

$$\hat{k} < 5 \cdot 53 < \left(\frac{n}{m}\,\frac{\alpha}{1-\alpha}+1\right)\hat{k}. \tag{35}$$

With values of m and n as in the following paragraph and with $\alpha = 0 \cdot 4$ (derived from Sperber et al., 1977, assuming $\beta = 0 \cdot 8$ for $f = 0 \cdot 6$) we get: $2 \cdot 91 < \hat{k} < 5 \cdot 53$ (temperature is 20°C). Ursin (1967) estimated $\hat{k}$ from size-at-age data for 81 fish species and from weight loss data for 12 species and found $\hat{k} = 4 \cdot 13$ after adjusting to 20°C. The confidence intervals were $3 \cdot 6$ to $4 \cdot 7$. Most species considered are from temperate areas with an annual mean temperature considerably below 20°C. Adjusting to 10°C may be more realistic. Assuming $Q_{10} = 2$ we obtain $\hat{k} \approx 2$ as an estimate valid for these animals in their natural environment. Because the gills are oxygen's most important access to the body, k is likely to be proportional to the gill area. Gray (1954) measured the gill surface in 31 marine fishes. These can be classified crudely as active, ordinary or sluggish. The mean gill area is six times bigger for active species than for sluggish ones. With $\hat{k} = 2$ in temperate waters we therefore can put $k = 5$ in active species, $k = 2$ in ordinary species and $k = 0.8$ in sluggish ones. Further work on gill surface area in fishes has been reviewed by Hughes & Morgan (1973).

Parameter Estimates for Brown Trout

Elliott (1976), in a study of the energetics of brown trout, determined most of the quantities necessary for the estimation of the parameters of the present model.

Elliott (1976) with reference to Ricker describes the energy budget as

$$C = F + U + \Delta B + R,$$

where $R = R_s + R_a + R_d$; C the energy value of food consumed; F the energy value of faeces; U the energy value of excretory products; ΔB the energy value of growth or loss, including spawning; R the total energy of metabolism; R_s the energy of standard metabolism (unfed and resting fish); R_a the energy of activity and R_d the energy required for digesting, moving and depositing food.

This model differs from the one described in this paper in the partitioning of metabolic losses. The difference is partly caused by the use of energy units instead of wet weight equivalents. This calls for a special account of unmetabolized energy in waste products (urine, etc.). The term for energy of activity gives some trouble because in this paper activity is partitioned into "normal behaviour" and activity caused by feeding. The quantities listed above including the growth rate are measured in calories and developed as functions of body wet weight. The mean energy content of 1 g of fish tissue can be calculated as equivalent to 1412 cal. The figures given below are all recalculated to body wet weight equivalents. Elliott hesitated to use mathematical expressions which were not linear or could not be made linear by taking logarithms. More complicated relationships are represented by a set of expressions each covering an arbitrary range of an independent variable. For instance, food consumption at satiation is described by the expression

$$C_{\max} = aW^{b_1} \exp(b_2 T) \tag{36}$$

where $C_{\max}$ is the energy value of satiation food, W the body wet weight of the trout and T the temperature in centigrades. a, b_1 and b_2 are parameters estimated separately for each of the temperature ranges 3.8–6.6°C, 6.6–13.3°C, 13.3–17.8°C and 17.8–21.7°C. The temperature coefficient b_2 decreases when temperature increases and is negative for the highest temperature range. This recalls the more or less bell-shaped curve describing anabolic processes as a function of temperature in the present paper. For convenience we shall assume a temperature of 10°C throughout.

There are nine estimates of exponents which in terms of this paper are either m, n or intermediate. All are in the interval 0·731–0·770 with 95% confidence intervals of about 0·04. The differences are probably not statistically significant although this is difficult to tell because of the above-mentioned adoption of arbitrary temperature ranges. There seems to be a tendency towards low exponents for observations referring to fasting animals or animals on low rations which would indicate $n < m$ as found by Sperber et al. (1977) for rainbow trout. In the present case, the difference, if any, is small and, neglecting it, we shall recalculate from Elliott's Table 2 to adjust the coefficients to a mean exponent value of 0·75.

As an example, consider the expression for satiation ration quoted above where we shall use as an accessory in the process of recalculation a body weight of 50 g because much of Elliott's work was done with fish of this size. We have $a = 15 \cdot 018$; $b_1 = 0 \cdot 759$; $b_2 = 0 \cdot 171$; $T = 10°C$; $W = 50$ g; cal g$^{-1} = 1412$ and find

$$C_{max} = aW^{b_1} \exp(b_2 T) = 1 \cdot 14535 \text{ g day}^{-1}. \tag{37}$$

Introducing $b_1 = n = m = 0 \cdot 75$ gives $w^{0 \cdot 75} = 18 \cdot 8030$ and $C_{max} = (1 \cdot 14535/18 \cdot 8030)w^{0 \cdot 75} = 0 \cdot 060913 w^{0 \cdot 75}$. The coefficient is fh in the notation of this paper. The fish being fed to satiation, we put $f = 1$ and get $h = 0 \cdot 060913$ g$^{0 \cdot 75}$ day$^{-1} = 22 \cdot 25$ g$^{0 \cdot 75}$ year^{-1}. The following results are obtained

$$C_{max} = 0 \cdot 060913 w^{0 \cdot 75};$$

$$F = P_F C; \ P_F = 0 \cdot 23899 \text{ (i.e. } \beta = 1 - P_F = 0 \cdot 76101);$$

$$U = P_U C; \ P_U = 0 \cdot 073020;$$

$$R = 0 \cdot 022912 w^{0 \cdot 75};$$

$$R_s = 0 \cdot 013904 w^{0 \cdot 75};$$

$$R_a + R_d = R - R_s = 0 \cdot 009008 w^{0 \cdot 75};$$

and

$$\Delta B = C - F - U - R_s - R_a - R_d = 0 \cdot 018996 w^{0 \cdot 75}$$

[i.e. $(1 - \alpha)\beta h - k = 0 \cdot 018996$]. Integrating $dw/dt = aw^n$ we get

$$w(t) = [w_0^{1-n} + (1-n)at]^{1/(1-n)} \tag{38}$$

This is in Table I, assuming $w_0 = 0 \cdot 09$ g. Elliott's test animals were immature. Assuming a momentaneous annual spawning cost of 40% of the body weight from four years on leads to the second column of Table I.

TABLE I

Calculated weights of brown trout

Age (years)	Weight	
	No spawning	With spawning (pre-spawning weight)
0	0·09 g	0·09 g
1	27·1 g	27·1 g
2	260 g	260 g
3	1·09 kg	1·09 kg
4	3·14 kg	3·14 kg
6	14·4 kg	6·74 kg
10	103 kg	15·9 kg
40	23·9 tonnes	43·0 kg
41	26·4 tonnes	43·1 kg

The first column assumes no spawning losses. The second column assumes annual spawning losses of 40% of the fish's weight from four years of age.

These results are quite sensible when it is remembered that brown trout seldom reach more than 10 years old.

The parameters m, n, h and β were estimated above. There remain α and k to be estimated from observations on feeding catabolism and fasting catabolism respectively. Elliott's Fig. 5 describes the weight change of trout of an initial weight of 50 g as a function of feeding level and temperature. For 10°C and $f = 0$, we find a weight loss of $k \times 50^{0.75} = 0.265581$ g day^{-1} from which $k = 0.014124$ g$^{0.25}$ day^{-1}. In order to compare this with observations of standard metabolism the latter must be multiplied by its proportional share of U, the uncombusted metabolic waste. Thus, we find the weight loss due to standard metabolism (the metabolism of an unfed and resting fish) to be $R_s(1 + U/R) = 0.016603 w^{0.75}$ which is slightly more than the figure of $0.014124 w^{0.75}$ found for an unfed fish behaving normally. The difference must be ascribed to variance. Within the accuracy of the observations we therefore can put $R_s(1 + U/R) = kw^n$ and assume that all activity of a fish fed to satiation is due to feeding so that $(R_a + R_d)(1 + U/R) = \alpha\beta hw^m = 0.010757 w^{0.75}$ from which $\alpha = 0.2320$. Using the second estimate of k the full list of parameter estimates becomes: $m = n = 0.75$; $\beta = 0.7610$; $\alpha = 0.2320$; $h = 0.060913$ g^{1-m} day$^{-1} = 22.25$ g^{1-m} year^{-1} and $k = 0.016603$ g^{1-n} day$^{-1} = 6.064$ g^{1-n} year^{-1}. The parameter estimates can be utilized when calculating the various quantities for trout fed below satiation level $(0 < f < 1)$. For $m = n$ we have in the notation of this paper:

$$dR/dt = fhw^m \tag{39}$$

$$\mathrm{d}U/\mathrm{d}t = (\alpha\beta fh + k)w^m. \tag{40}$$

$$\mathrm{d}w/\mathrm{d}t = [(1-\alpha)\beta fh - k]w^m \tag{41}$$

Note that Elliott uses U (for metabolic waste) differently to myself (total metabolism measured as weight loss).

It would have been more interesting in the present context if Elliott had used a fish with notably different values of m and n. Then the hypotheses on which exponents to expect in the various expressions could have been tested. On the other hand many things become simpler and clearer when all quantities are proportional to the same power of body weight. For instance, we find irrespective of body size the following estimates of the relative importance of the fasting catabolism (kw^n) of trout fed to satiation. Fasting catabolism as a fraction of

1. ingested food, $k/fh = 0\cdot27$;
2. absorbed food, $k/\beta fh = 0\cdot36$;
3. food available for growth, reproduction and maintenance, $k/(1-\alpha)\beta fh = 0\cdot47$;
4. total catabolism, $k/(k+\alpha\beta fh) = 0\cdot61$.

Some Computed Growth Curves

Detailed observations on the seasonal variation of growth in fishes are scarce in literature. The herring material of Fig. 1 is rather exceptional, but is not satisfactorily described by the model presented here because seasonal variation of food concentration is quite important. Instead, North Sea plaice, *Pleuronectes platessa* L., was chosen for the examples of computation because it is a classic population in studies of population dynamics (notably by Beverton & Holt, 1957). Figure 4 shows five computed curves of growth of North Sea plaice from birth to seven years old. Complexity increases from left to right.

Curve A represents a simple Pütter-von Bertalanffy expression with the parameter estimates made by Beverton & Holt (1957). Weight-at-age data from the same source are plotted. We have $\mathrm{d}w/\mathrm{d}t = Hw^{2/3} - kw$; $w(t) = W_\infty [1 - \exp(-(t-t_0)k/3]^3$; $H = 4\cdot049\,\mathrm{g}^{1/3}$ year^{-1}; $k = 0\cdot285$ year^{-1}; $t_0 = 0\cdot815$ years; $W_\infty = (H/k)^3 = 2867$ g. The part of the curve representing time before birth ($t_0 \leqslant t < 0$) is omitted. The estimated weight at birth is $1\cdot19$ g which is unrealistic because the hatching weight is about $0\cdot3$ mg, but later on and even up to 20 years old the fit is satisfactory and W_∞ is indeed like the size of a very old plaice.

Curve B is similar except for the exponents: $\mathrm{d}w/\mathrm{d}t = Hw^m - kw^n$: $H = 4.3\,\mathrm{g}^{1-m}$ year^{-1} for $t < 1$ year; $H = 8\cdot6\mathrm{g}^{1-m}$ year^{-1} for $t \geqslant 1$ year; $k = 1\cdot62\,\mathrm{g}^{1-n}$ year^{-1}; $m = 0\cdot58$; $n = 0\cdot78$; $W_\infty = (H/k)^c = 4216$ g and $c = (1/(n-m)) = 5$. The value of n is fairly realistic with respect to metabolic rates as a function of body size. The value of m is close to an estimate of $m = 0\cdot56$ from size-at-age data for 81 fish species (Ursin, 1967). The

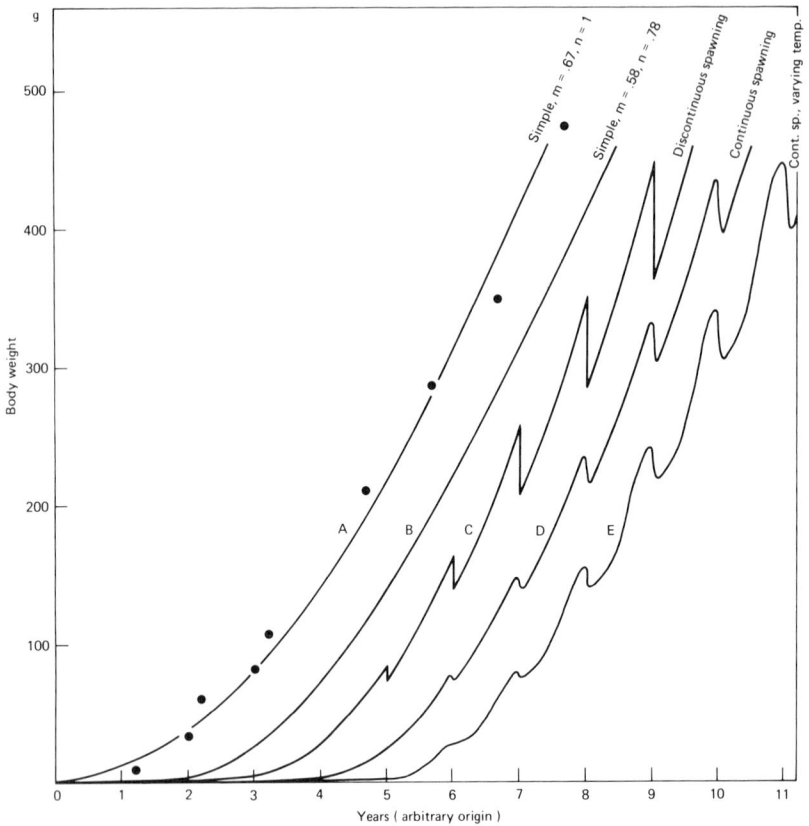

Fig. 4. North Sea plaice, *Pleuronectes platessa*. Five growth curves of increasing complexity from left to right. Curve A: Pütter-von Bertalanffy curve from Beverton & Holt (1957). Curves B–E: exponents adjusted to coincide with respiration experiments. Curve B: spawning implicit in catabolism. Curve C: spawning momentaneous once a year. Curve D: continuous spawning over a couple of months. Curve E: as curve D, but with account of seasonal temperature variation.

equation is integrated numerically beginning with $w = 0.0003$ g for $t = 0$. Using a constant value of H throughout leads to too fast growth in the first year, hence the reduction of H to one-half of its normal value. The failure of the model to describe early growth in a realistic way is discussed on p. 69.

Curve C differs from curve B by the introduction of spawning by subtracting a fraction $\pi(I)$ from the body weight once a year as described on p. 77. $dw/dt = Hw^m - kw^n$ in the continuous phase; $w_{after} = [1 - \pi(I)]w_{before}$ at spawning; $\pi(1) = 0$; $\pi(2) = 0.04$; $\pi(3) = 0.11$; $\pi(4) =$

$\pi(5)\ldots = 0\cdot15$; $H = 3\cdot5$ for $t < 1$ year; $H = 7\cdot0$ for $t \geq 1$ year; $k = 0\cdot50$; m and n as in curve B. The asymptotic size found by numerical integration is about 2000 g. The traditional $W_\infty = (H/k)^5 = 538$ kg is not very useful. The adoption of increasing values of π until an age of four years acknowledges the sought curve as the growth curve of a population of plaice some of which mature early, others late.

Curve D is similar to curve C except that spawning is continuous and follows a Gauss curve as described above: $\mathrm{d}w/\mathrm{d}t = Hw^m - kw^n - \varphi(I, \sigma, t)\pi(I)w$; $H = 3\cdot65$ for $t < 1$ year; $H = 7\cdot3$ for $t \geq 1$ year; $k = 0\cdot70$; $\sigma = 0\cdot03$ years; m, n and $\pi(I)$ as in curve C. The value of σ indicates that 68% of the spawning is assumed accomplished in $2\sigma = 0\cdot06$ years = 22 days and 95% in $2 \times 1\cdot96\sigma = 0\cdot118$ years = 43 days.

In curve E a temperature dependence of H and k as described above is superimposed on curve D: $\mathrm{d}w/\mathrm{d}t = H(\tau)w^m - k(\tau)w^n - \varphi(I, \sigma, t)\pi(I)w$; $H(\tau) = H_m/\cosh p_h(\tau - \tau_m)$; $H_m = 11\cdot7$; $p_h = 0\cdot186$; $\tau_m = 14\cdot2°C$; mean $H = 7\cdot44$: annual range: $4\cdot1 < H < 10\cdot8$; $k(\tau) = k_0 \exp (p_k\tau)$; $k_0 = 0\cdot38$; $p_k = 0\cdot07$; mean $k = 0\cdot710$; annual range: $0\cdot54 < k < 0\cdot88$; m, n and $\pi(I)$ as in curves C and D. The parameter values are from Ursin (1963, 1967). The annual temperature variation is described by: $\tau(t) = 3\cdot5 \sin (2 \times 3\cdot1416(t + 0\cdot67)] + 8\cdot5$ so that the maximum (12°C) is on 1 September and the minimum (3·5°C) on 1 March.

To summarize, the H and k estimates are in the five cases as follows

Curve	H	k
A	4·05	0·285
B	8·60	1·620
C	7·00	0·500
D	7·30	0·700
E	7·44	0·710

It was found above that, for a sluggish fish like the plaice, a k value of about 0·8 is expected in respiration experiments. The estimates from curves C, D and E, in which spawning is explicitly accounted for, are in fair agreement with this. The two simple curves, A and B, do not produce physiologically relevant values of k although they fit annual observations of weight-at-age. Curve A, however, is based on a different set of exponents. Its k value is therefore not directly comparable.

For comparison with plaice ("sluggish"), similar estimates were made for herring ("active") and cod ("ordinary") using the curve C expression with discontinuous spawning. The herring material was that of Fig. 1. For cod data was used from Daan (1974). Values of m and n were again 0·58 and 0·78. As for plaice H was reduced for cod to one-half of its value in the first year of life. The π values for cod increased through ages one to five: 0, 0·01, 0·04, 0·17, 0·19. For herring, they increased through ages one to four: 0, 0·01, 0·16, 0·20. The estimated values of k can be compared to values expected from respiration data (see p. 80).

Estimated "Expected"

	H	k	k
Plaice	7·0	0·5	0·8
Cod	31·0	2·0	2·0
Herring	15·1	4·0	5·0

The results are good enough to go on with. So here we stop.

REFERENCES

Andersen, K. P. & Ursin, E. (1977). A multispecies extension to the Beverton and Holt theory of fishing, with accounts of phosphorus circulation and primary production. *Meddr Danm. Fisk.-og Havunders.* N.S. **7**: 319–435.

Beamish, F. W. H. (1972). Ration size and digestion in largemouth bass, *Micropterus salmoides* Lacepède. *Can. J. Zool.* **50**: 153–164.

Beamish, F. W. H. (1974). Apparent specific dynamic action of largemouth bass, *Micropterus salmoides*. *J. Fish. Res. Bd Can.* **31**: 1763–1769.

Beverton, R. J. H. & Holt, S. J. (1957). On the dynamics of exploited fish populations. *Fishery Invest. Lond.* (2) **19**: 1–533.

Brody, S. (1945). *Bioenergetics and growth.* New York: Reinhold.

Daan, N. (1973). A quantitative analysis of the food intake of North Sea cod, *Gadus morhua*. *Neth. J. Sea Res.* **6**: 479–517.

Daan, N. (1974). Growth of North Sea cod, *Gadus morhua*. *Neth. J. Sea Res.* **8**: 27–48.

Ege, R. & Krogh, A. (1914). On the relation between temperature and the respiratory exchange in fishes. *Int. Rev. Hydrobiol.* **7**: 48–55.

Elliott, J. M. (1976). The energetics of feeding, metabolism and growth of brown trout (*Salmo trutta* L.) in relation to body weight, water temperature and ration size. *J. Anim. Ecol.* **45**: 923–948.

Fonds, M. (1975). The influence of temperature and salinity on growth of young sole *Solea solea* L. *Europ. Symp. Mar. Biol.* **10** (1): 109–125.

Gibson, M. B. & Hirst, B. (1955). The effect of salinity and temperature on the pre-adult growth of guppies. *Copeia* **1955**: 241–243.

Gray, I. E. (1954). Comparative study of the gill area of marine fishes. *Biol. Bull. mar. biol. Lab. Woods Hole* **107**: 219–225.

Hartnoll, R. G. (1978). The effect of salinity and temperature on the post-larval growth of the crab *Rhithropanopeus harrisii*. In *Physiology and behaviour of marine organisms*: 349–358. (Proceedings of the 12th Europ. Symp. Mar. Biol.) McLusky, D. S. & Berry, A. J. (eds). Oxford: Pergamon Press.

Hemmingsen, A. (1960). Energy metabolism as related to body size and respiratory surfaces, and its evolution. *Rep. Steno Mem. Hosp.* **9** (2): 1–110.

Hughes, G. M. & Morgan, M. (1973). The structure of fish gills in relation to their respiratory function. *Biol. Rev.* **48**: 419–475.

Ishibashi, N. (1974). Feeding, starvation and weight changes of early fish larvae. In *The early life history of fish*: 339–344. Blaxter, J. H. S. (ed.). Berlin, Heidelberg, New York: Springer-Verlag.

Job, S. V. (1955). The oxygen consumption of *Salvelinus fontinalis*. *Univ. Toronto Biol. Ser.* No. 61: 1–39.

Jones, R. (1973). Density dependent regulation of the numbers of cod and haddock. *Rapp. P.-v. Réun. Cons. perm. int. Explor. Mer* **164**: 156–173.

Jones, R. & Johnston, C. (1977). Growth, reproduction and mortality in gadoid fish species. In *Fisheries mathematics*: 37–62. Steele, J. H. (ed.). London & New York: Academic Press.

Kinne, O. (1963). Über den Einfluss des Salzgehaltes auf verschiedene Lebensprozesse des Knochenfisches. *Veröff Inst. Meeresf. Bremerhaven* **1963** (Sonderband): 49–66.

Laurence, G. C. (1977). A bioenergetic model for the analysis of feeding and survival potential of winter flounder, *Pseudopleuronectes americanus*, larvae during the period from hatching to metamorphosis. *Fish. Bull., U.S.A.* **75**: 529–546.

Parker, R. R. & Larkin, P. A. (1959). A concept of growth in fishes. *J. Fish. Res. Bd Can.* **16**: 721–745.

Pütter, A. (1920). Studien über physiologische Ähnlichkeit. VI. Wachstumsähnlichkeiten. *Pflügers Arch. Ges. Physiol.* **180**: 298–340.

Raitt, D. F. S. (1968). The population dynamics of the Norway pout in the North Sea. *Mar. Res.* **5**: 1–24.

Rashevsky, N. (1960). *Mathematical biophysics*, 3rd edn. New York: Dover Publications.

Saunders, R. L. (1963). Respiration of the Atlantic cod. *J. Fish. Res. Bd Can.* **20**: 373–386.

Sperber, O., From, J. & Sparre, P. (1977). A method to estimate the growth rate of fishes, as a function of temperature and feeding level, applied to rainbow trout. *Meddr Danm. Fisk.-og Havunders.* N.S. **7**: 275–317.

Ursin, E. (1963). On the incorporation of temperature in the von Bertalanffy growth equation. *Meddr Danm. Fisk.-og Havunders.* N.S. **4**: 1–16.

Ursin, E. (1967). A mathematical model of some aspects of fish growth, respiration and mortality. *J. Fish. Res. Bd Can.* **13**: 2355–2453.

Ursin, E. (In press.) Population dynamics and the behaviour of fishes. *Investigacion pesq.*

von Bertalanffy, L. (1934). Untersuchungen über die Gesetzlichkeit des Wachstums. *Roux' Arch.* **131**: 613–653.

Warren, C. E. & Davis, G. E. (1967). Laboratory studies on the feeding, bioenergetics, and growth of fish. In *The biological basis of freshwater fish production*: 175–214. Gerking, S. D. (ed.). Oxford: Blackwell.

Weiss, P. & Kavanau, J. Lee (1957). A model of growth and growth control in mathematical terms. *J. gen. Physiol.* **41**: 1–47.

de Wilde, P. A. W. J. & Berghuis, E. M. (1978). Laboratory experiments on the spawning of *Macoma balthica*; its implication for production research. In *Physiology and behaviour of marine organisms*: 375–384. (Proc. 12th Europ. Symp. Mar. Biol.) McLusky, D. S. & Berry, A. J. (eds). Oxford: Pergamon Press.

Winberg, G. G. (1956). [*Rate of metabolism and food requirements of fishes*] Minsk: Belorussian State Univ. [In Russian.] (*Fish. Res. Bd Can. Transl. Ser.* No. 194: 1–253).

Zeuthen, E. (1947). Body size and metabolic rate in the animal kingdom. *C. r. Trav. Lab. Carlsberg* (Sér. Chimique) **26**: 17–161.

Symp. zool. Soc. Lond. (1979) No. 44, 89–103

Endocrine Aspects of Metabolic Coordination in Teleosts

BRIDGET I. BAKER and T. WIGHAM

Bath University, Bath, Avon, England
University of Wales Institute of Science and Technology, Cardiff, Wales

SYNOPSIS

This review considers the influence of hormones on the control of general body growth in teleosts, the effects of individual hormones on mobilization or deposition of food stores, and also the synergistic co-operation between hormones in the seasonal control of lipid stores.

Growth more or less ceases in hypophysectomized fish but is restored by injections of growth hormone, while seasonal variation in growth rate can be associated with changes in the production and release of growth hormone. A number of other factors, including increased temperature and thyroxine, can enhance the response to growth hormone. Stress and starvation, which are normally associated with impaired growth, have also been found to stimulate the secretion of growth hormone in some species. These results are considered in the light of the possible involvement of a somatomedin-like factor in controlling skeletal growth in teleosts.

Growth hormone and thyroxine stimulate amino-acid metabolism in fed fish while cortisol can have a catabolic effect on muscle protein and liver glycogen in starved fish. The different effects of the catecholamines, glucagon and insulin on fat and carbohydrate metabolism in various species is discussed.

Both oestrogen and prolactin affect lipid mobilization or deposition in liver and muscle. Their effects are variable, apparently depending on the hormonal status of the fish. Many hormones show diurnal changes in plasma concentration and evidence is discussed which suggests that phase-shifts in the diurnal secretory pattern of hormones, bringing them in or out of phase with one another, may contribute to the seasonal control of deposition or mobilization of lipids.

INTRODUCTION

Since this symposium is concerned with phenology and with annual or diurnally recurring events in anabolism, we have decided to consider hormonal involvement in three main areas of relevance to this topic, of which two, at least, show a certain cyclical periodicity. These aspects are general body growth, the involvement of individual hormones in short-term metabolic responses such as those following feeding or stress and the synergistic action of hormones in more long-term events such as the deposition or mobilization of fat stores.

Fish do not usually show a constant rate of growth throughout the year but exhibit phases of fast and slow growth, related to environmental conditions and to reproductive events. In temperate climates, growth in length and body weight often occurs in spring and summer under the influence of increasing daylength, higher temperatures and abundant food supplies. (Le Cren, 1951; Swift, 1955, 1961; Ball & Jones, 1960; Cragg-Hine & Jones, 1969; Mann, 1973, 1974). Increase in growth and protein content may also be associated with enhanced glycogen and lipid stores (Shul'man, 1974) prior to their utilization during reproduction or during periods of overwinter starvation. Growth and metabolism are heavily influenced by hormones which in turn are subject to environmental control. It has been claimed that some fish, e.g. the brown trout, *Salmo trutta* L., will show persistent annual cycles of growth even when they are maintained under constant environmental conditions (Brown, 1946) but a more recent study by Swift (1961) indicates that, while fluctuations in growth certainly occur under these conditions, they are random and asynchronous between fish.

HORMONAL INFLUENCES ON BODY GROWTH

Pickford (1954) was the first to show that hypophysectomized fish do not grow but that length, weight and scale growth can be restored by injections of either bovine or teleost growth hormone (= somatotrophic hormone or STH). The stimulatory effect of growth hormone has since been demonstrated in hypophysectomized *Poecilia latipinna* (LeSueur) (Ball & Hawkins, 1976) and hypophysectomized *Ictalurus melas* (Rafinesque) (Kayes, 1977a,b), while the hormone will also promote growth in intact fish (Swift, 1954; Higgs *et al.*, 1976; Komourdjian, Saunders & Fenwick, 1976; Adelman, 1977; Craig-Clarke, Walker-Farmer & Hartnell, 1977). The increase in length and weight in hypophysectomized fish is dose dependent and also temperature sensitive (Pickford, 1957; Kayes, 1977b). Intact fish do not grow well above an optimal temperature and it has been suggested that high temperatures may impair the release of endogenous growth hormone (Adelman, 1977). However, both Pickford and Kayes found that growth is also retarded in hypophysectomized fish at high temperatures given a standard amount of exogenous growth hormone. Moreover, the reduced growth rate at these upper temperatures is difficult to interpret in view of the depressive effect which high temperatures may exert on feeding (other authors, this volume) and on the metabolic rate.

    Swift & Pickford (1965) were able to correlate annual changes in growth rate in the perch, *Perca fluviatilis* L., with changes in the growth hormone content of the pituitary gland. They observed a marked increase in hormone content following the reproductive period and immediately prior to the onset of rapid growth in June. This was followed by a sharp decline in hormone content during the period of active growth which presumably reflects enhanced release of hormone from the pituitary. Cytological studies of the teleost pituitary in relation to the growth rate are scarce but tend to support the view that the pituitary somatotrophic (growth hormone) cells become active during periods of rapid growth (Zanuy & Carillo, 1976). Nothing is known of the factors which control the secretory activity of the somatotrophs—whether photoperiod, temperature or other endocrine factors—but these are likely to be different in different species, depending on their ecological needs.

The rate of growth can be modified by factors other than the circulating level of growth hormone. Thus, thyroxine will enhance growth and the incorporation of radioactive sulphate into cartilage in intact fish, while, conversely, growth is impaired by thiourea treatment or radiothyroidectomy (Hopper, 1952; Barrington, Barron & Piggins, 1961; Piggins, 1962; La Roche et al., 1966; Barrington & Rawdon, 1967; Massey & Smith, 1968; Gorbman, 1969; Barber & Barrington, 1972). The effects of thyroxine are apparently demonstrable only in the presence of growth hormone. In hypophysectomized fish, injections of the pituitary thyrotrophic hormone, TSH, which stimulates endogenous thyroxine production, will not alone stimulate growth but will enhance the growth-promoting effect of injected growth hormone (Pickford, 1957). Since thyroid activity increases in several species with increase in temperature (see Gorbman, 1969), this might partially contribute to the enhanced growth rate at these temperatures. It is also possible that thyroxine can affect the synthesis and release of growth hormone itself in some species. Thus, Sage (1967) noted that, in the guppy Poecilia reticulata Peters, thiourea appeared to prevent the release of growth hormone from the pituitary and this was corrected by administering thyroxine. In pituitaries of the eel, Anguilla anguilla (L.), cultured in vitro, the reverse is observed: the addition of 1 μg ml^{-1} dl-thyroxine to the culture medium significantly reduced the release of growth hormone into the medium while the somatotrophs remain intensely granulated (Baker & Ingleton, 1975). Nevertheless, since this concentration of thyroxine is in excess of that normally found in the circulation, these results must be regarded as more suggestive than conclusive.

Certain conditions will impair the growth-promoting effects of growth hormone. Both stress and starvation will stimulate the release of growth hormone in certain species (Olivereau, 1970; McKeown, Leatherland & John, 1975); such conditions, however, are normally associated with a reduction of growth and Ottoway & Simkiss (1977) also showed that they reduce scale growth, as assessed by the rate of radioactive glycine incorporation by scales in vitro—a sensitive method which appears to measure "instantaneous" growth rates. It is possible to suggest several theoretical reasons to account for the reduction in growth under these conditions. It may be attributable to the antagonistic, catabolic action of corticosteroids, since stress and starvation both increase plasma corticosteroid levels at least in some species (Dave et al., 1975; Donaldson & McBride, 1967). Reduced growth may also be a consequence of a low level of insulin release during starvation (Patent & Foa, 1971; Thorpe & Ince,

1976). The phenomenon of growth cessation, despite high growth hormone titres, is well known in certain mammals, where growth hormone does not directly affect the skeletal cartilage but acts indirectly by stimulating the production of somatomedin by the liver. This it does in conjunction with other hormones such as insulin so that somatomedin production is reduced under conditions such as starvation when insulin secretion is also low (Phillips & Harvey, 1976; Daugherday, Phillips & Mueller, 1976). Corticosteroids will also cause a decline in plasma soma-tomedin levels (Mosier *et al.*, 1976). A somatomedin-like factor has been demonstrated in the plasma of several teleosts when tested on mammalian cartilage (Shapiro & Pimstone, 1977; van den Brande *et al.*, 1974), while mammalian serum, known to be rich in somatomedin, will consistently stimulate the incorporation of radioactive sulphate into teleost cartilage *in vitro* (Ash, 1977). However, in this latter work, fish serum failed to stimulate fish cartilage sulphation and since it was also observed that mammalian growth hormone could exert a direct, albeit inconsistent effect on teleost cartilage, it would be unwise to press the comparison with mammals too far.

In view of the mobilization of food stores and the reduced rate of growth seen in many teleosts during the reproductive period, the metabolic effects of sex steroids are of some interest. In both the coho and the chinook salmon, *Oncorhynchus kisutch* (Walbaum) and *O. tshawytscha* (Walbaum), the addition of 17α-methyltestosterone to the food stimu-lated a gain in body length and weight (McBride & Fagerlund, 1973; Fagerlund & McBride, 1975). Katz, Abraham & Echstein (1976) added the steroid adrenosterone to the water of developing *Tilapia* during the first three months of life. Levels of 5 mg litre^{-1} caused a 21% increase in length and a 61% increase in weight; lower doses were ineffective while other oestrogenic and androgenic steroids proved fatal. Other workers investigating the effects of oestrogens on growth have found variable responses: stimulation, inhibition or no effect have all been reported in one or another species (Ashby, 1957; Ghittino, 1970; Cowey *et al.*, 1973). The available data suggest that low growth rates during the reproductive season are probably not directly attributable to any inhibitory effect of the sex steroids. They more probably arise from the rechannelling of metabolites from growth to gamete production. In some species, also, they may arise from a change in the pattern of behaviour and feeding activity.

METABOLIC RESPONSES TO INDIVIDUAL HORMONES

The ability of growth hormone and thyroxine to stimulate growth is associated with the improved utilization of amino acids and decreased nitrogen excretion which follow the injection of these hormones into fed fish (Narayansingh & Eales, 1975; Smith & Thorpe, 1977). The hormones have no such effect in starved fish. Cortisol, on the other hand, has the reverse result; while it does not antagonize the anabolic effects of growth hormone and thyroxine in fed fish, it will enhance nitrogen excretion in starved rainbow trout, *Salmo gairdneri* Richardson, and goldfish (Storer, 1967; Smith & Thorpe, 1977). This can be related to its gluconeogenic action in *Oncorhynchus*, *Salmo gairdneri* and *Anguilla anguilla* (Robertson *et al.*, 1963; Butler, 1968; Chester-Jones *et al.*, 1974). These gluconeogenic responses are evident during the anadromous, reproductive migration of *Oncorhynchus* when plasma cortisol is very high and there is a 60% loss of body protein but an increase in liver glycogen (Roberston *et al.*, 1961; see Chester-Jones *et al.*, 1974). In the starved eel, plasma cortisol levels also became slightly but significantly increased (Dave *et al.*, 1975) but without alteration in muscle protein over two months' starvation and a decrease in liver glycogen content. The metabolic involvement of cortisol at this relatively early stage of starvation is uncertain, especially in view of the increase in hepatic glycogen found as a response to acute injections of cortisol in the eel (Butler, 1968). In other species, e.g. *Poecilia latipinna* (Ball, Giddings & Hancock, 1966), *Tilapia mossambica* (Peters) (Swallow & Fleming, 1966) and *Carassius auratus* (L.) (Umminger & Gist, 1973), cortisol exerts a glycogenolytic effect on the liver.

Other hormones capable of stimulating glycogenolysis or hyperglycaemia in teleosts include the catecholamines and glucagon. Both adrenaline and, to a lesser extent, noradrenaline can induce hyperglycaemia in several teleost species (Falkmer, 1961; Mazeaud, 1969; Farkas, 1967; Perrier, Perrier & Gras, 1971; Larsson, 1973), while incubations *in vitro* of liver tissue from *Fundulus heteroclitus* (L.) or *Ictalurus nebulosus* (Le Sueur) show that adrenaline acts on the liver directly to stimulate glycogen phosphorylase activity (Umminger, Benziger & Levy, 1975; Umminger & Benziger, 1975). Thus, either catecholamines or cortisol could be responsible for the hyperglycaemic response to stress. In several teleosts, plasma glucose increases markedly when fish are subjected to near zero temperatures (Umminger, 1969). This response has been studied most thoroughly in *F. heteroclitus* in which the high level of glucose seems to be maintained by the stimulatory effects of glucagon on hepatic glycogenolysis. Thus, in *Fundulus* held at $-1.5°C$, the pancreatic α (glucagon) cells are hypertrophied while the insulin-producing, β cells regress (Umminger & Bair, 1973); hepatic glycogen phosphorylase activity increases (Benziger & Umminger, 1973) and glycogen stores decline in the liver but not in the muscles (Umminger, 1970). That glucagon has a direct effect on liver glycogen phosphorylase was demonstrated by incubations *in vitro* of liver slices with the hormone (Umminger *et al.*, 1975). Glucagon has a similar effect *in vitro* on the liver of the catfish, *Ictalurus nebulosus* (Umminger & Benziger, 1975).

Both catecholamines and glucagon will also affect lipid mobilization in certain teleosts but their effect on plasma free fatty acids (FFA) varies with the species. Thus glucagon will increase plasma FFA in the pike, *Esox lucius* L. (Ince & Thorpe, 1975) but has no effect on the eel (Larsson & Lewander, 1972). Adrenaline, but not noradrenaline, will increase plasma FFA levels in the eel (Larsson, 1973) and the scorpion fish, *Scorpaena porcus* L. (Leibson, Plisetskaya & Mazina, 1968), while noradrenaline has a transient lipolytic effect in the pike (Ince & Thorpe, 1975) but then, as with adrenaline, plasma FFA levels are reduced. In *Cyprinus* and *Carassius*, adrenaline and noradrenaline injections and handling stress similarly lead to a reduction in plasma FFA levels (Farkas, 1967; Minick & Chavin, 1972). Further investigations on goldfish showed that adrenaline was effective in this respect only in the presence of functional pancreatic β cells and failed to lower plasma FFA levels in alloxan-treated, diabetic goldfish (Minick & Chavin, 1973). This demonstrates that the adrenaline effect is an indirect one, depending on insulin release. This can be related to the observation that glucose injections result in a lowering of plasma FFA levels, presumably also by stimulating the release of insulin (Minick & Chavin, 1972; Ince & Thorpe, 1974).

Injections of insulin have a pronounced effect on serum lipids, rapidly reducing the levels of free fatty acids, cholesterol and phospholipids (Minick & Chavin, 1972; Leibson *et al.*, 1968; Ince & Thorpe, 1974, 1975; Lewander *et al.*, 1976). Blood glucose levels may also be reduced but this response may be less striking than for the lipids (Young, 1970; Chavin & Young, 1970; Minick & Chavin, 1972). Insulin release is reduced by starvation and stimulated by feeding, both glucose and certain amino acids—leucine, arginine and lysine—being potent secretagogues in toadfish (*Opsanus*) and *Anguilla* (Watkins *et al.*, 1964; Patent & Foa, 1971; Ince & Thorpe, 1977). It is of interest to recall here that cold-induced hyperglycaemia in *Fundulus heteroclitus* involved the regression of the pancreatic β cells as well as the hypertrophy of the α cells (Umminger & Bair, 1973). Epple & Lewis (1977) found that surgical pancreatectomy of the eel increased blood glucose levels but, surprisingly, reduced plasma free fatty acids. The interpretation of these findings is not easy; the decline cannot easily be attributed to the simultaneous removal of the glucagon-producing cells in view of the failure of mammalian glucagon to modify plasma lipids in *Anguilla* (Larsson & Lewander, 1972) but the results serve to emphasize that lipid metabolism in teleosts is under multiple hormonal control.

The effects of oestrogens on lipid deposition have been examined by de Vlaming, Shing *et al.* (1977) in the golden shiner, *Notemigonus crysoleucas* (Mitchill). Oestradiol-17β increased the hepatosomatic index and modified both carcass and liver fat reserves, the response depending on the daylength under which the fish were kept. On long or intermediate (12-light/12-dark) photoperiods, the hormone induced fat deposition, but caused lipid mobilization in fish on a short daylength. Under natural conditions, endogenous sex hormones are highest during the pre-spawning and spawning season, attained in this species under conditions of long photoperiod and warmer temperatures (de Vlaming, 1975). At this stage of ovarian maturation there is normally a depletion of carcass fat reserves and an increase in hepatic lipids so that the data from the effect of oestrogen injections during a long photoperiod regime might appear to indicate that oestrogens play no part in the mobilization of muscle lipids during egg maturation. However, the fact that oestrogen can induce different effects, depending on the photoperiod, indicates that the response depends also on the endogenous hormonal milieu. As de Vlaming himself points out, the effect of oestrogen was tested in fish held at low temperatures which normally suppress gonadal development and which might also modify this hormonal background in other ways; the response to oestrogens could well be different at the higher temperatures which normally obtain during the period of reproductive activity. The different effects of hormones, depending on environmental factors which in turn modify hormonal secretion, are discussed below.

In goldfish, oestrogen administration increased hepatic and plasma lipid levels at all times except during the spawning season, when the effect of injected oestrogens was probably masked by the high circulating levels of endogenous sex steroids (de Vlaming, Vodicnik et al. 1977). This interpretation is supported by the fact that the administration of the oestrogen antagonist CI 628 (Parke Davis) at this time reduced both plasma and hepatic lipid levels.

SYNERGISTIC HORMONAL EFFECTS ON LIPID STORES

Recent investigations suggest that some metabolic events, such as seasonal changes in lipid deposition or mobilization, may be controlled not by a single hormone but by several hormones acting synergistically. Many hormones show diurnal changes in plasma concentration and both basal plasma hormone levels and the diurnal pattern of hormone secretion are susceptible to environmental control. The available data suggest that synergism between hormones may arise as a result of phase-shifts in the diurnal peak of secretion such that different hormones are brought in or out of phase with one another at particular times in the annual cycle.

Meier and his colleagues were the first to suggest that prolactin, injected over a period of several days, could induce either lipogenesis or lipolysis from muscle and liver stores, depending on the time of day when it was injected (Meier, 1969, 1972; Joseph & Meier, 1971). In *Fundulus grandis* Baird & Girard, carcass and liver fat stores showed peak lipid contents when prolactin was injected 8 h after first light. It has since been confirmed for several other cyprinodont species that prolactin injections induce intense lipid loss from total body stores when injected soon after the beginning of the photoperiod but lipid deposition if injected 8–10 h after the onset of light (Mehle & Fleming, 1970; de Vlaming & Sage, 1972; de Vlaming, Sage & Tiegs, 1975; Pardo & de Vlaming, 1976). In some species, however, the lipogenic response was only seen under the appropriate conditions of temperature and daylength (Pardo & de Vlaming, 1976; de Vlaming, Sage et al., 1975). This variation in response suggests that prolactin must be acting in co-operation with one or more other hormones which fluctuate diurnally.

In *F. grandis* and *F. chrysotus* Holbrook, held in constant light, Meier *et al.* (1971) found that prolactin no longer induced any significant change in lipid stores. However, if thyroxine was injected for two days prior to prolactin injections, a lipogenic response became established 18 h after the period of thyroxine administration (Meier, 1970). If, instead, cortisol was injected daily at a fixed time of day, prolactin injections made 6 to 12 h after the cortisol injection were now associated with a reduction in total body lipid stores (Meier *et al.*, 1971). Thus, both cortisol or thyroxine may be associated with the prolactin-induced changes in lipids.

Both cortisol and prolactin show diurnal changes in plasma concentration but nothing is yet known about variations in thyroxine levels. Prolactin has been measured in goldfish (McKeown & Peter, 1976); *Oncorhynchus* (Leatherland, McKeown & John, 1974); grey mullet, *Mugil cephalus* L., (Spieler, Meier & Loesch, 1976) and *Fundulus grandis* (Spieler, Meier & Noeske, 1978). In *F. grandis*, the time of the peak can be shifted by changes in temperature. In goldfish, the troughs and peaks of plasma concentration seem to be linked to the photoperiod while changes in temperature can modify the diurnal range in concentration. In *Mugil*, the diurnal pattern was different at different times of year, which did not seem to be correlated to the photoperiod. Little is known about the factors affecting the diurnal pattern of cortisol secretion but since different patterns have been described by separate investigators for the same species (e.g. goldfish—Fryer, 1975; Singley & Chavin, 1975), the timing of the peaks and troughs are probably susceptible to environmental modification. Garcia & Meier (1973) report a different pattern between male and female *F. grandis*. As Spieler, Meier & Noeske (1978) have pointed out, the mechanism used to control the pattern of hormone release in different fish probably depends more on the species' particular ecological needs rather than on any phylogenetic relatedness.

In summarizing these data, it appears that seasonal difference in the mobilization or deposition of food stores depends not only on the nutritional status of the fish and the action of individual hormones such as insulin, growth hormone and thyroxine, but also on the synergistic co-operation between hormones. Such synergism could theoretically be brought into play as a result of environmental influences on the diurnal secretory pattern of hormones such as prolactin, cortisol and thyroxine, so that the diurnal peaks of these hormones are brought in or out of phase with one another at particular times of the year. In addition to these shifts in their diurnal secretory pattern, the hormones may also exhibit, at certain times of year, an overall increase in their plasma concentration in response to environmental factors such as the photoperiod, temperature or salinity. For instance, increasing daylength can stimulate prolactin synthesis in the marine three-spined stickleback, *Gasterosteus aculeatus* L., form *trachurus* Cuvier, (Lam, 1972) while in other species prolactin secretion may be stimulated by decreasing salinity (Ingleton, Baker & Ball, 1973; Leatherland, Ball & Hyder, 1974; Holmes & Ball, 1974). As already stated, thyroxine and oestrogen levels may be enhanced in some species under conditions of increased temperature or daylength. However, these suggestions on mechanisms of metabolic control must at this stage be regarded as largely theoretical, being based on the experimental manipulation of hormones and fat reserves. The demonstration of such hormonal changes associated with changes in lipid reserves under natural conditions remains to be made.

REFERENCES

Adelman, I. R. (1977). Effects of bovine hormone on growth of carp (*Cyprinus carpio*) and the influences of temperature and photoperiod. *J. Fish. Res. Bd Can.* **34**: 509–515.

Ash, P. A. (1977). Incorporation of (^{35}S) sulphate into mucopolysaccharide by teleost cartilage *in vitro*: the influence of mammalian growth hormone, teleost plasma and mammalian plasma. *Gen. comp. Endocr.* **32**: 187–194.

Ashby, K. R. (1957). The effect of steroid hormones on the brown trout (*Salmo trutta* L.) during the period of gonadal differentiation. *J. Embryol. exp. Morph.* **5**: 225–249.

Baker, B. I. & Ingleton, P. M. (1975). Secretion of prolactin and growth hormone by teleost pituitaries *in vitro*. II. Effect of salt concentration during long-term organ culture. *J. comp. Physiol.* **100**: 269–282.

Ball, J. N., Giddings, M. R. & Hancock, M. P. (1966). Pituitary influence on hepatic glycogen stores in the teleost *Poecilia latipinna*. *Am. Zool.* **6**: 595.

Ball, J. N. & Hawkins, E. F. (1976). Adrenocortical (interrenal) responses to hypophysectomy and adenohypophysial hormones in the teleost *Poecilia latipinna*. *Gen. comp. Endocr.* **28**: 59–70.

Ball, J. N. & Jones, J. W. (1960). On the growth of the brown trout of Llyn Tegid, *Proc. zool. Soc. Lond.* **134**: 1–41.

Barber, S. & Barrington, E. J. W. (1972). Dynamics of uptake and binding of ^{35}S-sulphate by the cartilage of Rainbow trout (*Salmo gairdneri*) and the influence of thyroxine. *J. Zool., Lond.* **168**: 107–117.

Barrington, E. J. W., Barron, N. & Piggins, D. J. (1961). The influence of thyroid powder and thyroxine upon the growth of rainbow trout (*S. gairdnerii*). *Gen. comp. Endocr.* **1**: 170–178.

Barrington, E. J. W. & Rawdon, B. B. (1967). Influence of thyroxine upon the uptake of ^{35}S labelled sulphate into the branchial arch skeleton of the rainbow trout (*Salmo gairdnerii*). *Gen. comp. Endocr.* **9**: 116–128.

Benziger, D. & Umminger, B. L. (1973). Role of hepatic glycogenolytic enzymes in the cold-induced hyperglycemia of the killifish, *Fundulus heteroclitus*. *Comp. Biochem. Physiol.* **45A**: 767–772.

Brown, M. E. (1946). The growth of brown trout (*Salmo trutta*, Linn). II. The growth of two year old trout at a constant temperature of 11.5°C. *J. exp. Biol.* **22**: 130–144.

Butler, D. G. (1968). Hormonal control of gluconeogenesis in the North American eel (*Anguilla rostrata*). *Gen. comp. Endocr.* **10**: 85–91.

Chavin, W. & Young, J. E. (1970). Factors in the determination of normal serum glucose levels in goldfish, *Carassius auratus* L. *Comp. Biochem. Physiol.* **33**: 629–653.

Chester-Jones, I., Ball, J. N., Henderson, I. W., Sandor, T. & Baker, B. I. (1974). Endocrinology of fishes. In *Chemical zoology* **8**: 524–593. Florkin, M. & Sheer, B. T. (eds). New York & London: Academic Press.

Cowey, C. B., Pope, J. A., Adron, J. W. & Blair, A. (1973). Studies on the nutrition of marine flatfish. The effect of oral administration of diethylstilboestrol and cyproheptadine on the growth of *Pleuronectes platessa*. *Mar. Biol.* **19**: 1–6.

Cragg-Hine, D. & Jones, D. W. (1969). The growth of dace *Leuciscus leuciscus* (L), roach *Rutilus rutilus* (L) and chub *Squalus cephalus* (L) in Willow Brook Northamptonshire. *J. Fish Biol.* **1**: 59–82.

Craig-Clarke, W., Walker-Farmer, S. & Hartnell, K. M. (1977). Effect of teleost pituitary growth hormone on growth of *Tilapia mossambica* and on growth and sea water adaptation of sockeye salmon (*Oncorhynchus nerka*). *Gen. comp. Endocr.* **33**: 174–178.

Daugherday, W. H., Phillips, L. S. & Mueller, L. S. (1976). The effects of insulin and growth hormone on the release of somatomedin by the isolated rat liver. *Endocrinology* **98**: 1214–1219.

Dave, G., Johansson-Sjobeck, M. L., Larsson, A., Lewander, K. & Lidman, U. (1975). Metabolic and hematological effects of starvation in the European eel, *Anguilla anguilla* L. I. Carbohydrate, lipid, protein and inorganic ion metabolism. *Comp. Biochem. Physiol.* **52A**: 423–430.

de Vlaming, V. L. (1975). Effects of photoperiod and temperature regimes on gonadal activity in the cyprinid teleost, *Notomegonus crysoleucas*. *Biol. Bull. mar. biol. Lab. Woods Hole* **143**: 402–415.

de Vlaming, V. L. & Sage, M. (1972). Diurnal variation in fattening response to prolactin treatment in two cyprinodontid fishes, *Cyprinodon variegatus* and *Fundulus similis*. *Contr. Mar. Sci.* **16**: 59–63.

de Vlaming, V. L., Sage, M. & Tiegs, R. (1975). A diurnal rhythm of pituitary prolactin activity with diurnal effects of mammalian and teleostean prolactin on total body lipid deposition and liver lipid metabolism in teleost fishes. *J. Fish Biol.* **7**: 717–726.

de Vlaming, V. L., Shing, J., Paquette, G. & Vuchs, R. (1977). *In vivo* and *in vitro* effects of oestradiol-17β on lipid metabolism in *Notemigonus crysoleucas*. *J. Fish Biol.* **10**: 273–285.

de Vlaming, V. L., Vodicnik, M. J., Bower, G. & Murphy, T. (1977). Estradiol 17B effects on lipid and carbohydrate metabolism and on the induction of a yolk precursor in goldfish *Carassius auratus*. *Life Sci.* **20**: 1945–1952.

Donaldson, E. M. & McBride, J. R. (1967). The effects of hypophysectomy in the rainbow trout *Salmo gairdneri* (Rich.) with special reference to the pituitary-interrenal axis, *Gen. comp. Endocr.* **9**: 93–101.

Epple, A. & Lewis, T. L. (1977). Metabolic effects of pancreatectomy and hypophysectomy in the yellow American eel *Anguilla rostrata* Le Sueur. *Gen. comp. Endocr.* **32**: 294–315.

Fagerlund, U. M. M. & McBride, J. R. (1975). Growth increments and some flesh and gonad characteristics of juvenile coho salmon receiving diets supplemented with 17α-methyltestosterone. *J. Fish Biol.* **7**: 305–314.

Falkmer, S. (1961). Experimental diabetes research in fish. *Acta Endocrinol.* **37**: (*Suppl. 59*) 1–122.

Farkas, T. (1967). The effect of catecholamines and adrenocorticotrophic hormone on blood and adipose FFA levels in the fish *Cyprinus carpio*. *Progr. Biochem. Pharmacol.* **3**: 314–319.

Fryer, J. N. (1975). Stress and adrenocorticosteroid dynamics in the goldfish *Carassius auratus*. *Can. J. Zool.* **53**: 1012–1020.

Garcia, L. E. & Meier, A. H. (1973). Daily rhythms in concentration of plasma cortisol in male and female gulf killifish *Fundulus grandis*. *Biol. Bull. mar. biol. Lab. Woods Hole* **144**: 471–479.

Ghittino, P. (1970). Riposta della trote d'allevamento al dietilstilbestrole e metiltiuracile. *Riv. ital. Piscic. Ittopat.* **5**: 9–11.

Gorbman, A. (1969). Thyroid function and its control in fishes. In *Fish physiology* **2**: 241–274. Hoar, W. S. & Randall, D. J. (eds). New York & London: Academic Press.

Higgs, D. A., Donaldson, E. M., Dye, H. M. & McBride, J. R. (1976). Influence of bovine growth hormone and L-thyroxine on growth, muscle composition and histological structure of the gonads, thyroid, pancreas and pituitary of the coho salmon (*Oncorhynchus kisutch*). *J. Fish. Res. Bd Can.* **33**: 1585–1603.

Holmes, R. L. & Ball, J. N. (1974). *The pituitary gland. A comparative account.* Cambridge: University Press.

Hopper, A. F. (1952). Growth and maturation response in *Lebistes reticulatus* to treatment with mammalian thyroid powder and thiouracil. *J. exp. Zool.* **119**: 205–219.

Ince, B. W. & Thorpe, A. (1974). Effects of insulin and of metabolic loading on blood metabolites in the European silver eel (*Anguilla anguilla* L.). *Gen. comp. Endocr.* **23**: 460–471.

Ince, B. W. & Thorpe, A. (1975). Hormonal and metabolite effects on plasma free fatty acids in the northern pike *Esox lucius* L. *Gen. comp. Endocr.* **27**: 144–152.

Ince, B. W. & Thorpe, A. (1977). Glucose and amino acid-stimulated insulin release in the European silver eel (*Anguilla anguilla* L.). *Gen. comp. Endocr.* **31**: 249–256.

Ingleton, P. M., Baker, B. I. & Ball, J. N. (1973). Secretion of prolactin and growth hormone by teleost pituitaries *in vitro*. I. Effect of sodium concentration and osmotic pressure during short-term incubations. *J. comp. Physiol.* **87**: 317–328.

Joseph, M. M. & Meier, A. H. (1971). Daily variations in the fattening response to prolactin in *Fundulus grandis* held on different photoperiods. *J. exp. Zool.* **178**: 59–62.

Katz, Y., Abraham, M. & Echstein, B. (1976). Effects of adrenosterone on gonadal and body growth in *Tilapia nilotica* (Teleostei, Cichlidae). *Gen. comp. Endocr.* **29**: 414–418.

Kayes, T. (1977a). Effects of hypophysectomy, beef growth hormone replacement therapy, pituitary autotransplantation and environmental salinity on growth in the black bullhead (*Ictalurus melas*). *Gen. comp. Endocr.* **33**: 371–381.

Kayes, T. (1977b). Effects of temperature on hypophysial (growth hormone) regulation of length, weight and allometric growth and total lipid and water concentrations in the black bullhead (*Ictalurus melas*). *Gen. comp. Endocr.* **33**: 382–393.

Komourdjian, M. P., Saunders, R. L. & Fenwick, J. C. (1976). The effect of porcine somatotrophin on growth and survival in seawater of Atlantic salmon (*Salmo salar*) parr. *Can. J. Zool.* **54**: 531–535.

Lam, T. J. (1972). Prolactin and hydromineral regulation in fishes. *Gen. comp. Endocr.* Suppl. **3**: 328–338.

La Roche, G., Woodall, A. N., Johnson, C. L. & Halver, J. E. (1966). Thyroid function in the rainbow trout (*Salmo gairdnerii* Rich.) II. Effects of thyroidectomy on the development of young fish. *Gen. comp. Endocr.* **6**: 249–266.

Larsson, A. L. (1973). Metabolic effects of epinephrine and norepinephrine in the eel *Anguilla anguilla* L. *Gen. comp. Endocr.* **20**: 155–167.

Larsson, A. & Lewander, K. (1972). Effects of glucagon administration to eels (*Anguilla anguilla* L.). *Comp. Biochem. Physiol.* **43A**: 831–836.

Le Cren, E. D. (1951). The length-weight relationship and seasonal cycle in gonad weight and condition in the perch (*Perca fluviatilis*). *J. Anim. Ecol.* **20**: 201–219.

Leatherland, J. F., Ball, J. N. & Hyder, M. (1974). Structure and fine structure of the hypophyseal pars distalis in indigenous African species of the genus *Tilapia. Cell Tiss. Res.* **149**: 245–266.

Leatherland, J. F., McKeown, B. A. & John, T. M. (1974). Circadian rhythm of plasma prolactin, growth hormone and free fatty acids in juvenile kokanee salmon. *Comp. Biochem. Physiol.* **47A**: 821–828.

Leibson, L. G., Plisetskaya, E. M. & Mazina, T. I. (1968). Concentration of nonesterified fatty acids in blood plasma of cyclostomata and fishes and its changes under the influence of adrenalin and insulin. *Zh. Evol. Biokhim. Fiziol.* **4**: 121–127 [in Russian, with English summary].

Lewander, K., Dave, G., Johansson-Sjobeck, M. J., Larsson, A. & Lidman, U. (1976). Metabolic effects of insulin in the European eel *Anguilla anguilla* L. *Gen. comp. Endocr.* **29**: 455–467.

Mann, R. H. K. (1973). Observations on the age, growth, reproduction and food of the roach (*Rutilus rutilus* L.) in two rivers in southern England. *J. Fish Biol.* **5**: 707–736.

Mann, R. H. K. (1974). Observations on the age, growth, reproduction and food of the dace, *Leuciscus leuciscus* (L.) in two rivers in southern England. *J. Fish Biol.* **6**: 237–253.

Massey, B. D. & Smith, C. L. (1968). The action of thyroxine on mitochondrial respiration and phosphorylation in the trout (*Salmo trutta fario* L.). *Comp. Biochem. Physiol.* **25**: 241–255.

Mazeaud, F. (1969). Evidence for pituitary control on the blood sugar regulation of the carp by means of epinephrine hyperglycemia. *C.r. Séanc. Soc. Biol.* **163**: 24–28.

McBride, J. R. & Fagerlund, U. H. M. (1973). The use of 17α methyltestosterone for promoting weight increases in juvenile Pacific salmon. *J. Fish. Res. Bd Can.* **30**: 1099–1104.

McKeown, B. A., Leatherland, J. F. & John, T. M. (1975). The effect of growth hormone and prolactin on the mobilisation of free-fatty acids and glucose in the kokanee salmon, *Oncorhynchus nerka. Comp. Biochem. Physiol.* **50**: 425–430.

McKeown, B. A. & Peter, R. E. (1976). The effects of photoperiod and temperature on the release of prolactin from the pituitary gland of the goldfish *Carassius auratus* L. *Can. J. Zool.* **54**: 1960–1968.

Mehle, P. M. & Fleming, W. R. (1970). The effect of early and midday prolactin injection on the lipid content of *Fundulus kansae* held on a constant photoperiod. *Comp. Biochem. Physiol.* **36**: 597–604.

Meier, A. H. (1969). Diurnal variations of metabolic responses to prolactin in lower vertebrates. *Gen. comp. Endocr.* Suppl **2**: 55–62.

Meier, A. H. (1970). Thyroxin phases the circadian fattening response to prolactin. *Proc. Soc. exp. Biol. Med.* **133**: 1113–1116.

Meier, A. H. (1972). Temporal synergism of prolactin and adrenal steroids. *Gen. comp. Endocr.* Suppl. **3**: 499–508.

Meier, A. H., Trobec, T. N., Joseph, M. M. & John, T. M. (1971). Temporal synergism of adrenal steroid and prolactin controlling fat storage. *Proc. Soc. exp. Biol. Med.* **137**: 408–415.

Minick, M. C. & Chavin, W. (1972). Effect of vertebrate insulins upon serum FFA and phospholipid levels in the goldfish, *Carassius auratus* Linnaeus. *Comp. Biochem. Physiol.* **41A**: 791–804.

Minick, M. C. & Chavin, W. (1973). Effect of catecholamines upon serum FFA levels in normal and diabetic goldfish, *Carassius auratus*. *Comp. Biochem. Physiol.* **44**: 1003–1009.

Mosier, H. D., Jansons, R. A., Hill, R. R. & Dearden, L. K. (1976). Cartilage sulphation and serum somatomedin in rats during and after cortisone-induced growth arrest. *Endocrinology* **99**: 580–589.

Narayansingh, T. & Eales, G. (1975). Effects of thyroid hormones on *in vivo* 1-^{14}C L-leucine incorporation into plasma and tissue protein of brook trout (*Salvelinus fontinalis*) and rainbow trout (*Salmo gairdneri*). *Comp. Biochem. Physiol.* **52B**: 399–406.

Olivereau, M. (1970). Stimulation des cellules somatotropes de l'hypophyse de la carpe après un jeune prolongé. *C.r. hebd. Séanc. Acad. Sci., Paris* **270**: 2343–2346.

Ottoway, E. M. & Simkiss, K. (1977). A method for assessing factors influencing "false check" formation in fish scales. *J. Fish Biol.* **11**: 681–688.

Pardo, R. J. & de Vlaming, V. L. (1976). *In vivo* and *in vitro* effects of prolactin on lipid metabolism in the cyprinid teleost *Notemigonus crysoleucas*. *Copeia* **1976**: 563–573.

Patent, G. J. & Foa, P. P. (1971). Radioimmunoassay of insulin in fishes: experiments *in vivo* and *in vitro*. *Gen. comp. Endocr.* **16**: 41–46.

Perrier, H., Perrier, C. & Gras, J. (1971). Etude de l'hyperglycemie adrénalique chez la truite arc-en-ciel d'èlevage (*Salmo gairdnerii* Richardson): action des substances adrénolytique. *C.r. Séanc. Soc. Biol.* **165**: 2124–2144.

Phillips, L. S. & Harvey, S. Y. (1976). Nutrition and somatomedin I. Effect of fasting and refeeding on serum somatomedin activity and cartilage growth activity in rats. *Endocrinology* **99**: 304–314.

Pickford, G. E. (1954). The response of hypophysectomised male killifish to purified fish growth hormone as compared with the response to purified beef growth hormone. *Endocrinology* **55**: 274–287.

Pickford, G. E. (1957). The growth hormone. In *The physiology of the pituitary gland of fishes*: 84–99. Pickford, G. E. & Atz, J. (eds). New York: Zoological Society.

Piggins, D. J. (1962). Thyroid feeding of salmon parr. *Nature, Lond.* **195**: 1017–1018.

Robertson, O. H., Krupp, M. A., Thomas, S. F., Favour, C. B., Hane, S. & Wexler, B. C. (1961). Hyperadrenocorticism in spawning migratory and non-migratory rainbow trout (*Salmo gairdnerii*). Comparison with Pacific salmon (genus *Oncorhynchus*). *Gen. comp. Endocr.* **1**: 473–484.

Robertson, O. H., Hane, S., Wexler, B. C. & Rinfret, A. P. (1963). The effect of hydrocortisone on immature rainbow trout (*Salmo gairdnerii*). *Gen comp. Endocr.* **3**: 422–426.

Sage, M. (1967). Responses of pituitary cells of *Poecilia* to changes in growth induced by thyroxine and thiourea. *Gen. comp. Endocr.* **8**: 314–319.

Shapiro, B. & Pimstone, B. L. (1977). A phylogenetic study of sulphation factor activity in 26 species. *J. Endocr.* **74**: 129–135.

Shul'man, G. E. (1974). *Life cycles of fish.* Translated from Russian by N. Kaner. New York, Toronto: John Wiley & Sons.

Singley, J. A. & Chavin, W. (1975). Serum cortisol in normal goldfish (*Carassius auratus* L.). *Comp. Biochem. Physiol.* **50A**: 77–82.

Smith, M. A. K. & Thorpe, A. (1977). Endocrine effects of nitrogen excretion in the euryhaline teleost *Salmo gairdnerii. Gen. comp. Endocr.* **32**: 400–406.

Spieler, R. E., Meier, A. H. & Loesch, H. C. (1976). Seasonal variations in circadian levels of serum prolactin in mullet. *Gen. comp. Endocr.* **29**: 156–160.

Spieler, R. E., Meier, A. H. & Noeske, T. A. (1978). Temperature-induced phase shift of daily rhythm of serum prolactin in gulf killifish. *Nature, Lond.* **271**: 469–470.

Storer, J. H. (1967). Starvation and the effects of cortisol in the goldfish (*Carassius auratus* L.). *Comp. Biochem. Physiol.* **20**: 939–948.

Swallow, R. L. & Fleming, W. R. (1966). Effects of starvation, ACTH and glucose injections on liver glycogen levels of *Tilapia mossambica. Am. Zool.* **6**: 562.

Swift, D. R. (1954). Influence of mammalian growth hormone on rate of growth of fish. *Nature, Lond.* **173**: 1096.

Swift, D. R. (1955). Seasonal variations in the growth rate, thyroid gland activity and food reserves of brown trout (*Salmo trutta* Linn). *J. exp. Biol.* **32**: 751–764.

Swift, D. R. (1961). The annual growth-rate cycle in brown trout (*Salmo trutta* Linn.) and its cause. *J. exp. Biol.* **38**: 595–604.

Swift, D. R. & Pickford, G. E. (1965). Seasonal variations in the hormone content of the pituitary gland of the perch *Perca fluviatilis. Gen. comp. Endocr.* **5**: 354–365.

Thorpe, A. & Ince, B. W. (1976). Plasma insulin levels in teleosts determined by a charcoal-separation radioimmunoassay technique. *Gen. comp. Endocr.* **30**: 332–339.

Umminger, B. L. (1969). Physiological studies on super-cooled killifish (*Fundulus heteroclitus*). II. Serum organic constituents and the problem of supercooling. *J. exp. Zool.* **172**: 409–424.

Umminger, B. L. (1970). Physiological studies on supercooled killifish (*Fundulus heteroclitus*) III. Carbohydrate metabolism and survival at subzero temperatures. *J. exp. Zool.* **173**: 159–174.

Umminger, B. L. & Bair, R. D. (1973). Role of islets in the cold-induced hyperglycemia of the killifish *Fundulus heteroclitus. J. exp. Zool.* **183**: 65–70.

Umminger, B. L. & Benziger, D. (1975). *In vitro* stimulation of hepatic glycogen phosphorylase activity by epinephrine and glucagon in the brown bullhead *Ictalurus nebulosus. Gen. comp. Endocr.* **25**: 96–104.

Umminger, B. L., Benziger, D. & Levy, S. (1975). *In vitro* stimulation of hepatic glycogen phosphorylase activity by epinephrine and glucagon in the killifish, *Fundulus heteroclitus. Comp. Biochem. Physiol.* **51C**: 111–115.

Umminger, B. L. & Gist, D. H. (1973). Effects of thermal acclimation on physiological responses to handling stress, cortisol and aldosterone injections in the goldfish (*Carassius auratus*). *Comp. Biochem Physiol.* **44A**: 967–977.

van den Brande, J. L., Koote, F., Tielenburgh, R., van der Wilk, M. & Huyser, T. (1974). Studies on plasma somatomedin activity in different animal species. *Acta Endocr.* **75**: 243–248.

Watkins, D., Leonards, J., Dixit, P. K., Cooperstein, S. J. & Lazarow, A. (1964). Glucose stimulation of insulin release from toadfish islets tissue *in vitro. Biol. Bull. mar. biol. Lab. Woods Hole* **127**: 395–396.

Young, J. E. (1970). The relative effects of insulin and glucagon upon serum glucose levels of goldfish, *Carassius auratus* L. *Am. Zool.* **10**: 499.

Zanuy, S. & Carillo, M. (1976). Some observed correlations of the histophysiological and environmental factors of two types of marine teleost. *Gen. comp. Endocr.* **29**: 264.

Symp. zool. Soc. Lond. (1979) No. 44, 105–132

Environmental Timing and the Control of Reproduction in Teleost Fish

D. B. C. SCOTT

The University, St. Andrews, Fife, Scotland

SYNOPSIS

Reproduction is a cyclical phenomenon. In habitats where seasonal fluctuation in environmental conditions does not occur, reproductive cycles may recur uninterruptedly, at intervals determined by the finite time required for the completion of a cycle. Few natural habitats can provide such constancy and it is more usual for the periodicity of the reproductive cycle to be geared to that of the environment, ultimately to variations in, for example, food supply.

Coordination of the environmental and the reproductive cycles is achieved by proximate timing factors, regularly recurring environmental events which elicit specific physiological responses in the physiological status of the animal. These proximate factors (like the cycles which they regulate) are adaptive, and few generalizations are possible. Daylength and temperature are commonly important variables, but many others are involved; and it is the interplay of many such factors, including those stimulating gonad regression, which achieves the regulation of the cycle and the coordination of the cycles of individuals in a population.

The relay of environmental information by way of the hypothalamus–hypophyseal axis is well established, and induced spawning in commercially cultured fish is now routine practice. Less well established is the role of the epiphyseal complex, which in at least some vertebrates secretes the gonad-inhibiting hormone, melatonin, during the hours of darkness. If the epiphysis acts as a biological clock with a circadian rhythm, it may play a significant part in the fine timing of the reproductive cycle in fish, perhaps in association with the phases of the moon.

INTRODUCTION

Reproduction in teleost fish, as in other vertebrates, is characteristically cyclical. This cyclicity is ultimately imposed by the fact that environmental conditions tend to recur cyclically. In the course of their evolution, species have become adapted to perform their various reproductive processes at the most favourable phases of the environmental cycles. It is no simple matter to identify these ultimate determinants of reproductive cycles. Conventionally, it is usual to state that reproduction is so timed as to ensure that breeding periods are "suitable for rearing offspring" (de Vlaming, 1974), but this is surely an oversimplification. The relationship between biological cycles and their environmental determinants is subtle, as other papers in this symposium indicate, and the timing of a species' reproductive cycle is certainly a compromise involving many environmental considerations.

It is not the purpose of this paper to analyse the ultimate determinants of reproductive cycles, but to consider the means by which these cycles— whatever their form—are regulated so that the appropriate stages of reproduction do coincide with the appropriate phases of the environmental cycles. An understanding of how reproductive cycles are controlled is not merely intellectually rewarding, but has also practical application. Reproduction often becomes deranged when fish are transferred from their natural habitats, earning them the reputation of being "difficult to breed in captivity". Examples in pisciculture include the Asiatic riverine carps such as *Ctenopharyngodon idella* (C. and V.), which fail to reproduce in tropical fish-farm ponds (Hickling, 1967) and (happily) in English canals. The artificial induction of spawning by hormone administration is a widespread practice; its induction by environmental manipulation would be more advantageous in certain circumstances. Suitable manipulation of the environmental conditions which control reproduction has induced species to breed more often than usual, to provide a ready stock of experimental animals (Boyd & Simmonds, 1974).

The investigation of reproduction is an interdisciplinary study. There is a mass of published literature on teleost reproduction, as reference to a recent bibliography for 1963–74 (Donaldson, 1977) will show, but it is widely dispersed in physiological, ecological, genetical, ethological, fisheries and aquarium hobby journals. Because of the different approaches of the investigators in these diverse fields, it is often difficult to coordinate information. The physiologist, for example, may ignore the ecological context of his experimental animals; the ecologist may associate reproductive processes with environmental events which happen at the appropriate time, without confirming a causal relationship experimentally; the fisheries biologist may assess reproductive cycles in such vague terms as "ripe" or "spent" which do not correspond with physiologically discrete processes; and only an ethologist may realize that a fish strung up in a gill-net is a very different physiological system from the same fish in nature.

A further problem in considering reproductive control derives from the fact that reproductive cycles are adaptive. Each species has evolved a unique reproductive cycle, depending on its evolutionary/ecological niche. The means by which each reproductive cycle is synchronized with the environmental cycles are also liable to be species specific. So, although the reproductive timing of many species of teleosts has been studied, it is not feasible to transfer results obtained in one species wholesale to another. Reviews of this subject tend consequently to become lengthy catalogues of basically incompatible data, from diverse species. There is clearly a need for a comprehensive study of a single species, from as many points of view (ecological, physiological, ethological, etc.) as possible. This single species, moreover, should be one with as few reproductive specializations as possible; this review will be primarily concerned with "conventional" teleosts, disregarding those which are viviparous or ovoviviparous (Hoar, 1969), and those with complicated hermaphrodite life histories (Yamamoto, 1969).

THE REPRODUCTIVE CYCLE

In the course of a typical reproductive cycle, the gonads are matured, and the ova fertilized. More or less directly associated with these central processes is a wide range of accessory activities, such as migration, various forms of social behaviour (hierarchy formation, territory establishment, and the like), courtship and, in some species, parental care. These activities involve far-reaching changes in virtually every physiological system. Since this paper is concerned with the timing of reproduction, rather than with the reproductive processes themselves, the reader is referred to the many recent reviews of teleost reproductive physiology, such as Pickford & Atz (1957), Atz & Pickford (1964), Hoar (1969), Liley (1969), Donaldson (1973), and de Vlaming (1974), for a detailed treatment of the subject. The following summary of the processes involved in a reproductive cycle is mainly intended to stress that they are many, diverse, and controlled by a variety of factors. To consider a reproductive cycle as consisting of but two stages, "gonad recrudescence" and "spawning", is a misleading oversimplification.

Intragonadal Processes

The gonads are central to any study of reproductive periodicity. In most teleost species, gametogenesis ("recrudescence") extends over the major part of the reproductive cycle, whereas "spawning" is of relatively short duration. Although the timing of spawning is presumably of critical importance, aberrations in the timing of the lengthy processes of gametogenesis would also be detrimental to successful reproduction.

Ovary

The ovaries of teleosts are derived, like those of other vertebrates, from a pair of ridges along the dorsal peritoneal wall. Various degrees of fusion occur, resulting in species with a single ovary or asymmetrical ovaries. Most teleosts differ from other vertebrates in that the oviducts are continuous with the connective tissue layers that surround the ovary, so that ova do not pass into the coelomic cavity (the gymnovarian condition) but remain within the ovarian tunic (the cryptovarian condition). The ovary may have a central lumen into which the ova are shed, or the oviduct may be paraovarian, with the ova being shed outwards, the core of the ovary being solid. In salmonoids (e.g. *Coregonus*, see below) the oviducts degenerate, so that ova pass into the coelom, and thence to the exterior via pores adjacent to the urinary opening and anus.

Oogenesis. Follicles develop in the germinal epithelium which lines the connective tissue framework of the ovary. A follicle comprises a single layer of epithelial cells, the granulosa, surrounding an oogonium. External to the granulosa is a layer of connective tissue cells, the theca. During vitellogenesis, the follicular layers become separated from the oocyte by a non-cellular layer, the zona radiata or oolemma.

Oogonia multiply in the ovary by mitotic division. When an oogonium enters the prophase of the first meiotic division, it is called a primary oocyte. The primary oocyte passes through two discrete growth phases, the first non-vitellogenic, the second vitellogenic. In the first phase of vitellogenesis, vesicles appear initially in the cortical region of the cytoplasm, extending centripetally; in the final phase yolk platelets (globules) appear near the centre of the oocyte and extend centrifugally until only a thin peripheral shell of cytoplasm remains. The ovary may remain at this stage for some time, with yolk-laden primary oocytes whose nuclei (germinal vesicles) are in the first meiotic prophase.

Maturation and ovulation. Maturation and ovulation generally occur in quick succession. The nucleus migrates to the animal pole and breaks down, and the first meiotic division is completed, forming a secondary oocyte and a polar body. The second meiotic division converts the secondary oocyte into the ovum, plus another polar body. These maturation changes are generally revealed macroscopically by increasing translucency of the yolk. At ovulation, the ovum is released and the ruptured follicular membranes remain as calyces in the ovarian stroma. The size of the ripe ovum varies—in *Scleropages formosus* (Müller & Schlegel) it is as great as 1·9 cm in diameter (Scott & Fuller, 1976). In most species the ovary usually represents 10–20% of the total weight of the fish, regardless of individual ovum size.

Atresia. Previtellogenic oocytes seem to be remarkably independent of the teleost's reproductive hormones, and persist for a long time even in hypophysectomized fish. Vitellogenic oocytes, by contrast, degenerate immediately after hypophysectomy, and similar atretic degeneration occurs in response to noxious stimuli, though the degree of responsiveness varies from species to species. The transfer of minnows, *Phoxinus phoxinus* (L.), to aquarium tanks elicits atresia within 48 h. These corpora atretica are characterized by the breakdown of the oolemma and its penetration by phagocytic granulosa cells.

It has been suggested that, in the normal course of events, a proportion of the vitellogenic oocytes in teleost ovaries are transformed into steroidogenic structures called preovulatory corpora lutea, morphologically akin to corpora atretica (Chieffi & Botte, 1970). It may be that endocrine preovulatory corpora lutea exist in some species, but in many it seems certain that they are simply oocytes undergoing resorption (see p. 114). Postovulatory corpora atretica also are probably not endocrine, the follicle itself being the main source of oestrogens (Nagahama, Chan & Hoar, 1976).

Testis

As in the case of the ovaries, the testes of teleosts may be single or paired. The vas deferens of teleosts differs from almost all other vertebrates in having no connection with the mesonephros in the adult: the testis duct and the ureter are separate.

Spermatogenesis. In most vertebrates there is a continuous germinal epithelium lining the seminiferous tubules. In teleosts, resting single cells (primary spermatogonia) in the tubule walls proliferate to form clusters of secondary spermatogonia, each cluster enclosed in a cyst. The secondary spermatogonia in each cyst divide synchronously, mitotically, to form primary spermatocytes, sometimes in immense numbers, 2^{15} or 2^{16} from one spermatogonium in cyprinodonts, but sometimes without much multiplication, as in *Scleropages formosus* (Scott & Fuller, 1976). Meiotic division of the primary spermatocytes produces secondary spermatocytes, and the second meiotic division produces haploid spermatids.

Spermiogenesis. The metamorphosis of spermatids to spermatozoa occurs in the lumen of the testis tubules, after the cyst has burst. In some species, there is a concentration of mature cysts near the vas deferens, so that sections taken in different regions of the testis show different degrees of progress in gametogenesis. In other species, development is uniform throughout the testis. An apparent reduction in testis weight at this stage (Fig. 1) may be due to the small mass of the spermatozoa relative to earlier spermatocyte stages.

Sertoli cells. The cysts contain not only the gonocytes, but also Sertoli cells, which are supportive and nutritive. Spermatids (and perhaps earlier stages) are associated with the Sertoli cells, which may form a conspicuous layer just inside the basement membrane. Sertoli cells may also be phagocytic, resorbing unshed spermatozoa (Drance *et al.*, 1976). Androgens are secreted by interstitial cells, as in other vertebrates (Billard, Meusy-Dessolles & Fléchon, 1971).

Extragonadal Processes

In terms of time, gametogenesis usually occupies the major part of a reproductive cycle. Successful reproduction, however, also involves a gamut of accessory activities which, because they occur in a relatively short space of time, are often grouped together under the blanket term of "spawning". It is much more revealing from the point of view of timing the reproductive cycle, to consider each component separately. The nature of these associated activities varies from species to species, but they generally include the following.

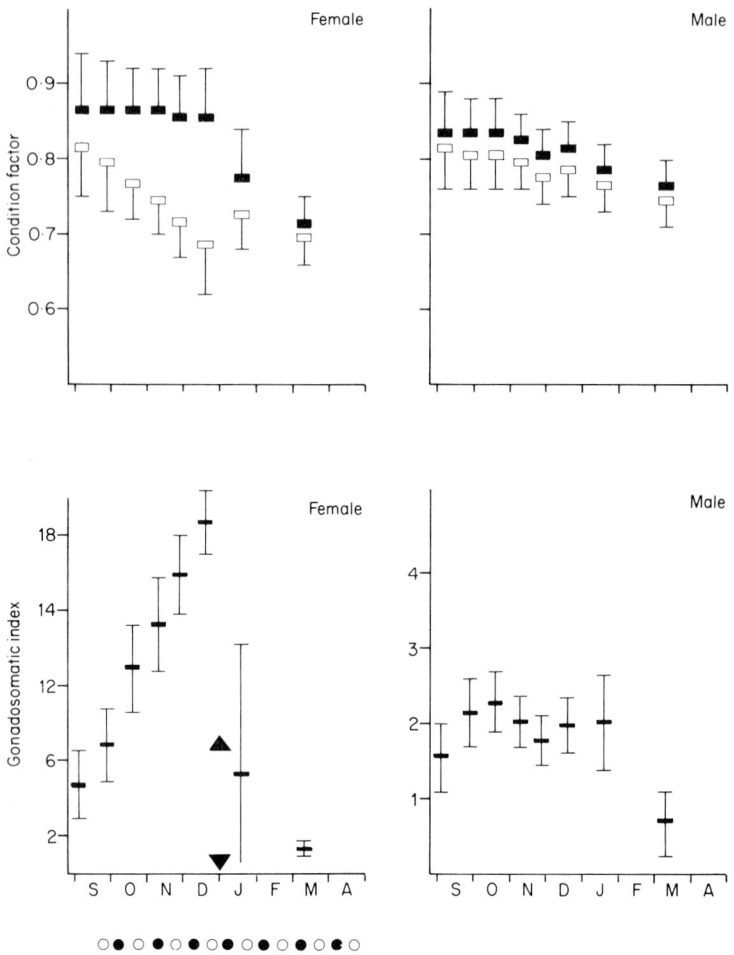

FIG. 1. *Coregonus lavaretus*, Loch Lomond, 1977–78. Monthly mean condition factor (black rectangles), somatic condition factor (open rectangles) and gonadosomatic index, for male and female fish taken by gill-netting off the spawning grounds from September to March. Minimum of 50 fish of each sex per sample; vertical lines, one s. d. above and/or below mean; lunar phases below time axis for females.

Migration

Pre- and post-spawning migrations are commonplace amongst teleosts, some of them extending over considerable distances (Harden-Jones, 1968). Population structure may be drastically affected even by small-scale migrations, and sampling techniques may have to be adjusted accordingly (see p. 117). Longer migrations, such as those of the anadromous salmonids, may involve far-reaching physiological adjustments (see Woodhead, 1975). Species with such complications are best avoided in timing studies.

Social behaviour

Some form of social behaviour involving hierarchy formation or territory establishment is often associated with spawning, though it may occur at other times. Such behaviour is particularly conspicuous in certain groups, and it is likely that it is of widespread occurrence, though not always visually conspicuous (Baerends, 1971).

Ovulation

Although already described as an intragonadal process, strictly speaking ovulation is the release of the oocyte from the body tissue proper. Ovulation is of particular practical significance; until it is completed, the ovum cannot be fertilized (except in some specialized viviparous species, see Miller this volume p. 263). Oviposition generally follows rapidly upon ovulation.

Spermiogenesis

Likewise, in the male, spermiogenesis is strictly a process outwith the gonadal tissue, the spermatids having escaped from the cysts into the lumen of the seminiferous tubules. Unlike ovulation, spermiogenesis may be completed long before the spermatozoa are shed at spawning.

Oviposition

In "conventional" teleosts, oviposition follows closely upon ovulation, and is associated with courtship behaviour. Oviposition is of less practical significance than ovulation, as ovulated fish can be "stripped" and the ova artificially fertilized.

Spermiation

In males, gonad hydration, sometimes called spermiation (Yamazaki & Donaldson, 1968), occurs immediately before the spermatozoa are shed. The hydration may be apparent as a terminal rise in testis weight (Fig. 1). Spermiation may be comparable to ovulation in females, when gonadal hydration also occurs (Hirose, Hirano & Ishida, 1974), the ejaculation of the spermatozoa being the equivalent of oviposition in females.

Parental care

Some degree of provision for the young is widespread, ranging from simple nest building to complex forms of viviparity (Hoar, 1969).

Refractory period

After spawning, in many teleosts, there supervenes a period during which the gonads are unresponsive to any of the usual stimuli for recrudescence.

It has been called the "refractory period" (Bissonette & Wadlund, 1932), a regrettably negative title since this is an important stage of reproduction in its own right (see p. 123). Increasing attention has recently been directed to its investigation (de Vlaming & Paquette, 1977).

Associated with these many activities is a vast host of phenological adaptations, ranging from the senescence of Pacific salmon to a loss of the alarm-substance cells in the skin of certain cyprinids with abrasive spawning behaviour (Smith, 1976). From the point of view of studying the timeous control of reproductive cycles, the fewer such complications a species possesses, the simpler the analysis is likely to prove.

Periodicity

Three main biologically significant cyclical periodicities occur in nature: diel (circadian), lunar (circalunar) and annual (circannual). Some workers further distinguish between solar and sidereal cycles, and, of course, there are many subsidiary cycles based upon subdivisions of the main cycles: tidal cycles, for example, or those based on twice-yearly rainy seasons in the tropics (Lowe-McConnell, this volume p. 219). Aspects of reproductive cycles are associated with each of these periodicities (Schwassmann, 1971).

Diel

Complete reproductive cycles within a 24-h period do not occur in teleosts. Certain stages of the reproductive cycles, however, follow a diel cycle. In particular, oviposition takes place at specific hours of night or day in many species; self-fertilization in *Rivulus marmoratus* Poey follows a diel cycle (Harrington, 1963). Diel cycles in many teleost activities, more or less implicated in reproduction, are well established, and similar cycles in hormone levels are also now recognized (Baker & Wigham, this volume p. 89). Although diel cycles do not encompass entire reproductive cycles in teleosts, there is increasing evidence that they may be critically important in the timing of the longer-term cycles (see p. 125).

Lunar

Lunar cycles in reproductive activity are particularly conspicuous in marine teleosts, where it is not unlikely that moon-induced cycles—such as tides—rather than the moon phases themselves are the ultimate determinants (Schwassmann, 1971). Grunion (*Leuresthes tenuis* (Ayres)), for example, oviposit (at night) at 14- to 16-day intervals when the high spring tides are receding (Walker, 1949). There is increasing evidence that spawning in freshwater teleosts, too, may follow lunar periodicity (Lowe-McConnell, this volume p. 219).

As in the case of diel cycles, lunar periodicity is associated predominantly with stages within the reproductive cycle rather than the whole cycle; the spawning period of the grunion extends over seven months of an annual cycle. Like diel cycles, it seems that lunar cycles may nevertheless play a part in determining the timing of the longer-term cycle (see p. 124).

Annual

The reproductive cycles of the vast majority of teleosts are based on an annual periodicity. In practice, the preponderance may be due to the fact that annual reproductive cycles are conspicuous, and hence preferentially studied. Nevertheless, since most research on the timing of reproductive cycles has been concerned with such species, this paper will concentrate upon them.

Reproductive cycles are adaptive, and it is not feasible to make generalizations on a taxonomic basis. It is slightly safer to make ecological generalizations. In habitats where the range of the cyclical environmental conditions is extreme, reproductive cycles tend to be regularly-recurring, accurately repetitive from year to year, and with short, sharply delimited spawning periods. Such habitats are typified by fresh waters in the cold-temperate zones of this planet, habitats which are dominated by annual cycles of such things as daylength, temperature and the availability of food. The timing of the reproductive cycles of species from these habitats is conspicuously accurate, and they have been much studied as a consequence.

As a typical example, Fig. 2 shows the reproductive cycle in females from a population of the European minnow, *Phoxinus phoxinus*, sampled in Loch Walton, Scotland, from 1961–63. Maximum and minimum temperature at 1m depth. The annual maximum seldom exceeds 20°C, and ice up to 20cm thick regularly covers the surface during much of the winter. Gonadosomatic index, the weight of the gonad as a percentage of total weight, is a much-used criterion of general gonad "recrudescence" (see p. 116) and, for these female minnows, is minimal in August, after spawning. The index rises somewhat in autumn but remains static throughout winter. Another increase occurs again in early spring and, finally, a rapid increase (to 12–14%) takes place in late spring, immediately prior to spawning. Females ovulate during May and June, in the loch, and then migrate up the tributary streams for spawning with the males which have ascended earlier.

The use of gonadosomatic index as an indication of gonad development ment conceals the fact that several physiologically discrete processes are taking place within the gonad. More exact information can be obtained by histological study of the gonad, and Fig. 2(c) shows the percentages of four oocyte stages as counted in longitudinal sections of ovaries: previtellogenic primary oocytes, primary oocytes in the first phase of vitellogenesis, primary oocytes in the final phase of vitellogenesis, and atretic oocytes. Previtellogenic oocytes are abundant throughout the year. The first phase of vitellogenesis occurs in autumn and resumes in spring. The final vitellogenic phase is restricted to late spring, though a few yolk-laden

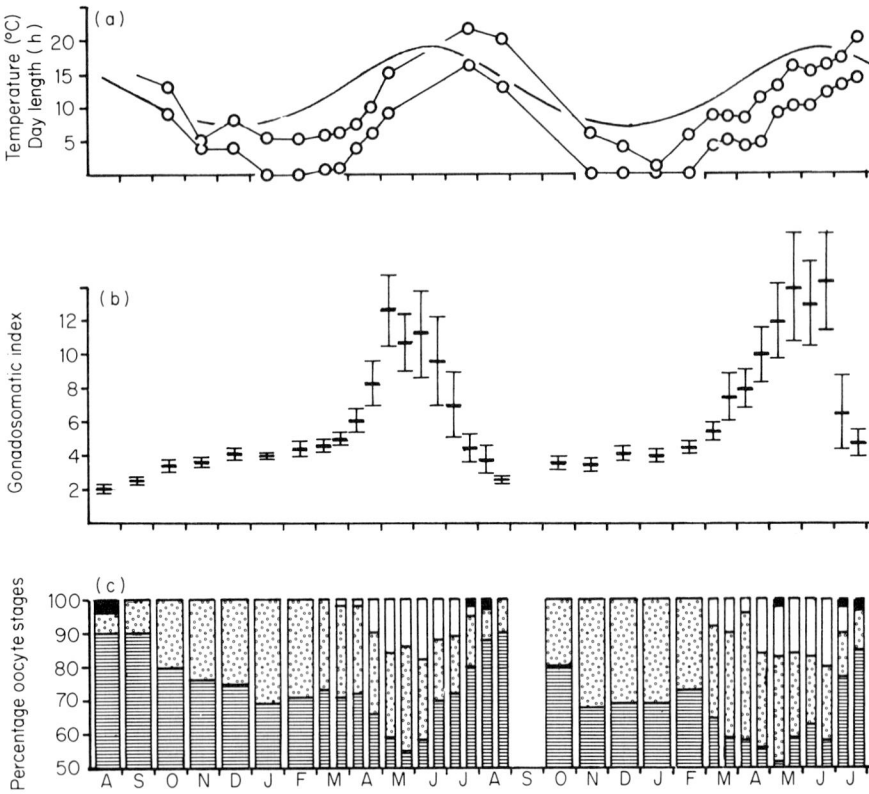

FIG. 2. *Phoxinus phoxinus*. Loch Walton, 1961–63. (a) Daylength (hours from sunrise to sunset) (continuous line) and monthly maximum and minimum water temperatures (open circles); (b) monthly mean gonadosomatic index (±1 s.d.) of females and (c) percentage of primary oocyte stages in ovarian sections: previtellogenic (crosslined); at first (stippled) and final (open) stages of vitellogenesis; and atretic (black). Minimum of 20 fish per sample.

oocytes do appear in some fish in the previous autumn. Atretic oocytes appear after spawning.

It is obvious, even from a cursory examination, that the reproductive cycle of the minnow is regularly repetitive from year to year. What is more, this accuracy in timing does not apply only to the culmination of the cycle—spawning—but applies to each stage composing the cycle. So, each stage of oocyte maturation occurs at its appropriate season. Likewise (though it is not illustrated here) each of the extragonadal processes takes place in its due order. Aberrations at any stage may disrupt the reproductive cycle. We are concerned in this paper with understanding how fish maintain this precise synchrony.

In habitats where environmental cycles are less marked, reproductive cycles are less rigidly organized, and spawning periods more protracted. At 56°N, near the northern limits of its range, *Phoxinus phoxinus* spawns in Loch Walton during May and June. In the Carpathians the same species spawns from March to October (Frost, 1943). Similarly Dahlberg & Conyers (1973) point out that the spawning seasons of many marine fishes become longer towards the south along the Atlantic coast of the USA, beginning earlier and finishing later. It does not require a change in latitude to achieve this effect; the sea is generally a more homeostatic environment than fresh water, and at equivalent high latitudes spawning seasons of marine species tend to be longer than those of freshwater species. Such prolongation of the spawning period may be achieved by repeat-spawning of successive batches of gonadal products or by only a part of the available gametes being shed at a time; the grunion, which spawns over a seven-month period, has already been noted (p. 112 ; see also Miller, this volume p. 263).

In habitats where there are no reproductively significant cyclical fluctuations in environmental conditions to dictate periodicity, reproduction might equally well take place at any time of the year. There may be such habitats: deep sea teleosts are obvious candidates for consideration (Gordon, this volume p. 327). Many equatorial freshwater teleosts are described as aseasonal breeders, but even here there are hints of an underlying cyclicity. *Tilapia*, in the equatorial Lake Naivasha, do not spawn during the coldest and driest months of the year (Hyder, 1970). It might be more profitable to regard such species as having lax annual reproductive cycles involving a much-extended spawning season, rather than as being non-cyclical. Other tropical freshwater species have clearly-defined reproductive cycles, but with ultimate environmental determinants different from those of temperate-zone species. Perhaps most conspicuous are the many species which spawn during rainy seasons either annually or at shorter intervals (Lowe-McConnell, this volume p. 219).

More difficult to account for are equatorial species which maintain circannual reproductive cycles without apparent relevance to any annual environmental cycle. In a preliminary survey, which still awaits confirmation, Scott (1974) gill-netted monthly samples of *Mormyrus kannume* Forskål in Lake Victoria, Uganda, close to the Equator. Samples caught on a feeding ground comprised individual fish with an annual reproductive cycle as exactly synchronized as in minnow populations at 56°N. Samples on a spawning ground, by contrast, comprised fish in ripe spawning condition in all months except July and August. Scott's tentative explanation was that individual populations of *M. kannume* followed an annual reproductive cycle, but populations were out of phase with each other, and moved to spawning grounds on reaching maturity. A similar situation has been described in the same locality for cormorants (Marshall & Roberts, 1959).

Assessment

Before attempting to analyse the factors involved in controlling reproductive cycles, it is essential to have accurate and detailed information on the nature of the cycle itself. Such information is remarkably scarce. In "aseasonal" breeders, each fish is likely to be at a different reproductive stage, so that statistically valid samples are difficult to obtain. Temperate-zone "seasonal" breeders are more amenable in this respect, but even so assessments of their reproductive cycles are often vaguely expressed.

Assessments of gonad recrudescence include macroscopic examination of the gonads, using such systems as those of Nikolsky (1963) or Kesteven (1960), still widely employed, particularly in fisheries research. Although convenient, they are inevitably subjective and less informative than assessments based on gonad weight. Absolute gonad weight is of value only in cases where the population sampled is of uniform size. In the absence of such uniformity, gonad weight must be assessed relative to some other parameter, and gonadosomatic index is widely used. Even gonadosomatic index is open to misinterpretation, however, as it is influenced not only by changes in gonad weight, but also by change in somatic weight. It is thus necessary to have an estimate of change in somatic weight, and this is usually expressed relative to length as the Somatic Condition Factor

$$\text{Somatic Condition Factor} = \frac{\text{total weight} - \text{gonad weight}}{\text{length}^3}.$$

The Somatic Condition Factor may be compared with the conventional Condition Factor

$$\text{Condition Factor} = \frac{\text{total weight (including gonad)}}{\text{length}^3}$$

to give an indication of changes in gonad weight. The relationship between condition factor, somatic condition factor and gonadosomatic index is exemplified in Fig. 1.

Gonadosomatic index may not increase linearly with size (or age) of the fish. In such species, either allowance should be made for the age composition of samples, or sampling should be restricted to a suitable age-group. For example, Fig. 1 is derived from samples of powan, *Coregonus lavaretus* (L.), caught in gill-nets of 39-mm mesh (knot to knot), which catch mostly fish in the size range 28–38 cm total length (three to four years old). Over this range, gonad weight increases linearly with total weight. Furthermore, in comparing gonadosomatic indices, it must be remembered that at least three different criteria of length are in use: standard, fork and total lengths, and gonadosomatic index may be given as gonad weight relative to total weight (including gonad) or somatic weight (excluding gonad).

Gonadal weight, however measured, gives only a crude overall estimate of activity without any indication of the diverse processes involved. More precise assessment of gonadal development demands histological examination. At its simplest, this involves counting the numbers of oocytes within certain arbitrary size ranges, and it is popular, particularly in fisheries studies, because of its convenience. The method suffers when the size ranges selected may not be related to physiologically distinct gametogonic stages. It is preferable to identify specific oocyte and spermatocyte stages from histological sections, as exemplified in Fig. 2.

Even when adequate methods for gonadal assessment are used, it is possible to obtain misleading results by inadequate sampling of the populations. The behaviour of teleosts alters significantly during the course of their reproductive cycles. This is particularly evident in migratory species, but even in non-migrants changes in diel activity patterns, changes in feeding behaviour and the like may demand an appropriately wide range of sampling methods and locations to get a balanced survey. Finally, of course, the sampling technique itself may alter the reproductive state of the fish. The transfer of *Phoxinus phoxinus* females to aquarium tanks results in massive atresia of vitellogenic oocytes within a few days (Scott, unpublished). In a study on plasma cortisol in relation to reproduction in *Coregonus lavaretus*, different netting and killing techniques result in widely different cortisol concentrations (Fuller, Scott & Fraser, 1976).

ENVIRONMENTAL TIMING

It is inconceivable that reproductive cycles of such long duration and complexity could be wholly endogenously timed. Since pioneer investigations almost half a century ago, it has been apparent that reproductive cycles, although essentially self-sustaining, are synchronized ("entrained") with environmental cycles by means of regularly recurring environmental events which act as "timing cues". These environmental timing cues have become physiologically significant to animals in that they stimulate (or perhaps inhibit) specific stages of gametogenesis or other reproductive processes. The first such timing cue to be positively identified was photoperiod (or daylength) and there is now an enormous body of published work on the photoperiodic control of reproduction, most of it concerned with birds and mammals.

There is no reason *a priori* why other regularly recurring environmental events should not act as timing cues, provided that they are within a species' sensory competence, and that the species has the physiological equipment to transduce this environmental information into reproductive responses. Poikilotherms such as fish, in the Earth's temperate zones, are subject to a regular cycle of temperature change (cf. Fig. 2). For some teleosts, temperature seems to replace photoperiod as the primary environmental timing cue. It has been suggested that there may be taxonomically based "preferences" in this respect; cyprinodonts for example using temperature, gasterosteids using photoperiod and cyprinids using both (de Vlaming, 1972a). As Marshall pointed out in an early symposium in this series, "Light is important only in species for which it is important that light shall be important" (Marshall, 1960).

The importance ascribed to photoperiod and temperature as environmental timing cues may derive from the fact that most of the species favoured for this kind of research are from habitats where the cyclical changes in these factors happen to provide reliable calendar information. Little is known of the timing cues of tropical teleosts in habitats where daylength changes become negligible towards the Equator and temperature changes are irregular. Hyder (1970) suggests that light intensity changes regulate reproduction in *Tilapia* in Lake Naivasha. Many tropical species spawn at the time of seasonal flooding, but the exact stimulus is seldom clear: changes in water chemistry, flow rates, food supply, availability of spawning sites, etc. may all accompany flooding (Okedi, 1969, 1970; Payne, 1975). In any case, it seems to be only the final stage of the reproductive cycle, spawning, which is associated with flooding, and the question remains of how such species regulate the earlier stages of their cycle so that they are physiologically ready for spawning when the floods come (de Vlaming, 1974). Numerous environmental factors have been invoked as regulators of reproductive cycles, but much of the evidence is anecdotal and experimentally unconfirmed. In the absence of such confirmation, investigation of the mechanism of action of the environmental cues is probably best restricted to the well-worn lines of photoperiod.

Nevertheless, in practice, it is clear that for the completion of a normal reproductive cycle, a range of stimuli are necessary. The cycles of teleosts transferred from their natural habitats are not always restored to normal by the provision of appropriate photoperiod and temperature regimes. *Phoxinus phoxinus*, for example, will not spawn in still-water aquarium tanks.

The total complement of environmental stimuli required for a species to complete its normal reproductive cycle may be called the "species requirement", a phrase introduced by Marshall (1960), though he restricted it to the culminating stages of reproduction only. There have been a few attempts to analyse the special requirements of a particular species as comprehensively, for example, as in the heroic series of papers on the goby, *Gillichthys mirabilis* Cooper (de Vlaming, 1971, 1972b, c, d, e). It is, however, more convenient to treat each component of the species requirement as a separate entity, and to test the role of photoperiod, for example, alone. This is conventional practice. While such studies may reveal the physiological potential of the animals, they can prove misleading in terms of what happens in nature.

For example, Bullough (1939, 1940, 1942) established experimentally that the final vitellogenesis in *Phoxinus phoxinus* in late spring is stimulated by increasing photoperiod, which he equated with increasing daylength in nature. Scott (unpub.) subjected minnows in aquarium tanks to controlled conditions of photoperiod and temperature, as did Bullough. The fish were caught at about the autumn equinox by electrofishing, and 50–100 fish were maintained in tanks of about 1 m³. The fish were fed daily on commercial dog-food and fish-food, and *Tubifex* were available at all times. Samples of 5–10 females were killed at intervals.

At low temperature and low photoperiod (Fig. 3), there was little gonad recrudescence, with much the same results at high temperature and low photoperiod (Fig. 3), and at low temperature and increasing

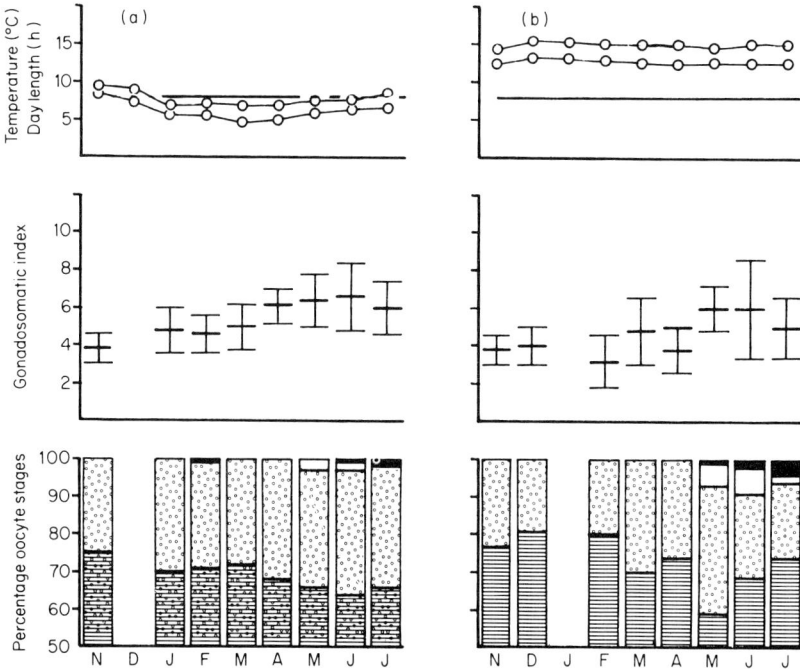

FIG. 3. *Phoxinus phoxinus*: mean gonadosomatic index (±1 s.d.) and percentage of oocyte stages (as Fig. 2) obtained from November to June at experimental temperatures (maximum and minimum values circled) and daylength (continuous line). (a) Low daylength and low temperature; (b) low daylength and high temperature.

photoperiod, following natural daylength change (Fig. 4a). However, at high temperature and increasing photoperiod (Fig. 4b), the gonadosomatic index rose to 10·5%, and the percentage of yolk-laden oocytes to 10%. Photostimulation clearly does stimulate final

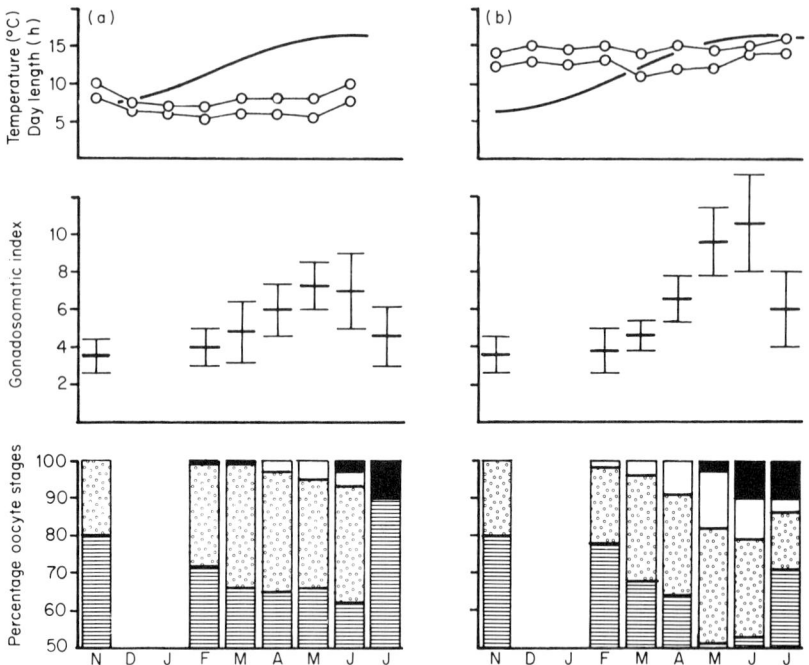

FIG. 4. *Phoxinus phoxinus*: mean gonadosomatic index and percentage of oocyte stages at experimental temperatures and daylength (see Fig. 3). (a) Gradually increasing daylength and low temperature; (b) gradually increasing daylength and high temperature.

vitellogenesis, at any rate at high temperature. There remains, however, a significant difference between the experimental results and the situation in nature. At best in aquaria the final gonadosomatic index reached only 10·5%, far short of the 12–14% in nature. Likewise, the percentage of yolk-laden oocytes is lower, at 10% instead of 20%.

Natural levels of gonadosomatic index and vitellogenesis can be achieved by exposing aquarium-maintained minnows to a sudden increase in photoperiod, a rise in daylength from 8 to 16 h within one week (Fig. 5a). Under these conditions, gonadosomatic index reaches 12% and yolk-laden oocytes 20%. Increasing temperature does not have the same effects (Fig. 5b). This sudden increase in photoperiod may seem artificial, but examination of the ecology of the minnows in nature reveals a different picture. In Loch Walton, in winter, minnows spend the daylight hours under piles of stones, in relative darkness. They emerge to swim in open water only after dark. When, in spring, water temperature reaches about 8°C (Fig. 2), their behaviour patterns change, and they begin to swim in open water in daylight, when their shoals are a conspicuous feature of the loch. These behavioural changes can readily be

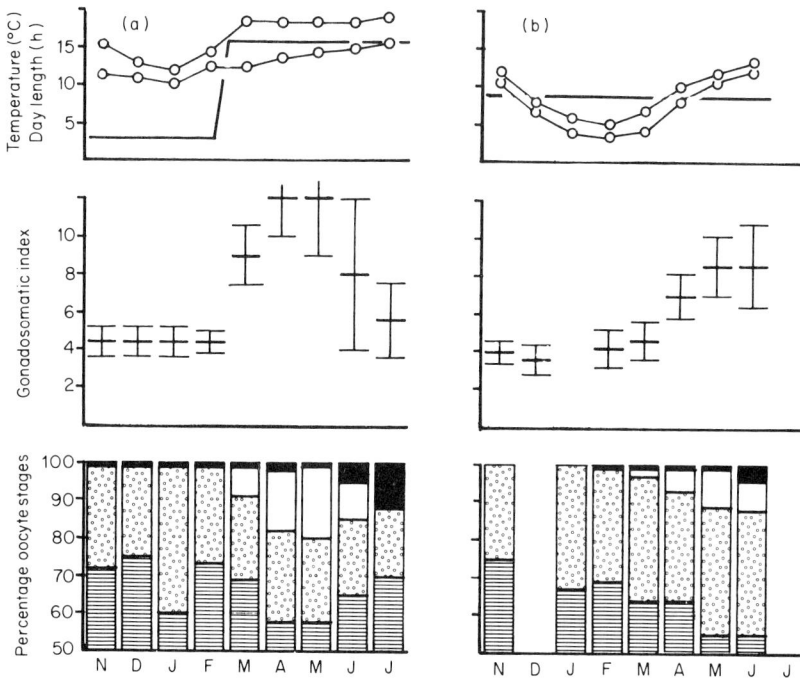

FIG. 5. *Phoxinus phoxinus*: mean gonadosomatic index and percentage of oocyte stages at experimental temperatures and daylength (see Fig. 3). (a) Increasing daylength (8 to 16 h) within one week, with gradually increasing temperature; (b) low daylength, and gradually increasing temperature.

duplicated in aquaria. The light regime to which they are exposed consequently changes dramatically. So, although it is indeed photo-stimulation which induces final vitellogenesis, the timing of this photo-stimulation is the result of behavioural changes which are in turn induced by temperature change in the water. The time of final vitellogenesis in Loch Walton does indeed vary from year to year, depending on when the temperature reaches 8°C. As experimental confirmation, Fig. 6 shows the effect of rising photoperiod and rising temperature on minnows without shelter in their aquarium tanks, a typical laboratory configuration, and with shelter in the form of drainpipes. In the former case (Fig. 6a) vitellogenesis occurs, but gradually and to a low level: gonadosomatic index 8–5%; yolk-laden oocytes 10%. In the latter case (Fig. 6b), vitel-logenesis is rapid, and occurs when water temperature reaches 8°C; gonadosomatic index reaches 12%, yolk-laden oocytes 20%.

It may therefore be worth questioning whether the overwhelming importance of photostimulation in the timing of reproductive cycles may not refer more to experimental situations than to real life. Experimenters

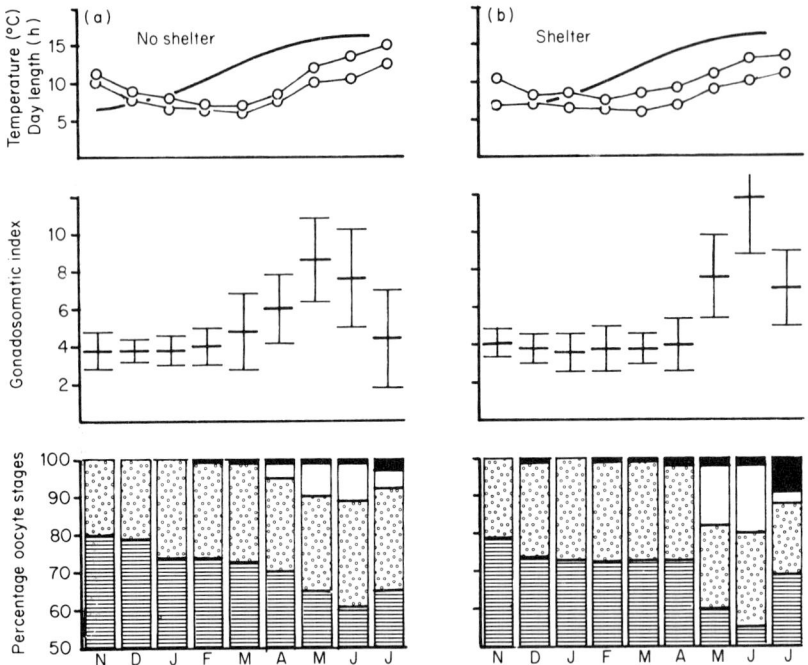

FIG. 6. *Phoxinus phoxinus*: mean gonadosomatic index and percentage of oocyte stages at experimental temperatures and daylength (see Fig. 3). (a) Gradually increasing daylength and temperature, without provision of shelter; (b) as (a), but shelter (drainpipes) provided.

tend to ignore the ecological context of their experimental animals, and assume that they are exposed to "textbook" environmental conditions. In practice, on the contrary, fish select preferred temperature and light-intensity ranges, and the environmental conditions experienced by an observer on the bank are not necessarily those experienced by a fish in the water. Changes in its behaviour may expose a fish to novel environmental conditions, and the fact that daylength has been increasing since December may be physiologically irrelevant to a minnow which remains in darkness until March.

Whatever the nature of the environmental timing cues, their function is to synchronize the reproductive cycle with the annual environmental cycle, and, as a corollary, to synchronize the individuals of a population reproductively with one another. The timing cues are generally not essential to gametogenesis; under constant environmental conditions gonad maturation is often completed, though it may be delayed (Pang, 1971). Indeed, under suitable conditions reproduction may occur more frequently than usual (p. 106). In experiments where withdrawal of environmental cues has resulted in reproductive failure, it is questionable whether the failure may not have been less due to the lack of cues than to the fact that the conditions imposed were noxious and induced a generalized stress response, a symptom of which is gonad degeneration. Although not essential to successful gametogenesis, the environmental cues may well be essential to successful reproduction, because individuals which mature out of phase with the environment—or each other—will be ineffectual. So, in *Phoxinus*, ovarian maturation occurs under virtually any non-noxious conditions, but at inappropriate times. Accurate synchronization is provided by the sudden (temperature-mediated) photostimulation in late spring, in that final vitellogenesis affects the whole population. Such synchronization can only be effective if the material upon which the environmental stimuli are acting is uniform. Not all oocytes in the minnow ovary reach full maturity in spring, and late growth-phase oocytes remaining in the ovary after spawning would probably reach maturity in the autumn, as environmental stimuli are not essential for the process. This situation is avoided by the atretic resorption of all vitellogenic oocytes remaining in the ovary after spawning, reducing the ovary to a uniform datum on which the next year's cycle can be based. The importance of this post-spawning synchronization has only relatively recently been recognized; previously it was considered merely as a "refractory period" in the reproductive cycle. In some species such as *Phoxinus*, this stage appears to be endogenously timed, and atresia follows spawning or (after a short interval) failure to spawn. In other species the post-spawning synchronization is timed, like other synchronizing stages, by environmental cues such as high summer temperatures (de Vlaming & Paquette, 1977).

A synchronizing stage at which environmental cues might be expected to be critically important is the final maturation and ovulation of ova, processes which usually immediately precede spawning. It would be logical to expect a high degree of temporal coordination at such a critical stage of the reproductive cycle. In many teleosts, maturation and ovulation are reported not to occur spontaneously, even in the presence of males (Sundararaj & Goswami, 1977), and failure of the reproductive cycle at this stage is commonplace in pisciculture. In the experiments with minnows described above, although gametogenesis can be induced in aquaria, ovulation does not occur and the vitellogenic oocytes become atretic shortly afterwards. These observations imply that an environmental stimulus induces ovulation, but it is worth considering that even though gametogenesis occurs in aquaria, it may not be comparable with the situation in nature (cf. Fig. 2 and Fig. 5a). If ovulation ensues spontaneously upon gonadal maturation, subnormal gonad recrudescence might well be inhibitory. On the other hand, in species which do ovulate spontaneously (for example, rainbow trout, *Salmo gairdneri* Richardson, in fish-farms), it is questionable whether environmental stimuli may not in fact be available, perhaps in the form of olfactory stimuli in through-flow water supplies.

Although the endocrine control of maturation and ovulation has been extensively studied, strangely little information is available on environmental aspects. Most studies invoke rather vague environmental stimuli such as "a consortium of factors" (Sundararaj & Vasal, 1976). In fish which spawn in association with rainy seasons, flooding is widely assumed to elicit ovulation, but exactly what aspect of flooding is seldom specified, nor is it always clear whether the associated activity is ovulation or oviposition. Minnows in Loch Walton oviposit in fast-flowing water in the upper reaches of tributary streams, but ovulation takes place in the loch itself. After ovulating, individual females migrate to the spawning areas, where the males are already congregated.

Spawning in association with lunar phases (or some derived phenomenon, such as tides) is well known in marine species (p. 112) and it is becoming increasingly apparent that the same applies to many freshwater species (Lowe-McConnell, this volume p. 219). In such cases, the absence of lunar cues in experimental aquaria might well explain failure in ovulation. Scott and various associates have studied the reproductive cycle of *Coregonus lavaretus*, the powan of Loch Lomond, for several years. Powan are landlocked glacial relicts, and no anadromous migration is involved. They spawn annually in mid-winter on shallow gravel banks in Loch Lomond. Males congregate on the spawning grounds in mid-October; females form more or less unisexual shoals in deep water at this time until they ovulate at about the winter solstice, when they migrate, individually, to the spawning banks (Fig. 1). Spawning is completed within a four-week period (Fuller *et al.*, 1976). The spawning period (defined as the period during which actively ovulating females are present) may begin up to two weeks early, towards the beginning of December, or up to two weeks late, at the beginning of January, but its total duration of four weeks is unaltered. There is little change in the environmental conditions in Loch Lomond at this time of year. Daylength is minimal and its rate of change negligible; water temperature falls from 9 to 4°C in the two-month period preceding spawning. Neither factor seems likely to permit accurate synchronization. Scott & O'Connell (unpub.) speculate that powan may spawn in response to lunar phases. In 1977–78, spawning began on 22 December and finished on 18 January. The moon was full on 25 December. In 1976–77 spawning was about two weeks earlier; the moon was full on 6 December. In 1971–72 spawning was two weeks late; the moon was full on 31 December. A short-term (lunar) cycle would thus be involved in the regulation of an annual reproductive cycle, the lunar cycle only becoming physiologically effective when the fish reach an appropriate gametogenic stage. It does not follow, of course, that the nearest lunar cycle to spawning would necessarily be the only one with physiological significance; the fish would presumably be entrained to all lunar cycles in the year. Any one, or several lunar phases might provide the critical stimuli, as Walker (1949) has suggested may be the case in the grunion (p. 112). A similar explanation was postulated for *Mormyrus kannume* (Scott, 1974), populations of which have an approximately annual reproductive cycle but are out of phase with each other (p. 115). If each population spawns at the first lunar phase after its gameto-genesis is complete, the spread of spawning throughout the year would be accounted for. In this case, it seems likely that changes in the availability of insect food, which follow a lunar periodicity (MacDonald, 1956) rather than moon phases themselves, may be the effective cues. Most of the mormyrids are anadromous spawners, the stimuli for their annual or twice-yearly spawning being flood-associated factors, perhaps including changes in food supply (Okedi, 1969). It may be that, in adapting to lacustrine conditions, *M. kannume* has found itself with spawning stimuli which are similar, but which recur more frequently and have thus permitted an extension of the spawning season.

Evidence for the involvement of even shorter-term cycles in the regulation of annual reproductive cycles has recently become available, in the form of a diel rhythm in photosensitivity which may be the basis of a teleost's ability to assess change in daylength. That such a diel rhythm of responsiveness to photostimulation exists in teleosts was first demonstrated by Baggerman (1972). Vasal & Sundararaj (1975) and Sundararaj & Vasal (1976) have shown that *Heteropneustes fossilis* (Bloch) responds maximally to single-hour light periods (1-h light/23-h dark) about midnight, and that additional light periods at other hours serve only to attenuate the response. They suggest that a circadian cycle of cellular function exists, with a photophil (light-preferring) and scotophil (dark-preferring) phase (Bünning, 1960, 1969). When natural photoperiod light intrudes into the scotophil phase, photostimulatory effects are elicited. The diel phases themselves may be endogenous, or entrained by the onset of either the dark or the light period.

TRANSDUCERS

Of the established environmental timing stimuli only one, temperature, has the potential to affect gonadal cells directly, by its action on enzyme systems. Light, and the less well-established stimuli generally, can only affect the gonad and other reproductive processes through some sort of transducing system. Temperature effects, indeed, are also likely to be so mediated. Part of this transducing system, the hypothalamus–pituitary complex, has been extensively investigated, and many reviews are available (Ball & Baker, 1969; Perks, 1969; and see Baker & Wigham, this volume p. 89).

The pituitary gland (hypophysis) is derived partly from a stomodaeal invagination (the adenohypophysis) and partly from a downgrowth of the floor of the third ventricle of the embryonic brain (the neurohypophysis). In teleosts, the neurohypophysis ramifies extensively in the adeno-hypophysis to form the adult pituitary, immediately posterior to which, in some species, is a structure of uncertain function, the saccus vasculosus.

The morphology of the adenohypophysis varies from species to species, but in general it is recognizably of three zones, the proadenohypophysis (pars distalis rostralis), mesoadenohypophysis (pars distalis proximalis) and metaadenohypophysis (pars intermedia). Gonadotrophic hormones are secreted in the mesoadenohypophysis, while luteotropin (prolactin) and adrenocorticotropin are characteristic of the proadenohypophysis. Thyrotropin and somatotropin-secreting cells may occur in either zone. Pituitary activity is under the control of neurosecretory cells in the hypothalamus, with major concentrations in the nucleus lateralis tuberis and the nucleus preopticus (Peter & Nagahama, 1974). These neurosecretory cells are neurally controlled by appropriate receptors for environmental (external or internal) stimuli.

In recent years the pineal system (epiphysis) has emerged from relative obscurity, and has been credited with a major role in the control of reproduction as an integral part of a pineal–hypothalamus–pituitary complex. General reviews of pineal structure and function are available (Fenwick, 1970; Wolstenholme & Knight, 1971; Oguri & Omura, 1973; Reiter, 1973, 1974; Axelrod, 1974; Ralph, 1975; Ellis & Reiter, 1976). The morphology of the pineal system of *Coregonus* is typically teleostean. The main pineal sac lies in a recess in the cranium which is at this point transparent, so that the pineal is directly exposed to light from above. The sac is much infolded, and is connected to the third ventricle by the pineal stalk. Ventral to the pineal sac (and in the adult surrounding the pineal stalk) is the thin-walled dorsal sac. The cells lining the pineal sac are of several kinds: some are glandular, some supportive and some photoreceptive. There is a copious vascular supply, and massive nerve tracts run along the dorsal side of the pineal stalk. The pineal nerve tract passes close to the habenular commissure and then ramifies into the subcommissural organ adjacent to the ventricle.

Much of our information on pineal function is derived from studies on mammals, which are only doubtfully relevant to teleosts. Mammals and birds, for example, lack pineal photoreceptors, and in these classes the eyes are the main source of photic information for the pineal. The pineal of teleosts is photosensitive, but it is not clear whether or not the eyes represent its main source of photic information (Urasaki, 1976; Smith & Weber, 1976). Whatever the light-sensory pathways may be, it seems established that in low light intensities the pineal system secretes indoleamines such as melatonin, which are "antigonadal" (a regrettably vague word). There is evidence that the secretion rates of follicle-stimulating hormone, luteinizing hormone, and luteotropin are affected by indoleamines in mammals, as is the electrical activity of the brain. It may be, however, that the inhibitory effects of the pineal on the pituitary are mediated by pineal polypeptides rather than the pineal indoleamines themselves (Reiter *et al.*, 1976).

If light inhibits pineal secretion, then, in short daylengths, gametogenesis should be inhibited and the pineal active. Not all the evidence for this in teleosts is wholly convincing. Pineal activity is often assessed simply on histological appearance of the gland, a method liable to subjective misinterpretation. There are also problems in experimental manipulation of an organ which is essentially inhibitory. Pinealectomy should result in gametogenesis, but in many experiments such effects are not apparent (Reiter, 1973). This may be due to the maintenance of experimental animals in long photoperiods prior to pinealectomy, in which case they will have already been physiologically pinealectomized, or because of unspecified seasonal variations in pineal responsiveness. The balance of evidence, nevertheless, supports the view that photoperiod, and temperature, affect pineal activity (Vodicnik, Kral & de Vlaming, 1978). The pineal is presumed to be the seat of the diel rhythmicity in photosensitivity already referred to (Vasal & Sundararaj, 1975), and there is considerable evidence that it shows a diel cycle of activity (Smith & Weber, 1976; Yates & Herbert, 1976; and others). There can be no doubt that the pineal system "acts as a neuroendocrine transducer of photoperiod information" (de Vlaming, Sage & Charlton, 1974), but more details on its relationship with the hypothalamus–pituitary system, and its light sensitivity in terms of both intensity and wavelength, are required.

Although the hormones of the pineal–hypothalamus–pituitary complex are the main transducers of environmental information to the gonads, a great many other endocrine processes are more or less directly involved in the series of reproductive activities which make up a reproductive cycle. The thyroid and adrenocortical hormones, among others, are implicated. A problem exists similar to that encountered in correlating environmental changes accurately with the reproductive cycle: it is difficult to be sure exactly with which reproductive stage endocrine activity is associated, especially if experimental studies are not correlated with studies in nature. Moreover, it is extremely difficult to analyse the interactions of the many hormone systems. Essentially gonadotrophic hormones may also play a major role in non-reproductive processes, while hormones not generally considered to be primarily concerned with reproduction may nevertheless be deeply involved, as in the case of the control of fat metabolism by luteotropin (Baker & Wigham, this volume p. 89). There is clearly a need for an integrated study of the endocrine cycles during the course of the reproductive cycle in a single, amenable, species and for the exact correlation of these endocrine activities with specific stages of its reproductive cycle (and hence with the corresponding environmental cues). The task is not easy: measurement of the hormones involved is difficult, and the need to measure rate of secretion and utilization, rather than instantaneous concentration, exacerbates the problem. In many studies, such biochemical refinements are simply not feasible, and it is necessary to estimate endocrine activity on the basis of the histological appearance of the tissues. At worst, such assessments are subjective; at best, they are questionable. As de Vlaming (1974) points out, cellular changes may be too subtle to be observed at light microscope level. In a study of cortisol concentration in the plasma of *Coregonus lavaretus*, Scott & Rennie (in preparation) measured cortisol level by gas–liquid chromatography and nuclear diameter of the adreno-cortical cells in the same fish, fixed immediately after blood withdrawal. The correlation coefficient was only 0·55, yet nuclear diameter is widely accepted as a useful criterion of adrenocortical activity. Fine structure changes of the endocrine cells may give more reliable indications of activity (Scott, Al-Asgah & Mackie, in preparation) but electron micro-scope studies are probably as impracticable for most workers as bio-chemical ones.

CONCLUSIONS

It is still not possible to give a comprehensive answer to the question "How do teleost fish time their reproductive cycles?" That they do, at any rate in habitats where timing confers a selective advantage, there is no doubt. That regularly recurring environmental events regulate the timing of the cycles, there is no doubt, but the nature of these cues is far from clear, especially during the complex of activities called spawning. That neuro-endocrine systems provide the transducers between the environmental stimuli and the physiological responses is certain, but how the actual systems act, and how and when the various hormones interact to control the reproductive organs is not clear. There is a need for carefully coordinated studies, simultaneously from ecological, ethological and physiological viewpoints, dealing with a single species deliberately chosen for its suitability for research into all these aspects.

REFERENCES

Atz, J. W. & Pickford, G. E. (1964). The pituitary gland and its relation to the reproduction of fishes in nature and in captivity. An annotated bibliography for the years 1956–1967. *F.A.O. Fish. Biol. Tech. Pap.* No. 37: 1–61.

Axelrod, J. (1974). The pineal gland: a neurochemical transducer. *Science, N.Y.* **184**: 1341–1348.

Baerends, G. P. (1971). The ethological analysis of fish behavior. In *Fish physiology* **6**: 279–370. Hoar, W. S. & Randall, D. J. (eds). London & New York: Academic Press.

Baggerman, B. (1972). Photoperiodic responses in the stickleback and their control by a daily rhythm of photosensitivity. *Gen. comp. Endocr.* Suppl. **3**: 466–476.

Ball, J. N. & Baker, B. I. (1969). The pituitary gland: anatomy and histo-physiology. In *Fish physiology* **2**: 1–110. Hoar, W. S. & Randall, D. J. (eds). London & New York: Academic Press.

Billard, C., Meusy-Dessolles, N. & Fléchon, J. E. (1971). Les cellules interstitielles de quelques poissons téléostéens. *J. Microsc., Paris* **11**: 30.

Bissonette, J. H. & Wadlund, A. P. (1932). Duration of testis activity of *Sturnus vulgaris* in relation to type of illumination. *J. exp. Biol.* **9**: 339–350.

Boyd, J. F. & Simmonds, R. C. (1974). Continuous laboratory production of fertile *Fundulus heteroclitus* (Walbaum) eggs lacking chorionic fibrils. *J. Fish Biol.* **6**: 389–394.

Bullough, W. S. (1939). A study of the reproductive cycle of the minnow in relation to the environment. *Proc. zool. Soc. Lond.* **109A**: 79–102.

Bullough, W. S. (1940). The effect of the reduction of light in spring on the breeding season of the minnow (*Phoxinus laevis* Linn.). *Proc. zool. Soc. Lond.* **110A**: 149–157.

Bullough, W. S. (1942). Gametogenesis and some endocrine factors affecting it in the adult minnow (*Phoxinus laevis* L.) *J. Endocr.* **3**: 211–219.

Bünning, E. (1960). Circadian rhythms and time-measurement in photoperiodism. *Cold Spring Harb. Symp. quant. Biol.* **25**: 249–256.

Bünning, E. (1969). Common features of photoperiodism in plants and animals. *Photochem. Photobiol.* **9**: 219–228.

Chieffi, G. & Botte, V. (1970). The problem of luteogenesis in non-mammalian vertebrates. *Boll. Zool.* **37**: 85–102.

Dahlberg, M. D. & Conyers, J. C. (1973). An ecological study of *Gobiosoma bosci* and *Gobiosoma ginsburgi* (Pisces, Gobiidae) on the Georgia coast. *Fish. Bull. U.S. natn. ocean. atmos. Admn* **71**: 279–287.

de Vlaming, V. L. (1971). The effects of food deprivation and salinity changes on reproductive functions in the estuarine gobiid fish, *Gillichthys mirabilis*. *Biol. Bull. mar. biol. Lab., Woods Hole* **141**: 458–471.

de Vlaming, V. L. (1972a). Environmental control of teleost reproductive cycles: a brief review. *J. Fish Biol.* **4**: 131–140.

de Vlaming, V. L. (1972b). Reproductive cycling in the estuarine gobiid fish, *Gillichthys mirabilis*. *Copeia* **1972**: 278–291.

de Vlaming, V. L. (1972c). The effects of temperature and photoperiod on reproductive cycling in the estuarine gobiid fish, *Gillichthys mirabilis*. *Fish. Bull. U.S natn. ocean. atmos. Admn* **70**: 1137–1152.

de Vlaming, V. L. (1972d). The effects of diurnal thermoperiod treatments on reproductive function in the estuarine gobiid fish, *Gillichthys mirabilis* Cooper. *J. exp. mar. Biol. Ecol.* **9**: 155–164.

de Vlaming, V. L. (1972e). The role of the endocrine system in temperature-controlled reproductive cycling in the estuarine gobiid fish, *Gillichthys mirabilis*. *Comp. Biochem. Physiol.* **41A**: 697–713.

de Vlaming, V. L. (1974). Environmental and endocrine control of teleost reproduction. In *Control of sex in fishes*: 13–83. Schreck, C. B. (ed.). Blacksburg, Virginia: Department of Fisheries and Wildlife Sciences, Virginia Polytechnic Institute and State University.

de Vlaming, V. L. & Paquette, G. (1977). Photoperiod and temperature effects on gonadal regression in the golden shiner, *Notemigonus crysoleucas. Copeia* **1977**: 793–796.

de Vlaming, V. L., Sage, M. & Charlton, C. B. (1974). The effects of melatonin treatment on gonosomatic index in the teleost, *Fundulus similis*, and the tree frog, *Hyla cinerea. Gen. comp. Endocr.* **22**: 433–438.

Donaldson, E. M. (1973). Reproductive endocrinology of fishes. *Am. Zool.* **13**: 909–928.

Donaldson, E. M. (1977). *Bibliography of fish reproduction* 1963–1974. (3 parts). Research and Resource Services, 4160 Marine Drive, West Vancouver, British Columbia U7V 1N6: *Fisheries and Marine Service Technical Report* No. 732.

Drance, M. G., Hollenberg, M. J., Smith, M. & Wylie, V. (1976). Histological changes in trout testis produced by injections of salmon pituitary gonadotropin. *Can. J. Zool.* **54**: 1285–1293.

Ellis, L. C. & Reiter, R. J. (1976). (eds). The endocrine role of the pineal. *Am. Zool.* **16**: 1–104.

Fenwick, J. C. (1970). The pineal organ. In *Fish physiology* 4: 91–108. Hoar, W. S. & Randall, D. J. (eds). London & New York: Academic Press.

Frost, W. E. (1943). The natural history of the minnow, *Phoxinus phoxinus. J. Anim. Ecol.* **12**: 139–162.

Fuller, J. D., Scott, D. B. C. & Fraser, R. (1976). The reproductive cycle of *Coregonus lavaretus* (L.) in Loch Lomond, Scotland, in relation to seasonal changes in plasma cortisol concentration. *J. Fish Biol.* **9**: 105–117.

Harden-Jones, F. R. (1968). *Fish migration.* London: Arnold.

Harrington, R. W. (1963). Twenty-four hour rhythms of internal self fertilisation and oviposition by hermaphrodites of *Rivulus marmoratus. Physiol. Zool.* **36**: 325–341.

Hickling, C. F. (1967). On the biology of a herbivorous fish, the white amur or grass carp, *Ctenopharyngodon idella. Proc. R. Soc. Edinb.* B **70**: 62–81.

Hirose, K., Hirano, T. & Ishida, R. (1974). Effects of salmon gonadotropin on ovulation in the ayu, *Plecoglossus altivelis*, with special reference to water balance. *Comp. Biochem. Physiol.* **46A**: 283–289.

Hoar, W. S. (1969). Reproduction. In *Fish physiology* 3: 1–72. Hoar, W. S. & Randall, D. J. (eds). London & New York: Academic Press.

Hyder, M. (1970). Gonadal and reproductive patterns in *Tilapia leucosticta* (Teleostei: Cichlidae) in an equatorial lake, Lake Naivasha, Kenya. *J. Zool., Lond.* **162**: 179–195.

Kesteven, G. L. (1960). (ed.). Manual of field methods in fisheries biology. *F.A.O. Man. Fish. Sci.* No.1 : 1–152.

Liley, N. R. (1969). Hormones and reproductive behaviour in fishes. In *Fish physiology* 3: 73–116. Hoar, W. S. & Randall, D. J. (eds). London & New York: Academic Press.

MacDonald, W. W. (1956). Observations on the biology of chaoborids and chironomids in Lake Victoria and on the feeding habits of the "elephant snout fish" *Mormyrus kannume. J. Anim. Ecol.* **25**: 36–53.

Marshall, A. J. (1960). The environment, cyclical reproductive activity and behaviour in birds. *Symp. zool. Soc. Lond.* No. 2: 53–67.

Marshall, A. J. & Roberts, J. D. (1959). The breeding biology of equatorial vertebrates: reproduction of cormorants (Phalacrocoridae) at latitude 0°21′N. *Proc. zool. Soc. Lond.* **132**: 617–625.

Nagahama, Y., Chan, K. & Hoar, W. S. (1976). Histochemistry and ultrastructure of pre- and post-ovulatory follicles in the ovary of the goldfish, *Carassius auratus. Can. J. Zool.* **54**: 1128–1139.

Nikolsky, G. V. (1963). *The ecology of fishes.* London & New York: Academic Press.

Oguri, M. & Omura, Y. (1973). Ultrastructure and functional significance of the pineal organ of teleost. In *Responses of fish to environmental changes*: 412–434. Chavin, W. (ed.). Springfield, Illinois: Thomas.

Okedi, J. (1969). Observations on the breeding and growth of certain mormyrid fishes of the Lake Victoria Basin (Pisces: Mormyridae). *Revue Zool. Bot. afr.* **79**: 34–64.

Okedi, J. (1970). A study of the fecundity of some mormyrid fishes from Lake Victoria. *E. Afr. Agric. For. J.* **35**: 436–442.

Pang, P. K. T. (1971). The effects of complete darkness and vitamin C supplement on the killifish, *Fundulus heteroclitus* adapted to sea water. 1. Calcium metabolism and gonadal maturation. *J. exp. Zool.* **178**: 15–22.

Payne, A. I. (1975). The reproductive cycle, condition and feeding in *Barbus liberiensis*, a tropical stream-dwelling cyprinid. *J. Zool., Lond.* **176**: 247–269.

Perks, A. M. (1969). The neurohypophysis. In *Fish physiology* **2**: 111–205. Hoar, W. S. & Randall, D. J. (eds). London & New York: Academic Press.

Peter, R. E. & Nagahama, Y. (1974). A light and electron microscopic study of the structure of the nucleus preopticus and nucleus lateral tuberis of the goldfish, *Carassius auratus*. *Can. J. Zool.* **54**: 1423–1437.

Pickford, G. E. & Atz, J. W. (1957). *The physiology of the pituitary gland of fishes.* New York: New York Zoological Society.

Ralph, C. L. (1975). The pineal complex: a retrospective view. *Am. Zool.* **15**: 105–116.

Reiter, R. J. (1973). Comparative physiology: pineal gland. *A. Rev. Physiol.* **35**: 305–329.

Reiter, R. J. (1974). Circannual reproductive rhythms in mammals related to photoperiod and pineal function: a review. *Chronobiologia* **1**: 365–395.

Reiter, R. J., Lukaszyk, A. J., Vaughan, M. K. & Blask, D. E. (1976). New horizons of pineal research. *Am. Zool.* **16**: 93–101.

Schwassmann, H. O. (1971). Biological rhythms. In *Fish physiology* **6**: 371–428. Hoar, W. S. & Randall, D. J. (eds). London & New York: Academic Press.

Scott, D. B. C. (1974). The reproductive cycle of *Mormyrus kannume* Forsk. (Osteoglossomorpha, Mormyriformes) in Lake Victoria, Uganda. *J. Fish Biol.* **6**: 447–454.

Scott, D. B. C., Al-Asgah, N. & Mackie, J. (In preparation). *Fine structure of the head kidney of teleost fish.*

Scott, D. B. C. & Fuller, J. D. (1976). The reproductive biology of *Scleropages formosus* (Müller & Schlegel) (Osteoglossomorpha, Osteoglossidae) in Malaya, and the morphology of its pituitary gland. *J. Fish Biol.* **8**: 45–53.

Scott, D. B. C. & Rennie, S. (In preparation). *Histological criteria of cortisol secretion in* Coregonus lavaretus.

Smith, R. I. F. (1976). Seasonal loss of alarm substance cells in North American cyprinoid fishes and its relation to abrasive spawning behaviour. *Can. J. Zool.* **54**: 1172–1182.

Smith, J. R. & Weber, L. J. (1976). The regulation of day-night changes in hydroxy-indole-O-methyltransferase activity in the pineal gland of steelhead trout (*Salmo gairdneri*). *Can. J. Zool.* **54**: 1530–1534.

Sundararaj, B. I. & Goswami, S. V. (1977). Hormonal regulation of *in vivo* and *in vitro* oocyte maturation in the catfish, *Heteropneustes fossilis* (Bloch). *Gen. comp. Endocr.* **32**: 17–28.

Sundararaj, B. I. & Vasal, S. (1976). Photoperiod and temperature control in the regulation of reproduction in the female catfish, *Heteropneustes fossilis*. *J. Fish Res. Bd Can.* **33**: 959–973.

Urasaki, H. (1976). The role of pineal and eyes in the photoperiodic effect on the gonad of the medaka, *Oryzias latipes*. *Chronobiologia* **3**: 228–234.

Vasal, S. & Sundararaj, B. I. (1975). Responses of the regressed ovary of the catfish, *Heteropneustes fossilis* (Bloch) to interrupted-light photoperiods. *Chronobiologia* **2**: 224–239.

Vodicnik, M. J., Kral, R. E. & de Vlaming, V. L. (1978). The effects of pinealectomy and pituitary on plasma gonadotrophin levels in *Carassius auratus* exposed to various photoperiod and temperature regimes. *J. Fish Biol.* **12**: 187–196.

Walker, B. W. (1949). *Periodicity of spawning in the grunion, Leuresthes tenuis.* Ph.D. Thesis, University of California, Los Angeles, California.

Wolstenholme, G. E. W. & Knight, J. (eds). (1971). *The pineal gland.* [CIBA Foundation Symposium.] London: Churchill.

Woodhead, A. D. (1975). Endocrine physiology of fish migration. *Oceanogr. Mar. Biol. Ann. Rev.* **13**: 287–382.

Yamamoto, T-O. (1969). Sex differentiation. In *Fish physiology* **3**: 117–175. Hoar, W. S. & Randall, D. J. (eds). London & New York: Academic Press.

Yamazaki, F. & Donaldson, E. M. (1968). The spermiation of goldfish *Carassius auratus* as a bioassay for salmon (*Oncorhynchus tshawytscha*) gonadotropin. *Gen. comp. Endocr.* **10**: 383–391.

Yates, C. A. & Herbert, J. (1976). Differential circadian rhythms in pineal and hypothalamic 5-HT induced by artificial photoperiods and melatonin. *Nature, Lond.* **262**: 219–220.

Symp. zool. Soc. Lond (1979) No. 44, 133–159

Energy Costs of Egg Production and Environmental Determinants of Fecundity in Teleost Fishes

R. J. WOOTTON

University College of Wales, Aberystwyth, Dyfed, Wales

SYNOPSIS

Although fecundity is related to the size and in some species to the age of the fish, and is further constrained by egg size, variations in the fecundity of females at a particular age and size are found. These variations take the form of inter-individual, inter-year and inter-population differences and they reflect variations in the investment of energy and materials in the ovaries.

The temporal pattern of investment in ovaries varies so that in some species the ovaries increase in weight and energy content in spring and summer but in others the increase occurs during the winter. The mean energy content of eggs and ripe ovaries from 50 species was $23·48 \text{ kJ g}^{-1}$ dry wt. The energy cost of egg production and measures of reproductive effort, for a range of marine and freshwater species of varying lifespans, are described. The proportion (energy content of eggs spawned/energy content of food consumed) varied from 1% in *Sardinops caerulea* to 11% in *Gadus morhua* when calculated on an annual basis. Over short time periods, especially during an extended breeding season, higher proportions occurred, e.g. *Gasterosteus aculeatus*. Other indices of the cost of egg production include the effect on somatic growth and the degree of depletion of the soma during ovarian maturation.

Field and experimental observations indicate that food availability is the most important proximate factor determining fecundity. A shortage of food may increase the proportion of atretic oocytes or reduce the proportion of oocytes maturing. The effects of temperature, light and "stressors" on fecundity are also considered.

The relationship between the annual feeding cycle and ovarian cycle is discussed. A cycle of storage and transfer links the two cycles when the optimal time for ovarian maturation and spawning does not correspond with favourable feeding conditions.

INTRODUCTION

At the centre of contemporary hypotheses on the adaptive significance of life-history patterns is the concept that there is a pay-off between reproduction and the maintenance and growth of the soma. Resources of energy and time spent on the one are not available to be spent on the other. An animal that reproduces here and now does so at the risk of reducing by a significant amount its future reproductive output, so that the greater the current reproductive effort, the poorer the future expected reproductive output (Williams, 1966; Stearns, 1976). Reproductive effort is measured as the proportion of the resources available that are used for reproduction (Calow & Woolhead, 1977). Theoretical studies on the adaptive significance of life histories are well developed, but empirical studies have lagged behind (Stearns, 1977). Analyses of the reproductive biology of teleosts may offer some progress in closing the gap between theory and data, and this review considers one aspect, the fecundity of teleosts.

DEFINITION OF FECUNDITY

Fecundity in this review means the number of eggs produced by a female per year. Where a species has a well-defined annual breeding season, the year can be considered as the period between the start of one breeding season and the start of the next. In species that spawn several times within a breeding season, fecundity is the product of the number of spawnings and the mean number of eggs per spawning. Egg production refers to the weight or its energy equivalent of eggs spawned in a year, unless otherwise qualified.

Although fecundity should be measured as the number of eggs spawned, in practice it is usually measured as the number of mature eggs present in the ovary immediately before spawning, on the assumption that few mature eggs are retained. This method will underestimate the fecundity of species that have multiple spawnings which involve the rapid recruitment of oocytes into a maturing batch.

CONSTRAINTS ON FECUNDITY

Size

The relationship between fecundity, F, and length of fish, L, is usually curvilinear

$$F = aL^b$$

or, in the linear form

$$\log F = \log a + b \log L$$

(Bagenal, 1967, 1973).

Differences in fecundity of females can reflect differences in length and differences in the parameters a and b.

The effect of an increase in length on fecundity implies that if, at any time, a female invests energy in growth rather than egg production, this will subsequently be reflected in a greater fecundity. Such an effect is likely to be an important factor in moulding the life histories of teleosts in contrast to groups such as insects, birds and mammals which usually stop growing at sexual maturation and produce a relatively constant clutch or litter size thereafter. If differences in fecundity between populations of a teleost species merely reflect differences in the length of the females, then the analysis is reduced to considering those factors which influence growth rates and age at maturity.

Differences in fecundity are found even when females of a similar length are compared which implies differences in the parameters a and b. If a varies but not b, the rate of change in fecundity with length is the same, but the level about which the change takes place is different, e.g. *Salmo salar* L. (Pope, Mills & Shearer, 1961). If b varies, the rate of increase in fecundity with length differs. The exponent b could be restricted to particular values by geometric constraints, and it is usually argued that fecundity should increase as the cube of length (Simpson, 1951). To test for this, the frequency distribution of some published values of b was obtained (Fig. 1). Although the values do cluster around 3·0, they vary from about 1·0 to 7·0 with the modal class of 3·250–3·749.

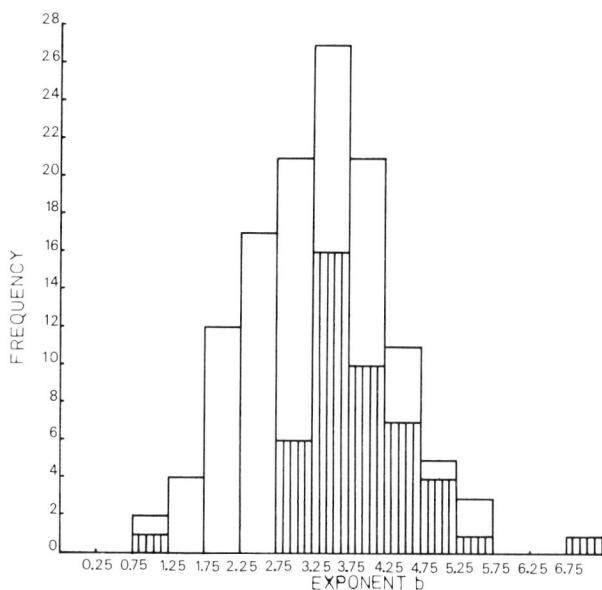

FIG. 1. Frequency distribution of the exponent b from the relationship: $F = aL^b$. Based on 124 observations from 62 species. Hatched portion: marine species.

There is a tendency for the exponents for marine species to be higher than for freshwater species, but this may reflect systematic bias in the samples with the marine species dominated by clupeids and the fresh-water species by salmonids and cyprinids. Short-lived species or those with poor post-spawning survival tend to have lower values of b than longer-lived species with good post-spawning survival. The cause and effect relationship is obscure but such a relationship would be explicable, for species with a high value of b are likely to profit more in terms of lifetime fecundity by maintaining some investment in somatic growth and survivorship than species with a relatively low b.

Within a species the range of b is more restricted than shown in Fig. 1, but may still show significant variation. In herring, *Clupea harengus* L., b varies from about 3·0 to 7·0 (Hodder, 1972; Schopka & Hempel, 1973; Messieh, 1976), while for the bream, *Abramis brama* (L.), values of b from 1·77 to 4·88 are recorded (Brylinska, 1971; Bialokoz, 1973).

The relationship between fecundity and weight of fish, W, is usually close to linear, i.e. $F = cW^d$ where $d = 1·0$ approximately. The use of total weight will partially confound the variables fecundity and weight, since a more fecund fish will weigh more than a less fecund fish because of the weight of the extra eggs (Bagenal, 1967). This problem can be avoided by using somatic weight, i.e. total weight less weight of ovaries, or by weighing the fish immediately after spawning (Wootton, 1973b). When these precautions are taken, fecundity is still usually greater in heavier fish. Thus factors which favour the growth in weight of the fish will usually lead to an increase in fecundity. But as with the relationship between length and fecundity, the parameters c and d may also vary so that fish of the same weight may have different fecundities. Factors affecting growth and the parameters may be environmental or genetic, but this review is concerned only with the former.

Age

Fecundity may also be related to the age of the fish. In most species, age and size are closely related so that any effects of age on fecundity can only be detected if the effects of size are eliminated by the appropriate statistical techniques. When this is done, the effect of age on fecundity can be small or non-existent, e.g. *Rutilus rutilus* (L.) (MacKay & Mann, 1969), *Cottus gobio* L. (Abel, 1973) and *Gadus morhua* L. (May, 1967) or highly significant, e.g. *Leuciscus leuciscus* (L.) (Wilkinson & Jones, 1977), *Cottus bairdi bairdi* Girard (Ludwig & Lange, 1975) and *Sprattus sprattus* (L.) (de Silva, 1973) (see Bagenal, 1967, for earlier references), but the effect of age is not consistent across species. In *Tilapia* species there is a tendency for the frequency of spawnings to decrease with age (Lowe-McConnell, 1955). In females becoming senescent, the proportion of connective tissue in the ovary may increase, with a concomitant reduction in the proportion of germinal tissue (J. F. Craig, pers. comm.; see also Woodhead, this volume p. 179).

Egg Size

A given weight of ovary could produce many small eggs or few large eggs, so that variations in fecundity could reflect variations in egg size. The limits of this variation will depend on the constraints on egg size, which will be set by the optimal size of the larvae. The latter will be related to factors such as the size spectrum of food particles, the size and abundance of predators and the abundance of competitors (Svardson, 1949). Such constraints are suggested by a size frequency analysis of the eggs of marine and freshwater species from northern Europe (Fig. 2). For both

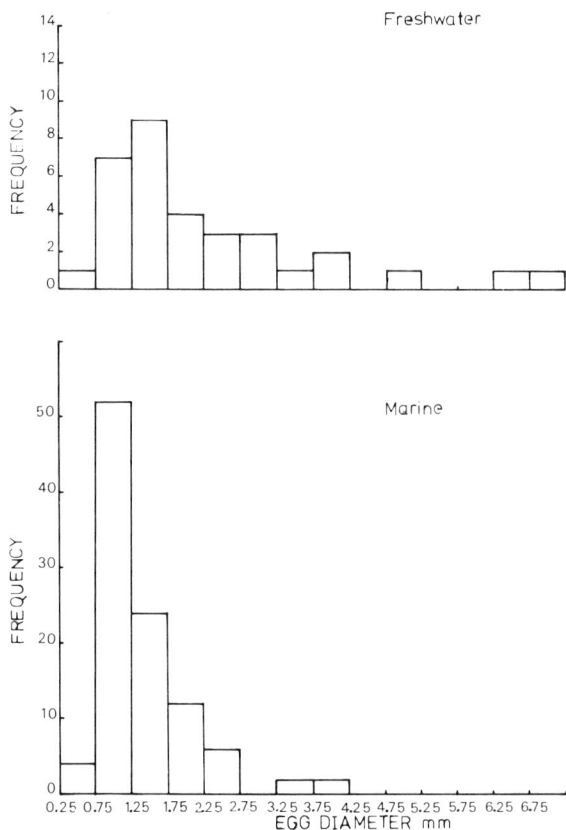

FIG. 2. Frequency distribution of egg diameters of species from European waters. 101 marine species, 33 freshwater species.

groups, the size distribution is strongly skewed. Variations of egg size within a species occur and their significance is discussed by Bagenal (1971) and Ware (1975). A clear relationship between fecundity and egg size is shown in *Clupea harengus*, for late winter and spring spawners are less fecund but produce larger eggs than late summer and autumn spawners (Hempel & Blaxter, 1967; Messieh, 1976). Jones (1974) noted that the fecundities of 10 species of flatfish varied considerably but the volume of eggs g^{-1} body wt varied much less. Inter-specific differences in number of eggs g^{-1} body wt were primarily a function of egg size. In some species there is a positive correlation between egg size and fish size, e.g. *Salmo salar* (Pope *et al.*, 1961) but no correlation in other species, e.g. *Gadus morhua* (Oosthuizen & Daan, 1974). Better fed *Salmo trutta* L. produced more but smaller eggs than trout on poorer rations (Bagenal, 1969). But Abel (1973) found that *Cottus gobio* at any particular length varied egg size and number independently, so there is not always a strict inverse relationship between egg size and number.

VARIATION IN FECUNDITY

Inter-Individual Variation

A plot of fecundity against size usually shows considerable scatter of points about the fitted curve; in a population, similar sized females will produce different numbers of eggs in the same year. Part of this may reflect the effects of age and egg size, but the rest represents the effects of genetic and environmental factors on fecundity.

Inter-Year Variation

Significant inter-year variation in the fecundity of females of a given size in a population occurs, e.g. *Pleuronectes platessa* L. (Bagenal, 1966). Since these variations are expressed within a population, it is likely that environmental rather than genetic changes are the cause.

Geographical Variation

Significant inter-population differences in the fecundity of similar-sized females are frequently recorded, e.g. *Pleuronectes platessa* (Bagenal, 1966), *Gadus morhua* (Schopka & Hempel, 1973), *Oncorhynchus* spp. (Rounsefell, 1957), *Coregonus clupeaformis* (Mitchill) (Healey & Nichol, 1975) and *Abramis brama* (Brylinska, 1971).

The relative importance of environmental and genetical factors in producing such geographical variation is not known but is clearly open to experimental study, and would be directly relevant to studies on the adaptive significance of life-history patterns (Fox, 1978).

REPRODUCTIVE CYCLES

A partial picture of the temporal pattern of investment in ovarian tissue by females in a population can be obtained by following changes in the gonadosomatic index. This index is usually calculated as: (weight of ovaries/total weight) × 100 or as (weight of ovaries/weight of body less ovaries) × 100. Most studies consider only wet weights and neither changes in the dry matter content nor energy content of the ovaries are revealed.

In northern temperate species, three broad patterns of ovarian development can be seen. In autumn and early winter spawners, the gonadosomatic index is low from the post-spawning period until mid-summer, but then shows a rapid increase to a maximum just prior to spawning, e.g. in the brook trout, *Salvelinus fontinalis* (Mitchill) (Wydoski & Cooper, 1966). In such species, somatic maintenance and growth has priority during winter, spring and early summer with the priority switching to ovarian development during late summer and autumn.

Species that spawn in late winter and spring usually have low gonadosomatic indices throughout the summer, but then ovarian development continues steadily throughout autumn and winter, so that maximum gonadosomatic indices are reached in late winter, e.g. *Esox lucius* L. (Frost & Kipling, 1967) and *Leuciscus leuciscus* (Hellawell, 1974). In such species, the major increase in ovarian size occurs during the period of low temperatures and short daylengths and probably low rates of food consumption.

In species that spawn in late spring and summer, the female gonadosomatic index remains low throughout the winter, but then shows a rapid increase in the months just prior to spawning, e.g. *Lepomis gibbosus* (L.) (Burns, 1976), *Ericymba buccata* Cope (Hoyt, 1971) and *Gasterosteus aculeatus* L. (Wootton, Evans & Mills, 1978). The rapid increase in ovarian size takes place in a period of increasing daylengths and temperature and is probably associated with high rates of food consumption (Glenn & Williams, 1976).

A rapid increase in ovary size in summer is shown by some cyprinids of the Indian subcontinent, e.g. *Labeo* spp. (Parameswaran, Selvaraj & Radhakrishnan, 1970). The gonadosomatic index reaches 20–35% and all the eggs are spawned over a short period. Other groups of subtropical and tropical species have an extended breeding with the female spawning several times (see Lowe-McConnell, this volume p. 219). Such species show changes in the gonadosomatic index of a much smaller amplitude. In mouth-brooding cichlids, the gonadosomatic index of a mature female may be only 3% (Welcomme, 1967) and low gonadosomatic indices occur in South American characids of the genus *Astyanax* (Nomura, 1975). Some species spawn a few eggs at daily or nearly daily intervals for an extended period. In such a species, *Cyprinodon nevadensis nevadensis* Eigenmann & Eigenmann, the gonadosomatic index of spawning females ranged between 2 and 14% (Shrode & Gerking, 1977).

Changes in gonadosomatic index for a population will be misleading as an index of the degree of investment where females spawn several times in a breeding season. The gonadosomatic index of female *Gasterosteus aculeatus* increases from about 8% to 20–30% in as few as three days, then returns to 8% after spawning (Wootton, 1974). This cycle can be repeated 15–20 times in favourable conditions. The number of spawnings in a breeding season is difficult to measure for natural populations. On the basis of a frequency analysis of oocyte sizes, Shackley & King (1977) argued that the inter-tidal shanny, *Blennius pholis* L., may spawn eight or more times in a season. The minnow, *Phoxinus phoxinus*, may lay four or five batches of eggs at intervals of about 15 days (Papadopol & Weinberger, 1975), while Texas darters, *Etheostoma* spp., may spawn 20–40 times in a breeding season of six months (Hubbs, Stevenson & Peden, 1968). In any assessment of annual fecundity and reproductive effort, the possibility of multiple spawnings must be considered.

The variety of patterns of ovarian development suggests that factors which cause variations in fecundity may operate in different ways and at different times in the ovarian cycle, so that inter-specific generalizations should be made with care.

ENERGY COST OF EGG PRODUCTION

Energy Content of Eggs

A first step in determining the energy costs of egg production is to measure the energy content of the eggs. The frequency distribution of values for the energy content of eggs or ripe ovaries is shown in Fig. 3. The overall mean was $23 \cdot 48$ kJ g^{-1} dry wt (s.e. = $0 \cdot 363$) based on 60 values from 50 teleost species of which 35 spawned in fresh water.

Energetics of Ovarian Development and Egg Production

When seasonal changes in average ovarian and somatic weight and energy content are known, the rates of energy accumulation or loss during the life history of the fish can be described. The partitioning of energy between somatic growth and reproduction can be compared both intra- and inter-specifically, as the following examples indicate.

Three-spined stickleback, *Gasterosteus aculeatus*

Aspects of the energy partitioning in this species were studied both in the laboratory and in two natural populations in Wales—one from an upland lake, Llyn Frongoch, the other from the backwaters of the River Rheidol almost at sea level. The upland fish were smaller and in poorer condition than the river fish, presumably reflecting a poorer food supply (Wootton *et al.*, 1978). In both populations, most fish died after a year.

The total energy content of the ovaries of average females from the two populations increased during the year to the onset of the breeding season, with a very rapid increase between March and May. The total energy content of the somatic component showed periods of stability or decline in the winter months and again during the breeding season (Fig.

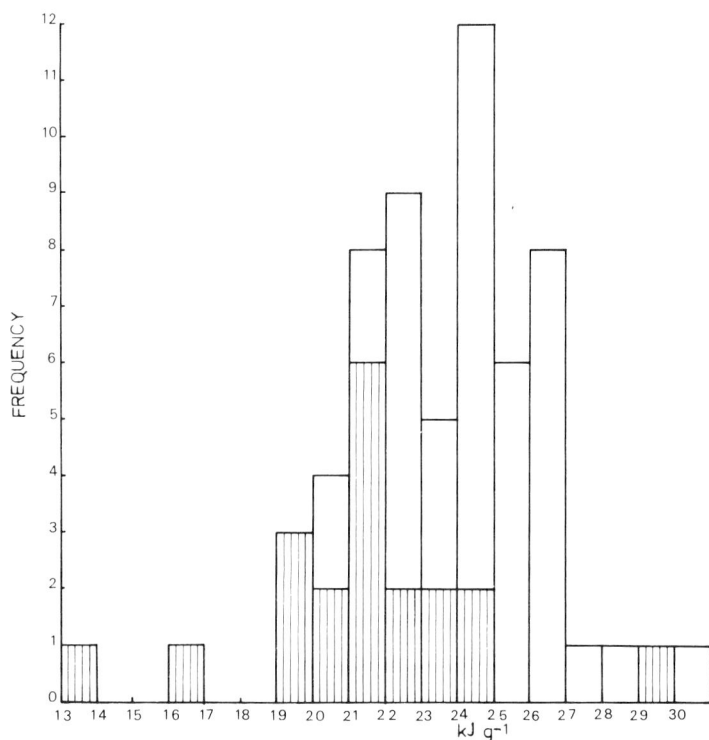

FIG. 3. Frequency distribution of energy content of eggs or mature ovaries in kJ g^{-1} dry wt. Based on 60 observations from 50 species. Hatched portion: marine species.

4). Two indices of reproductive effort were calculated. Figure 5 shows changes in the ratio of energy in the ovaries to energy in the soma, while Fig. 6 shows the ratio of the change in energy content of the ovaries to the energy of food consumed per unit time. The latter was estimated on the basis of the growth rate of the fish (Allen, unpub.). Both indices suggest that until the start of spawning, the reproductive effort of an average female in the two populations was similar, although the fish of one population were significantly bigger at a given age.

Once the breeding season has started, the number of spawnings is related to the food supply (Wootton, 1973a, 1977), so it is not possible to predict total egg production in a natural population without knowing the rate of food consumption. Experimental studies have provided estimates of the energy costs of egg production during the breeding season (Wootton & Evans, 1976; Wootton, 1977). Table I gives estimates of the ration in kJ day^{-1} required by a female if she was to spawn without showing a net loss of weight. This ration depended on the weight of the female, which

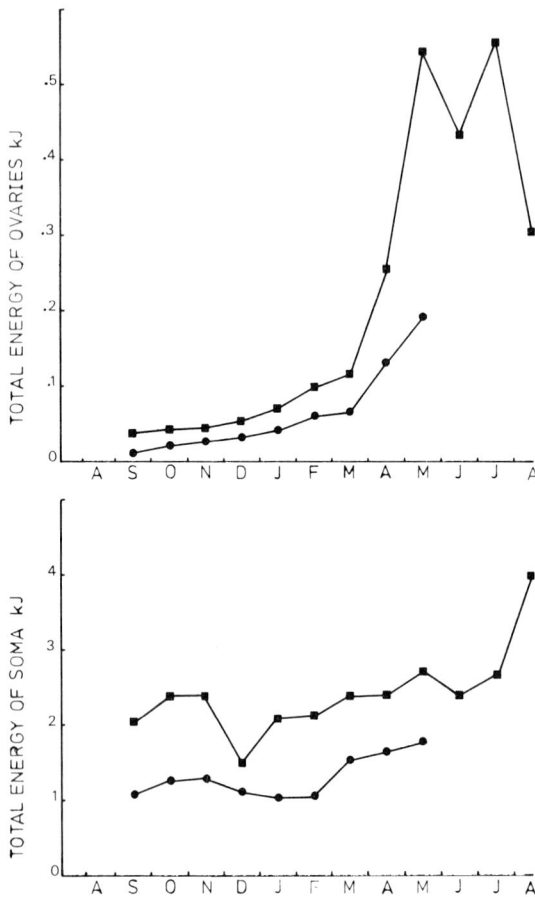

FIG. 4. Changes in total energy of soma and ovaries of average female *Gasterosteus aculeatus* from Llyn Frongoch (●) and River Rheidol (■), September 1974–August 1975.

determined the weight of eggs spawned, and on the interval between successive spawnings. Females that received a smaller ration spawned but less often and they lost weight. The gross efficiency of egg production measured as: (energy content of eggs/energy content of food consumed) × 100 was high when compared with values for the gross growth efficiency of *Gasterosteus aculeatus* reported (Walkey & Meakins, 1970; Wootton, 1976).

The river population contained ripe females between May and August, but in the upland lake, ripe females were found only in May. This difference probably reflects the lower rates of food consumption by the lake population.

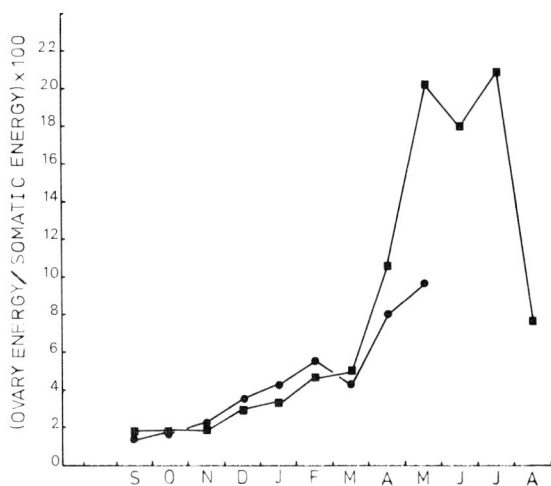

FIG. 5. Changes in ratio of energy in ovaries to energy in soma of female *Gasterosteus aculeatus* from Llyn Frongoch (●) and River Rheidol (■), September 1974–August 1975.

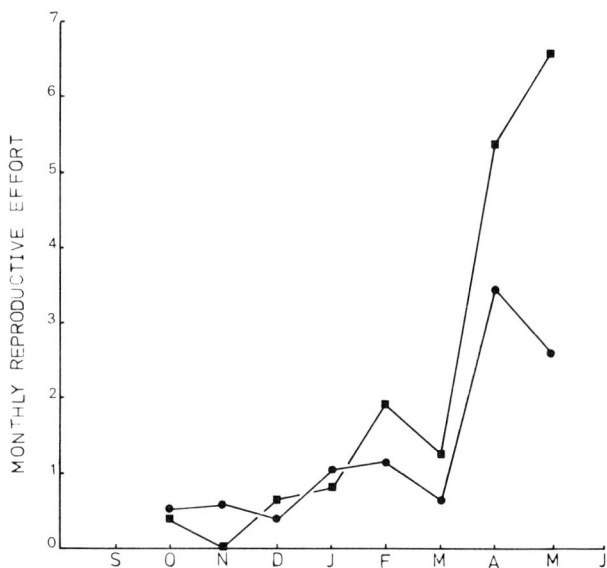

FIG. 6. Changes in monthly reproductive effort of average female *Gasterosteus aculeatus* from Llyn Frongoch (●) and River Rheidol (■), September 1974–June 1975. Reproductive effort measured as ratio of net energy change in ovaries to energy content of food consumed per unit time expressed as a percentage.

144   R. J. WOOTTON

TABLE I

Predicted egg production per spawning, ration required for no somatic weight loss, and efficiency of egg production of female Gasterosteus aculeatus *during the breeding season*

Fresh wt female (g)	Inter-spawning interval (days)	Egg production per spawning (kJ)	Ration (kJ day⁻¹)	Efficiency of egg production
	4	0·501	0·683	18·3
0·8	5	0·470	0·597	15·8
	6	0·447	0·512	14·5
	4	0·789	0·862	22·9
1·2	5	0·741	0·777	19·1
	6	0·704	0·691	17·0
	4	1·089	1·041	26·6
1·6	5	1·023	0·956	21·4
	6	0·972	0·870	18·6

Both field and experimental studies on the stickleback suggest that in this short-lived fish, investment in egg production is maintained even when rates of food consumption, and so energy input, are unfavourable. Ovarian development and egg production can both take place at the cost of declines in the weight and energy content of the soma.

Common minnow, *Phoxinus phoxinus*

The minnow is often found in the same freshwater habitats as the stickleback, but it reaches a larger body size and usually has a longer lifespan (Frost, 1943). In a population studied in an upland Welsh lake (Brays Pool), the females did not become sexually mature until their second year and there were three year-classes with sexually mature females. In these, the period of rapid ovarian development and spawning, April to June, coincided with a decline in the total energy content of the soma. Once spawning was completed there was rapid growth and an increase in the total energy content of the soma (Fig. 7). Reproductive effort measured as the ratio of ovarian energy to somatic energy is shown in Fig. 8. There is a suggestion that the older fish showed a greater reproductive effort than the youngest year-class, which is compatible with the prediction of Williams (1966) that reproductive effort should increase with age.

The energy costs of egg production during the spawning period have not been measured, but a comparison of Figs 5 and 8 suggests similar patterns and levels of reproductive effort in *P. phoxinus* and *G. aculeatus*.

Perch, *Perca fluviatilis*

In this long-lived, freshwater species, the bulk of the recrudescence of the ovaries is completed over the winter months (Craig, 1974). Energy changes in the soma and ovaries of perch in Lake Windermere were measured by Craig (1977), who considered large fish that showed little net somatic growth in a year so that energy was being partitioned between maintenance and ovarian development. This development over the autumn and winter was at the expense of the soma, which declined in weight between October and January, but recovered sharply in the

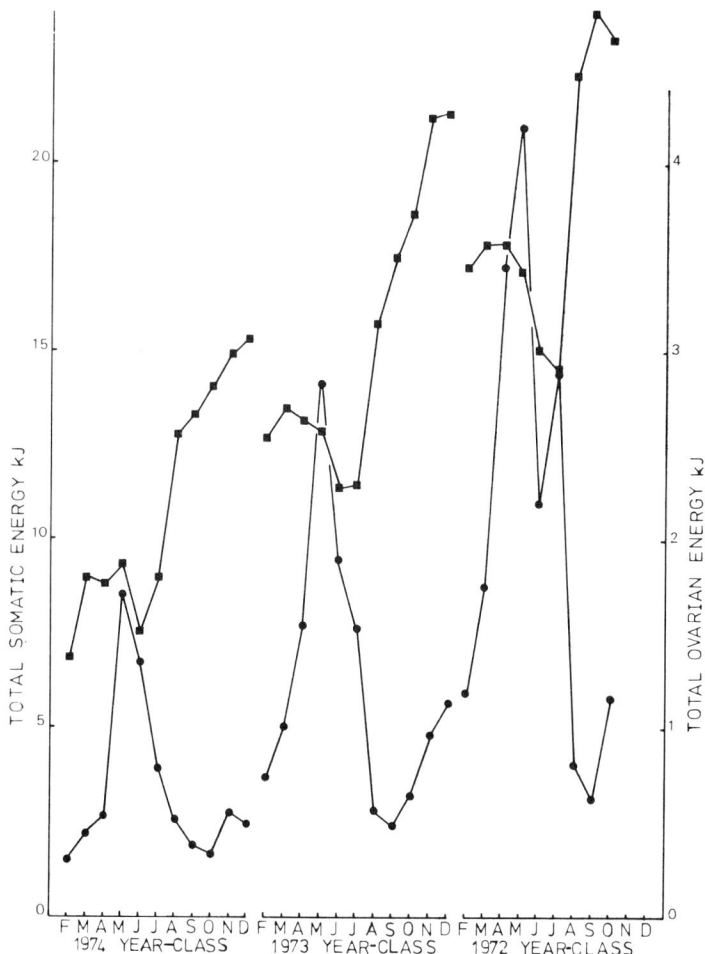

FIG. 7. Changes in total energy of soma and ovaries of average female *Phoxinus phoxinus* from three year-classes of Brays Pool population, 1976 (■), soma; (●), ovaries.

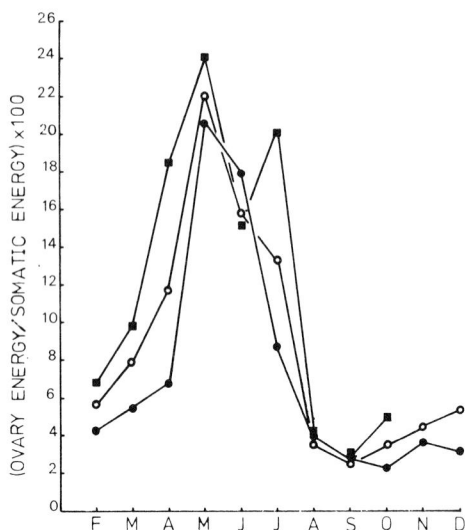

FIG. 8. Changes in ratio of energy in ovaries to energy in soma in the 1974 (●), 1973 (○) and 1972 (■) year-classes of *Phoxinus phoxinus* from Brays Pool, 1976.

post-spawning period of May to July. The energy lost as eggs by an average, 260-mm long female was 168·4 kJ, equivalent to 87·1% of the energy lost by the soma in a year. Thus, there was an annual cycle of storage in the soma with subsequent transfer to the ovaries. The ratio of ovary weight to total weight increased with the age of the fish, again supporting the hypothesis that reproductive effort increases with age (J. F. Craig, pers. comm.).

American plaice, *Hippoglossoides platessoides*

A similar pattern of energy partitioning to the perch occurs in the marine flatfish, the American plaice, *Hippoglossoides platessoides* (Fabricius), (MacKinnon, 1972, 1973). In mature females, the weight of the ovaries increased steadily from a post-spawning minimum of 1·6% of body weight in June to 10% just before spawning in late spring. The increase in weight and energy content of the ovaries was maintained during the winter period when food consumption was low and the soma decreased in weight. In the two periods when American plaice were actively feeding, a 350-mm female on average stored 86·6 kJ in her ovaries, 51·5 kJ prior to spawning and 35·1 kJ in the recovery period, June to December. Since egg production represented 170·3 kJ, the balance must have been transferred from the soma during the winter months. The net decrease in energy of the soma during the winter months was about sufficient to cover the costs of ovarian development and metabolic maintenance. Egg production by a mature female represented about 7·5% of the energy of the food ingested per year. The amount of energy diverted to egg production was relatively greater in the larger and older fish.

Cod, *Gadus morhua*

In a study of the cod in the North Sea, Daan (1975) developed predictive models for growth, egg production and food consumption and used these to estimate the gross efficiency of egg production on a yearly basis, i.e. (energy of eggs produced per year/energy of food consumed per year) × 100. This varied from 1·3% for two-year-old fish to 11–12% for 8- to 25-year-old fish. As the proportion of energy diverted into egg production increased with age, the proportion diverted into somatic growth decreased.

Pacific sardine, *Sardinops caerulea*

In this pelagic species, ovarian development did not begin until late winter and the summer spawning period extended over several months. In winter, the fat content of the sardines was a maximum but declined during springtime as the ovaries developed and was minimal during the spawning period. At its peak, the stored fat represented 12–15% of the annual energy requirements of the fish. Mature fish probably fed throughout the spawning season, though perhaps at a reduced rate with the deficits met from the fat store. Lasker (1970) estimated that annual egg production represented only about 1% of the assimilated energy, which is a much lower percentage than in the cod or American plaice. It is not clear whether this is a true difference reflecting the modes of life of the species or simply reflects methodological weaknesses of studies in which results obtained in laboratory conditions are extrapolated to field situations.

Other Indices of Cost of Egg Production

When a detailed energy budget of ovarian development is not calculated, the cost of egg production may be indicated indirectly.

Several studies have estimated the proportion of the annual production by a fish population that is represented by gonadal products. In many populations, a high proportion of the total production is due to the fast-growing, immature fish so that gonadal production represents only a small proportion of the total. In a multi-species cyprinid community in the River Thames, gonadal production accounted for 3·2% of total annual production (Mann *et al.*, 1972). Staples (1975) estimated that in a population of the upland bully, *Philypnodon breviceps* Stokell, gonadal production represented about 1% of the annual total. The bulk of the energy flow through a fish population is partitioned into somatic growth and maintenance rather than reproduction. But when only production by sexually mature fish is considered, gonadal production, especially of eggs, can form a high proportion of total adult production. In *Perca fluviatilis* of

Lake Windermere, gonadal production almost equalled somatic production by adults (Le Cren, 1951), while in *Salmo trutta*, gonadal production in some populations may be 10–24% of the production by adults (Le Cren, 1962). Egg production by female *Philypnodon breviceps* in their third and fourth years equalled 14–50% of the total (Staples, 1975). Gonadal production by *Hippoglossoides platessoides* represented 13% of the net production by fish over a year old (MacKinnon, 1973).

Abel (1973) noted that gonadal production is normally measured as the weight of eggs and sperm released, but this does not take account of the gonadal production represented by the gonads of fish that die or retain eggs after spawning. He estimated that the total ovarian production by females in the second year of life in a stream population of *Cottus gobio* represented 30% of their total production, while egg production represented 41% of ovarian production. This assumes one spawning a year, but *C. gobio* may show multiple spawnings (Fox, 1978) which means that egg production was underestimated.

An inverse relationship between somatic growth and egg production has been shown clearly in several studies (Lasker, 1970; MacKinnon, 1972; Wootton, 1973a; Daan, 1975). Hislop (1975) measured the food consumption of whiting, *Merlangius merlangus* (L.), during its prolonged spawning period, then compared the weight changes of the spawning females with the changes predicted for non-spawning fish eating the same amount. All the spawners lost weight, with the losses greater than predicted from the rate of food consumption. This weight loss was relatively greater in the larger fish.

Ovarian development and spawning are often associated with depletion of the soma (Woodhead, 1960; Love, 1970). For example, as the gonads of the haddock, *Melanogrammus aeglefinus* (L.), began to mature, the weight increase of the females was retarded. Final stages of maturation were marked by a reduction in muscle protein, while the lipid content and weight of the liver were at a minimum immediately after spawning (Shevchenko, 1972). The sites of storage may differ; in *Trachurus mediterraneus ponticus* Aleev the lipids of the muscles were depleted during the maturation of the ovaries, while in *Scorpaena porcus* L. the lipid in the liver declined as the ovaries developed (Shchepkin, 1971a,b). Even in subtropical species, spawning may be associated with the depletion of the soma. *Tilapia zillii* (Gervais), a substrate-brooding cichlid, spawns in June and September in Egypt (El-Maghraby, Ezzat & Saleh, 1972). Lipid from the liver was mobilized during the ovarian maturation leading to the June spawning, while the second spawning was associated with a depletion of the fat of the muscles as well as the liver.

Although depletion of the soma provides an indication of the cost of egg production, the depletion does not normally represent a pathological situation, but forms part of the suite of adaptive traits that characterize the life history of the species (Iles, 1974). The transfer of materials from the soma to the ovaries means that the maturation of the ovaries and spawning can take place at a time that is optimal for the eggs and larvae, even though in terms of food availability it may be unfavourable for the female. Iles (1974) also noted that rapid somatic growth and rapid ovarian development are often incompatible so there tends to be a seasonal division between the period of growth, particularly in length, and the period of ovarian development. Thus the energy partitioning has a temporal component.

ENVIRONMENTAL DETERMINANTS OF FECUNDITY

Introduction

This section is concerned solely with proximate factors and not with the ultimate factors that lead to the evolution of a particular level of fecundity (see Mann & Mills, this volume p. 161). Some variation in fecundity will reflect genetic variation, but the relative importance of this is unknown, though variation in size at maturity in *G. aculeatus* has been shown to have a strong genetic component (McPhail, 1977).

Food

Introduction

Given the energy costs of egg production discussed above, food is likely to be a major environmental factor determing fecundity. Evidence for this comes from both field and laboratory studies. Fecundity increases with the length and weight of the fish (p. 134), so that better fed fish which grow to a larger size will generally be more fecund than poorly fed fish. But variations in food supply may also cause differences in the fecundity of similar-sized females.

Field observations on the relationship between fecundity and food supply

Constantz (1974) compared some indices of reproductive effort of the viviparous cyprinodont, *Poeciliopsis occidentalis* (Baird & Girard), from two regions of a stream where food quantity and quality differed. Greater food availability was associated with higher fecundity and energy g^{-1} dry wt of egg, but not with mean egg weight, energy per egg or embryo weight. The fecundity of *Abramis brama* in lakes in Poland was correlated with indices of food resources (Brylinska, Platt & Skinsmont, 1974). In the same species, Tsyplakov (1969) found that as unfavourable feeding conditions developed in a new reservoir the fecundity at a given length declined. Low fecundity in the roach, *Rutilus rutilus*, has been associated with low availability or poor quality of food (Titova, 1965; MacKay & Mann, 1969).

In salmonids, food supply can affect fecundity and egg size, as well as the proportion of fish that become sexually mature at a given age. In Pennsylvania, *Salmo trutta* from fertile streams produced a greater weight of eggs than similar-sized fish from infertile streams. Variations in egg size meant that the former were not always more fecund than the latter (McFadden, Cooper & Andersen, 1965). Scott (1962) compared low and high density populations of lake-dwelling rainbow trout, *S. gairdneri* Richardson. Females at high density produced a smaller total weight of eggs and were less fecund but had larger eggs than low density females. Density was assumed to be inversely correlated with food availability. A population of *Salvelinus namaycush* (Walbaum) in an Ontario lake showed an increase in fecundity, egg size and ovary weight following a change in food availability (Martin, 1970). Vladykov (1956) argued that, in *S. fontinalis*, better feeding conditions reduced the degree of atresia in maturing, yolk-containing oocytes and so led to higher fecundity, but when populations from relatively rich and relatively poor areas of the Matamek River, Quebec, were compared, no differences between the fecundities of females of a given size were found (Gibson, Kerkhoven & Haedrich, 1976). A comparison of the fecundity of coho salmon, *Oncorhynchus kisutch* (Walbaum), from the relatively productive Lake Michigan and the relatively sterile Lake Superior indicated that the Lake Michigan coho produced slightly fewer but larger eggs than Lake Superior coho of a similar size. The weight of the ovaries of the Lake Michigan females was also higher (Stauffer, 1976).

Amongst marine species, Bagenal (1966) has argued that most of the variation in fecundity of *Pleuronectes platessa* in the seas of western Europe probably reflected variation in the food supply, which in turn was related to population density.

Experimental studies on the relationship between fecundity and food supply

Scott (1962) subjected hatchery-reared *Salmo gairdneri* to a series of feeding schedules so that in their third year, between May and November, they experienced up to three periods on one-half rations. Until the following May they were on full rations, then were killed. *S. gairdneri* spawns in spring, so the periods of food restriction were imposed during the first one-half of the period when the ovaries were maturing. Only 40 mature fish were obtained. Of these, females of a given length produced fewer mature eggs the longer the period of diet restriction experienced. This was because a higher proportion of the oocytes became atretic, but there was no significant effect on the wet weight of individual eggs. *Salmo trutta* were kept at different food levels from winter to the following autumn when they would normally have spawned (Bagenal, 1969). A higher proportion of the fish on high rations became sexually mature, and these better fed females were more fecund at a given length but their eggs had a lower mean dry weight than those of poorly fed fish. The number of atretic eggs was very low and could not account for the fecundity differences at that stage of maturity.

Food limitation affected the number of offspring produced by the viviparous guppy, *Poecilia reticulata*, during three gestation cycles (Hester, 1964). A restriction in food supply during a cycle reduced the number of young born in that cycle and the next. The restriction limited the recruitment of oocytes into a stage at which they could be fertilized after the birth of the current brood, but did not reduce the size of newborn fish nor alter the period separating successive births.

A study of the winter flounder, *Pseudopleuronectes americanus* (Walbaum), gave further evidence that food limitation can lower fecundity by restricting the recruitment of oocytes rather than by increasing atresia of maturing oocytes (Tyler & Dunn, 1976). Females experienced different rates of feeding between July and December, and were killed between September and December. They would have spawned the following spring. The percentage of females with ovaries that developed yolk increased with meal frequency and fish on higher rations had heavier ovaries. Ration size was positively correlated with the percentage of yolk-bearing oocytes per ovary, but not with the percentage of atretic oocytes. Starved females lacked yolky oocytes entirely. Reduced rations also reduced the weight and fat content of the liver, which is significant because ovarian maturation takes place at the expense of liver fat. The winter flounder adopts a strategy of favouring somatic growth and maintenance at the expense of ovarian development when food is short.

The response to food shortage may vary depending on when in the ovarian cycle it occurs. Starvation for 40 and 80 days did not block the initial increase in relative size of the ovaries of the goby, *Gillichthys mirabilis* Cooper, at the start of the cycle in July, but in January, when active vitellogenesis was occurring, 23 days' starvation resulted in ovarian regression (de Vlaming, 1971).

The ovarian cycle of *Gasterosteus aculeatus* divides into three phases: a relatively slow increase in size during autumn and winter, a rapid increase in spring and thirdly the breeding season with spawning at intervals of a few days. Under winter conditions of low temperatures and short photo-period maintained between September and November, ration size had no effect on relative ovary size. In spring conditions of high temperatures and long photoperiod, maintained through February and March, the female gonadosomatic index was positively correlated with ration size, females on higher rations matured more quickly (Wootton & Evans, unpub.). Once spawning started, fecundity was strongly food dependent (Wootton, 1973a), the number of spawnings being highly correlated with ration size (Wootton, 1977). When starvation or low rations were imposed, females spawned once or twice and then stopped. This was not simply because the interval between spawnings became very long but because the ovaries regressed. There was also a slight lengthening of the interval between successive spawnings at low rations. The weight of eggs produced per spawning was determined primarily by the weight of the female, not by the amount of food consumed. But if the amount consumed was not sufficient to meet the cost of egg production, the female lost weight and, if she spawned again, produced a proportionately smaller weight of eggs. A net loss of about 30% of body weight could occur before spawning ceased, so although egg production was related to food supply, there could be a considerable subsidy from the somatic tissue. The strategy of the short-lived sticklebacks is to maintain investment in the ovaries at the expense of the somatic tissue (p. 144). There is usually a high post-spawning mortality and, in many populations, few if any fish survive beyond 18 months (Wootton, 1976).

Even when the food supplies an adequate energy input, it may be nutritionally inadequate to support spawning. The common sole, *Solea vulgaris* Quensel, failed to spawn when fed cooked mussel, but when this was supplemented by casein some females spawned. The casein probably supplied amino acids essential for the final oocyte maturation that were lacking in the mussel (Fluechter & Trommsdorf, 1974).

Temperature

While temperature can influence the rate of ovarian maturation given permissive photoperiods and food supply (Baggerman, 1957; Sarsembaev, 1975), there is less evidence that it can cause variations in fecundity. The fecundity of pink salmon, *Oncorhynchus gorbuscha* (Walbaum), was inversely correlated with sea temperature in the year of spawning (Rounsefell, 1957). In *Esox lucius*, a drop in water temperature at the time of spawning was correlated with high levels of atresia so that fewer eggs were spawned (June, 1970). But in the same species, Kipling & Frost (1969) could detect no effect on fecundity of water temperatures experienced in the periods 24–18 and 12–6 months before spawning, so temperature may have different effects at different phases in the ovarian cycle. In *Cyprinodon n. nevadensis* the optimal temperature range for the percentage of days on which spawning occurred and for number of eggs per spawning was 24–32°C. Outside this range, egg production was curtailed. If small departures from the tolerance limits have large effects on fecundity, the temperature experienced by female fish during the period of egg maturation may be one of the factors determining year-class strength (Shrode & Gerking, 1977).

Rates of food consumption are temperature dependent so low temperatures could reduce fecundity indirectly by a reduction in food consumption. The interactions between food supply and temperature and their effects on fecundity require experimental analysis.

Light

Although photoperiod is often crucial in the control of maturation of the ovaries, there is no evidence that variations in light conditions cause variations in the fecundity of natural populations. In experimental conditions, control of photoperiod can shorten or lengthen the breeding season. An 8-h light/16-h dark regime imposed at the start of the breeding season greatly reduced the number of spawnings by *Gasterosteus aculeatus* (Baggerman, 1957). Multiple spawnings were obtained in the catfish, *Heteropneustes fossilis* (Bloch), by maintaining a regime of 14-h light/10-h dark at 25°C and inducing spawning with ovine luteinizing hormone (Sundararaj & Vasal, 1976). Catfish normally spawn once in a breeding season.

Other Determinants of Fecundity

Parasitic infestation can inhibit ovarian maturation. The gonadosomatic index of female *Gasterosteus aculeatus* infested with the cestode *Schisto-cephalus solidus* (Müller) reached a maximum of only 5% and there was evidence that the infested females failed to spawn (Meakins, 1974). This was probably due to the energy demands of the parasite rather than interference with the hormonal control of oogenesis (Arme & Owen, 1967). Infestation by *Diphyllobothrium* retarded the maturation of *Salvelinus fontinalis* (Vladykov, 1956), but it is not clear from these examples whether infestations cause a graded effect on fecundity or have an all or nothing effect on maturation.

High population densities, with a corresponding increase in behavioural interactions, may cause a reduction in fecundity (Kipling & Frost, 1969; Bagenal, 1973), but the evidence is weak. Crowding *Gasterosteus aculeatus* inhibited ovarian maturation (Schneider, 1969), but some females may have received insufficient food. A drop in water level was correlated with an increase in atresia in spawning *Esox lucius* (June, 1970).

Some environmental contaminants can reduce fecundity but often only at relatively high doses. Carbaryl at 0·68 mg litre^{-1} reduced the number of eggs spawned in nine months by fathead minnows, *Pimephales promelas* Rafinesque (Carlson, 1972). *Salvelinus fontinalis* fed high sublethal doses of DDT produced fewer mature oocytes than untreated fish (Macek, 1968).

FEEDING AND REPRODUCTIVE CYCLES

Although food availability is probably the most important environmental factor determining fecundity, the relationship between the temporal patterning of feeding and ovarian development varies considerably.

In some species, the periods of ovarian maturation and spawning are times of complete or partial fast. The most extreme examples of this are the anadromous salmonids, but the haddock provides another (Homans & Vladykov, 1954; Shevchenko, 1972). For other species, the period of spawning is a time of fasting, sandwiched between periods of intensive feeding, e.g. *Osmerus mordax* (Mitchill) (Foltz & Norden, 1977), *Scorpaena porcus* L. (Shchepkin, 1971a). In some species the breeding season is a time of voracious feeding, e.g. *Gasterosteus aculeatus* (Wootton & Evans, 1976).

The temporal pattern of ovarian development has at least two potentially incompatible requirements to meet. The eggs should be laid at a size and time that maximizes post-spawning survival, but the energy demands of egg production require that the female has a favourable period of feeding to meet this cost. For some species, the period of favourable feeding at least partially corresponds with the optimal spawning period, e.g. *Gasterosteus aculeatus*. But, for other species, both the times and places for optimal feeding and spawning may differ, so that ovarian maturation and spawning take place at a time that is energetically unfavourable. In these cases a cycle of storage links the feeding cycle with the ovarian cycle, e.g. *Hippoglossoides platessoides* (MacKinnon, 1972, 1973) and *Perca fluviatilis* (Craig, 1977). The presence of a store should allow the fish to partially insulate itself from the immediate effects of fluctuations in food availability and so perhaps maintain an optimal partitioning between the soma and the ovaries in the face of fluctuations.

A fast at spawning may minimize cannibalism by the spawners of their own offspring. *Gasterosteus aculeatus*, which feeds during the breeding season and includes eggs in its diet, shows nest-guarding behaviour by the male (Wootton, 1976). The fast may also reflect competition for the available time between spawning activity and feeding, with the former having motivational priority.

CONCLUSIONS

This review has discussed studies on the energy costs of egg production together with the effects of environmental factors, particularly food supply, on fecundity. But it has ignored another aspect of the cost of reproduction, the reduction in life expectancy and future reproductive output resulting from current reproductive effort. In future studies, patterns of mortality should be determined together with estimates of current reproductive effort; the teleosts, as Williams (1966) noted, are a particularly favourable group for such studies.

ACKNOWLEDGEMENTS

My research on *Gasterosteus aculeatus* and *Phoxinus phoxinus* was supported by a grant from the Natural Environment Research Council. I wish to thank Drs R. Abel and J. F. Craig for permission to quote from unpublished manuscripts.

REFERENCES

Abel, R. (1973). *The trophic ecology of* Cottus gobio. D. Phil. Thesis: Oxford University.

Arme, C. & Owen, R. W. (1967). Infections of the three-spined stickleback, *Gasterosteus aculeatus* L. with the plerocercoid larvae of *Schistocephalus solidus* (Müller, 1776), with special reference to pathological effects. *Parasitology* **57**: 301–314.

Bagenal, T. B. (1966). The ecological and geographical aspects of the fecundity of plaice. *J. mar. biol. Ass. U.K.* **46**: 161–186.

Bagenal, T. B. (1967). A short review of fish fecundity. In *The biological basis of freshwater fish production*: 89–111. Gerking, S. D. (ed.). Oxford: Blackwell.

Bagenal, T. B. (1969). The relationship between food supply and fecundity in brown t. out *Salmo trutta* L. *J. Fish Biol.* **1**: 167–182.

Bagenal, T. B. (1971). The interrelation of the size of fish eggs, the date of spawning and the production cycle. *J. Fish Biol.* **3**: 207–219.

Bagenal, T. B. (1973). Fish fecundity and its relations with stock and recruitment. *Rapp. P.-v. Reun. Cons. int. Explor. Mer* **164**: 186–198.

Baggerman, B. (1957). An experimental study on the timing of breeding and migration in the three-spined stickleback (*Gasterosteus aculeatus* L.). *Archs néerl. Zool.* **12**: 105–317.

Bialokoz, W. (1973). [Fecundity in chosen fish species from a few Mazurian Lakes prepared for fertilization]. *Roczn. Nauk roln. (Ser. H.)* **95**: 7–34. [In Polish].

Brylinska, M. (1971). [Factors regulating absolute fecundity and absolute bream (*Abramis brama* L.) population fecundity]. *Zesz. nauk. wyzsz. Szk. roln. Olsztyn.* (Seria C.) Suppl. **2**: 1–104 [In Polish].

Brylinska, M., Platt, C. & Skinsmont, W. (1974). [Analysis of the relation between the selected fecundity indices in bream and the indices of environmental conditions]. *Roczn. Nauk roln. (Ser. H.)* **93**: 155–170. [In Polish].

Burns, J. R. (1976). The reproductive cycle and its environmental control in the pumpkinseed, *Lepomis gibbosus* (Pisces: Centrachidae). *Copeia* **1976**: 449–455.

Calow, P. & Woolhead, A. S. (1977). The relationship between ration, reproductive effort and age-specific mortality in the evolution of life history strategies—some observations on freshwater triclads. *J. Anim. Ecol.* **46**: 765–782.

Carlson, A. R. (1972). Effects of long-term exposure to carbaryl (Sevin) on survival, growth and reproduction of the fathead minnow (*Pimephales promelas*). *J. Fish. Res. Bd Can.* **29**: 583–587.

Constantz, G. D. (1974). Reproductive effort in *Poeciliopsis occidentalis* (Poeciliidae). *SWest. Nat.* **19**: 47–52.

Craig, J. F. (1974). Population dynamics of perch, *Perca fluviatilis* L. in Slapton Ley, Devon. I. Trapping behaviour, reproduction, migration, population estimates, mortality and food. *Freshwat. Biol.* **4**: 417–431.

Craig, J. F. (1977). The body composition of adult perch, *Perca fluviatilis* in Windermere, with reference to seasonal changes and reproduction. *J. Anim. Ecol.* **46**: 617–632.

Daan, N. (1975). Consumption and production in North Sea cod, *Gadus morhua*: an assessment of the ecological status of the stock. *Neth. J. Sea Res.* **9**: 24–55.

de Silva, S. S. (1973). Aspects of the reproduction biology of the sprat, *Sprattus sprattus* (L.) in inshore waters of the west coast of Scotland. *J. Fish Biol.* **5**: 689–705.

de Vlaming, V. L. (1971). The effects of food deprivation and salinity changes on reproductive functions in the estuarine gobiid fish, *Gillichthys mirabilis*. *Biol. Bull. mar. biol. Lab. Woods Hole* **141**: 458–471.

El-Maghraby, A. M., Ezzat, A. & Saleh, H. H. (1972). Fat metabolism in *Tilapia zillii* Gerv. *Bull. Inst. Oceanogr. Fish. Egypt* **2**: 297–332.

Fluechter, J. & Trommsdorf, H. (1974). Nutritive stimulation in the common sole (*Solea solea*). *Ber. Dtsch. Wiss. Komm. Meeresforsch.* **23**: 352–359.

Foltz, J. W. & Norden, C. R. (1977). Seasonal changes in food consumption and energy content of smelt (*Osmerus mordax*) in Lake Michigan. *Trans. Am. Fish. Soc.* **106**: 230–234.

Fox, P. J. (1978). Preliminary observations on different reproduction strategies in the bullhead (*Cottus gobio*) in northern and southern England. *J. Fish Biol.* **12**: 5–11.

Frost, W. E. (1943). The natural history of the minnow (*Phoxinus phoxinus*). *J. Anim. Ecol.* **12**: 139–162.

Frost, W. E. & Kipling, C. (1967). A study of reproduction, early life, weight-length relationship and growth of pike, *Esox lucius* L., in Windermere. *J. Anim. Ecol.* **36**: 651–693.

Gibson, J. R., Kerkhoven, P. C. & Haedrich, R. L. (1976). The fecundity of unexploited brook trout populations in the Matamek River, Quebec. *Naturaliste can.* **103**: 417–424.

Glenn, C. L. & Williams, R. G. (1976). Fecundity of mooneye, *Hiodon tergisus*, in the Assiniboine River. *Can J. Zool.* **54**: 156–161.

Healey, M. C. & Nichol, C. W. (1975). Fecundity comparisons for various stocks of lake whitefish, *Coregonus clupeaformis*. *J. Fish. Res. Bd Can.* **32**: 404–407.

Hellawell, J. M. (1974). The ecology of populations of dace, *Leuciscus leuciscus* (L.), from two tributaries of the River Wye, Herefordshire, England. *Freshwat. Biol.* **4**: 577–604.

Hempel, G. & Blaxter, J. H. S. (1967). Egg weight in Atlantic herring. *J. Cons. perm. int. Explor. Mer* **31**: 170–195.

Hester, F. J. (1964). Effects of food supply on fecundity in the female guppy *Lebistes reticulatus* (Peters). *J. Fish. Res. Bd Can.* **21**: 757–764.

Hislop, J. R. G. (1975). The breeding and growth of whiting, *Merlangius merlangus* in captivity. *J. Cons. int. Explor. Mer* **36**: 119–127.

Hodder, V. M. (1972). The fecundity of herring in some parts of the Newfoundland area. *Res. Bull. int. Commn NW Atlant. Fish.* No. 9: 99–107.

Homans, R. E. S. & Vladykov, V. D. (1954). Relation between feeding and the sexual cycle of the haddock. *J. Fish. Res. Bd Can.* **11**: 535–542.

Hoyt, R. D. (1971). The reproductive biology of the silverjaw minnow, *Ericymba buccata* Cope, in Kentucky. *Trans. Am. Fish. Soc.* **100**: 510–519.

Hubbs, C., Stevenson, M. M. & Peden, A. E. (1968). Fecundity and egg size in two central Texas darter populations. *SW. Nat.* **13**: 301–324.

Iles, T. D. (1974). The tactics and strategy of growth in fishes. In *Sea fisheries research*: 331–345. Harden Jones, F. R. (Ed.). London: Elek Scientific.

Jones, A. (1974). Sexual maturity, fecundity and growth of the turbot, *Scophthalmus maximus* L. *J. mar. biol. Ass. U.K.* **54**: 109–125.

June, F. C. (1970). Atresia and year-class abundance of northern pike *Esox lucius*, in two Missouri River impoundments. *J. Fish. Res. Bd Can.* **27**: 587–591.

Kipling, C. & Frost, W. E. (1969). Variations in the fecundity of pike, *Esox lucius* L. in Windermere. *J. Fish Biol.* **1**: 221–237.

Lasker, R. (1970). Utilization of zooplankton energy by a Pacific sardine population in the California current. In *Marine food chains*: 265–284. Steele, J. H. (ed.). Edinburgh: Oliver & Boyd.

Le Cren, E. D. (1951). The length-weight relationship and seasonal cycle in gonad weight and condition in the perch (*Perca fluviatilis*). *J. Anim. Ecol.* **20**: 201–219.

Le Cren, E. D. (1962). The efficiency of reproduction and recruitment in freshwater fish. In *The exploitation of natural animal populations*: 286–296. Le Cren, E. D. & Holdgate, M. W. (eds). Oxford: Blackwell.

Love, M. R. (1970). *The chemical biology of fishes*. London & New York: Academic Press.

Lowe-McConnell, R. H. (1955). The fecundity of *Tilapia* species. *E. Afr. agric. J.* **21**: 45–52.

Ludwig, G. M. & Lange, E. L. (1975). The relationship of length, age, and age-length interaction to the fecundity of the northern mottled sculpin, *Cottus b. bairdi*. *Trans. Am. Fish. Soc.* **104**: 64–67.

Macek, K. J. (1968). Reproduction in brook trout (*Salvelinus fontinalis*) fed sublethal concentrations of DDT. *J. Fish. Res. Bd Can.* **25**: 1787–1796.

McFadden, J. T., Cooper, E. L. & Andersen, J. K. (1965). Some effects of environment on egg production in brown trout (*Salmo trutta*). *Limnol. Oceanog.* **10**: 88–95.

MacKay, I. & Mann, K. H. (1969). Fecundity of two cyprinid fishes in River Thames, Reading, England. *J. Fish. Res. Bd Can.* **26**: 2795–2805.

MacKinnon, J. C. (1972). Summer storage of energy and its use for winter metabolism and gonad maturation in American plaice (*Hippoglossoides platessoides*). *J. Fish. Res. Bd Can.* **29**: 1749–1759.

MacKinnon, J. C. (1973). Analysis of energy flow and production in an unexploited marine flatfish population. *J. Fish. Res. Bd Can.* **30**: 1717–1728.

McPhail, J. D. (1977). Inherited interpopulation differences in size at first reproduction in threespine stickleback, *Gasterosteus aculeatus* L. *Heredity* **38**: 53–60.

Mann, K. H., Britton, R. H., Kowalczewski, A., Lack, T. J., Mathews, C. P. & McDonald, I. (1972). Productivity and energy flow at all trophic levels in the River Thames, England. In *Productivity problems of freshwater*: 579–596. Kajak, Z. & Hillbricht-Ilkowska, A. (eds). Warszawa-Krakow: PWN-Polish Scientific Publishers.

Martin, N. V. (1970). Long term effects of diet on the biology of the lake trout and the fishery in Lake Opeongo, Ontario. *J. Fish. Res. Bd Can.* **27**: 125–146.

May, A. W. (1967). Fecundity of Atlantic cod. *J. Fish. Res. Bd Can.* **24**: 1531–1551.

Meakins, R. H. (1974). A quantitative approach of the effects of the plerocercoid of *Schistocephalus solidus* Müller 1776 on the ovarian maturation of the threespined stickleback *Gasterosteus aculeatus* L. *Z. Parasitenk.* **44**: 73–79.

Messieh, S. (1976). Fecundity studies on Atlantic herring from the southern Gulf of St. Lawrence and along the Nova Scotia coast. *Trans. Am. Fish. Soc.* **105**: 384–394.

Nomura, H. (1975). Fecundity, sexual maturation, and gonadosomatic index of minnows of the species *Astyanax* Baird & Girard, 1854 (Osteichthyes, Characidae) in relation to environmental factors. *Revta bras. Biol.* **35**: 775–798.

158   R. J. WOOTTON

Oosthuizen, E. & Daan, N. (1974). Egg fecundity and maturity of North Sea cod, *Gadus morhua. Neth. J. Sea Res.* **8**: 378–397.

Papadopol, M. & Weinberger, M. (1975). On the reproduction of *Phoxinus phoxinus* (Linnaeus, 1758) (Pisces: Cyprinidae) with notes on other aspects of its life history. *Věst. čsl. Spol. zool.* **39**: 39–52.

Parameswaran, S., Selvaraj, C. & Radhakrishnan, S. (1970). Observations on the maturation and breeding season of carp in Assam. *J. Inl. Fish Soc. India* **2**: 16–29.

Pope, J. A., Mills, D. H. & Shearer, W. M. (1961). The fecundity of the Atlantic salmon (*Salmo salar* Linn). *Freshwat. Salm. Fish. Res.* **26**: 1–12.

Rounsefell, G. A. (1957). Fecundity of North American Salmonidae. *Fishery Bull. Fish. Wildl. Serv. U.S.* **57**: 451–468.

Sarsembaev, Zh. G. (1975). [Effects of various ecological conditions of ponds on the reproductive system of silver carp]. *Izv. Akad. Nauk kazakh. SSR* (Biol.) **13**: 31–38. [In Russian].

Schneider, L. (1969). Experimentelle Untersuchungen über den Einfluss von Tageslänge und Temperatur auf die Gonadenreifung beim Dreistachligen stichling (*Gasterosteus aculeatus*). *Oecologia* **3**: 249–265.

Schopka, S. A. & Hempel, G. (1973). The spawning potential of populations of herring (*Clupea harengus* L.) and cod (*Gadus morhua* L.) in relation to the rate of exploitation. *Rapp. P.-v. Reun. Cons. int. Explor. Mer* No. 164: 178–185.

Scott, D. P. (1962). Effect of food quantity on fecundity of rainbow trout *Salmo gairdneri. J. Fish. Res. Bd Can.* **19**: 715–731.

Shackley, S. E. & King, P. E. (1977). The reproductive cycle and its control; frequency of spawning and fecundity in *Blennius pholis. J. exp. mar. Biol. Ecol.* **30**: 73–83.

Shchepkin, V. Ya. (1971a). The dynamics of the lipid composition in scorpion fish *Scorpaena porcus* L. in relation to maturation and spawning. *J. Ichthyol.* **11**: 262–267.

Shchepkin, V. Ya. (1971b). The dynamics of lipid composition of the Black Sea horsemackerel (*Trachurus mediterraneus ponticus* Aleev) in relation to gonadal maturation. *J. Ichthyol.* **11**: 587–591.

Shevchenko, V. V. (1972). The dynamics of protein and fat content in the organs and tissues of the North Sea haddock *Melanogrammus aeglefinus* L. in the process of seasonal growth and gonad maturation. *J. Ichthyol.* **12**: 830–837.

Shrode, J. B. & Gerking, S. D. (1977). Effects of constant and fluctuating temperatures on reproductive performance of a desert pupfish, *Cyprinodon n. nevadensis. Physiol. Zool.* **50**: 1–10.

Simpson, A. C. (1951). The fecundity of plaice. *Fish Invest., Lond.* (2) **17**: 1–27.

Staples, D. J. (1975). Production biology of the upland bully *Philypnodon breviceps* Stockell in a small New Zealand lake. III. Production, food consumption and efficiency of food utilization. *J. Fish Biol.* **7**: 47–69.

Stauffer, T. M. (1976). Fecundity of Coho salmon (*Oncorhynchus kisutch*) from the Great Lakes and a comparison with ocean salmon. *J. Fish. Res. Bd Can.* **33**: 1150–1155.

Stearns, S. C. (1976). Life-history tactics: a review of the ideas. *Q. Rev. Biol.* **51**: 3–47.

Stearns, S. C. (1977). The evolution of life history traits: a critique of the theory and a review of the data. *Ann. Rev. Ecol. Syst.* **8**: 145–171.

Sundararaj, B. I. & Vasal, S. (1976). Photoperiod and temperature control in the regulation of reproduction in the female catfish *Heteropneustes fossilis. J. Fish. Res. Bd Can.* **33**: 959–973.

Svardson, G. (1949). Natural selection and egg number in fish. *Rep. Inst. Freshwat. Res. Drottningholm* No. 29: 115–122.

Titova, K. N. (1965). [Contributions to the biology of roach (*Rutilus rutilus* L.) in southern and northern U.S.S.R.] *Nauch. Dokl. vyssh. Shk* (Biol. Nauki) **2**: 27–31. [In Russian].

Tsyplakov, E. P. (1969). Variation in reproduction of the bream (*Abramis brama*) population in the Kuybyshev Reservoir. *Probl. Ichthol.* **9**: 66–75.

Tyler, A. V. & Dunn, R. S. (1976). Ration, growth and measures of somatic and organ condition in relation to meal frequency in winter flounder, *Pseudopleuronectes americanus*, with hypotheses regarding population homeostasis. *J. Fish. Res. Bd Can.* **33**: 63–75.

Vladykov, V. D. (1956). Fecundity of wild speckled trout (*Salvelinus fontinalis*) in Quebec Lakes. *J. Fish. Res. Bd Can.* **13**: 799–841.

Walkey, M. & Meakins, R. H. (1970). An attempt to balance the energy budget of a host-parasite system. *J. Fish Biol.* **2**: 361–372.

Ware, D. M. (1975). Relation between egg size, growth and natural mortality of larval fish. *J. Fish. Res. Bd Can.* **32**: 2503–2512.

Welcomme, R. L. (1967). The relationship between fecundity and fertility in the mouthbrooding cichlid fish *Tilapia leucostica. J. Zool., Lond.* **151**: 453–468.

Wilkinson, D. R. & Jones, J. W. (1977). The fecundity of dace, *Leuciscus leuciscus* (L.) in Emral Brook, Clwyd, North Wales. *Freshwat. Biol.* **7**: 135–145.

Williams, G. C. (1966). *Adaptation and natural selection.* Princeton: University Press.

Woodhead, A. D. (1960). Nutrition and reproductive capacity in fish. *Proc. Nutr. Soc.* **19**: 23–28.

Wootton, R. J. (1973a). The effect of size of food ration on egg production in the female three-spined stickleback, *Gasterosteus aculeatus* L. *J. Fish Biol.* **5**: 89–96.

Wootton, R. J. (1973b). Fecundity of the three-spined stickleback, *Gasterosteus aculeatus* L. *J. Fish Biol.* **5**: 683–688.

Wootton, R. J. (1974). The inter-spawning interval of the female three-spined stickleback, *Gasterosteus aculeatus. J. Zool., Lond.* **172**: 331–342.

Wootton, R. J. (1976). *The biology of the sticklebacks.* London & New York: Academic Press.

Wootton, R. J. (1977). Effect of food limitation during the breeding season on the size, body components and egg production of female sticklebacks (*Gasterosteus aculeatus*). *J. Anim. Ecol.* **46**: 823–834.

Wootton, R. J. & Evans, G. W. (1976). Cost of egg production in the three-spined stickleback (*Gasterosteus aculeatus* L.). *J. Fish Biol.* **8**: 385–395.

Wootton, R. J., Evans, G. W. & Mills, L. 1978. Annual cycle in female three-spined sticklebacks (*Gasterosteus aculeatus* L.) from an upland and lowland population. *J. Fish Biol.* **12**: 331–343.

Wydoski, R. S. & Cooper, E. L. (1966). Maturation and fecundity of brook trout from infertile streams. *J. Fish. Res. Bd Can.* **23**: 623–649.

Symp. zool. Soc. Lond. (1979) No. 44, 161–177

Demographic Aspects of Fish Fecundity

R. H. K. MANN and C. A. MILLS

Freshwater Biological Association, River Laboratory, East Stoke, Wareham, Dorset, England

SYNOPSIS

The relevance of current theoretical ideas on life-history tactics is examined with respect to teleost fish. Although fish are extremely versatile in their reproductive tactics, few of these tactics can be predicted from the theories of r- and K-selection. Instead, repeat reproduction and increased longevity are the traits used to offset the problems of reproductive uncertainty. These traits are embodied in the theory of bet-hedging. Examples are given of intra-specific variation in life-history tactics, although the relative importance of proximate and ultimate influences is often not clear. The problem is more acute when inter-specific comparisons are attempted, and more experimental studies are required.

INTRODUCTION

Teleost fish employ a wide range of life-history tactics to ensure that the maximum number of progeny, summed over the lifespan of the parent, reach sexual maturity. The characteristic combination of biological traits such as fecundity, size of offspring, reproductive lifespan, spawning season and spawning pattern, which is evolved by each species or population, is an adaptation to environment. The mechanisms involved in the selection of these traits have been the subject of much theoretical discussion, and many of the ideas have been embodied in the concepts of r- and K-selection (MacArthur & Wilson, 1967).

In brief, r-selection describes selection in unstable environments where the size of a population is controlled largely by density-independent factors. Characteristic life-history tactics include early maturity, high fecundity and high reproductive effort, even though the last trait may be at the cost of an increased adult mortality rate. In contrast, K-selection describes selection in stable environments where populations are subject to density-dependent constraints. Here, characteristic tactics include late maturity, multiple broods, fewer but larger offspring, a low reproductive effort and, on occasion, parental care. There exists, of course, an r-K continuum, with most organisms having a combination of traits which are a compromise between the two extremes. Pianka (1970) suggests that, whereas insects tend to be r-selected and terrestrial vertebrates K-selected, fish (and other aquatic organisms) span the range of the r–K continuum.

More recently there has been a re-examination of the trends explained by r- and K-selection. It is claimed that increased fluctuations in environmental conditions do not always cause selection for increased reproductive effort and a trend towards a single reproduction in an organism's lifetime (semelparity), as would be predicted by r- and K-selection. Theoretical studies indicate that increased fluctuation in the mortality of immature fish can favour reproduction over several years (iteroparity) (Murphy, 1968) and also reduced reproductive effort in all individuals (Schaffer, 1974). However, where the fluctuations are largely in the sexually mature stages, then increased reproductive effort and a shorter lifespan will be selected (Schaffer, 1974), as would be predicted by the r and K theory. For a semelparous organism with fluctuations in pre-reproductive mortality, it is predicted that only a fraction of the population should reproduce annually (Schaffer, 1974). This alternative set of predicted responses to environmental conditions has been termed bet-hedging (Stearns, 1976) because of the implied trade-off between lower reproductive effort and greater longevity when pre-reproductive survival is uncertain. Calow (1977) presented a similar idea, stating that it is better to breed than grow, unless breeding endangers the adult and the adult has better chances of survival than its progeny.

In this paper we describe some of the reproductive strategies which have been evolved by teleost fish in various habitats. In particular we examine the relative advantages of high fecundity and large egg size, and also the trade-off between reproductive effort and adult survival.

First, two definitions are required. Absolute fecundity describes the number of developing eggs in the ovary just prior to spawning (Bagenal, 1973), and includes the eggs about to be laid and those which, in batch spawners, will develop further before being released later in the same spawning season.

If absolute fecundity (F) is plotted against fish length (L) the points will usually lie about a curve described by the function

$$F = aL^b \qquad (1)$$

which can be transformed to the logarithmic function

$$\text{Log } F = \text{Log } a + b \text{ Log } L. \qquad (2)$$

Comparisons between the fecundity of populations in different years, or in different habitats, can be made by calculating the expected fecundity of a fish of some arbitrarily chosen length in each population using eqn (2). Alternatively, the relative fecundity may be calculated. This describes the numbers of eggs g^{-1} total wt of fish, and assumes that the number does not alter with the size of the fish. Bagenal (1973) suggests that relating fecundity to total weight may be misleading as ovaries with more eggs will probably weigh more. For this reason, comparisons between populations in this paper are all based upon eqns (1) and (2) to give the fecundity of a standard animal.

REPRODUCTIVE STRATEGIES

Options

Before examining the tactics employed by particular species, it is pertinent to consider the options open to them with regard to their egg production. Svärdson (1949), following earlier work on clutch size in birds (Lack, 1947, 1948a,b,c), suggested the existence of an optimal reproductive effort for fish which is derived from a trade-off between present and future spawnings. Thus a very high reproductive effort might endanger future spawnings by decreasing the parent's chances of survival through diverting some of its energy resources away from maintenance and somatic growth. As predation and starvation are the prime causes of larval mortality (Hempel, 1965), there are, within the limits of the optimal reproductive effort, two conflicting selection pressures: to increase the number of eggs in order to overcome the effects of predation and to increase the size of the eggs (assuming larval size is related to egg size) to reduce larval starvation. The result is a compromise which is not uniform to all populations of fish but which, through natural selection, is closely related to the conditions met by the newly hatched larvae. This relationship is most evident in species living in relatively stable (or predictable) environments, whereas fish inhabiting less stable habitats may have to provide a wider range of reproductive possibilities to ensure their survival.

Semelparity versus Iteroparity

Cole (1954) questioned the predictions later embodied in the concepts of r- and K-selection that a trend towards semelparity would be favoured in an unstable environment, and iteroparity in a stable environment. He argued that an annual species would achieve the same gain in its intrinsic population growth by becoming iteroparous, as it would by adding just one to its litter size (i.e. fecundity in fish) in the semelparous state. This idea has been the subject of much argument by, among others, Murdoch (1966), Gadgil & Bossert (1970), Bryant (1971), Charnov & Schaffer (1973) and Stearns (1976). Whatever the validity of Cole's theories, iteroparity is the option most often selected in fish life-history tactics. An example of its value is shown by the Pacific sardine, *Sardinops caerulea* (Girard). Normally this species has seven or eight year-classes spawning together, but overfishing in the 1930s and early 1940s effectively reduced this to two year-classes. Following poor recruitment in 1949 and 1950 the population collapsed, clearly demonstrating the importance of iteroparity in cushioning the effects of highly variable juvenile mortality caused by environmental fluctuations. Holgate (1967) and Murphy (1968) emphasized the importance of this bet-hedging characteristic by stating that there will be selection for iteroparity when there is a significant risk of total reproductive failure in any one year. Under these conditions, most teleost fish have evolved bet-hedging traits, but an exception is the pink salmon, *Oncorhynchus gorbuscha* (Walbaum), which is an *r*-strategist. Its eggs and fry are subject to a variable, and often very high, mortality from several proximate factors including low oxygen concentration, movement of bottom sediments, freezing and overcutting of their redds (McNeil, 1964). In this extremely unpredictable environment, *O. gorbuscha* has opted for a short lifespan of two years, with the adults dying after they have spawned.

Not all species have the same mechanism to spread their reproductive effort over several years. The Atlantic salmon, *Salmo salar* L., is essentially semelparous, with a high reproductive effort and fecundity. However, individuals in each year-class become sexually mature at different ages, thus realizing the advantages of iteroparity. A similar phenomenon occurs in the Pacific salmon, *Oncorhynchus nerka* (Walbaum) (Murphy, 1968). In contrast, the anadromous form of the trout, *Salmo trutta* L., which often occurs in the same river as *S. salar*, has a perennial spawning habit with individuals in each year-class reproducing at the same age. Schaffer (1974) argues that the different reproductive strategies of such co-existing and closely related species indicate that there can be more than one stable equilibrium in the relationship between reproductive effort at one age and the next (see also Schaffer, this volume p. 307).

Trade-Off between Reproductive Effort and Longevity

Reproductive effort has been shown to increase with age in several fish species. Hislop (1975) demonstrated this for the whiting, *Merlangius merlangus* (L.). From feeding experiments he was able to calculate the theoretical increase in somatic weight which would have occurred for each fish had spawning not occurred. Most of the other documented examples use the ratio of gonad weight to total fish weight as a measure of reproductive effort. However, few examples demonstrate unequivocally that a high reproductive effort increases adult mortality. One such case is the cyprinid, *Pimephales promelas* Rafinesque, in which adults spawning at age I have a lower survival rate than those which do not spawn until age II (Markus, 1934). In addition, Calow (1977) reported that gonadectomized salmon do not spawn and are able to return to the sea. The stickleback, *Gasterosteus aculeatus* L., as shown by Wootton (1976), can increase the number of egg batches produced in one season in response to increased food levels. When food levels are reduced, fecundity levels are still maintained at a level near to the maximum, even though adult mortality increases. In most populations the majority of *G. aculeatus* appear to die after their first spawning, even though the age at first maturity may be from one to four years according to their growth rate.

Most species, however, do not develop all their oocytes when food is limited, and the trout, *Salmo trutta*, is able to reabsorb some of its eggs under conditions of starvation (Scott, 1962). In addition, some evidence exists of the trade-off between reproductive effort and longevity in two species of Cyprinidae. The chub, *Leuciscus cephalus* (L.), has a lifespan of 20+ years in some European rivers. It is a batch spawner whose reproductive effort has little effect on its cycle of relative condition[a] (Mann, 1976). In contrast the dace, *L. leuciscus* (L.), has a lifespan of eight to 10 years in the same rivers, and each female lays one batch of eggs each year with a pronounced decrease in relative condition occurring after spawning (Mann, 1974).

Murphy (1968) plotted the variation in spawning success of five populations of schooling, plankton-feeding fish against their reproductive lifespan. He argued that long-lived species could survive reproductive uncertainty, but that most short-lived species would not vary greatly in their spawning success. His data supported this hypothesis and we have expanded his graph to include data from a range of other species, both marine and freshwater (Table I, Fig. 1). Despite the tendency of data to be

TABLE I

Relationship between the range in spawning success and reproductive lifespan in some teleost fish

Serial No.	Species	Variation in spawning success	Reproductive lifespan (years)	Source
1.	*Engraulis mordax*	×2	2	Murphy, 1968
2.	*Clupea harengus*—Baltic	×3	4	Murphy, 1968
3.	*Pleuronectes platessa*	×3	11	Beverton & Holt, 1957 and Simpson, 1951
4.	*Morone saxatilis*	×4	*c* 15	Stevens, 1977
5.	*Esox lucius*	×5	*c.* 14	Kipling & Frost, 1969
6.	*Stizostedion v. vitreum*	×5	*c.* 13	Hile, 1954
7.	*Rutilus rutilus*—River Stour	×5	12	Mann, 1973
8.	*Coregonus albula*	×5	10	Aass, 1972
9.	*Leuciscus leuciscus*	×7	6	Authors, unpubl. data
10.	*Gobio gobio*	×12	4	Authors, unpubl. data
11.	*C. harengus*—North Sea	×9	10	Murphy, 1968
12.	*Sardinops caerulea*	×10	10	Murphy, 1968
13.	*R. rutilus*—River Frome	×10	12	Mann, 1973
14.	*Leuciscus cephalus*	×17	16	Mann, 1976
15.	*Micropterus salmoides*	×19	*c.* 15	Kramer & Smith, 1962
16.	*C. harengus*—Atlanto-Scandian	×25	18	Murphy, 1968
17.	*Perca fluviatilis*	×400	10	LeCren *et al.*, 1977
18.	*Perca flavescens*	×70	*c.* 9	Forney, 1971

a Relative condition Kn is measured as $\hat{W}/W_0$ where W_0 is the observed weight, and $\hat{W}$ is the expected weight calculated from the length/weight relationship (LeCren, 1951).

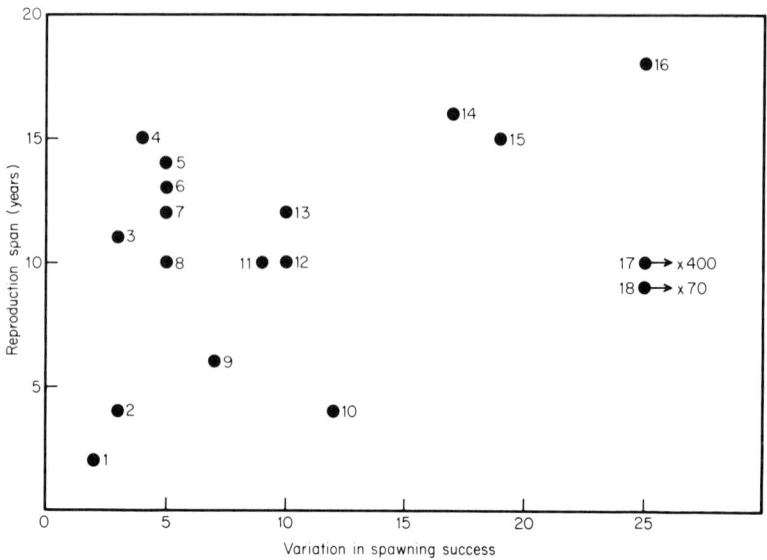

FIG. 1. Relationship between variation in spawning success and reproductive lifespan in some teleost fish. Data from Table I.

biased by the length of the study period, the points generally fit the pattern predicted by Murphy. Two exceptions are the perch, *Perca fluviatilis* L., in Windermere (LeCren, Kipling & McCormack, 1977) and the yellow perch, *P. flavescens* (Mitchill), in Oneida Lake, New York (Forney, 1971). Both show extremely high variation in the strengths of their year-classes. The Windermere population has been subjected to heavy fishing pressure and to heavy predation by pike. The latter is a result of the removal of large numbers of pike with gill-nets, which effectively reduced the mean size of pike in the lake, and in Windermere it is the smaller pike which eat the perch. Clark (1974) modelled the effects of schooling and he concluded that a small increase in either natural or fishing mortality could switch a population from a relatively stable situation, to one subject to violent fluctuations. This may explain the anomalously high variability in the spawning success of these two perch populations.

Trade-Off between Egg Number and Egg Size

In most teleost fish, both absolute fecundity and egg size increase with age or size (length, weight) of fish. However, when account has been taken of such trends, an inverse correlation between fecundity and egg size can often be demonstrated, as would be expected if selection pressures limit the overall reproductive effort. Moreover, intra-specific variations in the fecundity/egg size relationship may be found in populations caught in different years or different localities.

It has been shown for the herring, *Clupea harengus* L., (Blaxter & Hempel, 1963; Hempel, 1965) and trout, *S. trutta*, (Bagenal, 1969) that the larvae from large eggs are bigger than those from small eggs. In addition, their mouth gapes are larger and they can survive for a longer period when starved because of their larger yolk sacs. However, Ciechomski (1966) found no differences between the survival rates of different sizes of starved anchovy larvae, *Engraulis anchoita* Hubbs & Marini, in an environment in which food was scarce. Nevertheless, in most species it is likely that the larvae from the largest eggs are the best equipped to survive under difficult conditions. Added to this, Ware (1975) concluded that the mortality rate of eggs, particularly marine eggs, varies inversely with their size. Therefore eggs which are incubated during the colder months of the year tend to be larger than those incubated during warmer months. In contrast to the benefits accruing from large egg size, the production of larger numbers of eggs will increase the chances of an individual reaching sexual maturity when the juvenile stages are subject to heavy predation. This tends to occur mostly in very productive habitats, especially during the summer months when food organisms are abundant.

LIFE-HISTORY TACTICS

Inter-Specific Variation

The effects of proximate and ultimate factors are often difficult to distinguish in demographic studies, and this difficulty is further complicated in inter-specific investigations. As Stearns (1976) has pointed out, many of the hypotheses explaining the differences between species are plausible, but they cannot be tested experimentally.

Rass (1941) attempted to show the existence of a broad trend in the fecundity/egg size relationship of fish living in arctic waters. He showed that the populations of several different species which lived farthest north produced fewer and larger eggs than more southerly populations of the same species. Moreover, the larger size of eggs occurred despite the slower growth rate and smaller size of the parents. Rass therefore argued that this trend is evidence of parallel evolution, even though the species involved comprised seven different families. Svärdson (1949) took these results a stage further by suggesting a stronger intra-specific competition in the more northerly and cold waters than in the warmer arctic waters further south, although he admitted to a scarcity of supporting field data.

Svärdson (1949), followed by others, also suggested that parental care in teleost fish is associated with reduced fecundity and increased egg size, as later predicted among the tenets of K-selection. Certainly, many fish showing parental care (e.g. Cichlidae, Cottidae, Gasterosteidae, Syngnathidae) produce relatively few eggs, but it is difficult to prove a causal relationship. However, one piece of evidence from the Cichlidae does lend some weight to the argument. Lowe (1955) noted that species of East African *Tilapia* could be separated into two groups; those which built and guarded nests and those which were mouth-brooders. The "brooders" had a lower fecundity and larger egg size than the "guarders" and, as other evidence showed the brooders to be the farthest away from the parental *Tilapia* stock, Lowe suggested that natural selection had been towards increased parental care and an associated reduction in fecundity and increase in egg size.

Williams (1959) claimed the existence of increased fecundity with increased egg protection in three species of darter *Etheostoma* (Percidae), after comparing their relative ovary weights (ovary weight/total weight). However, the specimens were obtained from several habitats over a three-month period and, as the species are batch spawners, it is unlikely that relative ovary weight is a reliable measure of fecundity. It has been shown for several species (Wootton, 1976; Ware, 1977; Fox, 1978) that mean egg size usually decreases with each successive batch laid by an individual female during one spawning season.

Ware (1977) found a close association between larval size in the mackerel, *Scomber scombrus* L., and the size of their planktonic prey. Egg (hence larval) size decreases through the two-month spawning season, as does the size of the zooplankton which are eaten by the newly hatched larvae. In addition, the peak hatching time coincides with the time that the zooplankton are most abundant. Such an adaptation could only have occurred in a predictable environment which enables the laying of the size of eggs to be synchronized with the presence of the optimal size of zooplankton.

In less predictable environments, alternative reproductive strategies have been evolved. Thus, in the cyprinid *Leuciscus leuciscus* (L.), egg size increases with the size (or age) of the parent. Therefore, as reproductive effort is spread over several age-groups, a wider range of egg size occurs than within a single age-group. In addition there can be considerable variation in the relative fecundity and egg size of the same age-groups in different years, and also in the size range of eggs laid by individuals of the same age in different years.

Meien (1940), quoted by Nikolskii (1969), suggested that the size range of eggs increases when the food supply is limited, only oocytes developing close to the main blood vessels in the ovary obtaining an optimal amount of food. Thus eggs along the minor blood vessels will receive less food and therefore will be smaller. When the overall food supply is high, then all the developing oocytes will obtain sufficient food and will therefore grow to approximately the same size. Evidence for this is given by Anokhina (1960) who found a greater variability in egg size in *C. harengus* in the Baltic Sea in years when food was less abundant.

What adaptive advantage does this range of egg size have on individuals in each of the component age-groups? In particular, if large egg size results in the production of larger and more competitive larvae, what selective advantage is there for the smallest (youngest) females to produce a certain number of small eggs instead of fewer, larger eggs? One possibility, which would operate equally well on variation in egg size within an individual female, is that variation in the size of newly hatched larvae would increase the size range of appropriate food organisms. Therefore intra-specific competition between larvae would be reduced, thus increasing the survival chances of each individual.

In some species, e.g. the freshwater bullhead, *Cottus gobio*, the older (larger) fish spawn earlier than the younger age-groups. Incubation of the first spawned eggs is therefore at a lower temperature than those laid later, and we have already mentioned the suggestion by Ware (1975) that mortality rates are inversely correlated with particle size. Thus there is a selective advantage for earlier spawners to produce larger eggs than later spawners. In addition, larvae from later spawners will hatch into an environment containing more smaller food organisms than will be encountered by larvae which, in the case of *C. gobio*, hatch early in the spring.

Intra-Specific Variation

Herring, *Clupea harengus*

The demography of the herring is probably better known than that of any other species of fish, and it is worth examining in some detail. The herring occurs throughout the neritic zone of the northern Atlantic, North Sea and Baltic Sea as several identifiable stocks. Each stock has a specific spawning ground and spawning season, even though adults from different stocks can be found on the same feeding grounds. It is thought that the separate stocks are reproductively isolated, which leads to the possibility of genetic differences between them. Blaxter (1955) crossed spring spawners from the Scottish west coast with autumn spawners from the east coast, and obtained viable offspring. He therefore concluded that these two groups were not completely separated, either physiologically or genetically. However, because of the unlikelihood of significant gene flow between the two stocks, some progress towards allopatric speciation had occurred. Later (Blaxter, 1958) he considered that either the two stocks have only recently diverged, hence their close morphological similarity, or geographical isolation had resulted in insufficient competition between the stocks to cause a greater divergence.

The eggs of each stock are laid, and the larvae hatch, into different environmental conditions. Some experimental studies have been made to determine how far the differences in reproductive effort/longevity and fecundity/egg size, between the stocks, are due to proximal factors and how far environmental differences have resulted in the selection of genetically distinct life-history tactics, although generally the results are not conclusive. Bibov (1960) transferred herring eggs from the Baltic Sea to the Aral Sea and found that the progeny had a faster growth rate in the Aral. The mean absolute fecundity was also higher in the Aral population, but this could be explained entirely in terms of their greater adult size. As the fecundity/length relationship was the same in the two populations, this suggests that it is controlled by ultimate factors. Blaxter & Holliday (1963) suggested that the maximum absolute fecundity of a fish is genetically determined, but is attained only under ideal environmental conditions. Proximal factors, such as water temperature and food availability, were postulated as influences which could reduce this optimal fecundity.

Herring of the same size in the various stocks put approximately the same amount of energy into reproduction although, within each population, reproductive effort increases with age. An exception is the Norwegian stock which has a much lower reproductive effort and a greater longevity, as predicted by a reproductive effort/longevity trade-off. Cushing (1967) suggested that fluctuations in the recruitment of herring are correlated with fluctuations in the timing and amplitude of the production cycle (i.e. zooplankton abundance), which in turn increases with depth. Thus stocks which live in deeper waters will show greater fluctuations in their year-class strengths. The Norwegian stock exemplifies this (Murphy, 1977). The increase in maximum longevity to 23 years, compared with 12 to 16 years in other Atlantic stocks (Cushing, 1967), plus a reduced reproductive effort, is the response that the bet-hedging theory would predict under conditions of highly variable juvenile mortality.

As a species the herring spawns throughout the year, but each stock has a short, well-defined spawning season. Figure 2 shows the fecundity and mean dry weight of eggs laid throughout the year by different stocks (Blaxter, 1969).

Hempel (1965) speculated that the different compromises reached in the trade-off between egg size and number, implied by Fig. 2, are mainly a result of selection rather than proximal factors. In a new environment, only slight differences in the fecundity/egg size relationship can have a strong selective advantage and an optimal relationship should be reached quickly. There is a convincing basis to support the existence of such selective pressures. The winter and early spring spawners have a larger mean egg size and lower relative fecundity than the summer and autumn spawners. The explanation which is generally accepted is that, because the winter and spring spawners lay their eggs in colder water, their larvae will hatch into an environment providing a less abundant food supply than in the summer and autumn. Therefore there will be selection for greater food reserves. Furthermore, in the winter and spring, the zooplankton organisms tend to be relatively large and therefore selection in these stocks has favoured the production of eggs with sufficient resources to

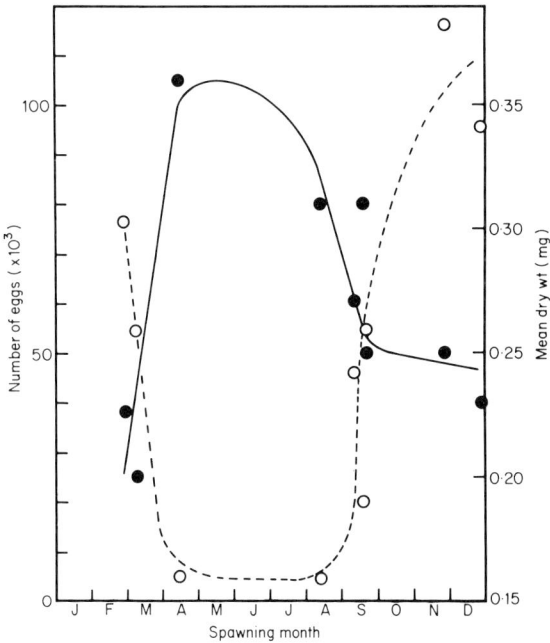

FIG. 2. Fecundity (●) and mean dry weight of ripe *Clupea harengus* eggs (○) in relation to the spawning season (redrawn from Blaxter, 1969).

produce larvae which are large enough to find and ingest them. Conversely, the summer and autumn spawned progeny hatch into more favourable feeding conditions but face higher predation pressure, e.g. from medusae through which the larvae pass on their way from the demersal eggs to feed on the surface zooplankton (Blaxter & Holliday, 1963). Therefore selection will push the compromise between egg size and number in the direction of higher relative fecundity, even at the cost of smaller egg size. An added complication to all this arises from work by Anokhina (1960) on the White Sea herring which suggested that the fat content of the mother influences the range in egg size. Lean fish produced the widest range and Anokhina considered this to be favourable for the survival of the largest larvae. However, Hempel (1965) could find no such effect in North Sea herring.

Plaice, *Pleuronectes platessa*

Many other species, as well as herring, show geographic variations in fecundity. Bagenal (1966) concluded that such variations in the plaice could mostly be explained as adaptations by individual fish to such proximal factors as water temperature and food supply. However, plaice in the Baltic Sea and Trondheim Fjord did have a much higher relative fecundity and he concluded that a racial or genetic explanation was required. Data given by Simpson (1951) show that Baltic plaice have a smaller mean weight per egg associated with their higher fecundity. Both Simpson (1951) and Bagenal (1966) discount food availability as influencing fecundity, the latter because Baltic plaice have not increased their fecundity level even though their population density has been considerably reduced by fishing. Marking experiments (Bagenal, 1966) have shown that the Baltic and Trondheim plaice do not mix with other North Sea stocks, and this has facilitated the evolution of their sub specific fecundity characteristics. The selection pressures involved, however, remain uncertain although one possibility may be that the larvae are subject to a higher level of predation than occurs in other plaice populations. Nikolskii (1969) considered this to be the reason for the high fecundity of *C. harengus* in the White Sea, and it might explain the high fecundity of other species in the Baltic Sea and Trondheim Fjord.

Bullhead, *Cottus gobio*

A simple trade-off between egg number and egg size is not the only mechanism adopted by a species living in a variety of environments. The freshwater bullhead, *Cottus gobio* L., inhabits streams and lakes throughout England and Wales, and exhibits a range of reproductive strategies associated with its potential to be a batch spawner (Fox, 1978). In the relatively warm, very productive, southern chalk streams, *C. gobio* has a fast growth rate, a short lifespan (two to three years) and individual females lay up to four or five batches of eggs in one spawning season, which lasts from late February into June. In the acid moorland streams of the north Pennines, which represent the northern limit of the species in Britain, spawning is confined to a two- to three-week period in April when each female lays only one batch of eggs. Recruitment is highly variable owing to the occasional catastrophic mortalities of eggs or larvae caused by severe spates (Crisp, Mann & McCormack, 1975). If the lowland reproductive lifespan of two to three years was maintained, the chance of an individual female's progeny surviving to maturity would clearly be reduced, especially if environmental conditions allowed only a single batch of eggs to be laid each year. Thus the much greater longevity (eight to 10 years) of the northern population may have been an adaptive response to spread reproductive effort over several generations.

This trend to greater longevity, like all adaptive mechanisms, can only operate at the level of the individual. However, it will have the consequence of enabling the population to persist in a fluctuating environment. The price of this increased survival involves a diversion of energy resources away from reproduction, i.e. from multiple broods to a single brood.

Smyly (1957) found that *C. gobio* in Windermere had more and larger eggs than fish of the same size in the afferent river Brathay. This appears to be an exception to the usual inverse correlation between fecundity and egg size. In fact, Smyly found that females of the same size in the two habitats had the same number of eggs at an early maturation stage of the ovary (ignoring the very small, immature oocytes <0·5 mm in diameter), but the Windermere fish ripened more of these eggs than did the river population. Windermere bullheads have a faster growth rate than Brathay fish and therefore differences in their ovary development may be associated with differences in water temperature and abundance of food organisms between the two habitats.

Again there is no satisfactory evidence as to the extent to which the different spawning strategies of river and lake, and northern and southern, bullhead populations are only a result of proximal influences, or to what extent (if any) the populations differ genetically.

Brown trout, *Salmo trutta*

Differences between the fecundities of trout from fertile and infertile streams were observed by McFadden, Cooper & Anderson (1965). Trout from the infertile streams had fewer eggs and a lower total weight of eggs compared with trout of the same size in the more productive streams. Differences in egg size did not affect the fecundity differences, except in one fertile stream in which significantly larger eggs were produced. Earlier, Miller (1957) had concluded that there was little evidence of changes in trout populations due to alterations in their gene pools, but the data given by McFadden *et al.* (1965) suggest that genetic differences do exist. However the latter did state that any genetic difference could be considered environmental, in the sense that selection pressures led to its establishment and maintenance.

DISCUSSION

Teleost fish have successfully colonized most of the world's marine and freshwater habitats and, to a large extent, they have done so because of their ability to adapt their life-history tactics in response to environmental conditions. However, it is difficult to gain an insight into the development of such tactics by comparing those of different species, even where the species are closely related. Account must be taken of too many variables to make such comparisons meaningful. A more promising approach is to examine one species living under different environmental conditions. In this paper, we have looked at four such species, namely *C. harengus*, *P. platessa*, *C. gobio* and *S. trutta*. Here the stumbling block is the separation of the influences of proximate and ultimate factors, and experimental work, utilizing species which exhibit variations in life-history tactics over the range of their natural habitats, is very much needed. Svärdson (1949) made the same observation in his review of natural selection and egg number in fish, and little progress appears to have been made since then. The majority of observations have been correlative but, as emphasized by

Stearns (1976), for any set of correlative observations an infinite number of theoretical hypotheses can be constructed to predict the same correlation.

The choice by a fish species of a particular set of life-history tactics cannot usually be predicted from the theories of r- and K-selection. Instead, when pre-reproductive survival is uncertain, and the fluctuations in that survival rate are greater than those in adult fish, then the reverse of r- and K-predictions occurs. Thus selection is not towards a single "big-bang" reproduction (semelparity), involving a high reproductive effort, but is towards iteroparity, with lower reproductive effort and increased longevity, as seen in *Clupea harengus*. This has been termed bet-hedging (Stearns, 1976). Under natural conditions, such a strategy protects populations against catastrophic population crashes of the type experienced by the Pacific sardine, when overfishing removed the insurance of having several spawning generations.

In predictable environments, fish often become highly specialized in their reproductive tactics. Reduced fecundity in association with parental care, which appears to occur in the Cichlidae, may make such populations less able to survive unexpected changes in their environment, because of the close relationship which exists between stock and recruitment. Other species, such as *Scomber scombrus*, which are highly dependent upon the timing and amplitude of the zooplankton cycle, may also be vulnerable to environmental changes.

In less predictable environments, fish are generally less specialized and many have the ability to modify their reproductive tactics in accordance with environmental fluctuations. Thus, *Cottus gobio* can produce one or more batches of eggs during one season, depending upon the water temperature and food availability. In addition, individuals of some species (e.g. *Leuciscus leuciscus*) may produce a wider range of egg sizes than occurs in fish in more predictable habitats. A further modification, which appears to be widespread, is the trade-off which can occur between egg number and egg size, as demonstrated by the work by Anokhina (1960) on Baltic herring.

ACKNOWLEDGEMENTS

The authors wish to thank Dr J. H. S. Blaxter for his valuable comments on the preparation of this paper.

REFERENCES

Aass, P. (1972). Age determination and year-class fluctuations of cisco, *Coregonus albula* L., in the Mjosa hydroelectric reservoir, Norway. *Rep. Inst. Freshwat. Res. Drottningholm* **52**: 5–22.

Anokhina, L. E. (1960). Interrelations between fecundity, variability of the size of the eggs and fatness of mother fish in Onega herring. *Dokl. Akad. Nauk SSSR* **133**: 960–963.

Bagenal, T. B. (1966). The ecological and geographical aspects of fecundity of plaice. *J. mar. biol. Ass. U.K.* **46**: 161–186.

Bagenal, T. B. (1969). The relationship between food supply and fecundity in brown trout *Salmo trutta* L. *J. Fish Biol.* **1**: 167–182.

Bagenal, T. B. (1973). Fish fecundity and its relations with stock and recruitment. *Rapp. P.-v. Réun. Cons. perm. int. Explor. Mer* **164**: 186–198.

Beverton, R. J. H. & Holt, S. J. (1957). On the dynamics of exploited fish populations. *Fishery Invest., Lond.* (2) **19**: 1–533.

Bibov, N. E. (1960). Acclimatization of salaka (Baltic herring) *Clupea harengus membras* L. in the Aral Sea. *I.C.E.S. Herring Committee, Paper* No. 135 (mimeo.) 1–9.

Blaxter, J. H. S. (1955). Herring rearing I. The storage of herring gametes. *Mar. Res.* No. 3: 1–12.

Blaxter, J. H. S. (1958). The racial problem in herring from the viewpoint of recent physiological, evolutionary and genetical theory. *Rapp. P.-v. Réun. Cons. perm. int. Explor. Mer* **143**: 10–19.

Blaxter, J. H. S. (1969). Development: Eggs and larvae. In *Fish physiology* **3**: 177–252. Hoar, W. S. & Randall, D. J. (eds). New York & London: Academic Press.

Blaxter, J. H. S. & Hempel, G. (1963). The influence of egg size on herring larvae (*Clupea harengus* L.). *J. Cons. perm. int. Explor. Mer* **28**: 211–240.

Blaxter, J. H. S. & Holliday, F. G. T. (1963). The behaviour and physiology of herring and other clupeids. *Adv. mar. Biol.* **1**: 261–293.

Bryant, E. H. (1971). Life historical consequences of natural selection: Cole's result. *Am. Nat.* **105**: 75–77.

Calow, P. (1977). Evolution, ecology and energetics: a study in metabolic adaptation. *Adv. ecol. Res.* **10**: 1–61.

Charnov, E. L. & Schaffer, W. M. (1973). Life history consequences of natural selection: Cole's result revisited. *Am. Nat.* **107**: 791–793.

Ciechomski, J. D. de (1966). Development of the larvae and variations in the size of the eggs of the Argentine anchovy *Engraulis anchoita* Hubbs and Marini. *J. Cons. perm. int. Explor. Mer* **30**: 281–290.

Clark, C. W. (1974). Possible effects of schooling on the dynamics of exploited fish populations. *J. Cons. perm. int. Explor. Mer* **36**: 7–14.

Cole, L. C. (1954). The population consequences of life history phenomena. *Q. Rev. Biol.* **29**: 103–137.

Crisp, D. T., Mann, R. H. K. & McCormack, Jean C. (1975). The populations of fish in the River Tees system on the Moor House National Nature Reserve, Westmorland. *J. Fish Biol.* **7**: 573–593.

Cushing, D. H. (1967). The grouping of herring populations. *J. mar. biol. Ass. U.K.* **47**: 193–208.

Forney, J. L. (1971). Development of dominant year classes in a yellow perch population. *Trans. Am. Fish. Soc.* **100**: 739–749.

Fox, P. J. (1978). Preliminary observations on different reproduction strategies in the bullhead (*Cottus gobio* L.) in northern and southern England. *J. Fish Biol.* **12**: 5–11.

Gadgil, M. & Bossert, W. (1970). Life-historical consequences of natural selection. *Am. Nat.* **104**: 1–24.

176   R. H. K. MANN and C. A. MILLS

Hempel, G. (1965). On the importance of larval survival for the population dynamics of marine food fish. *Rep. Calif. coop. oceanic. Fish. Invest.* **10**: 13–23.

Hile, R. (1954). Fluctuations in growth and year-class strength of the walleye in Saginaw Bay. *Fishery Bull. Fish Wildl. Serv. U.S.* **56**: 7–59.

Hislop, J. R. G. (1975). The breeding and growth of whiting, *Merlangius merlangus* in captivity. *J. Cons. perm. int. Explor. Mer* **36**: 119–127.

Holgate, P. (1967). Population survival and life-history phenomena. *J. theoret. Biol.* **14**: 1–10.

Kipling, C. & Frost, W. E. (1969). Variations in the fecundity of pike *Esox lucius* L. in Windermere. *J. Fish Biol.* **1**: 221–237.

Kramer, R. H. & Smith, L. L. (1962). Formation of year classes in largemouth bass. *Trans. Am. Fish. Soc.* **91**: 29–41.

Lack, D. (1947). The significance of clutch-size. *Ibis* **89**: 302–352.

Lack, D. (1948a). The significance of clutch-size. *Ibis* **90**: 25–45.

Lack, D. (1948b). The significance of litter-size. *J. Anim. Ecol.* **17**: 45–50.

Lack, D. (1948c). Natural selection and family size in the starling. *Evolution, N.Y.* **2**: 95–110.

LeCren, E. D. (1951). The length-weight relationship and seasonal cycle in gonad weight and condition in the perch (*Perca fluviatilis*). *J. Anim. Ecol.* **20**: 201–219.

LeCren, E. D., Kipling, Charlotte & McCormack, Jean C. (1977). A study of the numbers, biomass and year-class strengths of perch (*Perca fluviatilis* L.) in Windermere from 1941 to 1966. *J. Anim. Ecol.* **46**: 281–307.

Lowe, Rosemary H. (1955). The fecundity of *Tilapia* species. *E. Afr. agric. J.* **21**: 45–52.

MacArthur, R. H. & Wilson, E. O. (1967). *Theory of island biogeography.* Princeton: Princeton Univ. Press.

Mann, R. H. K. (1973). Observations on the age, growth, reproduction and food of the roach *Rutilus rutilus* (L.) in two rivers in southern England. *J. Fish Biol.* **5**: 707–736.

Mann, R. H. K. (1974). Observations on the age, growth, reproduction and food of the dace, *Leuciscus leuciscus* (L.) in two rivers in southern England. *J. Fish Biol.* **6**: 237–253.

Mann, R. H. K. (1976). Observations on the age, growth, reproduction and food of the chub *Squalius cephalus* (L.) in the River Stour, Dorset. *J. Fish Biol.* **8**: 265–288.

Markus, H. C. (1934). Life history of the black-head minnow, *Pimephales promelas. Copeia* **1934**: 116–122.

McFadden, J. T., Cooper, E. L. & Anderson, J. K. (1965). Some effects of environment on egg production in brown trout (*Salmo trutta*). *Limnol. Oceanogr.* **10**: 88–95.

McNeil, W. J. (1964). Redd superimposition and egg capacity of pink salmon spawning beds. *J. Fish. Res. Bd Can.* **21**: 1385–1396.

Meien, V. A. (1940). [Causes of the fluctuations in the year class strength of teleost fishes.] *Dokl. Akad. Nauk SSSR* **28**: 653–656. [In Russian.]

Miller, R. B. (1957). Have the genetic patterns of fishes been altered by introductions or by selective fishing? *J. Fish. Res. Bd Can.* **14**: 797–806.

Murdoch, W. W. (1966). Population stability and life history phenomena. *Am. Nat.* **100**: 45–51.

Murphy, G. I. (1968). Pattern in life history and the environment. *Am. Nat.* **102**: 390–404.

Murphy, G. I. (1977). Clupeoids. In *Fish population dynamics*: 283–308. Gulland, J. A. (ed.). Bath: The Pitman Press.

Nikolskii, G. V. (1969). *Fish population dynamics*. Edinburgh: Oliver & Boyd.

Pianka, E. R. (1970). On "r" and "K" selection. *Am. Nat.* **104**: 592–597.

Rass, T. S. (1941). [Analogous or parallel variations in structure and development of fishes in northern and arctic seas.] *Moskv. Obshch. Ispyt. Prir. 1805–1940*: 1–60. [In Russian.]

Schaffer, W. M. (1974). Optimal reproduction in fluctuating environments. *Am. Nat.* **108**: 783–790.

Scott, D. P. (1962). Effects of food quantity on fecundity of rainbow trout *Salmo gairdneri*. *J. Fish. Res. Bd Can.* **19**: 715–731.

Simpson, A. C. (1951). The fecundity of plaice (*Pleuronectes platessa* L.). *Fishery Invest., Lond.* (2) **17**: 1–27.

Smyly, W. J. P. (1957). The life-history of the bullhead or miller's thumb (*Cottus gobio* L.). *Proc. zool. Soc. Lond.* **128**: 431–453.

Stearns, S. C. (1976). Life history tactics: a review of the ideas. *Q. Rev. Biol.* **51**: 3–47.

Stevens, D. E. (1977). Striped bass (*Morone saxatilis*) year class strengths in relation to river flow in the Sacramento–San Joaquin estuary, California. *Trans. Am. Fish. Soc.* **106**: 34–42.

Svärdson, G. (1949). Natural selection and egg number in fish. *Rep. Inst. Freshwat. Res. Drottningholm* No. 29: 115–122.

Ware, D. M. (1975). Relation between egg size, growth and natural mortality of larval fish. *J. Fish. Res. Bd Can.* **32**: 2503–2512.

Ware, D. M. (1977). Spawning time and egg size of Atlantic mackerel, *Scomber scombrus*, in relation to the plankton. *J. Fish. Res. Bd Can.* **34**: 2308–2315.

Williams, G. C. (1959). Ovary weights of darters: a test of the alleged association of parental care with reduced fecundity in fishes. *Copeia* **1959**: 18–24.

Wootton, R. J. (1976). *The biology of the sticklebacks*. London: Academic Press.

Symp. zool. Soc. Lond. (1979) No. 44, 179–205

Senescence in Fishes

A. D. WOODHEAD

Brookhaven National Laboratory, Upton, New York, USA

SYNOPSIS

A long-standing theory, that there is a fundamental difference in aging between fishes and higher vertebrates, is still alive in the minds of many. In 1932, Bidder proposed that aging was causatively related to the cessation of growth at sexual maturity. Fish, which continue to grow throughout their lives, would not age, and therefore were potentially immortal. His ideas were clearly disproven by Comfort (1961), who established that the survival curves of a laboratory population of guppies, *Poecilia reticulata*, were very similar to those of a small mammal population under laboratory conditions. Recent data from field and laboratory studies, including histological evidence, amply confirm the occurrence of senescence in fishes.

Natural death in fish has been associated with reproduction. There is good evidence for a number of species which shows that, with increasing size, the gonad forms a greater proportion of total body weight. In older, larger fish, extensive energy depletion for reproduction is suggested as an important factor in mortality. Reproductive modifications in older fish are also noted.

INTRODUCTION

The concept that fish may be potentially immortal has existed in the literature for more than a century. This suggestion, first made by Ray Lankester, was elaborated by Bidder (1932), who believed that senescence was a result of the cessation of growth. This idea seems to fit mammals well. Mammals have a well-defined lifespan, growing to attain an adult size characteristic of the species; their growth then ceases or declines dramatically and changes associated with aging[a] start to appear. Many fish do not show this pattern. They continue to grow throughout their lifespan and do not exhibit a sharp fall in growth rate at maturity, nor do they show obvious and marked signs of aging. Bidder (1932) considered that fish with continued growth throughout life and indeterminate size would not age, being potentially immortal. He based his arguments upon his studies with the female plaice, *Pleuronectes platessa* L., which shows continuous slow growth over a long period and no apparent senescence (Bidder, 1925).

It is, perhaps, not surprising to find that Bidder's ideas are still advanced today (Kohn, 1971), although senescence in fish is known to fisheries biologists or, indeed, to anyone who has kept small fish in home aquaria. The subject has, however, been considered only on a very limited

[a] Current usage indicates that "aging" relates to senescence, and "ageing" to estimation of age (Ed.).

basis. There are few experimental data, and senescence in wild populations of fish is rarely seen unless the population is unexploited.

EVIDENCE FOR AGING IN FISH

Bidder's hypothesis was clearly disproven by Comfort (1961), who made
studies with laboratory populations of guppies, *Poecilia reticulata* Peters,
to find out whether the mortality rate increased with increasing age. At
that time, there were few field data on fish mortality available, and no
captive population of any cold-blooded vertebrate had been kept under
observation for long enough to determine the form of the age-mortality
curve. These studies still remain the most detailed to have been made.
The findings were decisive: under all experimental conditions the rate of
mortality rose with age. As the environment in which the fish were kept
was improved, the survival curves progressively approached a rectan-
gular configuration, i.e. more individuals in the population lived for a
longer time, but the maximum lifespan for the species was not altered
(Fig. 1). This work clearly established that fish show increasing mortality
with age. At the same time, they may continue growing, although the
growth rate may be slight during the latter phases of the lifespan.

Since that time, there have been few attempts to trace the aging
process through the lifespan of any other species. Walford & Liu (1965)

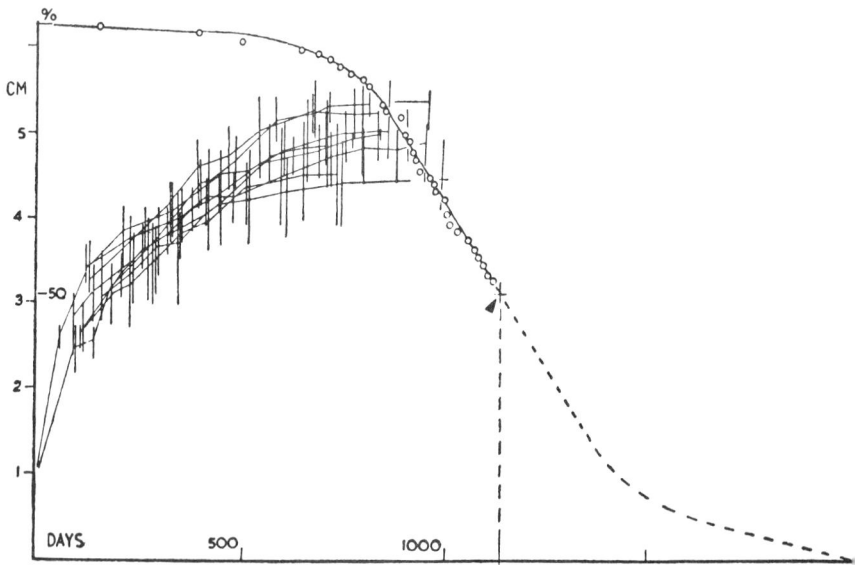

FIG. 1. Growth and mortality curves for female *Poecilia reticulata* (from Comfort, 1964).

have given survival curves for aquarium populations of the annual fish, *Cynolebias adloffi* Ahl. There was almost 100% survival of the females until the age of 10 months; thereafter mortality increased, and all of the females were dead by 14 months. The mortality of male fish increased from six to nine months and, by 13 months, there were no survivors. Accompanying the rise of the mortality rate, the fish showed evidence of senility, including gradual curvature of the spine, clouding of the cornea, exophthalmos and "generally ragged appearance". For the rice medaka, *Oryzias latipes* (Schlegel), another small oviparous cyprinodont, Egami & Etoh (1969) found that the mortality curve of fish (kept in outdoor tanks) resembled that shown by the female guppy, except that seasonal fluctuations in mortality rate were considerable under the more natural conditions of maintenance and that lifespan was shorter in *Oryzias* (Egami, 1971).

Other information on aging in fish comes from papers which are principally concerned with the growth dynamics of fish populations. Amongst these, there are relatively few instances in which direct estimates are available of the natural mortality, since most stocks are subject to commercial fisheries and differences in natural mortality with age are small compared with mortality due to fishing. Values have, however, been obtained from data collected at times when fishing was curtailed as during wartime, or when sampling of the population was begun before heavy fishing started. These data show that mortality increases throughout the lifespan as in mammals, although there are considerable differences in the form of the survival curves between species. In some, the survival rate is almost linear over the whole of the observed range. Thus, in many long-lived fish, such as the sturgeon, *Acipenser nudiventris* Lovetzky, and the plaice, *Pleuronectes platessa*, mortality seems to be almost constant at about 5–10% per year over a considerable span of the life history (Probst & Cooper, 1955; Alm, 1951; LeCren, 1958). For sturgeon older than 30 years, however, the mortality rate increases rapidly. Cushing (1975) has shown that, for plaice, specific growth rates and mortality rates become equal at a critical age of 16 years. After this "critical" age, senescent mortality takes place.

At the other extreme, some fish show a sharp rise in mortality rate at the onset of maturity. This reaches its extreme form in semelparous species in which all, or nearly all, of the population die after their first spawning. The well-known examples of so-called "parental death" are freshwater eels, *Anguilla* spp.; Pacific salmon, *Oncorhynchus* spp.; the Atlantic salmon, *Salmo salar* L.; the lampreys, *Lampetra* spp.; and the capelin, *Mallotus villosus* (Müller). In the majority of these fish, the males suffer heavy post-spawning mortality whilst a number of females may survive to spawn again. These species are particularly interesting because of the suggestion that their death may represent accelerated aging. In the space of a few months, or even weeks, the condition of the salmon migrating in fresh water changes drastically, and the spawning fish is a very poor counterpart of the lively, healthy individual that entered the river. Migrating salmon show histological evidence of deterioration of the stomach, liver, spleen, thymus, thyroid, pituitary, kidney, and cardiovascular system. The skin, and the islets of the pancreas, also exhibit hypertrophy and hyperplasia. Some investigators believe that the postspawning death of the salmon is directly related to greatly elevated levels of circulating adrenocorticosteroids (Robertson & Wexler, 1960) whilst others have related death to elevated gonadal hormones (Van Overbeeke & McBride, 1971). Childs & Law (1972) suggest that varying maximum lifespans seen in male fish within a population of Pacific coho salmon, *Oncorhynchus kisutch* (Walbaum), may reflect differences in their early rate of growth and differentiation.

Between these two extreme forms of the survival curve there are many species in which the mortality rate increases steadily with age. Analyses of the natural mortality rate of the Pacific herring, *Clupea pallasi* Valenciennes, throughout its lifespan (Table I), provide a good example of an

TABLE I

The increase in natural mortality with age in the Pacific herring, Clupea pallasi

Age interval	0–1	1–2	2–3	3–4	4–5	5–6	6–7	7–8	8–9
Mortality	0·12	0·25	0·38	0·51	0·64	0·77	0·90	1·03	1·16

From Taylor *et al.* (1958).

increase in mortality with age, rising from a value of 0·12 from the post-larval stage to one year, to 1·16 to ages eight and nine years (Taylor *et al.*, 1958). A similar pattern of increased mortality with age has been reported by Kennedy (1954) for lake trout, *Cristivomer namaycush* (Walbaum), by Wohlschlag (1954) for Alaskan whitefish, *Leucichthys sardinella* (Valenciennes), and by Mann (1973) for the roach, *Rutilus rutilus* (L.). Williams (1967) found the same relationship in four species of freshwater fish from the River Thames, England.

In summary, data from populations of fish in the wild, together with the experimental findings, show that aging occurs in fish, despite their continued growth (Comfort, 1964). There would seem to be no justification for considering that fish are potentially immortal.

ANATOMICAL CHANGES WITH AGE

The view that aging in fish is similar to that in higher vertebrates has been most strongly advocated by comparative pathologists but their claims have often been made on the basis of rather few observations. There seems little doubt that the demonstration of aging changes in fish tissues, comparable to those seen in mammals, would provide strong evidence indicative of a common process (Comfort, 1964). The lack of information for fish and for other cold-blooded vertebrates becomes particularly apparent when the situation is compared with that for mammals and domestic animals, where the literature is very detailed. But death from senescence is rare in fish in the wild, except perhaps in a few unexploited situations. Furthermore, as Comfort (1957) has pointed out, "biologists have been surprisingly incurious about the fate which finally overtakes the animals they investigate". Most of the evidence available comes from a limited number of histological surveys of captive, small, short-lived fish. Under optimal conditions in aquaria, these fish have often lived beyond the end of their reproductive period, and show clear anatomical evidence of senility.

The Gonads

The ovary

The ovary has been an important object for aging studies in mammals, and, in fish, it has received more attention than any other organ. We have made a histological study of the ovaries of a laboratory population of guppies, *Poecilia reticulata*, throughout their lifespan, distinguishing three phases of development (Woodhead & Ellett, 1969b). Young fish, about six months, had ovaries closely packed with small oogonia, which had recently differentiated from the germinal epithelium; a number of larger primary oocytes, which had undergone a minor cytoplasmic growth phase, were also present. As the fish approached sexual maturity, the primary oocytes began to show cytoplasmic differentiation, and, shortly after, oil droplets and small discrete granules of yolk were deposited within the differentiated cytoplasmic ring. The eggs rapidly increased in size and the yolk granules filled the entire cytoplasmic area. Successive waves of oogonia entered the growth cycle as earlier ones were spawned.

Guppies reached full reproductive capacity between the ages of 10 and 12 months, after which there was a gradual fall in the numbers of ripe eggs in the ovary. This depletion became marked after 30 months and, in older fish, there were very few ripe eggs. At the same time, ripe eggs present in the ovary became atretic and were gradually resorbed. Initially, there was no decline in the numbers of primary oocytes in the ovaries, but, in old fish, oocytes in all stages of development were affected by atresia.

Failure of vitellogenesis and atrophy of ripe eggs were the principal and the most conspicuous signs of aging in the ovary of the guppy, but there was a notable infiltration and proliferation of connective tissue and stoma throughout the ovary, as well as marked thickening of the ovarian wall (Fig. 2a). There was an increase in the numbers of "yellow" cells containing deposits of brightly staining pigment, which appeared similar to those described in the aging ovaries of women and rodents (Thung, 1961).

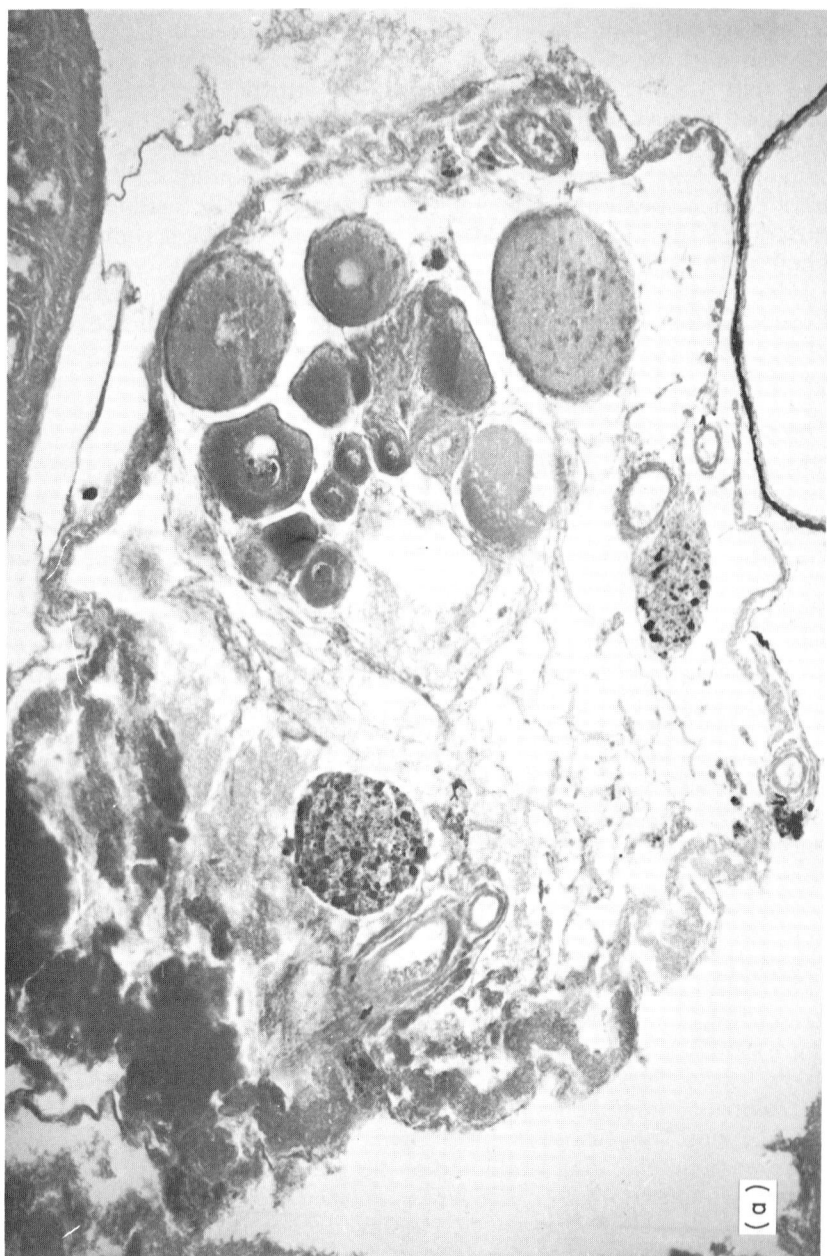

(a)

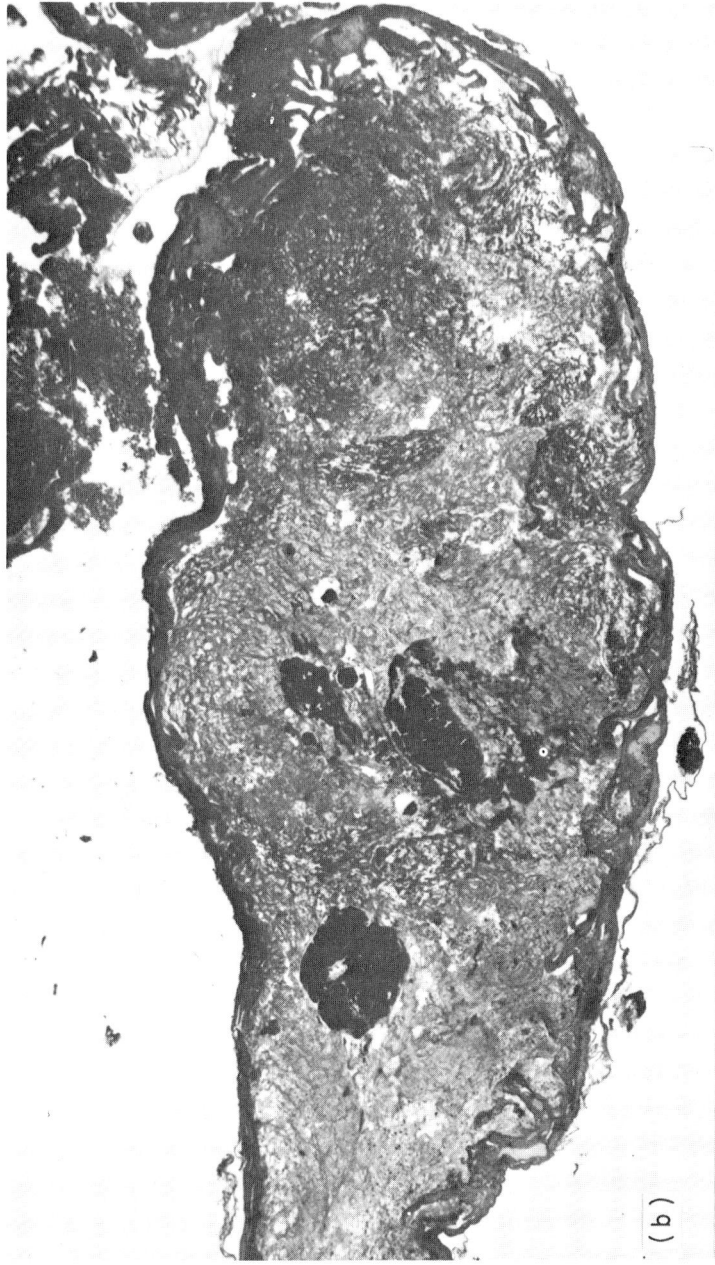

Fig. 2 (a) Ovary of old guppy, *Poecilia reticulata*, showing degenerate eggs, infiltration of connective tissue, and thickening of the ovarian wall, ×74. (b) Ovary of senile fighting fish, *Betta splendens*; the ovary is very shrunken, consisting of intermingled stroma, connective tissue and remains of eggs, ×40.

Gonadal senescence regularly precedes somatic senescence in captive Siamese fighting fish, *Betta splendens* Regan, and the fish may live for up to a year after the complete cessation of reproductive activity. The post-reproductive period is much more strongly defined than in the guppy, and fighting fish may remain in good physical condition throughout this phase, until shortly before death. Aging changes in the ovary were much more extreme and dramatic than those seen in guppies; they first became apparent in fish of about 16 months of age (Woodhead, 1974b). The most obvious signs were, again, failure of vitellogenesis and atrophy of ripe eggs present in the ovaries. There was no impairment of the growth and development of earlier stage eggs at first, but, after 20 months, atretic changes were seen in growing oocytes, leaving only the primary oocytes unaffected. The ovaries of fish older than 30 months contained no yolky eggs and all the development stages showed atresia. There was a progressive increase with age in the connective tissue and in the thickness of the ovarian walls. In the oldest fish (50 months), the ovaries had become much shrunken, and consisted principally of intermingled stroma and connective tissue, enclosing a few atretic eggs (Fig. 2b). Considerable individual variation was found in the rate and progress of aging. We have observed some decline in ovarian function in aged Amazon mollies, *Poecilia formosa*, which is manifested in a similar way—by a reduction in vitellogenesis and progressive infiltration of the gland by connective tissue (Woodhead & Setlow, in preparation). Haranghy and his colleagues (Haranghy *et al.*, 1977) studied reproduction and aging in the bitterling, *Rhodeus sericeus amarus* (Bloch), and failed to observe any marked deteriorative change in the ovary during the course of the lifespan ($3\frac{1}{2}$ years), other than the presence of a few atretic ova in older females.

An interesting finding, which emerged from fecundity studies with the haddock, *Melanogrammus aeglefinus* (L.); the herring, *Clupea harengus* L.; the plaice, *Pleuronectes platessa*, and the long rough dab, *Hippoglossoides platessoides* (Fabricius), was that the weight of the ovaries increased with age at a rate more rapid than that of increase in egg number. Since there was no concomitant increase in egg size, Hickling (1940) concluded that the permanent tissue of the ovary increased disproportionately as the fish grew older. Gerking (1959) sustained this view, suggesting that if the reproductive elements of the ovary are replaced by connective tissue in old age, then aging changes in the fish ovary would be comparable to those seen in the higher vertebrates. Unfortunately, this has not been verified histologically.

The changes in the aging ovary parallel those seen in fish after the removal of the pituitary gland. Hypophysectomy results in the failure of yolk deposition and any yolk-filled eggs in the ovary at the time of the operation become degenerate (Barr, 1963). The similarities between senile ovaries and the ovaries of hypophysectomized fish suggest that there has been decline in pituitary function in old age. But degeneration of early phase oocytes, infiltration of the ovary by connective tissue and thickening of the ovarian wall are not found after hypophysectomy; these features probably represent autonomous aging processes in the ovary itself.

The testis

Aging changes in the testes of mammals are minor ones compared to those in the ovary; normal spermatogenesis usually continues until the end of the lifespan. Woodhead & Ellett (1969a) followed the histological changes in the testes of guppies, *Poecilia reticulata*, aged two to 59 months. In the youngest individuals, the testes consisted almost entirely of cysts filled with large spermatogonia. Secondary spermatogonia were produced in large numbers as the fish approached first maturity at about four to five months of age, and shortly afterwards, primary spermatocytes and secondary spermatocytes appeared, initially localized in isolated bundles. Spermatogenesis was rapid and continuous in fish from six to 12 months. After this, there was a very gradual loss of spermatogenic tissue, infiltration of connective tissue into the body of the testis and thickening of the testis wall. Deposits of yellow "aging" pigment, melanin, and adipose tissue were common in older fish, and atrophic cysts were quite frequently observed side by side with normal cysts. Despite these aging changes, considerable areas of normal tissue were found in the testes of most senile males and normal spermatozoa were produced in old age (Fig. 3a).

Aging changes were observed in the testes of Siamese fighting fish, *Betta splendens*, from about the age of 14 months, when a few atretic cysts were noted; thereafter, the number of atretic cysts gradually increased (Woodhead, 1974a). There was progressive infiltration of the gland by connective tissue elements, and pigmentation was prominent in older fish. Adipose tissue also increased slightly with age. In the oldest fish examined (50 months), atrophy of the testis had progressed much further than in senile male guppies, and, in one or two individuals, the testes had been greatly reduced in size and were almost completely atrophic (Fig. 3b).

In their study of age changes in the testis of the characin, *Astyanax mexicanus* (Filippi), Rasquin & Hafter (1951) have described progressive infiltration of connective tissue into the testis from its outer capsule and an increase of testicular connective tissue. The testis of old characins contained much adipose tissue and large numbers of hyperchromic cells. There were many insoluble calcified "concentrations" which were strikingly similar to the concentrations in the aging prostate of man and other mammals. In parts of the testis, the epithelium of the spermatic tubules had degenerated, yet a large part of the gland remained functional, producing normal spermatozoa. Krumholz (1948) reported somewhat similar findings in the western mosquito fish, *Gambusia affinis affinis*, (Baird & Girard). There were no marked alterations with age seen in the structure of the testes of the bitterling, *Rhodeus sericeus amarus*, (Haranghy

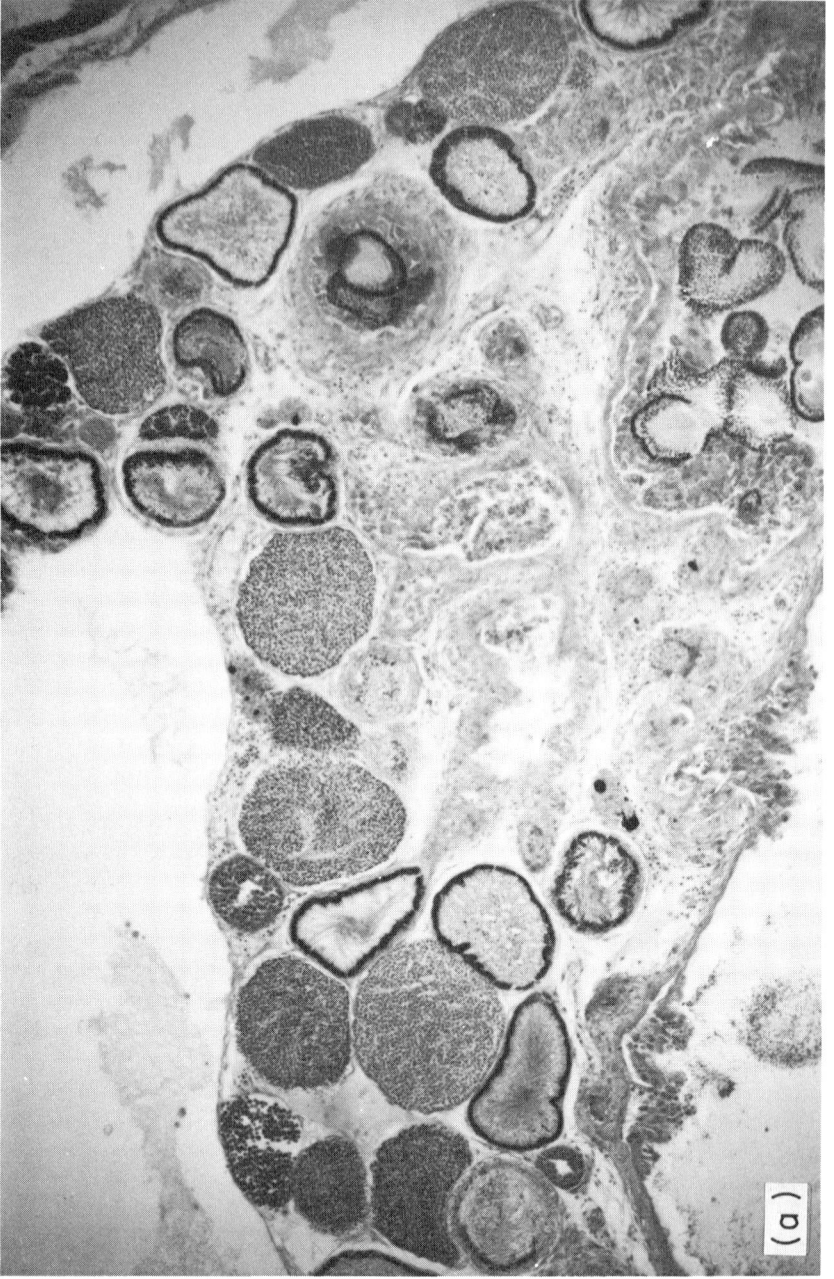

(a)

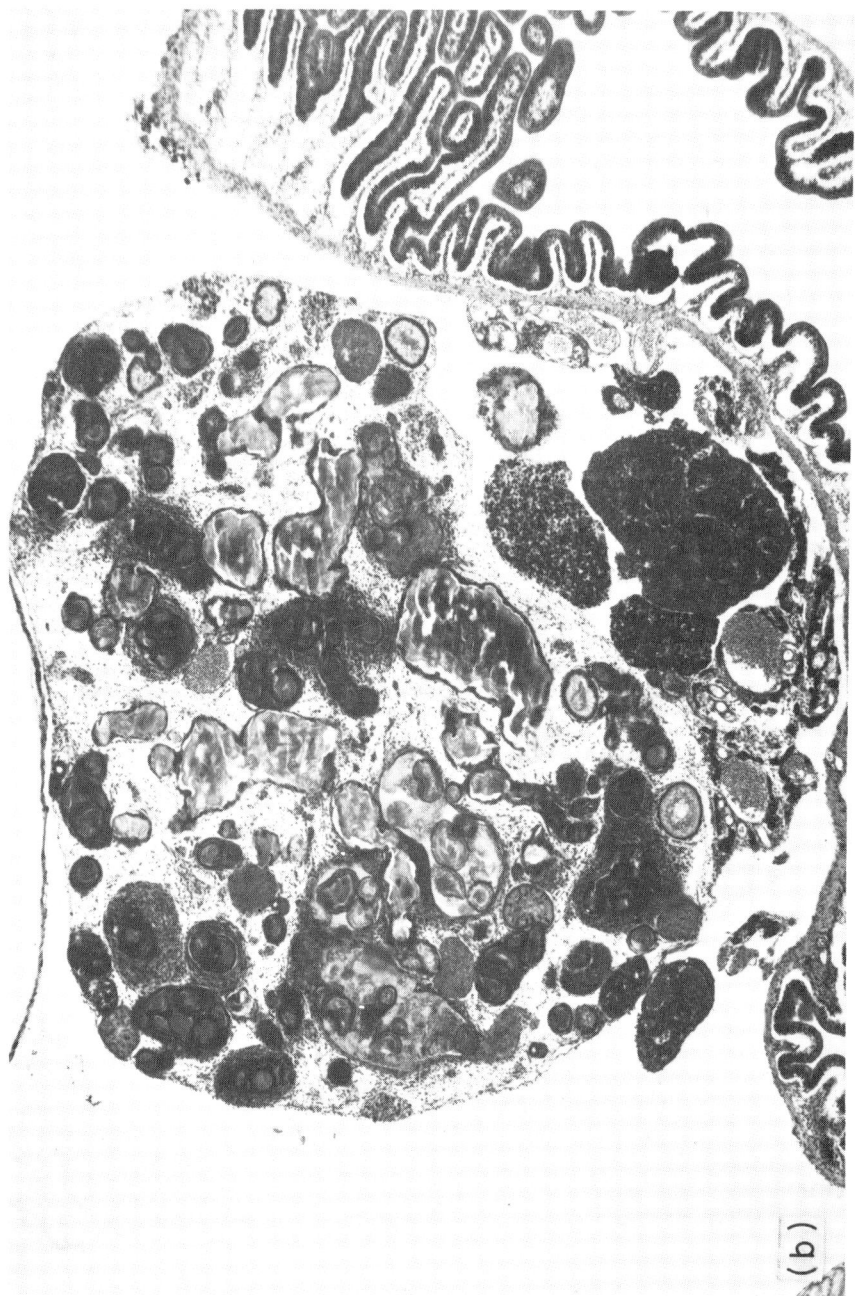

FIG. 3. Ageing testis of (a) guppy, ×50 and (b) Siamese fighting fish, ×125.

(b)

et al., 1977) other than a slight accumulation of connective tissue and a reduction in the number of germ cells in older animals. The amount of lipofuscin granules in the gonads had no clear relationship to the age of the bitterling in either sex.

The Endocrine Glands

The thyroid gland

Many of the features which characterize senescence in higher vertebrates are similar to those of a hypothyroid state. Studies of the aging thyroid of man and a number of small laboratory mammals have not, however, revealed any pronounced histological difference between the glands of young and old individuals. There are limited changes with age. Principally, these involve an increase in the fibrous tissue of the gland. The aged thyroid has a considerable functional reserve and retains the capacity to respond to increased demands with increased hormone secretion.

Woodhead & Ellett (1966) have followed histological changes with age in the thyroid gland of the guppy, *Poecilia reticulata*, throughout its lifetime. In this species, as in the majority of teleosts, the thyroid gland consists of numerous discrete follicles lying in the connective tissue around the ventral aorta. Each follicle consists of epithelial cells which enclose colloid, in which the thyroid hormone is stored. In resting glands, the follicular cells are low and stretched around the stored colloid which has a dense laminated appearance, whilst in active glands the follicular cells are high and columnar, and the colloid appears granular in texture. Using these criteria, they found that the activity of the gland gradually decreased after the age of 12 months until, in fish of three years, it had become almost completely inactive. Extra-pharyngeal thyroid tissue was never abundant in young fish, but, with advancing age, thyroid follicles were found in other sites, particularly in the choroid gland and kidneys. Several fish developed thyroid tumours in old age.

A preliminary study of the thyroid gland in fighting fish, *Betta splendens*, similarly revealed declining activity, until after about 30 months, the gland was inactive, the follicular cells were low and the follicles filled with dense stored colloid (Woodhead, unpub.).

The interrenal (adrenal) gland

Woodhead & Ellett (1967) provided evidence of some aging changes in the interrenal gland of the guppy. In young females, the interrenal tissue was disposed in long chords of polygonal or cuboidal cells with sparse cytoplasmic granulation, lying close to the walls of the posterior cardinal vein. With increasing age, there was a tendency for the volume of the gland to increase, while there was a steady fall in the height of the interrenal cells, and a decline in the volume of the cell nucleus. There was also a marked increase with age in the cytoplasmic granulation of the interrenal cells and in the intensity of the staining reaction of the nuclei.

In young male guppies, the gland was somewhat differently arranged, and was composed principally of groups of polygonal cells with pale staining granules. With advancing age, there was a marked increase in the volume of the gland, but there was no change in the size of the interrenal cells with age, and only a slight increase in cytoplasmic granulation. Interrenal cells with pycnotic nuclei were, however, more numerous in old male fish than in old females. We considered that the changes which we saw in both the thyroid and the interrenal indicated a decline in function with advancing age (Woodhead & Ellett, 1966, 1967).

Conclusions

Earlier workers tended to view aging changes in the endocrine system of mammals as almost entirely the result of a decline in the activity of the endocrine glands themselves. There is now evidence to show that the endocrine glands of older animals retain a considerable reserve capacity, and are able to produce greatly increased amounts of hormone when required. Decreased peripheral utilization of hormones appears to contribute to aging in the endocrine system, possibly with some alteration in the metabolism and excretion of hormones by the liver and the kidney.

Other Organs

There have been very few studies of structural changes in other organs throughout the lifespan of any fish. I have recently described changes in the anatomy of the liver of the guppy and the Amazon molly (Woodhead, 1977). In common with mammalian findings, the differences between the livers of young and old fish were small; only in the livers of the two oldest guppies (which were post-reproductive) were there signs of change in the tissue which might have caused impairment of liver function (Fig. 4). Any age derangements in liver function in older fish might present considerable disadvantages, since the liver is closely involved in the transfer of large quantities of yolk to the developing eggs and, with increasingly heavy commitments of metabolic reserves to reproduction as the fish ages, there is a correspondingly greater mobilization of metabolites through the liver.

Preliminary surveys of other tissues and organs of the guppy, Amazon molly and Siamese fighting fish suggest that the aging changes conform to the common vertebrate pattern, and that death is due to causes similar to those found in other vertebrates. Chronic renal disease was common in senile fish, but they died from many causes including neoplasia, dropsy, tuberculosis, extreme spinal curvature and bacterial and viral infections. Parasitic infections were not uncommon in some senile mollies and fighting fish. Older fish in wild populations often carry a greater number of parasites than young individuals.

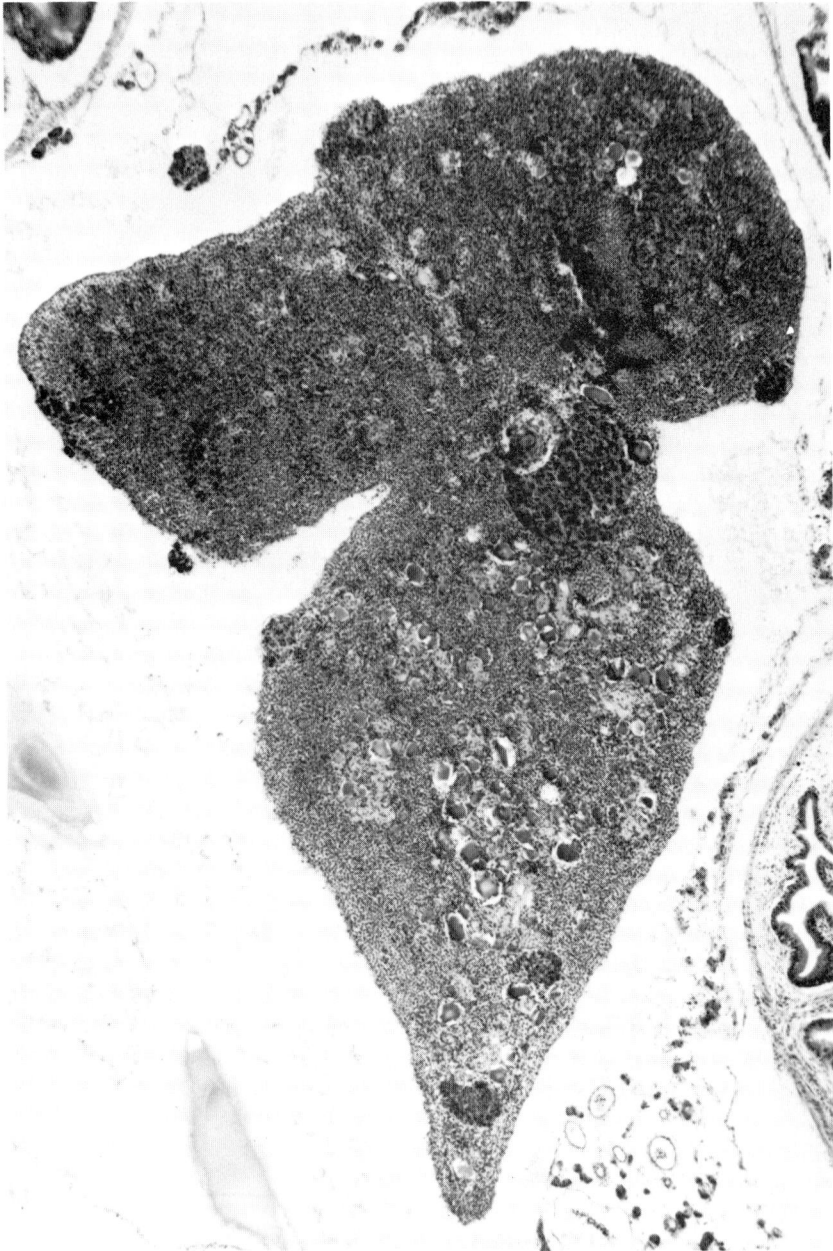

FIG. 4. Liver of a post-reproductive female guppy, showing limited areas of degeneration, ×125.

REPRODUCTION AND MORTALITY

Gonadal growth in fish, after the age and size of sexual maturity, depends upon the accumulation of impressive quantities of metabolites. Ripe ovarian weight in a number of species may thus attain at least 20% of body weight, and sometimes twice this value (Ursin, this volume p. 63; Wootton, this volume p. 133). It has generally been considered that the onset of sexual maturation in fishes is accompanied by a change of growth pattern, as the energy needs of the growing gonads divert metabolites which would otherwise be available for somatic growth (Brown, 1957). However, rather than viewing these two anabolic processes as competitive, Iles (1974) has noted that they may be regarded as alternative pathways whose peaks differ seasonally. This pattern is well demonstrated, for example, by Griswold & Smith (1973) for the stickleback, *Pungitius pungitius* L., (see also Miller, this volume p. 1). Decline in

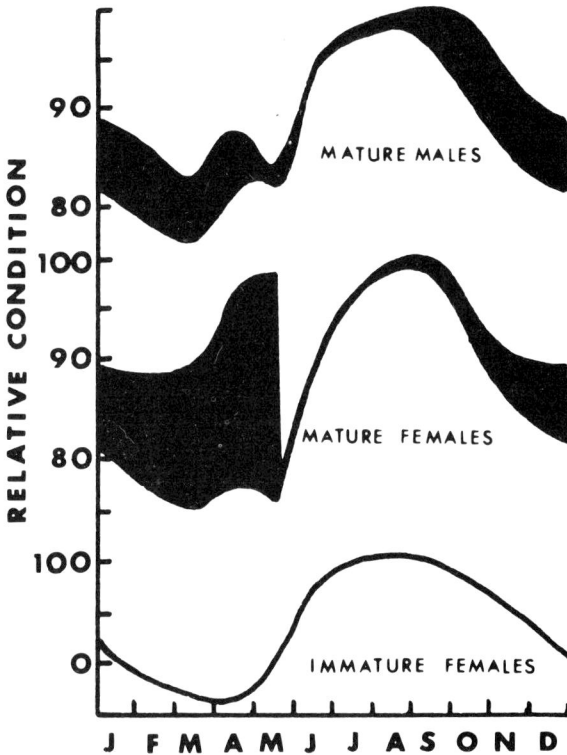

FIG. 5. Seasonal changes in relative condition in the perch, *Perca fluviatilis*, of Lake Windermere, England. The solid black denotes gonad weights; the upper edge of the line is relative condition with gonads, the lower edge relative condition without gonads (from LeCren, 1951).

194
A. D. WOODHEAD

body condition with reproduction is also widely reported for fishes (Fig. 5), and is indicative of the mobilization of stored material for gonad maturation and other reproductive activities (Le Cren, 1951; Shul'man, 1974; Woodhead, 1975). Such observations emphasize the impact of reproduction on somatic anabolism, and have long supported the concept of "reproductive stress", in which reproductive commitment and "effort", in the widest sense, is seen as a component of senescence, being an age-related source of changes deleterious for body maintenance (see Calow, 1973). The magnitude of reproductive effort, in relation to spawning frequency and longevity, has been regarded as an essential component of overall reproductive success (Stearns, 1976; Schaffer, this volume p. 307).

Gonadosomatic Changes with Age

Increasing loss of body weight in older fish during gonadal maturation was demonstrated by Orton (1929) for North Sea haddock, *Melanogrammus aeglefinus*. Using the data of Russell (1914) for a range of sizes of fish, Orton was able to show that a seasonal fall in gutted weight of haddock, associated with the annual cycle of maturation and spawning, became progressively greater as the weight of the fish increased. He suggested that, in larger haddock, the gonad forms a relatively greater percentage of the total body weight than in smaller individuals. These findings were confirmed by Raitt (1932). Similar results are shown in Fig. 8 for testis growth in the cod. If this tendency continued, the expenditure of metabolic reserves upon reproduction might "overbalance normal metabolism and result in death" (Orton, 1929).

There is good evidence for a number of species, including Atlantic and Pacific herring, to show that, with increasing size of the fish, the gonad forms a greater proportion of the total body weight (Gerking, 1959). MacKinnon (1972) found in female American plaice, *Hippoglossoides platessoides*, that the storage of metabolites for reproduction and for overwintering somatic maintenance in young mature plaice is at least equal to the metabolites which contribute to overall body growth, but, in older, larger fish, egg production assumes increasing importance. Thus, production for body growth decreases from 37% of total production of a 30-cm fish to 27% at 40 cm.

Fecundity and Age

Since the length and weight of fish increase with age, a relationship between age and fecundity, a function of size, will necessarily be found. In some species, however, age has a real effect upon fecundity. Thus in whitefish, *C. clupeaformis* (Mitchill) (Berg & Grimaldi, 1965); flounders (Kändler & Pirwitz, 1957); haddock (Raitt, 1932; Hodder, 1963); roach (Mackay & Mann, 1969) and capelin (Winters, 1970, 1971), there are positive correlations with age, even after length has been considered; that is, older fish have a higher fecundity than younger individuals of the same size. Usually, the variation in fecundity between fish of any age is greater than that between fish of the same weight or length. For example, in the haddock, the correlation coefficient "r" of age to fecundity is 0·66 compared to an "r" value of 0·83 for the relationship of fecundity to weight (Hodder, 1963). Hudson River shad, *Alosa sapidissima* (Wilson), however, show much less variability and a closer correlation between fecundity and age, where "r" is 0·98 (Lehman, 1953). There is also some evidence that egg size may tend to increase with parental size and age in some populations. Graumann (1973) noted there was a marked increase in egg diameter with increasing age and size of cod in Baltic waters.

Reproductive Costs in Older Fish

The combination of an increase in egg size with an increase in egg number must add considerably to reproductive expenditure in older, larger fish. Blaxter & Hempel (1963) compared the total egg mass spawned by female herring, *Clupea harengus*, of the same size, from races of herring which show significant differences in egg size. The eggs of herring in the Moray Firth, Scotland, are small, and, at a single spawning, a female measuring 27·5 cm sheds 5·0 g in total dry weight of eggs. Races of herring from the southern North Sea have larger eggs and the total dry weight shed was 7·3 g for a female of the same body length. Generally, the total egg mass in herring of a given size is higher in fish which spawn in autumn than in those spawning in the spring. Schopka & Hempel (1973) compared several different races of autumn-spawning herring (Fig. 6). In Norwegian spring-spawning herring the total egg mass is low and it is interesting to find that this race has the greatest longevity and reaches the largest size. Furthermore, they mature later in their lifespan, thus reducing the energy expenditure on reproduction. Autumn-spawning herring from the Nova Scotia coast and southern Gulf of St. Lawrence have a lesser expenditure on reproduction than do the spring spawners, and Messieh (1976) has suggested that the lower burden of reproduction in the autumn spawners is related to their greater longevity (Fig. 7). Baltic races of cod, *Gadus morhua*, are about twice as fecund (per unit of gutted weight) as North Sea or Icelandic races of the same size. Baltic cod live a maximum of 10 years, compared to about 16 years and about 20 years respectively for the other two races.

   Love & Robertson (1967) regard the annual extensive depletion of energy reserves for reproduction as a normal state of affairs to which the fish are well adapted. Indeed, Love (1970) cites evidence to show that older, larger fish lay down greater energy reserves than do smaller individuals. But fish are unusual amongst vertebrates in that fecundity increases with size. Further, the gonads form an increasingly greater proportion of the total weight with increasing size (Fig. 8). Iles (1974) has

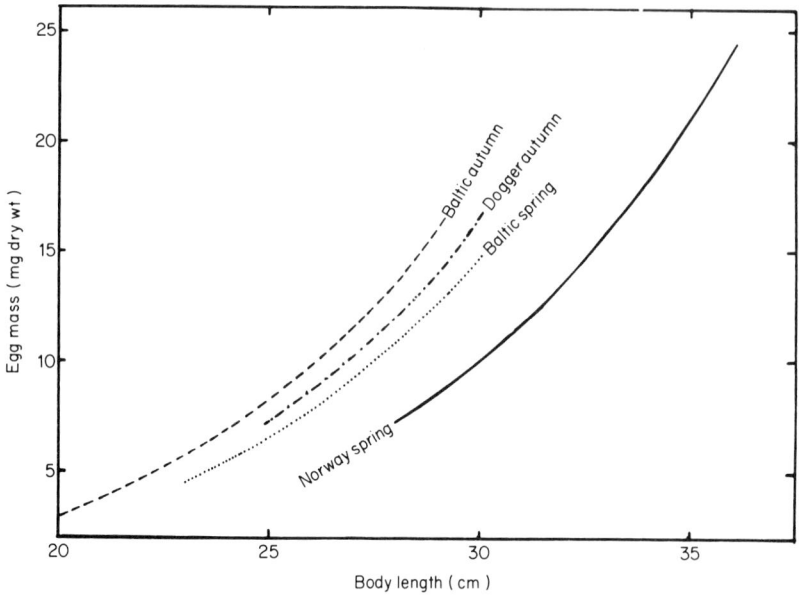

FIG. 6. Egg mass and size in different races of autumn-spawning herring (from Schopka & Hempel, 1973). In the Norwegian race, the total egg mass is low and body size is greatest.

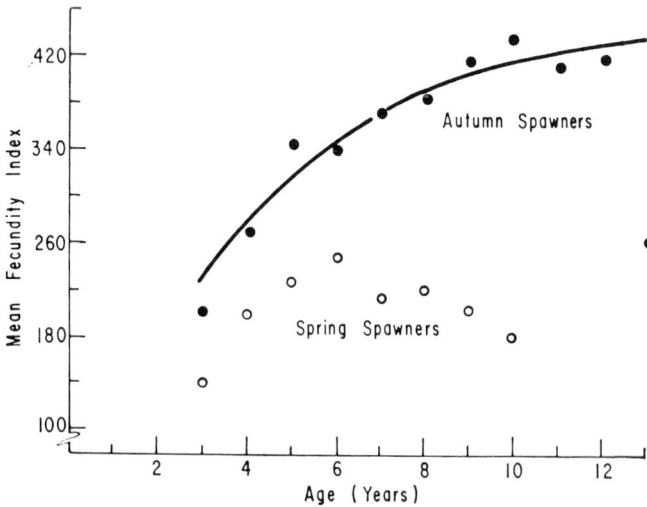

FIG. 7. The relationship between the mean fecundity index ($F = L^3$) and age for spring- and autumn-spawning Atlantic herring (from Messieh, 1976).

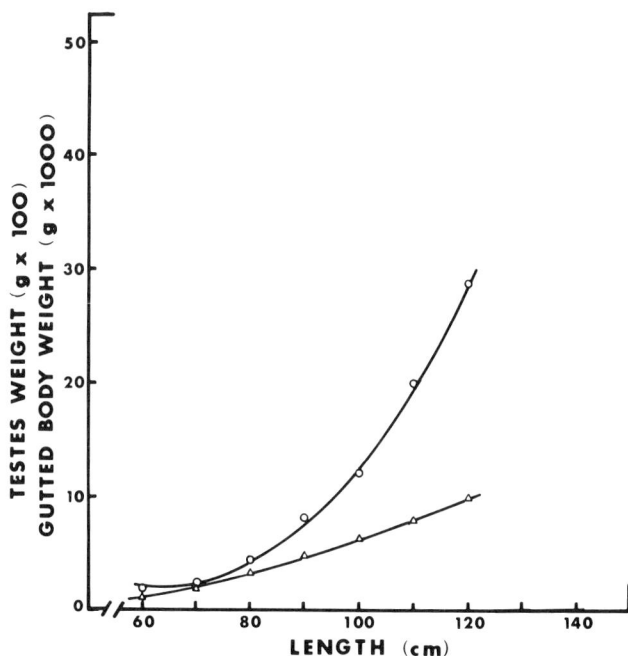

FIG. 8. Relation between somatic growth and testis growth with age for cod, *Gadus morhua*, in the Barents Sea.

pointed out that the seasonal excess of stored material will depend partially upon growth rate, so that as growth naturally declines in older fish, correspondingly, more will be available for gonad growth. It seems likely that stored metabolites will be sufficient to provide the bulk of the material for gonad growth throughout the lifespan of the fish. But in larger, older individuals the gonad forms a far greater percentage of body weight (Fig. 8). In a resource-limited environment or under adverse environmental conditions, the extensive energy depletion associated with gonadal ripening in old fish may be an important factor in mortality.

In female American plaice, MacKinnon (1972) suggested that the increased metabolic requirements for gonadal maturation in large, old fish may result in a "jellied" condition of the flesh (with a decreased metabolite content and higher water content), as was proposed by Templeman & Andrews (1956), and that this may be a contributory factor in the death of old individuals. Adult American shad, *Alosa sapidissima*, on their spawning grounds may feed on planktonic food, but older, larger fish do not obtain sufficient energy to prevent dramatic weight loss and death. Adult females of 421-mm length showed a fall of 38% in body weight which had risen to a value of 56% for females of 531 mm. Comparable values for male shad were a 24% loss at 359 mm to 46% at

493 mm (Chittenden, 1976). Chittenden (1969) has related the low percentage of repeat-spawners in Delaware River shad (0 to 6·5%), compared with populations from other rivers in the mid Atlantic Bight (20 to 25%), to the much longer migration upriver to spawning beds in the Delaware River. The additional energy expenditure on migration, combined with the energy needs of gonadal maturation, results in higher mortalities in this population. Hislop (1975) has clearly demonstrated that spawning causes an increasing percentage weight loss with increasing body size in female whiting, *Merlangius merlangus*. The values for daily weight loss due to maturation are shown in Fig. 9.

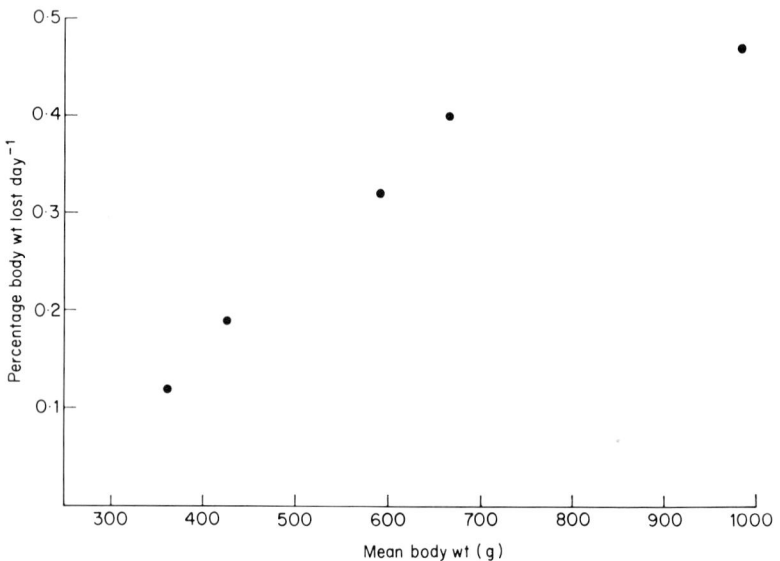

FIG. 9. Daily percentage loss in body weight due to spawning in whiting, *Merlangius merlangus* (from Hislop, 1975).

Although the data are not extensive, they imply that the increased energy requirements of reproduction in older individuals might well contribute to unstable homeostasis and so predispose them to death. This may be particularly important if the fish cease to feed during maturation, or during years when there is little food available. Body reserves may fall to extremely low levels after spawning, and against the background of such an impoverished physical state, the fish may well succumb to adverse environmental conditions. Thus, Wilkins (1967) found that the lipids in the tissues of autumn-spawning herring, *Clupea harengus*, in the Clyde, Scotland, fell to low levels after spawning, and declined further to levels of

2% during the subsequent winter fast. This level represented only the structural fats in the body. An increased mortality rate in female yellow perch, *Perca fluviatilis*, in two Laurentian lakes has been related to depletion of fats below a critical level of 2%. During the winter months, the body reserves of females are depleted as the ovaries ripen, leaving little available for body maintenance; feeding may be drastically reduced because the enlarging ovaries occlude the intestines. In some females, the fall in reserves to this critical level occurs several months prior to spawning (Newsome & Leduc, 1975).

Reproductive Modifications in Older Fish

In species which spawn many young, fecundity rates are often adjusted to environmental resources so that fitness is maximized. Such adaptive reproductive strategy was shown in the winter flounder by Tyler & Dunn (1976). When food was scarce, the egg production was curtailed so that body weight was maintained. When food was abundant again, the body was large, and able to support a large gonad. Hislop, Robb & Gauld (1978) have shown that, for haddock, *Melanogrammus aeglefinus*, when food energy is restricted, a balance is achieved between somatic growth and reproduction. Spawning is not postponed, but, on the other hand, somatic tissues are not depleted to lethal levels in order to maintain a high level of fecundity.

Reproductive longevity provides a spawning stock of fish consisting of a broad spectrum of survivors from a multitude of progeny. These fish will be "winners" in the sense that they have survived the vicissitudes of environmental extremes for some years. They are at the peak of distribution of general habitat fitness (Williams, 1975). If the greatly increased energy allocation for reproduction in older fish reduces their chances of survival and further spawning through a reduction in the amount of energy available for maintenance, we might expect to see adjustments in fecundity to ensure the survival of these older individuals. This might take the form of a reduction in egg number or in the frequency of spawning, countering the trend towards increased fecundity noted earlier in other species. Llewellyn (1974) studied the fecundity of the southern pygmy perch, *Nannoperca a. australis* Günther, from inland waters in eastern Australia, sampling fish over a length of 40–70 mm and weight range from 1 to 4 g. Fish of 55 mm had about 4000 ripening eggs in the ovary, but in 60-mm fish the number had fallen to about 2500. There was a decline in the number of eggs shed by older white perch, *Roccus americanus* (Gmelin), from about 600 in three-year-old fish to an average of 450 in six year olds (Taub, 1969). Data for the Downs stock of herring, *Clupea harengus*, in the North Sea show that egg number falls after the fish have reached the ages of eight and nine years (Bridger, 1961). The fecundity index ($F = L^3$) of Atlantic herring from the Nova

Scotia coast decreased with age after reaching a maximum (Fig. 7), indicating that the fish were approaching senility (Messieh, 1976).

Older fish may reduce egg size rather than egg number. Svärdson (1949) suggested that an evolutionary premium on egg number in older fish would be limited by the selective advantages of larger eggs which produce larger young. This may well apply to freshwater fish, where the young have to compete for limited territories, and Belding (1940) has shown that some older salmon do limit egg number rather than egg size. Svärdson's idea may not be wholly applicable to marine fish. In the sea, fertilization and embryonic development take place in a more extensive external environment compared to the close pairing of fish in fresh water and the sex products are spread over a wider area. Under these conditions in the sea, there may be a greater advantage in the production of larger numbers of eggs after the optimal egg size has been reached.

Other species reduce the frequency with which they spawn in old age. Comparison of the numbers of spawning lake trout, *Salvelinus alpinus* (L.), in Keller Lake, Canada, with non-spawning fish in several length groups showed a greater percentage of spawners in the size range of 500 to 599 mm, but this declined rapidly as the fish increased in size to 900 to 999 mm (Johnson, 1973). Adult white fish, *Coregonus clupeaformis*, do not spawn each year (Johnson, 1973; Power, 1978), though any relationship between spawning frequency and age is not clear.

In the live-bearing guppy, *Poecilia reticulata*, there is a reduction in ovarian size in older fish (Woodhead & Ellett, 1969b). Fraser & Renton (1940) found a diminished fecundity during the last few months of life in *Heterandria formosa* Agassiz, the mosquito-fish. During a lifespan of 25 months, one female produced a total of 180 young in successive broods, but 150 of the young were born during the first eight months of life. Krumholz (1948) provided a detailed series of observations on the reproductive capacity of the western mosquito fish, *Gambusia a. affinis* (Baird & Girard), throughout its lifespan, both in the laboratory and in the wild. He found that the average number of young increased in each successive brood as the length of the female increased. But, at large sizes, the number of young produced was drastically reduced. One very large old female had no eggs in the ovary, indicating that there may be a period of reproductive sterility in *Gambusia* towards the end of the lifespan.

It should also be noted that older females of both freshwater and marine species may produce qualitatively better eggs in terms of their lipid content (Nikolsky, 1969; Graumann, 1973). The survival of splake hybrids (*Salvelinus fontinalis* × *S. namaycush*) was increased during the developmental stages from "eyed" ova to yolk sac absorption, as the age of the female parent increased from three to six years (Ayles, 1974). V. P. Ponomarenko (1967) and I. Ya. Ponomarenko (1973) suggested that older spawners in stocks of cod, *Gadus morhua*, lay eggs of a higher quality than fish spawning for the first time.

CONCLUDING REMARKS

In this paper, I have discussed evidence for senescence in fishes, and have supported the concept that the increasing energy demands of reproduction are an important factor in predisposing older fish to death. There is direct, though limited, experimental evidence that fish show a pattern of mortality similar to that in mammals. Fish in the wild seldom live long enough to become senile, but data are gradually accumulating from field studies, corroborating these laboratory findings and, also, providing evidence for a relationship between increasing reproductive effort and mortality in old fish. More field observations and laboratory studies have yet to be made to put this theory on a sound footing.

Gerking (1959) considered that it would be unprofitable to continue fecundity studies on oviparous fishes, for gathering evidence to support or discount an aging process, because of great individual variability in fecundity and the difficulty of obtaining old fish. His views were discouraging. I see a real need to continue to collect evidence, where possible, for aging in wild fish, and to make further laboratory studies which express, in quantitative terms, partition of energy for reproductive and somatic growth, as has been done by MacKinnon (1972) and Hislop (1975). Comfort (1964) has strongly presented the case for comparative studies of aging, since they can provide systems in which to screen many of the theories of aging. It is particularly important to demonstrate that fish and other lower vertebrates conform to the general vertebrate pattern of aging; if they did not, many of the current aging theories would immediately become untenable (Comfort, 1964). Kohn (1971) has discussed the problem of whether the evolutionary origins of aging were in processes that restrict growth and period of reproductive activity. The extent to which all of these parameters are integrated or separated in fishes suggests that comparative studies would be most profitable in giving a good indication of when aging processes are initiated.

ACKNOWLEDGEMENTS

Research on this topic has been carried out at the Brookhaven Nation Laboratory under the auspices of the US Department of Energy and the National Cancer Institute (contract YOL-CP-50202).

REFERENCES

Alm, G. (1951). Year class fluctuations and span of life of perch. *Rep. Inst. Freshwat. Res. Drottningholm* **33**: 1–17.

Ayles, G. B. (1974). Relative importance of additive genetic and maternal sources of variation in early survival of young splake hybrids (*Salvelinus fontinalis* × *S. namaycush*). *J. Fish. Res. Bd Can.* **31**: 1499–1502.

Barr, W. A. (1963). The endocrine control of the sexual cycle in the plaice, *Pleuronectes platessa* (L). 1. Cyclical changes in the normal ovary. *Gen. comp. Endocr.* **3**: 197–204.

Belding, D. L. (1940). The number of eggs and pyloric appendages as criteria of river varieties of the Atlantic salmon (*Salmo salar*). *Trans. Am. Fish. Soc.* **69**: 285–289.

Berg, A. & Grimaldi, E. (1965). Biologia delle due forme di coregone (*Coregonus* sp.) del Lago Maggiore. *Memorie Inst. ital. Idrobiol.* **18**: 25–196.

Bidder, G. P. (1925). The mortality of plaice. *Nature, Lond.* **115**: 495.

Bidder, G. P. (1932). Senescence. *Br. Med. J.* **1932** (*ii*): 583–585.

Blaxter, J. H. S. & Hempel, G. (1963). The influence of egg size on herring larvae (*Clupea harengus* L.). *J. Cons. perm. int. Explor. Mer* **28**: 211–240.

Bridger, J. P. (1961). On fecundity and larval advance of Downs herrings. *Fishery Invest., Lond.*, (2) **23**(3): 1–30.

Brown, M. E. (1957). Experimental studies on growth. In *The physiology of fishes* **1**: 361–400. Brown, M. E. (ed.). New York & London: Academic Press.

Calow, P. (1973). The relationship between fecundity, phenology, and longevity: a systems approach. *Am. Nat.* **107**: 559–574.

Childs, E. A. & Law, D. K. (1972). Growth characteristics of progeny of salmon with different maximum lifespans. *Expl Geront.* **7**: 405–407.

Chittenden, M. E. (1969). *Life history and ecology of the American shad*, Alosa sapidissima, *in the Delaware River*. Ph. D. Thesis: Rutgers Univ.

Chittenden, M. E. (1976). Weight loss, mortality, feeding and duration of residence of adult American shad, *Alosa sapidissima*, in freshwater. *Fish. Bull., U.S.* **74**: 151–157.

Comfort, A. (1957). The duration of life in molluscs. *Proc. malacol. Soc. Lond.* **32**: 219–241.

Comfort, A. (1961). Age and reproduction in female *Lebistes*. *Gerontologia* **5**: 146–149.

Comfort, A. (1964). *Ageing, the biology of senescence*. New York: Holt, Rinehart and Winston.

Cushing, D. H. (1975). The natural mortality of the plaice. *J. Cons. int. Explor. Mer* **36**: 150–157.

Egami, N. (1971). Further notes on the lifespan of the teleost, *Oryzias latipes*. *Expl Geront.* **6**: 379–382.

Egami, N. & Etoh, H. (1969). Lifespan data for the small fish, *Oryzias latipes*. *Expl Geront.* **4**: 127–129.

Fraser, E. A. & Renton, R. M. (1940). Observations on the breeding and development of the viviparous fish, *Heterandria formosa*. *Q. Jl micr. Sci.* **81**: 479–520.

Gerking, S. D. (1959). Physiological changes accompanying ageing in fishes. *Ciba Fed. Colloq. on Ageing* **5**: 181–207.

Graumann, G. B. (1973). Investigations of factors influencing fluctuations in abundance of Baltic cod. *Rapp. P.-v. Réun. Cons. perm. int. Explor. Mer* **164**: 73–76.

Griswold, B. L. & Smith, L. L. (1973). The life history and trophic relationships of the ninespine stickleback, *Pungitius pungitius* in the Apostle Islands area of Lake Superior. *Fishery Bull., U.S.* **71**: 109–160.

Haranghy, L., Penzes, L., Kerenyi, T. & Penzes, B. (1977). Sexual activity and aging in the teleost fish, *Rhodeus serviceus amarus*. *Expl Geront.* **12**: 17–25.

Hickling, C. F. (1940). The fecundity of the herring in the southern North Sea. *J. mar. biol. Ass. U.K.* **24**: 619–632.

Hislop, J. R. G. (1975). The breeding and growth of whiting *Merlangius merlangus* in captivity. *J. Cons. perm. int. Explor. Mer* **36**: 119–127.

Hislop, J. R. G., Robb, A. P. & Gauld, J. A. (1978). Observations on effects of feeding level on growth and reproduction in haddock, *Melanogrammus aeglefinus* (L.) in captivity. *J. Fish Biol.* **13**: 85–98.

Hodder, V. M. (1963). Fecundity of Grand Bank haddock. *J. Fish. Res. Bd Can.* **20**: 1465–1487.

Iles, T. D. (1974). The tactics and strategy of growth in fishes. In *Sea fisheries research*: 331–346. Jones, F. R. H. (Ed.). New York: John Wiley and Sons, Inc.

Johnson, L. (1973). Stock and recruitment in some unexploited Canadian Arctic Lakes. *Rapp. R. -v. Réun. Cons. perm. int. Explor. Mer* **164**: 219–227.

Kändler, R. & Pirwitz, W. (1957). Über die Fruchtbarkeit der Plattfische im Nordsee-Ostee-Raum. *Kieler Meeresforsch.* **13**: 11–34.

Kennedy, W. A. (1954). Growth, maturity and mortality in the relatively unexploited lake trout of Great Slave Lake. *J. Fish. Res. Bd Can.* **11**: 827–852.

Kohn, R. R. (1971). *Principles of mammalian aging.* Edgewood Cliffs: Prentice Hall.

Krumholz, L. A. (1948). Reproduction in the western mosquito fish, *Gambusia affinis affinis* (Baird and Girard) and its use in mosquito control. *Ecol. Monogr.* **18**: 1–43.

LeCren, E. D. (1951). The length-weight relationship and seasonal cycle in gonad weight and condition in perch (*Perca fluviatilis*). *J. Anim. Ecol.* **20**: 201–219.

LeCren, E. D. (1958). Observations on the growth of perch (*Perca fluviatilis* L.) over twenty-two years with special reference to the effects of temperature and changes in population density. *J. Anim. Ecol.* **27**: 287–334.

Lehman, B. A. (1953). Fecundity of Hudson River shad. *Res. Rep. U.S. Fish Wildl. Serv.* No. 33: 1–8.

Llewellyn, L. C. (1974). Spawning, development and distribution of the Southern Pigmy Perch, *Nannoperca australis australis* Guenther from inland waters in Eastern Australia. *Aust. J. mar. Freshwat. Res.* **25**: 121–149.

Love, M. R. (1970). *The chemical biology of fishes.* London & New York: Academic Press.

Love, K. M. & Robertson, I. (1967). Studies on the North Sea cod. 1. Effects of starvation. 2. Changes in the distribution of muscle protein fractions. *J. Sci. Fd Agric.* **18**: 217–220.

Mackay, I. & Mann, K. H. (1969). Fecundity of two cyprinid fishes in the River Thames, Reading, England. *J. Fish. Res. Bd Can.* **26**: 2795–2805.

Mann, R. H. K. (1973). Observations on the age, growth, reproduction and food of the roach (*Rutilus rutilus* (L.)) in two rivers in southern England. *J. Fish Biol.* **5**: 707–736.

MacKinnon, J. C. (1972). Summer storage of energy and its use for winter metabolism and gonad maturation in American plaice (*Hippoglossoides platessoides*). *J. Fish. Res. Bd Can.* **29**: 1749–1759.

Messieh, S. N. (1976). Fecundity studies on Atlantic herring from the Southern Gulf of St. Lawrence and along the Nova Scotia coast. *Trans. Am. Fish. Soc.* **105**: 384–394.

Newsome, G. E. & Leduc, G. (1975). Seasonal changes of fat content in the yellow perch (*Perca flavescens*) of two Laurentian lakes. *J. Fish. Res. Bd Can.* **32**: 2214–2221.

Nikolsky, G. V. (1969). *Theory of fish population dynamics as the biological background for rational exploitation and management of fishery resources.* Edinburgh: Oliver and Boyd.

Orton, J. H. (1929). Reproduction and death in invertebrates and fishes. *Nature, Lond.* **123**: 14–15.

Ponomarenko, I. Ya. (1973). The effects of food and temperature conditions in the survival of young bottom dwelling cod in the Barents Sea. *Rapp. P-v. Réun. Cons. perm. int. Explor. Mer* **164**: 199–207.

Ponomarenko, V. P. (1967). *Reasons of changes in the rate of growth and maturation of the Barents Sea cod.* ICES, C.M. 1967/F: 16 (mimeo).

Power, G. (1978). Fish population structure in arctic lakes. *J. Fish. Res. Bd Can.* **35**: 53–59.

Probst, R. T. & Cooper, E. L. (1955). Age, growth and production of the lake sturgeon (*Acipenser flavescens*) in the Lake Winnebago region, Wisconsin. *Trans. Am. Fish. Soc.* **84**: 207.

Raitt, D. S. (1932). The fecundity of the haddock. *Scient. Invest. Fishery Bd Scotl.* **1**: 1–42.

Rasquin, P. & Hafter, E. (1951). Age changes in the testes of the teleost, *Astyanax mexicanus. J. Morph.* **89**: 397–404.

Robertson, O. H. & Wexler, B. C. (1960). Histological changes in the organs and tissues of migrating and spawning Pacific salmon (genus *Oncorhynchus*). *Endocrinology* **66**: 222–239.

Russell, E. S. (1914). Report on market measurements in relation to the English haddock fishery during the years 1901–1911. *Fishery Invest., Lond.* (2) **1**: 1–134.

Schopka, S. A. & Hempel, G. (1973). The spawning potential of populations of herring (*Clupea harengus* L.) and cod (*Gadus morhua* L.) in relation to the rate of exploitation. *Rapp. P.-v. Réun. Cons. int. Explor. Mer.* **164**: 178–185.

Shul'man, G. E. (1974). *Life cycles of fish.* New York: Wiley.

Stearns, S. C. (1976). Life history tactics: a review of ideas. *Q. Rev. Biol.* **51**: 3–47.

Svärdson, G. (1949). Natural selection and egg number in fish. *Rep. Inst. Freshwat. Res. Drottningholm* **29**: 1–115.

Taub, S. H. (1969). Fecundity of the white perch. *Progr. Fish. Cult.* **31**: 166–168.

Taylor, F. H. C. *et al.* (1958). The status of the major herring stocks in British Columbia in 1956–57. *Rep. Br. Columb. Dep. Fish.* **1956**: K45–K77.

Templeman, W. & Andrews, G. L. (1956). Jellied condition in the American plaice, *Hippoglossoides platessoides* (Fabricius). *J. Fish. Res. Bd Can.* **13**: 147–182.

Thung, P. J. (1961). Ageing changes in the ovary. In *Structural aspects of aging.* Bourne, G. H. (ed.). New York: Hafner Publishing Co.

Tyler, A. V. & Dunn, R. S. (1976). Ration, growth and measures of somatic and organ condition in relation to meal frequency in winter flounder, *Pseudopleuronectes americanus*, with hypotheses regarding population homeostasis. *J. Fish. Res. Bd Can.* **33**: 63–75.

Van Overbeeke, A. P. & McBride, J. R. (1971). Histological effects of 11-ketotestosterone, 17α-methyltestosterone, estradiol, estradiol cypionate and cortisol on the interrenal tissue, thyroid gland, and pituitary gland of gonadectomized sockeye salmon (*Oncorhynchus nerka*). *J. Fish. Res. Bd Can.* **28**: 477–484.

Walford, R. L. & Liu, R. K. (1965). Husbandry, lifespan, and growth rate of the annual fish, *Cynolebias adloffi, Expl Geront.* **1**: 161–171.

Wilkins, N. P. (1967). Starvation of the herring, *Clupea harengus* L. Survival and some biochemical changes. *Comp. Biochem. Physiol.* **23**: 503–518.

Williams, G. C. (1975). *Sex and evolution*. (Monographs in Population Biology 8.) Princeton: University Press.

Williams, W. P. (1967). The growth and mortality of four species of fish in the River Thames at Reading. *J. Anim. Ecol.* **36**: 695–720.

Winters, G. H. (1970). Biological changes in coastal capelin from the overwintering to the spawning condition *J. Fish. Res. Bd Can.* **27**: 2215–2224.

Winters, G. H. (1971). Fecundity of the left and right ovaries of Grand Bank capelin (*Mallotus villosus*). *J. Fish. Res. Bd Can.* **28**: 1029–1033.

Wohlschlag, D. E. (1954). Mortality rates of whitefish in an arctic lake. *Ecology* **35**: 388–396.

Woodhead, A. D. (1974a). Ageing changes in the Siamese fighting fish, *Betta splendens*. I. The testis. *Expl Geront.* **9**: 75–81.

Woodhead, A. D. (1974b). Ageing changes in the Siamese fighting fish, *Betta splendens*. II. The ovary. *Expl Geront.* **9**: 131–139.

Woodhead, A. D. (1975). Endocrine physiology of fish migration. *Oceanogr. mar. Biol.* **13**: 287–382.

Woodhead, A. D. (1977). Ageing changes in the liver of two poeciliid fishes, the guppy, *Poecilia* (*Lebistes*) *reticulatus* and the Amazon molly, *P. formosa*. *Expl Geront.* **13**: 37–45.

Woodhead, A. D. & Ellett, S. (1966). Endocrine aspects of ageing in the guppy, *Lebistes reticulatus* Peters—I. The thyroid gland. *Expl Geront.* **1**: 315–330.

Woodhead, A. D. & Ellett, S. (1967). Endocrine aspects of ageing in the guppy, *Lebistes reticulatus* (Peters)—II. The interrenal gland. *Expl Geront.* **2**: 159–171.

Woodhead, A. D. & Ellett, S. (1969a). Endocrine aspects of ageing in the guppy *Lebistes reticulatus* (Peters)—III. The testis. *Expl Geront.* **4**: 17–25.

Woodhead, A. D. & Ellett, S. (1969b). Aspects of ageing in the guppy, *Lebistes reticulatus* (Peters)—IV. The ovary. *Expl Geront.* **4**: 197–205.

Symp. zool. Soc. Lond. (1979) No. 44, 207–217

Genetics of Growth and Reproduction in Teleosts

C. E. PURDOM

MAFF Fisheries Laboratory, Lowestoft, Suffolk, England

SYNOPSIS

The genetic bases for growth and reproductive phenomena in teleosts are noted. The genetic determination of growth rate itself has been studied extensively in only one species, the carp. Genetic differences appear to exist between races and even families but additive genetic variance seems to be low. Environmental variation in growth rate is a major problem in the understanding of the genetic determination of growth rate in fish and the establishment of hierarchies in populations is a component of this.

Many facets of reproduction appear to be under some genetic control. The development of the sexes is genetically determined in the majority of teleosts which have been studied in this context, and environmental influences seem minor except, perhaps, in the case of hermaphrodite species. Other important aspects of reproduction, such as the time of first maturity, the season of spawning, fecundity and egg size are influenced both by genetic and environmental factors, each of which may be manipulated.

In a practical context, genetic control of aspects of the reproductive processes may be more relevant to growth rate *per se* than attempts to modify growth rate directly. Gonad development frequently takes place at the expense of somatic tissue after a main annual period of feeding is completed. Less well documented is the concept that sex hormones may accelerate somatic growth during some part of the sexual cycle. Thus steroids administered in food may increase growth rate and a comparison of the growth of triploid (sterile) and diploid fish shows that a spurt in growth occurs in the latter after spawning.

INTRODUCTION

Ideas about growth in fishes stem largely from preoccupation with the practical problems of managing either natural stocks or cultivated stocks of fish, the former for exploitation by fishing, the latter for development by farming. For natural fish stocks, the principal concern has been to measure the growth rate and abundance of fish in relation to the rate at which they are removed by fishing. In a fish-farming context, a more experimental approach has concentrated on the implication of environmental or management factors in growth rate, for example the effects of temperature and feeding rate, and the consequences of selective improvement or hybridization.

Of the two approaches, that from the aspect of natural stock management has been the more quantitative, but also the more simple. Thus the organic growth concept of von Bertalanffy has been found to fit well with observations of a relatively crude nature that derive from sampling of natural populations (Beverton & Holt, 1957), and has been widely used in fish stock assessment programmes.

The von Bertalanffy general formula $\left(\dfrac{dy}{dt} = \eta y^{n} - xy^{m}\right)$, describing growth rate as the balance of anabolic profit and catabolic loss, where each is dependent on size, stemmed from experimental observation, particularly in relation to respiration rates, but it does not appear to have furthered the experimental approach to the study of fish growth-rate phenomena. The common grounds for criticism are that the curve expresses a lifelong trend, where all seasonal and other short-term fluctuations are smoothed out (Parker & Larkin, 1959; Ursin, this volume p. 63), and does not take account of transformations, such as migration, in the lifetime of fish (Ricker, 1958). Neither do growth curves of this sigmoid form show any relationship between growth rate and sex, whether in terms of juvenile versus adult or male versus female changes, nor are the consequences of preparing for and completing spawning embraced.

Sex itself is a feature with strong genetic determinants. Genetic influence can also be detected in events consequential on sex, namely secondary sexual characters and the spawning act itself, and on growth patterns generally. This brief review covers the field of the genetic control of reproduction and growth in fish.

GENETICS OF GROWTH RATE

The most comprehensive study of the genetics of growth rate in fish is that performed by Moav and Wohlfarth on common carp, *Cyprinus carpio* L., within the Israeli programme of pisciculture (summarized by Moav & Wohlfarth, 1976). This work was begun in 1959 and one of the first features of carp growth to be recognized was that, within a population of fish, a very few grew so quickly that they attained weights far beyond the normal range, producing a markedly skew distribution with a long tail to the right. These were termed "jumpers" (Moav & Wohfarth, 1973) but similar observations had been made earlier by the Japanese investigators Nakamura & Kasahara, who called the fish "shooters" and described their characteristics in four papers (1955, 1956, 1957 and 1961). English translations of these papers, and a summary of the findings, are given by Wohlfarth (1977).

"Shooters" appear to arise only when there is competition for food. Initially, a newly hatched group of fish has a normal size-frequency distribution but, within 20 days, a skewness can be detected. If the fish are grown individually in tanks, no skewness develops and, if abundant food is given, little skewness develops even at high stocking densities. The fast-growing "shooters" do not retain this status when placed with larger fish and, when "shooters" are removed from a population, a new batch develops in their place. Clearly, the superior performance of the "shooters" is an hierarchic event with little genetic significance as far as growth rate is concerned except, perhaps, that the fast growth rate is an indication of what is physiologically, if not always psychologically, possible.

The principal genetic finding in the work of Moav and Wohlfarth, and their collaborators, was that selection over five generations for improved growth rate was ineffective although selection for reduced growth was marginally effective. Different families and, even more so, different strains, did show differences in growth rate and this character itself was very sensitive to inbreeding depression. In conclusion, the authors felt that genetic control of growth rate was important but restricted to non-additive genetic events. Additive genetic variance was absent possibly because of its elimination through generations of natural or artificial selection.

Additional evidence for strain differences comes from the work of Kirpichnikov (1962) using two strains of carp of different geographic origin and with different growth rates to produce a hybrid, the Ropsha carp, with intermediate growth characteristics and temperature tolerances.

Nothing like so comprehensive an analysis has been made of the genetic control of growth rate in any other species of fish but a considerable amount of selective breeding has been carried out with rainbow trout, *Salmo gairdneri* Richardson, and some other salmonids. Thus, Davis (1934) and Donaldson & Olson (1957) report on very large improvements over short histories of selection in brook trout, *Salvelinus fontinalis* (Mitchill), and rainbow trout respectively, but in neither case can husbandry improvements be distinguished from genuine genetic gain. More sophisticated selection experiments were conducted recently by Kincaid, Bridges & von Limback (1977). Rainbow trout were selected over three generations for fast growth on a family selection basis and, by the fourth generation, an improvement of 161% over the first generation was recorded. One-third of this improvement was attributed to genetic gain and an estimate of the heritability of growth rate on these data gave a figure of 0·06. This is low in relation to heritabilities for traits which have been selectively improved in other domesticated animals. In addition, a cautionary note should be taken of the feeding regime used by Kincaid *et al.*, which entailed an assessment of the amount of feed to be fed according to the weight of fish receiving it.

Selection programmes, or other means to assess heritability of growth rate, are notoriously difficult to design. Much easier is the comparison of strains or geographic races. Four strains of rainbow trout were found to differ significantly from each other in growth rate with the fastest increasing in length more than twice as fast as the slowest grower (Reinitz *et al.*, 1978). Significant geographical differences have also been reported for growth rate in Atlantic salmon, *Salmo salar* L., (Gjedrem, 1976).

It is perhaps surprising that more quantitative genetic study has not been undertaken with aquarium fish but an operational problem may reduce the validity of extrapolating results from these to fish of economic importance. This is the contrast between the determinate growth pattern expressed by many aquarium fish as opposed to the indeterminate nature of size in others. Thus selection may be for final size rather than growth rate and it might be supposed that this would be more responsive to selection. Selection for growth rate increase and decrease in guppies, *Poecilia reticulata* Peters, by Ryman (1972, 1973) failed to demonstrate significant heritability for this trait.

Interest in marine fish-farming of flatfish in the United Kingdom stimulated an examination of the prospects in selection for growth rate in these fish (Purdom, 1974). Instead of attempting a full genetic analysis of the situation, which would have been time-consuming and very difficult, a measure of the genetic status of growth rate was attempted by measuring the "repeatability" for incremental growth in length of young flatfish and by assessing the degree to which hierarchies contribute to size variation. Heritability estimates on the basis of repeatability were low and in the region of 0·1. Hierarchies were assessed by measurement of the coefficient of variance $[V/(\bar{x})^2]$ for length in various populations of fish. The outcome of several trials was that the coefficient of variance reached high levels where hierarchical interaction was possible and a very low level where fish were segregated individually in tanks. Hierarchies are environmental phenomena, not genetic.

In general, growth rate itself does not appear to be genetically determined in a way that responds to selection although the results for trout appear more positive than those for carp and other fish. There is one big difference which distinguishes carp and trout culture. The former is extensive while the latter is intensive. Carp feed in a more or less natural way whereas trout feed artificially at the whim of the husbandryman. Growth rate is clearly very dependent on feeding rate and, where there are possibilities for behavioural responses to feeding stimuli, there will be great variation in growth rate. Among the salmonids, it is possible to rank four taxa in which ease of management and growth rate are closely linked to behavioural patterns. Thus fingerling sea trout, *Salmo trutta* L., are extremely nervous, Atlantic salmon, *S. salar*, slightly less so, brown trout, *S. trutta*, reasonably placid and rainbow trout, *S. gairdneri*, completely at ease during feeding time. The growth rates of these fish are in the same order. Behavioural responses, or perhaps neurological patterns, might be more objective criteria for selection than growth rate *per se*.

GENETICS OF SEX AND REPRODUCTION

Sex Determination

Study of the genetic basis for sex determination in fish has a long history. Sex-linked inheritance of colour patterns was demonstrated independently in three small cyprinodonts in the 1920s. Winge (1927) described the male to male Y-linked mode of inheritance of many colour patterns in the guppy, *Poecilia reticulata* Peters, while Aida (1921) observed a similar phenomenon in the medaka, *Oryzias latipes* (Schlegel). In both cases, the implied genetic control of sex was vested in an XX female XY male chromosome arrangement. A quite different basic chromosomal plan was suggested in the case of the third species, the platy, *Xiphophorus maculatus* (Günther), in which Bellamy (1928) observed that, in the inheritance of melanophore patterns, females only ever had one characteristic whilst males could have two, and that females transmitted their pattern to sons but not to daughters. Bellamy's interpretation was that sex in the platy was XY female and XX male. Gordon (1937) later showed that, in some platies, an XY male situation prevailed and, finally, Kallman (1965) demonstrated that complex sex-chromosomal arrangements characterized most natural populations of platies and proposed the chromosomal structure whereby females could be XX or WY whilst males were XY or YY.

Sex-reversal techniques complement the sex-linkage studies. Thus Yamamoto (1953, 1958) demonstrated functional sex-reversal techniques in *Oryzias* by feeding sex hormones to sexually indifferent fish. Males or females could be produced and, in appropriate crosses, Yamamoto was able to confirm the XX female XY male type of sex control. Similar work with carp by Yamamoto & Kajishima (1968) and in the guppy by Dzwillo (1962), demonstrated male heterogamety in these fish. Clemens & Inslee (1968) also demonstrated male heterogamety in *Tilapia mossambica* (Peters) by crossing sex-reversed male fish with normal females and a similar result was obtained for *Tilapia nilotica* (L.) by Jalabert, Moreau *et al.* (1974). In the latter study, *Tilapia macrochir* Boulenger did not respond in the same way as *T. nilotica* and sex-reversed males were sterile; the authors discuss the possibility that this means that males are homogametic in *T. nilotica*.

Hybridization has also given clues to the nature of the genetic control of sex determination in *Tilapia* species. Hickling (1960) reported all-male broods from a cross between an unidentified species and *T. mossambica* and predicted a parallel situation to that believed at the time to represent the platy system, with male heterogamety and female heterogamety coexisting but in different populations. Jalabert, Kammacher & Lessent (1971) also found all-males amongst the offspring of the cross *T. macrochir* males and *T. nilotica* females and postulated female heterogamety for *T. macrochir* and male heterogamety for *T. nilotica*.

Sex-ratio characteristics following parthenogenesis have also yielded information on genetic control of sex. Thus, all-female broods indicate female homogamety in common carp (Golovinskaya, 1968) and grass carp (Stanley, 1976), while offspring of both sexes preclude female homogamety in plaice (Purdom & Lincoln, 1973). In the latter case, the prospect of non-chromosomal sex determination cannot be ruled out. Such lack of control must be the case with the many hermaphrodite species belonging to the Sparidae, Serranidae and other families, and has also been proposed for gonochoristic species such as the swordtail, *Xiphophorus helleri* Heckel (Kosswig, 1964) and the Siamese fighting fish, *Betta splendens* Regan (Lucas, 1968).

Direct evidence for the existence of sex chromosomes in fish is somewhat controversial. A number of instances of cytological observation of dissimilar chromosome pairs has been reported where confirmation or corroboration is lacking. The most definite description of chromosomal specialization in relation to sex, however, comes from the work of Chen and his colleagues (Chen, 1969; Ebeling & Chen, 1970; Chen & Reisman, 1970), on a variety of deep sea and shallow sea teleosts. Of the deep sea fish, 12 out of 25 species showed evidence of male heterogamety whilst five of 30 shallow water species showed male (three) or female (two) heterogamety. So far, no genetic confirmation is available on the cases where differential sex chromosomes have been observed. In rainbow trout, Thorgaard (1977) reports heteromorphic chromosomes in males, and studies on the sex of gynogenetic fish (Purdom, 1969), and on the sex of offspring of sex revertants, should soon supply the missing links.

In general, the main feature of the genetic sex determination mechanisms in fish is that, unlike the situation in birds, mammals, insects and many other animals, the process is very variable and therefore presumably polyphyletic and not too highly developed (Ohno, 1974).

Reproduction

The actual manner in which the sex ratio is controlled may be of little relevance to the phenology of reproduction although some powerful forces must favour the existence of a primary sex ratio close to one. The links with adaptiveness may be more apparent in other aspects of reproduction which include secondary sexual characteristics of colour and form, age at first maturity, season of spawning and features of egg size and fecundity.

Secondary sexual characters, such as coloration, clearly have a role during spawning and events leading up to spawning but, in view of their almost universally temporary nature, they must be a handicap outside the spawning season. Genetic studies of secondary sexual characteristics are limited to work on colour patterns in aquarium fish such as the guppy and Siamese fighting fish, where the permanent nature of the sex distinction is atypical of fish in general. Overall, the development of secondary characteristics seems to be controlled by the production of steroids in the gonad and is therefore likely to be subject to the genetic control of the maturation of the gonad itself.

The timing of the age at which fish mature must be under genetic control in the sense that individual species of fish have characteristic ages at first maturity. Within-species variation is not well documented. Donaldson & Olson (1957) report a decrease from four years to two years for first spawning in a selection programme with rainbow trout but the fish were also subject to other factors and size with age also changed dramatically. Inherited differences in size at maturity between wild populations of the stickleback, *Gasterosteus aculeatus* L., have been described by McPhail (1977). Size, and hence growth rate, are of clear importance to the onset of sexual maturity and early maturity after rapid growth has frequently been observed in salmonids and flatfish. In a commercial sense, the desirable features to develop in a fish are high growth rate and late sexual maturity. Testing individual strains of such fish as rainbow trout for maturity rate should present no technical problem.

The seasonal time of spawning is of more importance adaptively than the age at which a fish spawns. The distinctness of the spawning times of individual fish species suggests strong forces of natural selection. The timing itself may often be by photoperiod (de Vlaming, 1974; Scott, this volume, p. 105) but what controls the clock setting? Thus, plaice females spawn over a period of about three weeks but in the English Channel this spawning season occurs in December, in the Southern Bight in January, later still in the north of the North Sea and in April and May south of Iceland. The fish are all exposed to the same relative changes in photoperiod and hence some genetic adaptiveness must be assumed for the clock setting.

Much more varied spawning times are found in rainbow trout. In their natural habitat, the distinction appears to be between the coastal or anadromous forms, which spawn in late autumn, and the lacustrine forms, which spawn later in early spring (Behnke, 1972). Much of the natural distribution of rainbow trout has now been obliterated by the ubiquitous use of this fish in farming and in managed sport-fishing. Hatchery developments over the past 100 years have produced strains which are early and others which are late, so that rainbow trout spawning now covers almost every month of the year. The existence of this diversity suggests a highly plastic genetic control of spawning time but few precise data are available except for the general consensus that about five generations of selection are required to shift spawning time by about two months in this species.

Fecundity and egg size are important features of reproduction but we have little direct evidence on the extent of genetic control for either. These characters are presumably inversely related and certainly must be subject to a considerable level of environmental variation particularly in relation to factors affecting the availability of food (see Wootton, this volume p. 133; Mann & Mills, this volume p. 161). Many studies have shown the great variability of fecundity (Bagenal, 1967). Egg size is not so variable and may show remarkable consistency. Wimpenny (1953) describes the diameter of plaice, *Pleuronectes platessa* L., eggs as 1·8–1·9 mm in the Southern Bight and 1·65–1·70 mm off the east coast of Scotland. On the other hand, salmonid eggs can vary enormously in size.

In wild brook trout (*Salvelinus fontinalis*), egg diameters varied from 3·2 to 4·6 mm (Vladykov, 1956) and in cultivated rainbow trout, from 3·0 to 6·5 mm (Higgs, 1942). Some theoretical possibilities for egg size variation in salmonids are described by Purdom (1977). It is postulated that maximum egg number is defined before the onset of the somatic growth phase and that superabundance of food can over-extend the supply of eggs leading to large egg size and low relative fecundity.

The relative roles of genetic and environmental influences in egg size and fecundity are not known but it might be predicted that fecundity will largely be a matter of food supply and hence of limited dependence on genetics whilst egg size, in species for which this character shows little variation, will be more heavily dependent on genetic factors. Where egg size is variable, it might then be presumed that genetic control would be exerted only over the range of variation.

REPRODUCTION AND GROWTH

The material needs for reproduction on the one hand and growth on the other must occasionally be in conflict. In general, it seems that seasonally reproducing fish feed and grow in a somatic sense for most of the year with the development of gonads occurring rapidly, often associated with a period of fasting, just before spawning. Development of the gonad thus becomes almost entirely at the expense of somatic tissue. Since spawning is usually preceded by migration and/or courtship, under conditions quite distinct from those which obtain during the rest of the year, it is not surprising that the habit of feeding should be changed dramatically.

The influence of genetic and environmental agencies on these inter-actions must be very complex. A simple genetic means to bypass the conflict of reproduction and growth for fish cultivation purposes was to produce triploid fish (Purdom, 1972). That these sterile triploids continued to feed and grow whilst their diploid sibs stopped feeding prior to the spawning season was established with plaice (Lincoln & Purdom, unpub.). More surprisingly, however, the diploid fish showed a spurt of growth immediately after spawning and grew past the size attained by the triploids. In this sense, therefore, reproduction and growth appeared to be positively associated and a possible mechanism may lie in the anabolic effect of some steroids.

CONCLUSION

Growth and reproduction are linked in a complex competing and supporting cycle. Genetic influences are apparent in many aspects of sexuality but seem to be of little importance in growth so far as selection experiments can show. Non-additive genetic variance for growth may be more important than the additive type normally revealed by selection progress but the evidence in support of it rests only with strain differences and the observation of hybrid vigour in outcrossed fish. Huge differences in growth rate can be seen between closely related species but it seems as if genetic variance for this trait is largely fixed within individual species. Possibly the selective advantage of a specific growth rate is closely linked to average food supply situations. A fish must satisfy the basic maintenance needs of its somatic tissue before it grows and reproduces. Limits on growth might therefore be envisaged as a consequence of one year's growth being the next year's somatic debt.

REFERENCES

Aida, T. (1921). On the inheritance of color in a freshwater fish *Aplocheilus latipes* Temminck and Schlegel, with special reference to sex-linked inheritance. *Genetics* **6**: 554–573.

Bagenal, T. B. (1967). A short review of fish fecundity. In *The biological basis of freshwater fish production*: 89–111. Gerking, S. D. (ed.). Oxford and Edinburgh: Blackwell Scientific Publications.

Behnke, R. J. (1972). The systematics of salmonid fishes of recently glaciated lakes. *J. Fish. Res. Bd Can.* **29**: 639–671.

Bellamy, A. W. (1928). Bionomic studies on certain teleosts (Poeciliinae). 2. Color pattern inheritance and sex in *Platypoecilus maculatus* (Gunth.). *Genetics* **13**: 226–232.

Beverton, R. J. H. & Holt, S. J. (1957). On the dynamics of exploited fish populations. *Fishery Invest. Lond.* (2) **19**: 1–533.

Chen, T. R. (1969). Karyological heterogamety of deep-sea fishes. *Postilla* No. 130: 1–29.

Chen, T. R. & Reisman, H. M. (1970). A comparative chromosome study of the North American species of sticklebacks (Teleostei = Gasterosteidae). *Cytogenetics* **9**: 321–332.

Clemens, H. P. & Inslee, T. (1968). The production of unisexual broods by *Tilapia mossambica* sex-reversed with methyl testosterone. *Trans. Am. Fish. Soc.* **97**: 18–21.

Davis, H. S. (1934). Growth and heredity in trout. *Trans. Am. Fish. Soc.* **64**: 197–202.

de Vlaming, V. L. (1974). Environmental and endocrine control of teleost reproduction. In *Control of sex in fishes*: 13–83. Schreck, C. B. (ed.). Blacksburg, Virginia, U.S.A.: Sea Grant Extension Division, Virginia Polytechnic Institute and State University.

Donaldson, L. R. & Olson, P. R. (1957). Development of rainbow trout broodstocks by selective breeding. *Trans. Am. Fish. Soc.* **85**: 93–101.

Dzwillo, M. (1962). Über künstliche Erzeugung funktioneller Münnchen weiblichen Genotyps bei *Lebistes reticulatus. Biol. Zbl.* **81**: 575–584.

Ebeling, A. W. & Chen, T. R. (1970). Heterogamety in teleostean fishes. *Trans. Am. Fish. Soc.* **99**: 131–138.

Gjedrem, T. (1976). Possibilities for genetic improvements in salmonids. *J. Fish. Res. Bd Can.* **33**: 1094–1099.

Golovinskaya, K. A. (1968). Genetics and selection of fish and artificial gyno-
  genesis of the carp (*Cyprinus carpio*). *FAO Fish. Rep.* No. 44: 215–222.
Gordon, M. (1937). The production of spontaneous melanotic neoplasms in fishes
  by selective matings. *Am. J. Cancer* **30**: 362–375.
Hickling, C. F. (1960). The Malacca *Tilapia* hybrids. *J. Genet.* **57**: 1–10.
Higgs, A. (1942). Big trout from big eggs. *Salmon Trout Mag.* **104**: 216–230.
Jalabert, B., Kammacher, P. & Lessent, P. (1971). Déterminisme du sexe chez les
  hybrides entre *Tilapia macrochir* et *Tilapia nilotica*. Etude de la sex-ratio dans
  les recroisements des hybrides de première génération par les espèces
  parentes. *Annls Biol. Anim. Biochim. Biophys.* **11**: 155–165.
Jalabert, B., Moreau, J., Planquette, P. & Billard, R. (1974). Déterminisme du sexe
  chez *Tilapia macrochir* et *Tilapia nilotica*: action de la méthyltestostérone dans
  l'alimentation des alevins sur la différenciation sexuelle; proportion des sexes
  dans la descendance des mâles "Inversés". *Annls Biol. Anim. Biochim. Biophys.*
  14: 729–739.
Kallman, K. D. (1965). Genetics and geography of sex determination in the
  poeciliid fish, *Xiphophorus maculatus. Zoologica, N.Y.,* **50**: 151–190.
Kincaid, H. L., Bridges, W. R. & Limback, B. von (1977). Three generations of
  selection for growth rate in fall-spawning rainbow trout. *Trans. Am. Fish. Soc.*
  106: 621–628.
Kirpichnikov, V. S. (1962). Hybridization among carps. *Coll. Rep. Plenary Sess.
  Commn Fish. Res. W. Pacif. Ocean* **2**: 160–169.
Kosswig, C. (1964). Problems of polymorphism in fishes. *Copeia* **1964**: 65–74.
Lucas, G. A. (1968). Factors affecting sex determination in *Betta splendens. Genetics*
  60: 199–200 (Abstract only).
McPhail, J. D. (1977). Inherited interpopulation differences in size at first
  reproduction in threespine stickleback, *Gasterosteus aculeatus* L. *Heredity* **38**:
  53–60.
Moav, R. & Wohlfarth, G. (1973). Carp breeding in Israel. In *Agricultural
  genetics—selected topics*: 295–318. Moav, R. (ed.). New York: J. Wiley.
Moav, R. & Wohlfarth, G. (1976). Two-way selection for growth rate in the
  common carp (*Cyprinus carpio* L.). *Genetics* **82**: 83–101.
Nakamura, N. & Kasahara, S. (1955). A study on the phenomenon of the tobi-koi
  or shoot carp. I. On the earliest stage at which the shoot carp appears. *Bull.
  Jap. Soc. scient. Fish.* **21**: 73–76.
Nakamura, N. & Kasahara, S. (1956). A study on the phenomenon of the tobi-koi
  or shoot carp. II. On the effect of particle size and quantity of the food. *Bull.
  Jap. Soc. scient. Fish.* **21**: 1022–1024.
Nakamura, N. & Kasahara, S. (1957). A study on the phenomenon of the tobi-koi
  or shoot carp. III. On the results of culturing the modal group and the
  growth of carp fry reared individually. *Bull. Jap. Soc. scient. Fish.* **22**: 674–678.
Nakamura, N. & Kasahara, S. (1961). A study on the phenomenon of the tobi-koi
  or shoot carp. IV. Effects of adding a small number of larger individuals to
  the experimental batches of carp fry and culture density upon the occurrence
  of shoot carp. *Bull. Jap. Soc. scient. Fish.* **27**: 958–962.
Ohno, S. (1974). *Animal cytogenetics* **4**. Chordata. **I**. Protochordata, Cyclostomata
  and Pisces. Berlin & Stuttgart: Gebruder Borntraeger.
Parker, R. R. & Larkin, P. A. (1959). A concept of growth in fishes. *J. Fish. Res. Bd
  Can.* **16**: 721–745.
Purdom, C. E. (1969). Radiation-induced gynogenesis and androgenesis in fish.
  Heredity **24**: 431–444.

Purdom, C. E. (1972). Induced polyploidy in plaice (*Pleuronectes platessa*) and its hybrid with the flounder (*Platichthys flesus*). *Heredity* **29**: 11–24.

Purdom, C. E. (1974). Variation in fish. In *Sea fisheries research*: 347–355. Harden Jones, F. R. (ed.). London: Elek Science.

Purdom, C. E. (1977). Management of brookstock. In *The Two Lakes Ninth Fishery Management Training Course Report, Two Lakes, Romsey, Hampshire, 7–9 Oct. 1977*: 165–173. London: Janssen Services.

Purdom, C. E. & Lincoln, R. F. (1973). Chromosome manipulation in fish. In *Genetics and mutagenesis of fish*: 83–89. Schröder, J. H. (ed.). Berlin: Springer Verlag.

Reinitz, G. L., Orme, L. E., Lemm, C. A. & Hitzel, F. N. (1978). Differential performance of four strains of rainbow trout reared under standardized conditions. *Progve Fish. Cult.* **40**: 21–23.

Ricker, W. E. (1958). Handbook of computations for biological statistics of fish populations. *Bull. Fish. Res. Bd Can.* No. 119: 1–300.

Ryman, N. (1972). An attempt to estimate the magnitude of additive genetic variation of body size in the guppy-fish, *Lebistes reticulatus*. *Hereditas* **71**: 237–244.

Ryman, N. (1973). Two-way selection for body weight in the guppy-fish, *Lebistes reticulatus*. *Hereditas* **74**: 239–246.

Stanley, J. G. (1976). Female homogamety in grass carp (*Ctenopharyngodon idella*) determined by gynogenesis. *J. Fish. Res. Bd Can.* **44**: 1372–1374.

Thorgaard, G. H. (1977). Heteromorphic sex chromosomes in male rainbow trout. *Science, Wash.* **196**: 900–902.

Vladykov, V. D. (1956). Fecundity of wild speckled trout (*Salvelinus fontinalis*) in Quebec Lakes. *J. Fish. Res. Bd Can.* **13**: 799–841.

Wimpenny, R. S. (1953). *The plaice*. London: Edward Arnold.

Winge, O. (1927). The experimental alteration of sex chromosomes into autosomes and vice versa, as illustrated by *Lebistes*. *C.r. Trav. Lab. Carlsberg* (Physiol.) **21**: 1–49.

Wohlfarth, G. W. (1977). Shoot carp. *Bamidgeh* **29**: 35–40.

Yamamoto, T. (1953). Artificially induced sex-reversal in genotypic males of the medaka (*Oryzias latipes*). *J. exp. Zool.* **123**: 571–594.

Yamamoto, T. (1958). Artificial induction of functional sex reversal in geno-typic females of the medaka (*Oryzias latipes*). *J. exp. Zool.* **137**: 227–260.

Yamamoto, T. & Kajishima, T. (1968). Sex hormone induction of sex reversal in the goldfish and evidence for male heterogamety. *J. exp. Zool.* **168**: 215–221.

Symp. zool. Soc. Lond. (1979) No. 44, 219–241

Ecological Aspects of Seasonality in Fishes of Tropical Waters

ROSEMARY H. LOWE-McCONNELL

Streatwick, Streat, nr Hassocks, Sussex, England

SYNOPSIS

In tropical waters, seasonality, caused mainly by seasonal injections of nutrients, varies greatly from marked annual rhythms in floodplain rivers to relatively aseasonal conditions in equatorial lakes and some coral reefs. At the "seasonal" end of the spectrum, fish populations fluctuate greatly, both through the year and from year to year; at the "aseasonal" end, populations remain stable. This is achieved by phenological responses of the fishes: in seasonal conditions by migration, seasonal breeding and growth rhythms, high fecundity, rapid development, early maturity and short life-cycles, giving high production/biomass (P/B) ratios and few age-groups in the populations; seasonal mortalities are high and the fishes have to be facultative feeders. Under aseasonal conditions, fishes may spawn throughout the year, but biotic pressures (e.g. competition for nest sites) may impose seasonality. Species with demersal eggs produce small broods of guarded eggs and young. Maturity tends to be delayed and fecundity reduced. Marine reef species with pelagic eggs are more fecund, whether total or fractional spawners. Aseasonal conditions permit great trophic specialization (adaptive radiations) and produce the most diverse communities. These fishes show the most complex behaviour and interactions (territoriality, complex social systems, symbioses in reef fishes, anti-predator devices such as camouflage, poisons, etc.); predation pressures are high and availability of living space with cover helps to limit fish numbers.

Man-made lake studies have shown how seasonal riverine communities become changed to less seasonal lacustrine ones.

Ecological theory suggests that the fast-turnover, *r*-selected populations produced under seasonal conditions in the tropics should be very resilient, whereas the communities characteristic of the less seasonal habitats may be very fragile. This has important implications for the development of fisheries and conservation of fish stocks.

INTRODUCTION

Phenology was defined by the US/IBP Phenology Committee as "the study of the timing of recurring biological events, the causes of their timing with regard to biotic and abiotic forces, and the interrelation among phases of the same or different species" (Lieth, 1974: 4). In Lieth's volume *Phenology and seasonality modeling*, no consideration was given to fishes. In the temperate zone, we are used to thinking of seasonality being determined mainly by temperature and daylength. But, in the tropics, climatic seasonality may be much less marked and seemingly governed by other factors, such as flooding in rivers, and, in the sea, the two tradewind seasons and associated upwellings. As yet, hardly anything is known about physiological mechanisms controlling biological seasonality or triggering responses to environmental seasonality in tropical waters. However, a good deal of ecological information is available about the phenology of tropical fish, as manifest in their seasonality of reproduction and growth in various types of aquatic habitat. To review this briefly, and to examine some of the implications arising from it, are the aims of this paper.

Within the tropics, conditions become increasingly seasonal with increasing latitude both north and south of the equator: temperature and daylength differences become more marked, and rainfall and flooding increasingly annual following summer rains. In equatorial regions, where rain falls throughout the year (with two equinoctial peaks) and there is little seasonal change in temperature or light, the supply of nutrient salts often limits production cycles. Seasonal injections of nutrients then impose a seasonal biological response. This is very rapid at the prevailing high temperature, its effects passing quickly through the food webs (to plankton, to herbivores and thence to carnivores). Injections of nutrients are brought about mainly by flooding in rivers and wind-induced current changes in large deep lakes and tropical oceans (especially in upwelling areas). Wind-induced turbulence, currents, etc. may also have direct effects on fish, especially those with delicate planktonic larvae. Flooding in rivers also enlarges the aquatic environment seasonally available to the fishes.

Where temperature and food conditions permit, extended breeding and growth seasons can occur, but when, where and how often a fish species does in fact spawn will be decided by selection pressures affecting the survival of eggs and young or adult fish. Tropical communities are characteristically very diverse. Biotic pressures, including competition for food and living space, are likely to be great, and predation pressures are notoriously high. There may be behavioural and social pressures for seasonality as well as abiotic ones.

Within the tropics, a great range of seasonality is encountered. Where conditions fluctuate seasonally, fish populations are found to fluctuate greatly, both through the year and from year to year. Under relatively aseasonal conditions, fish populations are found to remain very stable, both through the year and from year to year. How is this achieved?

Before considering responses of fishes to seasonality in different aquatic systems, we should note that, as environmental conditions influence the species composition of a community, we are not necessarily dealing with the same kinds of fishes in different communities, though there is some overlap. For example, clupeoid fishes predominate in the open waters of upwelling areas (both in the sea and some large lakes), ostariophysan fishes (cyprinids, characoids, nematognath catfishes) in rivers, cichlids in tropical lakes and other percomorphs on marine reefs, where they can make full use of the substratum.

This paper deals essentially with the seasonality of reproduction. According to spawning pattern, the fishes under review fall into two main

categories: total spawners, which shed all their eggs in one batch each year
and multiple spawners, which produce several batches over an extended
period (see Bagenal, 1978). This latter group includes both fractional
(partial) spawners, which produce several (two, three or more) fairly large
batches of unguarded eggs and small brood spawners which produce
batches of up to several hundred (to a few thousand) eggs at frequent
intervals, often throughout the year, and which practise some form of
parental care.

RESPONSES TO SEASONALITY IN VARIOUS FISH COMMUNITIES

Riverine Communities

The fish community of a floodplain river may be taken as an example of
an extremely seasonal one. Within the savanna zone across the tropics,
huge areas flood annually (e.g. 90 000 km^2 in the Lake Chad basin,
30 000 km^2 in the Central Niger delta). Floodplains support important
fisheries and so the ecology of their fishes has been much studied (see
summaries and bibliographies in Lowe-McConnell, 1975; Welcomme,
1975, 1979). In such rivers, floods may increase the size of the aquatic
environment by up to 50% annually, and also bring in nutrients which
stimulate rapid growth of micro-organisms, invertebrates and plants,
giving abundant food and cover for the fish during the high-water season.

In these rivers, the whole biology of the fishes is geared to the flood
cycle. Most of the larger fishes (many ostariophysan) spawn just prior to
or during the floods, and many make long migrations up river for this
purpose (see Lowe-McConnell, 1975). Many species spawn in grass
swamps at the edge of the advancing floods, though some may spawn in
the river channel before the water overflows onto the floodplain. These
fishes are mostly total spawners, with very high fecundity. Egg number
increases with size of female, for example, from 32 000 to 111 000 in
Alestes baremose (Joannis) (quoted by Welcomme, 1979) and from
16 800 to 163 000 in *Clarias gariepinus* (Burchell) of 40 cm and 89 cm
long, respectively (Bruton, 1977). The high-water season is the main
feeding and growing time for the fish which then lay down fat stores to last
through the ensuing dry season, when they have to retreat to the main
rivers where there is little food, or remain in floodplain pools. Mortality is
very high as the waters recede, both from stranding and from predation
by fish, birds and men.

On the floodplain, losses due to eggs being stranded, deoxygenation
and predation are very great, providing great pressures for rapid
development and growth. Many of these floodplain fishes mature in one
or two years. Populations contain few age-groups and very high proportions of young-of-the-year. Age determinations are relatively easy to

make as fish scales and bones bear seasonal growth checks and the well-defined spawning season allows growth estimates from length-frequency mode progressions (Petersen's method). Both the intensity of flooding (height and duration of flood) and amount of water retained at low water may affect fish numbers in subsequent years (as discussed by Welcomme, 1975, 1979). The dependence of these fishes on the arrival of floods for spawning and the effects of floods on growth rates of individual fish, was well shown by lack of spawning and poor growth rates during the recent Sahelian drought. The recovery of stocks after such declines has also given some indication of the resilience of these flood-plain fish populations.

Many equatorial rivers have two floods a year. In parts of large systems, such as the Zaire and Amazon, these come from tributaries north and south of the equator flooding at different times; in smaller rivers, such as those flowing into the northern end of Lake Victoria, they result from equinoctial rains. Double floods may also be caused by rain far upriver taking a long time to work through these vast river systems (as in the Niger, with its "white" flood from local rains and "black" flood from rain elsewhere). Where there are two floods a year, fish spawning runs generally occur in both seasons (though it is not known whether the same individuals take part in both runs) or spawning may be less seasonal (Matthes, 1964; Roberts & Stewart, 1976). Okedi (1965) thought that some of the potamodromous mormyrids migrating up rivers at the north end of Lake Victoria might spawn at both seasons, but the situation may vary from year to year.

In a small stream environment, a single discrete breeding season, coinciding with the early rains, has been reported for *Barbus liberiensis* Steindachner by Payne (1975). However, many small fish of such streams have dry season spawning peaks, as do small clupeids which have plank-tonic larvae (Reynolds, 1974) and also certain small *Barbus* species from West African forest streams (Loiselle & Welcomme, 1971; Loiselle, 1977; Reynolds, 1973). Dry season spawning avoids the risk of sudden spates sweeping away planktonic larvae and also exploits the greater abundance of zooplankton, as food for young fish, in dry season pools. In Nicaragua, Baylis (1976) found that the small cichlid, *Herotilapia multispinosa* (Günther), breeds in the dry season in small ponds cut off from the river, where it is then free from competition from larger cichlid species; *Herotilapia* use the river as a highway for wider distribution in the wet season. There are thus many reasons why small fish may breed in the dry season.

However, a number of other factors may influence the time of spawning in tropical riverine and fluviatile fish. In *Barbus sylvaticus* Loiselle & Welcomme, of Dahomeyan streams, the ovary condition suggested continuous spawning over several months, an unusual occurrence in fish of this genus, and Loiselle & Welcomme (1971) believed that this was related to the small size of this fish—making the production of but few ova at a time possible. In a mildly seasonal stream in Panama, Kramer (1978) found that six small characin species had very different breeding regimes, seasons of only one or two days tied to the start of the rains in two species, *Bryconamericus emperador* (Eigenmann & Ogle) and *Piabucina panamensis* Gill, of over two months in *Brycon petrosus* Meek & Hildebrand and of four months in *Hyphessobrycon panamensis* Durbin, both in the dry season, and more or less throughout the year in *Roeboides guatemalensis* (Günther) (with a dry season peak) and *Gephyrocharax atricaudata* (Meek & Hildebrand). For those with extended breeding seasons, a wide range of oocyte sizes indicated that individual fish spawn repeatedly. The three species with most similar diets had spawning peaks at different times, suggesting maximum use of stream resources.

Finally, the Okavango delta in southern Africa (Botswana) presents an interesting case in that, over much of the area, the flood arrives at the coldest part of the year (the July water temperatures range 13–19°C), and breeding activity of much of the fish fauna does not appear to be tied to floods. Though some species ripen at the start of the flood, most species spawn in the warmer months between September and March (Fox, 1977).

Lacustrine Communities

Fishes in lakes with a high inflow to storage ratio will still be affected by floods, but conditions in large deep lakes are much more stable than in rivers, less affected by rains and inflowing rivers than by wind-induced mixing and upwelling from below a very stable thermocline. Most is known about fishes from the Great Lakes of East and Central Africa, which support important fisheries. From their fish communities, a number of examples of seasonality may be drawn.

Many lacustrine ostariophysan and mormyrid fishes continue to migrate up inflowing rivers and streams to spawn, responding to annual or biannual floods (Lowe, 1952, 1953; Whitehead, 1959; Jackson *et al.*, 1963; Badenhuizen, 1965). Large species ascend main rivers for long distances (approximately 8–25 km) up other rivers (e.g. *Labeo* species purpose, e.g. *Barilius microlepis* (Günther) from Lake Malawi, *Barbus altianalis* Boulenger from Lake Victoria. Many other species run lesser distances (approximately 8–25 km) up other rivers (e.g. *Labeo* species from these lakes, also *Schilbe* catfish and some mormyrids) while some small species (e.g. *Alestes, Barbus*) and *Clarias* catfish ascend short distances up spate streams in enormous numbers, whenever these happen to flood, taking advantage of the short-lived conditions (Greenwood, 1955; Welcomme, 1969).

A few ostariophysan and mormyrid species spawn in lakes but less is known about time and locality. In the African catfish *Clarias gariepinus*, populations inhabiting lakes with large rivers have a restricted breeding season (immediately following the first floods), whereas those inhabiting lakes with no inflowing rivers (as in Lake Sibaya, southern Africa) have an

(p. 223)
Line 30 should read: distances (80km or so), entering them over an extended period for this

extended breeding season (Bruton, 1977, in preparation). In Lake Sibaya, ripe *Clarias gariepinus* can be found between September and January each year, awaiting the right conditions for a spawning run, generally into flooded marginal areas after heavy rain on dark calm nights, with peak activity between 2000 and 0230 h. Although total spawners, courtship and pairing (a loose amplexus) are shown, and one female may mate several times on a spawning run. The *Bagrus* catfish species appear to have retained some seasonality of spawning in various lakes (in Malawi, Victoria and Turkana, according respectively to Jackson *et al.*, 1963; Chilvers, 1969; Hopson, 1974).

The best-developed pelagic fish community occurs in Lake Tanganyika, and consists of endemic clupeids (two species) and their centropomid predators, which live above the very stable thermocline in this very deep rift valley lake. In all these species, ripe females may be found at any time of year, but the clupeids show spawning peaks following wind-induced seasonal upwellings of nutrients and resulting phytoplankton growth (Coulter, 1970). Their pelagic larvae also survive best at the calmest time of year (the months of high plankton growth). Peak spawning is staggered within this period with a June–July maximum in the more inshore-living, larger, *Limnothrissa miodon* Boulenger (growing to 17 cm), and an August–December maximum in the offshore-living, smaller, *Stolothrissa tanganicae* Regan (10 cm).

Their main predators, four endemic Nile perch (*Lates*) species, were found to have seasonal maxima both in breeding and in peak condition between September and November–December (with a minor peak in March). These maxima, synchronous in all the *Lates* species and reflected in the numbers of young *Lates* in the weedbeds where they first live, were thought by Coulter (1976) to be related to the seasonal peaks in clupeid biomasses, which, at the south end of the lake, generally occur September–October and April in *Stolothrissa* and March–April in *Limnothrissa*. Thus, in the pelagic zone, seasonality in the predatory fish appears to be influenced by food-induced cycles of their prey fish. Temperatures remain very constant throughout the year in this lake. In Lake Chad (13°N), where seasonal temperature changes are much greater, seasonality of spawning in *Lates niloticus* (L.) (a total spawner) appears to be related to increased water temperature, and ripe fish are most abundant between January and June (Hopson, 1972).

Cichlid fishes dominate these lacustrine faunas, with species flocks of over 300 species in Lake Malawi, over 200 in Lake Victoria and 126 in Lake Tanganyika, nearly all endemic to the particular lake. These cichlids spawn in the lakes, producing small broods which are mouth-brooded by the females in all except a few *Tilapia* species and some groups in Lake Tanganyika which are substratum spawners, with both parents guarding eggs and young. In aquaria, most cichlids produce successions of broods throughout the year, but they do not necessarily do this in natural waters (see data for *Etroplus maculatus* (Bloch) p. 228). The mouth-brooding cichlids in the African lakes produce from less than 50 to several hundred eggs at a time (rarely a few thousand in very large females, the number increasing with size of fish, as discussed by Welcomme, 1967b), but substratum spawners may lay up to several thousand eggs (Lowe, 1955; Fryer & Iles, 1972).

In the equatorial African Lakes George and Victoria, ripe individuals of most cichlid species can be found at any time of year, but seasonal peaks in numbers spawning do occur; these peaks may be more marked in some years than others. These peaks are in wet seasons for indigenous tilapias in both lakes (Lowe-McConnell, 1956, 1958; Gwahaba, 1973; Welcomme, 1967a,b), and in the dry season for some *Haplochromis* species in Lake George (Dunn, 1975). In Lake Victoria, the tilapia *Sarotherodon esculentus* (Graham) has two peaks a year at the north end, and one at the south, in accordance with patterns of rainfall in these areas. Ovary condition suggested that several broods are produced in succession, and returns of tagged fish confirmed this (Lowe–McConnell, 1956). Fryer (1961) thought that the indigenous *Sarotherodon variabilis* (Boulenger) in Lake Victoria produced three, possibly five, broods in eight months, but that numbers spawning and survival of the young might vary acyclically from year to year (as his Fig. 4 suggests); this species declined after the introduced substratum spawning *Tilapia zillii* (Gervais) moved into its nursery grounds (Welcomme, 1966). The abnormally high level of Lake Victoria in 1962 had an important role in the establishment of the introduced tilapias (Welcomme, 1970). Once established, the introduced species, *Sarotherodon niloticus* (L.), *S. leucostictus* (Trewavas) and *T. zillii*, spawned throughout the year, as shown by Welcomme (1967a: Fig. 5).

Less is known about cichlid spawning seasons in Lake Tanganyika, where cichlids are not the main commercial fish. Matthes (1960, 1961) suggested that most spawn throughout the year and that the largest cichlid, the predatory *Boulengerochromis microlepis* (Boulenger), had three spawning peaks a year. Annual oscillations in lake level (of approximately 1 m) create lakeside pools wherein *Haplochromis burtoni* (Günther) spawns undisturbed by larger species (Fernald & Hirata, 1977).

Lake Malawi, lying farther from the equator (9°–14°S), has better-defined seasons: a cool, dry but windy season from March to August, which causes some mixing and resultant phytoplankton growth, a hot dry season, in October–November before the rains, and the annual rains, falling from December to February. In this lake the mbuna rockfish (mainly *Aufwuchs* feeders) were said by Fryer & Iles (1972) to spawn throughout the year; these produce less than 50 eggs at a time, which the female mouth-broods for three weeks to a month. In aquaria, the mbuna *Labeotropheus* spp. can produce five to seven broods a year (Balon, 1977). However, in the lake, many of the other cichlids have surprisingly restricted breeding seasons (Table I) and, among those which have, many appear to produce but one brood a year, i.e. to have very reduced

TABLE I

Seasonality of spawning in cichlids in Lake Malawi

	J	F	M	A	M	J	J	A	S	O	N	D
Sarotherodon squamipinnis	+	+	+	+	−	−	−	−	−	−	−	+
S. saka	−	−	−	−	−	−	−	+	+	+	+	−
S. lidole	+	−	−	−	−	−	−	−	−	+	+	+
S. shiranus	+	−	−	−	−	−	−	−	+	+	+	+
Haplochromis virginalis	−	−	+	+	+	−	−	−	−	−	−	−
H. quadrimaculatus	−	··	−	+	+	+	+	−	−	−	−	−
H. pleurostigmoides	−	−	−	+	+	+	+	+	−	−	−	−
H. borleyi	+	+	+	+	+	+	+	+	+	+	+	+
H. eucinostomus	+	+	−	−	+	−	+	−	−	−	−	−
H. mloto	−	−	−	−	−	−	−	+	+	+	−	−
H. intermedius	−	−	−	−	−	+	+	+	−	−	−	−
Lethrinops parvidens	−	−	−	−	−	−	−	−	+	+	−	−
L. longipinnis	−	−	−	−	+	+	+	+	+	+	−	−
Mbuna	+	+	+	+	+	+	+	+	+	+	+	+

Data from Lowe (1952); Iles (1959, 1971); Fryer & Iles (1972); Tweddle & Turner (1977).

fecundity. From aquarium studies Berns, Chave & Peters (1978) estimate that the endemic tilapia *Sarotherodon squamipinnis* (Günther) has a six-week "caring period" under natural conditions (mouth-brooding for four weeks, then guarding young for two weeks), but that females may be able to produce a second brood in the four-month breeding season. Among the tilapias at the south end of the lake, *S. saka* (Lowe) and *S. lidole* (Trewavas) spawn in shallow water before the rains (the hottest, calmest time of year), *S. squamipinnis* spawns in deeper water during the rains and the most inshore-living species, *S. shiranus* (Boulenger), has the least restricted season (September–January). Time and depth of spawning, reinforced by differences in male breeding colour, keep separate *S. saka* and *S. squamipinnis*, the most similar in appearance and ecology (Lowe, 1952, 1953; Lowe-McConnell, 1959, 1969).

Among the utaka zooplankton-feeding group of *Haplochromis* living in the open waters of Lake Malawi, some have more restricted seasons than others. Several species spawn between March and July (Iles, 1959, 1971), the time when mixing is greatest. Spawning season peaks are staggered for the various *Haplochromis*. The utaka probably have to come close inshore to spawn, where suitable places may be limited. In the southwest arm of the lake, two bottom-living *Lethrinops* species also spawn at the end of the cool windy season, one species having a more restricted season than the other (Tweddle & Turner, 1977). The staggering of spawning peaks in species sharing resources suggests that non-synchronization helps to maximize resource use.

In Lake Sibaya, at the southern border of the tropics on the southeast coast of Africa, the cichlid *Sarotherodon mossambicus* (Peters) has a well-defined breeding season which lasts from September to February (Bruton & Boltt, 1975). Males establish territories and nests in shallow water, and engage in brief courtship with females which mouth-brood eggs while remaining in sheltered, vegetated areas. The fry are released into shallow water in mid or late summer when food is abundant as a result of flooding and decay of plant matter and the development of invertebrate populations. Furthermore, water temperatures are so high that most other fish species in the lake are excluded from the extreme shallows.

Underwater observations of cichlids living in Lake Jiloá, a small crater lake in Nicaragua, Central America, by McKaye (1977), have illuminated factors regulating the timing and distribution of breeding in species which can be bred throughout the year in the laboratory. This lake has nine cichlid species, in all of which both parents guard eggs and young, and also houses a predatory eleotrine goby. The seasonal pattern of breeding is bimodal, with a different species complex breeding in wet and dry seasons. Proximate cues which trigger breeding are unknown, but for two relatively short periods, mid-wet and mid-dry seasons, competition for breeding sites was found to be intense. Over 90% of all territories were lost prior to the completion of a breeding cycle, either to conspecifics or to members of other species. Territorial conflicts allowed predators to dart into the area and eat the young. Pairs in shallow water were most successful in rearing young. Seasonality of spawning was apparently determined by the regime in a biomass-dominant species, *Cichlasoma citrinellum* (Günther). In the wet season, this aggressively excluded all but the two smallest species from breeding. In the dry season, when the dominant species did not breed (probably because of food limitation), all the other species were able to breed, separated both by depth and time of breeding. The dominant species, unlike the others, does not feed while guarding eggs and young, and so has to build up lipid reserves to last eight to 10 weeks. In the dry season it feeds on substrate infauna (snails and eggs) but turns to adult and larval insects when these become abundant at the onset of the rains. In 1972, when there was a drought, insects were scarce and breeding pairs of *C. citrinellum* were then much less abundant than in 1973. Thus, it seems that year to year variations in numbers of the dominant species breeding will have repercussions on the other species. The two smaller species which do manage to breed in the wet season, *Neetroplus nematopus* (Günther) and *Cichlasoma nigrofasciatum* (Günther), are herbivores and feed while guarding their young. One of these (*N. nematopus*) breeds at the same time as the dominant species, the other a month later; were they to start earlier, the general disruption as the dominant fish fight for territories might lead to brood losses. Breeding outside peak periods allows predators to wipe out broods, while synchrony of intraspecific breeding appears to an anti-predator strategy. Such synchrony was particularly marked in *Cichlasoma rostratum* (Gill &

Bransford), but also shown in *C. citrinellum*, a species with communal defence of the young (McKaye & McKaye, 1977) (as in *Etroplus suratensis* (Bloch) in Sri Lanka lagoons (Ward & Wyman, 1977)). In Lake Jiloá, the predatory cichlids, *C. dovii* (Günther) and *C. managuense* (Günther), spawn late in the dry season, their young then having young of other cichlids as prey when they turn from zooplankton to a diet of young fish. The neighbouring Lake Apoyo lacked *C. dovii*, and here *C. managuense* was found to have a broader niche than in Lake Jiloá.

In lagoons of Sri Lanka, the cichlid *Etroplus maculatus* continues to brood young until they are almost sexually mature. Spawning is continuous through the year and asynchronous. Ward & Wyman (1977) suggested that it is the cessation of brooding, when the young are lost to the parents, that controls the start of a new ovarian cycle in this species. In these lagoons, a pair has probably only two or three broods a year, though in an aquarium, a pair may produce up to 12 broods a year.

Man-made Lake Communities

Man-made lakes provide large scale experiments wherein to study the changes from seasonal riverine faunas to less seasonal lacustrine ones. Studies in the big new African lakes suggest that relaxation of breeding seasons is important for successful lake exploitation by a colonizing species. Initially, once the barrage is closed, flood-spawning fishes may spawn very successfully as the lake fills, and survival of their young is particularly high as predator populations have not yet built up. But these species generally decline in numbers within a year or so if they must ascend rivers to spawn. This happened for *Alestes* in Lake Volta (Petr, 1968), for *Citharinus* and other characoids at Kainji on the River Niger (Lewis, 1974) and for *Labeo* and other migrant species at Cabora Bassa on the Zambezi (Jackson & Rogers, 1976). In all these new lakes, cichlids, preadapted to breed in still water, have become the dominant fishes once the lake level has stabilized enough to allow them to nest in shallow water. Within a few years after dam closure, the ostariophysan-dominated faunas have become replaced by cichlid-dominated ones.

The pelagic zone is much enlarged as a lake forms, offering opportunities for plankton feeders. Reynolds (1974) found that Lake Volta was colonized by five small pelagic species, all fractional spawners (and with females larger than the males). Of these, two clupeid species and a cyprinid were dry-season spawners in the river, and two schilbeid catfishes wet-season spawners. One clupeid, *Pellonula afzeliusi* (Johnels), extended its breeding season to spawn throughout the year in the lake, where high water no longer presented a danger to its planktonic larvae (the other, larger, clupeid, *Cynothrissa mento* Regan, probably migrated to rivers to spawn). The wet-season spawning schilbeids both extended their breeding seasons, throughout the year in *Physailia pellucida* Boulenger and into the early dry season in *Siluranodon auritus* Geoffroy St-Hilaire;

for these species, lacustrine conditions provided a continued high-water season. The species, which extended their breeding seasons rapidly, became abundant in the lake.

In Lake Kariba, the replacement of a small characin, *Myletes* (= *Brachyalestes*) *imberi* (Peters), by the closely related *Brycinus* (= *Alestes*) *lateralis* (Boulenger) was apparently due to conditions in the new lake favouring the breeding regime of the immigrant species (Balon & Coche, 1974). Whereas *M. imberi* spawned off shores which became subject to irregular man-made changes in water level, *B. lateralis* spawned on the roots of the floating water plants which became so abundant in the new lake.

Marine Shelf Communities

In tropical oceans, the two monsoon (tradewind) seasons induce seasonal changes in current systems, leading to upwellings in certain areas (e.g. off Peru, Southwest Africa, Ghana). These have profound effects on fish cycles, as witnessed by the dramatic failures of fisheries, such as that for the Peruvian anchovy, when upwellings fail to occur. The small clupeoids in the upwelling areas respond to the effects of seasonal increases in nutrients by increased breeding and rapid growth following the enhancement of the planktonic food supply (Longhurst, 1971). These small fishes spawn several times during their short lives (few Peruvian anchoveta, *Engraulis ringens* Jenyns, survive beyond 18 months).

On the continental shelves, discharges from the many large rivers add a seasonality to that imposed by wind-induced currents, turbulence, water temperature changes, etc. During a trawl-fish survey off Guyana (6°–9°N on the Atlantic coast of South America), great diversity in the spawning rhythms of these fishes was found. Common species of at least four families (Sciaenidae, Carangidae, Gerridae, Pomadasyidae), and including the commonest species, the sciaenid croaker, *Micropogon furnieri* (Desmarest), had ripe females present in the catches at all times of year. Others, including members of the same families, such as the sciaenid *Macrodon ancylodon* (Bloch & Schneider), had much more restricted breeding seasons (Lowe-McConnell, 1962: Table 2; 1966; 1977). Young *Micropogon* were taken, all year round, entering brackish swamps from the sea along the open coast, but were never found in estuaries, unlike the young *Macrodon*, which were caught in Chinese seines in the estuaries but never from the open coast. Possibly the estuary-visiting species have better-defined seasons: seasonality in a tropical estuary in Costa Rica is discussed by Nordlie & Kelso (1975).

Water temperatures, as far as is known, remain high throughout the year on the Guyana continental shelf. On the other side of the Atlantic, off West Africa, there is greater seasonal variation. Longhurst, who studied West African trawl catches, found that, for the three commonest sciaenids (*Pseudotolithus* spp.), ripe fish were present in the populations throughout the year, but there was, nevertheless, a cycle of spawning intensity, the numbers of ripe females falling when the mean surface temperature fell below about 27·5°C, well shown in Fig. 4 of Longhurst (1964) for *P. senegalensis* (Valenciennes) and *P. typus* Bleeker off Nigeria. The third common species, *P. elongatus* (Bowdich), spawned in the Sierra Leone estuary with a peak in the dry season, the time of least river effluent and highest water temperatures (Longhurst, 1969). Among polynemid fish also common in the trawl here, *Pentanemus quinquarius* L. (which has a normal sexual cycle) and *Galeoides decadactylus* (Bloch) (a partial protan-drous hermaphrodite), ripe individuals of both sexes occurred in all months, the intensity being less cyclical in *Pentanemus* than in *Galeoides* which peaks in the dry season and almost ceases to spawn in the rains. The *Pentanemus* mature when less than six months old (at approximately 15 cm) and rarely survive the second year of life, but *Galeoides* of three years old appeared in catches (Longhurst, 1965). Longhurst stressed the significance of so few age-groups in these tropical marine fish; fluctua-tions resulting from spawning success or failure are reflected very quickly in the catches, although the large number of discrete broods from each year present in the stocks might help to dampen down any instability in stock strength from having so few year classes.

Marine Reef Communities

In the Caribbean, seasonality of spawning has been studied in 35 species on Jamaican reefs (18°N) by Munro *et al.* (1973), and the spawning patterns and seasonal number of juveniles in 350 species around Puerto Rico (18°N) by Erdman (1977). These reef fishes comprise (1) small species, with demersal eggs or oral incubation, whose larval young never enter the plankton and (2) larger species, which produce pelagic eggs hatching into a pelagic larva with either a short pelagic life, rapidly metamorphosing to the adult and never found in oceanic plankton, or with a long oceanic-pelagic larval or postlarval life in which the majority of larvae may drift far from the spawning site, as exemplified elsewhere by the Pacific surgeon fish, *Acanthurus triostegus sandvicensis* Streets (Randall, 1961a,b).

The small species with demersal eggs may spawn continuously throughout the year, as do the pomacentrid anemone commensals at Eniwetok Atoll in the Pacific (Allen, 1975), and the pomacentrid *Abudef-duf saxatilis* (L.) with slight equinoctial peaks, on Jamaican reefs. In the Red Sea, the numerous pomacentrid species, with their very varied types of social spawning behaviour, spawn over an extended season from March–April to September (Fishelson, Popper & Avidor, 1974).

On Jamaican reefs, among the larger species with a short pelagic larval stage, some lutjanid snappers and pomadasyid grunts spawned more or less throughout the year, but with a peak from February to April, the months when water temperatures are minimal (26.5°C in March); the *Haemulon* grunts showed some staggering of peak spawning times. In scarids, spawning appeared to be confined to January–June (with a February–March peak). Among those with a long pelagic larval stage, carangids spawned throughout the year, but, again, most spawned in the cooler water months; acanthurid spawning was continued to January–June (peak February–March). The serranid groupers here had an even more restricted season, from January to May (peak February–March). Off Florida, the red grouper, *Epinephelus morio*, a protogynous hermaphrodite (like many serranids), is a total spawner with breeding confined to May (Moe, 1969). The Nassau grouper, *Epinephelus striatus* (Bloch), spawns in late January off the Bahamas; Smith (1972) described a spawning aggregation here of well over 30 000 individuals, many of which must have travelled long distances (25 + km) to the spawning site. Captain Cousteau has filmed a similar seasonal aggregation of large groupers off Honduras. Data on seasonality of spawning in other groupers are given by Randall & Brock (1960) and Thompson & Munro (1978).

In the western Pacific (Palau), Johannes (1978) distinguished between:
1. migrating spawners (serranids, mugilids and possibly some carangids, lutjanids, scarids and leiognathids);
2. non-migrating spawners with pelagic eggs comprising smaller species, which remain close to their usual habitats to spawn, probably because small fish are more vulnerable to predation, e.g. some scarids, labrids, mullids, acanthurids and
3. non-migrating spawners with demersal eggs, found among pomacentrids, siganids, balistids, tetraodontids, gobiids, blenniids, clinids, apogonids, in most of which the eggs are guarded against predators.

He considered that the main selection pressure for an offshore pelagic larval existence has been to escape high predation on the reef, rather than to effect dispersal of the young, or to crop food from the open ocean, for plankton in tropical oceans is sparse and varies little seasonally.

It was somewhat surprising to find that spawning peaks coincided with lowest water temperatures on Jamaican reefs since maximum spawning occurs at times of highest water temperatures at the southern end of the Great Barrier reef. Johannes (1978), who has collated data on seasonality of spawning in coastal fishes, made a good case for the view that there are selection pressures for spawning at the calmest times of year, when pelagic larvae will be least endangered by turbulent surface waters, and also when inshore gyres have the best chance of bringing larval young back to the reef. Johannes (1978) also points out that nearly 50 species of taxonomically widely distributed tropical marine fish have lunar spawning rhythms, the majority of them spawning around the new or full moon. He suggests that there may be selective advantages associated with spawning on spring tides. Randall & Randall (1963), when describing year-round spawning in the sparid *Sparisoma rubripinne* (C. & V.) in the Virgin Islands, and the lunar spawning cycle of the labrid *Thalassoma bifasciatum* (Bloch), stressed that the reproductive potential of a fish is greatly enhanced when large groups assemble to spawn. Lunar cycles should help to synchronize spawning.

DISCUSSION

This brief survey has shown that, in tropical waters, the spawning seasons may be either

1. restricted, as for many total spawners such as riverine Ostariophysi and for certain marine groupers, as well as for some small-brood cichlids found in Lake Malawi or
2. extended, sometimes throughout the year (depending on latitude), as for
   a. total spawners, which produce eggs all in one batch, as in *Lates niloticus* L. of Lake Chad (Hopson, 1972), in *Clarias gariepinus* of Lake Sibaya (Bruton, 1977) and in the milkfish, *Chanos chanos* (Forskål) in the sea (Schuster, 1960);
   b. multiple-spawning reef-fish with pelagic eggs, as in many labrids, scarids and *Acanthurus* (Sale, 1978: table 7), and marine pelagic fish, such as Indian mackerels, *Rastrelliger* species, and the scombroid skipjack, *Katsuwonus pelamis* (L.) (Jones & Rosa, 1965; Raju, 1964); also in freshwater clupeids, which produce two or three batches of demersal eggs (Reynolds, 1974);
   c. small-brood spawners, with parental care, exemplified by cichlids in fresh water and pomacentrids on marine reefs, broods being produced for all or part of the year, though generally not as often in natural waters as in aquaria.

Sale (1978: Table 7) has collated information on the duration of the breeding period for a number of reef species, and he also gives the frequency of spawning by individual fish. But, for many species, we do not know whether they are total or multiple spawners, as few studies of oocyte size-frequencies have been made. In the surgeon fish, *Acanthurus triostegus sandvicensis*, which exhibits lunar spawning periodicity, ova diameters suggested multiple spawning, and Randall (1961a) found a 123-mm long female with approximately 40 000 large eggs ready for one spawning; in Hawaiian waters (21°N), the relative gonad length (GL/SL × 100) of these females remained high from November to June, but ripe females were found throughout the year in more equatorial waters. This indicates that this fish, with a lunar-spawning cycle, spawns several times between November and June. For West African sciaenids (*Pseudotolithus* spp.), Longhurst (1969) commented that the patterns of individual spawning within the stock spawning cycle remain obscure.

We do not know the total fecundity of a species until we know how many batches of eggs are produced in a year. For this, ova size-frequency studies should be helpful, though, in tropical waters, the number of batches may be found to vary from year to year.

The Adaptive Value of Extended Spawning Seasons

For reef fishes, Johannes (1978) has suggested that the selective value of an extended spawning season may be related to the spread through the year of vacancies in reef communities which are taken up by larval fish on their return to the reef. Vacancies arise as resident fish disappear from the reef in an aseasonal manner, many picked off by predators. The piecemeal and random nature of reef repopulation has been stressed by experiments on the Great Barrier Reef including the use of artificial reefs (Russell, Talbot & Domm, 1974; Sale, 1974, 1978); these studies suggested that it is often possible for one of several ecologically similar species to slip into a vacant place (but see discussions in papers by Sale, Dale, Smith, and Helfman, in Helfman, 1978). An extended spawning season should allow a particular species a greater chance of doing so.

In fresh waters, where water levels fluctuate and eggs and young may be endangered by stranding, deoxygenation, etc., the production of two or three batches of eggs would seem to have obvious adaptive value. It is surprising that so many floodplain ostariophysan fishes are total spawners. What are the selective advantages of this? Conditions do change very rapidly as rivers flood and perhaps total spawning is more effectively synchronized. It occurs in many long-range migrants. But the Brazilian *Prochilodus scrofa* Steindachner is said by de Godoy (1959) to be a partial spawner, depositing numerous eggs—approximately 1 300 000 in a 4-kg female—in batches as it moves up river, with many residual "immature and mature" ova being resorbed after spawning.

The staggering of peak spawning times in sympatric, closely related species, or among those sharing the same resources (food or living space), has been noted in many cases—among cichlids in Lakes Malawi and Jiloá, small characins in Panama streams, *Haemulon* grunts on Jamaican reefs—and has been suggested for other reef fish (Smith & Tyler, 1972). These cases all stress the importance of biotic pressures in determining seasonality in these very diverse tropical communities. They suggest that there must be competition for food or living space. In Lake Victoria, availability of spawning and nursery grounds in shallow water appeared to limit tilapia numbers (Lowe-McConnell, 1956; Fryer, 1961).

In the very diverse, less seasonal communities, predation and living space with cover seem to be more limiting to numbers than food supply. The high numbers of predators in these communities may keep numbers of prey fish below the level at which they would compete for food (as discussed by Greenwood, 1974; Lowe-McConnell, 1969, 1975).

There are, of course, many other factors, both abiotic and biotic, which may affect seasonality of spawning: for example, effects of turbulence on survival of planktonic young or possibly differential predation pressures at different times of year (about which very little is yet known). Furthermore, all the many factors must be interacting.

The effect of environmental conditions on the number of batches of young produced is well shown in cichlids bred in aquaria and ponds, where they produce many more broods per year than under natural conditions in lakes and rivers. The precise reasons for this are not clear and may vary for different species. A social factor, the removal of broods of young earlier in aquaria than in the field, has been suggested for *Etroplus maculatus* (Ward & Wyman, 1977). The ability to breed at a reduced size and with greater frequency, according to circumstance, has an adaptive value, enabling populations of tilapia, for example, to survive in small pools and then to repopulate lakes and rivers when conditions permit (Lowe-McConnell, 1958; Fryer & Iles, 1969, 1972).

The "Seasonality Spectrum" and Attributes of Seasonal and Aseasonal Fish Communities

In summary, Table II lists some of the attributes of fish populations in the most and least seasonal communities of tropical waters. We have seen how, when conditions fluctuate seasonally, fluctuations in fish populations are brought about by migration, seasonal spawning and mortality.

TABLE II

Attributes of extreme types of seasonality in tropical waters

Conditions	Very seasonal	Aseasonal
Fish populations	Fluctuating	Very stable
Migrations	+ +	− −
Spawning	Seasonal, total	Aseasonal, multiple
Fecundity	High	Reduced (brooded or demersal eggs); high (pelagic eggs)
Life cycles	Short	Longer
P/B ratio	High	Lower
Feeding	Facultative	Specialized
Behaviour	Simple	Complex
Selection	*r* type, by abiotic agents	Mainly *K* type, by biotic agents
Community	Rejuvenated	Very mature
Implications	?Resilient	?Fragile

Under these conditions, strong selection pressures exist for high fecundity (and, connected with this, females are often larger than males, the egg number increasing with size of female), as well as for rapid development and growth. Populations contain few age-groups, life-cycles are short, and population overturn is rapid (high P/B ratio), with little time or opportunity for the development of very complex behaviour. As conditions change seasonally so the fish have to change food eaten, and must remain rather generalized feeders. The predominant type of selection here seems to be r-selection, for rapid rate of increase, as in pioneer communities. Much of the floodplain is indeed a new habitat opened up for colonists to exploit every year. The communities, though diverse, are rejuvenated. The abiotic factors governing spawning success (such as those associated with the flood regime, stranding, deoxygenation), interacting with intense predation, vary from year to year and great fluctuation in numbers of a particular species also occurs from year to year. Ecological theory predicts that such communities will be resilient, but this question remains to be answered.

Where conditions are less seasonal, fish populations remain very stable throughout the year and from year to year, as many tagging experiments have shown (e.g. on marine reefs, by Fishelson *et al.*, 1974; Ehrlich, 1975; Goldman & Talbot, 1976). Many fish are territorial or have home ranges; repopulation happens in a piecemeal way, vacancies arising as individual fish disappear. In lakes, fecundity of fish species is reduced, few young being produced at a time, though, in some cases, over a relatively long lifespan. On marine reefs, fecundity also appears to be low among demersal-spawning fishes, but is much higher in fishes with pelagic larval stages which have to withstand the exigencies of life in the very different environment of open waters. In these species, numbers may be limited more by recruitment to the reef fauna than by fecundity of the adults. In some marine fish (e.g. serranids), protogynous sex changes decrease potential fecundity. Males are often larger than females. There is less information on growth rates than is available for species belonging to the seasonal communities, since it is much more difficult to determine age and consequently growth rates, under aseasonal conditions where growth is continuous throughout the year and breeding seasons not well defined. The presence of the same food sources throughout the year allows great trophic specialization, and spectacular examples of adaptive radiation are found in such communities (e.g. among the cichlids of African lakes). "Stores of information" (Margalef, 1968) are high: there is complex intra- and inter-specific behaviour, including symbioses with other fish (such as cleaners) and invertebrates in the sea; predators are abundant and anti-predator devices, such as camouflage or possession of poison, are common. These less seasonal communities have many of the attributes of mature, predominantly "K-selected" ones. Ecological theory, awaiting confirmation, suggests that they may be very fragile (May, 1975).

Implications of Seasonality

What evidence is there that fish populations living in the seasonal environments are resilient, and those in aseasonal ones fragile? In seasonal habitats, where there are few age-groups in the populations, breeding success or failure is manifested very rapidly in exploited populations (as noted by Longhurst (1965), see p. 230). Recoveries can be very rapid after decline due to natural causes, as shown, for example, by recovery after the recent Sahelian drought (discussed by Welcomme, 1979). Many of these fishes are migratory, and recovery may depend on repopulation from outside the affected area. Where there are few age-groups in the population, heavy fishing over very few years can make very serious inroads into stocks. Such populations can be exploited beyond recovery, as in the case of *Labeo altivelis* Peters overfished during spawning runs up the Luapula River from Lake Mweru (de Kimpe, 1964) and as appeared to be happening for *Labeo victorianus* Boulenger from Lake Victoria (Fryer, 1973: Fig. 3).

For the reef ecosystems, Munro *et al.* (1973) noted that fish were scarce in their samples the second year of sampling, which they suggested might be an effect of their own fishing, though, for reef species with pelagic larvae, the authors could not be certain that events well away from the reef had not affected reef populations. We know as yet very little about what really controls numbers in these fishes, although predation is certainly very important in the aseasonal communities. Data on growth rates are sparse, but some evidence suggests that fishes living under relatively aseasonal conditions grow more slowly or mature later than those under more seasonal regimes, as certainly seems to obtain for lake cichlids. The demersal spawning, small-brood spawners are much less fecund than types of fish living in more seasonal environments. Low fecundity only succeeds where there is parental care; the survival of the species depends on parents being present to guard young, and, once parent fish are removed, whole broods are lost to predators. The most colourful and exotic "tropical fish", much fished for the aquarium trade, both from freshwater and coral reefs, are nearly all small-brood spawners from relatively aseasonal communities. Conservation measures to protect these fish populations are likely to be much needed.

In conclusion, it seems from this brief survey that, in tropical waters, where temperatures do not limit fish spawning, seasonality is imposed mainly by

1. factors leading to injections of nutrients (affecting the fish through food webs), though some (such as turbulence affecting fish larvae) may influence the species directly, and
2. by biotic pressures (such as competition for spawning grounds or living space) which may impose seasonality in the relatively aseasonal environments with their very diverse fish communities.

ACKNOWLEDGEMENTS

I am very grateful to the Trustees of the British Museum (Natural History) for working space and excellent library facilities while studying these problems, to my colleagues in the Fish Section there and M. Bruton for many helpful discussions and also to D. L. Kramer and R. E. Johannes for allowing me to quote their work in press.

REFERENCES

Allen, G. R. (1975). *The anemone fishes.* (2nd edn). T. F. H. Publs Inc.: Neptune City, New Jersey, U.S.A.
Badenhuizen, G. R. (1965). Lufubu River research notes. *Fish. Res. Bull. Zambia* **1963–64**: 11–41.
Bagenal, T. (ed.) (1978). *Methods for assessment of fish production in fresh waters.* (3rd edn). (IBP Handbook No. 3). Oxford: Blackwell Scientific Publication Ltd.
Balon, E. K. (1977). Early ontogeny of *Labeotropheus* Ahl, 1927 (Mbuna, Cichlidae L. Malawi) with a discussion on advanced protective styles in fish reproduction and development. *Envirl Biol. Fish.* **2**: 147–176.
Balon, E. K. & Coche, A. G. (1974). *Lake Kariba: a man-made tropical ecosystem in Central Africa.* The Hague: W. Junk.
Baylis, J. R. (1976). The behaviour and ecology of *Herotilapia multispinosa* (Teleostei, Cichlidae). In *Investigations of the ichthyofauna of Nicaraguan lakes*: 477–508. Thorson, T. B. (ed.). Lincoln: School of Life Sciences, University of Nebraska.
Berns, S., Chave, E. H. & Peters, H. M. (1978). On the biology of *Tilapia squamipinnis* (Günther) from Lake Malawi (Teleostei: Cichlidae). *Arch. Hydrobiol.* **84**: 218–246.
Bruton, M. N. (1977). *The biology of* Clarias gariepinus *(Burchell, 1822) in L. Sibaya, Kwazulu, with emphasis on its role as a predator.* Ph.D. thesis: Rhodes University, Grahamstown, S. Africa.
Bruton, M. N. (In prep.). *The breeding biology and early development of* Clarias gariepinus *(Pisces: Clariidae) in L. Sibaya, S. Africa, with a review of breeding in* Clarias.
Bruton, M. N. & Boltt, R. E. (1975). Aspects of the biology of *Tilapia mossambica* Peters (Pisces: Cichlidae) in a natural freshwater lake (L. Sibaya, S. Africa). *J. Fish Biol.* **7**: 423–445.
Chilvers, R. M. (1969). A method of age estimation from length frequency data for larger fish with reference to *Bagrus docmac* Forskahl. *Rep. E. Afr. Freshw. Fish Res. Org.* **1968**: 32–38.
Coulter, G. W. (1970). Population changes within a group of fish species in Lake Tanganyika following their exploitation. *J. Fish Biol.* **2**: 329–353.
Coulter, G. W. (1976). The biology of *Lates* species (Nile perch) in Lake Tanganyika, and the status of the pelagic fishery for *Lates* species and *Luciolates stappersii* (Blgr). *J. Fish Biol.* **9**: 235–259.
Dunn, I. G. (1975). Ecological notes on the *Haplochromis* (Pisces: Cichlidae) species-flock of Lake George, Uganda (East Africa). *J. Fish Biol.* **7**: 651–666.
Ehrlich, P. R. (1975). The population biology of coral reef fishes. *A. Rev. Ecol. Syst.* **6**: 211–247.
Erdman, D. S. (1977). Spawning patterns of fish from the northeastern Caribbean. In *Symposium on progress in marine research in the Caribbean and adjacent regions, Caracas, July 1976*: 145–169. Stewart, H. B. Jr (ed.). (*FAO Fish Rep.* No. 200).

Fernald, R. D. & Hirata, N. R. (1977). Field study of *Haplochromis burtoni*: habitats and co-habitant. *Envirl Biol. Fish.* **2**: 299–308.

Fishelson, L., Popper, D. & Avidor, A. (1974). Biosociology and ecology of pomacentrid fishes around the Sinai Peninsula (northern Red Sea). *J. Fish Biol.* **6**: 119–133.

Fox, P. J. (1977). Preliminary observations on fish communities of the Okavango delta. *Proc. Symp. Okavango delta and its future utilization, Botswana Society, National Museum, Gaberones, Botswana* August 30–September 2, 1976.

Fryer, G. (1961). Observations on the biology of the cichlid fish *Tilapia variabilis* Blgr. in the northern waters of L. Victoria (E. Africa). *Revue Zool. Bot. afr.* **64**: 1–33.

Fryer, G. (1973). The Lake Victoria fisheries: some facts and fallacies. *Biol. Conserv.* **5**: 304–308.

Fryer, G. & Iles, T. D. (1969). Alternative routes to evolutionary success as exhibited by African cichlid fishes of the genus *Tilapia* and the species flocks of the Great Lakes. *Evolution,Lancaster, Pa* **23**: 359–369.

Fryer, G. & Iles, T. D. (1972). *The cichlid fishes of the Great Lakes of Africa.* Edinburgh: Oliver & Boyd.

Godoy, M. P. de (1959). The age, growth, sexual maturity, behaviour, migration, tagging and transplantation of the curimbata (*Prochilodus scrofa* Stdr, 1881) of the Mogi-Guassu R., Sao Paulo State, Brasil. *An. Acad. bras. Cienc.* **31**: 447–477.

Goldman, B. & Talbot, F. H. (1976). Aspects of the ecology of coral reef fishes. In *Biology and geology of coral reefs* **3** Biology 2: 125–154. Jones, O. A. & Endean, R. (eds). New York & London: Academic Press.

Greenwood, P. H. (1955). Reproduction in the catfish *Clarias mossambicus*, Peters. *Nature, Lond.* **176**: 516.

Greenwood, P. H. (1974). The cichlid fishes of Lake Victoria, East Africa: the biology and evolution of a species flock. *Bull. Br. Mus. nat. Hist. Lond.* (Zool.) Suppl. **6**: 1–134.

Gwahaba, J. S. (1973). Effects of fishing on the *Tilapia nilotica* (L. 1757) population in Lake George, Uganda, over the past twenty years. *E. Afr. Wildl. J.* **11**: 317–328.

Helfman, G. S. (ed.) (1978). Patterns of community structure in fishes. Proceedings of a mini-symposium held at Cornell University, Ithaca, New York, May 1976. *Envirl Biol. Fish.* **3**: 1–152.

Hopson, A. J. (1972). A study of the Nile Perch in Lake Chad. *Overseas Res. Publs* No. 19: 1–93.

Hopson, A. J. (1974). *Lake Rudolf Fisheries Research Project. Progress Report, June, 1974* (cyclostyled).

Iles, T. D. (1959). A group of zooplankton feeders of the genus *Haplochromis* (Cichlidae) in Lake Nyasa. *Ann. Mag. nat. Hist.* (13) **2**: 257–280.

Iles, T. D. (1971). Ecological aspects of growth in African cichlid fishes. *J. Cons. perm. int. Explor. Mer* **33**: 362–384.

Jackson, P. B., Iles, T. D. Harding, D. & Fryer, G. (1963). *Report on the survey of northern Lake Nyasa, 1954–55.* Zomba: Govt. Printer.

Jackson, P. B. & Rogers, K. H. (1976). Cabora Bassa fish populations before and during the first filling phase. *Zoologica Afr.* **11**: 373–397.

Johannes, R. E. (1978). Reproductive strategies of coastal marine fishes in the tropics. *Envirl Biol. Fish.* **3**: 141–160.

Jones, S. & Rosa, H. Jr. (1965). Synopsis of biological data on Indian mackerel *Rastrelliger kanagurta* (Cuvier) 1817 and short-bodied mackerel, *Rastrelliger brachysoma* (Bleeker) 1851. *FAO Fish. Biol. Synops.* No. 29: 1–42.

Kimpe, P. de (1964). Contribution à l'étude hydrobiologique du Luapula-Moero. *Annls Mus. r. Afr. Centr.* (8vo, Sci. zool.) No. 128: 1–238.

Kramer, D. L. (1978). Reproductive seasonality in the fishes of a tropical stream. *Ecology* **59**: 976–985.

Lewis, D.S.C. (1974). The effects of the formation of Lake Kainji (Nigeria) upon the indigenous fish population. *Hydrobiologia* **45**: 281–301.

Lieth, H. (ed.) (1974). *Phenology and seasonality modeling.* Ecological studies, analysis and synthesis **8**. Berlin: Springer-Verlag.

Loiselle, P. V. (1977). Description of new species of *Barbus* (Pisces, Cyprinidae) from West Africa. *Revue Zool. Bot. afr.* **83**: 1–15.

Loiselle, P. V. & Welcomme, R. (1971). Two new species of *Barbus* (Pisces, Cyprinidae) from southern Dahomey. *Revue Zool. Bot. afr.* **83**: 1–15.

Longhurst, A. R. (1964). Bionomics of the Sciaenidae of tropical West Africa. *J. Cons. perm. int. Explor. Mer* **29**: 93–114.

Longhurst, A. R. (1965). The biology of West African polynemid fishes. *J. Cons. perm. int. Explor. Mer* **30**: 58–74.

Longhurst, A. R. (1969). Synopsis of biological data on West African croakers *Pseudotolithus typus, P. senegalensis* and *P. elongatus. FAO Fish. Biol. Synops.* No. 35, Rev. 1: 1–48.

Longhurst, A. R. (1971). The clupeoid resources of tropical seas. *Oceanogr. Mar. Biol. Rev.* **9**: 349–385.

Lowe, R. H. (1952). Report on the tilapia and other fish and fisheries of Lake Nyasa. *Fishery Publs Colon. Off.* **1** (2): 1–126.

Lowe, R. H. (1953). Notes of the ecology and evolution of Nyasa fishes of the genus *Tilapia*, with a description of *T. saka*, Lowe. *Proc. zool. Soc. Lond.* **122**: 1035–1041.

Lowe, R. H. (1955). The fecundity of *Tilapia* species. *E. Afr. agric. J.* **11**: 45–52.

Lowe-McConnell, R. H. (1956). Observations on the biology of *Tilapia* (Pisces-Cichlidae) in Lake Victoria, East Africa. *E. Afr. Fish. Res. Org.* Suppl. Publ. No. 1: 1–72.

Lowe-McConnell, R. H. (1958). Observations on the biology of *Tilapia nilotica* L. in E. African water. *Revue Zool. Bot. afr.* **57**: 129–170.

Lowe-McConnell, R. H. (1959). Breeding behaviour patterns and ecological differences between *Tilapia* species and their significance for evolution within the genus *Tilapia. Proc. zool. Soc. Lond.* **132**: 1–30.

Lowe-McConnell, R. H. (1962). The fishes of the British Guiana continental shelf, Atlantic coast of South America, with notes on their natural history. *J. Linn. Soc. Lond.* (Zool.) **44**: 669–700.

Lowe-McConnell, R. H. (1966). The sciaenid fishes of British Guiana. *Bull. mar. Sci.* **16**: 20–57.

Lowe-McConnell, R. H. (1969). Speciation in tropical freshwater fishes. *Biol. J. Linn. Soc.* **1**: 51–75.

Lowe–McConnell, R. H. (1975). *Fish communities in tropical freshwaters.* London: Longman.

Lowe-McConnell, R. H. (1977). *Ecology of fishes in tropical waters.* (Studies in Biology No. 76) London: Edward Arnold.

240   ROSEMARY H. LOWE-McCONNELL

Margalef, R. (1968). *Perspectives in ecological theory.* Chicago: University of Chicago Press.
Matthes, H. (1960). Note sur la reproduction des poissons au Lac Tanganyika. *Symp. Hydrobiol. Major Lakes* **3**: 107–112.
Matthes, H. (1961). *Boulengerochromis microlepis,* a Lake Tanganyika fish of economical importance. *Bull. aquat. Biol.* **3** (24): 1–15.
Matthes, H. (1964). Les poissons du lac Tumba et de la région d'Ikela. *Annls Mus. r. fr. cent.* (Sci. Zool.) No. 126: 1–204.
May, R. M. (1975). Stability in ecosystems: some comments. In *Unifying concepts in ecology*: 161–168. van Dobben, W. H. & Lowe-McConnell, R. H. (eds). The Hague: W. Junk.
McKaye, K. R. (1977). Competition for breeding sites between the cichlid fishes of Lake Jiloá, Nicaragua. *Ecology* **58**: 291–302.
McKaye, K. R. & McKaye, N. M. (1977). Communal care and kidnapping of young by parental cichlids. *Evolution* **31**: 674–681.
Moe, M. A. Jr. (1969). Biology of the red grouper *Epinephelus morio* (Val.) from the eastern Gulf of Mexico. *Prof. Pap. Fla State Bd Cons.* No. 10: 1–95.
Munro, J. L., Gaut, V. C., Thompson, R. & Reeson, P. H. (1973). The spawning seasons of Caribbean reef fishes. *J. Fish Biol.* **5**: 69–84.
Nordlie, F. G. & Kelso, D. O. (1975). Trophic relationships in a tropical estuary. *Revue Biol. Trop.* **23**: 77–99.
Okedi, J. (1965). The biology and habits of the mormyrid fishes. *Rep. E. Afr. Freshwat. Fish. Res. Org.* **1964**, Appendix F: 58.
Payne, A. I. (1975). The reproductive cycle, condition and feeding in *Barbus liberiensis,* a tropical stream-dwelling cyprinid. *J. Zool., Lond.* **176**: 247–269.
Petr, T. (1968). The establishment of lacustrine fish population in the Volta Lake in Ghana during 1964–1966. *Bull. Inst. fr. Afr. noire* **30A**.: 257–269.
Raju, G. (1964). Studies on the spawning of oceanic skipjack *Katsuwonus pelamis* (Linn.) in Minicoy waters: 744–768. In *Proc. Symp. Scombroid Fishes, Mandapam Camp, 1962,* pt II, MBAI Sympos. Series I, Mandapam Camp, India.
Randall, J. E. (1961a). A contribution to the biology of the convict surgeonfish of the Hawaiian Islands, *Acanthurus triostegus sandvicensis. Pacif. Sci.* **15**: 215–272.
Randall, J. E. (1961b). Observations on the spawning of surgeon fishes (Acanthuridae) in the Society Islands. *Copeia* **1961**: 237–238.
Randall, J. E. & Brock, V. E. (1960). Observations on the ecology of epinephaline and lutjanid fishes of the Society Islands, with emphasis on food habits. *Trans. Am. Fish Soc.* **89**: 9–16.
Randall, J. E. & Randall, H. A. (1963). The spawning and early development of the Atlantic parrot fish, *Sparisoma rubripinne,* with notes on other scarid and labrid fishes. *Zoologica, N.Y.* **48**: 49–59.
Reynolds, J. D. (1973). Biological notes on *Barbus* species (Pisces: Cyprinidae) in the Volta Lake, Ghana. *Revue Zool. Bot. afr.* **87**: 815–821.
Reynolds, J. D. (1974). Biology of small pelagic fishes in the new Volta Lake in Ghana. Pt. III. Sex and reproduction. *Hydrobiologia* **45**: 489–508.
Roberts, T. & Stewart, D. J. (1976). An ecological and systematic survey of fishes in the rapids of the Lower Zaire or Congo River. *Bull. Mus. comp. Zool. Harv.* **47**: 239–317.

Russell, C., Talbot, F. H. & Domm, S. (1974). Patterns of colonization of artificial reefs by coral fishes. *Proc. Int. Coral Reef Symp.* **2**: 207–215.

Sale, P. F. (1974). Mechanisms of co-existence in a guild of territorial fishes at Heron Island. *Proc. Int. Coral Reef. Symp.* **2**: 193–206.

Sale, P. F. (1978). Coexistence of coral reef fishes—a lottery for living space. *Envirl Biol. Fish.* **3**: 85–102.

Schuster, W. H. (1960). Synopsis of biological data on milkfish *Chanos chanos* (Forskål) 1775. *FAO Fish. Biol. Synops.* No. 4: 1–63.

Smith, C. L. (1972). A spawning aggregation of the Nassau grouper *Epinephelus striatus* (Bloch). *Trans. Am. Fish. Soc.* **101**: 257–261.

Smith, C. L. & Tyler, J. C. (1972). Space resources sharing in a coral reef community. *Bull. nat. Hist. Mus. Los Angeles* **14**: 125–178.

Thompson, R. & Munro, J. L. (1978). Aspects of the biology and ecology of Caribbean reef fishes: Serranidae (hinds and groupers). *J. Fish Biol.* **12**: 115–146.

Tweddle, D. & Turner, J. L. (1977). Age, growth and natural mortality rates of some cichlid fishes of Lake Malawi. *J. Fish Biol.* **10**: 385–398.

Ward, J. A. & Wyman, R. L. (1977). Ethology and ecology of cichlid fishes of the genus *Etroplus* in Sri Lanka: preliminary findings. *Envirl Fish. Biol.* **2**: 137–145.

Welcomme, R. L. (1966). Recent changes in the stocks of *Tilapia* in Lake Victoria. *Nature, Lond.* **212**: 52–54.

Welcomme, R. L. (1967a). Observations on the biology of the introduced *Tilapia* in Lake Victoria. *Revue Zool. Bot. afr.* **76**: 249–279.

Welcomme, R. L. (1967b). The relationship between fecundity and fertility in the mouth-brooding cichlid fish *Tilapia leucosticta*. *J. Zool., Lond.* **151**: 453–468.

Welcomme, R. L. (1969). The biology and ecology of the fishes of a small tropical stream. *J. Zool., Lond.* **158**: 485–529.

Welcomme, R. L. (1970). Studies of the effects of abnormally high water levels on the ecology of fish in certain shallow regions of Lake Victoria. *J. Zool., Lond.* **160**: 405–436.

Welcomme, R. L. (1975). The fisheries ecology of African floodplains. *CIFA/TA, FAO, Rome*: 1–51.

Welcomme, R. L. (1979). *The fisheries ecology of floodplain rivers.* London: Longman.

Whitehead, P. J. P. (1959). The anadromous fishes of Lake Victoria. *Revue Zool. Bot. afr.* **59**: 329–363.

Symp. zool. Soc. Lond. (1979) No. 44, 243–261

The Phenology of Annual Killifishes

BETTY R. C. SIMPSON

University of Bristol, Bristol, Avon, England

SYNOPSIS

"Annual" killifishes (Teleostei:Cyprinodontidae), of several African and South American genera, are small fishes inhabiting temporary pools in tropical and subtropical areas. These pools provide an abundant invertebrate food resource but exist for only part of the year. The phenology of annual killifishes is considered in relation to the certainty of adult death after a relatively short period, usually some months, whose precise duration may vary. Survival of the population is in the form of eggs remaining in the dried bed of the pool. Reproductive modifications include drought-resistant eggs, embryonic diapause, hatching response to rainfall, early sexual maturity after rapid growth of young fishes achieved within two months, daily production of eggs and moderately high primary reproductive effort. Reproductive behaviour involves burial of eggs more or less deeply in the pool substrate. Adults exhibit sexual dichromatism. In captivity, lifespan in *Cynolebias* is usually no longer than 18 months but can be prolonged to 44 months at a lower temperature. Senescence is indicated by changes in soluble to insoluble collagen ratios, but adult life in captivity is long in relation to early maturation and attainment of limiting size. Experimental work on growth of *Nothobranchius guentheri* and a non-annual cyprinodont, *Rivulus milesi*, does not indicate better growth rate at lower temperatures, although estimated asymptotic length is higher. Economic aspects of annual killifishes are noted.

INTRODUCTION

The egg-laying toothcarps or killifishes (Teleostei:Cyprinodontidae) form an almost world-wide tropical and warm temperate group of small teleosts, rarely exceeding 7·5–10·0 cm in length. The major subfamily, the Rivulinae, comprises about 300 species, mostly freshwater or euryhaline. Within this subfamily, several genera, by modification of life history (Fig. 1), are able to exploit temporary pools in tropical or subtropical areas and have achieved some fame as "annual" fishes (Myers, 1952). Balon (1975) also classes these fishes as xerophils on the basis of their reproductive biology (brood hider, A 2·5).

Their habitats, although of limited and, at times, unpredictable duration, must nevertheless hold some ecological attractiveness, since annualism may have been evolved by different lines of rivulins in both South America and Africa. However, Scheel (1972) states that "the most ancient and basic rivulin may be an annual fish". He also suggests that the origin of the rivulins may be traceable to dry periods during the Permian in Gondwanaland, that is, before South America and Africa became separated. Annual killifishes from Africa (Table I) are included in the genera *Fundulosoma*, *Aphyosemion* (although only relatively few of the

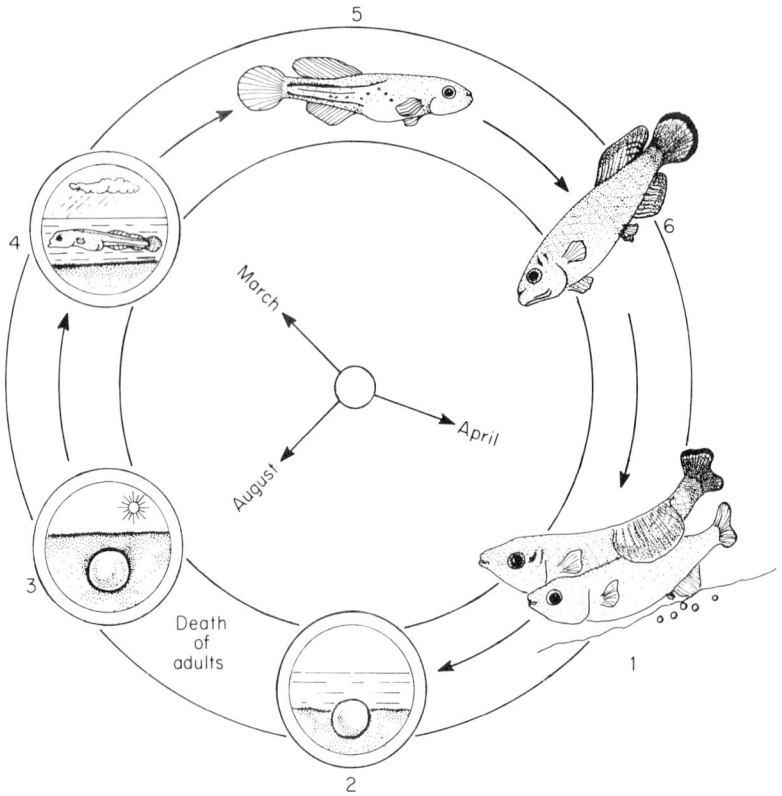

FIG. 1. Life-cycle of *Nothobranchius guentheri* (Pfeffer), based on data from Bailey (1972) and Haas (1976), after similar diagram for *Austrofundulus myersi* Dahl by Wourms (1972c). 1, spawning over several months; 2, eggs deposited in mud of pool bottom; 3, evaporation of pool and death of adults; 4, start of rainy season, flooding of pool basin and hatching of some eggs; 5, rapid growth of young fishes; 6, sexual maturity at from four to eight weeks from hatching.

bottom-spawning species are truly annual), *Roloffia* and *Nothobranchius*, with the last probably the most popular among aquarists. Genera of South American killifishes which include annual forms (Table II) are *Austro-fundulus*, *Cynolebias*, *Cynopoecilus*, *Rachovia*, *Pterolebias*, *Trigonectes*, *Simpsonichthys* and *Rivulus* (with only one truly annual species, *R. stellifer* but with at least another of intermediate lifestyle). The genus best known to fish keepers is probably *Cynolebias*, which has featured in the study of developmental modifications, especially the dispersion–aggregation pattern and the ability to diapause (Wourms, 1967).

ECOTOPE

Temporary pools tend to support a substantial, if transient, invertebrate population which supplies an excellent food source for small fish. The presence of such variety and numbers of small food organisms, such as mosquito larvae, copepods and ostracods, makes exploitation of these habitats worthwhile despite the certainty of early death, and the anabolic costs of life in this more or less unpredictable environment.

Adult annual fishes can live only as long as water is available in their isolated ponds, usually for about eight months, in contrast to a lifespan of three to four years often found in other rivulins. However, there is no one typical annual fish habitat, the single common factor being that water will be plentiful only during the rainy season. The rains do not come with entirely predictable regularity. There may be one wet and one dry season, as reported by Vanderplank (1940) and Wourms (1964) for *Nothobran-chius* habitats, or two wet and two dry periods, as experienced by *Rachovia* (Thomerson, 1971) and *Cynolebias* (Boschi, 1953). Occasionally, annuals have been found in permanently water-filled habitats, e.g. *Cynolebias* (Boschi, 1953; Vaz-Ferreira, Soriano & Paulete, 1964) and *Nothobranchius korthausae* (Meinken, 1973). Scheel (1962) has shown that eggs of *Cyno-lebias bellottii* can develop in permanent water. Erratic rainfall, "false rains" in the dry season, has been reported for *Nothobranchius* habitats (Walters, 1952). In contrast, year-long droughts may be encountered by populations of *Nothobranchius* (Pienaar, 1968) and an experimental population of *Cynolebias bellottii* survived an artificial drought lasting 10 months (Bay, 1966).

The somewhat variable chemistry of water from temporary ponds containing annual fishes is described by Geisler (1959), Jubb (1967), Haas (1969) and Taberner, Fernandez Santos & Castelli (1975).

REPRODUCTION

Developmental Modifications

The most obvious phenological modifications distinguishing annual killifishes from other short-lived teleosts are found in relation to individual survival over the dry season, from fertilization of the egg in the flooded basin of one year to sexual maturation of the resulting offspring in the re-flooded basin of the next wet season. Aestivation takes place, not in a cocoon, like lungfish, but in a drought-resistant egg, which is buried in the mud bottom of a temporary pool. However, it is of interest to consider the suggestion of Wourms (1972c) that, physiologically, the state of the prehatching embryo may be very similar to that of an aestivating lungfish.

The embryonic period can last from a few weeks to several months. Pienaar (1968) reports that one population of *Nothobranchius* was maintained by eggs which hatched after being dry for 18–24 months. Even

TABLE I

African annual killifishes for which reproductive data are available

Species	Distribution	Total length (cm)	Spawning site*; incubation time (d) in damp peat (p) or water (w)	Egg diameter (mm)	Nature of diapause[2]
Aphyosemion arnoldi Boulenger	SE Nigeria	5·5	B; p, 28–49; w, 20–40	1·0	No spontaneous D I and D III; D II prolonged (c. 60–90 d), with reversible bradycardia
A. deltaense Radda	S Nigeria	7·0–10·0	B; p, 84; w, nd	1·6	nd
A. fallax Ahl*	Ghana	4·0–6·0	B; p, 35–49; w, 25–45	nd	As arnoldi, but D II reported
A. lacustre Radda	W Cameroun	7·0–10·0	B; p, 84; w, nd	1·3	nd
A. nigerianum Clausen[3],*	N Nigeria	7·0–10·0	I; p, 42; w, nd	1·0–1·5	As fallax
A. robertsoni Radda & Scheel	W Cameroun	3·0–5·0	B; p, 112; w, nd	0·9	nd
A. rubrolabiale Radda	W Cameroun	3·0–5·0	B; p, 70; w, nd	0·9	nd
A. schwoiseri Scheel & Radda	W Cameroun	7·0–10·0	nd	nd	nd
A. seymouri Loiselle & Blair	Ghana	3·8	I; p, 56; w, nd	nd	nd
A. sjoestedti (Lönnberg)[4],*	W Cameroun	12·7	B; p, 42–56; w, 35–40	1·4–1·5	As arnoldi
A. walkeri (Boulenger)*	S Ghana	8·3	B; p, 28–42; w, 30–40	1·3	As fallax
Nothobranchius guentheri (Pfeffer)	E Africa	6·8	B; p, 42–84; w, nd	1·3	D I facultative, under stress; D II rare or obligate; incidence of D II and D III increased with partial drying

(Pfeffer)					As guentheri
N. orthonotus (Peters)	Mozambique	7·0	B; p, 168; w, nd	1·0	As guentheri
N. palmquisti (Lönnberg)	Burundi	4·0	B; p, 84–112; w, nd	1·0	As guentheri
N. rachovii Ahl	Mozambique	5·0	B; p, 112–196; w, nd	0·9–1·0	As guentheri
N. taeniopygus Hilgendorf	Lake Victoria region	5·2	B; p, 140–196; w, nd	1·0	As guentheri
Roloffia occidentalis Clausen[5]	Sierra Leone	9·0	B; p, 112; w, nd	1·5	D I not spontaneous in aerobically-incubated eggs; obligate D II (50 d) and D III (c.150–200 d)
R. toddi Clausen	Sierra Leone	7·0–10·0	B; p, 140; w, 49	1·4	nd

Main sources: Kluge (1961); Peters (1963, 1965); Scheel (1968); Wourms (1963, 1972c).

* semi-annual; [1] B, bottom spawning and I, intermediate/plant spawning; [2] see text for description of D I–III; [3] A. calliurum in Peters (1963); [4] formerly A. coeruleum Boulenger; [5] formerly A. sjoestedti Lönnberg; nd, no data.

TABLE II

South American annual killifishes for which reproductive data are available

Species	Distribution	Total length (cm)	Spawning site[1]; incubation time (d) in damp peat (p) or water (w)	Egg diameter (mm)	Nature of diapause[2]
Austrofundulus myersi Dahl	N Colombia	5·0–8·0	B; p, nd; 40–316	2·0	D I (embryonic stage 20) facultative; D II (st. 32) and D III (st. 43) obligate (both 105–120 d). About 10% of eggs escape D II and/or D III, hatching in 40 d
A. transilis Myers	Venezuela	8·0–11.5	B; p, nd; w, 40–316	nd	As *myersi*
A. dolichopterus Weitzman & Wourms	Venezuela	3·0–4·0	B; p, nd; w, 40–316	nd	As *myersi*, but D I arrest (20–30 d) may be obligate
Cynolebias bellottii Steindachner	Argentina	6·0–7·5	B; p, 112–168; w, nd	1·5	D I and D II facultative, induced by partial drying

C. nigripinnis Regan	Argentina	5·0	B; p, 140–196; w, nd	nd	D I and D II facultative, D III prolonged, variable
C. whitei Myers	Rio de Janeiro	5·0–10·0	B; p, 168; w, nd	1·25	Continuous development in water to D III (prolonged, variable); D I and D II as bellottii
C. melanotaenia (Regan)	SE Brazil	5·0	B; p, 84–112; w, nd	1·25	As whitei
Pterolebias longipinnis Garman	SE Brazil	7·0–8·0	B; p, 140–252; w, nd	3·0	As A. myersi
Pt. peruensis Myers	Peruvian Amazon	7·0–8·0	B; p, 112–308; w, nd	nd	nd
Pt. zonatus Meyers	Venezuela	7·5	B; p, 224; w, nd	nd	nd
Rachovia brevis Regan	Columbia	5·0–8·0	B; p, 140–196; w, nd	nd	As A. myersi, but sometimes obligate D I; "escape" eggs present
R. hummelincki De Beaufort	Venezuela	7·5	B; p, 168–224; w, nd	nd	As R. brevis
Rivulus stellifer Thomerson & Turner	Venezuela	3·5–5·0	B; p, nd; w, nd	1·5	D I observed

Main sources: Peters (1963); Wourms (1967, 1972a, b, c).

[1,2] as Table I; nd, no data.

longer dry periods may be experienced by eggs, and Scheel (1962) has collected viable eggs after a period of five and a half years. These data serve to illustrate that life in the egg may well be considerably longer than the time spent subsequent to hatching, "even if the individual lives to be an old fish" (Glut, 1961). To serve this need, the eggs of annual killifishes have developed thickened chorionic membranes, approaching 24 μm, and the chorionic filaments so characteristic of other rivulin eggs are either absent or modified into stiff, short structures, all features contributing to a hard, incompressible "shell" which will withstand severe mechanical stress and desiccation (Peters, 1963). Not only are the eggs protected in this way, but they show also unique and incredible embryological modifications.

First, embryogenesis occurs in a reaggregated mass of cells which have previously dispersed at the blastoderm stage (Wourms, 1972b). Subsequently, three periods of diapause, or developmental arrest, of varying duration, may occur (Peters, 1963; Wourms, 1963, 1964, 1967, 1972c), and, finally, competent eggs have an almost immediate hatching response to the rains of the next wet season. Originally, annual killifishes were defined by their ecology and the nature of their overt life history, but knowledge of their specialized development now permits more precise segregation from other teleosts.

The process of cleavage seems to be much shorter in annual fish eggs than in other teleosts, although there is no sign of embryological development until dispersed cells have reaggregated. Two populations of blastomeres are formed, those which disperse and later form the embryo, and others which produce an enveloping cell layer (extra-embryonic cell layer) and play no part in embryo formation. It is apparent that some of the dispersed cells may become damaged or destroyed during periods of stress without inhibiting the development of a normal embryo, and that, when conditions improve, these cells can be replaced by mitosis.

As previously mentioned, diapause may occur at three different stages and is remarkably similar to that found in insects. It is a period when morphological growth and development is suspended or at least retarded, and, as such, differs from quiescence, which is only a temporary inhibition directly influenced by environmental conditions. When diapause occurs spontaneously, without any noticeable change in surroundings, it is termed obligate. When external factors have a modifying effect, diapause is said to be facultative. A general review of diapause is given by Andrewartha (1952).

In annual killifish development, the first diapause (D I), usually facultative, occurs at the dispersed-cell phase (embryonic stage 20 of Wourms, 1972c), with the result that reaggregation may not occur for several weeks. For many annuals, the second period of diapause (D II) is obligate, and occurs at the long somite stage (stage 32) and the third period of diapause (D III), just prior to hatching (stage 43), seems to be obligate in all annuals. During diapause, the embryo is inactive, blood circulation stops and heart beats are infrequent (Wourms, 1972c), although vigorous activity has also been recorded (Peters, 1963). However, in many populations, there are "escape eggs" which avoid diapause at a particular stage. The same eggs are not always involved at each stage so that eight varieties of development cycle become possible. This is known as the "multiplier effect" (Wourms, 1972c), and ensures that at least some of the egg population will survive to reproduce at maturity in the next season. The multiplier effect compensates mainly for environmental unpredictability, such as the false cues of rainfall in the dry season and continuous flooding.

Eggs which have completed D III seem to have an almost immediate response to the rains of the next wet season, but not all these eggs may be competent to hatch (Bay, 1966). Peters (1965) suggested that the stimulus to break D III is given by a decrease in oxygen supply to the embryo, caused by decomposition in the soil after the first rainfall disturbs bottom mud. It is equally possible that hatching under these circumstances is merely induced in eggs which have already completed D III (Wourms, 1972c).

Sexual Maturity

After hatching, development to sexual maturity is characterized by an unusually rapid growth, supported by abundance of food, and virtually all annual killifishes are capable of spawning at an age of merely six to eight weeks (Vaz–Ferreira *et al.*, 1964; Bay, 1966; Weitzman & Wourms, 1967; Bailey, 1972). Haas (1976) has observed even earlier sexual maturity in *Nothobranchius guentheri*, at less than four weeks. As Myers (1952) remarked, the typical age at maturity is earlier than in most other teleosts and, for many annuals, sees spawning by fishes at a mere 1·0 cm or even less in length. For example, *N. rachovii* females may spawn at four weeks and a size of 0·9 cm (British Killifish Association, 1966). With the possibility of premature drought, there is an obvious selective advantage in commencement of spawning at as early an age as possible.

Spawning Pattern

Once mature, there is a pattern of daily repeat-spawning, as found in many cyprinodonts (Foster, 1967; Miller, this volume p.263), with production of a typically large (0·1–0·2 cm) rivulin egg. This is iteroparity with a vengeance, related here to an environment at best only semipre-dictable (Stearns, 1976), and also achieves a substantial reproductive effort in the sector of primary anabolism (Miller, this volume pp. 1 and 263). If females fail to spawn in any given day, economy operates and few if any eggs are added to the existing complement (Haas, 1976).

Reproductive Effort

The daily fecundity of annual killifishes would seem to range from a few eggs to at least 50, depending on species, size, level of feeding and age

(Bay, 1966; Walford & Liu, 1965; Liu & Walford, 1969; Wourms, 1972a). Bailey (1972) described in *Nothobranchius guentheri* a strongly positive allometric relationship between size of female and number of ripening and ripe ovarian eggs. For *Cynolebias bellottii*, Bay (1966) found that between 500 and 700 eggs were deposited by females in a period of 62 days, daily output being eight to 12 eggs, although young females produced a daily average of only 4·1 eggs in the first eight weeks of maturity. Using growth data from this author, and a wet weight of 1·3 mg for the relatively large egg (1·35 mm) of this species, primary reproductive effort (Miller, this volume p. 1) may be estimated at 5·33 for young females (weight 3·0 g) and 8·21–12·32 for larger individuals (3·8 g), as a percentage of maternal weight expended in 30 days. For *N. guentheri*, a mature female of 1 g, producing 20 eggs per day, each 0·45 mg, would achieve a higher value of about 27% in a month. This expenditure by annuals on reproduction is substantial, with, perhaps, a total egg production approaching maternal weight in a breeding season of four or five months. However, in comparison with the rice medaka, *Oryzias latipes* (Schlegel), an epibenthic cyprinodont of permanent waters, reproductive effort (Miller, this volume p. 263) seems appreciably less per month, and may represent a compromise with degree of habitat predictability. In larger female *C. bellottii*, a higher reproductive effort may be found than that of juveniles, yet Walford & Liu (1965) noted considerable decrease in egg production by this species after about five months of adult life at 22°C. If a cycle in reproductive effort relative to parent biomass does occur in annuals, this may reflect a corresponding change with time in probability of habitat desiccation as the wet season progresses, and deserves further investigation.

Behaviour

With significance in ethology, many annual fishes exhibit sexual dichromatism, males being more brightly coloured. In African forms, the predominant colours are blues and reds, with females having cryptic coloration. The coloration of the males renders them potentially more conspicuous to predators, but the extent of vertebrate predation on annual killifishes does not seem to be heavy. Nevertheless, selection of male *Nothobranchius* by herons is recorded (Haas, 1969). Sexual differences in coloration do not seem to be maintained by intra-sexual or inter-specific selection since annuals are rarely territorial and rarely live syntopically with other species of the same lifestyle. It is possible that inter-sexual selection could well be responsible, especially in the Darwinian sense of sexual selection, because females are known to choose the most brightly coloured males with whom to spawn (Haas, 1976). The environment may also influence coloration. Annual fishes often live in very muddy water and, since vision has an important role in the reproductive behaviour of these fish, there might be some selective pressure for easily visible male coloration. The cryptic coloration of female annuals may not only protect them from predation but also from persistent and aggressive spawning advances by males, when the female is not in a receptive condition. However, they may avoid males in other ways. In *Nothobranchius*, Rowe (1958) noticed that "males and females are clearly separate, often being found at opposite sides of the pool".

Reproductive behaviour is fairly simple, with pre-spawning advertisement reduced to a minimum (Haas, 1976). This behaviour is largely visual, but includes some tactile elements. Male fishes are thought to monitor position relative to the female using contact organs which are found on "regions in the males that come into most intimate contact with the female during the spawning act proper, or during the preliminary courtship . . . judging by the nerve supply, they must be very sensitive" (Newman, 1909). Males and females will spawn as soon as they encounter each other, provided that the females are receptive. Non-receptive females are usually soon ignored, so reproductive activity is channelled into maximizing egg deposition rather than into unsuccessful courtship procedure.

Although some *Aphyosemion* species lay eggs on vegetation on or near the pool bed, most annual killifishes are bottom spawners, eggs being buried in the substrate, where humidity may remain high and risk of mechanical damage may be lessened. In *Nothobranchius*, placement is superficial, but in *Cynolebias* and other South American forms, parents of only 5 cm in length burrow down to 15 cm in the mud to deposit eggs (Vaz–Ferreira *et al.*, 1964). Meder (1955) writes that "this deep placing of the eggs is surely not accidental, because no doubt those eggs which were left higher are sure to perish during the dry season due to complete drying". When the young of these South American annuals hatch, they can be seen to wriggle backwards, up through the soil, with pectoral fins folded over the head, in order to escape from the substrate (Vaz–Ferreira *et al.*, 1964).

LIFESPAN

Mortality

By the time most eggs have reached their first diapause stage, both pools and parents have ceased to exist. In nature, senescence may not generally occur before lifespan is curtailed by extrinsic factors, especially the onset of drought. Stewart (1976) reported dead or dying *Nothobranchius* under conditions of plentiful, oxygenated water but with temperatures of at least 35°C. Heat stress, rather than ultimate desiccation, would seem to have been the immediate cause of death. Reduction in the amount of food available in drying ponds has also been held responsible for adult death (Thomerson, 1971), or a combination of high temperatures and food shortage (Boschi, 1957; Vaz–Ferreira *et al.*, 1964). Although the start of drought conditions has been considered to speed up the onset of sexual maturity, and thus possibly senescence, it has also been linked with the production of increased numbers of "resting eggs". Roloff (1967) has noticed that such fishes will lay a greater proportion of eggs entering prolonged diapause than do presumably younger fishes under less stressful conditions.

Predation from other fishes is erratic and depends solely on the duration of temporary connections with standing water. Large catfishes, cichlids and characoids have been collected from temporary pools but only after flooding has brought them from surrounding bodies of water. Predation by birds, as noted earlier, may be of common occurrence; herons have been observed to feed on *Nothobranchius* and appear to selectively remove males (Haas, 1969). Bird predation on both sexes probably increases as water volume decreases, that is, with the onset of drought.

Aquarists have found that, in captivity, their annual fishes usually die after only 12–15 months of life, even with assured water supply. Consequently, *Cynolebias* species (Walford & Liu, 1965 and later papers) and *Nothobranchius guentheri* (Markofsky & Perlmutter, 1973) have come to feature in research on the process of senescence. Such work has shown that maximum lifespan may be greatly extended at lower temperatures within the overall tolerance range. Thus, at 21–23°C, *Cynolebias adloffi* can live from 13 to 17 months, but at 15–17°C, as long as 32–44 months; similarly, maximum longevity for *C. wolterstorffi* can be increased from 14–16 to 26–35 months (Liu & Walford, 1966, 1970).

Senescence

For vertebrates, it is possible to examine a number of parameters which may reflect, fairly closely, the rate of physiological aging or senescence. One such indicator is the relative increase in insoluble collagen in skin and other tissues as physiological aging occurs, obtained by comparing ratios of soluble to insoluble collagen determined by chemical analysis. Alteration in soluble to insoluble collagen ratios has been investigated in the annual fish *Cynolebias bellottii* (Walford, Liu, Troup & Hsiu, 1969). Populations of this species were maintained at 15 and 20°C for most of the lifespan. Fish at 15°C lived much longer, and it was suggested that physiological aging is actually retarded in these individuals. The difference in collagen ratios between fishes at the two temperatures was $0 \cdot 120 \pm 0 \cdot 036$ (effect $\pm$ standard error; $P > 0 \cdot 01$). A small effect ($0 \cdot 084 \pm 0 \cdot 040$), possibly due to differences in the early life history of populations at 20°C, was also found, but none attributable to sex ($0 \cdot 006 \pm 0 \cdot 022$). The soluble to insoluble collagen ratios declined greatly with age (Walford *et al.*, 1969: Table 1). These experiments do not appear to challenge the immune theory of aging (Walford, 1969).

In laboratory populations of another cyprinodontoid, the guppy, *Poecilia reticulata* Peters, Comfort (1961) found that senescence, as indicated by mortality rate, began in virgin females at an age when about 75% of limiting size had been reached, and that this age (about 800 days) represented approximately four-tenths of the observed maximum life-span (2000 days). If the same ratio is applied to *Cynolebias bellottii* reared at the higher temperature range by Liu & Walford (1970), the maximum potential longevity might be expected to be no more than eight to nine months, if 75% of limiting size is reached in about three months, as estimated from growth curves shown by these authors. Instead, as already noted, fishes under these conditions can live for 17–18 months. Using further data from Liu & Walford (1970), it can be shown that, in the related *C. adloffi*, the disparity between predicted and actual lifespan is even greater, being 6·75 and 13–17 months respectively. Values for *C. wolterstorffi* are roughly coincident at about 15 months. Thus, although potential lifespan in these annual killifishes may not normally exceed 18 months at tropical aquarium temperatures, some species appear to be unusually long-lived in relation to their early maturation and attainment of limiting size. The physiological ability to sustain a relatively long adult life, with moderately high reproductive effort, would seem to be a basic anabolic requirement in the phenology of annual fishes faced with uncertainty in habitat persistence.

GROWTH

Pattern

In the annual species studied, growth rate has been found to be high during the first seven to eight weeks in both sexes (Bay, 1966; Walford & Liu, 1965; Liu & Walford, 1966, 1969, 1970; Bailey, 1972). In *Nothobranchius guentheri*, limiting or asymptotic length was reached by most females at about eight weeks, with growth by males persisting at a reduced rate for a further month. Females of this population began to mature at five weeks and ripe eggs were present in the ovaries of fishes aged seven to eight weeks (Bailey, 1972). In captivity, the somewhat larger *Cynolebias* species take much longer to reach asymptotic length (Liu & Walford, 1970), although levelling of the growth curve at about ten weeks is suggested by the data of Bay (1966) for *C. bellottii*. In the wild, fast growth to a size for maturity must obviously have adaptive value in relation to the possibility of early drought and perhaps for avoidance of predation by invertebrates such as dragonfly nymphs, bugs and beetles. Arrest of further growth by early sexual maturity may indicate that the latter event may outweigh any advantages from reaching a larger, more fecund body size later in the season.

Experimental Studies

For *Cynolebias adloffi*, Walford & Liu (1965) found that growth rate and limiting size of fishes reared at 15–17°C were higher than those shown by fishes kept at 21–23°C. These results differed from those obtained by Kinne (1960) for a non-annual cyprinodont, *Cyprinodon macularius* Baird & Girard, in which, over a similar temperature range, growth rate and limiting size increased with temperature. Liu & Walford (1969) suggested that higher temperatures may stimulate growth in young fishes, although lower temperatures are more effective after sexual maturity has been reached. It could be speculated that enhanced growth rate and final size in *Cynolebias* under cooler conditions might be due to retarded gonad development. Although eventually laying more eggs, females at 15–17°C lived longer (Walford & Liu, 1965; Liu & Walford, 1969, 1970), and the critical effect on both growth and expectation of life might be one of rate of reproductive expenditure, rather than final total. In the wild, rapid growth at high temperatures has been associated with increased aging (Boschi, 1957; Vaz-Ferreira *et al.*, 1964).

The author has undertaken some experimental work on growth by the annual killifish, *Nothobranchius guentheri*, and for comparison, the related but larger, non-annual, *Rivulus milesi* Fowler. Results described here were obtained from fishes (aquarium stock) maintained in individual, aerated 3-litre jars at temperatures from 20 to 28°C and photoperiod of 8 h light/12 h dark, with twice-daily ration slightly in excess of food requirement. Frequent partial water changes were made to remove excess food and excretory products. The most suitable diet was found to be brine-shrimp (*Artemia salina*) nauplii for fry, progressing to *Daphnia*, white-worms (*Enchytraeus albidus*) and a commercial flake food (Aquarian carnivore and growth food).

The growth pattern of *Nothobranchius guentheri* over 130 days from hatching indicates higher growth rate at 28°C than at 20°C, with a similar effect suggested for *R. milesi* (Fig. 2). Using Ford-Walford plots (Ricker, 1975), estimates of asymptotic length gave much higher values for fishes kept at the lower temperature (Fig. 3). In *N. guentheri*, asymptotic length for 20°C fishes was 8·8 cm but only 4·3 cm for those at 28°C, while figures for *R. milesi* at these temperatures were 7·3 and 5·2 respectively. The value for asymptotic length in *N. guentheri* at the lower temperature is 2·0 cm greater than the maximum size recorded in wild fishes at an average temperature of 25°C (Bailey, 1972). In *R. milesi*, estimates[a] of asymptotic length for five temperatures show an inverse relationship with temperature, which may represent the apex as well as the descending limb of a reciprocal catenary curve which Ursin (1963) believed could represent the dependence of asymptotic length on temperature in fishes, including *Cyprinodon macularius*.

---

[a] At 20°C, 7·32 cm; 22°C, 7·89 cm; 24°C, 7·69 cm; 26°C, 6·54 cm; 28°C, 5·20 cm.

In both *N. guentheri* and *R. milesi*, male sexual coloration was attained at a shorter total length in the fishes kept at 28°C, and was often more intense. Females at the end of this temperature regime were found to possess ripening oocytes while fishes of similar length and age at 20°C were often immature. To assess the complicating effect of gonad maturation, it would appear that future work on the influence of temperature on growth in annual killifishes must involve numbers of experimental fishes sufficient to permit adequate sampling for gonad examination in the course of the growth period.

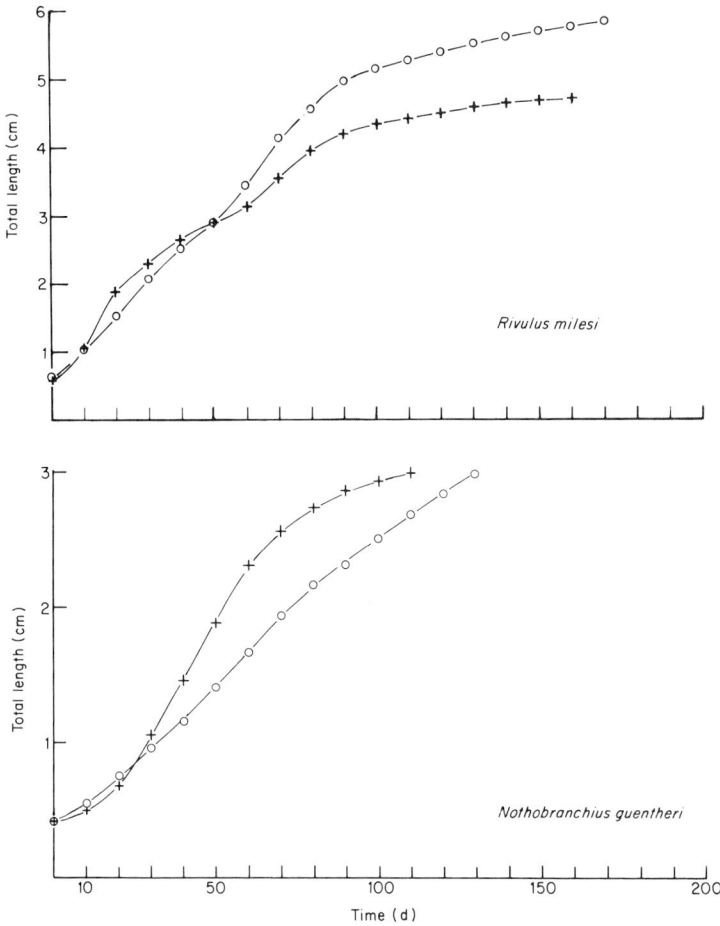

FIG. 2. Growth of *Nothobranchius guentheri* and *Rivulus milesi* at 20°C (open circles) and 28°C (crosses), under conditions described in text; each point is mean length of 12 fishes; curves fitted by eye.

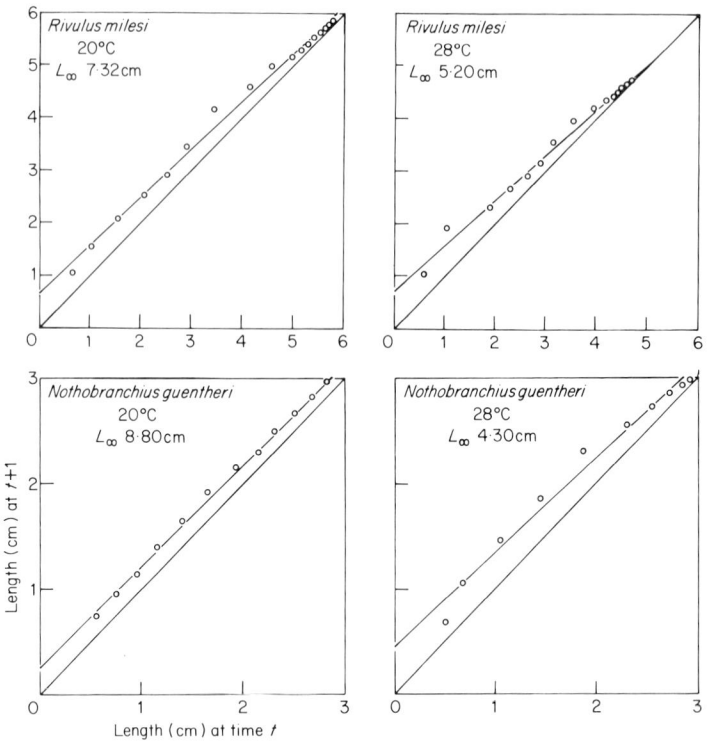

FIG. 3. Ford-Walford plots for growth data of *Nothobranchius guentheri* and *Rivulus milesi* shown in Fig. 2. L_∞, estimated asymptotic length; time interval 10 days.

CONCLUSION

Annual killifishes are not only of phenological interest for research into growth and aging, But also, because of their brilliant coloration, enjoy considerable popularity among aquarists.

In addition, wild populations of these fishes may be of some economic value as biological control agents for the eradication of malaria. At a very early age, annual killifishes will readily eat mosquito larvae (Bay, 1965) and, indeed, their readiness to eat such food was noticed by Vanderplank (1940), who suggested that *Nothobranchius taeniopygus* should be used in areas where malaria was prevalent. Hildemann & Walford (1963) compared the abundance of *Cynolebias* with rarity of mosquitoes in flooded areas of southern Brazil and Argentina. The adaptability of annuals for such a purpose has been shown in California rice fields, where *Cynolebias bellottii* can be successfully field-reared and propagated under climatic conditions which are the reverse of those experienced in its normal Argentinian habitat (Bay, 1966).

While experiments in Africa were in progress, testing the usefulness of *Nothobranchius* for mosquito control, it was noticed that large quantities of these fishes were being removed by local inhabitants as a tasty and easily available source of food. This prompted Vanderplank (1967) to suggest that "instant fish farms" should be created to utilize every available water source, however limited in size, for the production of this protein-rich foodstuff. The "instant fish" idea also made a temporary, but unsuccessful, appearance in the domestic toy/hobby market of the sixties, in the form of kits providing annual killifish eggs, brine-shrimp eggs and appropriate containers for their hatching. The vacuum-sealed sachets, in which the killifish eggs were supplied, did not promote long-term egg viability. However, killifish enthusiasts regularly exchange the eggs of annual species, packed in damp peat and sent through the post. These rarely fail to produce the next generation on the addition of water.

REFERENCES

Andrewartha, H. G. (1952). Diapause in relation to the ecology of insects. *Biol. Rev.* **27**: 50–107.

Bailey, R. G. (1972). Observations on the biology of *Nothobranchius guentheri* (Pfeffer) (Cyprinodontidae), an annual fish from the coastal region of East Africa. *Afr. J. Trop. Hydrobiol. Fish.* **1**: 33-43.

Balon, E. (1975). Reproductive guilds of fishes: a proposal and definition. *J. Fish. Res. Bd Can.* **32**: 821–864.

Bay, E. C. (1965). Instant fish! A new tool for mosquito control? *Pest Control Mag.* **33**: 14–16, 58.

Bay, E. C. (1966). Adaptation studies with the Argentine pearl fish, *Cynolebias bellottii*, for its introduction into California. *Copeia* **1966**: 839–846.

Boschi, E. E. (1953). Cinolebia o pavito. *Cynolebias bellottii* Steindachner 1881. *Ichthys, Argentina* **1**: 45–55.

Boschi, E. E. (1957). *Argentine Pearl Fish*, Cynolebias bellottii *Steindachner 1881*. New Jersey: T.F.H.

British Killifish Association. (1966). *Information Pamphlet* No. 8.

Comfort, A. (1961). The expected rate of senescence and age-dependent mortality in fish. *Nature, Lond.* **191**: 822–823.

Foster, N. R. (1967). Trends in the evolution of reproductive behaviour in killifishes. *Stud. Trop. Oceanogr.* **1**: 549–566.

Geisler, R. (1959). Zur Kenntnis des Lebensraumes Östafrikanischer Cyprinodontinae der Gattung *Nothobranchius*. *Bull. Aquatic Biol.* **1**: 33.

Glut, C. F. (1961). Breeding the *Nothobranchius rachovii*. *Tropicals* **5**(5): 7–9.

Haas, R. (1969). *Ethology and sexual selection in the annual fish*, Nothobranchius guentheri. Ph.D. thesis: University of California, Los Angeles.

Haas, R. (1976). Behavioural biology of the annual killifish, *Nothobranchius guentheri*. *Copeia* **1976**: 80–91.

Hildemann, W. H. & Walford, R. L. (1963). Annual fishes—promising species as biological control agents. *J. Trop. Med. Hyg.* **66**: 163–166.

Jubb, R. A. (1967). *Freshwater fishes of Southern Africa.* Cape Town: Balkema.

Kinne, O. (1960). Growth, food intake, and food conversion in a euryplastic fish exposed to different temperatures and salinities. *Physiol. Zool.* **33**: 288–317.

Kluge, K. (1961). Wo ich den Ghana-*Aphyosemion* fand. *Aquar. Terrar. Z.* **14**: 234–236.

Liu, R. K. & Walford, R. L. (1966). Increased growth and life-span with lowered ambient temperature in the annual fish, *Cynolebias adloffi. Nature, Lond.* **212**: 1277–1278.

Liu, R. K. & Walford, R. L. (1969). Laboratory studies on lifespan, growth, ageing, and pathology of the annual fish, *Cynolebias bellottii* Steindachner. *Zoologica, N.Y.* **54**: 1–16.

Liu, R. K. & Walford, R. L. (1970). Observations on the lifespans of several species of annual fishes and of the world's smallest fishes. *Expl Geront.* **5**: 214–246.

Markofsky, J. & Perlmutter, A. (1973). Growth differences in subgroups of varying longevities in a laboratory population of the male annual cyprinodont fish, *Nothobranchius guentheri* (Peters). *Expl Geront.* **8**: 65–73.

Meder, E. (1955). *Pterolebias longipinnis* Garman. *Aquarium* **24**: 346–350.

Meinken, H. (1973). Mitteilung der Fisch-bestimmungsstelle des VDA Nr 77. *Nothobranchius korthausae* spec. nov., eine hübsche Cyprinodonten-Neuheit von der Insel Mafia (Östafrika). *Aquarium Aqua Terra* **7**: 351–355.

Myers, G. S. (1952). Annual fishes. *Aquarium J.* **23**: 125–141.

Newman, H. H. (1909). Contact organs in killifishes of Woods Hole. *Biol. Bull. mar. biol. Lab. Woods Hole* **17**: 170–180.

Peters, N. (1963). Embryonale Anpassungen oviparer Zahnkarpfen aus periodisch austrocknenden Gewässern. *Int. Rev. ges. Hydrobiol.* **48**: 257–313.

Peters, N. (1965). Diapause und Embryonale Missbildung bei eierlegenden Zahnkarpfen. *Wilhelm Roux Arch. EntwMech. Org.* **156**: 75–87.

Pienaar, E. de V. (1968). The freshwater fishes of the Kruger National Park. *Koedoe* **11**: 1–82.

Ricker, W. E. (1975). Computation and interpretation of biological statistics of fish populations. *Bull. Fish. Res. Bd Can.* **191**: 1–382.

Roloff, E. (1967). Aphyosemions. Their way of life and their usefulness. *J. Am. Killifish Assn* **4**: 41–44.

Rowe, G. (1958). Lovely *Nothobranchius* toothcarps. *Fishkeeping*, March, 1958: 227–229.

Scheel, J. J. (1962). Factors governing the development of killie eggs. *Tropicals* **7**: 9–15.

Scheel, J. J. (1968). *Rivulins of the Old World.* Jersey City: T. F. H. Publications.

Scheel, J. J. (1972). Rivulin chromosomes: the genus *Pterolebias* Garman. *Adv. Aquar. Mag.*, May, 1972: 4–5.

Stearns, S. C. (1976). Life-history tactics: a review of the ideas. *Q. Rev. Biol.* **51**: 3–47.

Stewart, F. (1976). *Nothobranchius korthausae. J. Am. Killifish Assn* **9**: 33–36.

Taberner, R., Fernandez Santos, J. O., & Castelli, J. O. (1975). Some considerations about the morphology, habitat, and aquarium behaviour of the new species, *Cynolebias nonoiuliensis. J. Am. Killifish Assn* **8**: 95–102.

Thomerson, J. E. (1971). Distribution and biology of the annual cyprinodontid, *Rachovia hummelincki* in Venezuela. *J. Am. Killifish Assn* **7**: 21–28.

Ursin, E. (1963). On the incorporation of temperature in the von Bertalanffy growth equation. *Meddr Danm. Fisk. og Havunders.* (N.S.) **4**: 1–16.

Vanderplank, F. L. (1940). A study of *Nothobranchius taeniopygus* in its natural habitat. *Aquarist, Lond.* **10**: 247–249.

Vanderplank, F. L. (1967). Why not "instant fish farms"? *New Scient.* 5 Jan., 1967: 42.

Vaz-Ferreira, R., Soriano, S. de & Paulete, S. de (1964). Edoetologia de la reproduction en los peces del genero *Cynolebias* Steindachner 1876. *Archos Soc. Biol. Montev.* **26**: 44–49.

Walford, R. L. (1969). *The immunologic theory of aging.* Copenhagen: Munksgaard.

Walford, R. L. & Liu, R. K. (1965). Husbandry, lifespan and growth rate of the annual fish, *Cynolebias adloffi* E. Ahl. *Expl Geront.* **1**: 161–171.

Walford, R. L., Liu, R. K., Troup, G. M. & Hsiu, J. (1969). Alterations in soluble/insoluble collagen ratios in the annual fish, *Cynolebias bellottii*, in relation to age and environmental temperature. *Expl Geront.* **4**: 103–109.

Walters, M. W. (1952). A new presentation of the seasonal rainfall of East Africa. *E. Afr. Agric. J.* July, 1952: 11–20.

Weitzman, S. H. & Wourms, J. P. (1967). South American cyprinodont fishes allied to *Cynolebias* with a description of a new species of *Austrofundulus* from Venezuela. *Copeia* **1967**: 89–100.

Wourms, J. P. (1963). Naturally occurring developmental arrest in teleost fishes with associated modifications of epiboly and embryogenesis. *Int. congr. Zool.* **16(2)**: 264.

Wourms, J. P. (1964). Comparative studies on the early ambryology of *Nothobranchius taeniopygus* (Hilgendorf) and *Aplocheilichthys pumilus* (Boulenger) with especial reference to the problem of naturally occurring embryonic diapause in teleost fishes. *Rep. E. Afr. Freshwat. Fish. Inst.* **1964** (App. H): 68–73.

Wourms, J. P. (1967). Annual fishes. In *Methods in developmental biology*: 123–137. Wilt, F. W. & Wessells, N. K. (eds). New York: Thomas Y. Crowell Co.

Wourms, J. P. (1972a). The developmental biology of annual fishes. I. Stages in the normal development of *Austrofundulus myersi* Dahl. *J. exp. Zool.* **182**: 143–168.

Wourms, J. P. (1972b). The developmental biology of annual fishes. II. Naturally occurring dispersion and reaggregation of blastomeres during the development of annual fish eggs. *J. exp. Zool.* **182**: 169–200.

Wourms, J. P. (1972c). The developmental biology of annual fishes. III. Pre-embryonic and embryonic diapause of variable duration in the eggs of annual fishes. *J. exp. Zool.* **182**: 389–414.

Symp. zool. Soc. Lond. (1979) No. 44, 263–306

Adaptiveness and Implications of Small Size in Teleosts

P. J. MILLER

University of Bristol, Bristol, Avon, England

SYNOPSIS

Teleost fishes less than 10 cm in maximum length comprise at least 10% of species in this group; examples not exceeding 2·9 cm are tabulated. Adaptiveness of small size in fishes relates to efficiency of feeding on small prey and possibilities for exploitation of spatially restricted habitats. The significance of small size in resource partitioning and species diversification is discussed. Three basic types of ecotope for small fishes—nektonic, epibenthic and cryptobenthic—are described. Greater susceptibility to predation is a consequence of small size in at least nektonic and epibenthic habitats, and the significance of protective mechanisms is briefly noted. Sources of adult mortality are compared with patterns in the disposition of reproductive effort by small fishes whose life histories are shown to range from early maturation and short adult life to later maturation and enhanced longevity, as exemplified by certain eastern Atlantic gobiids. The adaptive value of various reproductive mechanisms, from highly fecund oviparity, via internal fertilization and simple viviparity, to superfoetation, is discussed and provisional estimates of reproductive effort made for several species contrasting in offspring size and number. The value of small fishes to mankind is summarized.

INTRODUCTION

From long before Charles Dickens and the consideration of this matter by the Pickwick Club, little fishes have received scornful treatment. However, the present speculations about the purpose and problems of small size in teleosts may show that their anabolic adaptiveness, in terms of growth and reproductive phenology will vindicate Mr Pickwick's interest in the "Theory of Tittlebats". Nowadays, popular enthusiasm for small fishes may be as widespread as that for larger fishes, with aquarists and anglers representing major hobbies in the Western world.

Human terms "small" and "large" relate ultimately to human physique and their application is much influenced by tradition and experience. In defining the size range covered by this review, lower limits are set for adult organization at about 0·75–0·9 cm, and a few milligrams, among the smallest teleosts listed in Table I. A more arbitrary upper limit has been drawn at a maximum body length of about 10 cm, corresponding to a weight of roughly 15 g in a fish of typical fusiform shape.

This size category coincides with the lowest subdivision for teleosts made by Lindsey (1966) in a comprehensive survey of body size among

TABLE I

Some teleost fishes not exceeding 2·0 cm in maximum standard length (exclusive of caudal fin)

Species*	Distribution	Habitat	Adult length (cm)	Sources
Cyprinidae				
Barbus lorenzi Loiselle & Welcomme	Dahomey	F	1·37–1·60	Loiselle & Welcomme (1971)
B. sylvaticus Loiselle & Welcomme	Dahomey	F	1·45–1·90	Loiselle & Welcomme (1971)
Horadandia atukorali Deraniyagala	Shri Lanka	F	1·90	Deraniyagala (1943)
Rasbora maculata Duncker	SE Asia	F	2·00	Brittan (1975)
Fluviphylax pygmaeus (Myers & Carvalho)	Amazonia	F	females 1·415–1·85 males 1·25–1·85	Roberts (1970)
Poeciliidae				
Neoheterandria elegans Henn	Columbia	F	females 2·00† males 1·5–1·8†	Jacobs (1971)
Poecilia minor (Garman)	Amazonia	F	females 2·00† males 1·70†	Jacobs (1971)
Phallostethidae				
Phenacostethus posthon Roberts	Thailand	F	females 1·23–1·80 males 1·27–1·70	Roberts (1971)
Ph. smithi Myers	Thailand	F	females 1·37–1·56 males 1·27–1·49 1·4–1·7†	Roberts (1971) Te Winkel (1939)
Schindleriidae				
Schindleria praematura (Schindler)‡	W Pacific	M	females 1·6–2·13 males 1·1–2·0	Schindler (1932); Bruun (1940)
Sch. pietschmanni (Schindler)	Hawaii	M	females 1·5–2·0 màles 1·15–1·7	Schindler (1932)

Gobiidae

Bryaninops ridens Smith	W Indian Ocean	M	2·0†	J. L. B. Smith (1959)
Eviota nebulosa Smith	W Indian Ocean	M	2·0†	J. L. B. Smith (1958)
E. zonura Jordan & Seale	Indo-W Pacific	M	2·0†	Koumans (1953)
Fagasa diaphana Harry	Guadalcanal	B	1·84	Harry (1949)
Garmannia pallens Ginsburg	tropical W Atlantic	M	1·60	Böhlke & Robins (1968)
Ginsburgellus novemlineatus (Fowler)	tropical W Atlantic	M	2·00	Böhlke & Robins (1968)
Lythrypnus elasson Böhlke & Robins	tropical W Atlantic	M	1·29	Böhlke & Robins (1960)
L. heterochrona Ginsburg	tropical W Atlantic	M	1·90	Böhlke & Robins (1960)
L. nesiotes Böhlke & Robins	tropical W Atlantic	M	1·40	Böhlke & Robins (1960)
L. phorellus Böhlke & Robins	tropical W Atlantic	M	1·25	Böhlke & Robins (1960)
Mirogobius lacustris Herre	Philippines	F	1·25– > 1·9	Herre (1927)
Mistichthys luzonensis Smith	Philippines	F	females 1·1–1·4 males 1·1–1·35	Herre (1927); Te Winkel (1935)
Pandaka lidwilli (McCulloch)	W Pacific	M	females 1·42–1·75 males 1·33–1·57	Dôtu (1957)
P. pusilla Herre	Philippines	M	females 1·45–1·55 males 1·35–1·65	Herre (1927)
P. pygmaea Herre§	Philippines	B	females 1·00–1·15† males 0·75–0·09	Herre (1927); Sarenas & Ronquillo (1954); Villadolid & Marquez (1960)
P. trimaculata Akihito & Meguro	W Pacific	B	1·28	Prince Akihito & Meguro (1975)
Psilotris alepis Ginsburg	tropical W Atlantic	M	2·00	Böhlke (1963)
Ps. batrachodes Böhlke	tropical W Atlantic	M	1·78	Böhlke (1963)

* Excluding species known from few specimens; F, freshwater; M, marine; B, brackish.
† May include caudal fin.
‡ Lightest teleost recorded (not > 0·008 g) (Bruun, 1940).
§ Shortest teleost (weight not > 0·0198 g) (Bruun, 1940).

poikilotherms, and also embraces the majority of familiar aquarium fishes, both of tropical and temperate fresh waters (Sterba, 1962). In all, at least 1800 species of Teleostei are no larger than 10 cm in maximum length, and must form at least 10% of this infraclass (Lindsey, 1966; Nelson, 1976).

ADAPTIVENESS OF SMALL SIZE

Feeding Efficiency

Recently, among ecologists, there has been much attention paid to the theoretical significance of specific size, the particulate distribution of biomass characterizing different species, and the adaptiveness of growth patterns followed by individuals. Relative size of an organism within an ecosystem is especially important for consideration of trophic niche and predator/prey relationships. In fishes, as well as other animals, body size and feeding behaviour should relate to the size range of food organisms taken in such a way as to maximize net energy gain per unit time spent feeding, and to minimize the role of mortality to the predator while so engaged (Schoener, 1971). Growth efficiency in fishes is known to decrease when prey becomes small in proportion to the consumer (Kerr, 1971) and a consequent failure to achieve optimal gonadal biomass or fecundity, together with longer exposure to the chance of mortality by protracted feeding, would adversely affect reproductive fitness. Reduction in size among fishes is thus an appropriate adaptation for increasing net energy gain by individual capture of items from a food resource composed of small organisms, and also enables pursuit of the latter in a complex substrate or spatially restricted environment.

Phylogeny

Despite Cope's Law, which refers to a widespread tendency for evolution towards larger physical size (Van Valen, 1973), all small teleosts would seem to have been derived from larger ancestors within the group, as a part of the adaptive radiation by this type of osteichthyan organization towards niche and ecotope opportunities awaiting suitably diminutive fishes (Whittaker, Levin & Root, 1973). It should be noted that the length category (up to 10 cm) considered here has an appreciably lower mode than that shown by recorded sizes from 5 to 30 cm for stem-teleost leptolepids (Patterson, 1974).

Whatever ecological resources may exist, the evolution of small size among teleosts must meet intrinsic curbs set by the limits of body organization characterizing this group. The effect of scaling on the functional capabilities of animals, including fishes, has recently been much discussed (Pedley, 1977). Earlier, Huxley (1941) described various

phyletic "problems" set by diminution in size, concerning space requirements for basic organ systems, and the inexorable rise in surface area to
body weight ratios for the entire body, gills and alimentary canal. In the
latter respect, fishes have the advantage of being poikilothermous in
evolving towards smaller body size. However, they may instead be
affected by greater osmoregulatory demands in an aqueous medium. For
the minute goby, *Mistichthys luzonensis* (Table I), Te Winkel (1935)
believed that a low value for the ratio of gill surface to body surface area,
and relatively small cell types (erythrocytes, Mauthner's cells, gametes,
etc.) were all features of size adaptation. Allometric growth of organs in
relation to small body size was discussed by Wellensiek (1953) for poeciliid
cyprinodonts, while minimal dimensions for functional competence
in the lens-eye of vertebrates have been estimated by Kirschfeld
(1976). Smaller fishes tend to have relatively larger eyes (Dobrinskaya,
1965) and a theoretical situation may be envisaged where increasing
allometry to obtain a requisite minimum absolute size for a body part
could result in excessive disproportion of this within reduced overall
dimensions. However, an effective lower limit to the evolution of adult
size in teleosts seems to be set by the fact that the vital function of
gametogenesis cannot be completed in a teleost frame of less than about
1 cm in length and weighing a few milligrams (Bruun, 1940), although
free-living, self-feeding existence is possible, at least for a short time, at a
size of the smallest postlarvae, about 0·2 cm in length (Breder & Rosen,
1966).

Ecology

Examination of data provided by Lindsey (1966) shows that the vast
majority of small teleosts occur in tropical and warm-temperate areas of
the world, especially in freshwater habitats of the tropics (Fig. 1). In fresh
water and the deep sea, small species also form a higher proportion of the
total fish fauna as latitude decreases. Most frequent occurrence of small
fishes nearer the equator would seem to result from the much discussed
situation of resource subdivision and niche proliferation found in the
long established, predictable ecosystems of tropical seas and many
freshwater habitats which form both Old and New World centres of
species diversity. A proliferation, for example, of 6000–8000 species of
fishes associated with coral reefs (Ehrlich, 1975) and such species flocks as
that of at least 150–170 taxa of the cichlid *Haplochromis* in Lake Victoria
(Greenwood, 1974) has been frequently accompanied by a spread in
maximum size between congeners and higher grades of organization.
Food-resource partitioning by simple size displacement, between closely
related and otherwise similar species, might be expected as a frequent
outcome of this process (MacArthur, 1972). This would certainly be the
case if food were moderately limited (Schoener, 1965), although excessive
scarcity might lead to a smaller species being displaced by larger forms

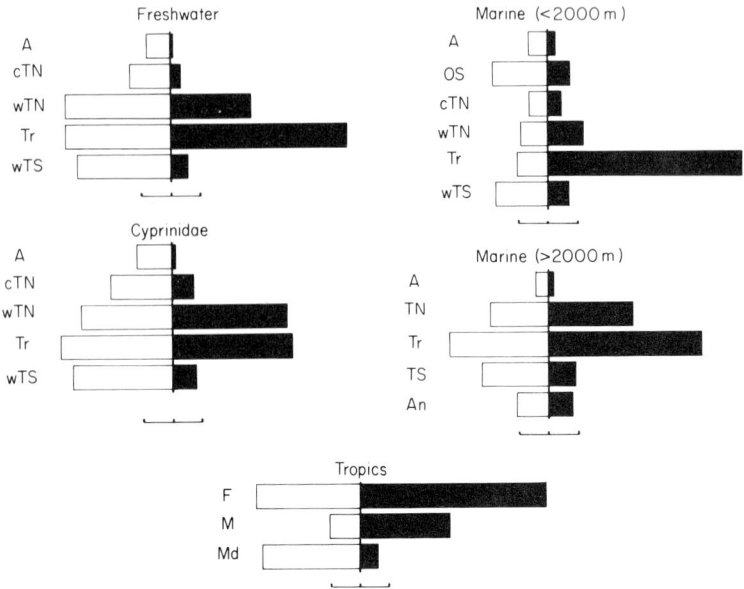

FIG. 1. Occurrence of small teleosts (less than 10 cm) as percentage of all small species (black) or all teleosts (open) in groupings indicated; regions: A, Arctic; An, Antarctic; c, cool; OS, Sea of Okhotsk; TN, north temperate; Tr, tropical; TS, south temperate; w, warm; habitats: F, freshwater; M, marine (< 2000 m); Md, marine (> 2000 m). Scale 10% from vertical axis. Data and definitions from Lindsey (1966).

(Wilson, 1975). With avoidance of competition at a K-selective premium in such closely integrated and saturated ecosystems, an evolutionary trend towards decrease in size would make available new sources of smaller food not only in open waters but also in a variety of spatially restricted habitats, even on or in other organisms. Access to these is mechanically possible only for fish of reduced dimensions, and yields further resources of cover and breeding terrain.

In practice, among the fishes of Caribbean reefs, C. L. Smith & Tyler (1975) and C. L. Smith (1978) concluded that size plays a vital role in the incorporation of species into the fish community, and viewed the environment as offering a linear series of ecotopes, with characteristic food dimensions, shelter sites and hunting territory, each of which was available only for fish of a certain size. C. L. Smith (1978) suggested that a difference in length of more than 12% was sufficient for elimination of competition over a size-related resource. The range and magnitude of body size achieved by individuals may be further advantageously lowered in phenotypic expression by competition with other species (Page & Schemske, 1978) or even by intra-specific competition for limited sites (Fricke, 1974).

Within a community of small fishes, adaptiveness of a species is determined not merely by size, but by a host of other morphological, physiological and behavioural peculiarities, so that a degree of spatial overlap is possible between fishes of contrasting structure and habits, but of comparable diminutive size (Zaret & Rand, 1971). Closeness of species packing is facilitated when these differ appreciably in niche width, as shown, for example, in the range of prey selected by sympatric specialist and generalist feeders (McMurtrie, 1976). This situation is well shown by the "mbuna" community of small cichlid fishes, endemic to Lake Malawi, whose trophic adaptations and inter-relationships have been detailed by Fryer (1959).

Such instances do not invariably relate to circumstances in which population size is controlled by inter-specific competition for some limiting resource such as food. If predation exerted greater influence over numbers in small sympatric species, the very fact of being small in size, and therefore at risk from a greater number of larger predators, should promote co-existence of more than one small species in the same ecotope, held below saturation level in total population size or in a "lottery" situation for randomly occurring living sites (see Fryer 1959; Fryer & Iles, 1972; Roughgarden & Feldman, 1975; Sale, 1978). Predation may also lead to selection for "aspect diversity" (Rand, 1967) among co-existing small fishes. Given the tropical diversity in predator species (Paine, 1966), the ability of generalized predators to "switch" from one co-existing prey species to another according to relative abundance (Murdoch, 1969), and the tendency for even specialized forms to take items smaller than their optimal prey size (Schoener, 1974), predation would seem to be a potentially important and widely imposed factor in the evolution of small fish under the organization of a crowded tropical ecosystem.

Relevant to an anabolic theme (Miller, this volume p. 1), Connell & Orias (1964), in comparing energy-flow patterns within the stable tropical community and those of unstable ecosystems elsewhere, found that stability was aided by increased recycling rate for nutrients. The evolution of small fish species could be viewed as a contribution to this process in that predation is potentially higher on these than on larger fish. However, the higher catabolic rate per unit weight in small fish would mean that a smaller proportion of energy could be devoted to productivity (anabolism of growth and reproduction) than Connell & Orias (1964) would regard as typical of the stable community. Perhaps small size in fish is symptomatic of the "overspecialization" which is envisaged as a later stage in the development of the tropical ecosystem, leading to smaller populations.

ECOTOPES FOR SMALL FISH

The great variety of ecotopes occupied by small fishes reflects a very wide distribution of potential food organisms and living spaces. On a basis of physical cover, the adult habitat and trophic niche of many small fishes may be classified as nektonic, epibenthic or cryptobenthic (Fig. 2). As Fig. 2 shows, these types grade into one another over the range of small species, within which ecological distribution may sometimes vary in temporal or geographical pattern. Choice of this aspect of ecotope is merely for convenience: other dimensions, such as niche breadth, resource limitation and environmental predictability, tend to be less well documented than those of food and occurrence.

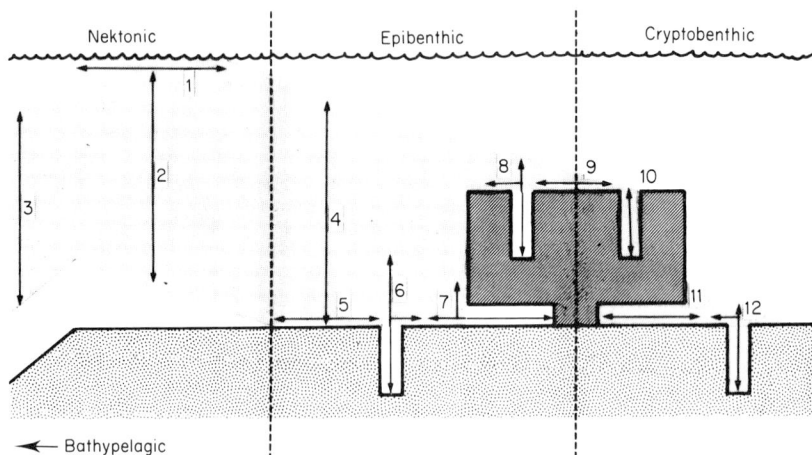

FIG. 2. Ecotopes of small fish, with feeding habitat (fine stipple) and range of movement (arrows) in relation to deposit/substrate (coarse stipple) and structured habitat/covering body/reef organism (cross-hatching). Numbers refer to examples in text.

Nektonic

The open nektonic habitat involves foraging in the water column, or above substrates, where habitat structure necessarily provides little or no cover apart from turbidity or other conditions of reduced illumination. Such habits characterize numerous tropical freshwater species familiar to aquarists. Many of these fishes are adapted for surface ("top") feeding in shallow waters, predominantly on aquatic insect larvae and also on surface insects of terrestrial origin, such as ants (see Knöppel, 1970). They include most of the highly successful and numerous cyprinodontoid fishes (both oviparous "killifishes" and viviparous "livebearers"), many small Oriental cyprinids (*Barbus, Danio, Rasbora*, etc.) and also the curious phallostethiform derivatives of the Atherinidae (Fig. 2, 1). In the New World, the glandulocaudine characins are surface feeders, as are another group of characoids, the highly modified freshwater hatchetfish (Gasteropelecidae). This is a style of feeding which lends itself to the rapid exploitation of new food sources and dispersal from predators in the surface waters of flooded areas resulting from heavy seasonal rainfall in many parts of the tropics. It culminates in the extreme lifestyle of annual species among rivulin cyprinodonts reviewed by Simpson (this volume p. 243). Under more pelagic conditions, small planktonivorous fishes occur in the lacustrine freshwater environment, such as the specialized African cyprinid, *Engraulicypris argenteus* (Pellegrin), which feeds on cladocerans, copepods, diatoms and surface insects (Corbet, 1961), and also in marine coastal waters, where such Indo-Pacific forms as the dussumierid *Spratelloides delicatulus* (Bennett) and the atherinid *Allanetta ovalaua* (Herre) take copepods, decapod larvae and other zooplankton (Hiatt & Strasburg, 1960). In temperate areas, small atherinids and gasterosteids may play a similar role (Fig. 2, 2).

Brief mention must here be made of what Murray & Hjort (1912) termed the "Lilliputian" fauna of the deep sea. This embraces fishes of the bathypelagic communities, where there are many small stomiatoids, myctophids, melamphaeids and ceratioids (Fig. 2, 3). Here, productivity limitations, reviewed by Marshall (1960), may play a role in selection for reduced body size. Distribution of prey seems sparse, and, under these circumstances, a common trend has been towards small size with considerable anatomical modification to permit the ingestion of food organisms up to at least twice the length of the predator (Marshall, 1965). By this means, the widest possible size range of prey can be exploited when perhaps infrequent opportunities for feeding arise. Bathypelagic melamphaeids achieve this versatility by retaining the gill filtering mechanisms of more planktonivorous epipelagic species in conjunction with increase in size of jaws (Ebeling & Cailliet, 1974). In this environment, small size is a requirement in the bizarre reproductive strategy of male parasitism found within at least three families of ceratioid angler fishes (Pietsch, 1976).

Epibenthic

These are patterns of occurrence and feeding, ranging from involvement with both substrate and overlying water layers (Fig. 2, 4) to exclusively benthic feeding but relatively superficial distribution (Fig. 2, 5). Many small fishes feed on both mid-water and bottom-living organisms, especially in shallower waters of streams, lake- and sea-margins. As an extreme example of versatility, hovering ptereleotrine gobies feed on zooplankton over sand and coral rubble, but take refuge in nearby burrows (J. L. B. Smith, 1958; Davis & Birdsong, 1973) (Fig. 2, 6).

Small, bottom-feeding teleosts in tropical fresh waters comprise a range of ostariophysan types, from characins, such as *Nannostomus*, *Neolebias* and *Nannaethiops*, to the little armoured catfishes (Callichthyidae) of South America, sometimes foraging on land, and a number of Old World loaches (Cobitidae). Among the smallest (Table I), a minute cyprinid, *Barbus sylvaticus*, from a forest stream of southeastern

Dahomey, is a bottom feeder, over peaty deposits, consuming copepods and ostracods as well as general detritus, while another, even tinier, form *B. lorenzi*, found along the edges of water-lily beds, browses on the "Aufwuchs" of plant stems in addition to taking mid-water particles (Loiselle & Welcomme, 1971). Perhaps the best documented of small benthophagous fishes are the "mbuna" cichlids of Lake Malawi, whose dependence on the algal flora and associated invertebrates has been studied by Fryer (1959) (Fig. 2, 8). Under much more rigorous physical conditions, highly modified homalopterid loaches graze algae and invertebrates from the surfaces of stones and boulders in hill-stream torrents (Hynes, 1970) (Fig. 2, 9) while amphibious blennies (*Andamia*) feed similarly on littoral splash-zone rocks (Gibson, 1969).

In the more fluctuating and generalized freshwater ecosystems of higher latitudes, trophic emphasis in many small fishes is also on demersal feeding, with more or less seasonal changes in extent of benthic concealment (Fig. 2, 7). Among these species, cyprinids are well represented by a variety of Nearctic shiner-like forms (*Notropis, Rhinichthys*, etc.) and Palearctic minnows (*Phoxinus, Alburnoides*, etc.) while the many percid darters of the USA and southern Canada include *Etheostoma microperca* Jordan & Gilbert, which does not exceed 3·8 cm (Berg, 1949; Scott & Crossman, 1973). More primitive teleosts, with predominantly larger species, are also represented among small fishes by the family Umbridae, comprising the mud-minnows (*Umbra*), with the related Alaska blackfish, *Dallia pectoralis* Bean, (7·6–15·2 cm) extending into muskeg swamp after the spring thaw (Blackett, 1962; Scott & Crossman, 1973).

In temperate seas, the partial unlocking of a rich food source, the meiobenthos of soft deposits, effected by small body size, may explain the success of Mediterranean–Atlantic gobies belonging to *Pomatoschistus* and neighbouring genera (Miller, 1963, 1976). However, a related species, *Gobiusculus flavescens* (Fabricius) (6·0 cm), has adopted a mid-water habitat over inshore weed beds and feeds to a large extent on plankton (Miller, 1963).

The hermatypic coral communities of tropical seas are renowned for their assemblages of small fishes. The general ecology and trophic relationships of coral fishes have been reviewed by Hiatt & Strasburg (1960), Randall (1967), C. L. Smith & Tyler (1972), Ehrlich (1975), Goldman & Talbot (1976), and C. L. Smith (1978). Part of the fauna occurs in superficial habitats, feeding on water-column plankton, other epifauna, detritus and even coral polyps, but retiring to shelter within the structurally complex substrate, transiently or on a regular diurnal basis (Hiatt & Strasburg, 1960; Hobson, 1975; Davis & Birdsong, 1973) (Fig. 2, 8). A much discussed element, often advertising their presence, are small cleaner wrasses and gobies (Ehrlich, 1975). Apart from picking food off other animals, further epifaunal ecotopes, for which small size is a necessity, involve life on or about the surface of larger invertebrates. The famous association between anemones and damsel-fishes (*Amphiprion*) has been well described by Mariscal (1970) and Edmunds (1974). Other small fishes, appropriately camouflaged, live on the stems of gorgonians or crinoids (Randall & Randall, 1960; Davis & Cohen, 1969; Briggs, 1976).

Cryptobenthic

Small body size permits exploitation of restricted habitats, where food and shelter are obtained in, or in relation to, conditions of substrate complexity and/or restricted living space, with a physical barrier likely to be interposed between the small fish and sympatric predators. Simpler forms of this lifestyle are shown by burrowers in soft substrates, such as the kraemeriine gobies or the coolie loaches (*Acanthophthalmus*), while commensalism with tunnelling invertebrates, especially decapod crustaceans, has been adopted by numerous gobiids (Polunin & Lubbock, 1977). Some commensal gobies hover or lie near the burrow of their partner, and the extent of residence and feeding under exposed or sheltered conditions must produce a gradation from epibenthic to cryptobenthic species (Fig. 2, 6 and 12). Residence under stones characterizes many small fishes of streams (Hynes, 1970) and the intertidal zone (Gibson, 1969) (Fig. 2, 11).

A variety of cryptobenthic ecotopes for small fishes is provided by the ramified, convoluted or porous nature of madreporan and soft-coral aggregations (Tyler, 1971; Patton, 1976) (Fig. 2, 10). Not surprisingly, one of the smallest fish species, the gobiid *Eviota zonura* (Table I), belongs to an Indo-Pacific genus whose members are commonly found in the interstices of coral (Herre, 1927). A related group, the flattened gobiodontine gobies, live only within Indo-Pacific corals, feeding on small invertebrates and sometimes coral polyps (Hiatt & Strasburg, 1960; Tyler, 1971; Patton, 1976).

Highly "structured" reef conditions are also presented by other sessile organisms, such as coralline algae, sponges, polychaetes, vermetid molluscs and bryozoans, as well as eroded rocks and boulder areas (Collete & Rützler, 1977). In the Caribbean, tiny species of another gobiine stock, belonging to *Evermannichthys*, *Risor*, *Pariah* and *Gobiosoma*, together with the apogonid *Phaeoptyx xenus* (Böhlke & Randall) (5·26 cm), live permanently inside sponges (Tyler & Böhlke, 1972). Gobies and blennies of temperate seas include several small species found in coarse grounds or reefs. The smallest European vertebrates are gobiids associated with coralline beds of calcareous red algae, *Lebetus* species in the eastern Atlantic (*L. scorpioides* (Collett) (4·0 cm)) and in the Mediterranean, *Odondebuenia balearica* (Pellegrin & Fage) (3·2 cm) and *Corcyrogobius liechtensteini* (Kolombatovic) (2·5 cm) (Miller & Tortonese, 1968; Miller, 1972).

The general advantages of life on or about the surface of echinoderms have been listed by Davenport (1966). For a number of small fishes, transient refuge is afforded by a commensal relationship with large sea urchins (Abel, 1960; Fricke, 1970), or even the crown-of-thorns starfish (Allen, 1972). Permanent residence between the spines of a large sea urchin (*Diadema*) provides a food source, initially other epifauna, such as harpacticoid copepods, in a relatively protected environment (Fig. 2, 10). Various common features of adaptation to this habitat are noted by Marshall (1965) and Edmunds (1974). Ultimately, some clingfish (*Diademichthys, Arcos, Cellichthys*) and gobies (*Ginsburgellus*) have become vertebrate ectoparasites, feeding on the tube feet of the urchin (Dix, 1969; Teytaud, 1970).

Finally, on the subject of parasitism by small fish, the famous "candiru" (*Vandellia*) of Amazonia must be mentioned. This is one of several small pygidiid catfish which enter the gill-chambers of larger fish to browse on the gill-filaments (Myers, 1944). The straying of the candiru into human orifices has generated some folklore (Norman, 1963).

PROBLEMS OF SMALL SIZE

Predation

Evolving down in size to suit a small prey resource—becoming a second-ary consumer rather than a tertiary one—brings the drawback of greater likelihood of capture by larger animals into whose size range of potential prey the small fish now fits. This danger is faced by all small develop-mental stages of fish, but, in the case of species with small adult size, it will also be manifest over the entire reproductive life. In the critical situation of pursuit, there is the simple scaling effect that larger fish can swim faster in absolute terms than smaller individuals. This will usually override a reverse trend that maximum speed, in anaerobic "burst" swimming by a small fish, may be much greater in terms of body lengths per second (at 10 cm, up to $25\,L\,s^{-1}$, against only $6\,L\,s^{-1}$ achieved at 100 cm) (Wardle, 1977). The importance of predation as a factor in the diversification of small fish has already been discussed. Not only other fish, and piscivorous birds, but a variety of larger invertebrates are physically capable of overpowering and ingesting fish of small size. Thus gobies may be swallowed by nemertine worms (Hunt, 1925), blennies speared by fish-eating cones (Kohn, 1956), minnows devoured by dytiscid water-beetles (Imms, 1957) and guppies sucked by giant water bugs (Cullen, 1969). Even the common shrimp, *Crangon crangon* (L.), may catch small fish, at least in captivity (Muus, 1967).

Many small species, abundant in open habitats, consequently form essential intermediate components in food-webs, including those of economic fishes. Thus, small cyprinodonts, moving with the tide, feature in the transfer of energy from detritus-producing saltmarsh to nearby coastal waters of New England (Valiela *et al.*, 1977; Kneib & Stiven, 1978), with large populations and high productivity. Other good examples of small fish as trophic intermediates are provided by New Zealand galaxiids (McDowall, 1968) and the pelagic cyprinid, *Engraulicypris*, of Lake Victoria (Corbet, 1961). There is less information about predation on small fish in more specialized cryptobenthic habitats, whose nature may be thought to ensure a high degree of safety. In these species, although numbers are likely to be more influenced by other biotic factors (see below), individuals are not entirely immune to capture by larger animals (Hobson, 1975). In their work on Marshall Island coral reefs, Hiatt & Strasburg (1960) recorded that a small blenniid, *Istiblennius*, despite the habit of concealment in crevices and a noticeable alertness, could still fall victim to a hawkfish, *Paracirrhites forsteri* (Bloch & Schneider), lying in wait on the surface of coral heads, while the little coral-dwelling gobiid *Eviota* was eaten by a small cardinal fish, *Apogon exostigma* (Jordan & Starks) (4·5–5·3 cm), which itself entered the interstices of coral masses. The need for cryptic striped coloration, shown by small fishes in such an apparently secure habitat as the surface of a sea-urchin, is revealed by the ability of a long-snouted predator (*Aulostomus*) to delve between urchin spines (Hiatt & Strasburg, 1960). Sometimes, the entire habitat may be destroyed when sea urchins, such as *Diadema*, despite their poisonous spines, are eaten by large fish (Randall, Schroeder & Starck, 1964).

Protection

To reduce this risk of predation attendant on diminutive size, numerous adaptations are shown by small fishes to minimize the efficiency of predators. They are manifest both before and during adult life and, in many cases, may resemble those seen in juvenile stages of species whose adults are much larger. Such mechanisms involve various patterns of energy utilization, with different emphasis on behavioural (catabolic) and structural (anabolic) components. They may also be divided functionally into avoiding (prepredatory) or escape (postpredatory) devices, according to their operation relative to the occurrence of attack. The magnitude and relative importance of the various anti-predator devices employed by a small species become of greater significance when the reproductive strategy of the species is iteroparous, with moderate but protracted reproductive effort. Many examples of protective modifications and mimicry in small fishes are described by Edmunds (1974).

FITNESS AND SMALL SIZE

Mortality Patterns

Over the range of ecotopes adopted by small fishes, three sources of mortality may be encountered, two of these (depensatory and compensatory) linked with population density and the third (extra-pensatory) independent of this factor (Neave, 1953). Their relative significance varies with ecotope and contrasting patterns of adult mortality result in a variety of phenological adaptations for development of gonadal products.

In open areas, where food for nektonic or epibenthic species may be abundant, risk of predation must usually be high, affecting not only juvenile stages but also the small adults, with unpredictable individual survival not typically aided by elaborate protective mechanisms. Such mortality is depensatory and likely to become proportionately heavier as numbers fall towards a level set by predator behaviour. In the present case, population abundance is more responsive to changes in predation pressure than in food level and equilibrium size of the population is below the carrying capacity of the habitat as determined by food and space resources (Southwood, 1977). For example, in Lake Tanganyika, biomass of the small clupeids *Limnothrissa miodon* Boulenger (usually <9·5 cm) and *Stolothrissa tanganicae* Regan (10 cm) greatly increased after their predators began to be exploited by a commercial fishery (Coulter, 1970). Selection for high reproductive effort in species of this category (see below), with intrinsic detriment to adult survival, introduces a more or less apparent component of mortality from "reproductive stress" (Woodhead, this volume p. 179). For a combination of factors, therefore, there are often few survivors beyond a single breeding season (as in many gobies, darters, shiners, cyprinodonts, sticklebacks, etc.) or, in some cases, a single act of spawning (semelparity). Deferment of reproduction may prolong life (Comfort, 1964) and absence of predation see the onset of reproductive senescence (Krumholz, 1963).

Adult survival may also be drastically affected in habitats—such as temporary pools or hill-streams—impassable to predators but subject to marked environmental changes of irregular periodicity. Such extrapensatory mortality is independent of age and population density. Between catastrophes, population growth, again associated with high reproductive effort (Heins & Clemmer, 1976), may reach or overshoot a saturation level (Southwood *et al.*, 1974).

In more restricted epibenthic or cryptobenthic conditions, with high environmental stability or predictably moderate fluctuation, the physical structure of the habitat contributes more or less effectively to protection. However, space and associated food resources, potentially limited in a confined or specialized ecotope, must curb population size at some equilibrium level. Overcrowding would lead to compensatory, density-dependent mortality from starvation or predation, as a result of resource depletion or abnormal behaviour prompted by hunger or social displacement. This situation is usually associated with a complex community, like that of a coral reef, but may be reached under harsh conditions in a very sparse ecosystem, as found, say, in hot springs (Southwood, 1977). At carrying capacity, mortality in a juvenile phase or at entry to the adult ecosystem may be much higher and more erratic than that experienced by the securely-lodged reproducers. Adults, despite often elaborate protective mechanisms, may succumb to random predation but mortality from this source is probably not great and an age-dependent component of senescence may eventually appear. Thus, the coral reef damsel fish *Eupomacentrus planifrons* Cuvier (12·5 cm) can live at least four years (A. H. Williams, 1978) and some temperate cryptobenthic species at least 10 years (see below).

Maturation Patterns

From numerous studies summarized by Stearns (1976), the adaptive response to a particular configuration of mortality factors must lie at some point in a balance between magnitude and distribution with time of reproduction effort. With predation as a major, unpredictable, source of mortality over the entire lifespan, the phenological response is towards early sexual maturity and high reproductive effort, with less regard for the effect of reproduction on the survival of adults. Shortening of lifespan by intrinsic factors connected with the physiology of reproduction (Jones & Johnston, 1977; Woodhead, this volume p. 179) would be of no disadvantage to net reproductive value. This type of life history provides the conventional example of *r*-selection, with the attributes favoured being those of a perpetually expanding population without density-dependent limitation.

Under this pattern of mortality, fitness is best ensured by commencing to breed at a younger age, once the physiologically minimum body size for gonad maturation has been reached. Early maturation has been shown to have a substantial influence on rate of numerical increase (Lewontin, 1965). As many aquarists have observed, sexual maturity is reached after only a few months of life in most cyprinodonts (Foster, 1967a; Kneib,1978), and as early as four weeks after birth in the poeciliid *Gambusia affinis* (Krumholz, 1948). For lacustrine populations of the three-spined stickleback on Vancouver Island, all overwintering before first spawning, reduced size (age) at maturity has been interpreted as a local genetic adaptation to abundance of larger predators (McPhail, 1977). It could be postulated that delay in gonad maturation caused by seasonality may prevent spread of certain small fish species into higher latitudes. Among temperate gobiids (Table III), epibenthic *Pomatoschistus* species, which are eaten by other fish and birds, reach sexual maturity after the first winter of life (Green, 1968; Swennen, 1971; Lee, 1974; Miller, 1975). By 18 months, a year-class of *P. microps* of *P. minutus* has already completed a lengthy breeding season and is mostly extinct (Lee, 1974; Miller, 1975). Indeed, one of the developmental changes by which small adult size may be achieved is "progenesis" (Gould, 1977), where ontogeny is truncated by accelerated gonad maturation, and body growth, perhaps initially enhanced, is terminated at a lower asymptotic length. At extremes of reduction in size, postlarval features and early maturation are shown by the lightest teleost, *Schindleria praematura*, and the second shortest, *Mistichthys luzonensis*, both found in nektonic habitats (Table I).

With a high degree of uncertainty in adult survival, genetic representation in the next generation can also be enhanced by an increase in material and energy allocated to the function of reproduction, "reproductive effort" as defined by Williams (1966). This has already been discussed by Miller (this volume p. 1) and Wootton (p. 133), and is most conveniently visualized in terms of gonadosomatic index. If density-independent sources of mortality removed any possibility of competition for a limiting resource at the same trophic level, the only constraints on reproductive effort by a small fish might be intrinsic ones of system maintenance and an increase in risk of predation stemming from the processes of reproduction. Williams (1966) believed that a high reproductive effort among smaller fish was indicated by more determinate growth patterns and shorter lifespan than are found in larger species, but this could be viewed as putting effect before cause.

In the context of imposed adult mortality and reproductive effort, semelparity, a single act of reproduction, unlimited in proportion to body maintenance and followed by death of participants, has higher success, in some circumstances, than the cumulative outcome of iteroparity, with reproductive effort expended at intervals by an adult whose viability is less impaired by breeding. Among small fish, semelparity is always associated with early maturation since their reproductive success is not likely to be improved by time-requiring growth-enhancement of fecundity, size or vigour. Semelparity would seem appropriate only under conditions of habitat predictability and high resource availability for young stages. Examples of small fish practising semelparity include the North American smelt, *Labidesthes sicculus* (Cope) (Nelson, 1968), and the much predated *Galaxias maculatus* (Jenyns) of New Zealand (McDowall, 1968). Semelparity is also found in a group of progenetic mid-water gobies, including the Atlantic–Mediterranean *Alphia* and *Crystallogobius*, Indo-Pacific *Gobiopterus* and the ice-goby, *Leucopsarion petersi* Hilgendorf, from Japan (Tamura & Honma, 1970; Miller, 1973).

As a means of enhancing reproductive effort, a direct increase in gonadosomatic index, especially for female fish, raises problems of hydrodynamic performance and predator attraction, in addition to intrinsic ones of maintenance and growth of excessive gonadal tissue at practicable levels of food intake. However, a high reproductive effort may be achieved by summation of repeat (partial, batch, heterochronal) spawning in which successive batches of eggs are produced during a lengthy period of reproduction (Williams, 1959).

This type of iteroparity, for fishes of any size, is supposedly attuned to the persistent but relatively low levels of productivity found in warmer marine, and some freshwater, habitats (Qasim, 1956; McConnell, this volume p. 219), providing food resources for both larval survival and repeated gonad maturation. Repeat-spawning has been frequently described for small tropical fishes, and many such species have been found in breeding condition throughout the year (Breder & Rosen, 1966). However, the duration of reproduction by individuals in the wild is usually unknown. Using what data is available from direct observation on such small fishes, total ovarian expenditure in a breeding season, whether by oviparity or viviparity, may prove surprisingly high (Williams, 1959; Hubbs, Stevenson & Peden, 1968), as suggested here by estimates for certain early maturing tropical to warm-temperate nektonic feeders (Table II). Among these species, differing in reproductive mechanism (see below), monthly primary anabolic expenditure during the long breeding seasons can reach from 50 to 160% of maternal dry somatic weight. The relatively low values for the guppy, *Poecilia reticulata*, highly predated in the wild (Farr, 1975), may be a feature of domestication in aquarium strains. I have examined an exceptional female guppy, 3·5 cm in standard length, carrying 74 early embryos whose total dry weight attained 30·17% of that of the parent.

The property of repeat-spawning, having originated within a phyletic line under warmer conditions, might enable derivatives to colonize appropriate niches in higher latitudes when reproductive effort might need to be maximized. If early maturation was delayed by seasonal climatic fluctuation, the value of repeat-spawning in promoting reproductive output could be proportionately greater than in a more stable physical environment. The most abundant small fishes of temperate areas, both marine and freshwater, are derived from essentially warm temperate or tropical groups; these shiners, darters, gobies, blennies and sticklebacks are nearly all repeat-spawners, as an extreme case found in Texas darters, *Etheostoma* spp., Hubbs & Strawn (1957) record spawning every five to seven days during a breeding season which may exceed six months. The small epibenthic gobiid *Pomatoschistus microps* spawns about six times during the usual breeding season of three months (Fig. 3). Dry weight of the ripe ovary in this species is equivalent to almost one-half of the somatic weight (Table III), and total expenditure in gonad anabolism (i.e. eggs spawned) over this period is at least twice the average adult body weight (Miller, unpub.). Monthly reproductive effort is 0·60, comparable to that of top feeders in Table II.

At higher latitudes, limitation of productivity to short periods of the year cannot support a long season of repeat-spawning, and consequently may bar nektonic and open epibenthic habitats to most small fishes, except highly armoured sticklebacks. In other small fishes, under warmer conditions, exigencies of habitat can restrict spawning, so that, among African *Barbus*, riverine species have a single short breeding season, in contrast to lacustrine, all-year-round spawners (Payne, 1975). However, the young of riverine species can be already mature by a later rainy season, if two such periods occur in the same year, so that early

TABLE II

Reproductive mechanisms and effort (primary anabolic expenditure) in small tropical or warm-temperate teleosts.

Species*	Reproductive mechanism (c)	Temperature (°C); natural habitat or aquaria (c)	Adult females: mean and range of L_S (cm)[1] W_{sd} (g)[2]	Brood (ovulation) frequency: usual/mean and range (d)	Fecundity per brood: mean usual range, extremes	Ripe egg: yolk diameter (mm), W_d (mg)[3]	Young at hatching/birth: L_T (mm)[4] W_d (mg)[3]	Overall season (bs)/duration of individual breeding (i) (days)	Reproductive effort per 30 d (total W_d offspring ÷ W_{sd} female)
Brachydanio rerio (Hamilton-Buchanan)	O[5]	26 (c)[6]	3·0, 0·1263 (2·5, 0·0595– 3·6 0·2684)[7]	5 (5–45)[6]	100–500 (78–1,109)[6]	0·625,[8] 0·0542[9]	3·0,[9] nd	→145 (i)[6]	0·7725[10]; 0·4910[11]; 0·2470[12]
Oryzias latipes (Schlegel)	O[5]	15–28 (c)[13]	2·93, 0·1534 (2·57, 0·0946– 3·24, 0·2223)[13,14]	1, in 30–80 d periods[13]	12–19 (1–67)[13]	1·078,[15] c. 0·28[16]	4·5–5·0,[15] nd	May–Aug (Apr–Oct) (bs), →153(i)[13]	0·7200 (0·0731–[17] 1·5364)[17]
Gambusia affinis (Baird & Girard)	Vs[18]	nd, woodland pool[19,23] nd, grass-land pool[19,27]	3·76, 0·2394 (2·59, 0·0515– 4·64 0·5695), 2·92, 0·0845 (2·44, 0·0403– 3·46, 0·1699)[19,21]	23·9 (21–28)[19]	116·23 (43–205)[19] 21–65 (9–30)[19]	1·6[22]–2·00[23], 1·93–1·97	8–9,[19] 1·47[23]– 2·0[24]	May–late Aug (bs); 95–105 (i)[19,25]	1·2010[26] 0·6336[26]
Gambusia	Vs[18]	18·9–	2·66,0·0575	24·5	6·4[28]	nd	nd	Mar–May	0·2685[31]

	pool[2,3,29]		
		2·98 0·0918)[28,30]	→ 150(i)[28]

	Vs[18]							
Poecilia reticulata Peters	22[32] (c)	3·0, 0·1543 (2·5, 0·0834– 3·6, 0·2854)[33,34]	34 (31–46)[32]	16·27 (3–25)[32]	1·6[35]– 2·1[22] 1·4[36]– 1·5[37]	6·08–6·5,[36] 0·9[36]– 1·7[24]	→ 212(i)[32]	0·1349[38]
	22·9[34] (c)		31·1 (33–37)[39]	11·7 (2–39)[39]				0·1061[38]
	22·5[33]		30 (29–33)[33]	15–16 (8–21)[33]			→ 229(c)[32]	0·1457[38]
	24·5[33] (c)							
	28 (c)		21·4 (16–25)[32]	11·42 (1–29)[37]				0·1504[38]

	Va[40]							
Heterandria formosa Agassiz	15–32, sandhill lake[41,42]	1·8, 0·0265 (1·12, 0·0069– 3·41, 0·1639)[41,43]	10 (3–10)[44]	1–11[44]	0·4, nd[22]	7·5, 0·9[45]	Mar-mid Nov (bs)[41], → 150[46]– 240[47](i)	0·5094[48], 0·7019[49], 1·1509[50], 0·1226[51](i)

Note that data for each species are compiled from various sources (nd, no data).

* Notes and sources. [1] standard length (exclusive of caudal fin); [2] dry somatic weight (exclusive of gonad, dried at 70°C for 48 h); [3] dry weight; [4] total length; [5] oviparous; [6] Hisaoka & Firlit (1962); [7] PJM; dried at 70°C for 48 h; [8] Roosen-Runge (1938); [9] PJM; dried at 70°C for 48 h; [10] estimates for female of 3·0 cm, based on usual spawning frequency, eggs recorded for 145 d (11 spawnings, total 5530)[11] or 107 d (5, 2053)[12] from restricted mating of individual females of unspecified size (Hisaoka & Firlit, 1962); [13] Egami (1959); [14] Kaufman & Beyers (1972); [15] Kamito (1928); [16] PJM, estimate; [17] estimated from egg-production by 28 females, of size range shown (Egami, 1959); [18] simple viviparity; [19] Krumholz (1948); [20] pool regarded as highly productive, North Illinois; [21] PJM; weights estimated from $W_{sd} = 0.00102 L_s^{4.1213}$, for females from Lake Idku, Egypt; [22] Scrimshaw (1946); [23] PJM; Idku material, dried at 70°C for 48 h; [24] Scrimshaw (1945); [25] overwintered females; [26] average female, using "offspring" $W_d = 1.97$ mg; [27] pool regarded as of low productivity; [28] Krumholz (1963); [29] tidal, brackish, with predators; [30] PJM; standard lengths estimated from Böhlke & Chaplin (1968), dry weights from [21], [31] for average female, using *G. affinis* "offspring" W_d; [32] Bowden (1970); [33] Hester (1964); [34] PJM; estimated, for length range studied by Hester, from $W_{sd} = 0.00379 L_s^{3.3730}$ for aquarium stock; [35] Stolk (1951); [36] Thibault & Schultz (1978); [37] PJM; dried at 70°C for 48 h; [38] estimated for average female, of size shown, using brood-frequency and fecundity data recorded for temperature given; [39] Rosenthal (1952); [40] advanced viviparity; [41] Colson (1969); [42] oligotrophic; Florida; [43] PJM; weight estimated, for length range of overwintered females during breeding season (Colson, 1969); from $W_{sd} = 0.00496 L_s^{2.8503}$ for aquarium stock; [44] Breder & Rosen (1966); [45] Scrimshaw (1944a); [46] Colson (1969); overwintered females; [47] Fraser & Renton (1940); [48-51] estimates for average female producing 5 young every 10 d[48], 53 in 77 d[49] and 87 in 77 d[50] (Breder & Rosen, 1966) and for female of $L_s = 3.21$ cm, $W_{sd} = 0.1379$ g, producing 150 in 240 d[51] (Fraser & Renton, 1940).

TABLE III

Comparative phenology of gobiid fishes around western British Isles

Species*	Usual habitat[1]	Maximum standard length (L_S) (cm)	$\bar{L}_S$ of breeding female (cm)	Maximum breeding age (years)	Age at maturity (years)	Breeding season (usual extent)	No. of broods	Gonadosomatic index (% wt of female)[2]	Relative fecundity at L_S of breeding females (g^{-1})[3]	Sources
Thorogobius ephippiatus (Lowe)	C: inshore; in or near rock crevices	11·8	c. 8·0	9	3–4	May–July	>1	nd	978·2[3]	Miller (1969); Dunne (1976)
Gobius paganellus L.	C: intertidal; under stones	9·25	7·5	10	2–3	Apr–June	≥2	15·6 (w) 24·3 (d)	686·8	Miller (1961 and unpub.)
Lesueurigobius friesii (Malm)	C: shelf; burrowing in mud	7·4	6·0	11	2	late May–Aug	≥2	→22 (w)	2662·6[3]	Gibson & Ezzi (1978)
Pomatoschistus minutus (Pallas)	E: inshore; on sand	7·3	5·5	1·3–1·6	0·6–1·0	Feb–May	→9–10	21·23 (d)	2823·5	Lee (1974); Fonds, (1973)
P. microps (Krøyer)	E: estuarine; on sand or mud	5·4	3·5	1·6–2·1	0·6–1·0	late Apr–early Aug	→9	→30·0 (w) 46·65 (d)	2364	Miller (1963, 1975, and unpub.)

* [1] C, cryptobenthic; E, epibenthic; [2] w, wet and d, dry weights; [3] using somatic weight (W_S) for average female estimated from
W_S 0·00007 $L^{3·28238}$ for C. paganellus

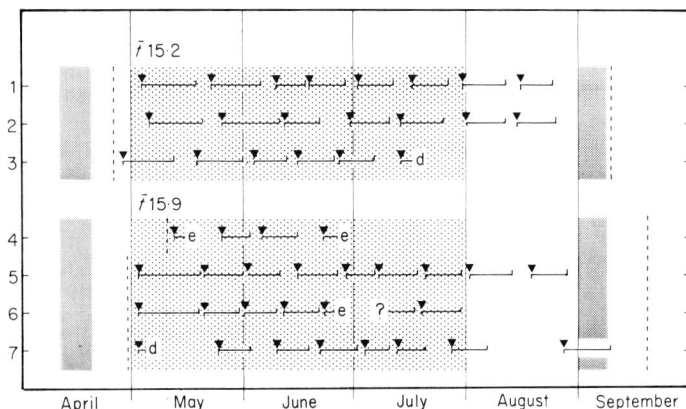

FIG. 3. Repeat-spawning in captivity by pairs of *Pomatoschistus microps* from Silver Burn estuary, Isle of Man (1–3) and Cardross, Clyde estuary (4–7), at natural photoperiod; mean temperature ($\bar{t}°C$) as indicated during period of captivity (vertical broken lines); spawning (black triangle) and incubation time (horizontal line) of each brood are shown in relation to natural occurrence of earliest and latest ripe females (dense stipple) and months with majority ripening or ripe (fine stipple) (Miller, 1963); ?, date of spawning uncertain; d, eggs died or e, eaten by parents.

maturation might compensate for any reduction in overall fecundity by less frequent spawning.

In habitats where environmental change is pronounced and, at best, only semi-predictable, there will be selection for early maturation, followed by iteroparous expenditure of a relatively high reproductive commitment. The phenology of annual cyprinodonts in transient savannah pools is described in detail by Simpson (this volume p. 243). Repeat-spawning, after early maturation, is also found in the Alaskan black fish, *Dallia pectoralis*, which matures after the first winter of life and spawns from May to August in muskeg swamp (Blackett, 1962) and in the silverjaw minnow, *Ericymba buccata* Cope, as an adaptation for streams of varying current and siltload (Wallace, 1973; Heins & Clemmer, 1976).

When adult mortality increases with population density, in a saturated ecosystem, optimal reproductive expenditure should form a smaller proportion of overall anabolism and lifespan be correspondingly extended. This trend is a characteristic feature of the "*K*-selection" supposed to operate under such circumstances (Stearns, 1976). Given a common reduction in reproductive effort, the pattern of deployment will depend on sources of juvenile mortality. In a complex community, opportunity for young to enter the adult habitat probably depends on random occurrence of vacancies (Sale, 1978). To meet a basic requirement for long-term availability of young, early maturation must be followed by repeat-spawning over a long breeding period, perhaps the entire adult life. Low primary reproductive effort should not impair longevity, although brood protection may be an important activity. Under tropical marine conditions, with sustained larval food supply, many small coral fish are repeat-spawners of planktotrophic larvae, such as *Abudefduf saxatilis* (L.) (Munro *et al.*, 1973), *Eupomacentrus planifrons* Cuvier (Williams, 1978) and other pomacentrids (Verwey, 1930; Fishelson, Popper & Avidor, 1974). Eleven spawnings in three and a half months were recorded by Verwey (1930) for a captive pair of *Amphiprion percula* (Lacépède). Where juvenile survival is less feasible or erratic in another ecosystem or even the parental environment, reproductive effort becomes apportioned among fewer but larger offspring which are, however, still produced by repeat-spawning. This occurs in the mouth-brooding "mbuna" cichlids of Lake Malawi, which spawn batches of large eggs throughout the year, although gonadosomatic index is less than 5% (Fryer & Iles, 1972; Balon, 1977), as well as in some "advanced" live-bearing poeciliids from fast, "harsh", streams (Thibault & Schultz, 1978).

Finally, a number of small fishes, more or less cryptobenthic, exploit the annual cycle of marine plankton in temperate seas via a minute pelagic postlarval stage in development. With a chance of year-class failure, emphasis in the life history of such species must be placed on annual iteroparity, i.e. breeding in more than one season, so that adult life can be prolonged over several years as a result of late maturation and lower reproductive effort (Schaffer, 1974). This reproductive strategy also relates to the probability that adult populations are at saturation for resources in the typically cryptic habitats. Thus, among cryptobenthic temperate gobiids (Table III), maturity is not reached until at least the third year of life, and reproduction may occur in as many as nine subsequent years. Repeat-spawning during a breeding season is probably limited to two occasions for most individuals, and, for average female *Gobius paganellus*, total ovarian expenditure over two months is somewhat less than one-half the dry body weight, with a low monthly reproductive effort estimated at 0·27. Duration of planktonic life is about six weeks in *G. paganellus* (Miller, 1961), and marked year-class fluctuations in recruitment have been noted for *Lesueurigobius friesii* by Gibson & Ezzi (1978). Certain intertidal blennids, such as the eastern Atlantic–Mediterranean *Blennius pholis* L. (Qasim, 1957) and the western Pacific *Halmablennius lineatus* (Valenciennes *in* Cuvier & Valenciennes) (Lee & Chang, 1977), also have life histories of this type, not maturing until two years old and having an adult life of as long as eight years. The blind *Typhlogobius californiensis* Steindachner, symbiotic with a decapod crustacean, is credited with a lifespan of at least 12 years (MacGinitie, 1939).

Much of the life-history data available for small fish concern those species found in nektonic or epibenthic habitats, where predation and an emphasis on reproduction (see below) combine to reduce longevity. It is therefore not surprising that Beverton & Holt (1959) were able to demonstrate a direct relationship between longevity and size in a variety of teleosts, However, there seems to be no intrinsic barrier to long life in small fishes, and, under conditions noted above, such potential longevity can be seen to be an integral component of fitness at small size. In relation to ecotope differences between two gobiids of similar body length, it is of interest to compare the early maturation, frequent spawning and short life of the epibenthic *Pomatoschistus minutus* with the later maturation, fewer spawnings, but much longer life in the cryptobenthic *Lesueurigobius friesii* (Table III).

REPRODUCTIVE MECHANISMS

The course of subdividing a given allocation of ovarian material and energy for the provisioning of young is directed by natural selection along one of two opposing routes, either towards increasing number of offspring per spawning (fecundity), but with limited investment in individual members of the batch, or towards increasing the quantity in each offspring, whose small number may be compensated for by increased size and chance of survival. The relative merits and adaptiveness of these contrasting mechanisms have been much discussed (Mann & Mills, this volume p. 161). Which point on the continuum between these two extremes confers fitness seems to depend on food availability and patterns of mortality in juvenile fish (see Price, 1974; Ware, 1975), and may be subject to seasonal variation within a population (Bagenal, 1971). Having already considered the timing and magnitude of reproductive effort in small fishes, the tactics of allocation relative to ecotope may be shown to comprise a wide range of reproductive modifications.

The secondary sphere of reproductive effort, involving the anabolism of secondary sexual characters and the catabolism of reproductive behaviour, supports a wide range of ethological adaptiveness in small fishes. Little is known about the quantities of energy and material involved in these processes, which complement primary anabolic commitment, and their description cannot be undertaken here.

Fecundity Enhancement

Reduced expenditure on individual offspring—but with a high number of these produced— is a mechanism of reproduction believed to derive from r-selection (Gadgil & Solbrig, 1972), and may seem appropriate for small fishes of nektonic or epibenthic habitats. An essential requirement is environmental suitability, especially in food sources, for survival of free-living young at a relatively early developmental stage. However, increase in fecundity within small adult size is limited by various other factors. Fecundity in teleosts is typically, but not invariably, a positive allometric function of body size, so that higher values may be achieved by growth of the female (Blaxter, 1969). The adaptiveness of small size in the fishes discussed here must preclude undue body growth to raise fecundity. Nevertheless, persistence of growth in female poeciliids after maturity, when growth ceases in males, may derive from this advantage (Krumholz, 1963; Comfort, 1964). There is certainly a well-marked correlation between size and fecundity in the oviparous cyprinodont *Nothobranchius* (Bailey, 1972) and here, too, it seems to denote continued reproductive commitment into adult life, rather than diversion of energy and materials towards survival and competition.

An alternative means of enhancing individual fecundity is by increase in relative fecundity (i.e. number of eggs per unit body weight of female). Higher relative fecundity, as a response to predation, has been found in a "black" population of *Gasterosteus aculeatus* (Moodie, 1972), as well as for *Gambusia manni* Hubbs (Krumholz, 1963). A similar trend with emphasis on reproductive effort is seen in the epibenthic *Pomatoschistus* species, whose relative fecundity is about four times that of the cryptobenthic *Gobius paganellus*. Although obtained mostly from much higher maternal expenditure on ovarian anabolism, oocyte diameter at fertilization is also smaller in the *Pomatoschistus* species, being 0·06–0·07 cm against 0·095–0·11 cm in *G. paganellus* (Miller, 1961, 1963; Lee, 1974). However, it should be noted that the other cryptobenthic species listed in Table II are much more fecund at the same size than *G. paganellus*. This may reflect greater reliance on planktotrophic nutrition for young, rather than difference in reproductive effort, and maternal investment per offspring is certainly very low in *Lesueurigobius friesii*, whose oocytes do not exceed 0·05–0·06 cm in diameter (Gibson & Ezzi, 1978).

With a given ovarian biomass, whose dimensions and weight may be set by other factors, there seem to be limits to the possibility of gaining in fecundity by further subdivision of this material into oocytes of smaller size at maturation. This must be due, at least partly, to increasing disadvantage from predation or starvation likely to be suffered by the smaller and less provisioned young which would hatch from such tiny eggs. Also, teleost eggs, in general, are probably small in comparison to those in which the embryological specializations of meroblastic cleavage originally evolved. Further reduction in dimensions might create an unsuitable housing for this type of development. The lowest value for an allegedly "ripe" oocyte in an oviparous teleost seems that of rather more than 0·01 cm estimated by Roberts (1970) for the cyprinodont *Fluviphylax pygmaeus* (Table I), with 30–40 such eggs in tiny females of 1·45–1·85 cm.

Several small gobies produce ripe eggs with a yolk diameter between 0·025 and 0·040 cm, and trend towards high fecundity. Thus, in the estuarine *Acentrogobius masago* (Tomiyama) (2·5 cm), from southern Japan, with eggs of 0·037 cm in diameter and size at hatching of 0·20 cm, a female merely 1·4 cm long contained 264 eggs (Dôtu, 1958b), five times as numerous as the much smaller egg of *Fluviphylax* at the same body length. In another estuarine species, *Tridentiger nudicervicus* Tomiyama (5·0 cm), whose eggs are 0·033 cm in diameter and hatch at 0·20 cm, fecundity may reach 13 000 (Dôtu, 1958a). The stream-dwelling sicydiine gobies, whose young are swept downstream on hatching to spend their postlarval life in estuaries, must be among the most fecund of small fishes with small eggs. Dôtu & Mito (1955) record 224 960 eggs from a female *Sicydium japonicum* Tanaka 10·5 cm long; the eggs of this species are 0·045 cm in diameter and yield a minute larva of 0·15 cm, yolk being absorbed by 0·19 cm.

At ovulation, oocytes of the zebrafish, *Brachydanio rerio*, a diminutive Indian cyprinid, average 0·0625 cm in diameter (Roosen–Runge, 1938). With small eggs and ovarian growth exceeding 25% of somatic weight at maturity, the maximum fecundity achieved by zebrafish is probably only about 500 eggs per spawning (Hisaoka & Firlit, 1962). By repeat-spawning, the individual can achieve a much higher total of eggs during adult life, constituting the high reproductive effort required by this top feeder of open nektonic habitats. Since the zebrafish is very easily bred in captivity, some records of fecundity potential are available for this species from the work of Hisaoka & Firlit (1962), and are summarized in Table II. Thus, even with restricted mating, a female produced 5530 eggs in five months, suggesting a potential fecundity of over several thousand eggs g^{-1} of adult somatic weight per season.

Small progeny are not invariably associated with high reproductive effort. Many small demersal marine fishes exploit the plankton resources of temperate waters by a more or less complex life history involving tiny planktotrophic postlarvae (Russell, 1976). Planktonic life for the young of small coral fishes may offer greater security from the numerous reef-dwelling predators (Johannes, 1978).

Offspring Size

If small young are at a disadvantage, there will be selection for increase in size at the commencement of self-feeding life, achieved most simply by greater yolk-provisioning of the egg (i.e. increased primary anabolic expenditure per offspring) but with the unavoidable reduction in number of offspring if ovarian mass relative to maternal body size remains unchanged. More elaborate techniques involving viviparity in small fish will be discussed later. In many oviparous fishes, there is a well established correlation between egg-size, size of young at hatching and chance of subsequent survival (Wootton, this volume p. 133). The elimination of a small larval phase may also be an adaptation against dispersal from the definitive habitat of the species, such as running fresh water (Hynes, 1970), rocky shores (Rosenblatt, 1963) or small coral reefs (Ehrlich, 1975). This developmental change brings in its train much higher genetic differentiation between populations, with presumably higher rate of speciation, and scope for further specialization (Rosenblatt, 1963). A trend towards larger young is often associated with density-dependent selection, and accompanied by an overall fall in reproductive effort (Stearns, 1976). However, for small species with high adult mortality from factors not derived from reproductive rate, this type of development may be the only successful approach to fitness if number of young per brood cannot be increased for ecological or morphogenetic reasons.

Increase in relative size of offspring seems to be a feature common to the smallest examples of most animal groups (Gould, 1977). Using freshwater cyprinids of the temperate Northern Hemisphere, it is possible to demonstrate that, within this group of basically similar ecology, eggs tend to be of similar diameter despite a great range in adult size (Fig. 4). Conversely, if we make the arbitrary assumptions that egg weight is a simple function of volume, and that the length/weight relationship in a generalized cyprinid (such as the Stour roach, of Mann, 1973) can be used to estimate body weights at the species' maximum sizes, then a much greater relative expenditure of primary reproductive effort per offspring

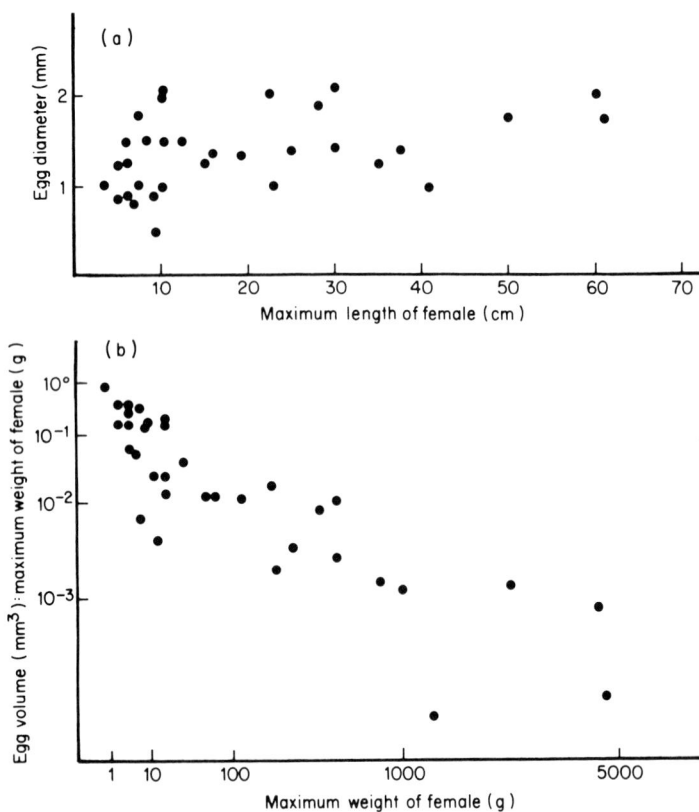

FIG. 4. Egg and body size in north temperate cyprinids; (a) diameter of egg against maximum length of female recorded for species; (b) egg volume ÷ estimated weight of female against estimated weight of female, using length/weight relationship for Stour roach (Mann, 1973). Other data mostly from Berg (1949) and Scott & Crossman (1973).

is indicated for the smaller species. The tendency for small species to have comparatively large eggs is also seen, for example, among cyprinodonts (Foster, 1967a), galaxiids (McDowall, 1968; Campos, 1972) and even *Schindleria* (Schindler, 1932).

A possible conflict between selection for larger size at hatching—but fewer eggs per unit ovarian biomass—and maximizing overall number of young, required by adult mortality from inter-specific rather than intra-specific events, is solved by the operation of repeat-spawning. In the minute forest-stream barbs already mentioned, both of which species have relatively very large eggs, only three to 10 may ripen at a time, and a long breeding season, perhaps of several months, was interpreted by Loiselle & Welcomme (1971) as an adaptation towards the small size of adult females, to permit eventual maturation of all 30–60 developing oocytes found in the ovaries. Among oviparous cyprinodonts, with relatively large eggs (0·1–0·2 cm), this process of egg deposition is often daily for long periods of reproductive activity (Foster, 1967b), and can be sustained for the entire year under artificial conditions (Boyd & Simmonds, 1974). Egami (1959) has recorded frequency of spawning and fecundity in the rice medaka, *Oryzias latipes* (4 cm), whose egg is over double the volume of that in zebrafish. Reproductive effort is estimated from these results in Table II. By frequent spawning, daily for long periods, this small fish can produce a high number of large eggs, far beyond its physical and metabolic capacity to contain and grow at the same time—a typical seasonal total of about 2000 eggs represents at least three and a half times average maternal dry weight (Egami, 1959; Kaufman & Beyers, 1972; Table II). Young cyprinodonts on hatching are usually longer than 0·4 cm.

In contrast, a low reproductive effort may also be expended by repeat-spawning of very large eggs. The mouth-brooding "mbuna" cichlids of Lake Malawi produce small batches of eggs all year round, with egg diameters in some species reaching 0·7 cm (Fryer & Iles, 1972; Balon, 1977).

Internal Fertilization

The basic teleostean practice of shedding the ovulated eggs for external fertilization can lead to loss of potential offspring, perhaps negligible in relation to other factors when fecundity is high but more significant when egg number is reduced with diminutive body size and a single egg comes to represent a greater proportion of primary reproductive anabolism. Elaborate reproductive behaviour seen in many small fishes, often in conjunction with coloration attractive to aquarists, and leading to close juxtaposition of the sexes, serves to eliminate gamete wastage. However, internal fertilization, with sperm introduced into the oviduct or ovary of the female, is not only a means to ensure fertilization but also allows salvage of defective eggs by resorption back into the maternal system.

This facility should become more advantageous as relative size of egg and stake of gonadal biomass increases.

Apart from increasing the efficiency of reproductive commitment, internal fertilization is useful in other aspects for small fishes under environmental conditions leading to alternate aggregations and dispersal of a population subject to predation. Such species include top feeders in tropical fresh waters whose volume and extent may show marked seasonal fluctuation (Lowe-McConnell, this volume p. 219). Among these fish, fertilization might be more easily achieved in crowded habitats during a dry season, but developing eggs or young would have better chance of survival if kept for release by females when the latter subsequently dispersed over flooded areas where predators are relatively infrequent (Nelson, 1964). Apart from occurrence in viviparous cyprinodonts of Central and South America, internal fertilization also precedes oviparity in the glandulocaudine characins, surface-feeding species of this area (Nelson, 1964). The ovi-oviparous cyprinodont, *Tomeiurus gracilis* Eigenmann, from South America has an oviparous Indian relative, *Horaichthys setnai* Kulkarni (males 1·88–2·34 cm, females 1·86–2·13 cm), which uses barbed spermatophores for this purpose (Kulkarni, 1940). In the phallostethiform fishes, small oviparous top feeders, inhabiting brackish and tidal waters of the tropical Indo-Pacific, some amazing structural modifications have appeared to effect internal fertilization (Aurich, 1937; Te Winkel, 1939). In this case, mating is believed to occur at tidal low water, with dispersal and oviposition at high water periods (Roberts, 1971). Sperm is stored by female phallostethiforms, *Horaichthys*, and the glandulocaudine characins, for several months in *Corynopoma risii* Gill (7·0 cm), belonging to the last group (Villadolid & Manacop, 1934; Kulkarni, 1940; Nelson, 1964). The technique of internal fertilization, especially with sperm storage, has general significance for permanent colonization of new areas. Each fertilized female carries the nucleus of a future population (Rosen, 1962). Among demersal small fishes, internal fertilization has been reported for certain littoral cottids and blennioid clinids (Breder & Rosen, 1966). Perhaps the most efficient means to this end is the self-fertilization which follows ovulation in the hermaphrodite cyprinodont *Rivulus marmoratus* Poey (Harrington, 1971).

Viviparity

Possession of relatively large eggs, and a means for their internal fertilization, would seem to have provided the starting requirements for viviparity in a number of groups among small fishes. Viviparity, in the wide sense, is retention and nurture of young within the female until their birth as free-living individuals, and is clearly distinguishable from the more or less transient stay of fertilized eggs within ovary or oviduct before deposition, recorded in some otherwise oviparous cyprinodonts (Kulkarni, 1940; Yamamoto, 1961; Harrington, 1971). Facultative ovoviviparity of longer duration has been described for *Tomeiurus* by Rosen & Bailey (1964), while hatching occurs on oviposition by the Celebes adrianichthyid *Xenopoecilus poptae* Weber & De Beaufort (20 cm) (Weber & De Beaufort, 1922). In its most elaborate form, viviparity can benefit survival of the female parent by spreading the temporal distribution of high reproductive effort, as well as that of young by providing the "most advanced hiding style" (Balon, 1977).

Among small fish, this phenomenon is best known in certain New World families of surface-feeding cyprinodonts (Poeciliidae, Goodeidae, Jenynsiidae), containing some of the smallest teleosts as well as many popular aquarium species. Viviparity is also found among hemirhamphid halfbeaks of similar habitat in fresh and brackish tropical waters. In marine coastal to bathyal regions, a number of small bottom-living ophidioid genera are viviparous, as also may be some clinids and cottids. The morphological aspects of viviparity, chiefly with reference to cyprinodonts among small fishes, have been reviewed by Turner (1940a, b, c, d, 1947), Tavolga & Rugh (1947), Rosen (1962), Rosen & Bailey (1964), Breder & Rosen (1966) and Amoroso (1968), while Jacobs (1971) describes many viviparous aquarium fishes and their natural history.

For the young of top-feeding cyprinodonts and halfbeaks, viviparity adds the further advantages of protection, nurture and aeration to those of dispersal obtained by merely internal fertilization (Nelson, 1964; Rosen & Bailey, 1964; Williams, 1966; Amoroso, 1968; Balon, 1975, 1977). As a means of brood-care, it is more appropriate for life at the surface than is the guarding of eggs at a fixed site. Johannes (1978) has also suggested that viviparity is more likely to evolve in fresh water because the range of trophic options for young fishes is more limited in this habitat than in the sea. In addition the "reclaim" of material from available young is extended to a later stage in viviparous species, a feature of possible value to repeat-breeders with fecundity limited by offspring size. These various benefits from viviparity presumably outweigh the traditional disadvantage of putting all one's offspring in the same basket.

Most poeciliids follow a relatively primitive version of this process which has been compared to ovoviviparity. Based on follicular gestation, this entails a large prezygotic commitment by the female, with yolky eggs typically of about $0 \cdot 19–0 \cdot 2$ cm in diameter when mature (Scrimshaw, 1946). Embryos may be capable of development even when prematurely released (Rosen & Bailey, 1964), and Dépêche (1962) believed that, in *Poecilia*, interchange between mother and offspring involved only minerals and gases. Scrimshaw (1945) found that maternal contribution during development was equivalent to at least the bulk of embryonic maintenance, without significant weight change during development in 18 species of poeciliids studied. However, recent work indicates a loss of over 36% in dry weight between ovum and full-term guppy embryo (Thibault & Schultz, 1978), and at least 15–25% in *Gambusia affinis* (Miller, unpub.), at or approaching the reduction of one-third in overall embryo weight which Scrimshaw (1945) regarded as demonstrating ovo-viviparity. Extent of loss may depend on maternal nutrition during the gestation period. This simpler type of viviparity does seem more suited to conditions of short-term fluctuation in parental food supply (Thibault & Schultz, 1978).

In a minority of poeciliids, a much higher degree of viviparity is based on eggs with little yolk and maternal investment, via more elaborate placentation, chiefly after fertilization (Turner, 1940b; Scrimshaw, 1944a, b, 1945). For example, in *Poeciliopsis turneri*, the young fish at birth is about 19 times as heavy as the mature egg (Thibault & Schultz, 1978). From separate oviparous stock, the Goodeidae, restricted to an area of central Mexico, and the Jenynsiidae, from Argentina, also follow elaborate modes of viviparity, involving ovarian gestation and embryonic nutrition by trophotaeniae or lappets from the ovary wall (Turner, 1940c, d).

Much remains to be learned about embryonic nurture in other small viviparous fishes. The convergent evolution of trophotaeniae in some marine zoarcids and ophidioids (Cohen & Wourms, 1976) suggests emphasis on postzygotic support, while the follicular gestation of rela-tively yolky eggs ($0 \cdot 14$ cm) in viviparous halfbeaks parallels the general-ized condition of most poeciliids (Turner, 1940b; Stolk, 1956).

The practice of viviparity in small fish results in the birth of relatively large young (Table II; Scrimshaw, 1945). By eliminating high mortality from extrinsic factors during the earlier course of development, viviparity should permit a saving in the number of offspring which need to be produced for representation in the next generation. However, retention of young until an increased size puts obvious mechanical and metabolic constraints on the possibility of using viviparity to increase "effective" fecundity (the number of offspring reaching adulthood) by imposing this mode of offspring care on the number of eggs produced by an oviparous ancestor of the same body size. For the same reasons, an increase in relative fecundity by virtue of the very small starting size of mature oocytes in the most viviparous forms would also seem unlikely.

Among poeciliids with less elaborate viviparity, fecundity may reach over 300 per brood in the larger *Gambusia affinis* (Baird & Girard) (males $3 \cdot 5$ cm, females $6 \cdot 5–8 \cdot 0$ cm); Krumholz (1948) noted 315 from a female of $5 \cdot 9$ cm, while Bonham (1946) found 354 in an individual of un-recorded size. Within species, great variation in fecundity occurs not only with size but also with locality (Krumholz, 1963; Stearns, 1978) or resource availability (Constantz, 1974). In cyprinodonts showing a high level of viviparity, number of young per brood is usually low, in cor-respondence with their relatively larger size at birth. Thus, between species of comparable length ($9 \cdot 0$ cm), the poeciliid *Xiphophorus helleri* Heckel may produce up to 150 young, born at $0 \cdot 83–0 \cdot 89$ cm, while the goodeid *Ameca splendens* Miller & Fitzsimons, whose young range from $1 \cdot 1$ to $1 \cdot 7$ cm (average $1 \cdot 4$ cm), carries no more than 17 (Tavolga, 1949;

Vallowe, 1953; R. R. Miller & Fitzsimons, 1971). In *Heterandria formosa* (Table II) and in *Ameca*, not infrequently only one offspring is produced, while in *Poeciliopsis turneri* (mature at 4·0 cm), mean fecundity is only 3·6, the young being born when 1·2–1·7 cm long (Thibault & Schultz, 1978).

Fecundity among viviparous cyprinodonts is always multiplied by repeat-breeding. The potentially rapid maturation and succession of oocytes in poeciliids was noted by Turner (1938). Any hindrance to brood production by delay between ripening and fertilization is overcome by sperm storage in the oviduct of the female, as also occurs in various oviparous top feeders and the viviparous halfbeaks. Even near the northern limits of present distribution, in Iowa, where breeding occurs only from May to August, *Gambusia affinis*, maturing in the first summer of life, produce two or three broods in eight to ten weeks, while those reaching maturity after their first winter have usually four broods, perhaps occasionally five, over 14–15 weeks; the usual interval between broods was found to be 23·9 days but elsewhere 27·7 days (Krumholz, 1948; Table II). In tropical surroundings at Barro Colorado in the Panama Canal Zone, gravid females of the poeciliid *Brachyrhaphis episcopi* (Steindachner) (males 3·5 cm, females 5·0 cm) were found throughout the year, although the duration of individual reproductive life is not known (Turner, 1938). Under long-term captivity, a modest performance of four to five broods in 132–140 days by *Xiphophorus maculatus* is easily outstripped by 17 broods from a female guppy over 344 days (Bowden, 1970).

In *Gambusia*, maturation of a new batch of oocytes does not begin until after the birth of young already carried in the ovary. Other poeciliids, such as *Mollienisia* and *Quintana*, commence maturation of the next group of oocytes during gestation, so that ripe oocytes are available for fertilization by stored sperm immediately after birth of the developing brood. The next step in increasing frequency of brood production is for new oocytes to reach maturity and be fertilized while developing young from the previous brood remain in the ovary. This phenomenon termed "superfetation" or "superfoetation" has been discussed in detail by Turner (1937, 1940a), Scrimshaw (1944b), Thibault (1974), Downhower & Brown (1975) and Thibault & Schultz (1978). Superfoetation leads to the presence in the ovary of batches of young at different stages in development, and seems possible only in poeciliids, where gestation is within the intact follicle. In *Poeciliopsis* species with advanced viviparity, such as *P. retropinna* (Regan) (males 6·0 cm, females 10·0 cm) and *P. elongatus* (Günther) (males 6·0 cm, females 15·0 cm), and also in the much smaller *Heterandria formosa*, up to nine broods may be present simultaneously (Turner, 1940d), perhaps reflecting increased frequency of ovulation by virtue of the very small size of the oocytes at maturation.

The success of superfoetation would seem to depend on assured levels of food availability for maternal consumption during gestation. Whatever the value for larger *Poeciliopsis* species, superfoetation, combined with advanced viviparity, offers a small fish the means to produce, over the reproductive life, a relatively large number of relatively large young, with a spreading of physiological demand on the maternal system but a minimal interval between these offspring. In the diminutive *Heterandria formosa* (males 1·75 cm, females 2·5–3·0 cm, rarely 4·0 cm), although gestation, depending on temperature, lasts 25–35 days (Colson, 1969), a superfoetatious female can give birth, every three to 10 days, to 1–11 babies, each almost one-third maternal length (Table II). The breeding season of *H. formosa* in Florida lasts from March to mid-November (Colson, 1969) and may be similarly protracted in captivity. Thus, Fraser & Renton (1940) recorded 150 young in eight months from an exceptionally large female of total length 4·0 cm. Here females may live two to three years (Fraser & Renton, 1940), although probably not beyond one and one-half years in the wild (Colson, 1969). An estimate of reproductive effort for *Heterandria formosa* is given in Table II, where this species marks the culmination in a series of increasingly modified reproductive physiology which starts with the simple oviparity of *Brachydanio*. Despite the progression in complexity of brood-care, and in allocation of resource per offspring, overall primary anabolic effort remains comparable between the species, with *H. formosa* retaining such characteristic traits as early maturation (35 days), repeat-breeding, increasing fecundity with size, and up to three generations per year (Colson, 1969). Although retiring habits confine this little fish to the vicinity of dense vegetation, there is predation on adults by other piscivorous species, especially during drought (Colson, 1969). However, in *Poeciliopsis*, superfoetation is associated with relatively delayed maturation (56–82 days) and, in two species, whose habitats are spatially limited, there is no increase in fecundity with body size (Thibault & Schultz, 1978). For *P. turneri* Miller (females 6·5 cm), the process leads to proportionately gigantic young (1·2–1·7 cm), whose size must have survival value in deep swift waters of the typical habitat.

Although, in general, viviparity is traditionally associated with reduced expenditure on reproduction, it is essentially a response to patterns of juvenile mortality, and may be used to deploy a wide range of primary anabolic commitment. In the marine environment, and another group of teleosts, reduced fecundity in some viviparous ophidioids could reflect selection for large young which would be immediately eligible for entry into a complex and packed benthic community (Wourms & Cohen, 1975). The high fecundity seen in other ophidioids, even in conjunction with the viviparous elaboration of trophotaeniae (Cohen & Wourms, 1976), might indicate higher juvenile mortality among these species.

In the open, top-feeding, ecotope, *Gambusia affinis* is a most successful opportunist, with a potentially high rate of population increase and a great propensity for colonization (Self, 1940). Reproductive anabolism in this poeciliid is comparable to that of the oviparous *Brachydanio*, even though the young *Gambusia* is relatively much larger than that of *Brachy-*

danio and produced in much smaller numbers per unit time (Table II). Nevertheless, in spite of repeat-breeding, the enhanced survival of larger young is associated with a birth-rate lower in viviparous species than in oviparous forms of comparable size. A low birth-rate—further reduced by seasonal effects—would render a population more susceptible to sudden environmentally induced increases in mortality (Brockelman, 1975), and may perhaps explain why viviparity in small fish, such as the cyprinodonts, is largely confined to tropical or subtropical forms. Species of *Gambusia*, among the most fecund for weight, penetrate farthest into temperate parts of North America, but the cyprinodonts found under more fluctuating cold-temperate conditions belong to the oviparous genus *Fundulus* (Krumholz, 1948; Jacobs, 1971; Scott & Crossman, 1973).

CONCLUSION

The phenology of most small fishes is not of direct use to mankind, except in the case of those species whose numerical abundance warrants consumption *en masse* like elvers or whitebait. A local Philippine fishery for even the tiny *Mistichthys luzonensis*, with about 70 000 individuals kg^{-1} (Bruun, 1940), has been described (Herre, 1927; Gudger, 1941). However, it has long been realized that many other small nektonic or epibenthic fishes play a very important ecological role as trophic intermediates below the level occupied by larger species of obvious economic importance, feeding the latter or sometimes feeding on their young.

As well as determining a position in the human food-chains based on fish, small size has rendered various species useful to man in other respects. The larviphagous feeding habits and reproductive potential of cyprinodonts have proved of value in mosquito control (Gerberich & Laird, 1968). The poeciliid *Gambusia affinis* has been transported for this purpose to many warm areas of the world from its native Gulf States of North America (Krumholz, 1948). Unfortunately, such introductions may have deleterious effects on local fish species (Laird, 1970), and even contribute towards eutrophication (Hurlbert, Zedler & Fairbanks, 1972).

For purposes of zoological research, small fishes, by virtue of their dimensions, provide excellent laboratory material. The ethology of cichlids, genetics of livebearers, growth of topminnows and gerontology of guppies are well known areas of research for which small teleosts have formed a profitable basis. Stearns (1976) has recently advocated the use of poeciliids in the difficult practical study of life-history evolution. Among subjects of the present volume, experimental analysis of reproductive timing and effort has been based on minnows (Scott, this volume p. 105) and sticklebacks (Wootton, this volume p. 133).

Other than for scientific use, the maintenance and propagation of small fishes in domestic aquaria has become increasingly popular. In the developed world, modern demand has created an aquarium industry of appreciable size. Thus, the annual retail value of fishes and accessories has been estimated at about four thousand million dollars world-wide, with the export of living fishes forming an important component in the trade of some developing countries in the tropics (Conroy, 1975). Scientific workers benefit from the resulting availability of exotic fishes and a variety of fish-keeping equipment. Many species, whose small size, coloration, behaviour and metabolism preadapt them for the artificial habitat of an aquarium, are now entering into a new symbiosis with man. As natural populations become depleted by over-collecting or environmental change, such species will come to be maintained by conservation or large-scale pisciculture for their aesthetic contribution to human welfare.

ACKNOWLEDGEMENTS

I am most grateful to Mr D. Kenwood and Mr R. James for the gift of *Heterandria* used in this work, and to Dr M. M. Fouda for help in collecting *Gambusia* from the marshy periphery of Lake Idku in Egypt, during a visit sponsored by the Royal Society and the Egyptian Academy of Scientific Research and Technology.

REFERENCES

Abel, E. F. (1960). Zur Kenntnis des Verhaltens und der Ökologie von Fischen an Korallenriffen bei Ghardaqa (Rotes Meer). *Z. Morph. Ökol. Tiere* **49**: 430–503.

Akihito, Prince & Meguro, K. (1975). *Pandaka trimaculata*, a new species of dwarf goby from Okinawa Prefecture, Japan and the Philippines. *Jap. J. Ichthyol.* **22**: 63–67.

Allen, G. R. (1972). Observations on a commensal relationship between *Siphamia fuscolineata* (Apogonidae) and the crown-of-thorns starfish, *Acanthaster planci. Copeia* **1972**: 595–597.

Amoroso, E. C. (1968). The evolution of viviparity. *Proc. R. Soc. Med.* **61**: 1188–1200.

Aurich, H. (1937). Die Phallostethiden (Unterordnung Phallostethoidea Myers). *Int. Revue ges. Hydrobiol. Hydrogr.* **34**: 263–286.

Bagenal, T. B. (1971). The interrelation of the size of fish eggs, the date of spawning and the production cycle. *J. Fish Biol.* **3**: 207–219.

Bailey, R. G. (1972). Observations on the biology of *Nothobranchius guentheri* (Pfeffer) (Cyprinodontidae), an annual fish from the coastal region of East Africa. *Afr. J. trop. Hydrobiol. Fish.* **2**: 33–43.

Balon, E. K. (1975). Reproductive guilds of fishes: a proposal and definition. *J. Fish. Res. Bd Can.* **32**: 821–864.

Balon, E. K. (1977). Early ontogeny of *Labeotropheus* Ahl, 1927 (Mbuna, Cichlidae, Lake Malawi), with a discussion on advanced protective styles in fish reproduction and development. *Envirl. Biol. Fish* **2**: 147–176.

Berg, L. S. (1949). [*Freshwater fishes of Soviet Union and adjacent countries.*] **2**, 4th edn. Moscow: Akademia Nauk SSSR. [In Russian.] (English translation, 1965. Jerusalem: Israel Program for Scientific Translations).

Beverton, R. J. H. & Holt, S. J. (1959). A review of the life spans and mortality rates of fish in nature, and their relation to growth and other physiological characteristics. *Ciba Fdn Colloq. Ageing* **5**: 142–180.

Blackett, R. F. (1962). Some phases in the life history of the Alaskan blackfish, *Dallia pectoralis. Copeia* **1962**: 124–130.

Blaxter, J. H. S. (1969). Development: eggs and larvae. *Fish Physiol.* **3**: 177–252.

Böhlke, J. E. (1963). The species of the West Atlantic gobioid fish genus *Psilotris. Notul. Nat.* No. 362: 1–10.

Böhlke, J. E. & Chaplin, C. C. G. (1968). *Fishes of the Bahamas and adjacent tropical waters.* Wynnewood, Pa.: Livingston Publishing Co.

Böhlke, J. E. & Robins, C. R. (1960). Western Atlantic gobioid fishes of the genus *Lythrypnus*, with notes on *Quisquilius hipoliti* and *Garmannia pallens. Proc. Acad. nat. Sci. Philad.* **112**: 73–101.

Böhlke, J. E. & Robins, C. R. (1968). Western Atlantic seven-spined gobies, with descriptions of ten new species and a new genus, and comments on Pacific relatives. *Proc. Acad. nat. Sci. Philad.* **120**: 45–174.

Bonham, K. (1946). Management of a small fish pond in Texas. *J. Wildl. Mgmt* **10**: 1–4.

Bowden, B. S. (1970). *The relationship of light and temperature to reproduction in the guppy*, Poecilia reticulata *Peters.* Ph.D. thesis: University of Connecticut.

Boyd, J. F. & Simmonds, R. C. (1974). Continuous laboratory production of fertile *Fundulus heteroclitus* (Walbaum) eggs lacking chorionic fibrils. *J. Fish Biol.* **6**: 389–394.

Breder, C. M. & Rosen, D. E. (1966). *Modes of reproduction in fishes.* New York: Natural History Press.

Briggs, J. C. (1976). A new genus and species of clingfish from the western Pacific. *Copeia* **1976**: 339–341.

Brittan, M. R. (1975). Rasbora. *A revision of the Indo-Malayan fresh-water fish genus* Rasbora. Hong Kong: T. F. H. Publications.

Brockelman, W. Y. (1975). Competition, the fitness of offspring, and optimal clutch size. *Am. Nat.* **109**: 677–699.

Bruun, A. F. (1940). A study of a collection of the fish *Schindleria* from South Pacific Waters. *Dana Rep.* No. 21: 1–12.

Campos, H. (1972). Breeding season and early development of *Brachygalaxias bullocki* (Osteichthyes: Galaxiidae). *Texas J. Sci.* **23**: 531–544.

Cohen, D. M. & Wourms, J. P. (1976). *Microbrotula randalli*, a new viviparous ophidioid fish from Samoa and New Hebrides, whose embryos bear trophotaeniae. *Proc. biol. Soc. Wash.* **89**: 81–98.

Collette, B. B. & Rützler, K. (1977). Reef fishes over sponge bottoms off the mouth of the Amazon River. *Proc. int. coral Reef Symp.* **3**: 305–310.

Colson, C. M. (1969). *Effects of daylength and temperature on the reproduction of* Heterandria formosa. Ph.D. thesis: University of Florida.

Comfort, A. (1964). *Ageing. The biology of senescence.* London: Routledge & Kegan Paul.

Connell, J. H. & Orias, E. (1964). The ecological regulation of species diversity. *Am. Nat.* **98**: 399–414.

Conroy, D. A. (1975). An evaluation of the present state of world trade in ornamental fish. *Fish. Circ. FAO.* No. 335: 1–120

Constantz, G. D. (1974). Reproductive effort in *Poeciliopsis occidentalis* (Poeciliidae). *SWest. Nat.* **19**: 47–52.

Corbet, P. S. (1961). The food of non-cichlid fishes in the Lake Victoria basin, with remarks on their evolution and adaptation to lacustrine conditions. *Proc. zool. Soc. Lond.* **136**: 1–101.

Coulter, G. W. (1970). Population changes within a group of fish species in Lake Tanganyika following their exploitation. *J. Fish Biol.* **2**: 329–353.

Cullen, M. J. (1969). The biology of giant water bugs (Hemiptera: Belostomatidae) in Trinidad. *Proc. R. ent. Soc. Lond.* (A) **44**: 123–136.

Davenport, D. (1966). Echinoderms and the control of behavior in association. In *Physiology of Echinodermata*: 145–156. Boolootian, R. A. (ed.). New York: Interscience Publishers.

Davis, W. P. & Birdsong, R. S. (1973). Coral reef fishes which forage in the water column. A review of their morphology, behavior, ecology and evolutionary implications. *Helgoländer wiss. Meeresunters.* **24**: 292–306.

Davis, W. P. & Cohen, D. M. (1969). A gobiid fish and a palaemonid shrimp living on an antipatharian sea whip in the tropical Pacific. *Bull. mar. Sci.* **18**: 749–761.

Dépêche, J. (1962). Le développement *in vitro* des oeufs de Poeciliidae (Cyprinodontes vivipares). *C. R. hebd. Séanc. Acad. Sci. Paris* **255**: 2670–2672.

Deraniyagala, P. E. P. (1943). A new cyprinoid fish from Ceylon. *J. Ceylon Branch R. Asiat. Soc.* **35**(4) No. 96: 1–2.

Dix, T. G. (1969). Association between the echinoid *Evechinus chloroticus* (Val.) and the clingfish *Dellichthys morelandi* Briggs. *Pacif. Sci.* **23**: 332–336.

Dobrinskaya, L. A. (1965). [Age changes in the relative weight of inner organs of fishes.] *Zool. Zh.* **44**: 72–80. [In Russian. English summary.]

Dôtu, Y. (1957). The life history of the small, transparent goby, *Gobius lidwilli* McCulloch. *Sci. Bull. Fac. Agric. Kyushu Univ.* **16**: 85–92.

Dôtu, Y. (1958a). The bionomics and life history of two gobioid fishes, *Tridentiger undicervicus* Tomiyama and *Tridentiger trigonocephalus* (Gill) in the innermost part of Ariake Sound. *Sci. Bull. Fac. Agric. Kyushu Univ.* **16**: 343–358.

Dôtu, Y. (1958b). The life history of the gobioid fish, *Acentrogobius masago* (Tomiyama). *Sci. Bull. Fac. Agric. Kyushu Univ.* **16**: 359–370.

Dôtu, Y. & Mito, S. (1955). Life history of a gobioid fish, *Sicydium japonicum* Tanaka. *Sci. Bull. Fac. Agric. Kyushu Univ.* **15**: 213–221.

Downhower, J. F. & Brown, L. (1975). Superfoetation in fishes and the cost of reproduction. *Nature, Lond.* **256**: 345–346.

Dunne, J. (1976). Littoral and benthic investigations on the west coast of Ireland—V. (Section A: faunistic and ecological studies). A contribution to the biology of the leopard-spotted goby, *Thorogobius ephippiatus* (Lowe) (Pisces: Teleostei: Gobiidae). *Proc. R. Irish Acad.* **76**(B): 121–132.

Ebeling, A. W. & Cailliet, G. M. (1974). Mouth size and predator strategy of midwater fishes. *Deep-Sea Res.* **21**: 959–968.

Edmunds, M. (1974). *Defence in animals.* Harlow: Longman Group.

Egami, N. (1959). Record of the number of eggs obtained from a single pair of *Oryzias latipes* kept in laboratory aquarium. *J. Fac. Sci. Tokyo* (Zool.) **8**: 521–538.

Ehrlich, P. R. (1975). The population biology of coral reef fishes. *A. Rev. Ecol. Syst.* **6**: 211–247.

Farr, J. A. (1975). The role of predation in the evolution of social behavior of natural populations of the guppy, *Poecilia reticulata* (Pisces: Poeciliidae). *Evolution* **29**: 151–158.

Fishelson, L., Popper, D. & Avidor, A. (1974). Biosociology and ecology of pomacentrid fishes around the Sinai Peninsula (northern Red Sea). *J. Fish Biol.* **6**: 119–133.

Fonds, M. (1973). Sand gobies in the Dutch Waden Sea (*Pomatoschistus*, Gobiidae, Pisces). *Neth. J. Sea Res.* **6**: 417–478.

Foster, N. R. (1967a). *Comparative studies on the biology of killifishes (Pisces, Cyprinodontidae).* Ph.D. thesis: Cornell University.

Foster, N. R. (1967b). Trends in the evolution of reproductive behaviour in killifishes. *Stud. trop. Oceanogr.* **5**: 549–566.

Fraser, E. A. & Renton, R. M. (1940). Observation on the breeding and development of the viviparous fish, *Heterandria formosa. Q. Jl microsc. Sci.* **81**: 479–520.

Fricke, H. W. (1970). Ein mimetisches Kollektiv-Beobachtungen an Fischschwärmen, die Seeigel nachahmen. *Mar. Biol.* **5**: 307–314.

Fricke, H. W. (1974). Öko-Ethologie des monogamen Anemonenfisches *Amphiprion bicinctus* (Freiwasseruntersuchung aus dem Roten Meer). *Z. Tierpsychol.* **36**: 429–512.

Fryer, G. (1959). The trophic interrelationship and ecology of some littoral communities of Lake Nyasa with especial reference to the fishes, and a discussion of the evolution of a group of rock-frequenting Cichlidae. *Proc. zool. Soc. Lond.* **132**: 153–281.

Fryer, G. & Iles, T. D. (1972). *The cichlid fishes of the Great Lakes of Africa.* Edinburgh: Oliver & Boyd.

Gadgil, M. & Solbrig, O. T. (1972). The concept of "r" and "K" selection: evidence from wild flowers and some theoretical considerations. *Am. Nat.* **106**: 14–31.

Gerberich, J. B. & Laird, M. (1968). Bibliography of papers relating to the control of mosquitoes by the use of fish. *Fish. Tech. Pap. FAO* No. 75: 1–70.

Gibson, R. N. (1969). The biology and behaviour of littoral fish. *Oceanogr. mar. Biol.* **7**: 367–410.

Gibson, R. N. & Ezzi, I. A. (1978). The biology of a Scottish population of Fries' goby, *Lesueurigobius friesii. J. Fish Biol.* **12**: 371–389.

Goldman, B. & Talbot, F. H. (1976). Aspects of the ecology of coral reef fishes. In *Biology and geology of coral reefs.* **3**: Biology 2, 125–154. Jones, O. A. & Endean, R. (eds). London & New York: Academic Press.

Gould, S. J. (1977). *Ontogeny and phylogeny.* Cambridge, Mass: Harvard University Belknap Press.

Green, J. (1968). *The biology of estuarine animals.* London: Sidgwick & Jackson.

Greenwood, P. H. (1974). The cichlid fishes of Lake Victoria, East Africa: the biology and evolution of a species flock. *Bull. Br. Mus. (Nat. Hist.)* (Zool. suppl.) **6**: 1–134.

Gudger, E. W. (1941). The quest for the smallest fish. *Nat. hist. Mag.* **48**: 216–223.

Harrington, R. W. Jr. (1971). How ecological and genetic factors interact to determine when self-fertilizing hermaphrodites of *Rivulus marmoratus* change into functional secondary males, with a reappraisal of the modes of intersexuality among fishes. *Copeia* **1971**: 389–432.

Harry, R. R. (1949). A new species of goby and new records of fishes from the Solomon Islands. *J. Wash. Acad. Sci.* **39**: 140–146.

Heins, D. C. & Clemmer, G. H. (1976). The reproductive biology, age and growth of the North American cyprinid, *Notropis longirostris* (Hay). *J. Fish Biol.* **8**: 365–379.

Herre, A. W. (1927). Gobies of the Philippines and the China Sea. *Monogr. Philipp. Bur. Sci.* No. 23: 1–352.

Hester, F. J. (1964). Effects of food supply on fecundity in the female guppy, *Lebistes reticulatus* (Peters). *J. Fish. Res. Bd Can.* **21**: 757–764.

Hiatt, R. W. & Strasburg, D. W. (1960). Ecological relationships of the fish fauna on coral reefs of the Marshall Islands. *Ecol. Monogr.* **30**: 65–127.

Hisaoka, K. K. & Firlit, C. F. (1962). Ovarian cycle and egg production in the zebrafish, *Brachydanio rerio. Copeia* **1962**: 788–792.

Hobson, E. S. (1975). Feeding patterns among tropical reef fishes. *Am. Scient.* **63**: 382–392.

Hubbs, C., Stevenson, M. M. & Peden, A. E. (1968). Fecundity and egg size in two central Texas darter populations. *SWest. Nat.* **13**: 301–324.

Hubbs, C. & Strawn, K. (1957). The effects of light and temperature on the fecundity of the greenthroat darter, *Etheostoma lepidum* (Girard). *Ecology* **38**: 596–602.

Hunt, O. D. (1925). The food of the bottom fauna of the Plymouth fishing grounds. *J. mar. biol. Ass. U.K.* **13**: 560–599.

Hurlbert, S. H., Zedler, J. & Fairbanks, D. (1972). Ecosystem alteration by mosquitofish (*Gambusia affinis*) predation. *Science, Wash.* **175**: 639–641.

Huxley, J. (1941). *The uniqueness of man.* London: Chatto & Windus.

Hynes, H. B. N. (1970). *The ecology of running waters.* Liverpool: University Press.

Imms, A. D. (1957). *A general textbook of entomology* 9th Edn. (revised by Richards, O. W. & Davies, R. G.). London: Methuen.

Jacobs, K. (1971). *Livebearing aquarium fishes.* London: Studio Vista.

Johannes, R. E. (1978). Reproductive strategies of coastal marine fishes in the tropics. *Envirl Biol. Fish.* **3**: 65–84.

Jones, R. & Johnston, C. (1977). Growth, reproduction and mortality in gadoid fish species. In *Fisheries mathematics*: 736–62. Steele, J. H. (ed.). London & New York: Academic Press.

Kamito, A. (1928). Early development of the Japanese killifish (*Oryzias latipes*), with notes on its habits. *J. Coll. Agric. Imp. Univ. Tokyo* **10**: 21–38.

Kaufman, G. A. & Beyers, R. J. (1972). Relationships of weight, length and body composition in the medaka. *Am. Midl. Nat.* **88**: 239–245.

Kerr, S. R. (1971). Prediction of fish growth efficiency in nature. *J. Fish. Res. Bd Can.* **28**: 809–814.

Kirschfeld, K. (1976). The resolution of lens and compound eyes. In *Neural principles in vision*: 354–360. Zettler, F. & Weiler, R. (eds). Berlin: Springer.

Kneib, R. T. (1978). Habitat, diet, reproduction and growth of the spotfin killifish, *Fundulus luciae*, from a North Carolina salt marsh. *Copeia* **1978**: 164–168.

Kneib, R. T. & Stiven, A. E. (1978). Growth, reproduction, and feeding of *Fundulus heteroclitus* (L.) on a North Carolina saltmarsh. *J. exp. mar. Biol. Ecol.* **31**: 121–140.

Knöppel, H.-A. (1970). Food of central Amazonian fishes. Contribution to the nutrient-ecology of Amazonian rain-forest-streams. *Amazonia* **2**: 257–352.

Kohn, A. J. (1956). Piscivorous gastropods of the genus *Conus. Proc. natn. Acad. Sci.* **42**: 168–171.

Koumans, F. P. (1953). Gbioidea. *The fishes of the Indo-Australian Archipelago* **10**: 1–423. Weber, M. & Beaufort, L. F. de (eds). Leiden: E. J. Brill.

Krumholz, L. A. (1948). Reproduction in the western mosquitofish, *Gambusia affinis affinis* (Baird & Girard), and its use in mosquito control. *Ecol. Monogr.* **18**:1–43.

Krumholz, L. A. (1963). Relationships between fertility, sex ratio, and exposure to predation in populations of the mosquitofish *Gambusia manni* Hubbs at Bimini, Bahamas. *Int. Revue ges. Hydrobiol.* **48**: 201–256.

Kulkarni, C. V. (1940). On the systematic position, structural modifications, bionomics and development of a remarkable new family of cyprinodont fishes from the province of Bombay. *Rec. Indian Mus.* **42**: 379–423.

Laird, M. (1970). Integrated control of mosquitoes. *Am. Zool.* **10**: 573–578.

Lee, S-C. (1974). *Biology of the sand goby* Pomatoschistus minutus (*Pallas*) (*Teleostei*: *Gobioidei*) *in the Plymouth area.* Ph.D. thesis: University of Bristol.

Lee, S-C. & Chang, K-H. (1977). Food and reproduction of the blenny *Halmablennius lineatus* (Valenciennes). *Bull. Inst. zool. Acad. Sinica* **16**: 1–7.

Lewontin, R. C. (1965). Selection for colonizing ability. In *The genetics of colonizing species*: 77–91. Baker, H. G. & Stebbins, G. L. (eds). New York & London: Academic Press.

Lindsey, C. C. (1966). Body size of poikilotherm vertebrates at different latitudes. *Evolution* **20**: 456–465.

Loiselle, P. V. & Welcomme, R. L. (1971). Two new species of *Barbus* (Pisces: Cyprinidae) from southeastern Dahomey. *Revue Zool. Bot. afr.* **83**: 1–15.

MacArthur, R. H. (1972). *Geographical ecology.* New York: Harper & Row.

MacGinitie, G. E. (1939). The natural history of the blind goby, *Typhlogobius californiensis* Steindachner. *Am. Midl. Nat.* **21**: 489–505.

Mann, R. H. K. (1973). Observations on the age, growth, reproduction and food of the roach (*Rutilus rutilus* (L.)) in two rivers in southern England. *J. Fish. Biol.* **5**: 707–736.

Mariscal, R. N. (1970). The nature of the symbiosis between Indo-Pacific anemone fishes and sea anemones. *Mar. Biol.* **6**: 58–65.

Marshall, N. B. (1960). Swimbladder structure of deep-sea fishes in relation to their systematics and biology. *Discovery Rep.* **31**: 1–122.

Marshall, N. B. (1965). *The life of fishes.* London: Weidenfeld & Nicolson.

McDowall, R. M. (1968). *Galaxias maculatus* (Jenyns), the New Zealand whitebait. *Fisheries Res. Bull. N. Z.* (N.S.) No. 2: 1–84.

McMurtrie, R. (1976). On the limit to niche overlap for non uniform niches. *Theoret. Popul. Biol.* **10**: 96–107.

McPhail, J. D. (1977). Inherited interpopulation differences in size at first reproduction in threespine stickleback, *Gasterosteus aculeatus* L. *Heredity* **38**: 53–60.

Miller, P. J. (1961). Age, growth, and reproduction of the rock goby, *Gobius paganellus* L., in the Isle of Man. *J. mar. biol. Ass. U.K.* **41**: 737–769.

Miller, P. J. (1963). *Studies on the biology and taxonomy of British gobiid fishes.* Ph.D. Thesis: Liverpool University.

Miller, P. J. (1969). Systematics and biology of the leopard-spotted goby, *Gobius ephippiatus* (Teleostei: Gobiidae), with description of a new genus and notes on the identity of *G. macrolepis* Kolombatovic. *J. mar. biol. Ass. U.K.* **49**: 831–855.

Miller, P. J. (1972). Generic status and redescription of the Mediterranean fish *Gobius liechtensteini* Kolombatovic, 1891 (Teleostei: Gobioidea), and its affinities with certain American and Indo-Pacific gobies. *J. nat. Hist.* **6**: 395–407.

Miller, P. J. (1973). The species of *Pseudaphya* (Teleostei: Gobiidae) and the evolution of aphyiine gobies. *J. Fish Biol.* **5**: 353–365.

Miller, P. J. (1975). Age-structure and life-span in the common goby, *Pomato-schistus microps. J. Zool., Lond.* **177**: 425–448.

Miller, P. J. (1976). Predation of meiofauna by the goby *Pomatoschistus microps. Bull. est. br.-w. Sci. Ass.* No. 12: 10.

Miller, P. J. & Tortonese, E. (1968). Distribution and systematics of the gobiid fish *Odondebuenia balearica* (Pellegrin Fage). *Annali Mus. civ. Stor. nat. Giacomo Doria* **77**: 342–358.

Miller, R. R. & Fitzsimons, J. M. (1971). *Ameca splendens*, a new genus and species of goodeid fish from western Mexico, with remarks on the classification of the Goodeidae. *Copeia* **1971**: 1–13.

Moodie, G. E. E. (1972). Morphology, life history, and ecology of an unusual stickleback (*Gasterosteus aculeatus*) in the Queen Charlotte Islands, Canada. *Can. J. Zool.* **50**: 721–732.

Munro, J. L., Gaut, W. C., Thompson, R. & Reeson, P. H. (1973). The spawning seasons of Caribbean reef fishes. *J. Fish Biol.* **5**: 69–84.

Murdoch, W. M. (1969). Switching in general predators: experiments on predator specificity and stability of prey populations. *Ecol. Monogr.* **39**: 335–354.

Murray, J. & Hjort, J. (1912). *The depths of the ocean.* London: Macmillan.

Muus, B. J. (1967). The fauna of Danish estuaries and lagoons. Distribution and ecology of dominating species in the shallow reaches of the mesohaline zone. *Meddr Danm. Fisk. Havunders.* (N.S.) **5**(1): 1–316.

Myers, G. S. (1944). Two extraordinary new blind nematognath fishes from the Rio Negro, representing a new subfamily of Pygidiidae, with a rearrange-ment of the genera of the family, and illustrations of some previously described genera and species from Venezuela and Brazil. *Proc. Calif. Acad. Sci.* (4) **23**: 591–602.

Neave, F. (1953). Principles affecting the sizes of pink and chum salmon popu-lations in British Columbia. *J. Fish. Res. Bd Can.* **9**: 450–491.

Nelson, K. (1964). Behavior and morphology in the glandulocaudine fishes (Ostariophysi, Characidae). *Univ. Calif. Publs Zool.* **75**: 59–152.

Nelson, J. S. (1968). Life history of the brook silverside, *Labidesthes sicculus*, in Crooked Lake, Indiana. *Trans. Am. Fish. Soc.* **97**: 293–296.

Nelson, J. S. (1976). *Fishes of the world.* New York: Wiley.

Norman, J. R. (1963). *A history of fishes.* 2nd edition (edited by P. H. Greenwood). London: Ernest Benn.

Page, L. M. & Schemske, D. W. (1978). The effect of interspecific competition on the distribution and size of darters of the subgenus *Catonotus* (Percidae: *Etheostoma*). *Copeia* **1978**: 406–412.

Paine, R. T. (1966). Food web complexity and species diversity. *Am. Nat.* **100**: 65–75.

Patterson, C. (1974). The braincase of pholidophorid and leptolepid fishes, with a review of the actinopterygian braincase. *Phil. Trans. R. Soc.* **269**(B): 275–579.

Patton, W. K. (1976). Animal associates of living reef corals. In *Biology and geology of coral reefs.* **3**: Biology 2: 1–36. Jones, O. A. & Endean, R. (eds). London & New York: Academic Press.

Payne, A. I. (1975). The reproductive cycle, condition and feeding in *Barbus liberiensis*, a tropical stream-dwelling cyprinid. *J. Zool. Lond.* **176**: 247–269.

Pedley, T. J. (ed.) (1977). *Scale effects in animal locomotion.* New York: Academic Press.

Pietsch, T. W. (1976). Dimorphism, parasitism and sex: reproductive strategies among deepsea ceratioid angler fishes. *Copeia* **1976**: 781–793.

Polunin, N. V. C. & Lubbock, R. (1977). Prawn-associated gobies (Teleostei: Gobiidae) from the Seychelles, Western Indian Ocean: systematics and ecology. *J. Zool., Lond.* **183**: 63–101.

Price, P. W. (1974). Strategies for egg production. *Evolution* **28**: 76–84.

Qasim, S. Z. (1956). Time and duration of the spawning season in some marine teleosts in relation to their distribution. *J. Cons. perm. int. Explor. Mer* **21**: 144–155.

Qasim, S. Z. (1957). The biology of *Blennius pholis* L. (Teleostei). *Proc. zool. Soc. Lond.* **128**: 161–208.

Rand, A. S. (1967). Predator-prey interactions and the evolution of aspect diversity. *Atas Simp. Biota Amazôn.* (Zoologia) **5**: 73–83.

Randall, J. E. (1967). Food habits of reef fishes of the West Indies. *Stud. trop. Oceanogr.* **5**: 665–847.

Randall, J. E. & Randall, H. A. (1960). Examples of mimicry and protective resemblance in tropical marine fishes. *Bull. Mar. sci. Gulf Caribb.* **10**: 444–480.

Randall, J. E., Schroeder, R. E. & Starck, II, W. A. (1964). Notes on the biology of the echinoid *Diadema antillarum*. *Caribb. J. Sci.* **4**: 421–433.

Roberts, T. R. (1970). Description, osteology and relationships of the Amazonian cyprinodont fish *Fluviphylax pygmaeus* (Myers and Carvalho). *Breviora* **347**: 1–28.

Roberts, T. R. (1971). The fishes of the Malaysian family Phallostethidae (Atheriniformes). *Breviora* No. 374: 1–27.

Roosen-Runge, E. C. (1938). On the early development—bipolar differentiation and cleavage—of the zebrafish, *Brachydanio rerio*. *Biol. Bull. mar. biol. Lab., Woods Hole* **75**: 119–133.

Rosen, D. E. (1962). Egg retention: pattern in evolution. *Nat. Hist., N.Y.* **71**: 46–53.

Rosen, D. E. & Bailey, R. M. (1964). The poeciliid fishes (Cyprinodontiformes), their structure, zoogeography, and systematics. *Bull. Am. Mus. nat. Hist.* **126**: 1–176.

Rosenblatt, R. H. (1963). Some aspects of speciation in marine shore fishes. *Publs Syst. Assoc.*, No. 5: 171–180.

Rosenthal, H. L. (1952). Observations on reproduction of the poeciliid *Lebistes reticulatus* (Peters). *Biol. Bull. mar. biol. Lab., Woods Hole* **102**: 30–38.

Roughgarden, J. & Feldman, M. (1975). Species packing and predation pressure. *Ecology* **56**: 489–492.

Russell, F. S. (1976). *The eggs and planktonic stages of British marine fishes.* London & New York: Academic Press.

Sale, P. F. (1978). Coexistence of coral reef fishes—a lottery for living space. *Envirl Biol. Fish.* **3**: 85–102.

Sarenas, A. M. & Ronquillo, I. A. (1954). Discovery of living specimens and re-description of *Pandaka pygmaea* Herre. *Philipp. J. Sci.* **83**: 257–261.

Schaffer, W. M. (1974). Optimal reproductive effort in fluctuating environments. *Am. Nat* **108**: 783–790.

Schindler, O. (1932). Sexually mature larval Hemirhamphidae from the Hawaiian Islands. *Bull. Bern. Bish. Mus.* No. 97: 1–28.

Schoener, T. W. (1965). The evolution of bill size differences among sympatric congeneric species of birds. *Evolution* **19**: 189–213.

Schoener, T. W. (1971). Theory of feeding strategies. *A. Rev. Ecol. Syst.* **2**: 369–404.

Schoener, T. W. (1974). Resource partitioning in ecological communities. *Science, Wash.* **185**: 27–39.

Scott, W. B. & Crossman, E. J. (1973). Freshwater fishes of Canada. *Bull. Fish. Res. Bd Can.* No. 184: 1–966.

Scrimshaw, N. S. (1944a). Embryonic growth in the viviparous poeciliid, *Heterandria formosa*. *Biol. Bull. mar. biol. Lab., Woods Hole* **87**: 37–51.

Scrimshaw, N. S. (1944b). Superfetation in poeciliid fishes. *Copeia* **1944**: 180–183.

Scrimshaw, N. S. (1945). Embryonic development in poeciliid fishes. *Biol. Bull. mar. biol. Lab., Woods Hole* **88**: 233–246.

Scrimshaw, N. S. (1946). Egg size in poeciliid fishes. *Copeia* **1946**: 20–23.

Self, J. T. (1940). Notes on the sex cycle of *Gambusia affinis affinis* and on its habits and relation to mosquito control. *Am. Midl. Nat.* **23**: 393–398.

Smith, C. L. (1978). Coral reef fish communities: a compromise view. *Envirl Biol. Fish.* **3**: 109–128.

Smith, C. L. & Tyler, J. C. (1972). Space resource sharing in a coral reef fish community. *Bull. Nat. hist. Mus. Los Angeles Cty* **14**: 125–170.

Smith, C. L. & Tyler, J. C. (1975). Succession and stability in fish communities of dome-shaped patch reefs in the West Indies. *Am. Mus. Novit.* No. 2572: 1–18.

Smith, J. L. B. (1958). The fishes of the family Eleotridae in the Western Indian Ocean. *Ichthyol. Bull. Rhodes Univ.* No. 11: 137–163.

Smith, J. L. B. (1959). Gobioid fishes of the families Gobiidae, Periophthalmidae, Trypauchenidae, Taenioididae and Kraemaeriidae of the western Indian Ocean. *Ichthyol. Bull. Rhodes Univ.* No. 13: 185–225.

Southwood, T. R. E. (1977). Habitat, the templet for ecological strategies? *J. Anim. Ecol.* **46**: 337–365.

Southwood, T. R. E., May, R. M., Hassell, M. P. & Conway, G. R. (1974). Ecological strategies and population parameters. *Am. Nat.* **108**: 791–804.

Stearns, S. C. (1976). Life-history tactics: a review of the ideas. *Q. Rev. Biol.* **51**: 3–47.

Stearns, S. C. (1978). Interpopulational differences in reproductive traits of *Neoheterandria tridentiger* (Pisces: Poeciliidae) in Panama. *Copeia* **1978**: 188–190.

Sterba, G. (1962). *Freshwater fishes of the world.* London: Vista Books.

Stolk, A. (1951). Histo-endocrinological analysis of gestation phenomena in the cyprinodont *Lebistes reticulatus* Peters. IV. The oocyte-cycle during pregnancy. *Proc. K. Ned. Akad. Wet.* (C) **54**: 574–578.

Stolk, A. (1956). Histo-endocrinological analysis of gestation phenomena in the hemirhamphid *Dermogenys pusillus* van Hasselt. I. Thyroid activity during pregnancy. *Acta morph. neerl-Scand.* **1**: 1–11.

Swennen, C. (1971). Het voedsel van de Groenpootruiter *Tringa nebularia* tijdens het verblijf in het Nederlandse Waddengebied. *Limosa* **44**: 71–83.

Tamura, E. & Honma, Y. (1970). Histological changes in the organs and tissues of the gobiid fishes throughout the life-span—III. Hemopoietic organs in the icegoby, *Leucopsarion petersi* Hilgendorf. *Bull. Jap. Soc. scient. Fish.* **36**: 661–669.

Tavolga, W. N. (1949). Embryonic development of the platyfish (*Platypoecilus*), the swordtail (*Xiphophorus*), and their hybrids. *Bull. Am. Mus. nat. Hist.* **94**: 161–230.

Tavolga, W. N. & Rugh, R. (1947). Development of the platyfish, *Platypoecilus maculatus. Zoologica, N.Y.* **32**: 1–15.

Te Winkel, L. E. (1935). A study of *Mistichthys luzonensis* with special reference to conditions correlated with reduced size. *J. Morph.* **58**: 463–535.

Te Winkel, L. E. (1939). The internal anatomy of two phallostethid fishes. *Biol. Bull. mar. biol. Lab.*, *Woods Hole* **76**: 59–69.

Teytaud, A. R. (1970). Food habits of the goby, *Ginsburgellus novemlineatus*, and the clingfish, *Arcos rubiginosus*, associated with echinoids in the Virgin Islands. *Caribb. J. Sci.* **11**: 41–45.

Thibault, R. E. (1974). Genetics of cannibalism in a viviparous fish and its relationship to population density. *Nature, Lond.* **251**: 138–140.

Thibault, R. E. & Schultz, R. J. (1978). Reproductive adaptations among viviparous fishes (Cyprinodontiformes: Poeciliidae). *Evolution* **32**: 320–333.

Turner, C. L. (1937). Reproductive cycles and superfetation in poeciliid fishes. *Biol. Bull. mar. biol. Lab.*, *Woods Hole* **72**: 145–164.

Turner, C. L. (1938). The reproductive cycle of *Brachyraphis episcopi*, an ovoviviparous poeciliid fish in the natural tropical habitat. *Biol. Bull. mar. biol. Lab.*, *Woods Hole* **75**: 56–65.

Turner, C. L. (1940a). Superfetation in viviparous cyprinodont fishes. *Copeia* **1940**: 88–91.

Turner, C. L. (1940b). Pseudoamnion, pseudochorion, and follicular pseudoplacenta in poeciliid fishes. *J. Morph.* **67**: 59–89.

Turner, C. L. (1940c). Pericardial sac, trophotaeniae, and alimentary tract in embryos of goodeid fishes. *J. Morph.* **67**: 271–283.

Turner, C. L. (1940d). Adaptations for viviparity in jenynsiid fishes. *J. Morph.* **67**: 291–297.

Turner, C. L. (1947). Viviparity in teleost fishes. *Scient. Mon., N.Y.* **65**: 508–518.

Tyler, J. C. (1971). Habitat preferences of the fishes that dwell in shrub corals on the Great Barrier Reef. *Proc. Acad. nat. Sci. Philad.* **123**: 1–26.

Tyler, J. C. & Böhlke, J. E. (1972). Records of sponge-dwelling fishes, primarily of the Caribbean. *Bull. Mar. Sci.* **22**: 601–642.

Valiela, I. Wright, J. E., Teal, J. M. & Volkmann, S. B. (1977). Growth, production and energy transformations in the salt-marsh killifish *Fundulus heteroclitus*. *Mar. Biol.* **40**: 135–144.

Vallowe, H. H. (1953). Some physiological aspects of reproduction in *Xiphophorus maculatus*. *Biol Bull. mar. biol Lab.*, *Woods Hole* **104**: 240–249.

Van Valen, L. (1973). Body size and numbers of plants and animals. *Evolution* **27**: 27–35.

Verwey, J. (1930). Coral reef studies. I. The symbiosis between damselfishes and sea anemones in Batavia Bay. *Treubia* **12**: 305–366.

Villadolid, D. V. & Manacop, P. R. (1934). The Philippine Phallostethidae, a description of a new species, and a report on the biology of *Gulaphallus mirabilis* Herre. *Philipp. J. Sci.* **55**: 193–220.

Villadolid, D. V. & Marquez, J. (1960). On the *Pandaka pygmaea*, the smallest known fish or vertebrate. *Comm. 1ᵉʳ Congr. Int. Aquariol. Monaco* **A**: 149–152.

Wallace, D. C. (1973). Reproduction of the silverjaw minnow, *Ericymba buccata* Cope. *Trans. Am. Fish. Soc.* **102**: 786–793.

Wardle, C. S. (1977). Effects of size on the swimming speeds of fish. In *Scale effects in animal locomotion*: 299–313. Pedley, T. J. (ed.). New York: Academic Press.

Ware, D. M. (1975). Relation between egg size, growth, and natural mortality of larval fish. *J. Fish. Res. Bd Can.* **32**: 2503–2512.

Weber, M. & De Beaufort, L. F. (1922). *The fishes of the Indo-Australian Archipelago.* IV. Heteromi, Solenichthyes, Synentognathi, Percesoces, Labyrinthici, Microcyprini. Leiden: Brill.

Wellensiek, U. (1953). Die Allometrie verhältnisse und Konstruktionsänderung bei dem kleinsten Fisch in Vergleich mit etwas grösseren verwandten Formen. *Zool. Jb.* (Anat.) **73**: 187–228.

Whittaker, R. H., Levin, S. A. & Root, R. B. (1973). Niche habitat, and ecotope. *Am. Nat.* **107**: 321–338.

Williams, A. H. (1978). Ecology of threespot damselfish: social organization, age structure, and population stability. *J. exp. mar. Biol. Ecol.* **34**: 197–213.

Williams, G. C. (1959). Ovary weights of darters: a test of the alleged association of parental care with reduced fecundity in fishes. *Copeia* **1959**: 18–24.

Williams, G. C. (1966). *Adaptation and natural selection.* Princeton: Princeton University Press.

Wilson, D. S. (1975). The adequacy of body size as a niche difference. *Am. Nat.* **109**: 769–784.

Wourms, J. P. & Cohen, D. M. (1975). Trophotaeniae, embryonic adaptations, in the viviparous ophidioid fish, *Oligopus longhursti*: a study of museum specimens. *J. Morph.* **147**: 385–402.

Yamamoto, T. (1961). Progenies of sex-reversal females mated with sex-reversal males in the medaka, *Oryzias latipes. J. exp. Zool.* **146**: 163–179.

Zaret, T. M. & Rand, A. S. (1971). Competition in tropical stream fishes: support for the competitive exclusion principle. *Ecology* **52**: 336–342.

Symp. zool. Soc. Lond. (1979) No. 44, 307–326

The Theory of Life-History Evolution and its Application to Atlantic Salmon

W. M. SCHAFFER

University of Arizona, Tucson, Arizona, USA

SYNOPSIS

Recent advances in the theory of life-history evolution make possible the testing of *a priori*, deductive hypotheses regarding inter-population variation in demographic parameters on assumption that the differences are adaptive. Salmonid fishes are appropriate subjects for such investigations because of the large number of semi-isolated populations within single species and the great diversity of reproductive strategies within and between species. In the case of *Salmo salar* L., it has been possible to account for differences in the mean age of first spawning in terms of three environmental variables that theory suggests would affect the optimal allocation of energy to reproduction (*sensu lato*). These factors are river length, growth rates at sea and the intensity of estuarine fishing. A more dramatic variation in life-history phenology exists between the genera *Salmo* (iteroparous) and *Oncorhynchus* (semelparous). Several potential explanations are examined including the possibility that iteroparity and semelparity correspond to local optima with an intervening valley in fitness.

INTRODUCTION

This paper is divided into four parts. The first reviews the mathematical theory of life-history evolution as it has been developed since 1954. The second considers the relevance of this theory to variation in the age of first spawning in North American Atlantic salmon. In the next section, I consider potential applications to other aspects of salmon biology. The concluding discussion considers the alternative formalism of r– and K–selection.

THE THEORY

Preliminaries

Current interest in the evolution of life-history parameters can be traced to Lamont Cole's seminal paper *The population consequences of life history phenomena* which was published in the *Quarterly Review of Biology* in 1954. Cole approached the problem mathematically. Specifically, he considered the rate λ_1 at which an age structured population comes to multiply on achieving stable age distribution. Consider a population in which reproduction is confined to a discrete yearly breeding season. Let $x_i(t)$ be the number of individuals in the ith year of life alive during the breeding season in year t. Further suppose that i year olds produce m_i offspring of which c_i survive to be counted during the breeding season in their first year of life. The effective fecundity of an i year old can thus be defined as

$$B_i = c_i m. \tag{1}$$

Further suppose that, following the breeding season, an i year old survives with probability p_i to breed the following year at age $i + 1$. Then, if we agree to call the youngest age class censussed during the breeding season, i.e., the young of the year, zero year olds, and if there are $w + 1$ age classes

$$x_0(t) = \sum_{i=0}^{w} B_i x_i(t-1) \tag{2a}$$

and

$$x_i(t) = p_{i-1} x_{i-1}(t-1), \qquad i > 0 \tag{2b}$$

(Fig. 1). In this case, the population will, on attaining stable age distribution, multiply at an annual rate λ_1 which is the positive root of the

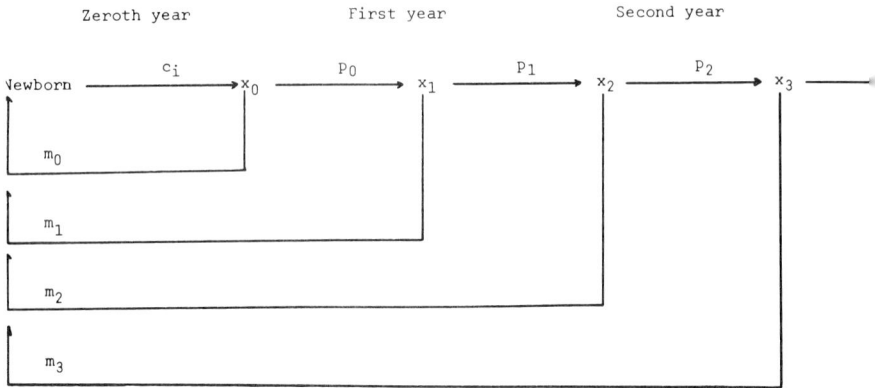

FIG. 1. Schematic representation of a population in which individuals reproduce at discrete (yearly) intervals. The number of individuals in each age class present during the breeding season is denoted x_i. Each of these produces m_1 offspring of which c_i survive to the breeding season in their first year of life (zeroth age class). The product $c_i m_i = B_i$ is termed the effective fecundity of an i-year-old individual. The p_i are post-breeding survival probabilities. Thus, p_0 is the probability that a zero-year-old individual alive during the breeding season at time t survives to become a one-year-old individual during the breeding season the following year. From Schaffer & Rosenzweig (1977).

stable age equation

$$1 = \sum_{x=0}^{w} \lambda^{-(x+1)} l_x B_x \tag{3}$$

(Leslie, 1945). Here, since survival from birth to the first breeding season has been absorbed into the B's

$$l_0 = 1 \tag{4a}$$

and

$$l_x = \prod_0^{x-1} p_k, \qquad x > 0. \tag{4b}$$

The relationship of λ_1, or $r = \ln \lambda_1$ in the case of continuous reproduction, to fitness has been discussed by several authors including Fisher (1958), Charlesworth (1973) and Charlesworth & Williamson (1975). Consider a population with phenotype $\phi = \bar{\phi}$ which has attained stable age structure and is at carrying capacity. Under these conditions, $r = \ln \lambda_1 = 0$. Now let us introduce a mutant with phenotype $\phi = \phi'$. In the absence of frequency-dependent selection, the probability u that the mutant will replace the wild type is proportional to its selective advantage s,[a] which is given by the relation

$$s = [r(\phi') - r(\bar{\phi})] \approx \Delta\phi (dr/d\phi)|_{\bar{\phi}}. \tag{5}$$

Consequently, changes in the life table, which increase the value of $r = \ln \lambda_1$, should be selected for (Fig. 2).

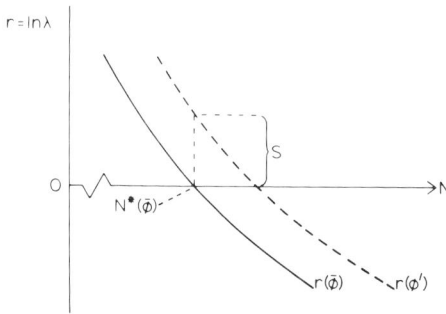

FIG. 2. Fitness, $r(N) = (1/N)(dN/dt)$, plotted against density for wild type and mutant phenotypes, $\bar{\phi}$ and ϕ'. The selective advantage, s, of the mutant is $r(\phi') - r(\bar{\phi})$, evaluated at $N^*(\bar{\phi})$.

Sensitivity Analysis

Unfortunately, the stable age equation cannot be solved explicitly for λ_1 except in certain special cases. Nevertheless, it is still possible to calculate the consequences to λ_1 of varying survival and fecundity at different ages

[a] For non-overlapping generations, the familiar "textbook" result is $u \approx 2s$ (Crow & Kimura, 1970). In the present case (generations overlapping) $u \approx 2sT/V$ (Charlesworth & Williamson, 1975), where V is the variance of the offspring distribution, and $T = \Sigma l_x B_x$.

by differentiating eqn (3) implicitly and rearranging terms.[a] Specifically, it can be shown (Hamilton, 1966; Emlen, 1970) that

$$\frac{\partial \lambda_1}{\partial B_i} = \frac{l_i/\lambda_1^i}{V_T} \tag{6}$$

and

$$\frac{\partial \lambda_1}{\partial p_i} = \frac{l_i/\lambda_1^i}{V_T} \frac{v_{i+1}}{v_0} \tag{7}$$

Here, v_i/v_0 is the reproductive value (Fisher, 1958) of an i year old, and V_T is the population's total reproductive value. Recall that

$$v_i/v_0 = (\lambda^i/l_i) \sum_{j=i}^{w} \lambda^{-(j+1)} l_j B_j \tag{8a}$$

and

$$V_T = \sum_{i=0}^{w} (i+1)\lambda^{-(i+1)} l_i B_i. \tag{8b}$$

Equations (6) and (7) suggest two conclusions: first, from eqn (6), we note that increased reproduction at earlier ages confers greater improvements in fitness than comparable increases at later ages. Secondly, Eqn (7) suggests that the advantages accruing from improved survivorship at a particular age depend on the reproductive value at that age class. In the case of man, and other higher vertebrates, reproductive value is a unimodal function of age, peaking at what is roughly the age of first reproduction (e.g. see Fisher, 1958). This observation suggests that selection will more likely "tolerate" increased mortality among the old or very young, if, in exchange for this increase, something else might be gained—for example, increased survival among sibs, enhanced fecundity, etc.

Cost Benefit Analysis

Implicit in a proper interpretation of the preceding results is the observation that selection cannot work to increase all the B's and p's simultaneously. Instead, we accept that there will be trade-offs. The resources available to an organism for reproduction, growth and maintenance at any particular age class are finite, Increasing the allocation to reproduction can be expected to yield benefits in the form of an immediate increase in effective reproduction. But this increase will, in general, be achievable only at a cost measured in currency of reductions in subsequent survival and fecundity. Given such constraints, the problem of maximizing λ_1 then

---

[a] Recently, equivalent results have been derived by Caswell (1979) using the technique of perturbation analysis (e.g. Franklin, 1968: 186–189).

becomes one of determining the schedule of age-specific reproductive allocations which maximizes the benefits relative to the costs.

Gadgil & Bossert (1970; see also Emlen, 1970) were the first authors to state the question in this form and to attempt a numerical solution. Subsequent authors, including Schaffer (1974a,b; Schaffer & Rosenzweig, 1977) and Taylor *et al.* (1974), have made further analyses. The basic model studied by these authors is shown in Fig. 3. Resources are harvested

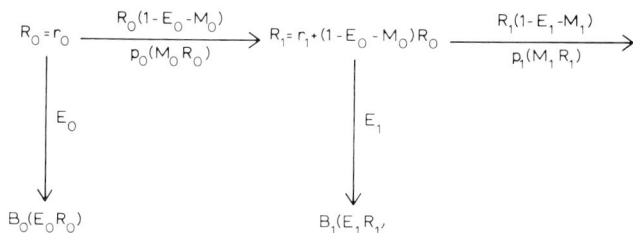

$$R_0 = r_0 \xrightarrow{\dfrac{R_0(1 - E_0 - M_0)}{p_0(M_0 R_0)}} R_1 = r_1 + (1 - E_0 - M_0)R_0 \xrightarrow{\dfrac{R_1(1 - E_1 - M_1)}{p_1(M_1 R_1)}}$$

$$\downarrow E_0 \qquad\qquad \downarrow E_1$$

$$B_0(E_0 R_0) \qquad\qquad B_1(E_1 R_1)$$

FIG 3. Schematic representation of age-specific availability of resources which can be allocated to reproduction, maintenance and growth. At each age class, resources are produced in amount r_x. Of the total, R_x, available at that age, one fraction, $E_x R_x$, is devoted to reproduction, and another, $M_x R_x$, is used for maintenance. The remainder $(1 - E_x - M_x)$ is used for growth, some of which will be available for future reproduction at ages $j > x$.

(produced in the case of plants) in amount r_x at age x. The total amount of resources R_x, available at that age for reproduction, maintenance, and growth is thus r_x plus any accumulation from preceding years. Of these, a fraction, $E_x R_x$, is allocated to reproduction. The remainder, $(1 - E_x)R_x$, are used either for maintenance or growth, or are passed on to the next age class in a form that can be used for future reproduction. We thus expect that increasing an organism's reproductive expenditure, E_x, at age x will result in reductions in subsequent survival, or reproduction, or both. The optimal schedule of allocation thus depends on the nature of the aforementioned trade-off and on the way in which λ_1 depends on the various quantities involved.

Consider, for example, the selective advantage associated with an increase in fecundity, dB_i, at age i. Recall that the selective advantage of a mutant with phenotype $\phi = \phi'$ is simply

$$s \approx \Delta\phi (dr/d\phi)|\bar{\phi} \tag{5}$$

where $\bar{\phi}$ is average phenotype in the population. Since $r = \ln \lambda_1$,

$$s_{B_i} = (dB_i/\lambda_1)\,(d\lambda_1/dB_i). \tag{9}$$

From our model of resource allocation (Fig. 3), we note that increasing reproductive expenditure at age i will affect the following quantities

1. B_i, which will generally increase in value,
2. $B_{j>i}$, which will usually decline, and
3. $p_{j \geq i}$, which will generally also decline.

Thus, we can write

$$(\mathrm{d}\lambda_1/\mathrm{d}B_i) = (\partial\lambda_1/\partial B_i) + (\partial\lambda_1/\partial p_i)(\mathrm{d}p_i/\mathrm{d}B_i) + \sum_{j=i+1}^{w}\left[\frac{\partial\lambda_1}{\partial B_j}\frac{\mathrm{d}B_j}{\mathrm{d}B_i} + \frac{\partial\lambda_1}{\partial p_j}\frac{\mathrm{d}p_j}{\mathrm{d}B_i}\right].$$
(10)

From (9) it then follows that

$$S_{B_i} = \lambda_1^{-1}\left\{(\partial\lambda_1/\partial B_i)\,\mathrm{d}B_i + (\partial\lambda_1/\partial p_i)\mathrm{d}p_i + \sum_{j=i+1}^{w}\left[\frac{\partial\lambda_1}{\partial B_j}\,\mathrm{d}B_j + \frac{\partial\lambda_1}{\partial p_j}\,\mathrm{d}p_j\right]\right\}.$$

Substituting for

$$\frac{\partial\lambda_1}{\partial B_j} = \frac{l_j/\lambda_1^j}{V_T}$$
(6)

and

$$\frac{\partial\lambda_1}{\partial p_j} = \frac{l_j/\lambda_1^j}{V_T}\frac{v_{i+1}}{v_0}$$
(7)

gives us

$$s_{B_i} = \frac{l_i/\lambda_1^i}{V_T}\left\{\mathrm{d}B_i + \frac{v_{i+1}}{v_0}\mathrm{d}p_i + p_i\left[\frac{\lambda_1^i}{l_{i+1}}\sum_{j=i+1}^{w}\frac{l_j}{\lambda_1^j}\left(\mathrm{d}B_j + \frac{v_{j+1}}{v_0}\mathrm{d}p_j\right)\right]\right\}$$
(11)

Now consider the case in which $B_i = \hat{B}_i(E_0,\ldots,E_w)$, which is the optimal value of B_i given fixed expenditures at ages $j \neq i$. Since our criterion of optimality is the maximization of λ_1, both $(\mathrm{d}\lambda_1/\mathrm{d}B_i)$ and s_{B_i} equal zero at $B_i = \hat{B}_i$. From eqn (8a) we can calculate

$$d(v_{i+1}/v_0)|_{\hat{B}_i} = (\lambda_1^i/l_{i+1})\sum_{j=i+1}^{w}\frac{l_j}{\lambda_1^j}(\mathrm{d}B_j + \frac{v_{j+1}}{v_0}\mathrm{d}p_j)$$
(12)

Hence, at $B_i = \hat{B}_i(E_0,\ldots,E_w)$

$$0 = \hat{s}_{B_i}$$
$$= (l_i/\lambda_1^{i+1}V_T)\,[\mathrm{d}B_i + (v_{i+1}/v_0)\,\mathrm{d}p_i + p_i d(v_{i+1}/v_0)]$$
$$= (l_i/\lambda_1^{i+1}V_T)\,[\mathrm{d}B_i + d(p_i v_{i+1}/v_0)].$$
(13)

We have thus shown that the value of B_i maximizing λ_1 for fixed expenditures at all other age classes maximizes the sum

$$B_i + p_i v_{i+1}/v_0.$$
(14)

This result was first conjectured by Williams (1966) and subsequently proved by Schaffer (1974a) and Taylor *et al.* (1974). Notice that since

$$\lambda_1(v_i/v_0) = B_i + p_i(v_{i+1}/v_0)$$

maximizing eqn (14) also maximizes reproductive value at age i. Notice also that, contrary to a suggestion by Caswell (in press), these results assume only that increasing reproductive expenditure at age i does not affect reproduction and survival at earlier ages. In particular, we have not restricted our analysis to trade-offs that occur within an age class as Caswell maintained.

In passing, we further observe that the optimality criterion eqn (14) also allows us to write down expressions for the benefit and cost associated with increasing reproductive expenditure at age i from $\bar{E}_i$ to E'_i (Schaffer & Gadgil, 1975). Thus

$$\text{Benefit} = B_i(E'_i) - B_i(\bar{E}_i) \approx \Delta E_i (\partial B_i / \partial E_i)|_{\bar{E}_i}$$

and

$$\text{Cost} = -\left\{ [p_i(E'_i)v_{i+1}(E'_i)/v_0] - [p_i(\bar{E}_i)v_{i+1}(E_i)/v_0] \right\}$$
$$\approx -\Delta E_i [\partial (p_i v_{i+1}/v_0)/\partial E_i]|_{\bar{E}_i}.$$

Next we allow the expenditures at the other age classes to vary. Consider our criterion of optimality (eqn 14)

$$\max \lambda_1 \leftrightarrows \max [B_i + p_i v_{i+1}/v_0].$$

If we now alter $E_{j \neq i}$, the optimal expenditure at age i will change, because

1. $B_i(E_i)$ can change,
2. so can $p_i(E_i)$, and the B's and p's contained in v_{i+1}/v_0 if $j < i$ and
3. because v_{i+1}/v_0 also depends on λ_1 which varies with all the p's and B's.

Consequently, for each set of age-specific expenditures, $\mathbf{E} = (E_0, \ldots, E_w)$, we obtain a different optimal value of $\hat{E}_i = E_i(\mathbf{E})$. Each such value satisfies criterion (eqn 14). This leads us to consider a $(w+1)$ dimensional state space whose axes are $(E_0, E_1, \ldots, E_w)$. In this space we plot surfaces of maximum fitness, $\hat{E}_0(\mathbf{E}), \hat{E}_1(\mathbf{E}), \ldots, \hat{E}_w(\mathbf{E})$.

Selection will then move the vector of expenditures at time t, $\mathbf{E}(t)$, toward the point or points where the isosurfaces intersect. We note that, at each intersection (there may be more than one), criterion (eqn 14) is maximized for all age classes. We have thus also demonstrated that an optimal life history is one in which reproductive value is maximal at every age. For a different proof of the same result, see Taylor *et al.* (1974).

Figure 4 gives some two-dimensional examples from Schaffer & Rosenzweig (1977). These are for a three age class system in which the expenditure at the oldest age class is fixed at the value maximizing fecundity at that age. Notice the importance of the shape of the trade-off function B_i versus $p_i v_{i+1}/v_0$. If the trade-off is convex (Fig. 4a), the optimal expenditures are generally less than 100%—an iteroparous life history is favored. Conversely, if $B_i(p_i v_{i+1}/v_0)$ is concave (Fig. 4b), selection will be for semelparity—0 or 100% effort at each age class. More complex trade-off functions (Figs 4c and 4d) can yield multiple and, in some cases, mixed optima.

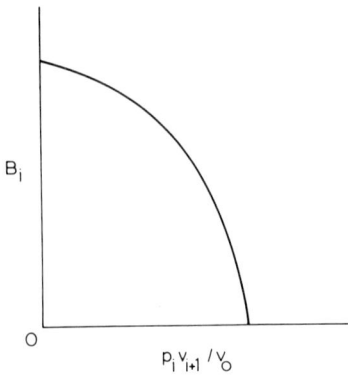
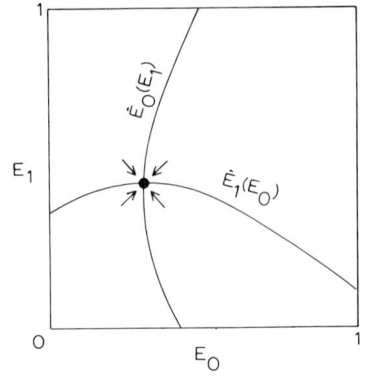

a.

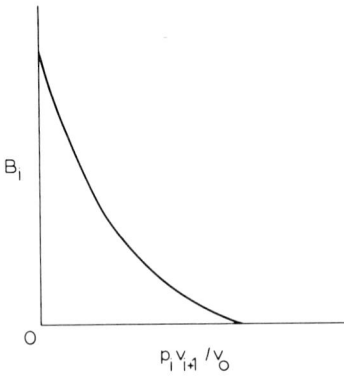
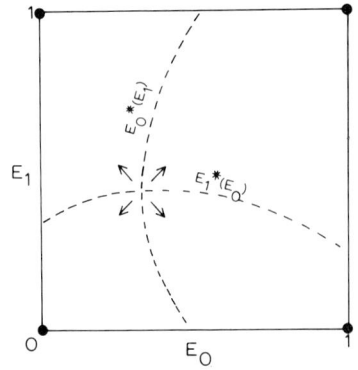

b.

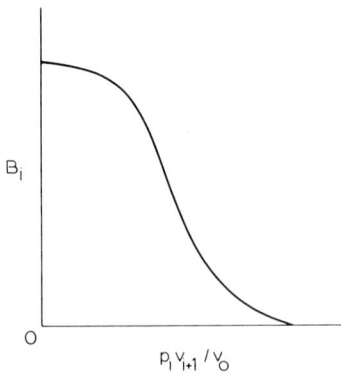
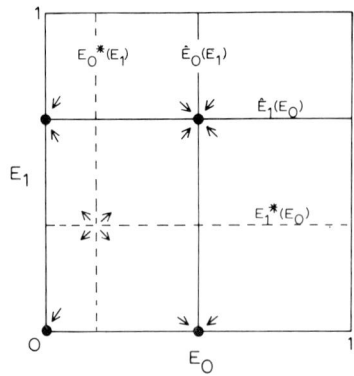

c.

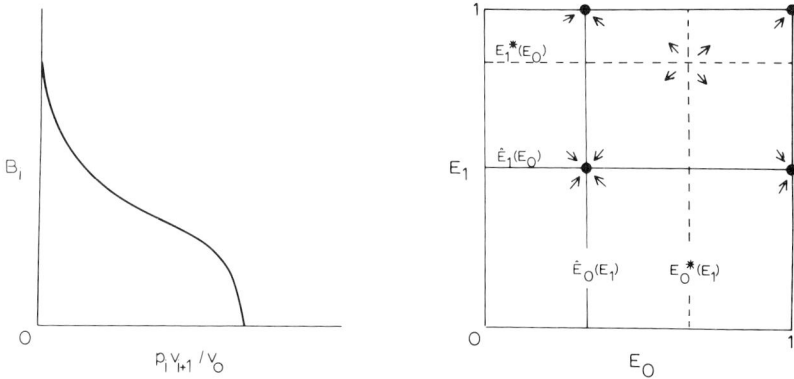

d.

FIG 4. Various shapes (a–d) of the trade-off function, $B_i(p_i v_{i+1}/v_0)$ (left), and the isoclines $\hat{E}_i(E_j)$ (right), that result in a three-stage life history with E_2 fixed at the value maximizing B_2 (right). For the sake of clarity, the isoclines in (c) and (d) have been represented as straight lines. After Schaffer & Rosenzweig (1977).

The concave-convex trade-off (Fig. 4d) is especially interesting since, in this case, one of the local optima corresponds to repeated reproduction whereas the others entail a maximum expenditure at some stage in the life-cycle.

APPLICATION TO SALMON

The theory developed in the preceding section makes several predictions which are susceptible to empirical test. Consider, first the effects of an environmental change which reduces effective fecundity ($B_i = c_i m_i$) per unit reproductive expenditure by a multiplicative constant. In this case, Schaffer (1974a) showed that the optimal expenditure at all age classes will be reduced and the optimal age of sexual maturity will consequently be delayed (Fig. 5a). Conversely, a similar reduction in survivorship per unit expenditure will select for increased reproductive expenditure and an earlier age of first breeding (Fig. 5b). Reducing the rate at which fecundity increases with age as a result of growth has the same effect.

Schaffer & Elson (1975) tested these predictions using data for populations of Atlantic salmon, Salmo salar L., spawning in various rivers of eastern North America.[a] These authors considered three environmental

[a] By way of reminder, we recall that most populations of Atlantic salmon are anadromous. Spawning occurs in freshwater streams where the young (fry and parr) grow to the smolt stage. The adult phase of the life cycle is spent at sea where the fish grow more rapidly. Unlike Pacific salmon, of the genus Oncorhynchus, Atlantic salmon do not necessarily die after spawning although post-spawning mortality is often high (Belding, 1934b). Evidence, suggesting that local populations are at least partly isolated from each other genetically, is summarized by Schaffer & Elson (1975).

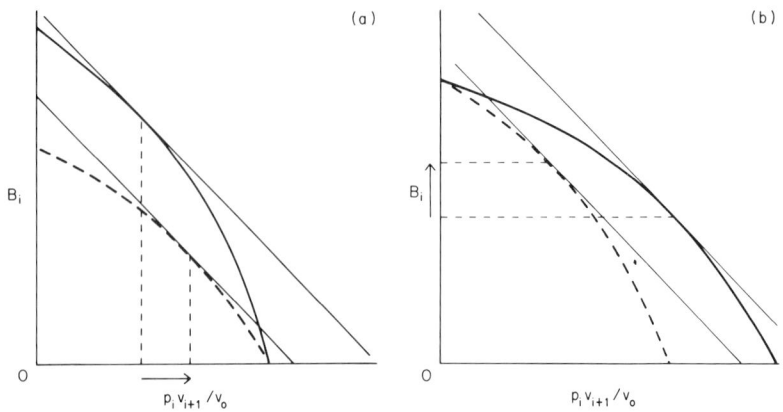

FIG. 5. Selective consequences of reducing fecundity per unit effort and post-breeding survival þer unit effort by a multiplicative constant. In the first case, the optimal expenditure is reduced; in the second, increased.

variables
1. the length of the river;
2. the rate at which fish from different rivers increased in weight while at sea and
3. the intensity of coastal and estuarine fishing.
In terms of the preceding theory, they predicted
1. that increased river length should select for delayed maturity—since the extra fuel consumed during migration would reduce fecundity per unit effort;
2. that increased growth at sea would have the same effect, by virtue of increasing the benefits derived from spending additional years feeding in the ocean and
3. that increased fishing pressure would select for an earlier age of return, since the fishery selectively takes the larger (= older) fish.

In general the available data support the predictions. Figure 6 illustrates the way in which the mean weight, Wt, of angled fish varies with the length of the river from which the fish were taken. For those rivers (10) for which both types of data were available, Schaffer & Elson (1975) showed that the mean weight of angled fish was significantly correlated ($r = 0.91$) with the average sea age at first spawning. Notice that, whereas Wt increases with river length in all four regions, the slope of the regression line and the closeness of fit vary from region to region. Not surprisingly, the importance of river length is greatest in regions of low fishing pressure and high growth rates at sea (Figs 7 and 8).[a] Figure 9

[a] The rivers of Newfoundland, whose fish experience the lowest growth rates at sea, show no correlation between river-length and weight.

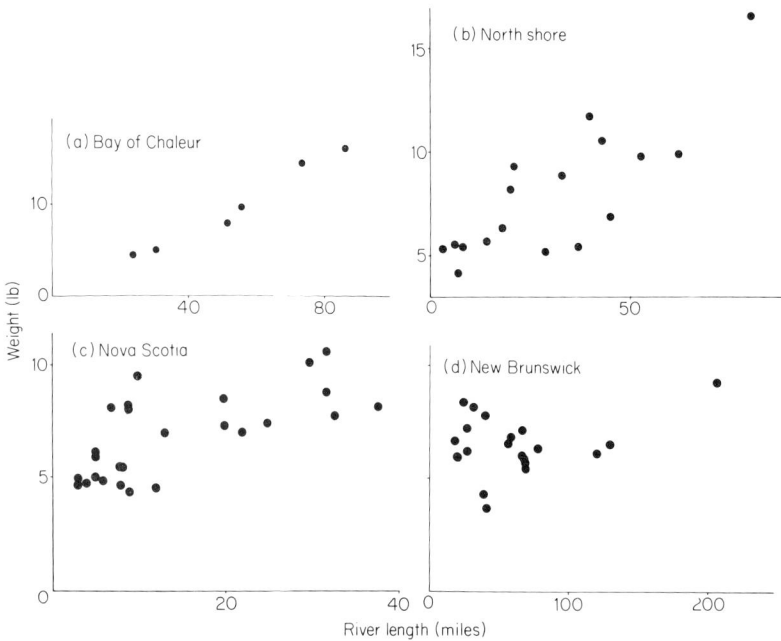

FIG 6. The mean weight of angled fish plotted against river length for four regions: (a) Bay of Chaleur (1949–60). $r = 0.98$; $P(r) < 0.001$. Slope of regression line, $m = 0.20$ lb mile^{-1}. (b) North Shore of Gulf of St. Lawrence (1964–69). $r = 0.87$; $P(r) < 0.001$; $m = 0.14$ lb mile^{-1}. (c) Nova Scotia (1949–60). $r - 0.69$; $P(r) < 0.001$; $m = 0.12$ lb mile^{-1}. (d) New Brunswick (1949–60). $r = 0.29$; $P(r) > 0.10$; $m = 0.01$ lb mile^{-1}. Data from Schaffer & Elson (1975).

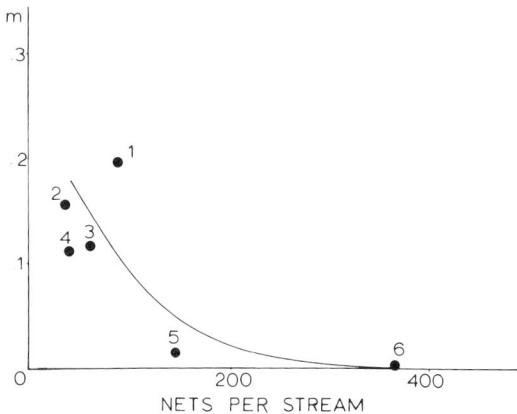

FIG. 7 Slope, m, of regression line: mean weight angled fish versus river length plotted against the number of estuarine nets for six regions: (1) Bay of Chaleur; (2) South Gaspé (Québec); (3) North Shore Gulf of St. Lawrence; (4) Nova Scotia; (5) St. John river system (New Brunswick); (6) Miramichi river system (New Brunswick). From Schaffer & Elson (1975).

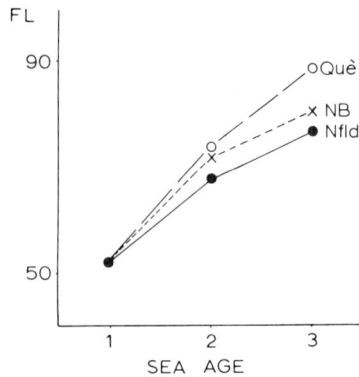

FIG. 8. Fork length (FL) versus sea age for rivers of different regions. Slopes of regression lines are—Québec, $18 \cdot 5$ cm year^{-1}; New Brunswick, $14 \cdot 8$; Newfoundland, 12.5. New Brunswick measurements adjusted to grilse fork length—52 cm by subtracting 2 cm from average fork length of each age class. From Schaffer & Elson (1975).

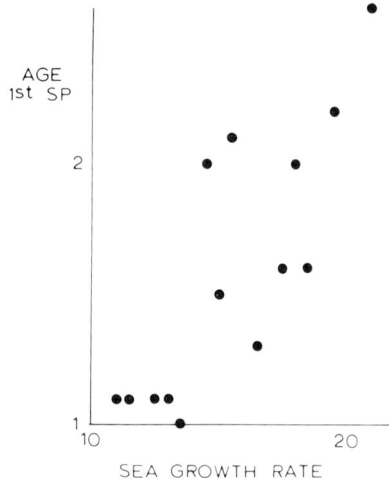

FIG 9. Mean age first spawning (SP) plotted against rate of sea growth (m) after the grilse stage; $r = 0 \cdot 81$; $P(r) < 0 \cdot 001$. From Schaffer & Elson (1975).

shows directly the effect of increasing growth rates in the ocean on the age of first spawning. For rivers for which the data were available, the effects of all three variables are summarized in Table I.

Schaffer & Elson (1975) also showed that delayed reproduction was associated with an increasing propensity of repeat-spawners to spend one or more complete summers at sea between spawning migrations, and further that the loss of growth due to spawning appeared to be greater on long rivers.

TABLE I

Correlation of mean weight of angled fish with river length, sea growth and number of commercial nets

| Sample | Sample size | F-value | River length | | | Sea growth | | | No. of commercial nets | | | Total Proportion var. determined |
			Regr. coef.	Partial corr. coef.	Proportion cum. var.	Regr. coef.	Partial corr. coef.	Proportion cum. var.	Regr. coef.	Partial corr. coef.	Proportion cum. var.	
Excluding Newfoundland	11†	7·21*	0·004	0·538§	0·07	0·11	0·77*	0·49	−0·002	−0·67*	0·20	0·76
Total	14‡	9·68*	0·001	0·15	0·12	0·13	0·77*	0·52	—‖	—‖	—‖	0·64

From Schaffer & Elson (1975).
* Significant at 0·05 level (one-sided).
† Rivers—Moise, P. Saguenay, Ste. Marguerite, Port Daniel, Big Salmon, St. John, NW Miramichi, West, Naraguagas, St. Jean, Mingan.
‡ The above plus Exploits, Sandhill, and L. Rattling Brook in Newfoundland.
§ $P(t) < 0.10$, one-sided.
‖ Bivariate analysis, fishing pressure for Newfoundland unavailable.

OTHER POTENTIAL APPLICATIONS OF LIFE-HISTORY THEORY TO SALMON PHENOLOGY

Differences in Age of First Return Between Males and Females

One of the more interesting patterns of life-history variation in Atlantic salmon not considered by Schaffer & Elson (1975) is the observation that in any particular river the average age of first return among males is usually less than that of females (Table II). In terms of the preceding

TABLE II

*Variation in age of first spawning among male and female Atlantic salmon**

| N | \multicolumn{5}{c}{Sea age} |
	1	2	3	4	$\bar{x}$
NW Miramichi (1968)†					
Males 268	0·95	0·05	—	—	1·05
Females 126	0·31	0·60	0·02	0·06	1·81
St. John (1970)‡					
Males 447	0·90	0·09	0·01	—	1·11
Females 433	0·38	0·61	0·02	—	1·66
Big Salmon (1968)‡					
Males 290	0·92	0·07	0·01	—	1·09
Females 723	0·86	0·12	0·02	—	1·16
P. Saguenay (1967–69)§					
Males 105	0·62	0·29	0·10	—	1·50
Females 126	0·44	0·40	0·17	—	1·75
Ungava Rivers (1956–60)‖					
Males 107	0·31	0·69	—	—	1·69
Females 282	0·01	0·99	—	—	1·99

* Virgin fish plus repeat spawners for which the age of first spawning is known.
† Counted at Curventon Fence. Data courtesy of P. F. Elson, Dept Environment, Fisheries Research Board of Canada, St. Andrews, N. B.
‡ Data courtesy of D. B. Lister and K. Smith, Dept. Environment, Resource Development Branch, Halifax, N. S.
§ Data courtesy of A. Ducharme, Dept. Tourism, Fish and Game, Fish and Game Branch, Québec, P. Q.
‖ Data for George, Whale and Koksoak Rivers, from Power (1969).

theory, one would expect such a state of affairs if fecundity increased more rapidly with sea age in females than in males. Regarding females, it is well known that egg count increases with size (and therefore sea age). Large males may also have an advantage both in terms of increased milt production and likelihood of pairing with a large female (e.g. Belding, 1934a; Jones, 1959). On the other hand, it is commonly observed that a mating pair of salmon will be joined by smaller "satellite" males, including sexually mature parr all of which dart in at the last moment and deposit their milt (Jones, 1949). Presumably the satellite males (sometimes? often?) fertilize at least a fraction of the eggs, thus tempering the rate at which male fecundity would otherwise increase with age, and selecting for an earlier age of first return.

Life in the River

As with any theory, the preceding mathematics constitute a drastic simplification of reality. In particular, our model life history (Fig. 1), having been devised to caricature a variety of organisms, says nothing about the salmon's life in the river before going to sea. A more realistic model is shown in Fig. 10. Here, the x's are the numbers of individuals of

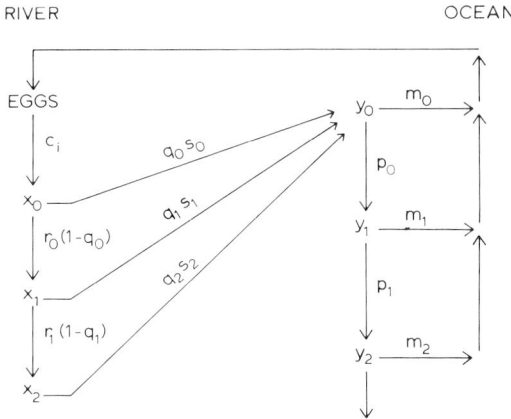

FIG. 10. Schematic representation of an anadromous life history. x_i is the number of parr of river age i. Of these, q_i go to sea. The remainder survive in the river to age $i + 1$ at rate r_i. Of those going to sea s_i survive to the spawning season in their first year of sea life. Fish of sea age i, y_i, reproduce at rate m_i and survive spawning at rate p_i. The fraction of eggs (produced by adults of age i) which survive to be counted in their first summer is c_i. Notice that provision in this model has not been made for reproduction of sexually mature male parr.

river age i, while the y's are the number of fish of sea age j. The r's, s's and p's give probabilities of survival (in the river, during the migration from river to ocean, and at sea). Finally, q_i is the fraction of parr of age i that become smolts and go to sea in that year. Thus, neglecting reproduction by precocious male parr, we have for the river

$$x_0(t+1) = \sum_0^{w_s} B_i y_i(t) \tag{15a}$$

$$x_i(t+1) = r_{i-1}(1 - q_{i-1})x_{i-1}(t), \qquad i > 0 \tag{15b}$$

while for the ocean

$$y_0(t+1) = \sum_0^{w_r} q_i s_i x_i(t) \tag{16a}$$

$$y_i(t+1) = p_{i-1} y_{i-1}(t), \qquad i > 0. \tag{16b}$$

An interesting question to ask is the way in which the q's should change in response to changes in the environment. To answer this question, we note that the rate of population growth, λ_1 is now the dominant root of the equation

$$1 = \left(\frac{B_0}{\lambda} + \frac{p_0 B_0}{\lambda_2} + \cdots \right) \left(\frac{q_0 s_0}{\lambda} + \frac{r_0(1-q_0)q_1 s_1}{\lambda_2} + \cdots \right). \tag{17}$$

If we differentiate this expression with respect to q_i, we obtain

$$\frac{d\lambda_1}{dq_i} \propto \left\{ s_i - \left[\frac{r_i q_{i+1} s_{i+1}}{\lambda} + \frac{r_i r_{i+1}(1-q_{i+1})q_{i+2}s_{i+2}, \ldots}{\lambda^2} \right] \right\}. \tag{18}$$

Hence, parr should go to sea at age i if

$$s_i > \max \{(R_j s_j \lambda^{i-j}/R_i)\}, \qquad j > i. \tag{19}$$

Here

$$R_j = \prod_0^{j-1} r_k$$

and the symbol $\max\{ \ \}$ is to be read the product $(R_j s_j \lambda^{i-j}/R_i)$ of greatest value. Since s_i depends positively on the size of seaward migrating smolts (Lindroth, 1965), this result is consistent with the observation that the age of smolts in North America increases with increasing latitude and reduced growth rates in the river—a result of colder temperatures (Elson, 1957; Power, 1969).

Notice that increased growth rates in the river, all else being equal, will also select for a reduced number of years spent in the ocean before the adults return to spawn. This is because fecundity per unit expenditure is increased for all age classes, thus favoring higher reproductive output at an earlier age. In this regard, Schiefer (1971) has suggested, for several rivers on the North Shore of the Gulf of St. Lawrence, that fast growing parr are more likely to return and spawn as grilse than their slower growing contemporaries. This situation is expected to hold within rivers or between similar streams and should not be confused with the results obtained by Schaffer & Elson (1975) who considered a large number of very different rivers.

"Big Bang" Reproduction versus Iteroparity

Atlantic salmon do not necessarily die after spawning. Indeed, on "easy" rivers, fish have been caught on their fifth and sixth spawning runs. By way of contrast, Pacific salmon (*Oncorhynchus*) almost always die after spawning. At present, the adaptive significance of this variation remains obscure. Certainly, it is not a matter of Pacific salmon having to make a more arduous upstream migration. Granted the demands of the Fraser, Columbia and other famous rivers of Western North America, Pacific salmon also spawn (and die) in the myriad shorter rivers along the coast. And steelhead trout *Salmo gairdneri* Richardson, which, like Atlantic salmon, are iteroparous, once penetrated far up the River Snake. These observations leave two possibilities.

1. Differences in physiology between the two genera make for concave trade-offs in *Oncorhynchus* and convex ones in *Salmo* (compare Figs 4a and 4b).
2. In both genera, the trade-off is concave-convex. In this case (Fig. 4d), iteroparity and semelparity correspond to alternative local optima, and the difference between the two genera is an historical one.

RELEVANCE OF THE PRESENT TREATMENT TO THE THEORY OF *r*- VERSUS *K*-SELECTION

At the same time that models of optimal life histories were being explored, other theorists (e.g. MacArthur & Wilson, 1967; Gadgil & Solbrig, 1972; Pianka, 1970; Roughgarden, 1971) were developing the theory of *r*- versus *K*- selection. This theory stems from the observation that, if populations are at carrying capacity, K, selection will act to increase equilibrium numbers (MacArthur, 1962), even at the expense of reducing the population's rate of increase when rare. Specifically, suppose that

$$\frac{dN}{dt} = rN(1 - N/K).$$

We compare the selective advantages s_r and s_K of mutants having higher values of r and K. Thus

$$s_r = \varepsilon r(1 - \bar{N}/K)$$

and

$$s_K = \varepsilon r(\bar{N}/K).$$

Here $\bar{N}$ is the population's average size and ε the units of evolutionary change, assumed equal, in r and K. Mutations resulting in improved r are thus more likely to be favored by selection when $\bar{N}/K$ is low and vice versa for mutations resulting in higher K. Furthermore, since increasing the amount of environmental instability will often reduce $\bar{N}/K$ (Levins, 1969), we expect increased *r*-selection in uncertain environments.

There is nothing in this argument with which one can take issue, since, when put in this fashion, the theory boils down to the statement that selection will act to improve $r(N) = (1/N)(dN/dt)$ in the vicinity of average numbers. The problem comes when one attempts to associate specific life history attributes with one selective regime or another. To assert, for example, that increasing average crowding necessarily selects for reduced reproductive expenditures can only be justified if crowding can be shown to primarily reduce fecundity or the survival of young of the year. Similarly, reductions in $\bar{N}/K$, whether the result of constant or fluctuating rates of density-independent mortality, will only select for increased reproduction if this mortality principally affects adults (see Schaffer, 1974b). The generalizations of the r-, K-literature fail logically because r is not justifiably equated with reproduction nor K with post-breeding survival. Rather, r and K are functions of both variables which, together with density, enter into the equation specifying λ_1 (Schaffer & Tamarin, 1973). Any theory of optimal reproductive expenditures, no matter how simplified, has at its heart the notion of a trade-off between current and future reproduction. But this amount of detail is not built into the theory of r- versus K-selection, which cannot therefore be properly applied to the problem of predicting the evolution of a species' life table. Other authors, e.g. Wilbur, Tinkle & Collins (1974), have come to the same conclusion on empirical grounds.

ACKNOWLEDGEMENTS

It is a pleasure to acknowledge the assistance of Paul Elson, with whom I collaborated during the course of the salmon study, and also that of Robert MacArthur, Egbert Leigh, and Henry Horn, under whose tutelage much of the work reported here was carried out. Discussions with Mike Rosenzweig contributed materially to my understanding of life history evolution. Figures 1, 4, 6, 7, 8, and 9 and Table I were reprinted from *Ecology*, **56** and **58**, Copyright 1975 and 1977 by the Ecological Society of America, with their permission. W. A. Cornell prepared Figs 2, 3, 5, and 10.

REFERENCES

Belding, D. I. (1934a). The spawning habits of Atlantic salmon. *Trans. Am. Fish. Soc.* **64**: 211–216.

Belding, D. I. (1934b). The cause of high mortality in Atlantic salmon after spawning. *Trans. Am. Fish. Soc.* **64**: 219–224.

Caswell, H. (1979). A general formula for the sensitivity of population growth rate to changes in life history parameters. *Theoret. Pop. Biol.* **14**: 215–230.

Caswell, H. (In press). On the equivalence of maximizing reproductive value and maximizing fitness. *Ecology*.

Charlesworth, B. (1973). Selection in populations with overlapping generations. V. Natural selection and life histories. *Am. Nat.* **107**: 303–311.

Charlesworth, B. & Williamson, J. A. (1975). The probability of survival of a mutant gene in an age-structured population and implications for the evolution of life-histories. *Genet. Res. Camb.* **26**: 1–10.

Cole, L. C. (1954). The population consequences of life history phenomena. *Q. Rev. Biol.* **29**: 103–137.

Crow, J. F. & Kimura, M. (1970). *An introduction to population genetics theory.* New York: Harper and Row.

Elson, P. F. (1957). The importance of size in the change from parr to smolt in Atlantic salmon. *Can. Fish Cult.* **21**: 1–6.

Emlen, J. M. (1970). Age-specificity and ecological theory. *Ecology* **51**: 588–601.

Fisher, R. A. (1958). *The genetical theory of natural selection.* New York: Dover Publ. (First published by Oxford Clarendon Press, 1930).

Franklin, J. N. (1968). *Matrix theory.* Englewood Cliffs, N. J.: Prentice Hall.

Gadgil, M. & Bossert, W. (1970). Life historical consequences of natural selection. *Am. Nat.* **104**: 1–24.

Gadgil, M. & Solbrig, O. T. (1972). The concept of r- and K-selection: evidence from wild flowers and some theoretical considerations. *Am. Nat.* **106**: 14–31.

Hamilton, W. D. (1966). The moulding of senescence by natural selection. *J. theoret. Biol.* **12**: 12–45.

Jones, J. W. (1949). Studies of the scales of young salmon *Salmo salar*. L. (juv.) in relation to growth, migration and spawning. *Fish. Invest., Lond.* **5**: 1–23.

Jones, J. W. (1959). *The salmon.* New York: Harper & Bros.

Leslie, P. H. (1945). On the use of matrices in certain population mathematics. *Biometrika* **35**: 213–245.

Levins, R. (1969). The effect of random variations of different types of population growth. *Proc. natn. Acad. Sci. U.S.A.* **62**: 1061–1065.

Lindroth, A. (1965). The Baltic salmon stock. Its natural and artificial regulation. *Mitt. Int. Ver. Limnol.* **13**: 163–192.

MacArthur, R. H. (1962). Some generalized theorems of natural selection. *Proc. natn. Acad. Sci. U.S.A.* **48**: 1893–1897.

MacArthur, R. H. & Wilson, E. O. (1967). *Theory of island biogeography.* Princeton, N.J.: Princeton Univ. Press.

Pianka, E. R. (1970). On "r" and "K" selection. *Am. Nat.* **104**: 592–597.

Power, G. (1969). The salmon of Ungava Bay. *Tech. Pap. Arct. Inst. N. Am.* No. 22: 1–72.

Roughgarden, J. (1971). Density-dependent natural selection. *Ecology* **52**: 453–468.

Schaffer, W. M. (1974a). Selection for optimal life histories: The effects of age structure. *Ecology* **55**: 291–303.

Schaffer, W. M. (1974b). Optimal reproductive effort in fluctuating environments. *Am. Nat.* **108**: 783–790.

Schaffer, W. M. & Elson, P. F. (1975). The adaptive significance of variations in life history among local populations in North America. *Ecology* **56**: 577–590.

Schaffer, W. M. & Gadgil, M. D. (1975). Selection for optimal life histories in plants. In *Ecology and evolution of communities*: 142–157. Cody, M. L. & Diamond, J. M. (eds). Cambridge, Mass.: Belknap Press.

Schaffer, W. M. & Rosenzweig, M. L. (1977). Selection for optimal life histories II: multiple equilibria and the evolution of alternative reproductive strategies. *Ecology* **58**: 60–72.

Schaffer, W. M. & Tamarin, R. H. (1973). Changing reproductive rates and population cycles in lemmings and voles. *Evolution* **27**: 114–125.

Schiefer, K. (1971). *Ecology of Atlantic salmon, with special reference to occurrence and abundance of grilse, in North Shore Gulf of St. Lawrence rivers.* Ph.D. Thesis: Univ. Waterloo, Ontario.

Taylor, H. M., Gourley, R. S., Lawrence, C. E. & Kaplan, R. S. (1974). Natural selection of life history attributes: an analytical approach. *Theoret. Pop. Biol.* **5**: 104–122.

Wilbur, H. M., Tinkle, D. W. & Collins, J. P. (1974). Environmental certainty, trophic level, and resource availability in life history evolution. *Am. Nat.* **108**: 805–817.

Williams, G. C. (1966). Natural selection, the costs of reproduction and a refinement of Lack's principle. *Am. Nat.* **100**: 687–690.

Symp. zool. Soc. Lond. (1979), No. 44, 327–359

Lifestyle and Phenology in Deep Sea Anacanthine Teleosts

J. D. M. GORDON

Scottish Marine Biological Association,

Dunstaffnage Marine Research Laboratory, Oban, Argyll, Scotland

SYNOPSIS

The phylogeny of the order Anacanthini and especially of the deep sea families Macrouridae and Moridae is briefly discussed and the current status of the fishery for macrourids is reviewed. Their lifestyle and phenology are considered in relation to age, growth, reproduction and feeding. Information on seasonal aspects of the biology of deep sea organisms is sparse and in this paper the published work is supplemented with some new data from a seasonal survey of slope-dwelling fish from the west of Scotland.

There is increasing evidence that, at least on the continental slopes at depths down to about 2000 m and in temperate latitudes, macrourids and morids exhibit many of the seasonal characteristics of shelf-dwelling species, such as changes in growth rate, well-defined reproductive cycles and seasonal variations in the intensity of feeding. In shallow waters, periodicity of growth and reproduction depends ultimately on the often complex interaction of changing environmental factors such as photoperiod, temperature and food supply. The relevance of these parameters to the deep sea environment is discussed and it is concluded that seasonal changes in food supply must be of prime importance. The possible mechanisms whereby energy from the euphotic zone is transmitted to the deep sea are considered.

INTRODUCTION

The phylogeny of the order Anacanthini (Gadiformes) has been discussed by, amongst others, Svetovidov (1948), Okamura (1970) and Marshall & Cohen (1973). Although there are differences of opinion on the status of some of the families there is general agreement on the family status of the Macrouridae and Moridae (Eretmophoridae). Unlike the commercially important Gadidae, which predominate in the shallow waters of the shelf, all the species of the Macrouridae and Moridae are deep sea dwellers.

In this paper, the term deep sea is used to include all species habitually living below a depth of about 500 m on the continental slope and rise and in abyssal depths.

Lepidion eques (Günther) and *Antimora rostrata* Günther are the only members of the Moridae included in this review; all the other species belong to the Macrouridae, the systematics of which have been discussed by Marshall (1973a), Okamura (1970) and Iwamoto & Stein (1974). The latter authors have proposed that the genera *Coryphaenoides*, *Nema-tonurus*, *Chalinura*, *Lionurus*, *Macrourus* and *Hyomacrurus* may eventually be accorded subgeneric status within the genus *Coryphaenoides*. Many of the species discussed below belong to this complex and, unless otherwise specified, the nomenclature follows that used by Marshall (1973a, b) for the Macrouridae and Cohen (1973) for the Moridae.

Since 1975, the Scottish Marine Biological Association at Oban has been investigating seasonal aspects of the biology of slope-dwelling fish from depths of 500 to 2000 m to the west of Scotland (56–57°N 9–11°W). The programme is continuing and the results presented in this paper are of a preliminary nature.

The status of the world-wide fishery for macrourids and morids has been reviewed by Suda (1973). Moiseev (1973) estimated that the world catch of macrourids increased from 0·1 to 0·3 million tonnes between 1966 and 1970 and has predicted that this could increase to 1·0 million tonnes annually. The FAO Yearbook of Fisheries Statistics for 1975 gives the total catch of macrourids for that year as slightly in excess of 100 000 tonnes but this is an underestimate since, in many cases, macrourid catches are included under the general heading of Gadiformes. The fishery for *Coryphaenoides rupestris* Gunnerus in the north Atlantic is now well established (Fig. 1). The main fishery is conducted by the USSR on the slopes off North Newfoundland, Labrador and Iceland. Parsons (1976) considered that stocks off Newfoundland and Labrador were fully

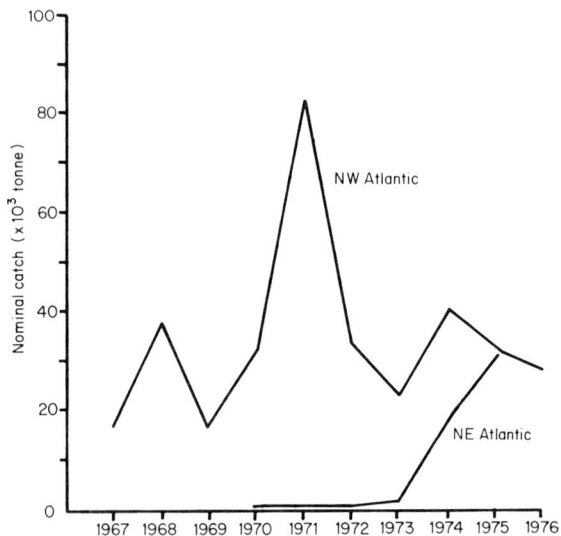

FIG. 1. The nominal catch (tonnes) of *Coryphaenoides rupestris* from the northwest Atlantic (ICNAF area) and the northeast Atlantic (ICES area). The data are from the ICNAF Statistical Bulletin for 1976 and the FAO Year Book of Fishery Statistics for 1975.

exploited and a preliminary estimate of the maximum sustainable yield had been put at between 24 000 and 37 000 tonnes. A quota system has been in operation since 1974 and this has increased from 32 000 to 43 000 tonnes in 1977. The importance of the macrourid fishery to the other deep water fisheries in the north Atlantic is discussed by Pechenik & Troyanovskii (1970) and Stanek (1971).

AGE AND GROWTH

Age

Introduction

The theoretical basis of age determination by growth rings on the scales, otoliths and other hard tissues of fish has been adequately reviewed by Bilton (1974), Liew (1974), Pannella (1974) Simkiss (1974) and Ottaway & Simkiss (1977a, b). It is fundamental to the technique that scale or otolith growth should be correlated with body growth and this has recently been convincingly demonstrated in the roach, *Rutilus rutilus* L., by Ottaway & Simkiss (1977a). The precise physiological basis of the correlation remains obscure but fluctuating levels of growth hormone have been implicated (Swift & Pickford, 1965; Ball, 1969; Simkiss, 1974). The growth rate and, consequently, the formation of annual rings on the scales and otoliths of shallow water fish in temperate waters is influenced by the seasonal variations in the environment. In the comparatively stable environment of parts of the tropics or the deep sea, growth rates might be expected to remain constant and no annual rings would be present.

Information on the age and longevity of deep sea animals is extremely sparse. In shallow waters, age determination of invertebrates by examination of growth rings on hard parts is limited to a few groups such as the molluscs. Recently, Turekian *et al.* (1975) have used radiometric techniques to age a population of a deep sea clam, *Tindaria callistiformis*, Verrill & Bush and tentatively suggest that bands on the shell are produced annually. If this is substantiated then the species reaches an age at first maturity of 50–60 years and lives to an age of about 100. Mauchline (1972) has predicted that the longevity of bathypelagic crustacea can be up to seven times that of epipelagic species by using a technique of extrapolating from the known growth rates of epipelagic species after making an allowance for slower growth due to lower temperature and decreased food availability in the bathypelagic zone.

Compared with those applied to invertebrates, techniques for ageing fish are well established and it is surprising that little work has been done on deep sea fish. In the mesopelagic and bathypelagic zones, Kulikova (1957), Halliday (1970) and Gjosaeter (1973) have aged myctophids by means of their otoliths. In the benthopelagic and benthic zones, only some macrourid species have been aged. The macrourid fishes have probably received most attention because of their abundance and their potential commercial importance.

Review of published work

Murray & Hjort (1912) were the first to notice that the scales of *Nematonurus armatus* (Hector) and *Bathygadus melanobranchus* Vaillant, caught by the *Michael Sars* at depths of 3120 and 1365 m respectively, had a ring structure. Farran (1924) gives ring counts and measurements from the scales of several species of macrourids from the west of Ireland but did not feel justified in drawing any definite conclusions regarding the age of the fish from his observations. Rannou (1975) has found rings on the otoliths of *Coryphaenoides guentheri* (Vaillant), *Chalinura leptolepis* (Günther) and *Nematonurus armatus*, all Macrouridae, and also in *Antimora rostrata* (Eretmophoridae), *Bathysaurus mollis* Günther (Bathysauridae) and *Histiobranchus bathybius* (Günther) (Synaphobranchidae). These fish were obtained from the Golfe de Gascogne in the north east Atlantic at depths ranging from 1800 to 4700 m.

Kulikova (1957) has used scales to age small samples of four Pacific species of *Coryphaenoides*. She found the greatest age of eight years in *Coryphaenoides pectoralis* (Gilbert) and the mean length of the eight-year-old fish was 96 cm. Novikov (1970), in a detailed study of *Chalinura pectoralis*[a] from the northern Pacific, aged a large number of specimens and concluded that this species lives for 15 to 17 years. The discrepancy between the results of Kulikova and Novikov may have arisen because of differences on the interpretation of which rings were the true annual rings. Common methods of establishing whether rings on a scale or other hard part are annual involve tagging or marking experiments and rearing experiments, none of which is appropriate to the deep sea.

Another method is to study the outer edge of a scale or otolith and determine whether there is a seasonal variation in the distribution of hyaline and opaque edges. This latter technique was used by Motais (1960) in a study of the otoliths of *Trachyrhynchus trachyrhynchus* (Risso) from the Mediterranean (700–1100 m). He found opaque edges in June and July and hyaline edges in November and December and concluded that growth occurred between June and November. Motais was able to show that there was a seasonal change in the phosphatase activity of the large rostral scales of this species which he attributed to growth. The phosphatase activity began to increase in May, reached a peak in July, and decreased until October. Motais was unable to compile a complete growth curve for this species because his fish were caught by long lines which were highly selective for fish in the 31 to 43-cm size range and only represented the III to VIII year-classes.

[a] A synonym for *Coryphaenoides* (*Nematonurus*) *pectoralis*, according to Iwamoto & Stein (1974).

The length-frequency (Petersen) method of age determination can often be used to separate the youngest age-groups of a fish population. Crespo, Rey & Caminas (1976) found that a population of *Trachyrhynchus trachyrhynchus* from the Mediterranean could be separated into two main groups and postulated that the first group, which represented 16% of the population with a length range of 30–35 cm, might represent the O or I group. The next group (83%) would then represent the older fish and had a mean length of 42·8 cm. However, a comparison with the results of Motais (1960), who worked on the same species, suggests that the first group might be the III group. Rannou (1976) has used this method to study a population of *Nezumia sclerorhynchus* (Valenciennes) from the Mediterranean. He measured head length and was able to separate the population into ten length-classes, which he found corresponded very closely with a frequency analysis of the number of rings on the otoliths. He concluded that the rings were a measure of relative age and might represent the spawning seasons. The length-frequency method may therefore be useful in determining whether the rings are annual, at least for the younger fish, but, before it can be used successfully, an unbiassed sample of the whole population must be obtained. The collection of unbiassed samples must take into account the complex separation of size groups and sexes by depth which has been observed in some macrourids and morids (p. 339).

The developing fishery for *Coryphaenoides rupestris*[a] in the north Atlantic has resulted in a number of studies of the age structure and growth of these populations. Savvatimskii (1969, 1971, 1972) attempted to age this species by conventional methods without success. He was able to demonstrate a clear ring structure in the outer edges in 10-μm sections of decalcified otoliths but the central portion was missing and the age could not be determined. He then adopted the method first used by Farran (1924) and examined the scales by polarized light. By this method, he was able to assign an age to the fish but his criterion for the validity of the method is not apparent in his papers. He found that this species can live to a great age; a female of 104 cm from Icelandic waters was 27 years old. Most of the specimens from which his growth curves were compiled ranged from 31 to 88 cm and were from three to 19 years old. Similar results were obtained by Kosswig (1974).

A new approach to ageing this species by otoliths has been described by Koch (1976). The otoliths were stored in formalin (*c.* 4%) and, before use, were briefly immersed in hydrochloric acid. The treated otoliths, when placed under water and illuminated by indirect transmitted light, showed a clear ring structure. He found that this method worked well and was probably easier than scale reading for

---

[a] *Coryphaenoides rupestris* is frequently referred to as *Macrourus rupestris* or *Macrurus rupestris* in the literature (especially Russian). The former name is used exclusively in this paper.

young fish up to 40 cm but later stages became progressively more difficult. He therefore advocated the use of both otoliths and scales for age-determination in *C. rupestris*.

Stanek (1971), quoting unpublished work by Zukowski, indicated that *C. rupestris* of length range 38–90 cm were seven to ten years old, *Macrourus berglax* Lacépède of 33–82 cm were three to 12 years and *Nezumia bairdii* (Goode & Bean) of 24–44 cm were three to seven years old. These fish were all taken from the waters of Labrador and Newfoundland.

Unpublished observations

A large number of otoliths has been collected by myself from benthopelagic species from the continental slope to the west of Scotland (500–2000 m). No ring structures were found in *Aphanopus carbo* Lowe (Trichiuridae) and *Alepocephalus bairdii* Goode & Bean (Alepocephalidae) but all the macrourids so far examined were found to have a ring structure. Only one species, *Coryphaenoides rupestris*, has been studied in detail and it has been possible to assign an age to 79·6% of 760 otoliths examined. The otoliths of young fish, up to about 30 cm, were read by placing them under terpineol in a black dish and illuminating them with direct light. Otoliths from larger fish could not be read in this way even after prolonged soaking in a variety of commonly used solvents. However, the standard technique for ageing gadoid otoliths (Williams & Bedford, 1974), by breaking the otolith and viewing the broken surface with light shone through the side of the otolith, was found to be successful. The appearance of the ring structure on difficult otoliths was often enhanced by gentle burning of the broken surface. As yet, no attempt has been made to verify the annual nature of the rings but it should be possible to study the edge of otoliths of the smallest fish to determine whether the conclusions of Motais (1960) also apply to *C. rupestris*. It was found that *C. rupestris* in this area lives in excess of 30 years which agrees with previous observations on the otoliths (Bridger, 1978).

Discussion

All the macrourid species mentioned above are from temperate latitudes where shelf-dwelling species also have annual rings. It is perhaps significant that Okamura (1970), in his study of the comparative anatomy of the scales of Japanese macrourids, has commented that "annual rings are limited to such northern forms as the fishes of the subgenus *Nematonurus* of *Coryphaenoides* while most of the macrourids which are southern forms lack rings". There is a clear need for studies on the scales and otoliths of tropical macrourids and also those species from temperate latitudes which inhabit the abyssal plains far from any possible seasonal influence of the continental slope.

Electron microscope studies of the otoliths of shallow water temperate and tropical fish have shown that daily, bimonthly and monthly growth patterns are present (Pannella, 1971, 1974). The daily patterns can probably be ultimately related to diurnal effects and it has been proposed that the bimonthly and monthly patterns are a lunar influence. Tidal cycles have been suggested as a cue for the synchronization of endogenous reproductive rhythms in deep sea invertebrates (Rokop, 1974) and deep sea fish may react behaviourally to semi-diurnal tidal currents at depths of 2000 and 4700 m in the Bay of Biscay (Guennegan & Rannou, in prep.). Electron microscope studies of otoliths from macrourids and other deep sea fish may reveal whether lunar cycles are of significance in the deep sea. Rannou & Thiriot–Quievreux (1975) studied the otoliths of *Coryphaenoides guentheri* with a scanning electron microscope and observed "lamelles épaisses" and "lamelles fines".

Growth in Length

Studies of the growth rate of macrourid fish have been limited to the relatively few species which have been aged and the results are summarized in Fig. 2. The curves have been computed from length measurements at known ages by counting the rings but, as yet, no attempt has been made to back-calculate growth rate from the scales or otoliths. Seasonal changes of growth rate are found in shallow water fish, living in temperate regions, but the only evidence to suggest that a similar phenomenon might exist in the deep sea is the statement that "*Chalinura pectoralis* like most shallow water fishes is characterised by distinctly periodic growth which is undoubtedly related to seasonal environmental variations in the sea surface horizons" (Novikov, 1970).

The growth curves shown in Fig. 2 are typical of the form of those for shallow water teleosts; indeed, Novikov (1970) has shown that the growth of *Coryphaenoides pectoralis* is similar to that of halibut, Pacific cod and rockfish from adjacent regions of the shelf. The growth curves, which Kulikova (1957) has obtained for *Coryphaenoides acrolepis* (Bean), *C. pectoralis*, *C. cinereus* (Gilbert) and *C. angustifrons* Rass, are based on small samples and, as noted above, her interpretation of the ring structure of *C. pectoralis* is in doubt. The rapid growth of *C. acrolepis*, if it is substantiated by further work, is more difficult to explain. According to Kulikova, this species dwells in the region of deep ocean trenches and her material was collected at depths of between 1430 and 9900 m. She further states that this species "undertakes considerable vertical migrations, rising to comparatively small depths, 1430 m". Iwamoto & Stein (1974) consider that *C. acrolepis* has a primary depth range of 600–2500 m and that records of capture at greater depths represent mid-water captures while the net was on passage to and from the bottom. They cite further evidence that this species has been caught in several thousands of metres from the bottom and conclude that it is probably a bathypelagic species. Other macrourids have been recorded from considerable depths off the bottom, e.g. *Coryphaenoides rupestris* (Pechenik & Troyanovskii, 1970; Haedrich,

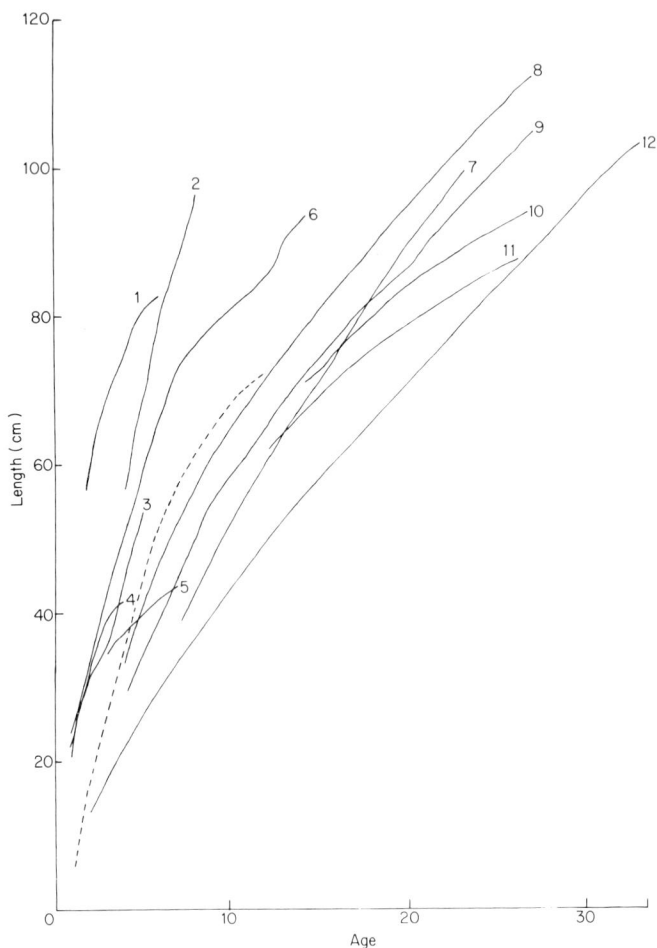

FIG. 2. Growth curves of macrourid fish. 1. *Coryphaenoides acrolepis*. 2. *Coryphaenoides pectoralis*. 3. *Coryphaenoides cinereus*. 4. *Coryphaenoides angustifrons* (Kulikova, 1957). 5. *Trachyrhynchus trachyrhynchus* (Motais, 1960). 6. *Coryphaenoides pectoralis* (Novikov, 1970). 7. *Coryphaenoides rupestris* (Kosswig, 1974). 8. *C. rupestris*, females, N, Newfoundland. 9. *C. rupestris*, male, N, Newfoundland. 10. *C. rupestris*, female, Iceland. 11. *C. rupestris*, male, Iceland (Savvatimskii, 1971). 12. *C. rupestris*, west of Scotland (Gordon, unpublished). The dashed line is the growth curve for Labrador/Newfoundland cod (Clayden, 1972).

1974), *C. pectoralis* (Novikov, 1970), and, by inference from stomach contents, *C. armatus* (Hector) (Haedrich & Henderson, 1974).

If *C. acrolepis* is primarily a bathypelagic species, then it is possible that this lifestyle might account for its rapid growth and shorter life span. It does not, however, have any of the characteristic morphological adaptations to the bathypelagic mode of life such as are evident in the truly bathypelagic macrourid genera *Cynomacrurus* and *Odontomacrurus* (Marshall, 1973a) and nothing is known of the age and growth of these species.

As a general rule, female teleosts grow faster than males and this also appears to be true for the macrourids (Novikov, 1970; Savvatimskii, 1971). Differences in growth rates between areas are well known in shallow water teleosts and can be attributed to a number of physical, biological or genetic factors. Similar differences have been found in *Coryphaenoides rupestris* (Savvatimskii, 1971) and *C. pectoralis* (Novikov, 1970). The differences in growth rate in the former have been attributed to genetics and in the latter to food availability.

Growth of Body Parts (Excluding Gonads)

Motais (1960) has shown that the relationship between rostral length and total length of *Trachyrhynchus trachyrhynchus* differs between age-groups and also between sexes after the age of first maturity. The rostrum of *Coryphaenoides armatus* becomes blunter, broader and shorter with increasing length (Iwamoto & Stein, 1974), and McLellan (1977) has proposed that this is an ontogenetic adaptation to a change in feeding habit.

Seasonal changes in the ratio of liver weight to body weight have been demonstrated in *Trachyrhynchus trachyrhynchus* (Motais, 1960) and *Coryphaenoides rupestris* (Podrazhanskaya, 1967, 1971; Savvatimskii, 1969). The seasonality has been attributed to endocrine cycles in *T. trachyrhynchus* and to changes in the intensity of feeding in *C. rupestris*.

Length/Weight Relationship

There have been very few studies of the length/weight relationship of deep sea anacanthine fishes. The published data, together with some unpublished results for fish from the west of Scotland slope, are given in Table I. A graph of the length/weight relationship of *Coryphaenoides carapinus* (Goode & Bean) is given by Haedrich & Polloni (1976). Female *Coryphaenoides rupestris* have a greater weight for a given length than the males (Savvatimskii, 1969). Savvatimskii also showed that there was no significant difference in the length/weight relationship of *C. rupestris* from different areas of the northwest Atlantic but that there was a significant difference between fish from the northwest Atlantic and from Icelandic waters, the latter being almost twice the weight for a given

TABLE I

The length/weight relationships of macrourid and morid fish (total length, cm; weight, mg)

Species	Length/weight relationship	Number of fish	Length range (cm)	Area	Reference
Coelorhynchus coelorhynchus	$W = 0{\cdot}00056L^{3{\cdot}5808}$	79	23–43	NE Atlantic	Gordon (New data)
Coelorhynchus occa	$W = 0{\cdot}00187L^{3{\cdot}1437}$	73	10–34	NE Atlantic	Gordon (New data)
Coryphaenoides armatus*	$W = 18{\cdot}7L - 0{\cdot}15L^2 + 0{\cdot}0005L^3 - 728$	79	c. 6–22	W Atlantic	Haedrich & Henderson (1974)
Coryphaenoides rupestris	$W = 0{\cdot}00491L^{2{\cdot}7979}$	1193	7–100	NE Atlantic	Gordon (New data)
Coryphaenoides rupestris—male	$W = 351{\cdot}98 - 14{\cdot}34L + 0{\cdot}28L^2$	—	c. 43–87	NW Atlantic	Savvatimskii (1969)
Coryphaenoides rupestris—female	$W = 587{\cdot}81 + 12{\cdot}54L + 0{\cdot}11L^2$	—	c. 43–85	NW Atlantic	Savvatimskii (1969)
Coryphaenoides rupestris—male	$W = 507{\cdot}515 - 2{\cdot}78L + 0{\cdot}16L^2$	—	c. 56–95	NE Atlantic	Savvatimskii (1969)
Coryphaenoides rupestris—female	$W = 1567{\cdot}45 - 32{\cdot}10L + 0{\cdot}395L^2$	—	c. 56–103	NE Atlantic	Savvatimskii (1969)
Nezumia aequalis	$W = 0{\cdot}00113L^{3{\cdot}3013}$	322	8–35	NE Atlantic	Gordon (New data)
Trachyrhynchus murrayi	$W = 0{\cdot}00062L^{3{\cdot}4566}$	174	10–45	NE Atlantic	Gordon (New data)
Trachyrhynchus trachyrhynchus	$W = 0{\cdot}000998L^{3{\cdot}589}$	99	14–50	Mediterranean	Crespo et al. (1976)
Halargyreus johnsonii	$W = 0{\cdot}00393L^{3{\cdot}2017}$	207	11–31	NE Atlantic	Gordon (New data)
Lepidion eques	$W = 0{\cdot}00068L^{3{\cdot}7579}$	509	8–36	NE Atlantic	Gordon (New data)

length. He uses this as evidence that the fish from these areas might represent distinct stocks.

Condition Factor

Introduction

The condition factor has frequently been used in fisheries research and Weatherley (1972) considers that it is most effective for (1) comparing monospecific populations living under different conditions, (2) determining the timing of the reproductive cycle and (3) determining changes in the feeding activity of a population. There are no published accounts of condition factor in macrourids or morids.

Unpublished observations

The condition factor (K) is often calculated as weight/length^3 but the cube law is seldom applicable and Le Cren (1951) has advocated the use of the "relative condition factor" (K_n), which is derived from the

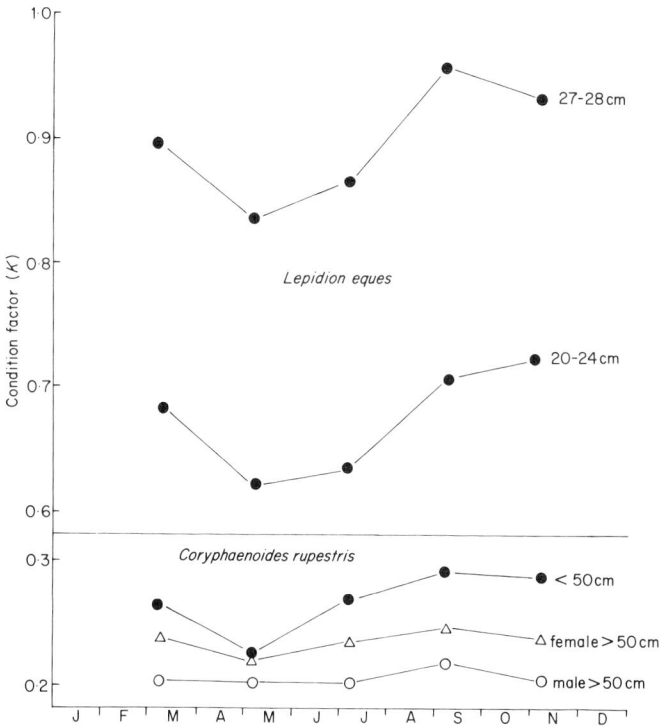

FIG. 3. Seasonal changes in the mean condition factor (K) of *Lepidion eques* and *Coryphaenoides rupestris* from 56–57°N 09–11°W in the eastern north Atlantic.

length/weight relationship. For the purposes of this preliminary study, K has been calculated for the macrourids *Coryphaenoides rupestris, Coelorhynchus coelorhynchus* (Risso), *Coelorhynchus occa* (Goode & Bean) and *Trachyrhynchus murrayi* Günther and for the morid *Lepidion eques*. In all these species, the cube law does not apply and K varies with length. However, comparisons of mean values of K for discrete length groups show a trend for a seasonal change in condition. Figure 3 shows the change in condition for two length groups of *Lepidion eques* and *Coryphaenoides rupestris*. It is interesting that the lowest condition appears to occur during the late spring and early summer, when condition is lowest in inshore teleosts at the same latitude (De Silva, 1973; Gordon, 1977). Gonad weights were included in the calculation of K and, since immature fish also show a tendency for seasonal change, it is possible that feeding activity could account for the observations. There is evidence from other areas for seasonal changes in the intensity of feeding of *Coryphaenoides rupestris* and *C. pectoralis* (p. 351). *C. rupestris* has a prolonged spawning season with different individuals maturing at different times (p. 345) and if further investigation confirms the trend for minimal seasonal changes of K in mature fish (Fig. 3), it is interesting to speculate whether changes caused by feeding are masked by an irregular reproductive cycle.

REPRODUCTION

Mate Location and Spawning Behaviour

Marshall (1971) has considered the problems of mate location in deep sea fish and, in general terms, he concludes that each of the three major groupings of deep sea fish uses different sensory mechanisms. Mesopelagic fish have evolved a system of communication with light organs and, in the bathypelagic zone, olfactory signals appear to be important in mate location, the males having well-developed olfactory organs enabling them to seek out scent-producing females. Sound production is common in the males of benthopelagic fish and is particularly well-developed in the macrourids and brotulids which comprise over one-half of the benthopelagic biomass.

Sound production of male macrourids is effected by drumming muscles on the swimbladder wall and is confined to those species which inhabit the upper slope (Marshall, 1965, 1971). Marshall concludes that sound is only of value as a directional aid in the acoustic near field and therefore is only important when the fish are not widely dispersed. Upper slope macrourids appear to meet these requirements but the more widely dispersed abyssal macrourids would gain little advantage in evolving a sound-producing capability. The method of mate location by abyssal macrourids is still a matter of conjecture. Light organs occur in some species of macrourids and may have a role in sexual activities but they are absent in many of the common abyssal forms which are unable to produce sound.

Spawning migrations are a feature of the Gadidae and, indeed, many other teleost families. No evidence of seasonal changes in abundance of any of the macrourid or morid species has been detected on the slope to the west of Scotland. In a much more detailed study of *Coryphaenoides pectoralis* in the north Pacific, Novikov (1970) found no aggregations of spawning fish but there was a low percentage of running and newly spent fish which suggested that, in some way, the females, at the time of spawning, were inaccessible to the trawl. On the evidence of the sex ratios in his catches, he has proposed that the males inhabit greater depths than the females and it is possible that spawning occurs at depths greater than were sampled. Makushok (1967) has suggested that the reported occurrence of large numbers of *Macruronus novaezelandiae* (Hector) and *Coryphaenoides denticulatus* (Regan) in shallow waters round New Zealand is evidence of a spawning migration. In an attempt to explain the apparent lack of mature *Coryphaenoides rupestris* on the slopes of the northwest Atlantic, Podrazhanskaya (1971) has proposed that these stocks are derived from spawnings in Icelandic waters. The eggs and larvae are carried by a series of currents to the North Newfoundland bank where they grow until they reach a length of 40–50 cm and then begin the migration back to Iceland. Savvatimskii (1972) considers that body shape of macrourids is not suited to undertaking such migrations and proposes that the apparent lack of mature fish can be more simply explained by the fact that they inhabit depths greater than have been sampled. He supports this view with the results from one deep trawl (1500 m) off Labrador from which larger fish in a more advanced state of maturity were obtained.

Nothing is known of the mating behaviour of macrourid fish but it has been suggested (see Moser, 1976) that the males of *Coryphaenoides acrolepis* may hold territories on the upper slope and that the females move up the slope in the spring to spawn.

Distribution by Depth and Sex

Review of published work

Savvatimskii (1969) has shown that, in the north Atlantic, male and female *Coryphaenoides rupestris* are often separated by depth and area. For example, at depths down to 1000 m, males were dominant in the northwest Atlantic, females were dominant at Iceland and equal numbers of each sex were taken northwest of Rockall. Pechenik & Troyanovskii (1970) have examined the seasonal catch rates of *C. rupestris* from different depths on the northwest Atlantic slope and have postulated a seasonal vertical migration linked to the vertical migration of zooplankton. They have also observed diurnal variations in catch rate which they propose are related to migrations of the food organisms.

Coryphaenoides pectoralis, in the north Pacific, shows sex separation by depth, the females tending to occur between 300 and 700 m and the males below 700 m (Novikov, 1970). Juvenile fish of less than 50–60 cm were absent from the bottom trawl catches, except in the Sea of Okhotsk, and he has proposed that they are pelagic at this stage. The depth range of this species is from 200 to 2170 m but Novikov trawled only to a depth of 1200 m. The possibility that the juvenile fish are distributed on the bottom at depths greater than 1200 m cannot be excluded.

Haedrich & Polloni (1976) have found a significant increase in size with depth in *Coryphaenoides carapinus* but they give no information on the sex ratios.

The distribution of morids by sex and size has received little attention. Iwamoto (1975), in reviewing the biology of the abyssal *Antimora rostrata*, has commented on the small size of the males and their relative paucity in research catches has suggested that there is a distinct difference in habitat preference between males and females.

Unpublished observations

Off the west coast of Scotland, *Coryphaenoides rupestris* has a complex distribution by depth and sex. Figure 4 shows the length-frequency distribution at different depths and the percentage of females of fish of 50 cm and over (50 cm is the approximate length at first maturity). These results were obtained from a total of 26 trawls between March and November. The smallest modal length of juvenile fish was found at depths of about 1000 m and the modal length increased with increasing depth. No *C. rupestris* was taken at depths exceeding 1800 m. At a length of about 60 cm and over, they become distributed over the whole depth range and there is a partial separation of the sexes, the males being concentrated on the upper slope. This pattern of distribution remained constant between March and November.

Trachyrhynchus murrayi, off the west of Scotland, has a depth distribution between 1000 and 1250 m (Ross & Gordon, 1978) and unpublished data have shown that, although there is no obvious separation of the sexes with depth, the smallest and largest fish appear to be concentrated at 1000 m and the intermediate sizes at 1250 m. *Lepidion eques* occurs at depths of 700–1250 m off the west coast of Scotland and there appear to be no sex or size differences with depth.

Nematonurus armatus has been taken at depths of 2400 to 4800 m in the Rockall Channel and the Porcupine Abyssal Plain and preliminary results have shown an increase in size with increasing depth.

Egg Size and Fecundity

Information on egg size and fecundity of macrourids and morids is sparse. Table II summarizes the published work.

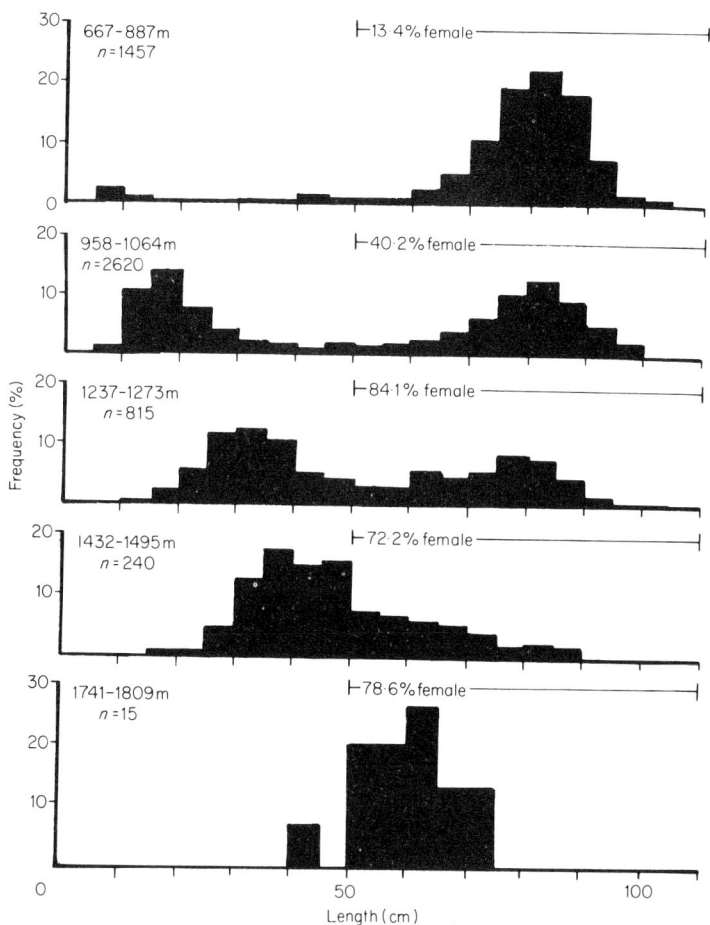

FIG. 4. Percentage length frequency of *Coryphaenoides rupestris* from different depth ranges in the area 56–57°N 09–11°W in the eastern north Atlantic. Data from 26 trawls between March 1975 and October 1977 have been included. The total number of fish from each depth range is shown together with the percentage of females for fish greater than 50 cm total length.

Egg size in fish is extremely variable between species and even within a species (Bagenal, 1971). For comparative purposes, ovarian eggs are of limited value since the eggs may not have reached the maximum pre-ovulation size and it is generally assumed that an increase in size follows fertilization. Table III shows the egg diameters of anacanthine fish which are known to occur in the northeast Atlantic between 56 and 57°N. The data on depth range, maximum length and egg diameter in A of Table III are from Svetovidov (1973), Wheeler (1969) and Russell (1976) respectively, but do not relate specifically to the area under consideration. The

TABLE II *Published data on fecundity and egg size in macrourid and morid fishes*

Species	Fecundity	Egg diameter (mm)	Area	Authority
Cetonurus globiceps	10350 (1 specimen, 32·5 cm)	c. 1·0 (ovarian)	Off Cuba	Mead et al. (1964)
Coelorhynchus coelorhynchus	—	1·15–1·21 (planktonic)	Mediterranean	Marshall (1973a)
*Coelorhynchus fasciatus**	—	1·15–1·21 (planktonic)	South Africa	Sanzo (1933) Gilchrist (1905)
*Coelorhynchus parallelus**	—	1·3–1·32 (ripe ovarian)	South Africa	Gilchrist (1905)
Coryphaenoides rupestris	12–16·5 thousand (up to 35·5)	1·8 (ovarian)	N Atlantic	Savvatimskii (1969)
Coryphaenoides carapinus	50–220 thousand	0·5 (ovarian)	NW Atlantic	Haedrich & Polloni (1976)
Hymenocephalus italicus	—	1·0–1·08 (planktonic)	Mediterranean	Sanzo (1933)
Macrourus berglax	25000 (1 specimen, 70·5 cm)	3·4–3·85 (ovarian)	N Atlantic	Yanulov (1962)
Nezumia aequalis	—	1·75–1·85 (transparent ovarian)	NE Atlantic	Farran (1924)
Nezumia sclerorhynchus	—	1·6 (planktonic)	Mediterranean	Sanzo (1933)
Sphagemacrurus grenadae	—	c. 1·5 (ovarian)	—	Marshall (1973a)
Lepidion eques	—	0·6 (ovarian)	N Atlantic	Templeman (1970)

* Gilchrist used the generic name of *Macrurus* (see Mead et al., 1964).

TABLE III

The egg diameters of anacanthine fish which occur at latitude 56 to 57°N in the northeastern Atlantic

Species	Depth range (cm)	Approx. maximum length (cm)	Egg diameter (mm)
A			
Trisopterus minutus	inshore	23	0·95–1·03
Pollachius pollachius	inshore	130	1·10–1.22
Merlangius merlangus	30–100	70	0·97–1.32
Melanogrammus aeglefinus	40–300	80	1·2–1·7
Pollachius virens	100–200	120	1·03–1·22
Trisopterus esmarki	100–250	24	1·0–1·19
Gadus morhua	150–220	150	1·16–1·60
Brosme brosme	150–450	110	1·29–1·51
Merluccius merluccius	150–550	99	0·94–1·03
Gadiculus argenteus	200–1000	9	0·91 (ovarian)
Micromesistius poutassou	300–400	41	1·04–1·275
Molva molva	300–400	200	0·97–1·13
B			
Coelorhynchus coelorhynchus	?–750	44	1·4–1·6
Lepidion eques	450–1250	35	1·1–1·2
Nezumia aequalis	600–1100	35	1·75–1·85
Coryphaenoides rupestris	650–1800	110	2·2–2·3
Trachyrhynchus murrayi	1000–1500	48	0·9–1·1 (Not ripe)
Coelorhynchus occa	1000–2000	38	0·8

data in B are taken from my own observations of the egg diameter in ripe ovaries, with the exception of the egg diameters of *Nezumia aequalis* (Günther) which is from Farran (1924). A rough correlation between egg size and the maximum size of the species in macrourids has been suggested by Marshall (1973a) and, if fish size is taken into consideration, the data in Table III, with a few exceptions, show a trend for an increase in egg size with depth. The measurements of the egg diameters in A were, with one exception, of fertilized planktonic eggs while those in B were of ovarian eggs. The trend for increasing size with depth would probably be more distinct if the ultimate size of the fertilized eggs of the deep sea specimens was known.

The fecundity of macrourids has been studied in detail only for *Coryphaenoides carapinus* by Haedrich & Polloni (1976) and the other information included in Table II consists of estimates from single specimens or very few fish. Visual examination of macrourid ovaries from the west of Scotland suggests that the fecundity is of a similar order of magnitude, but the morid species *Lepidion eques* may have a higher fecundity compared with macrourids of an equivalent size. Fecundity is generally correlated with fish length and weight (Bagenal, 1968), but Haedrich & Polloni (1976) have found that in *C. carapinus* there was only a weak correlation with weight and little correlation with length.

Bagenal (1973) has discussed the interrelationships between egg size and fecundity and concludes that "it seems likely that in most fish there is a negative correlation between number and size of eggs". Marshall (1953) has considered the ecological advantages of large egg size and consequently large larvae in the deep sea. The reproductive strategies of deep sea fish are many and varied but most fish can be placed into one of two categories. They can either produce large eggs at the expense of numbers and develop in the deep sea or produce large numbers of small eggs and develop in the productive epipelagic zone (Mead, Bertelsen & Cohen, 1964). The macrourid fish may fall into the former group although their adaptation is moderate compared with the extremes found in some deep-sea families.

Spawning Periodicity

Introduction

It has often been supposed that the constant nature of the physical environment of the deep sea would favour all-the-year-round reproduction. A number of benthic invertebrates from the San Diego Trough off Southern California show such a pattern (Rokop, 1974) but there is also evidence that some invertebrate species have predictable seasonal cycles of reproduction (George & Menzies, 1967, 1968; Schoener, 1968; Rokop, 1977). Two species of bivalve collected seasonally over a number of years at a depth of 2900 m in the Rockall Channel (54°40'N 12°16'W) have an annual spawning cycle, one maturing in January and the other in October (R. Lightfoot, Scottish Marine Biological Association, pers. comm.). In deep sea fish, seasonal cycles of reproduction appear to be of a more widespread occurrence (Mead *et al.*, 1964).

Review of published work

Marshall (1965, 1973a) has summarized what little is known of the spawning periods of macrourid fish. The seasonal occurrence of eggs and young larvae of *Coelorhynchus coelorhynchus*[a], *Nezumia sclerorhynchus*[a] and *Hymenocephalus italicus* Giglioli in the Mediterranean suggests a spawning period from December to March (Sanzo, 1933)). Larvae collected by the *Dana* expeditions have been examined by Marshall (1965) and spawning probably occurs from February to April in the Caribbean, February to March off West Africa and February to September in the Malayan and Indonesian area. Gilchrist (1905) obtained pelagic eggs of *Coelorhynchus fasciatus* (Günther)[a] off South Africa from July to September.

---

[a] The nomenclature follows Marshall (1973a). The original authors placed them in the genus *Macrourus*.

A summer and autumn spawning period for *Nezumia bairdii* in the Gulf of Maine has been proposed by Bigelow & Schroeder (1953). Matsui (quoted by Phleger, 1971) has found that *Coryphaenoides acrolepis* spawns between late February and early May off the coast of California. A seasonal study of the maturity stages of *Coryphaenoides pectoralis* in the north Pacific has shown that, while spawning occurs all the year round, it is most evident during the autumn and winter (Novikov, 1970). Seasonal changes in the gonadosomatic ratio (GSR) of *Coryphaenoides carapinus*, from latitude 39°N in the western Atlantic, have shown that this species spawns between November and March (Haedrich & Polloni, 1976). A similar study of *Trachyrhynchus trachyrhynchus* in the Mediterranean has shown that the females were ripe in February and spent by April (Motais, 1960).

Macrourus berglax, from the slopes north of Iceland, has a prolonged spawning season which may extend over the whole year but is most vigorous between the months of November and February (Magnusson, 1977). Yanulov (1962) has studied an ovary from a single specimen of this species and found eggs of three size groups, which suggests that the prolonged spawning season may be due to serial spawning.

There have been several studies on the spawning of *Coryphaenoides rupestris* in the north Atlantic. Collett (1905) found ripe ovaries in October in Norwegian fjords but Marshall (1973a) reports that this species must also spawn earlier in the year in the Norwegian Sea. Grigoryev (1972) found that, in the northwest Atlantic, all the males and all but the largest females were immature. The largest females were probably maturing for the first time. In contrast, he found that, in the region of Iceland, most of the males were capable of fertilizing spawned eggs at least from May to December, if not throughout the year. The females were sexually mature but they showed no clearly defined spawning season and he proposed that different individuals spawned at different times. Magnusson (1977) reached a similar conclusion and commented on the lack of spawning females and newly spent males, which suggested that, at the time of spawning, they were inaccessible to bottom trawling. Savvatimskii (1972) has found spawning fish on the slopes of the Hatton Bank in October and, recently, Geistdorfer (1977) found a brief spawning period between April and June on this bank and also at Rockall.

There is very little information on the spawning of the Moridae. Templeman (1970), quoting some unpublished data of Krefft on *Lepidion eques* from Iceland, has found that the largest females were close to spawning or had spawned in April.

Unpublished observations

The gonadosomatic ratio (GSR) of male and female *Coryphaenoides rupestris* from the west coast of Scotland has been calculated at two-monthly intervals between March and November 1975. The male ratio was constant throughout this period and preliminary histological studies have shown that the males appear to be capable of fertilizing eggs throughout this time (Gordon & McRae, unpublished). The female GSR showed considerable variation within each sample and the reason for this was apparent when the ovaries of mature fish of 50 cm and over were staged on a six-point maturity scale. Figure 5 shows that all stages of maturity

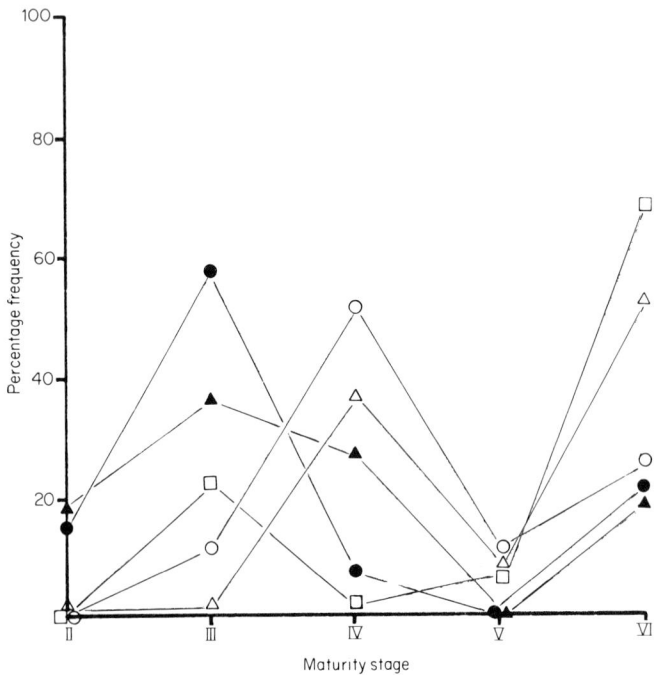

FIG. 5. Percentage frequency of female *Coryphaenoides rupestris* of 50 cm and over at different stages of maturity during March (●), May (▲), July (○), September (△) and November (□) 1975, at 56–57°N 09–11°W in the eastern north Atlantic. Stage II, resting; Stage III, early maturation; Stage IV, advanced maturation; Stage V, running ripe; Stage VI, spent.

occurred throughout the period but that there was evidence for a peak of autumn spawning. This conclusion has been confirmed in subsequent years and, although a full analysis has yet to be completed, there does not appear to be a correlation between depth of occurrence or size of fish and the time of spawning. A few ovaries have been dissected and the eggs were found to be of uniform size, which suggests that the prolonged spawning season is not due to serial spawning but rather to different individuals maturing at different times. The small percentage of stage V females could be due to their being inaccessible to the bottom trawl, as suggested by Magnusson, but, alternatively, this period may have a relatively short duration or the eggs may be extruded by pressure changes during the prolonged hauling from great depths.

The spawning periods of other macrourids from the west of Scotland have also been studied. *Trachyrhynchus murrayi* occurs at depths between 1000 and 1250 m and the females reach first maturity at about 32 cm. Ovarian eggs appear to be of uniform size and the mean GSR of mature females is shown in Fig. 6. Spawning must occur between November and March. *Coelorhynchus coelorhynchus* has a shallower distribution (500–750 m) and evidence from dissection of ovaries and calculations of the GSR suggests that this species is a serial spawner between March and September.

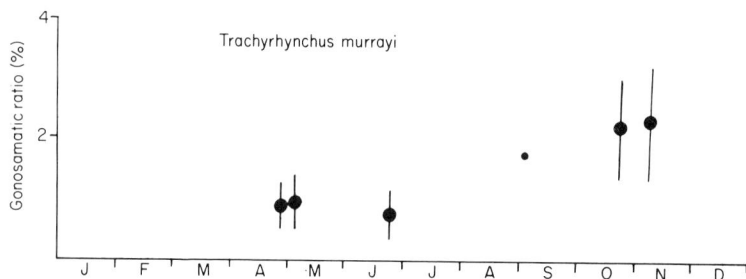

FIG. 6. The seasonal changes in the mean gonadosomatic index of female *Trachyrhynchus murrayi* from 56–57°N 09–11°W in the eastern north Atlantic. The vertical bars represent two standard deviations of the mean and the small circle less than five observations.

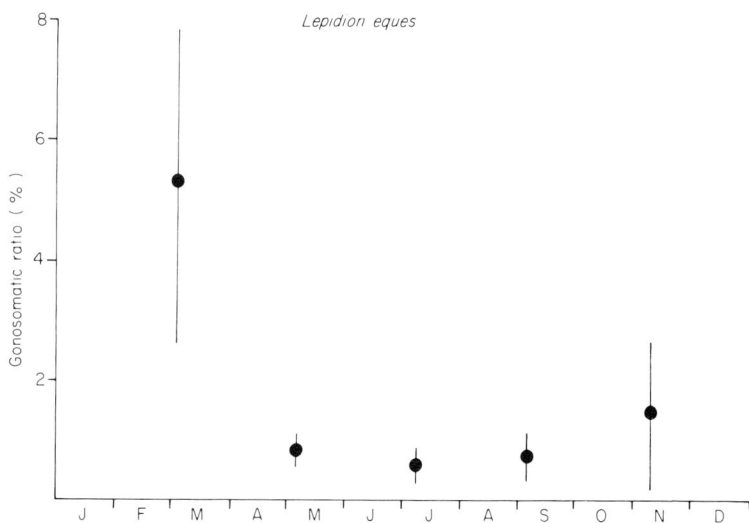

FIG. 7. The seasonal changes in the mean gonadosomatic index of female *Lepidion eques* from 56–57°N 09–11°W in the eastern north Atlantic. The vertical bars represent two standard deviations of the mean.

The morid *Lepidion eques* has a depth distribution from 700 to 1250 m and the females reach sexual maturity at about 27 cm. The seasonal changes in mean GSR of females of 27 cm and over (Fig. 7) show that *L. eques* spawns between March and May.

Egg and Larval Distribution

The eggs and larvae of macrourids have seldom been taken in any quantity by plankton nets and have presented considerable taxonomic problems. This is especially true of some species which have a prolonged bathypelagic existence and have a juvenile form which is unlike the adult. The earlier literature has been adequately reviewed by Mead *et al.* (1964) and Marshall (1973a). With improved sampling techniques, Merrett (1978) has successfully collected larval macrourids from the northeast Atlantic and has described the larval stages of several species.

Marshall (1965, 1971, 1973a) has proposed that macrourid eggs are spawned and fertilized near the bottom and that they develop as they float upward through the water column. The youngest larvae become concentrated below the seasonal thermocline and, as they grow, migrate into deep water. He has also proposed that those species with a restricted slope distribution have a rapid development whereas more widely dispersed species often have prolonged development with pelagic juveniles. Mead *et al.* (1964) and Phleger (1971) have proposed that the local endemism or absence of species in enclosed basins with a shallow sill is evidence that the eggs and larvae do not reach the epipelagic zone. Merrett (1978) has examined the vertical distribution of larval macrourids caught with a closing net at discrete depths at 60°N 20°W and 53°N 20°W during the period April and May. His data support Marshall's hypothesis that the larvae undergo an ontogenic migration into deeper water but he found a shallower distribution for the smallest larvae than has hitherto been observed. (see p. 350). In discussion following the present paper at the Symposium meeting, Professor Marshall advanced the further idea that the eggs and larvae of some macrourids may develop close to the bottom, without ascent into shallower waters. There is a growing realization that the near-bottom zone in the deep sea may have a distinctive fauna and be particularly rich in food for young macrourids. Merrett has shown that, at the 60°N station, juvenile *Coryphaenoides rupestris*, with a head length of 12–20 mm (*c*. 60–100 mm total length), were pelagic at 700–1100 m over a sounding of *c*. 2790 m. The smallest fish taken in the west of Scotland study area had a head length of 19 mm but significant numbers were not taken on the bottom until a head length of *c*. 30 mm was reached. The depth of occurrence of 1000 m (Fig. 4) agrees well with Merrett's data and no fish younger than 2+ have been found. The mean head length of 13 2+ fish was 21·6 mm. Direct comparison between the two sampling areas may not be valid because of their distance apart (400 miles) and their separation by the physical barrier of the Rockall and other banks but a tentative conclusion might be that *C. rupestris* has a prolonged pelagic phase.

Discussion

Deep sea anacanthine fish appear to differ little from their shallow water counterparts in their reproductive strategies. There is good evidence that many species show periodicity in their reproduction and factors which could synchronize periodicity will be discussed in detail below, but, if such a factor exists, it is most likely that it will in some way be related to seasonal variations in the surface waters. If this is so, then we might expect tropical species to show less seasonality than species inhabiting temperate waters. Unfortunately, there is only circumstantial evidence from the *Dana* larvae for seasonality in the tropics and this hypothesis remains untested. It is perhaps significant that Rokop (1974) considered all-year-round reproduction of invertebrates to be dominant in the San Diego Trench (32°N) while there is increasing evidence for seasonality in more northerly latitudes.

Shallow water anacanthine fish generally spawn during the spring and early summer and it is generally assumed that spawning is synchronized so that the larvae are produced when food is at a maximum in the euphotic zone. In the deep sea species, the somewhat limited evidence appears to show a trend for spawning to occur during the late summer, autumn or winter. As mentioned above, Marshall has proposed a working hypothesis that the young larval macrourids inhabit the waters beneath the seasonal thermocline and, by so doing, avoid dispersal by surface currents and have an adequate food supply. The occurrence of thermal discontinuities in the world's oceans is caused by many factors, but, in the simplest terms, there exist three classical temperature profiles. In tropical latitudes, there is a permanent thermocline which generally occurs in the upper 100 m. In temperate latitudes, seasonal heating and cooling of the surface waters cause a seasonal thermocline. The formation and decline of the seasonal thermocline at 57°06′N 09°25′W to the west of Scotland is shown in Fig. 8 (Ellett, D. J., S.M.B.A. Internal Report, October 1978). In polar latitudes, there is no marked thermal discontinuity. It therefore follows that, if macrourids of temperate latitudes are to gain advantage from the seasonal thermocline, spawning must be synchronized so that the larval stages coincide with the seasonal occurrence of the thermocline. Figure 8 shows that, in the northern hemisphere, the seasonal thermocline begins to form in May, is well established and has deepened by August, and begins to decline until, in December, it is weak but deep. It is apparent that many of the macrourids which occur in temperate latitudes do have a tendency to spawn during the period when the thermocline is present and the two species which have been studied in most detail, *Coryphaenoides rupestris* and *C. pectoralis*, appear to have the potential for year-round spawning but do so most intensively in the autumn when the

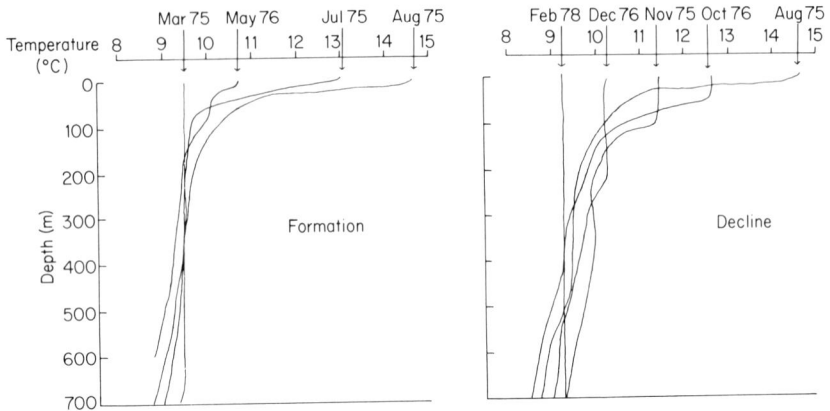

FIG. 8. The formation and decline of the seasonal thermocline at SMBA Hydrographic Station P (57°06′N 09°25′W); data from Ellett, D. J., SMBA Internal Report (October 1978).

seasonal thermocline is well established. As noted earlier there is no direct evidence for the periodicity of spawning of tropical species. The only polar species which has been studied (*Macrourus berglax*), shows all-the-year-round spawning. The synchronization of spawning with the development of a seasonal thermocline could be a useful preliminary hypothesis for future study but, before it can be developed fully, it will also be necessary to determine the incubation period of the eggs and the duration of the pre-feeding larval stages.

The typical temperate structure of the oceans outlined above can vary from place to place and from time to time. Indeed, the disruption of stable thermoclines by upwelling allows nutrients to be brought to the surface and is the basis for many of the important oceanic fisheries (see Garrod & Knights, this volume p. 361). The layering of water-masses of different origin by depth can cause temperature discontinuities and, in this respect, Merrett's (1978) data on larval *Coryphaenoides rupestris* in the northeast Atlantic may be significant. Twenty-eight larval *C. rupestris* were obtained at the 60°N station at depths from 25 to 800 m and, at 53°N, nine larvae of this species were taken between 300 and 900 m. Spot hydrographic data for these two stations at the time of sampling have been given by Badcock & Merrett (1976), and show that at 60°N, although there were slight temperature anomalies in the upper layers, there was no marked thermal discontinuity at least down to 1000 m. At 53°N, there was a thermal discontinuity at about 400–500 m. The observations were made during the period April/May when the seasonal thermocline at both stations should have been either absent or just beginning to form at the surface. The 53°N station was close to Ocean Weather Station Juliet and hydro-graphic observations at this station have shown considerable variability at depths of 400 m, probably due to the proximity of the polar front (Ellett, 1968). In view of the prevailing hydrographic conditions, it appears that the presence of most of the larvae in the upper 100 m at 60°N and deeper distribution at 53°N may be explained in terms of the presence of a non-seasonal thermocline at the latter station.

FOOD AND FEEDING

The food and feeding relationships of deep sea fish and especially the macrourids have recently been the subject of considerable interest. Publications by McLellan (1977), Marshall & Merrett (1977) and Sedberry & Musick (1978), are of particular interest and review most of the earlier work. There is a wide diversity of trophic types in benthopelagic fish but these have been subdivided into three main groups by Marshall & Merrett (1977). These are (1) species depending on a mixed diet of pelagic and benthic organisms, (2) species with a marked preference for pelagic animals and (3) species with a marked preference for benthic organisms. They place most members of the subfamily Macrourinae, which comprises about 90% of the species of the family, in (1); a few of the large adult Macrourinae and the subfamilies Bathygadinae and Trachyrhynchinae in (2) and only a few species in (3). Most of the species discussed in this paper fall into (1) and a few into (2), and, therefore, in considering food as a possible influence on seasonality of growth and reproduction (p. 353), it will be necessary to consider both benthic and pelagic sources.

Information on seasonal variation in feeding intensity is sparse partly because so few seasonal studies have been carried out. Any investigation of feeding in the deep sea is complicated by the problem of everted stomachs during recovery from depth, which results in the complete or partial loss of the contents, and also by the possibility of feeding in the net. Research on the abundant material from commercial catches of *Coryphaenoides rupestris* in the northwest Atlantic and at Iceland has shown a decrease in feeding intensity from June to August and an increase from August to December (Podrazhanskaya, 1967, 1971; Savvatimskii, 1969). Novikov (1970) recorded the percentage of empty stomachs in *Coryphaenoides pectoralis* from the Bering Sea and concluded that feeding occurred throughout the year but was most intense during the late autumn and in the spring.

DISCUSSION

In terms of growth, reproduction and feeding, deep sea anacanthine fish have much in common with their shelf counterparts but it is important to emphasize that almost all the evidence relates to species which are normally distributed on the upper 2000 m of the slope and in latitudes where seasonality exists in the euphotic zone. All the species are bentho-pelagic *sensu* Marshall (1965) and there is good evidence in the literature for a peak of biomass in the upper 1200 m (Marshall & Merrett, 1977). Studies of faunal assemblages on the slope have shown that two distinct zones can be distinguished, one coinciding with the shelf/slope transition and the other at depths betwen 500 and 1200 m. Most of the species considered in this paper belong to the latter assemblage.

Although there is no direct evidence for seasonal changes in growth rate, its occurrence can be inferred from the patterns of scale and otolith growth. Cyclical changes in liver weight and fat content have been observed and there is tentative evidence for cyclical changes in condition factor. Periodicity of gonad development and spawning appears to be a dominant feature of the group.

Periodicity of growth and reproduction of shelf-dwelling species depends ultimately on the often complex interaction of changing external factors such as photoperiod, temperature and food supply on the metabolic processes of the organism. The penetration of light and temperature in the deep sea have frequently been discussed in the literature and only a few comments are necessary in this paper. The penetration of light is influenced by many factors but Marshall (1971) has calculated that, in the clearest tropical waters, the threshold for fish vision is probably at about a mean depth of 1000 m. Particulate matter in the productive temperate waters is likely to reduce considerably the depth of penetration and this effect will be enhanced by turbidity on the continental slopes. A depth of 500 to 600 m might be a reasonable estimate of light penetration in these waters. Several species of macrourid are known to make migrations into mid-water (p. 333) and the larvae and juveniles, at least of some species, have a pelagic existence. It would appear, therefore, that although macrourids may experience photoperiodic changes at some stages in their life history, for most of their adult life they live in total darkness.

The possible role of thermoclines in ensuring reproductive success and the selective advantage of synchronizing spawning to take advantage of the seasonal thermocline in temperate latitudes have been discussed above. Most macrourids live at depths below the thermocline and therefore all except the youngest stages will not be subject to marked changes in temperature. For example, in the northeast Atlantic, fluctuations in temperature are of the order of $0.5°C$ although sudden aperiodic changes may occur at some locations caused by movements of the various water masses (Ellett, 1968, 1974; Ellett & Martin, 1973).

In the shallow water environment, the seasonal availability of suitable food can have a direct effect on growth and other metabolic processes but other environmental factors are often involved. For example, the effect of temperature on metabolism can cause changes in growth-rate even when food is in excess and changes in photoperiod can influence the fishes' ability to ingest food. In the deep sea, where temperature, light and other environmental parameters are constant, it would seem logical that seasonal availability and perhaps changes in quality of the food must be of prime importance.

There has been considerable speculation on the possible means whereby organic material from the euphotic zone or of terrestrial origin might reach the sea bed (see Sedberry & Musick, 1978, for a recent summary of the literature). In Fig. 9, an attempt has been made to summarize the various mechanisms of energy transfer. Preliminary estimates of the amount of energy reaching the sea-bed have occasionally been made (Riley, 1951; Menzies, 1962; Deuser, 1971) but, as yet, there is no good evidence for seasonal fluctuations in the rates of deposition. Many of the mechanisms shown in Fig. 9 could account for spasmodic pulses of energy reaching the benthopelagic zone but only a few, such as the supposed fallout from the euphotic zone and the energy transfer through interlocking food chains, could result in predictable cycles of energy transfer.

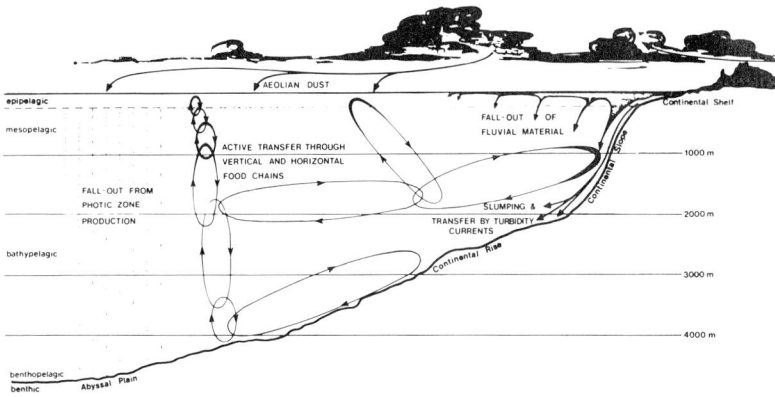

FIG. 9. The possible routes by which organic material either from the photic zone or of terrestial origin may reach the deep sea.

In the context of this paper, the food supply available to slope-dwelling species inhabiting a depth range of 500 to 2000 m is of particular interest. A study of the food and feeding habits of these fish has led Marshall & Merrett (1977) to propose that the extraordinary success of this assemblage of benthopelagic fish is linked to their ability to utilize planktonic food. Although benthic food cannot be ignored, the impingement of the rich mesopelagic fauna on the slope at these depths is of prime importance. Therefore, if food supply is a factor in inducing periodicity in the benthopelagic fauna, it is necessary to consider whether periodicity exists in the mesopelagic fauna. Unfortunately, there have been few comprehensive seasonal studies of the mesoplankton but there is evidence, widely scattered in the literature, to suggest that seasonal changes occur at least in temperate latitudes. The proceedings of a conference entitled *Oceanic sound scattering prediction*, edited by Andersen & Zahuranec (1977), contains much useful information. It is important that the term food-availability is used in its broadest sense since changes in biomass may not be as important as other factors such as change in the modal length frequency with season, and seasonal horizontal and vertical migrations. Mention has been made (p. 339) of both the seasonal and the diurnal depth distribution of *C. rupestris* in relation to the vertical migrations of the zooplankton.

Just as there is a lack of evidence to indicate whether seasonality occurs in benthopelagic fish of tropical latitudes, so there is a requirement to study mesopelagic organisms in these areas. Similarly, there is a clear need to investigate benthopelagic fish which occur at depths greater than 2000 m in temperate latitudes.

Whatever the external influence, there is little doubt that the endogenous control of the metabolic processes will be mediated by the endocrine system. There have been few studies on the endocrinology of deep sea fish but Bougis & Ruivo (1954, 1957) have suggested that thyroid activity in two abyssal fish, *Benthocometes robustus* (Goode & Bean) and *Bathypterois dubius* Vaillant, is feeble. Motais (1960), however, found evidence of a seasonal cycle of thyroid activity in the slope-dwelling *Trachyrhynchus trachyrhynchus*.

Endogenous rhythms of activity are well documented in fish (Schwassmann, 1971) and it is interesting to consider their possible role in the deep sea. All known biological rhythms require a physical cue to maintain synchrony and Rokop (1974, 1977) has speculated that factors such as lunar tidal cycles, seasonal currents and even specific metabolites in the food or the environment, acting as pheromones, might be utilized. The behaviour of deep sea fish in relation to tidal cycles (p. 333) may be significant.

Although it is becoming increasingly apparent that the phenology and lifestyle of deep sea benthopelagic fish, and especially the anacanthine fish, have much in common with their shelf counterparts, it is important not to generalize about the deep sea environment. The many and varied lifestyles of shallow water fish have their homologues in the deep sea.

ACKNOWLEDGEMENTS

I should like to thank my colleagues at the Scottish Marine Biological Association and especially Dr Mauchline for many stimulating discussions during the preparation of this paper. I am particularly grateful to Mr Ellett for providing hydrographic data, Dr Pearson for drawing Fig. 9 and Mr Lightfoot for allowing me to quote his unpublished results. My grateful thanks are also due to all who have assisted on the cruises of RRS

Challenger and especially to Mrs J. Duncan and the fishing skipper, Mr F. Dunning. Finally, I should like to thank Drs Barnett, Blaxter, Mauchline and Ross for their helpful comments on the manuscript.

REFERENCES

Andersen, N. R. & Zahuranec, B. J. (eds) (1977). *Oceanic sound scattering prediction.* (*Marine Science* 5.) New York: Plenum Press.
Badcock, J. & Merrett, N. R. (1976). Midwater fishes in the eastern North Atlantic. I. Vertical distribution and associated biology in 30°N, 23°W, with developmental notes on certain myctophids. *Progr. Oceanogr.* 7: 3–58.
Bagenal, T. B. (1968). Fecundity. In *Methods for assessment of fish production in fresh waters*: 160–169. Ricker, W. E. (ed.) (I.B.P. Handbook No. 3.)
Bagenal, T. B. (1971). The interrelation of the size of fish eggs, the date of spawning and the production cycle. *J. Fish Biol.* 3: 207–219.
Bagenal, T. B. (1973). Fish fecundity and its relations with stock and recruitment. *Rapp. P–V. Reun. Cons. perm. int. Explor. Mer* No. 164: 186–198.
Ball, J. N. (1969). Prolactin (fish prolactin or paralactin) and growth hormones. In *Fish physiology* 2: 207–240. Hoar, W. S. & Randall, D. R. (eds). New York & London: Academic Press.
Bigelow, H. B. & Schroeder, W. C. (1953). Fishes of the Gulf of Maine. *Fishery Bull. Fish. Wildl. Ser. U.S.* 53: 1–577.
Bilton, H. T. (1974). Effects of starvation and feeding on circulus formation on scales of young sockeye salmon of four racial origins, and of one race of young kokanee, coho and chinook salmon. In *The ageing of fish*: 40–70. Bagenal, T. B. (ed.) Old Woking: Unwin Brothers.
Bougis, P. & Ruivo, M. (1954). Recherches sur le poisson de profondeur *Benthocometes robustus* (Goode and Bean) (= *Pteridium armatum*, Doederlein) (Brotulidae). *Vie Milieu* Suppl. No. 3: 155–209.
Bougis, P. & Ruivo, M. (1957). Contribution à la connaissance de la morphologie et de la thyroide de *Bathypterois dubius* Vaillant. *Vie Milieu* Suppl. No. 6: 185–205.
Bridger, J. (1978). New deep-water trawling grounds to the west of Britain. *Lab. Leafl. MAFF Direct. Fish. Res. Lowestoft* No. 41: 1–40.
Clayden, A. D. (1972). Simulation of the changes in the abundance of the cod (*Gadus morhua* L.) and the distribution of fishing in the North Atlantic. *Fishery Invest., Lond.* (2) 27: 1–58.
Cohen, D. M. (1973). Eretmophoridae. In *Check list of fishes of the north-eastern Atlantic and of the Mediterranean* 1: 322–326. Hureau, J. C. & Monod, Th. (eds). Paris: Unesco.
Collett, R. (1905). Fiske, indsamlede under "Michael Sars" togter i Nordhavet 1900–1902. *Rep. Norw. Fishery mar. Invest.* 2: 1–151.
Crespo, J., Rey, J. C. & Caminas, J. A. (1976). *Trachyrhynchus trachyrhynchus* (Risso 1810) del mar de Alboran (Region Surmediterranea). *Boln Inst. esp. Oceanogr.* No. 218: 1–21.
De Silva, S. S. (1973). Abundance, structure, growth and origin of inshore clupeid populations of the west coast of Scotland. *J. exp. mar. Biol. Ecol.* 12: 119–144.
Deuser, W. G. (1971). Organic-carbon budget of the Black Sea. *Deep Sea Res.* 18: 995–1004.
Ellett, D. J. (1968). Subsurface temperature and salinity conditions at ocean weather stations Alfa, India and Juliett in 1964. *ICES C.M.* 1968/C:22 1–11.

Ellett, D. J. (1974). Data from ocean weather station India (59°N 19°W) 1964–1966. *ICES Oceanographic data lists and inventories* No. 15.

Ellett, D. J. & Martin, J. H. A. (1973). The physical and chemical oceanography of the Rockall Channel. *Deep Sea Res.* **20**: 585–625.

Farran, G. P. (1924). Seventh report of the fishes of the Irish Atlantic slope. The macrurid fishes (Coryphaenoidedae). *Proc. R. Ir. Acad.* **36**: 91–143.

Geistdorfer, P. (1977). Contribution à la biologie de *Coryphaenoides rupestris*. Repartition et reproduction dans l'Atlantique nord est. *ICES C.M.* 1977/F:45.

George, R. Y. & Menzies, R. J. (1967). Indication of cyclic reproductive activity in abyssal organisms. *Nature, Lond.* **215**: 878.

George, R. Y. & Menzies, R. J. (1968). Further evidence for seasonal breeding cycles in the deep-sea. *Nature, Lond.* **220**: 80–81.

Gilchrist, J. D. F. (1905). The development of South African fishes, part 2. *Mar. Invest. S. Afr.* **3**: 131–152.

Gjosaeter, J. (1973). Age, growth and mortality of the myctophid fish, *Benthosema glaciale* (Reinhardt), from Western Norway. *Sarsia* **52**: 1–14.

Gordon, J. D. M. (1977). The fish populations in inshore waters of the west coast of Scotland. The biology of the Norway pout (*Trisopterus esmarkii*). *J. Fish Biol.* **10**: 417–430.

Grigoryev, G. V. (1972). [On fecundity of rock grenadier of North Atlantic.] *Trudy polyar. nauchno-issled. proekt. Inst. morsk. ryb. Khoz. Okeanogr.* **28**: 107–115. [In Russian, English summary.] (Fish. Res. Bd Can. Transl. Ser. No. 2529. 1973.)

Guennegan, Y. & Rannou, M. (In preparation). *Semi-diurnal rhythmic activity in deep-sea benthic fishes.* [Abstract of a paper presented to the Kristeneberg Centenary Symposium on Deep-Sea Faunas. Kristeneberg, Sweden, August 1977.]

Haedrich, R. L. (1974). Pelagic capture of the epibenthic rattail *Coryphaenoides rupestris*. *Deep Sea Res.* **21**: 977–979.

Haedrich, R. L. & Henderson, N. R. (1974). Pelagic food of *Coryphaenoides armatus* a deep benthic rattail. *Deep Sea Res.* **21**: 739–744.

Haedrich, R. L. & Polloni, P. T. (1976). A contribution to the life history of a small rattail fish, *Coryphaenoides carapinus*. *Bull. Sth. Calif. Acad. Sci.* **75**: 203–211.

Halliday, R. G. (1970). Growth and vertical distribution of the glacier lantern fish, *Benthosema glaciale* in the Northwestern Atlantic. *J. Fish. Res. Bd Can.* **27**: 105–116.

Iwamoto, T. (1975). The abyssal fish *Antimora rostrata* Günther. *Comp. Biochem. Physiol.* **52B**: 7–11.

Iwamoto, T. & Stein, D. L. (1974). A systematic review of the rattail fishes (Macrouridae:Gadiformes) from Oregon and adjacent waters. *Occ. Pap. Calif. Acad. Sci.* **111**: 1–79.

Koch, H. (1976). A contribution on the methodics of age determination in Roundnose Grenadier (*Coryphaenoides rupestris* Gunn.). *ICNAF Res. Doc.* 76/VI/28 revised.

Kosswig, K. (1974). Alter und Wachstum des Grenadierfisches in Nordatlantik. *Inform. Fischwirtsh.* No. 1: 6–7.

Kulikova, E. B. (1957). [Growth and age of deep-water fishes]. *Trudy Inst. okean. Akad. Nauk.* **20**: 347–355 [In Russian.] (translated by Am. Inst. Biol. Soc. 1959: 284–290).

Le Cren, E. D. (1951). The length-weight relationship and seasonal cycle in gonad weight and condition in the perch (*Perca fluviatilis*). *J. Anim. Ecol.* **20**: 201–219.

Liew, P. K. L. (1974). Age determination of American eels based on the structure of their otoliths. In *The ageing of fish*: 124–136. Bagenal, T. B. (ed.) Old Woking: Unwin Brothers.

McLellan, T. (1977). Feeding strategies of the macrourids. *Deep Sea Res.* **24**: 1019–1036.

Magnusson, J. V. (1977). Some notes on the spawning habits of Macrouridae at Iceland. *ICES C.M.* 1977/F:49.

Makushok, M. (1967). [Whiptails (Family Macrouridae or Coryphaenoididae Auct)] In *Tikhiy Okean, Biologiya Tokhogo Okeana. Kn III, Ryby Otkrytylch Vod.* Kort, V. G. (ed.) Chapter IV. [In Russian.] (Translated by United States Naval Oceanographic Office. Trans 528, Washington D.C.)

Marshall, N. B. (1953). Egg size in arctic, antarctic and deep sea fishes. *Evolution* **7**: 328–341.

Marshall, N. B. (1965). Systematic and biological studies of the macrourid fishes (Anacanthini–Teleostii). *Deep Sea Res.* **12**: 299–322.

Marshall, N. B. (1971). *Explorations in the life of fishes*. Cambridge, Massachusetts: Harvard University Press.

Marshall, N. B. (1973a). Family Macrouridae. In *Fishes of the western North Atlantic*. Cohen, D. M. (ed.) *Mem. Sears Fdn mar. Res.* 1(6): 496–665.

Marshall, N. B. (1973b). Macrouridae. In *Check list of fishes of the north-eastern Atlantic and of the Mediterranean* 1: 287–299. Hureau, J. C. & Monod, Th. (eds). Paris: Unesco.

Marshall, N. B. & Cohen, D. M. (1973). Order Anacanthini (Gadiformes). In *Fishes of the western North Atlantic*, Cohen, D. M. (ed.) *Mem. Sears Fdn mar. Res.* 1(6): 479–495.

Marshall, N. B. & Merrett, N. R. (1977). The existence of a benthopelagic fauna in the deep sea. In *A voyage of discovery*: 483–497. Angel, M. (Ed.) Oxford: Pergamon Press.

Mauchline, J. (1972). The biology of bathypelagic organisms especially Crustacea. *Deep Sea Res.* **19**: 753–780.

Mead, G. W., Bertelsen, E. & Cohen, D. M. (1964). Reproduction among deep sea fishes. *Deep Sea Res.* **11**: 569–596.

Menzies, R. J. (1962). On food and feeding habits of abyssal organisms as exemplified by the Isopoda. *Int. Revue ges. Hydrobiol.* **47**: 339–359.

Merrett, N. R. (1978). On the identity and pelagic occurrence of larval and juvenile stages of rattail fishes (Family Macrouridae) from 60°N, 20°W and 53°N, 20°W. *Deep Sea Res.* **25**: 147–160.

Moiseev, P. A. (1973). Development of fisheries for traditionally exploited species. *J. Fish. Res. Bd Can.* **30**: 2109–2120.

Moser, M. (1976). Protozoa (Myxosporida) as biological tags in deep-sea macrourid fishes. In *Book of abstracts*: 145. Joint Oceanographic Assembly, Edinburgh, Scotland. 13–24 September 1976. Rome: F. A. O.

Motais, R. (1960). Quelques observations sur la biologie d'un poisson abyssal *Trachyrinchus trachyrinchus* Risso et sur les conditions de vie en mer profonde. *Bull. Inst. oceanogr. Monaco* No. 1165: 1–79.

Murray, J. & Hjort, J. (1912). *The depths of the ocean*. London: Macmillan.

Novikov, N. P. (1970). [Biology of *Chalinura pectoralis* in the North Pacific]. In *Soviet fisheries investigations in the north-east Pacific* Part V: 304–331. Moiseev, P. A. (ed.). [In Russian.] (Translated from Russian by Israel Progr.. Sci. Transl. Jersusalem 1972.)

Okamura, P. (1970). Studies on the macrourid fishes of Japan. Morphology, ecology and phylogeny. *Rep. Usa mar. biol. Stn Kochi Univ.* **17**: 1–189.

Ottaway, E. M. & Simkiss, K. (1977a). "Instantaneous" growth rates of fish scales and their use in studies of fish populations. *J. Zool., Lond.* **181**: 407–419.

Ottaway, E. M. & Simkiss, K. (1977b). A method of assessing factors influencing 'false check' formation in fish scales. *J. Fish. Biol.* **11**: 681–687.

Pannella, G. (1971). Fish otoliths: daily growth layers and periodical patterns. *Science, N. Y.* **173**: 1124.

Pannella, G. (1974) Otolith growth patterns: an aid in age determination in temperate and tropical fishes. In *The ageing of fish*: 28–39. Bagenal, T. B. (ed.) Old Woking: Unwin Brothers.

Parsons, L. S. (1976). Grenadiers. *Bull. Fish. Res. Bd Can.* **194**: 19–23.

Pechenik, L. N. & Troyanovskii, F. M. (1970). [*Trawling resources of the North Atlantic slope.*] Murmansk [In Russian] Transl: Israel Program for Scientific Translations, Jerusalem: 1–77.

Phleger, C. F. (1971). Biology of macrourid fishes. *Am. Zool.* **11**: 419–423.

Podrazhanskaya, S. G. (1967). Feeding of *Macrurus rupestris* in the Iceland area. *Annls biol., Copenh.* **24**: 197–198.

Podrazhanskaya, S. G. (1971). Feeding and migrations of the roundnose grenadier, *Macrurus rupestris* in the northwest Atlantic and Iceland waters. *ICNAF Res. Doc.* 71/89.

Rannou, M. (1975). Données nouvelles sur l'activité reproductrice cyclique des poissons benthiques bathyaux et abyssaux. *C.r. hebd. Séanc. Acad. Sci. Paris* **281** (D): 1023–1025.

Rannou, M. (1976). Age et croissance d'un poisson bathyal: *Nezumia sclerorhynchus* (Macrouridae Gadiforme) de la mer d'Alboran, *Cah. Biol. mar.* **17**: 413–421.

Rannou, M. & Thiriot-Quievreux, C. (1975). Structure des otolithes d'un Macrouridae bathyal (Poisson Gadiforme). Etude au microscope électronique à balayage. *Annls Inst. oceanogr. Paris* **51**: 195–201.

Riley, G. A. (1951). Oxygen, phosphate and nitrate in the Atlantic ocean. *Bull. Bingham oceanogr. Coll.* **13**(1): 1–126.

Rokop, F. J. (1974). Reproductive patterns in deep-sea benthos. *Science, N.Y.* **186**: 743–745.

Rokop, F. J. (1977). Seasonal reproduction of the brachiopod *Frieleia halli* and the scaphopod *Cadulus californicus* at bathyal depths in the deep sea. *Mar. Biol.* **43**: 237–246.

Ross, L. G. & Gordon, J. D. M. (1978). Guanine and permeability in the swimbladders of slope-dwelling fish. In *Physiology and behaviour of marine organisms*: 113–121. McLusky, D. S. & Berry, A. J. (Eds) Oxford: Pergamon Press.

Russell, F. S. (1976). *The eggs and planktonic stages of British marine fishes.* London & New York: Academic Press.

Sanzo, L. (1933). Macruridae. *Fauna Flora Golfo Napoli* **38**: 255–265.

Savvatimskii, P. I. (1969). [The grenadier of the North Atlantic.] *Trudy polyar. nauchno-issled. proekt. Inst. morsk, ryb. Khoz. Okeanogr.* **1969**: 3–72 [In Russian] (Fish. Res. Bd Can. Transl. Ser. No. 2879. 1974).

Savvatimskii, P. I. (1971). Studies on the age and growth of roundnose grenadier (*Macrourus rupestris* Gunn.) in the North Atlantic, 1967–1970. *ICNAF Redbook* 1971, part III: 125–138.

Savvatimskii, P. I. (1972). [The age of the rock grenadier in the north-west Atlantic and a possible influence of fisheries on its population numbers.] *Trudy polyar. nauchno-issled. proekt. Int. morsk. ryb. Khoz. Okeanogr.* **28**: 116–127. [In Russian]. (Fish. Res. Bd Can. Transl. Ser. No. 2491. 1973).

Schoener, A. (1968). Evidence for reproductive periodicity in the deep-sea. *Ecology* **49**: 81–87.

Schwassmann, H. O. (1971). Biological rhythms. In *Fish physiology* **6**: 371–428. Hoar, W. S. & Randall, D. T. (eds). New York & London: Academic Press.

Sedberry, G. R. & Musick, J. A. (1978). Feeding strategies of some demersal fishes of the continental slope and rise off the Mid-Atlantic coast of the U.S.A. *Mar. Biol.* **44**: 357–375.

Simkiss, K. (1974). Calcium metabolism of fish in relation to ageing. In *The ageing of fish*: 1–12. Bagenal, T. B. (ed.) Old Woking: Unwin Brothers.

Stanek, E. (1971). [Studies on the fish stock in waters off Labrador and Newfoundland]. *Proc. Mar. Fish. Inst. Jubilee Vol.*: 121–146. [Polish]. (Fish. Res. Bd Can. Transl. Ser. No. 2754, 1973.)

Suda, A. (1973). Development of fisheries for nonconventional species. *J. Fish. Res. Bd Can.* **30**: 2121–2158.

Svetovidov, A. N. (1948). [*Fauna of U.S.S.R. Gadiformes*]. [In Russian.] Israel Program for Scientific Translations, Jerusalem, 1962.

Svetovidov, A. N. (1973). Merlucciidae and Gadidae. In *Check list of fishes of the north-eastern Atlantic and of the Mediterranean*. **1**: 300–320. Hureau, J. C. & Monod, Th. (Eds). Unesco, Paris.

Swift, D. R. & Pickford, G. E. (1965). Seasonal variation in the hormone content of the pituitary gland of the Perch (*Perca fluviatilis*). *Gen. comp. Endocr.* **5**: 354–365.

Templeman, W. (1970). A review of the morid fish genus *Lepidion* of the North Atlantic with first records of *Lepidion eques* from the Western North Atlantic. *J. Fish. Res. Bd Can.* **27**: 457–498.

Turekian, K. K., Cochran, J. K., Kharkar, D. P., Cerrato, R. M., Vaišnys, J. R. Sanders, H. L., Grassle, J. F. & Allen, J. A. (1975). Slow growth rate of a deep-sea clam determined by ^{228}Ra chronology. *Proc. natn. Acad. Sci. USA* **72**: 2829–2832.

Weatherley, A. H. (1972). *Growth and ecology of fish populations*. London & New York: Academic Press.

Wheeler, A. (1969). *The fishes of the British Isles and North-West Europe*. London: Macmillan.

Williams, T. & Bedford, B. C. (1974). The use of otoliths for age determination. In *The ageing of fish*: 114–123. Bagenal, T. B. (Ed.). Old Woking: Unwin Brothers.

Yanulov, K. P. (1962). [On the reproduction of the rough headed grenadier (*Macrurus berglax* Lacépède).] *Zool. Zh.* **41**: 1259–1262.

Symp. zool. Soc. Lond. (1979), No. 44, 361–382

Fish Stocks: Their Life-History Characteristics and Response to Exploitation

D. J. GARROD and B. J. KNIGHTS

MAFF Fisheries Laboratory, Lowestoft, Suffolk, England

SYNOPSIS

The life-history strategies and characteristics of species have evolved to provide a population growth potential which will enable a species to persist against the severity and variability of its physical and biological environment. Harvesting generates an additional constraint on a resource and its response exploits the same mechanism: its resilience depends on its population-growth characteristics. A generalized stock and recruitment relationship is used to demonstrate how life-history characteristics, e.g. individual growth, mortality, age at maturity and fecundity, may combine to generate population growth rates characteristic of different species. These are discussed against a conceptual framework which defines a species "niche", in terms of the severity and variability of its "total" environment, to explain features of the global pattern of fish production and to characterize the response to exploitation of species with different population growth patterns.

INTRODUCTION

The review of primary and secondary production cycles shows that their distribution, and the global distribution of fish production per unit area, can be associated with latitude and the proximity of continental land masses (Cushing, 1975). In Table I, these two physical characteristics are used to categorize estimates of potential fish production reviewed by Gulland (1970) into six zones, namely Arctic shelf, temperate shelf, temperate boundary, upwelling, tropical boundary and tropical shelf waters. "Boundary zones" refer to localities where continental shelf waters are relatively narrow and contiguous with major oceanic current systems. The potential fish production in these zones has been summarized as tonnes km^{-2} of "shoaling pelagic" and "demersal" species defined by Gulland. These estimates are rounded to the nearest tonne to damp the approximations, in both quantity and area, which are inevitable in such a broad generalization, but a number of features can be seen in the data illustrated in Fig. 1. Two important points are that (1) the highest levels of potential fish production occur in the upwelling and boundary zones and (2) the increase is associated with a predominance of "shoaling pelagic" species.

TABLE I

Statistical characteristics of stock/recruitment regression model, Log R = A + B log E

| | Stock | | | | | | | |
| | Arcto-Norwegian | | North Sea | | | Atlanto-Scandian Herring | California Sardine | Grouped data |
	Cod	Haddock	Haddock	Plaice	Herring			
Observations	26	26	46	23	25	20	19	185
A^*	−0·33	−1·42	−0·47	−0·59	+0·77	−1·57	−1·17	−1·25
B	0·16	0·67	0·09	0·14	+	0·62	0·62	0·57
r	0·13	0·27	0·07	0·08	+	0·57	0·57	0·78
Percentage variance in regression	1·7	7·4	0·5	7·2	+	32·3	32·9	60·9
sd residuals	0·32	0·45	0·50	0·15	0·20	0·51	0·29	0·42
Probability of B	<0·5	<0·2	<0·7	<0·8	−	<0·01	<0·01	<0·01

* Differs from text by scaling factor used in regression analysis.

Zone	Locality	Tonnes km^{-2}	Percentage pelagic shoaling
Arctic Shelf	Sea of Okhotsk		41
	Bering Sea		46
	NE Arctic		37
	Labrador/Newfoundland		25
Temperate Shelf	Sea of Japan		32
	Nova Scotia/St Lawrence		41
	New England		37
	Argentine/Falkland		63
	North Sea/Westerly		63
Temperate Boundary	Greenland		29
	Iceland		40
	Faroe		19
	Gulf of Alaska		76
	NE Pacific Transition		61
	SE Pacific (Chile)		71
	South Africa		77
	NW Pacific (Kuroshio)		63
Tropical Boundary	E Central Atlantic		79
	E Central Pacific		89
Upwelling	SW Africa/Angola		73
	Peru		99
Tropical Shelf	W Central Atlantic		59
	Indonesia		9
	Philippines		27

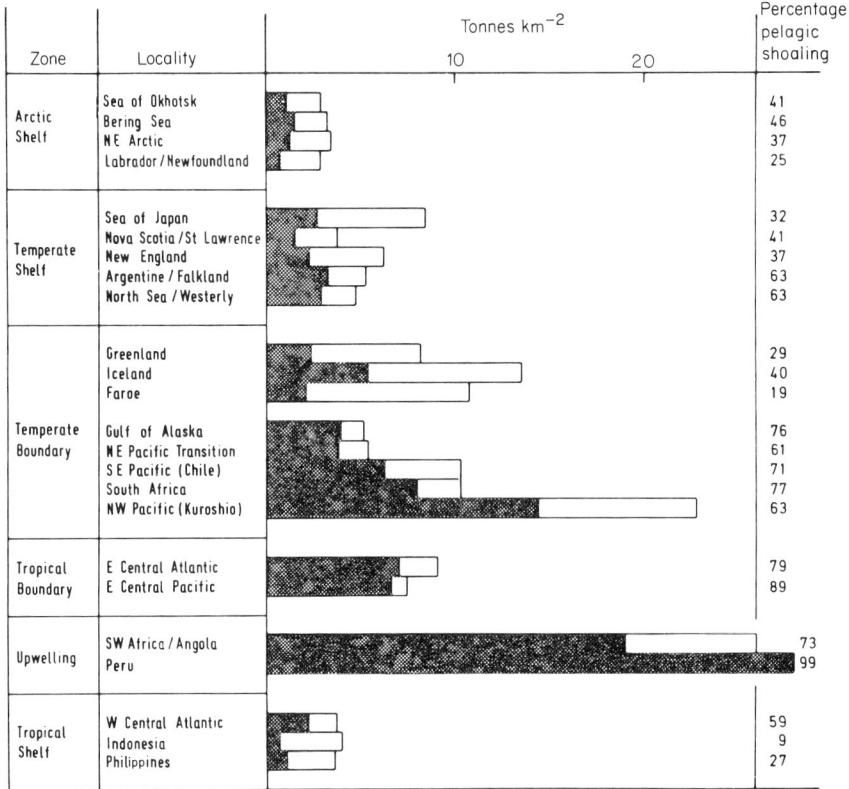

FIG. 1. Potential fish production per km^2 in selected geographic zones (percentage of "pelagic shoaling" species, ▓).

There are two other interesting aspects: the dominance of demersals over pelagics in the north Atlantic and *vice versa* in the north Pacific, in what would superficially appear to be two ecologically similar zones, and the low estimates of production for tropical shelf areas. It is possible (but unlikely) that Gulland's figures underestimate the potential of shoaling pelagics in the tropical shelf areas, and, certainly, the estimates for demersals will be low because of the inadequacy of statistics, but neither of these reasons, nor the exclusion of crustacean production, is sufficient to account for the difference in potential production between tropical shelf and tropical boundary or upwelling zones.

The variation in production with latitude undoubtedly reflects fundamental differences in the productivity of the ecosystems involved but the qualitative differences are equally interesting and point to some other characteristic which determines the relative importance of the shoaling pelagic and demersal categories. The classification of zones adopted in Fig. 1 may be broadly related to environmental variability and we suggest that it may play an important role in this context. The adaptive response of an organism, and hence the ability of populations to persist in variable environments, may involve a suite of life-history characteristics which differs from that of species adapted to a more stable environment, the adaptation being expressed in the changes in population growth rate required to offset the effect of variation at reduced population levels.

Exploitation is an analogous form of stress which can only be overcome by increased population growth. The response of a population to exploitation, which determines its fishery-productivity, is therefore intimately related to the adaptive response of a population to environmental stress and consequently to its life-history characteristics. This paper explores the influence of life-history characteristics on population growth rates and their relationship to the observed distribution of the major resource categories and their productivity.

POPULATION GROWTH

Recruitment

The potential production in Fig. 1 reflects the size of the stocks and the production to biomass ratios they can sustain. Both are determined by the population growth characteristics but, while the potential growth of fish species is well documented, population growth has received less attention because it depends on the relationship between stock and recruitment which cannot yet be specified with reliability for any fish stock. In Fig. 2, the number of one-year-old recruits is plotted against egg production for three north Atlantic stocks to illustrate the problem. The data are highly variable and, though customarily fitted by either an asymptotic (Beverton & Holt, 1957) or a dome-shaped (Ricker, 1954) relationship, there is little evidence of a functional relationship between recruitment and the number of eggs spawned.

Clearly, stock size is only one of a number of factors which influence recruitment. Physiological condition of the adults, success of fertilization, the distribution of spawning in time and space in relation to physical characteristics of the environment, and the relative abundance of prey or predator organisms appropriate to each phase of fish larval development may all contribute to the variability in Fig. 2.

It need not be surprising, then, that the influence of stock size alone should be difficult to detect even though the immediate cause of juvenile mortality might be associated with the local density of larval fish in a particular patch of organisms. Reddingius & den Boer (1970) have examined the effect of increasing numbers of environmental factors on net reproductive success and concluded that overall survival rate will tend to some average value implying recruitment proportional to stock size.

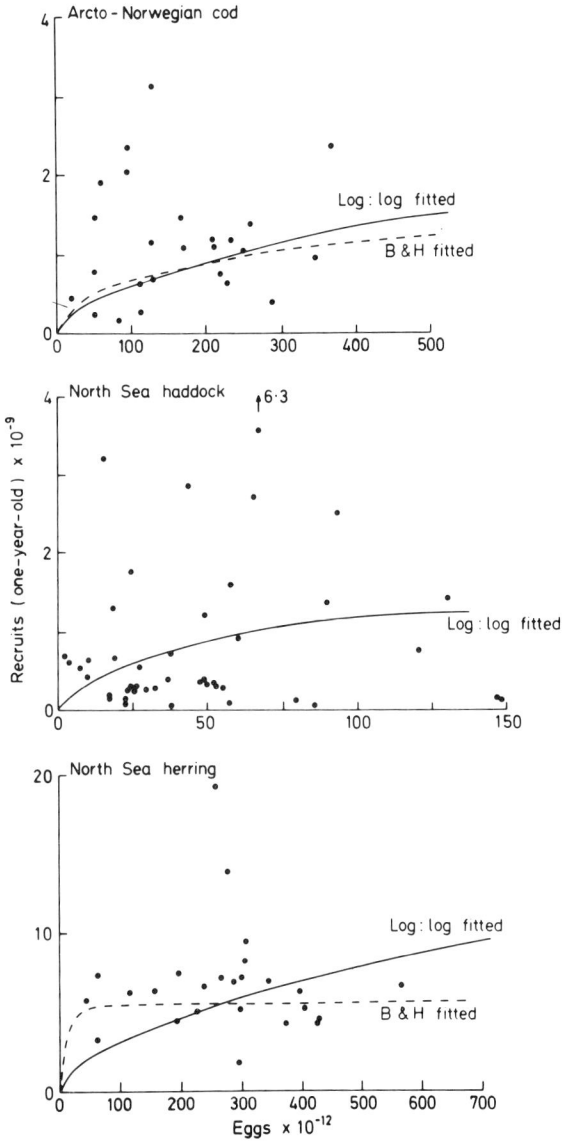

FIG. 2. Stock and recruitment data for selected north Atlantic species. B & H fitted, Beverton & Holt (1957) model.

Reddingius (1971) further observes that the sufficient conditions to ensure persistence of a population are very weak, being simply that the net rate of population increase per unit time should be greater than unity at low population numbers, and less than unity at high population numbers, and neither should lead to untenably low or high population numbers. In fact, there is no *a priori* necessity that recruitment should be rigorously dependent on stock density.

We also note that many life-history characteristics of fish, namely fecundity, age at maturity, growth, etc, will have been adjusted to the probability of egg/larval survival by long-term evolutionary and ecological processes. Stocks which are closely related and even adjacent exhibit fine distinctions in their growth, fecundity and maturation (Bagenal, 1973; Garrod, 1977), suggesting an ecological significance, which is easier to appreciate in a system where these characteristics exert a direct influence on recruitment rather than one in which it is determined at some subsequent phase of the life-cycle.

We have, therefore, re-examined stock and recruitment data to explore the implications of a relationship which is less rigorously determined by density-dependent processes, as defined by Cushing & Harris (1973), than in models by these authors or by Beverton & Holt (1957), or Ricker (1954) and to seek a generalization on which to estimate rates of population growth.

A Generalized Stock and Recruitment Relationship

The evolutionary adaptations referred to above imply that the relevant population parameters of a stock will be "internally" adjusted to each other to ensure that the unexploited stock will replace itself. On average, $R_{t+1} = R_t E_R \, e^{-Mo}$ where R_t, R_{t+1} are the numbers of one-year-old recruits in successive generations, E_R is the average number of eggs per recruit in the unexploited stock irrespective of sex and e^{-Mo} is the survival during the first year of life. At replacement $R_{t+1}/R_t = 1$ and hence $e^{Mo} = E_R$. The number of eggs per recruit is therefore a measure of the survival averaged over evolutionary time, which can be determined from the growth, sex ratio, age at maturity, fecundity and mortality in a cohort of a particular species, i.e.

$$E_R = \frac{\sum_{1}^{35} N_{t^*} \; \text{Sex ratio} \times \bar{W}_t \times \% \; \text{Maturity} \times \text{Fecundity}}{R_1}$$

where $R_1 = N_t$ where $t = 1$; $N_t = N_{t-1} \, e^{-M}$, where $t = 2 \ldots 35$ years; W_t is the mean weight at age and fecundity is defined as number of eggs g^{-1} female.

We have already noted that the underlying variation of survival of eggs to recruitment (R_1) between years is invariably sufficient to obscure its functional relationship to stock size (see Fig. 2). This difficulty can only be overcome by understanding the cause of variance, involving observations over many years, or by the combination of data from several stocks in the expectation that the relationship is driven by a mechanism common to each of them. We have followed the second approach, making use of the number of eggs per recruit, E_R. This defines the average number of eggs required to produce one R_1 recruit in the unexploited stock where the life-history characteristics are adjusted to ensure replacement. The ratio of egg per recruit of a species to some standard may then be used to scale the total egg production of that species at any stock level to the equivalent egg production by the standard.

Here, the standard has been based upon Arcto-Norwegian cod and haddock (*Gadus morhua* L., *Melanogrammus aeglefinus* L.), and North Sea haddock, plaice (*Pleuronectes platessa* L.), and herring (*Clupea harengus* L.), having a mean fecundity/recruit = $1·009 \times 10^6$ eggs estimated by the calculation described earlier. The scaling factor applied to the egg production of an individual stock is then $1·009 \times 10^6 / E_R$ (species). If the eggs per recruit ratio of a species is twice that of the standard, then the egg production of that species in terms of the standard will be one-half of the recorded egg production. This weighting procedure has been used to combine stock and recruitment data for the standard stocks and data for Atlanto-Scandian herring and California sardine shown in a log:log plot in Fig. 3.

Cushing (1969) and Paulik (1973) have shown that conventional stock and recruitment models may be approximated by a power function, here $R_1 = \alpha E^B$, over the limited range of stock sizes usually observed and, though there is no *a priori* reason to select a linear model, it can be seen in Fig. 3 that regression of the log-transformed data does provide an adequate summary.

Analysis of variance between regressions for the individual stocks (Table I) showed that the slopes of the regressions for Atlanto-Scandian herring and California sardine were significantly different from zero but not significantly different from each other. The slope for Arctic haddock was similar but not significantly different from zero and the slopes for other species (cod, haddock, plaice) were also non-significant. The total data set has therefore been approximated by the overall regression Log $R_1 = 1·251 + 0·574$ Log E), where $r = 0·78$, $P < 0·01$, giving the generalized stock and recruitment relationship $R_1 = 7·24 E^{0·574}$. It implies that, for all these stocks, a proportional increase in stock-size generates the same, but a less than proportional, increase in recruitment.

Strictly, the relationship must be at least slightly non-linear to provide a lower threshold of stock size where recruitment is zero but, with a regression slope $0·574$ i.e. <1, stocks governed by this relationship will stabilize. We note, however, that, although the pelagic stocks would stabilize at realistic levels, the asymptotic recruitment and stock size of the demersal stocks would be very high. This suggests an additional density-dependent reduction in recruitment beyond the upper limit of data

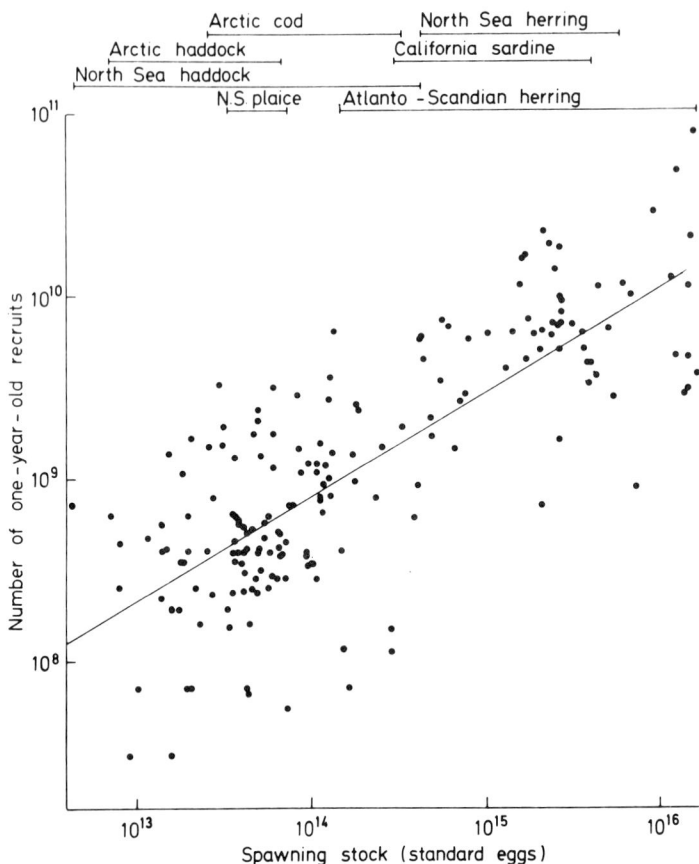

FIG. 3. Linear regression of standardized stock and recruitment data.

available here for each stock. The precise form of this non-linearity is likely to remain inaccessible because the stocks concerned will never be recovered to the appropriate level but, though it must be borne in mind, it need not concern comparisons of the growth potential of stocks at the observed stock levels.

This approach describes a generalized stock and recruitment relationship which contains an element of density-dependent reduction in the level of recruitment with increasing stock size which is implied by the coefficient 0·574. Stock and recruitment relationships for the individual stocks have been derived from it by retransformation of the stock weighting factor, the level of species stock appropriate to a specified recruitment being the number of standard eggs × 1/stock weighting factor. These are shown in Fig. 2 and compared with the fit achieved by the Beverton &

Holt (1957) model. Clearly, given the variability, the log-linear approach provides a statistical and biological summary of the data which is comparable to other models and which may be used as a basis for broad comparisons of population growth rates. The model itself is so simple, and as will be shown below, the implications in the summary of population growth are so interesting that we have assumed the approach to have wider application to species for which stock and recruitment data are not available. The results, outlined below for stocks other than those listed earlier, are entirely speculative but lend coherence to this review.

Population Growth Rates

The stock and recruitment relationships described above have been used to compare the rate of population growth by simulating their growth in numbers and biomass from low initial stock sizes. The simulations include the essential life-history characteristics and generate the stable population by allowing the stock to "grow" from low initial population numbers over a 200-year period, the recruits in each successive year being generated from the egg production of the annual spawning stock, using the species-specific stock recruitment relationship described earlier, i.e. $R_1 = 7 \cdot 24$ (egg production $\times$ species weighting factor)$^{0 \cdot 574}$.

Figure 4 shows the simulated growth against time for Arcto-Norwegian cod, North Sea herring and haddock, and North Sea sprat; *Sprattus sprattus* (L.), as a proportion of the equilibrium population size.

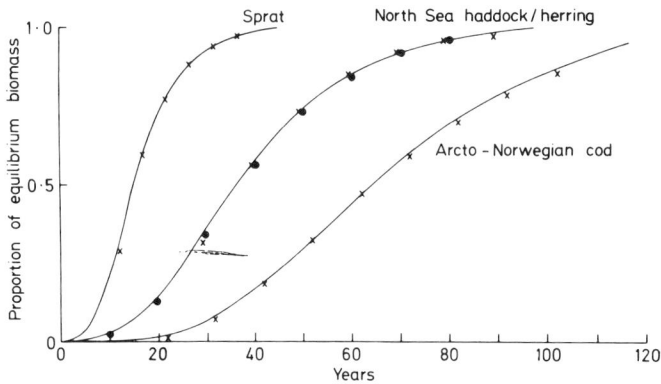

FIG. 4. Population growth curves of Arcto-Norwegian cod, North Sea haddock, herring and sprat.

These may be fitted almost exactly by Richards' growth function (Richards, 1959).

$$W_t^{1-m} = A^{1-m}(1 - b\, e^{-r't})$$

where W_t is the population biomass at time (t); A is the equilibrium biomass of the unexploited population; m is a constant related to the inflection of the growth curve; r' defines the rate of change in the weight function and b is a coefficient locating the time scale. (In Richards' nomenclature, the parameter r' is designated k: here it is redefined for convenience in later discussion of r- and K-strategies because it describes population growth rate though it is not formally the same as 'r' of the logistic growth curve.)

The growth parameters of Richards' equation, A, m and r', are given in Table II for a range of species. The estimates of A, the maximum

TABLE II

Population growth characteristics

	A	r'	m	$E/R \times 10^3$	P/B
Spurdog (*Squalus acanthias*)	70	0·02	1·03	$\cdot98 \times 10^{-3}$	0·03
North Sea plaice*	93	0·036	0·98	479	0·04
Pacific halibut	680	0·035	0·95	265	0·04
Arcto-Norwegian cod*	198	0·037	0·85	1970	0·04
Arctic haddock*	360	0·039	0·80	1981	0·05
Atlanto-Scandian herring*	86	0·044	0·77	91	0·05
North Sea haddock*	72	0·061	0·70	502	0·08
George's Bank haddock	412	0·053	0·67	212	0·07
North Sea herring*	26	0·053	0·65	111	0·09
California sardine*	1	0·094	0·47	144	0·17
North Sea sprat	0·4	0·131	0·41	17	0·26
Norway pout	1	0·184	0·27	10	0·44

A, r', m	Parameters of Richards' growth function $W_t^{1-m} = A^{1-m}(1 - b \, e^{-r't})$.
E/R	Eggs per recruit of unexploited stock.
P/B	Production/biomass ratio at maximum increment on population growth curve.
*	Species used as basis for generalized S/R relationship.

biomass, lie beyond the range of the stock and recruitment observations described earlier but do not alter the shape of the curves represented by m and r'. The values of the parameters follow a sequence from the slowest growing, long-lived species to the faster growing, short-lived species. Population growth is essentially similar to the growth characteristics of individual fish of each species but it should be noted that species with very different characteristics, e.g. North Sea haddock and herring, exhibit strikingly similar population growth rates. The time scale of population growth appears long for all species but it should be noted these are generated by a determined stock/recruitment relationship, without variance. In each species, development of the population extends over approximately three generations. The variations in population growth are determined by the population fecundity and the population biomass required to produce it. This can be illustrated by the growth of a hypothetical population where the asymptotic weight of individuals, their growth rate, sex ratio and fecundity (eggs g^{-1} female), are held constant and population growth varied by assumptions concerning natural mortality and age at maturity. The growth potential of three alternatives is shown in Fig. 5 as the annual increment in biomass (= potential yield)

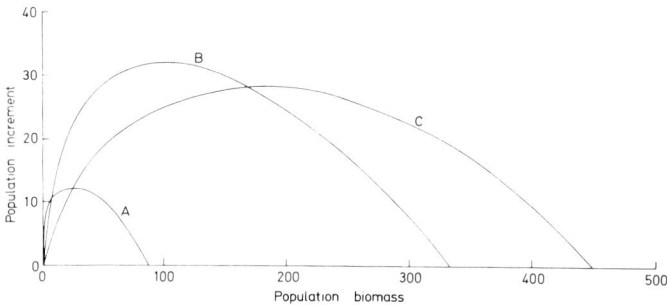

FIG. 5. Relative population growth of three hypothetical species to demonstrate a range of growth potential. A^{1-m}, the biomass of the unexploited population; m, r', parameters of Richards' equation (Table II); E/R, eggs per recruit; P/B (MSY), production/biomass ratio at the point of maximum sustainable yield (MSY); P_W(MSY)/P_W unexploited ratio of biomass of the population providing MSY to the biomass of the unexploited population.

	A^{1-m}	m	r'	E/R	P/B(MSY)	P_W(MSY)/P_W (unexploited)	Type
A	88	0·65	0·07	1·13	0·55	0·25	Short-lived, high growth rate
B	332	0·77	0·05	5·06	0·32	0·30	
C	426	0·90	0·03	1·15	0·16	0·43	Long-lived, slow growth rate

against biomass. There is an intermediate configuration of parameters providing population growth which may be modified in either of two directions. On the one hand, in A, an increase in natural mortality to a level where natural mortality/von Bertalanffy k, $M/K = 1·75$ (i.e. within the range of clupeid and engraulid species—Beverton, 1963), with age at maturity constant, will decrease the number of eggs per recruit. This leads to a population which is smaller but with more rapid growth (high r') and a production/biomass ratio which is higher at its maximum than in the other alternatives, and which occurs at a lower proportion of A (i.e. would be realized at a higher level of exploitation). Other things being equal, delayed maturity (C) also reduces the eggs per recruit but, in this case, it leads to a slower growing (low r') population which, though potentially larger in biomass, has a lower production/biomass ratio occurring at a higher proportion of the potential maximum.

These three examples capture the essential features of the growth patterns of species listed in Table II and demonstrate the rich potential for variation implicit in the stock and recruitment relationship used. The rapid population growth *A* is broadly representative of morphologically small, fast-growing pelagic species, e.g. sprat or Norway pout, *Trisopterus esmarki* (Nilsson), and California sardine, *Sardinops caerulea* (Girard), which mature at an early age (one to two years) and produce relatively few eggs because of their small adult size. They also suffer a high natural mortality so that, although individuals may be capable of spawning over several years, reproduction of a cohort is effectively concentrated almost to a single year. North Sea herring and haddock populations show similar growth potential with life-history characteristics which are intermediate between the sprat, Norway pout and California sardine group and the slow population-growth types, e.g. Arcto-Norwegian cod, North Sea plaice, Pacific halibut (*Hippoglossus stenolepis* Schmidt) or the elasmobranch, *Squalus acanthias* L. These last all have similar growth potential. Individuals are slow growing, they mature later in life (many as late as seven to eight years of age), and have a relatively low level of natural mortality so that the reproduction of a cohort spans several years. Fecundity is in many instances extremely high, e.g. in cod, but the same population growth potential can be achieved by the completely different, low-fecundity, ovoviviparous strategy of *Squalus acanthias*.

One of the most interesting theoretical features is that the population growth curves are asymmetric sigmoid and do not follow the symmetric logistic form. Indeed the influence of the life-history characteristics is expressed in the degree of asymmetry from the logistic form.

PRODUCTION/BIOMASS RATIOS, STOCK SIZE AND THE EFFECT OF EXPLOITATION

The relationship between growth potential, as represented by r', the production/biomass (P/B) ratio at the maximum yield level, and the population level at which this occurs is illustrated in Fig. 6 for a number of commercially important stocks.

The series reflect the intuitively logical sequence from the low to high r' described earlier. The P/B ratio used here expresses production (= potential yield) as a proportion of the biomass of the stock of fish (one year and older) to avoid the complexities of comparing the exploited stocks of different species which depend on the pattern of ages exploited in different fisheries. As a result, the P/B ratios of Table II are lower than one would normally expect in respect of the exploited stock. Figure 7 shows P/B ratios as a function of proportionate stock size. Here, again, the correspondence between the degree of depletion and level of exploitation will depend on the ages exploited but it serves to show the different scales of productivity implied by the three population growth options of Fig. 5.

We are conscious of having taken a liberal interpretation of available data to establish this framework relating the life-history strategies and potential yield of different species. It is therefore inappropriate to draw any conclusions concerning the precise effects of exploitation on particular species, or to seek specific reasons for the observed collapse of particular resources. Nevertheless, the population growth patterns do have characteristics of general interest.

Many of the great commercial fisheries are based on species with population growth characterized by intermediate values of m and r^1 in Table II, and reference to Fig. 6 will show that equivalent potential can be achieved by several species, each of which will exhibit unique life-history parameter combinations. The trade-off in terms of yield between high and low r'-strategies is, however, of considerable interest in determining exactly why species supporting the major fisheries show intermediate values.

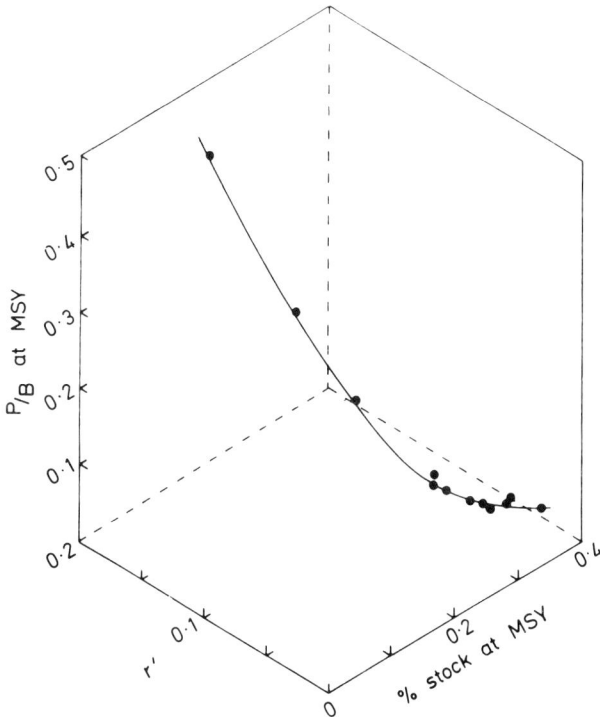

FIG. 6. Plot of population growth parameters for a range of species. P/B, production/biomass ratio; MSY, maximum sustainable yield. Descending order: Norway pout, sprat, California sardine, North Sea herring, North Sea haddock, George's Bank haddock, Atlanto-Scandian herring, Arctic haddock, Arcto-Norwegian cod, Pacific halibut, North Sea plaice, Spurdog (*Squalus acanthias*).

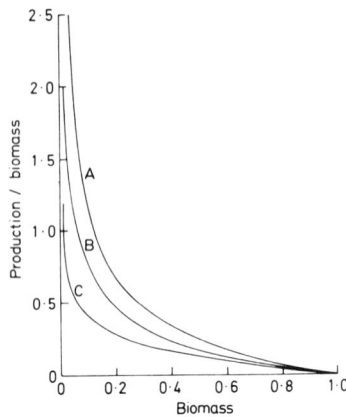

FIG. 7. Production/biomass ratios of three hypothetical species (Fig. 5). A, short-lived/high growth rate; B, intermediate; C, long-lived/slow growth rate.

High r' species, the opportunists, tend to be small fish, with maximum production at a higher level of exploitation than low r' species. Many of them are categorized as shoaling pelagics. Further, because of the short lifespan, the biomass accumulated in the unexploited stock is relatively low; the youngest age-groups predominate and hence they are intrinsically more variable. Exploitation evokes a rapid response but because of the low accumulated biomass and dominance of recruiting age-groups the decline in catch rates usually associated with increased exploitation will be masked by variations in recruitment. The consequence of these morphological, behavioural and dynamic characteristics is a resource capable of maintaining high but variable catch rates and a high but variable yield of small fish. The maximum P/B ratio is higher than that of low r' species and occurs at a lower proportion of the unfished stock, i.e. at a higher level of exploitation. They are an eminently suitable basis for an industrial fishery. But, as Fig. 5 shows, there will be a level of exploitation where a rapid decline in the potential yield will take place. High r' stocks will be susceptible to collapse.

At the other, low r' end of the scale, large long-lived species establish a large biomass in the unexploited state in which the recruiting year-class is relatively insignificant. The onset of exploitation leads to very high yields in the initial years as the stock moves towards equilibrium with the fishery. This adjustment is associated with a protracted decline in catch rates and an increase in variability as the average age of the stock declines and dependence on the recruit year-classes becomes relatively more important. These are the traditional human-consumption fisheries. Their productivity (P/B) is lower than that of high r' species (Fig. 7) and the yield/fishing mortality curve has a maximum at low levels of exploitation, which follows from the benefit of prolonged survival to the growth of individual fish. The shape of the production/biomass curve in Fig. 5 shows, however, that, although they may be less susceptible to sudden collapse as a result of exploitation than high r' species, they will be adversely affected by the slow expansion in fishing. Indeed, judging from records of earlier centuries, we may suspect that very low r' species in the north Atlantic, notably Atlantic halibut, *Hippoglossus hippoglossus* (L.), turbot, *Psetta maxima* (L.); brill, *Scophthalmus rhombus* (L.), and even sturgeon, *Acipenser sturio* L., might well have been overfished for many years. The potential productivity of these species is, in many respects, similar to the estimated productivity of whale resources.

The response of stocks to exploitation, therefore, may itself be seen as a continuum with different characteristics leading to fisheries with different purposes and histories. The fisheries for species with very low r' cannot sustain heavy exploitation and were reduced to relatively insignificant population levels in the earliest phases of fisheries development whereas fisheries for the high r' species are a comparatively recent development and already seen to be liable to collapse (e.g. Peruvian anchovetta, *Engraulis ringens* Jenyns). The enduring, high yield fisheries are those with intermediate population characteristics.

LIFE-HISTORY AND OTHER ECOLOGICAL FACTORS INFLUENCING GLOBAL DISTRIBUTION OF POTENTIAL FISH-PRODUCTION

So far, we have been concerned with population growth characteristics and their influence on the response of a stock to exploitation. The absolute stock size and potential yield in tonnage terms has at least three other dimensions: the productivity of the ecosystem, its variability and the species interactions which determine the structural stability and diversity of the community in which the stock occurs.

The stock and recruitment relationship used here can account for the numerical abundance of many species appropriate to highly productive systems, but not all. The ecological expectation is that adaptation to a lower (planktonic) trophic food-source would enhance population size purely as a result of energetic considerations and it is not immediately obvious how the postulated relationship might account for the very high abundance of some stocks, e.g. Peruvian anchovetta. We note, however, that stocks used in this analysis all have a restricted spawning season whereas high r' species include some which are characterized by extended spawning seasons, including perhaps serial spawning of eggs developed and matured over intervals of a few months, especially in tropical environments. In reality, these stocks may be composed of a number of breeding units, superimposed but phased in time in a manner analogous to that of the separate salmon stocks within rivers of the north Pacific but on a shorter time scale. Giesel (1974) discusses the adaptive significance of this strategy in a varying environment and one cannot dismiss the possibility that high stock size is generated by the overlay of breeding units each responding in the manner suggested for stocks with a restricted spawning season/area. It may even be an adaptation which is essential to fully utilize the carrying capacity of a very productive environment.

It is also apparent that population size is influenced by the variability of recruitment. Table III lists estimates of the standard deviation of $\log_e R_1$ in a number of north Atlantic stocks. The time series vary in length and no correction is made for stock size but the data show the recorded range with 95% confidence limits of, for example, 55–182% for Iceland cod ($\times 4$)

TABLE III

Standard deviation of year-class strength (Log_e) in selected stocks

Location	Species	σ	n
Gulf of St. Lawrence	Cod	0·27	30
Nova Scotia	Cod	0·32	15
South Newfoundland	Cod	0·34	17
Iceland	Cod	0·30	47
Irish Sea	Plaice	0·30	10
Irish Sea	Cod	0·36	11
Faroe	Saithe	0·38	15
North Sea	Plaice	0·40	43
Faroe	Cod	0·40	15
NE Arctic	Saithe	0·44	15
Faroe	Haddock	0·45	17
Iceland	Saithe	0·47	15
West Scotland	Saithe	1·48	15
North Sea (south)	Cod	0·50	11
Labrador	Cod	0·50	11
New England	Herring	0·51	16
Iceland	Haddock	0·55	20
Isle of Man	Herring	0·55	12
North Sea	Herring	0·61	47
Celtic Sea	Herring	0·63	11
West Greenland	Cod	0·68	48
North Sea	Saithe	0·76	15
North Sea	Sole	0·78	27
West Ireland	Herring	0·78	15
Nova Scotia	Haddock	0·87	10
Arcto-Norwegian	Cod	0·90	32
East Greenland	Cod	0·95	14
North Sea	Whiting	0·96	36
Arcto-Norwegian	Haddock	1·19	28
North Sea	Haddock	1·25	45
Atlanto-Scandian	Herring	1·33	20

n, number of years in time series.

and 10–1200% for North Sea haddock ($\times 100$). The effect of variance in recruitment on average population size is shown in Fig. 8, where the potential yield of high and low r' stocks is plotted against fishing mortality and the variability of recruitment as $\sigma \ln R_1$. The larger variance of

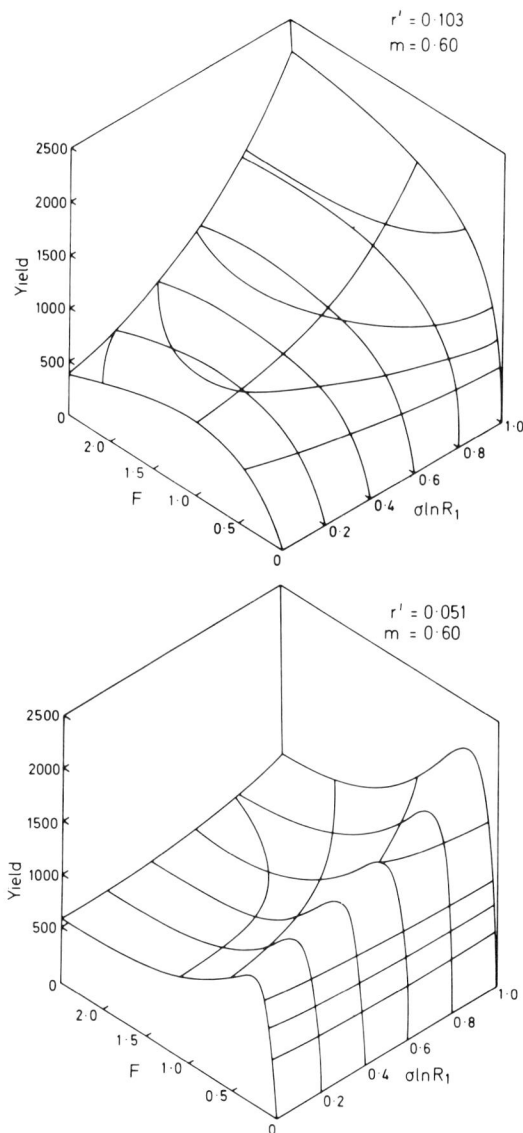

FIG. 8. Yield/fishing mortality curves of high and low r' species as a function of variation in recruitment ($\sigma \ln R_1$).

recruitment around the common mean of the stock/recruitment relationship will generate a higher average recruitment, stock size and
potential yield. The apparent mean stock size will be approximately
doubled within the range of recruitment variance observed. If this is
coupled with the response of stocks to the exploitation, it is evident that
high r' stocks (e.g. many shoaling pelagics), in an environment which
promotes high variability in recruitment, will appear to be very much
more productive than a low r' stock with a lower variation in recruitment.
The high potential yields of stocks within Gulland's (1970) shoaling
pelagic category may then be compounded from their population
characteristics which generate a predominantly high r' strategy, their
trophic relationships and spawning behaviour and the variability of
recruitment they experience.

   The summary of life-history characteristics of fish stocks, their variability and the productivity of the ecosystems in which they occur, can be
combined to attempt a broad rationale for the global pattern of fish
production summarized on p. 379. That identified three quantitative and
two qualitative aspects of potential yield. Quantitatively, there is a systematic variation in potential yield with latitude, including apparently low
potential yield in the tropical shelf areas and involving the variability of
the zones concerned. Qualitatively, zones of high potential are associated
with a high proportion of shoaling pelagic species and the balance
between shoaling pelagics and demersals is reversed in the north Atlantic
and north Pacific.

   The analysis of population growth has illustrated the two extremes of a
continuous spectrum of growth options, the short-lived, rapidly growing,
high r' type and the long-lived, slow-growing, low r' type. Southwood
(1976, 1977) and May (1976) develop the general consequences of these
alternatives and, drawing the analogy between r' and the intrinsic rate of
growth of the logistic, we may conclude that the high r' type will be better
adapted to tracking environmental fluctuation than the low r' population,
where the generation time tends to damp environmental effect. Inter-
preting environmental variability as referring to a range of periodic
frequencies as opposed to random fluctuation, one may speculate that
high r' species are opportunists able to take advantage of favourable
conditions with a short period. Low r' species, on the other hand, would be
better fitted to persist through long periods of adverse conditions that
occur in extreme environments.

   Both types occur within each of Gulland's (1970) resource categories
but one may associate zones of increased variability with conditions
favouring high r' species, and the predominance of high r' characteristics
amongst shoaling pelagic species. These relationships will explain the
predominance of shoaling pelagics in the most variable environments
which will therefore tend to be the most productive. Indeed, it may be that
the evolution of the extremes of the high r' characteristic is associated with
small size and a dietary dependence on the planktonic trophic level, so that

the high productivity implied by occupation of a lower trophic niche is enhanced by the life-history strategy required to exploit it.

At the other extreme, it is evident from the species considered earlier that many of the major commercial fisheries at high latitudes depend upon species with low r' characteristics.

These implications of periodic variation must be seen in conjunction with the fundamental productivity of an ecosystem. Periodic variation may be equated with Southwood's durational stability axis (Southwood, 1977) and productivity can be expressed in two dimensions, one dimension referring to environmental adversity and the second to biotic adversity, i.e. primary productivity per unit area. If biotic adversity is taken to increase from shelf waters toward oceanic systems, then the relationships described can be represented schematically as in Fig. 9. In effect a species niche is described by three dimensions of adversity—time, latitude and proximity to land. Diversity would be inversely related to adversity. The extremes of the durational axis have been associated with a predominance of high or low r'-strategists and within each the potential yield (as a level as opposed to a rate) is scaled from high to low according to the degree of adversity.

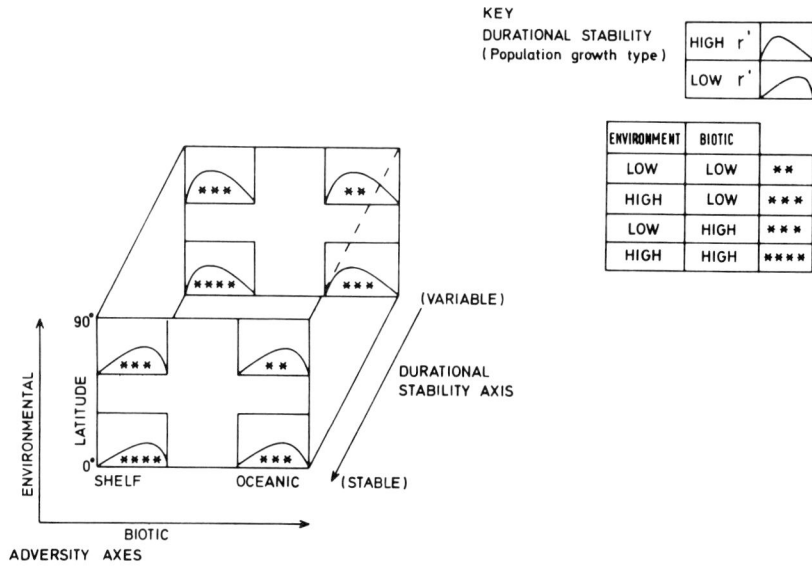

KEY
DURATIONAL STABILITY
(Population growth type)

HIGH r'	
LOW r'	

ENVIRONMENT	BIOTIC	
LOW	LOW	**
HIGH	LOW	***
LOW	HIGH	***
HIGH	HIGH	****

FIG. 9. Global patterns in potential fish production.

Relating this to known circumstances, variable habitats close to continental land mass at low latitudes may be expected to support high yields of predominantly high r' species as can be seen, for example, in tropical and subtropical upwelling zones. Conversely, variable habitats in the open ocean at high latitudes, if they can exist, would be less productive and we do not know of any fisheries that would meet this category though myctophids may be the appropriate species group. The intermediate circumstances of variable habitats at high latitudes on the shelf or at low latitudes in the open ocean are typified by the clupeid, engraulid and scombrid fisheries throughout the world.

At the stable end of the durational axis, little is known of the characteristics of fisheries in the open ocean at high latitudes but, if one adopts depth as an additional dimension of adversity instead of latitude, then the implied low potential of low r'-strategists may be seen in abyssal fish communities. The intermediate positions would apply to the great demersal fisheries of the north and south temperate zones.

The implied high production of shelf waters at low latitudes is less easy to reconcile unless one introduces the concept of diversity. These areas support fish communities with highly adaptive feeding and behavioural characteristics and, if these are typified by relatively low r' compared to, say, species in upwelling zones, their biomass may be high, but their potential yield would be low as described by May (1973) and in accordance with the data drawn from the review by Gulland (1970).

It must be emphasized that each axis is a continuous spectrum and species with both high and low r', both shoaling pelagic and demersal, occur in every habitat. This construction poses a number of questions on the relationships between species and ecosystems and it may suggest where some answers might lie. For example, it is possible to account for the predominance of shoaling pelagics in the north Pacific compared to the north Atlantic. These habitats lie near the shelf at high latitudes. Some evidence for their relative variability is provided by Moiseev (1956), who draws attention to the lower availability of shelf water in the north Pacific, the effect of the intensity of winter cooling on the physical characteristics of benthic habitats, and the dislocation between zones of planktonic production suitable for larval fish and areas suitable for other phases of the life history. The implication is that habitats in the north Pacific will be more favourable for high r' species normally associated with the shoaling pelagics. The north Pacific community may then lie further toward the "variable" extreme of the durational stability axis than the north Atlantic community.

The concepts of r'- and K'-strategists would then seem to apply to the two extremes of the durational stability axis. Southwood (1977: Table 1) lists contrasting suites of characteristics for the extremes of r- and K-selection which conform in most respects, e.g. generation time, size, dispersal, etc. But the fecundity characteristics of marine fish species are not easily reconciled with these ideas. The fecundity of very many teleosts is high but, within the group, fecundity per recruit is low for high r' species. Indeed, one might expect that the predominantly small size of opportunists necessitates low fecundity though it might equally require other devices to augment the number of eggs laid (serial spawning) or their survival (deposition of demersal attached eggs). The true 'K' strategy is best represented by the ovoviviparous and viviparous strategies of the elasmobranchs and it may be that the high-fecundity, low r' forms, e.g. many gadoids and pleuronectids, represent a third strategy, which is closer to that of the K-strategists, but require high fecundity as a consequence of their mode of reproduction and dispersal.

ACKNOWLEDGEMENTS

The study has been based on data for individual species contained in a very large number of papers, both published and unpublished. We are indebted to colleagues who have contributed to this body of data and, in particular, to Mr M. J. Holden and Dr R. C. A. Bannister who have made additional information available to us.

REFERENCES

Bagenal, T. B. (1973). Fish fecundity and its relations with stock and recruitment. *Rapp. P.-v. Cons. int. Explor. Mer* No. 164; 186–199.

Beverton, R. J. H. (1963). Maturation, growth and mortality of clupeid and engraulid stocks in relation to fishing. *Rapp. P.-v. Cons. int. Explor. Mer* No 154: 44–67.

Beverton, R. J. H. & Holt, S. J. (1957). On the dynamics of exploited fish populations. *Fishery Invest., Lond.* (2) **19**: 1–533.

Cushing, D. H. (1969). The fluctuation of year classes and the regulation of fisheries. *Fisk. Dir. Skr. (Havunders.)* **15**: 368–379.

Cushing, D. H. (1975). *Marine ecology and fisheries.* Cambridge: University Press.

Cushing, D. H. & Harris, J. G. K. (1973). Stock and recruitment and the problem of density dependence. *Rapp. P.-v. Cons. int. Explor. Mer* No. 164: 142–155.

Garrod, D. J. (1977). The north Atlantic cod. In *Fish population dynamics*: 215–242. Gulland, J. A. (Ed.). Oxford: John Wiley & Sons Ltd.

Giesel, J. T. (1974). Fitness and polymorphism for net fecundity distribution in iteroparous populations. *Am. Nat.* **108**: 1–321.

Gulland, J. A. (1970). The fish resources of the ocean. *FAO Fish. Biol. Tech. Pap.* No. 97, FIRS/T97.

May, R. M. (1973). *Stability and complexity in model ecosystems.* Princeton, New Jersey. Princeton Univ. Press.

May, R. M. (1976). Models for single populations. In *Theoretical ecology: principles and application*: 4–26. May, R. M. (Ed.). London: Blackwell. Sci. Publ.

Moiseev, P. A. (1956). Fluctuations in the commercial fish populations of the north-western Pacific in relation to environmental and other factors. In *International technical conference on the conservation of living resources of the sea*: 266–289. New York: U.N.

Paulik, G. J. (1973). Studies of the possible form of the stock recruitment curve. *Rapp. P.-v. Cons. int. Explor. Mer* No. 164: 302.

Reddingius, J. (1971). Gambling for existence. *Acta Biotheoret.* **20** Suppl. Primum XII.

Reddingius, J. & den Boer, P. J. (1970). Simulation experiments illustrating stabilization of animal numbers by spreading of risk. *Oecologia* **5**: 240–284.

Richards, F. J. (1959). A flexible growth function for empirical use. *J. exp. Bot.* **10**: 290–300.

Ricker, W. E. (1954). Stock and recruitment. *J. Fish. Res. Bd Can.* **11**: 559–623.

Southwood, T. R. E. (1976) Bionomic strategies and population parameters. In *Theoretical ecology, principles and application*: 26–48. May, R. M. (Ed.). London: Blackwell Sci. Publ.

Southwood, T. R. E. (1977). Habitat, the templet for ecological strategies. *J. Anim. Ecol.* **46**: 337–365.

Symp. zool. Soc. Lond. (1979), No. 44, 383–415

Physiological and Ecological Factors in the Development of Fish Culture

A. I. PAYNE

Lanchester Polytechnic, Coventry, West Midlands, England

SYNOPSIS

Current feeding practices in fish culture are compared with experimental work on feeding and growth in fishes. Progress in the substitution of plant or single-cell protein for animal proteins in artificial diets for primarily carnivorous fish is examined together with the possibility of improved feeds for herbivorous fish, to take advantage of the ability of these species to use plant rather than animal material. How the complementary properties of different fish species can be integrated into a mixed culture system, and thereby considerably improve yields, is discussed. Some extrapolation from experimental work is attempted to estimate an optimal feeding regime which takes into account economic considerations. The introduction of appetite stimulants to promote food processing and steroids to enhance growth offer further prospects. The application of steroids in this way leads to a consideration of their simultaneous use to effect sexual transformation or to repress sexual maturity in order to prevent reproduction in controlled populations and to reduce energy expenditure on reproduction. The techniques and role of induced spawning in fishes are discussed. The effect of salinity tolerance on growth in brackish-water fish is also examined.

The inter-relationships of respiration, appetite, growth and oxygen supply, and their implications for management, are considered.

INTRODUCTION

Fundamentally, fish culture involves the growth of fish under conditions over which we have some degree of control. A principal aim, therefore, is to create the optimal conditions for growth. Growth is, to some extent, a luxury in that energy and materials will only begin to accumulate after the energy requirements of catabolic processes, including those of standard metabolism, food processing and activity have been met (see Elliott, this volume p. 29). In deciding upon the optimal conditions, therefore, the interplay of the environment, particularly food supply, upon these other factors, as well as on growth itself, must be taken into account. Furthermore, growth is also regulated internally, largely by the endocrine system, and may depend on the stage of development of the fish so that, for example, additional effects associated with the degree of maturity and also seasonal spawning might be superimposed upon the general change in growth with age and size. Manipulation of the internal as well as the external environment must be considered, therefore, in relation to optimal conditions for growth.

Much work has been carried out in recent years, both in the laboratory and in the field, concerning the factors influencing fish growth. The aim, here, is to draw together the themes from this work and assess their prospective contributions to the development of fish culture. In doing this, the level of technology and expertise required in relation to the wide range of social and economic backgrounds under which the procedures will have to be applied must be a major consideration.

FOOD AND FEEDING

Diet Composition

Sophisticated fish diets are currently available which are largely a result of intensive work on fish nutrition in connection with salmonid culture (Halver, 1972; Cowey & Sargent, 1972; Halver, 1976). These diets are readily assimilated by fish, usually with an efficiency greater than 90%, and are converted into new fish tissue with a net growth efficiency (growth as percentage of energy assimilated) generally in excess of 30%. As the diets often include up to 40% by weight of fish meal, fish tend to process them as readily as natural animal food which, under optimal conditions, can be used with assimilation efficiencies greater than 85% (Winberg, 1956; Elliott, 1976; Beamish, 1972; Solomon & Brafield, 1972) and gross and net gross efficiencies of some 20% and 40% respectively (Pandian, 1967; Niimi & Beamish, 1974; Elliott, 1976; Winberg, 1956). Fish meal, however, although very effective in formulated diets, is becoming increasingly expensive and the supply is not entirely reliable. Consequently, it has become necessary to make more efficient use of this commodity or to find cheaper alternatives, usually based on plant products, in the diet of both carnivorous and herbivorous fishes.

The utilization by fish of plant and detrital food has received rather less attention than the use of animal sources, which is surprising bearing in mind the importance of herbivores and detritivores in extensive culture systems where natural food sources play a major role. Growth and assimilation efficiencies are both lower for fishes using plant material but precise values are scarce. The efficiency with which phytoplankton is assimilated by the cichlid fishes *Haplochromis nigripinnis* Regan and *Sarotherodon mossambicus* (Peters) varies from 40 to 70% depending upon the species of alga (Moriarty & Moriarty, 1973). The leaf-chewing grass carp, *Ctenopharyngodon idella* (Val.), has an assimilation efficiency of some 60% for a variety of higher plant types (Chiang, Ching & Ch'en, 1966; Hickling, 1966; Van Dyke & Sutton, 1977), whilst *Tilapia rendalli* Boulenger assimilated 53% of the protein and between 49 and 64% of the crude fibre from freshwater weeds (Mann, 1969). In browsing on mixed algal and detrital material, grey mullet have an efficiency of between 44 and 54% (Payne, 1975; J. E. Wilson, pers. comm.).

Estimates of the efficiency with which fish use plant food for growth are particularly scarce. The carp, *Cyprinus carpio* L, feeding on filamentous algae and detritus, was shown to have a net growth efficiency of 9% (Kevern, 1966). The maximum net growth efficiency achieved by the cyprinid *Barbus liberiensis* Steindachner, feeding on groundnut, was 15·1%, although, on average, young fish on optimal rations tended to have net efficiencies of 9–10% (Payne, 1973). In terms of nitrogen assimilated, grass carp had net efficiencies of 16% when fed on plant materials (Fischer, 1972). Chinese fish farmers generally reckon to give 60–70 kg leaves to obtain 1 kg of grass carp (Tapiador *et al.*, 1977) which, in bioenergetic terms, suggests a gross growth efficiency of some 2–3%.

The degree of difference in growth response to plant and animal diets is illustrated by the growth efficiencies observed in an omnivorous fish, *Barbus liberiensis*, fed on groundnut and shredded beef muscle (Fig. 1).

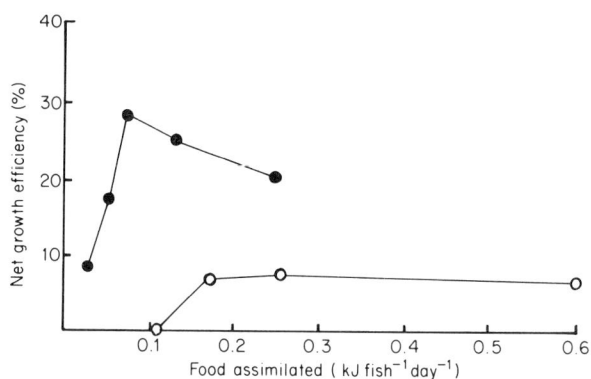

Fig. 1. The influence of diet quality and quantity on net growth efficiency in *Barbus liberiensis*; —●—, beef; —○—, groundnut (from Payne, 1973).

Whilst the maximum net growth efficiency on beef was 27·4%, a value comparable to those quoted above for other animal diets, the maximum efficiency for groundnut was only 6·9%. The peak gross efficiencies were 5·5% and 25·7% respectively (Payne, 1973).

Difficulty in the utilization of plant material is due partly to the relatively high level of indigestible substance in unprocessed plants and partly to a less satisfactory balance in the amino acid composition of plant proteins. Nevertheless, because they are cheaper, there is a great interest in using plant products to replace animal derivatives in fish diets. There have been two approaches in this direction; either the plant, or, in some cases, microbial material, has been used partially or entirely to replace fish meal in a pelleted diet or, alternatively, high grade pellets have been given along with a plant supplement such as grain, a popular procedure in extensive systems. In the first case, the plant material may be intended as a protein and/or energy source whilst, in the latter, the grain is intended mainly as an energy supplement so that the protein from the pelleted diet or from the natural food in the pond can be used more efficiently for growth. A further alternative for herbivorous types, of course, is to use unprocessed plant food entirely and accept the lower rates of production with the benefit of lower costs.

Paradoxically, much of the work on use of plant products in formulated diets has been carried out on carnivorous rather than herbivorous fish, mainly because these types have most commonly been used in the technologically sophisticated commercial systems of the developed countries. Because these fish tend to accept plant proteins less readily and also because only relatively small amounts of animal material are required for maintenance in fish, only partial replacement of fish meal with plant proteins is generally considered. Such mixtures can be used successfully by carnivorous fish so that, for example, the plaice, *Pleuronectes platessa* L., is able to utilize mixtures of fish/leaf protein concentrate from rye grass and fish/yeast protein extract almost as efficiently as fish alone (Cowey, Pope *et al.*, 1971). It was only when, in the first mixture, leaf protein exceeded 40% of the total protein content that efficiency of utilization declined markedly. It has also been found possible to substitute up to 25% of fish meal with soya in the diet of the rainbow trout, *Salmo gairdneri*, (Koops *et al.*, 1976) and up to 20% in that of the carp (Nomura & Fuji, 1969) without unfavourable effects on growth. In the carp, however, this was true only above 20°C as a marked relationship with temperature was observed. In the plaice, utilization of soya in a mixture with fish meal was relatively low partly because of poor assimilation but also because a proportion of the carbohydrates was unavailable (Cowey, Pope *et al.*, 1971; Cowey, Adron, Blair & Shanks, 1974).

Little work has been carried out on the use of plant proteins as the sole protein source of the diet. The biological values of a range of proteins have been determined for carp (Ogino & Chen, 1973a) as follows

Dried egg yolk	89
Casein	80
White fish meal	76
Wheat germ	78
Soybean meal	74
Petroleum yeast	73–79
Corn gluten meal	55

Thus, whilst animal proteins tend to have a slightly higher biological value than those of the plant, the differences are not very great. Ogino & Chen did note, however, that the biological value of all proteins declined as their percentage contribution to the diet increased beyond 10%. The plant proteins were also assimilated less well than the animal proteins (Ogino & Chen, 1973b). Work in progress at the University of Aston in Birmingham has shown that diets based on single-cell protein, blue-green algae concentrate or soybean meal are acceptable to both carp and rainbow trout and, perhaps surprisingly, utilized with equivalent efficiency by both species (T. Atack, pers. comm.). Soybean appeared to be the least effective.

The efficiency with which specific plant proteins are used for growth is found to be inferior to that for animal proteins because they are often deficient in one or more of the essential amino acids. For example, methionine is likely to be limiting in single-celled proteins and lysine in cereal and grass based diets (Halver, 1976). One obvious way around this would be to use a mixture of plant or microbial derivatives in the fashion recommended by human nutritionists, while an alternative is to supply the deficient amino acid along with the protein. Thus, for rainbow trout, Dabrowska & Wojno (1977) found that, with the addition of cysteine and trytophan, soybean protein could be used as efficiently as fish meal and allowed the substitution of 40% of the latter with soya. A significant enhancement was shown with the addition of cystein and lysine but not with lysine and arginine mixture. Similar work has also been carried out on augmentation of petroleum yeasts with amino acids (Nose, 1974a, b).

However, Koops et al. (1976) found that, while it was possible to substitute 25% of the fish meal with soya in the diet of rainbow trout, the addition of amino acids gave no further improvement. In carp, the addition of lysine, cystine and methionine along with the substituted soya meal gave improved growth only in young fish (Nomura & Fuji, 1969).

The use of mixed plant or single-celled protein sources to enhance growth and reduce dependence on fish meal has been attempted in a number of instances. A substitution of 25% of the maize meal by groundnut in an initial diet of 80% maize meal to 20% fish meal, given to *Sarotherodon mossambicus*, significantly improved both growth rate and food conversion efficiency (Mabaye, 1971). It is also notable that reasonable growth was obtained on the initial maize/fish meal diet bearing in mind the difficulties encountered elsewhere in substituting soya meal and other plant proteins for fish meal. *S. mossambicus* may, therefore, be able to process a relatively low-grade diet better than the other carnivorous or omnivorous fish discussed previously.

Meske & Pruss (1977) developed a basic fish-meal-free diet based on soybean meal and whey powder which they then mixed in various proportions with powdered algae. For the grass carp, an optimal diet was found to consist of 80% algal powder while a similar diet produced heavy mortality among the more naturally omnivorous common carp. For the common carp, however, a mixture of 68% basic diet plus 32% algal powder was found to be equivalent in quality to commercial fish foods.

There is some suggestion, therefore, that fish do differ in their ability to use plant proteins in accordance with their natural diet. Furthermore, it is apparent that, while mixtures of plant proteins can be effectively utilized for growth by some fishes, most of the diets developed still retain a small quantity of animal protein, most commonly fish meal or milk products. The use of plant mixtures alone to supply a full complement of amino acids, particularly for the more herbivorous fish, remains to be investigated.

Diets have been augmented with carbohydrates and lipids in order to exploit their protein-sparing capacity. In such cases, the digestibility of the diet as a whole can be reduced (Kitamikado, Morishita & Tachino, 1964; Koops et al., 1976; R. R. Smith, 1971). The digestibility of the protein component itself may not be interfered with, except when there is a high fibre or cellulose content, and the digestibility of the carbohydrate component is almost proportional to the molecular complexity, that of glucose, for example, being high whilst that of starch is somewhat lower (R. R. Smith, 1971; Halver, 1976). In several instances, it has been shown that the inclusion of a readily assimilated carbohydrate increases the efficiency with which protein is used for growth, by, for example, turbot, Psetta maxima (L.) (Adron, Blair, Cowey & Shanks, 1976), and, at least with high dietary levels of protein, in plaice (Cowey, Adron, Brown & Shanks, 1975) and rainbow trout (Lee & Putnam, 1973; Tiews, Gropp & Koops, 1975). For plaice, it seemed that, unlike in the turbot, an energy source of carbohydrate and lipid was more effective in increasing the efficiency of protein utilization than lipid alone. In the rainbow trout, lipid levels of 8–26% of the diet gave no increase in growth rate but gave improved food conversion efficiency (Lee & Putnam, 1973). Similar effects were observed when carbohydrate comprised 17–25% of the diet, although a level of 38% carbohydrate resulted in reduced growth and conversion efficiency (Edwards et al., 1977).

Improved Exploitation and Supplementation of Natural Food Sources

Similar approaches to the experimental work on diet formulation outlined above have been explored in pond culture. Here, however, there is the additional element of the natural food supply in the pond which itself can be encouraged with some form of fertilization. To obtain really high yields, however, some form of supplementary feed is generally required. In Israel, where extensive work on high density fish production has been carried out, supplementary feeding usually takes the form of sorghum grains or high protein pellets. An indication of the levels of production generally obtained from carp monoculture with three different types of feed is given in Table I. With intensive fertilization alone, daily increments in carp stocked at $1200\ ha^{-1}$ could be $3 \cdot 9\ kg\ ha^{-1}$ (Yashouv, 1957) whereas, when supplementary sorghum was given, increments of $11 \cdot 3$ and $16 \cdot 6\ kg\ ha^{-1}\ day^{-1}$ were attained when the fish were stocked at 2000 and $4000\ ha^{-1}$ respectively (Hepher, Chervinski & Tagari, 1971). The sorghum is given mainly as a carbohydrate energy source in order that the protein obtained from the natural food can be used more efficiently for growth in exactly the same way that carbohydrates were added to formulated diets in the experimental work quoted

TABLE I

The influence of diet on production and yields from carp monoculture

Species	Stock density ha^{-1}	Treatment	Daily increment (kg ha^{-1})	Growing season (days)	Total yield (kg ha^{-1})
Carp*	1200	inorg. fert.	3·9	172	670
Carp†	2000	sorghum	10·5	126	1323
Carp†	4000	sorghum	12·3	126	1550
Carp†	2000	pellets	16·5	90	1445
Carp†	4000	pellets	24·9	90	2241

inorg. fert. = inorganic fertilizer only (inorganic fertilizer applied in all treatments).
* Yashouv (1957).
† Hepher *et al.* (1971).

above. A combination of fertilization with the addition of protein-rich pellets gave further increases in fish production with values of 16·5 and 24·9 kg ha^{-1} day^{-1} (Hepher *et al.*, 1971) when stocked at similar densities to those above. The commercial carp pellets used in Israel tend to contain 25% protein of which 15% is from fish meal and the rest from grain derivatives.

The efficiency with which the total food supply in a pond is utilized can be further increased by stocking with more than one species of fish providing that there is little competition between the species, an approach the Chinese developed centuries ago (Table II). The Israelis have found that, for their purposes, the most effective mixture is the common carp, a tilapia, usually *Sarotherodon aureus* (Steindachner), and the Chinese silver carp, *Hypophthalmichthys molitrix* (Val.). The common carp is an

TABLE II

The influence of diet on production and yields from polyculture

Species	Stock density ha^{-1}	Treatment	Daily increment (kg ha^{-1})	Growing season (days)	Total yield (kg ha^{-1})
Carp, tilapia, silver carp*	4000	inorg. fert.	16·1	187	2980
Carp, tilapia, silver carp†	4500	sorghum	20·9	—	—
Carp, tilapia, silver carp*	8500	pellets	44·1	223	9710

inorg. fert. = inorganic fertilizer only (inorganic fertilizer applied in all treatments).
* Yashouv & Halevy (1972).
† Reich (1975).

omnivorous bottom feeder whilst *S. aureus* feeds mainly on algae and detritus with the result that, in mixtures of these two, there is little evident depression on the growth of carp, the most economically valuable fish, unless the tilapia are stocked at above $2\,500\ \mathrm{ha}^{-1}$. The production of tilapia, however, is often depressed in these mixtures (Reich, 1975). In combination with silver carp, a phytoplankton feeder, both tilapia and the common carp actually gave improved production compared to that in monoculture. The addition of the silver carp appears to increase the response of the other species to fertilization (Reich, 1975). Thus, carp stocked at $1000\ \mathrm{ha}^{-1}$ along with *S. aureus* and *H. molitrix* contributed $5 \cdot 23\ \mathrm{kg\ ha}^{-1}\ \mathrm{day}^{-1}$ to a total of $16 \cdot 14\ \mathrm{kg\ ha}^{-1}\ \mathrm{day}^{-1}$ (Yashouv & Halevy, 1972) compared to the $3 \cdot 9\ \mathrm{kg\ ha}^{-1}\ \mathrm{day}^{-1}$ when grown in monoculture as mentioned above. The total rate of production from this mixture, with only fertilization and no supplementary feed, was very similar to that of a carp monoculture at $2000\ \mathrm{ha}^{-1}$ which received protein-rich pellets, and is considerably in excess of the values for monoculture using only natural food sources (Tables I and II). It is thought that the particularly beneficial effect of the silver carp stems from increased primary productivity as a result of its grazing on the phytoplankton. In part, this could be due to increased light penetration as a result of the decrease in phytoplankton standing crop by grazing, which would enable primary production to take place throughout the water column rather than only close to the surface. In addition, as the assimilation efficiency of the silver carp is relatively low, large quantities of faecal material are deposited on the pond bottom to be used by tilapia and carp; substantial quantities of food are therefore made available to these fish (Reich, 1975). A further species, the grass carp, which feeds on leafy vegetation, can usefully be added to this combination (Moav, Wohlfarth *et al.*, 1977; Reich, 1975).

If this system of polyculture is used along with supplementary feeding, then very high rates of production can be achieved. Supplementation of sorghum grains to the fish stocked at a total density of $4000\ \mathrm{ha}^{-1}$ gave an increase from the rate with fertilizer alone of $16 \cdot 1\ \mathrm{kg\ ha}^{-1}\ \mathrm{day}^{-1}$ to $20 \cdot 9\ \mathrm{kg\ ha}^{-1}\ \mathrm{day}^{-1}$, whilst with pellets instead of sorghum the highest rate achieved was $49 \cdot 45\ \mathrm{kg\ ha}^{-1}\ \mathrm{day}^{-1}$ (Yashouv & Halevy, 1972). A similar rate of $49 \cdot 8\ \mathrm{kg\ ha}^{-1}\ \mathrm{day}^{-1}$ has also been attained with a mixture of common carp, silver carp, *Sarotherodon aureus* and grass carp (Moav, Wohlfarth *et al.*, 1977).

So it is clear that, whether in experimental situations, in monoculture or in polyculture, protein-rich pellets based on fish meal give the highest rates of production, although not all fish benefit from them. Tilapia (Yashouv & Halevy, 1972; Moav, Wohlfarth *et al.*, 1977) and silver carp (Moav, Wohlfarth *et al.*, 1977) benefit marginally, if at all, from protein-rich pellets and seem to be able to rely on natural food production for their protein requirements even at high densities. Nevertheless, protein-rich pellets have been used in some circumstances to induce very high production rates in tilapia monocultures (Rappoport & Sarig, 1975).

Sorghum grains have been found of little value in the case of tilapia (Rappoport & Sarig, 1975), grey mullet (Prugnin, Shilo & Mires, 1975) and grass carp (Moav, Wohlfarth *et al.*, 1977). In all of these instances, the basic problem may be in the particle size of the food since all except the grass carp are fundamentally microphagous.

Protein-rich pellets are, therefore, more effective in promoting growth than sorghum but, on the other hand, sorghum is only one-half of the price. The relative effectiveness of pellets and sorghum was recently examined by Rappoport & Sarig (1975) for very high density carp culture with forced aeration. The feed conversion ratio (FCR) was lowest at equivalent feeding rates for pellets and ranged from 3·1 to 4·2 compared to the range for sorghum of 4·9–8·5; i.e. less of the pellet feed was required per unit increase in growth. With high density polyculture, however, although the ranking was the same, the FCR was lower for both diets, being 2·46 for pellets and 3·22 for sorghum (Moav, Wohlfarth *et al.*, 1977), which indicates that the supplementary food was utilized more efficiently by a mixture of species. The use of a 50% pellet and 50% sorghum diet in the intensive carp monoculture gave a yield and FCR intermediate between those for sorghum and pellets alone. This presented the problem of whether the cheaper cost of the mixture compensated for its inferior performance compared to that of the pellets (Rappoport & Sarig, 1975). Moav, Wohlfarth *et al.* (1977) concluded that, in their polyculture experiments, although the FCR and yields from grain were inferior to those from pellets, the cost efficiency of their use was similar.

In order to dispense with grain or pelleted feeds as far as possible whilst still maintaining high yields, other approaches have been developed (Table III). Moav, Wohlfarth *et al.* (1977) used a mixture of common, silver and grass carps together with *Sarotherodon aureus* and fertilized the ponds intensively with liquid cow manure, adding from 250 to 1750 litres $ha^{-1} day^{-1}$, and some inorganic fertilizer. This was effectively recreating the Chinese traditional system with a slightly different mixture of fish and more precisely determined conditions. At the highest rate of fertilization, fish production attained a rate of 32·7 kg $ha^{-1} day^{-1}$ compared with 50 kg $ha^{-1} day^{-1}$ for control groups fed on protein-rich pellets and 29·9 kg $ha^{-1} day^{-1}$ for groups fed on grain pellets. Although the rate of production was lower than for the pellet group, it was still very high and FCR in terms of dry weight of manure added was calculated to be 2·7, just slightly greater than that for pellets. The total quantities of manure required to obtain substantial yields, however, are comparatively large. The Chinese generally apply 5000 kg ha^{-1} over a growing season whilst Moav, Wohlfarth *et al.* (1977) added up to 113 000 kg ha^{-1}. The Chinese normally expect to obtain some 0·5 kg silver carp or bighead for each 25 kg of undried manure supplied (Tapiador *et al.*, 1977).

At an Indian fish farm, Chaudhuri *et al.* (1975) used a mixture of partly indigenous, traditionally cultured species and partly exotic types to

TABLE III

The use of agricultural waste with polyculture

Species	Stock density ha^{-1}	Treatment	Daily increment (kg ha^{-1})	Growing season (days)	Total yield (kg ha^{-1})
Mixed Chinese carps*	approx. 15 000	org. manure plant waste	—	annual	3750 (standard) 11 430 (max)
Carp, tilapia, silver carp grass carp†	17 980	inorg. fert. org. manure	32·7	126	4121
Mixed Indian and exotic carps‡	7840	inorg. fert. org. manure vegetation	30·3	365	9389

inorg. fert. = inorganic fertilizer.
* Tapiador *et al.* (1977).
† Moav, Wohlfarth *et al.* (1977).
‡ Chaudhuri *et al.* (1975).
§ Southern China.

which they fed large quantities of a mixture of foodstuffs mainly derived from agricultural waste. The species involved and their mode of feeding is shown in Table IV. The ponds were heavily fertilized with both inorganic fertilizer and organic manure while supplementary feed consisted of groundnut oilcake, rice bran and chopped waterweeds given in large quantities. An effective means of distributing these foods was found to be mixing them into a dough and presenting them on trays at different depths. The greatest single contribution to the production came from the silver carp but it was evident that the processing of the water weeds by the grass carp had a particularly beneficial effect upon the bottom and marginal feeding common carp and mrigal. The result was a

TABLE IV

Experimental mixture of fish species used at Cuttack, India by Chaudhuri et al. *(1975)*

	Fish	Feeding niche
Major carps:	*Catla catla*	Surface: plankton, decaying vegetation
	Labeo rohita	Column: decaying vegetation
	Cirrhinus mrigala	Bottom: herbivore
Common carp		Bottom: omnivore
Silver carp		Phytoplankton
Grass carp		Leafy vegetation

rate of production of some $30 \cdot 3$ kg ha^{-1} day^{-1} when dry season inhibition is taken into account. This is similar to the results obtained by Moav, Wohlfarth et al. (1977) for the addition of liquid cow manure (Table III) and greater than most of the rates of production for monoculture, although it is rather lower than the rates achieved for polyculture experiments using protein-rich pellets (Yashouv & Halevy, 1972; Moav, Wohlfarth et al., 1977). The Indian experiments, however, unlike much of the Israeli work, continued over a whole year and so the actual yield gave an average of 8200 kg/ha^{-1} year^{-1} with a maximum of 9389 kg ha^{-1} year^{-1} (Table III), a total yield which substantially exceeds those obtained from the more traditional Asian polyculture systems. It has been sur-passed in experimental circumstances by, for example, a mixed system of carp, silver carp and tilapia, fed on protein-rich pellets, which gave a total yield of 8570–10 620 kg ha^{-1} (Yashouv & Halevy, 1972) and in high density monoculture, with forced aeration and protein-rich pellets, which produced 14 670–15 550 kg ha^{-1} (Rappoport & Sarig, 1975). In the latter case, the rate of production reached an astounding 142 kg ha^{-1} day^{-1} (Table V). However, the total duration of the growing season, as well as the rate of production, must be taken into account in assessing the productivity of the various systems, since there is evidence that an inhibitory crowding factor can severely curtail the period of growth in high density systems (Rappoport & Sarig, 1975).

TABLE V

Yields and production rates from intensive monoculture systems incorporating forced aeration and demand feeders

Species	Stock density ha^{-1}	Treatment	Daily increment (kg ha^{-1})	Growing season (days)	Total yield (kg ha^{-1})
Carp	45 000	pellets + forced aeration	142	110	15 550
Carp	45 000	sorghum + forced aeration	76	66	4990
Tilapia	80 000	pellets + forced aeration	167	100	16 750

Taken from Rappoport & Sarig (1975).

Feeding Regimes

There are other ways of obtaining the best return from food apart from altering its composition. It is apparent from Fig. 1 that the level of food intake, as well as the nature of the diet, influences the efficiency with which the food is used for growth. The relationships between food intake and growth efficiency and also body weight, based on factorial experiments using *Barbus liberiensis*, are shown more extensively in Figs 2 and 3. In all cases the growth efficiency increases from zero at the maintenance ration, where energy intake is in equilibrium with energy expenditure, to a maximum at some intermediate feeding level beyond which the efficiency declines progressively with higher rates of consumption. A similar pattern has been found in sockeye salmon, *Oncorhynchus nerka* (Walbaum) (Brett, Shelbourn & Shoop, 1969; Brett & Shelbourn, 1975); bluegill sunfish, *Lepomis macrochirus* Rafinesque (Gerking, 1971); brown trout, *Salmo trutta* L. (Elliot, 1975a); rainbow trout; and common carp (Huisman, 1976). The intermediate level of food intake, which is used most efficiently for growth, has been termed the optimal ration (Brett *et al.*, 1969; Elliott, 1975a). This can be estimated graphically (Brett *et al.*, 1969) or it can be calculated (Payne, 1973). The relationship between food intake and growth efficiency is derived from the curve describing the increase in growth rate with increasing food consumption (Fig. 4) which appears to have a characteristic form for a variety of fish and diets (Warren & Davis, 1967; Davis & Warren, 1968; Brett *et al.*, 1969; Payne, 1973; Elliot, 1975a). In terms of fish culture, this means that, although feeding fish at the maximum level will produce the highest growth rate (Fig. 4), the food will actually be used more wastefully than if fed at the optimal level (Figs 2 and 3). A greater economic return may be obtained by waiting a little longer to produce fish of a marketable size while using

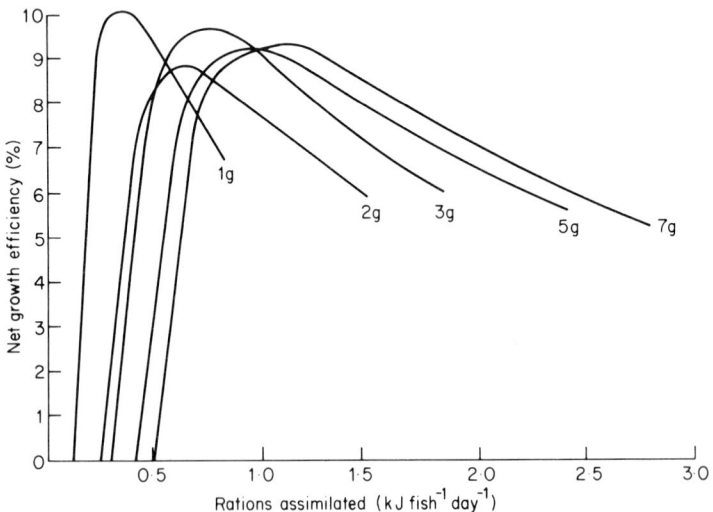

FIG. 2. Ration availability and net growth efficiency in relation to body weight (g) in *Barbus liberiensis* fed groundnut (from Payne, 1973).

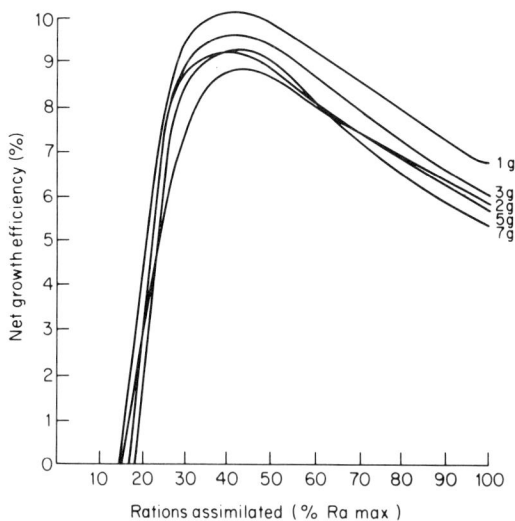

FIG. 3. Ration availability and net growth efficiency in relation to body weight (g) in *Barbus liberiensis* fed on groundnut with rations expressed as a percentage of the potential daily maximum quantity assimilated (% Ra max) at each body weight (from Payne, 1973).

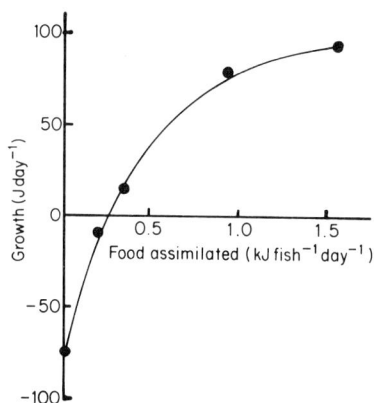

FIG. 4. The effect of ration availability on growth of *Barbus liberiensis* of 5 g body weight, fed groundnut (from Payne, 1973).

less food to achieve this, particularly if the food is a major item of expenditure. Zeitoun, Ullrey & Magee (1976) have devised a polynomial expression which takes into account both biological and economic considerations in determining optimal feeding levels.

The actual growth rate at the optimal ration can be quite high; Elliott (1975a) gives it as close to 80% of the maximum obtained at the highest ration level. Calculations from the data of other authors give equivalent values of 68% (Brett et al., 1969) and 64–74% (Payne, 1973).

The optimal ration is often considerably less than the maximum (Fig. 3). Thus, considering the 5-g fish, for example, 38·9% of the maximum ration gave 66·5% of the maximum growth rate. The ratio of optimal to maximum rations, however, appears to be dependent upon temperature (Brett et al., 1969; Elliott, 1975a) but, within the optimal temperature ranges, it can be calculated from the data of these two authors that the optimum is 59% and 60–72% respectively of the maximum ration.

Rappoport & Sarig (1975) tested the effect of reduced ration level in intensive pond culture of carp. For a 90-g fish, a 38% reduction from a feeding level near repletion gave a mean decrease in yield of only 22% and a 14% improvement in the conversion ratio. A similar procedure for 400-g fish produced an even greater improvement of 35% in the feed conversion ratio compared to that of the small fish. No direct control was carried out against which to compare the yield, although it appeared to be particularly high. The greater improvement in food utilization by larger fish demonstrated above agrees with the experimental pattern indicated in Fig. 3, which shows that there is the greatest divergence in growth efficiencies between small and large fish at maximum rations and progressively less towards the optimal ration. Rappoport & Sarig (1975) thought that to reduce the ration level even further could be worthwhile and, moreover, felt that there was a real possibility of economic benefit from using the reduced ration levels.

It is possible to define the inter-relationships of ration intake, growth and temperature, with some precision and, in fact, to derive an optimal temperature range which will give the best growth rate from the optimal ration (Brett et al., 1969; Elliott, 1975a). This could be of value in closed systems, where water temperature can be controlled but will be of less immediate use in open pond culture where water temperature is largely uncontrolled and varies with the environment.

When it is necessary to give rations at a known level to fish of different sizes, or when appreciable change in size is anticipated, it is inappropriate to give the food as a fixed proportion of body weight. Food consumption does not vary directly with body weight but as a function of W^b—where W is total body weight and the constant b is less than one. Estimates of b for Barbus liberiensis on different diets are 0·6–0·76 (Payne, 1973), for sockeye salmon 0·66 (Brett, 1971), for brown trout 0·76 (Elliott, 1975b) and for carp 0·65 (Hamada et al., 1975). As the value of b is <1, this means that the physiologically equivalent ration intake declines as a percentage of the body weight (Elliott, 1975b) and consequently, feeding on a fixed percentage of the body weight entails a disproportionate increase in rations as the fish gets older (Gerking, 1971).

The optimal ration follows a similar relationship to weight as the maximum ration. The weight exponent in this case is 0·63 for the brown trout (Elliott, 1975a) and 0·62 for B. liberiensis (Payne, 1973).

HORMONES AND OTHER CHEMICAL AGENTS

Growth Enhancement

A number of hormones are known to enhance growth in vertebrates. Perhaps the most familiar are the steroid androgens and oestrogens which, together with their synthetic substitutes, have been used extensively to increase nitrogen retention and therefore growth rate in cattle, sheep and poultry. Similar effects have been demonstrated in fish (Baker & Wigham, this volume p. 89). With reference to species used in fish culture, diethylstilboestrol, a steroid with oestrogenic properties, was shown to promote growth rate at low dosage in the plaice, *Pleuronectes platessa*, as it induced a higher voluntary food intake and also improved protein conversion efficiency. There was an inverse relationship between dose and growth rate, with the fishes receiving the smaller dose, $600 \mu g \, kg^{-1}$ moist diet, showing the highest growth rate (Cowey, Pope, Adron & Blair, 1973). An elevation of growth rate was observed in the salmon, *Salmo salar*, at doses of 0.5 and $2.5 \, mg \, kg^{-1}$ ethylestranol and a rather less marked effect at $12.5 \, mg \, kg^{-1}$ (Simpson, 1975/76). However, no positive effect on growth by a natural oestrogen, oestradiol-17β, could be demonstrated on the goldfish, *Carassius auratus* (L.), rainbow trout or sockeye salmon when fed at 1, 10 and 30 $mg \, kg^{-1}$ diet (Yamazaki, 1976). Similar experiments on the same three species, using methyltestosterone instead of oestradiol, gave accelerated growth in all three cases at $1 \, mg \, kg^{-1}$ diet but showed a positive reduction in growth at 10 and $30 \, mg \, kg^{-1}$ (Yamazaki, 1976). Thus the same inverse effect of dose on growth was obtained by both Yamazaki and Cowey, Pope *et al.* (1973) whilst increased voluntary food intake at low doses was also observed in the two cases. The efficacy of methyltestosterone in promoting growth has also been noted for the coho salmon, *Oncorhynchus kisutch* (Walbaum), although with a positive dose/response relationship up to $10 \, mg \, kg^{-1}$ diet (McBride & Fagerlund, 1973; Fagerlund & McBride, 1975).

It is convenient that these steroids can be effectively administered in the diet rather than by implantation as in cattle and this must improve the possibility of their widespread use in fish culture. In beef production, restriction on the use of steroids has often been imposed because of the residual action of the compounds although a second generation of compounds, some of which may be of value in fish culture, are now being used (Harvey, 1977).

Fish and mammalian growth hormones from the pituitary gland have both been shown to influence fish growth (Ball, 1969; Chester Jones *et al.*, 1974). Administration of bovine growth hormone (bGH) to coho salmon at doses between 5 and 100 μg hormone g^{-1} body wt^{-1} $week^{-1}$ by both injection and implantation resulted in growth two to six times greater than the controls (Higgs *et al.*, 1975, 1976). The younger fish generally showed the greatest response (Higgs *et al.*, 1976). The hormone did, however, tend to lower the condition factor and produce leaner fish than the controls. Carp also showed improved growth rates of between two and three and one-half times that of the control when given between 12·5 μg hormone g^{-1} body wt week^{-1} by intraperitoneal injection (Adelman, 1977). Unlike the situation in the coho salmon, however, where doses of 10–100 μg g^{-1} week^{-1} (Higgs et al., 1975) and 10–30 μg g^{-1} week^{-1} (Higgs et al., 1976) were found to be equipotent, a positive relationship between hormone dose and increased growth rate was demonstrated for carp (Adelman, 1977). Moreover, again in contrast to the coho salmon, bGH administration gave increased condition factors in the carp.

The enhanced growth caused by bGH can be correlated with increased voluntary intake and improved food and protein conversion efficiencies in treated fish (Markert et al., 1977). Temperature also influences the effectiveness of growth hormone and in carp has been found to promote the greatest response above the optimum for this factor (Adelman, 1977).

Although growth hormone is obviously effective its administration is not particularly convenient. Higgs et al. (1976) simplified the procedure by demonstrating that intramuscular (i.m.) treatment, whilst as effective as intraperitoneal, caused lower mortalities. Furthermore, i.m. injection need only be done every week or even two weeks, or i.m. implantation only every three weeks. Such a procedure could be viewed as applicable to only a comparatively small number of relatively valuable fish. Nevertheless, mass treatment by an oral route cannot be discounted even though growth hormone is a protein which is probably at least partially digested in the gut (Higgs et al., 1976). Markert et al. (1977) did conclude, however, that use of growth hormone is not economically viable at the moment.

The thyroid hormones have been implicated in the enhancement of growth rate (Dodd & Matty, 1964; Gorbman, 1969). Some inconsistencies which have appeared (Gorbman, 1969), could be attributable to experimental factors (Barrington, Barron & Piggins, 1961; Narayansingh & Eales, 1975a). Using hormone treatments within the physiological range, Narayansingh & Eales (1975a) obtained significant growth increases in the brook trout, Salvelinus fontinalis, when the fish were fed, and decreased weight loss when starved. The effect of thyroxine appears to entail the mobilization of lipid reserves, including a reduction in lipid around the gut and an increase in protein synthesis in some tissues (Narayansingh & Eales, 1975a, b). In the coho salmon, thyroxine treatment gave growth rates up to twice as high as those of controls although rather less than those of fish treated with bGH which were part of the same experiment (Higgs et al., 1976). Fish injected at 10 μg g^{-1} week^{-1} gave slightly higher growth rates than those receiving 1 μg g^{-1} week^{-1} but, at the higher dose, the fish tended to suffer from pronounced skeletal abnormalities. Consequently, the lower dose was thought to be more suitable. Higgs et al. (1976), however, emphasized the possible sources of variability in response to thyroxine by fishes whilst stating that their own methods of administration by i.m. injection and implantation optimized the release of the hormone. Thyroxine can be given more conveniently and with some success in water (Eales, 1974; Narayansingh & Eales, 1975a). Mixing thyroxine with the food may not be successful as there are indications that absorption from the gut is relatively poor (Eales & Sinclair, 1974).

The hormones of the thyroid do, therefore, appear to promote growth in some species of fish although probably to a lesser extent than the growth hormone from the pituitary. A convenient means of adminis-tration may be through the water, particularly in recycling systems, while the oral route remains to be investigated.

One method of promoting growth is to induce the animal to eat more. The appetite stimulant cyproheptadine was used on plaice but with no effect on weight gain or food conversion efficiency (Cowey, Pope et al., 1973). Main et al. (1976) examined a commercial appetite stimulant which they assumed to contain cobalamin and found that it did increase volun-tary intake by the blue-gill, although no measurements of growth were made. Appetite stimulation from the addition of certain amino acids, including alanine, tyrosine and serine, to the diet, has also been reported (Yone, Sakomoto & Furuichi, 1974).

Control of Reproduction

Many species of fish which previously would not spawn under conditions of culture can now be induced to do so by manipulation of the endocrine control system (Fontaine, 1976; Chaudhuri, 1976). The development of these techniques has reduced the dependence of the fish farmer on wild-spawned fry and also enabled the introduction of biologically valu-able types, such as the silver and grass carps, into culture systems beyond the normal range of these fish. The most generally successful method at the moment is to inject whole extracts of fish pituitary glands, not necessarily taken from the species in which spawning is to be induced. The efficacy of these extracts may be aided by the inevitable inclusion of growth and thyrotropic hormones, both of which have some influence on reproduction, along with the gonadotropic hormones (GTH) (Chaudhuri, 1976). However, the variability in the potency of pituitary extracts may make the use of purified fish GTH desirable to ensure the correct degree of response (Fontaine, 1976).

It would probably be more convenient to induce spawning using the more freely available mammalian GTH or the sex steroids, although results with these seem less certain than with fish pituitary extracts. Mammalian GTH, particularly luteinizing hormone (LH), can induce spawning in some fish, e.g. Heteropneustes fossilis (Bloch) (Sundararaj & Goswami, 1966), as can the placental hormone, human chorionic gonadotropin (HCG), which is structurally similar to LH (Shehadeh,

Madden & Dohl, 1973). Females are often less responsive to mammalian GTH than males (Fontaine, 1976).

With both HCG and sex steroids, some degree of concurrent treatment with fish pituitary hormones is often required. Evidence for the effectiveness of the steroids alone is contradictory but this may reflect the differences in experimental conditions such as the reproductive state of the animal and the quality and quantity of the compound tested (Fontaine, 1976). Yamazaki (1976) showed that, in male rainbow trout receiving 5 mg kg^{-1} methyltestosterone in the diet, maturation could be induced, although not as effectively as with piscine GTH or a combined treatment of methyltestosterone and GTH. In the females, by contrast, neither GTH nor the steroid, diethylstilboestrol, alone induced gonad maturation whilst a combination of the two did so. In both cases, therefore, a combination of the steroid with three injections per week of GTH were more effective, although less convenient, than the use of a steroid alone.

Induced spawning has an important role to play in fish culture. Successful techniques have been developed and the problem now is to simplify them. For example, Jalabert et al. (1977) report the effective use of the steroid 17α-hydroxy-20β-dihydroprogesterone to spawn carp which requires only a single priming dose of carp GTH. Nevertheless, Fontaine (1976) suggests that, because of the labour and expense involved in application of the hormone techniques, a close examination of the ecological and physiological factors controlling reproduction should now be made in order that they may be integrated to promote spawning. Such a study has been carried out recently on the minnow, Phoxinus phoxinus, (Scott, this volume p. 105).

Suppression of Gonad Development

Some fish, such as tilapia, reproduce too readily in ponds with the result that increasing competition interferes with production (Payne, 1971). Moreover, gonad development in general, when not essential for the spawning of new breeding stock, requires energy and materials which could otherwise be used for somatic growth. There are two main approaches to this problem: either gonad development can be suppressed directly or a sterile or single sex population can be produced which obviates reproduction.

The inhibitory effect of sex steroids, particularly oestrogens and their analogues, upon gonad maturation has been demonstrated on a wide variety of fish (Fontaine, 1976). The inhibition probably results from the negative feedback mechanism on GTH secretion by the pituitary (Sundararaj & Goswami, 1966). The precise effect, however, particularly with respect to androgens, may depend upon the dose, the age of the fish and the duration of treatment. Yamazaki (1976), for example, found that, while giving rainbow trout methyltestosterone at 50 mg kg^{-1} diet for five months after hatching suppressed gonad maturation even after three years, feeding fingerlings at 5 mg kg^{-1} for four weeks promoted it, as mentioned above.

It may be possible, by feeding steroids, to obtain both delayed maturity and the enhanced growth associated with these compounds as discussed previously. Improved growth, with delayed smolting in *Salmo salar* L., was obtained after feeding 2·5 mg ethylestranol kg^{-1} food (Simpson, 1975/76). Residues of the compound were also found to disappear from the muscle tissue within 10 days. Similarly, rainbow trout, receiving 10 mg kg^{-1} methyltestosterone for 72 weeks, gave a growth rate 125% greater than the controls whilst the testes of the males degenerated (Fagerlund & McBride, 1975).

Synthetic compounds such as methallibure have been shown to inhibit reproductive development. Methallibure, when added to the water, prevents development or causes resorption of tilapia gonads (Hyder, 1972). Both the addition of methallibure to the water and oral administration gave gonad regression in *Sarotherodon aureus* with the oral route being effective most rapidly (Dadzie, 1975). Furthermore, fish which had been treated initially with methallibure for 40 days in aquaria generally showed better growth and delayed spawning when stocked in ponds compared to controls, apparently indicating an improvement in growth at the expense of reproduction. The effectiveness of the oral route for methallibure means that it could be administered in the pond itself rather than in aquaria beforehand and the low concentrations required make the procedure an economic proposition (Dadzie, 1975).

The production of a monosex population can be accomplished either by chemical treatment or by hybridization. The latter has been used most extensively, particularly amongst tilapia where it has been found that crosses between certain species give 100% male offspring often showing a faster growth rate than either parent (Hickling, 1967).

Sex reversal in fish has been obtained by feeding steroid sex hormones. Rainbow trout given methyltestosterone at 1 mg kg^{-1} food for seven months starting one month after hatching resulted in 87% male fish; when begun four months after hatching the sex ratio was indistinguishable from that of the control (Yamazaki, 1976). It should be borne in mind that, when the concentrations of 1 mg kg^{-1} and 5 mg kg^{-1} were fed to older fish for shorter periods, growth enhancement and the promotion of gonad development respectively occurred. Consequently, with steroid treatment, dose, duration of treatment, age and sex of fish can all interact to produce apparently different effects, as emphasized earlier. Production of all male fish with methyltestosterone has been attained, for example, in *S. mossambicus* with doses of 10–40 mg kg^{-1} food (Clemens & Inslee, 1968) and in *Zebra fario*[a] at 1–100 mg kg^{-1} applied two days after hatching (Yamazaki, 1976). Sex reversal of male *Salmo salar* was obtained

[a] *Zebra fario* is not a valid name and therefore it is uncertain which species the author used.

using 17-β oestradiol at 20 mg kg^{-1} diet for the first 30 days after hatching but growth was markedly inhibited (Simpson, 1975/76). Similarly, sex reversal of males was induced by 17α-methyltestosterone at 3 mg kg^{-1} administered for the first 90 days.

Whilst hybridization in many animal types produces infertile offspring this is often not the case in fish. However, one method of producing a genetically sterile, non-reproducing population could be to induce polyploidy. Triploid fish can be induced by heat treatment of the eggs in some cases (Purdom, 1972, 1976) and attempts to produce polyploid fish using agents such as cytochalsin B have been made (Refstie, Vassvik & Gjedrem, 1977).

Growth Inhibition

Under crowded conditions there is evidence of reduced growth, decreased reproductive potential and high larval mortality associated with the production of a chemical crowding factor (Solomon, 1977). A common feature of this factor is that it is often the growth of smaller fish which is depressed. A major question is the nature of the factor; that is whether it is a pheromone-like compound or results merely from an accumulation of metabolic by-products such as ammonia. There is also the possibility of a social element such as the frequency of individual contact, although the inhibitory effect appears far less pronounced in systems with a large throughput of water where conditions would not allow the accumulation of a chemical agent. It is also possible to extract a growth-inhibiting factor in non-polar solvents, particularly chloroform (Yu & Perlmutter, 1970; Francis, Smith & Pfuderer, 1974) and some progress has been made in characterizing it (Francis et al., 1974). There has been some reference made to alarm factors (Solomon, 1977) which have been associated with certain secretory cells in the epidermis (R. J. F. Smith, 1976). The possibility of a relationship between alarm and crowding factors cannot be ignored while the epidermal cells may also be considered a possible site for secretion of the growth inhibitor. Nevertheless, it has also been demonstrated that ammonia itself inhibits growth (Brockway, 1950; Kawamoto, 1961) and so the influence of the excretory products must be taken into account.

The importance of growth inhibition under crowded conditions is emphasized in recent work on intensive high density systems. Here, exceptionally high rates of production can be obtained but effects of growth inhibition become apparent after 50–70 days rather than after 100–200 days as in the more conventional semi-intensive systems of Israel (Rappoport & Sarig, 1975). This may indicate that growth-inhibiting factors are the next barrier to be surmounted in attempts at further intensification. Rappoport & Sarig (1975) do mention that ammonia levels in their ponds ranged between 0·5 and 1·0 ml litre^{-1} and, rarely, up to 1·5 ml litre^{-1}, concentrations they considered insignificant. However, growth has been shown to be depressed in carp at between 0·3 and 1·2 ml litre^{-1} and this in tanks with a pH of 6·5 (Kawamoto, 1961). Above pH 7, the relatively non-toxic NH_4^+ becomes progressively converted into the extremely toxic NH_3 and it is likely that, in fertilized and productive fishponds, the pH will be alkaline. Stocking at high densities in closed systems tends to result in a lowered water pH and therefore reduced toxicity from NH_3 (Hampson, 1976). In ponds where natural productivity must be encouraged, the pH is often high; for example, in fertilized East African fish ponds, the pH fluctuated almost entirely within the range 8–9 (Payne, 1971), and consequently this presents the serious possibility of sub-lethal effects from un-ionized ammonia.

PHYSICO-CHEMICAL ENVIRONMENT

A growth response may also follow alteration in the physico-chemical background to fish metabolism. The influence of temperature on fish growth has been widely considered (Brown, 1957; Paloheimo & Dickie, 1966; Brett et al., 1969; Fry, 1971; Elliott, 1976). Other factors, such as oxygen and salinity, also have marked effects and these can be controlled to some degree even in extensive systems.

Oxygen

In fish ponds, there is a diurnal fluctuation in oxygen concentration with a maximum in the early evening due to oxygen production from photosynthesis and a minimum shortly after dawn resulting from total oxygen consumption by all pond organisms. The effect can be particularly pronounced in warm waters as oxygen solubility decreases with temperature while respiratory requirements increase. For example, oxygen concentrations in Tanzanian ponds containing *Sarotherodon esculentus* (Graham) and *Tilapia zillii* fluctuated from 0·23 to 1·21 mg litre^{-1} (2·6–15·7% saturation) in the morning to 6·3–8·5 mg litre^{-1} (91·6–123% saturation) in the evening (Payne, 1971). The same effect, however, can be seen in ponds in temperate regions particularly in the summer and under intensive culture conditions (Knoeshe, 1976). Low ambient oxygen concentrations can interfere with metabolism. Thus, below 2·3 mg litre^{-1}, oxygen concentration limits metabolism in *S. mossambicus* (Job, 1969), this value being rather higher, for example, than the minimum concentration to which the two tilapia species mentioned above were exposed. This interference includes an effect on growth. In the large-mouthed bass, *Micropterus salmoides*, a reduction in oxygen concentration from 8 mg litre^{-1} to 4 and perhaps 3 mg litre^{-1} led to a reduced growth rate which was probably attributable to decreased food consumption as the food conversion efficiency remained stable (Dahlberg, Shumway & Doudoroff, 1968). Similarly, growth rate and food consumption also declined with environmental oxygen concentration in *Esox lucius*, the reduction becoming extreme at 3–4 mg litre^{-1} (Adelman & Smith, 1970). Below a critical concentration of 2·9 mg litre^{-1} food conversion in *E. lucius* became less efficient, suggesting a direct effect on metabolism.

Under diurnally fluctuating conditions of oxygen concentration which emulated a pond situation, growth in brook trout suffered. Whilst these fish grew well at a constant concentration of 10·7 mg litre^{-1}, with diurnal changes of 10·6–5·3 mg litre^{-1} growth was negligible, at 10·7–3·6 it was negative and, at a range of 11·0–2·0, the fish died (Whitworth, 1968). A similar effect has been observed in carp ponds where large diurnal fluctuations can cause fish to lose weight (Yashouv, 1956).

Oxygen, therefore, must be a significant limiting factor in production particularly when concentrations are sufficiently low to cause substantial reduction of feeding or, beyond that, to limit metabolism and reduce the food conversion efficiency. The oxygen regime of a culture system should aim, therefore, not only to prevent mortality but also to increase production. In China, for example, yields have been increased on average by 14% and by up to 28% in some cases through the use of aerators in farm ponds (Tapiador *et al.*, 1977). By paying particular attention to oxygenation it has been possible to intensify fish culture substantially (Sarig & Marek, 1974). The use of aeration systems enables carp to be stocked at 50 000 ha^{-1}, mixed carp, silver carp and tilapia up to 32 000 ha^{-1} and tilapia up to 80 000 ha^{-1} (Rappoport & Sarig, 1975; Rappoport, Sarig & Marek, 1976). A survey of the efficiency of several aeration systems showed that the less effective methods gave oxygen saturation levels in the morning of 9–44% and yields about 20% less than the average of some 17 500 kg ha^{-1} 200 days^{-1} for other systems (Rappoport *et al.*, 1976). At these levels oxygen has no apparent effect on food conversion efficiency although values below 25% saturation were generally regarded as having detrimental effects on growth. Aerators which pump up lower layers of water and spray them on the surface were found to be more effective than those which inject air into the pond water (Rappoport *et al.*, 1976).

With forced aeration and the very high stocking densities this allows, extremely high yields have been obtained (Table V), with carp monoculture on a high protein diet giving 11 510–15 550 kg ha^{-1} and tilapia monoculture, 16 320–16 750 kg ha^{-1} (Rappoport & Sarig, 1975). In both cases the feed conversion ratio was good. It is remarkable that tilapia, even stocked at 80 000 ha^{-1}, showed no reduction in individual increment compared to that achieved when stocked at lower densities as would be found in carp. Tilapia appear to be less sensitive to density and might be stocked in still higher numbers (Rappoport & Sarig, 1975).

A comparison of an intensive system with a controlled oxygen regime, against a semi-intensive, both using a mixture of common carp, silver carp and tilapia in a commercially acceptable ratio produced a yield from the semi-intensive ponds of 56% less than the intensive, with negligible differences in the efficiency by which the supplementary food was used for growth (Rappoport *et al.*, 1976). The procedure was also successfully used in properly supervised, large commercial ponds.

The indications are, therefore, that manipulation of the oxygen regime, so that oxygen concentration does not interfere with growth via influence on food consumption or conversion efficiency, can lead to higher stocking densities and increased yields. However, if due attention is paid to the oxygen demands within a pond it is, in fact, possible to introduce large quantities of organic material, such as cow manure, into unaerated ponds without damaging the oxygen relations of the pond (Schroeder, 1975).

Salinity

The salinity of water may be expected to influence fish productivity since it is generally associated with an osmoregulatory response which must be supplied with energy at the expense of other metabolic parameters including growth. Brackish-water fish culture in estuaries is important as it does not compete for land with agriculture and also tidal fluctuations can be used to control water levels without use of pumps.

The interaction of growth with other metabolic components in relation to salinity is demonstrated, for example, by the responses of the marine fishes, *Bairdiella icista* (Jordan & Gilbert), *Cynoscion xanthulus* (Jordan & Gilbert) and *Anisotremus davidsoni* (Steindachner) subjected to a series of salinities between 29–45‰ (Brocksen & Cole, 1972). Here, optima were found for growth, efficiency of food utilization, assimilation efficiency and oxygen consumption at intermediate salinities within the range 33–37‰. To indicate the degree of effect that salinity can have on growth it can be estimated that, in juvenile *A. davidsoni*, there can be up to a 4% reduction in growth rate between the optimal salinity at 33‰ and the extremes of 29 and 45‰. An optimal salinity for growth has also been found in young striped bass, *Morone saxatilis*, where growth at 4 and 20‰ was some 10% less than at 12‰ (Otwell & Merriner, 1975). No discrete optimum was found in the growth efficiency of the rainbow trout in relation to salinity although there was a marked drop beyond 28‰ (MacLeod, 1977). There was, however, an optimal salinity range of 15–28‰ where food consumption was highest and, therefore, where growth rate might be expected to be greatest.

The influence of salinity on growth would appear to be a significant factor in brackish-water fish culture although Otwell & Merriner (1975) estimated that it was less important than temperature. Paloheimo & Dickie (1966) deduced that, whilst temperature affected the general rate of metabolism, salinity influenced the actual partition of energy between growth and other metabolic fractions and, from the values given above, it is apparent that variation in salinity can cause substantial differences in growth rate. The interplay of salinity with low concentrations of oxygen may cause additional reductions in energy availability for other metabolic parameters including growth (Fry, 1971).

Apart from deriving the optimal salinity for growth directly, it should be possible to infer it from alternative data on other metabolic factors. For example, osmotic stress has been associated with increased respiration even at the tissue level. Respiratory energy demand rose very sharply in a number of organs taken from acclimated *S. mossambicus* at salinities between 17·5‰ (the isosmotic point) and 26·25‰ (Bashamohideen & Parvatheswararao, 1976). Thus, salinities associated with lowest rates of oxygen consumption, which in a number of cases coincide with isosmotic concentrations with the fish blood, may generally represent the range most suitable for growth, as found by Brocksen & Cole (1972). However, after reviewing respirometric data, MacLeod (1977) concluded that the relationship of respiratory rate to osmoregulatory response was variable and it has been suggested that there could be several patterns of metabolic/osmotic relationships in teleosts depending upon their evolutionary history (Bashamohideen & Parvatheswararao, 1976). The effect of salinity on other traumatic factors may give some indication of the degree of osmotic stress. So, for example, in the estuarine tilapia *Sarotherodon melanotheron* Rüppell acclimation to salinities within the range 8·5–26·25‰ had no effect on the ability to respond to thermal stress whilst beyond these limits this capability declined progressively (Basimi, 1973).

CONCLUSIONS

During the past 10 years enormous increases in yields have been achieved by manipulation of the fish species used, with respect to their physiology and environment. For example, compared to the earlier apparent plateaux of production of $1000\,kg\,ha^{-1}\,yr^{-1}$ for fertilized ponds and 2500–3000 kg ha^{-1} year for ponds with supplementary feeding (Swingle, 1967), yields of $9389\,kg\,ha^{-1}\,year^{-1}$ (Chaudhuri *et al.*, 1975) and $10\,620\,kg\,ha^{-1}\,year^{-1}$ (Yashouv & Halevy, 1972) have been attained with polyculture and intensive feeding. Furthermore, up to 15 550 kg ha^{-1} and $16\,750\,kg\,ha^{-1}$ have been obtained, over a growing period of approximately 100 days in carp and tilapia monoculture respectively, using high densities and forced aeration (Table V). The fact remains, however, that, in many parts of the world, yields of $1000\,kg\,ha^{-1}\,year^{-1}$ or less are commonplace, particularly in areas with no great tradition of fish culture. If there were some relatively simple method which required little additional managerial expertise or technological input but which would result in even a doubling of the yield in many of the less developed areas, a substantial benefit could ensue. Such a system is that of polyculture, which, by mixing fish using different ecological niches, ensures maximum utilization of natural food sources in a pond and may even enhance the primary productivity (Reich, 1975). Thus, carp alone, using only inorganic fertilizer in the ponds, can give a yield of $670\,kg\,ha^{-1}\,season^{-1}$, while when mixed with tilapia and silver carp under similar conditions, a yield of some 2980 kg ha^{-1} may be obtained (Tables I and II). Initially, the optimal mixtures for each area must be established which could mean assessing the suitability of indigenous species or using exotic types of proven value in culture. The development of endocrine techniques to induce spawning has meant that species, whose use was once limited to their natural range because they would only reproduce in the wild, can now be cultured elsewhere in the world. For example, the silver carp now plays an important role in the development of fish culture in Israel and India whereas previously it was restricted to China and the Far East. Refinement of the induction techniques themselves should make the procedure simpler, cheaper and more predictable although induced spawning by more precise environmental control must remain a possibility. No matter how successful exotic species have been in other places, however, their response to a new area may be uncertain and consequently the possible superiority of indigenous species must be considered.

One major problem in the development of fish culture is the comparative failure to domesticate the animal itself. Extensive attempts at selective breeding have generally demonstrated a high variability in growth but a poor response to selection for faster growth rates (e.g. Moav & Wohlfarth, 1976). It does seem, however, as if races differ in their response to management methods so that, for example, the more traditional strains such as the Chinese Big Belly can cope well under rigorous conditions but use the high inputs from intensive management regimes rather less efficiently than do the recently developed, artificially selected breeds which, correspondingly, are much less hardy (Moav, Soller & Hulata, 1976). The identification of the most appropriate genotype for a particular management regime may, therefore, be worthwhile. In addition, the monitoring of primary and secondary effects of stress has opened up the possibility of selective breeding for low response to stress by fish under intensive conditions as has been accomplished for chickens and turkeys (Mazeaud, Mazeaud & Donaldson, 1977).

Supplementary feeding is necessary to obtain the higher yields and the highest, both in monoculture and polyculture, have been achieved using protein-rich pellets based on fish meal (Tables I, II, III and V). The reliance on expensive high-grade feed of this nature means that it is unlikely that these systems, developed in Israel, will be applicable on an extensive scale throughout the world. The system developed by Chaudhuri *et al.* (1975), which is partly traditional and partly experimental, and the conventional traditional Chinese system are both based on polyculture, using manure and agricultural waste as the major sources of supplementary food. Yields from these systems can approach the highest achieved on protein-rich pellets (Tables I and III) and the general procedure could probably be suitably adapted by any agrarian community. The major disadvantage is the enormous quantities of manure and waste required to sustain high levels of production in the ponds. For example, up to 113 500 kg ha^{-1} manure have been added to ponds when this was the sole feed (Moav, Wohlfarth *et al.*, 1977) and 5–10 000 kg ha^{-1} are regularly applied in China (Tapiador *et al.*, 1977). Consequently, in this situation, the fish farm must be integrated with a well-developed agricultural system capable of supplying the waste. Those parts of the world which could benefit most from aquaculture often do not have such intensive agricultural systems. A further difficulty is that the availability of agricultural waste is often seasonal and may not entirely coincide with the growing season of the fish.

A pelleted diet has advantages over agricultural waste in that it is more convenient to handle and it is of a controlled and predictable composition. Attempts to substitute plant material for fish meal in pelleted diets have been outlined elsewhere but relatively little work has been done on all-plant diets for use by herbivorous fish. Much of the work has been carried out in carnivorous fish and soybean meal has frequently been used. There are indications that soybean is not a particularly suitable nutrient for fish and, in any case, soya as a feed in fish culture would compete with its use by man and his domestic animals. Leaf protein extracts may have some potential in fish diets, however. In a crude fashion, these can be prepared fairly simply from agricultural waste, when this is available, or from the leaves of plants which at present have no economic value. They could even be prepared from agricultural waste in parts of the world which have intensive agricultural systems but no great commitment to aquaculture. In this way, a supply of plant material could be obtained throughout the year in a form which could also be incorporated into a pelleted diet. Leaf concentrate has been used effectively by the carnivorous plaice when it constituted up to 40% of the protein source (Cowey, Pope *et al.*, 1971), whilst a diet including 80% algal extract proved suitable for grass carp (Meske & Pruss, 1977). The use of leaf or plant protein extracts, therefore, remains a possibility.

An additional advantage of pelleted diets is that hormones and other compounds can be incorporated. Several steroids have been shown to enhance growth when given at low dosages in the diet. Their application in this way is, therefore, a practical possibility although numerous countries have severe restrictions on such compounds. In addition, the sex steroids in particular appear to show a remarkable variety of effects depending upon dose, duration of treatment and age of the fish. More information may be required before the steroids can make as important a contribution to fish culture as they have to beef production.

Thyroxine and growth hormone have both been shown to improve growth but, as yet, their long-term effects are unknown. Moreover, their method of administration is still relatively time-consuming and inconvenient so that, whilst they may be useful where the individual value of the fish is high, their widespread use in mass culture in the near future is doubtful.

The beneficial effect of temperature on growth rates in fish is enjoyed by virtue of geography in many parts of the world where the greater production of fish protein is a necessity. It has now been shown that other aspects of the physico-chemical environment can be profitably altered by relatively simple means. Thus, yield may be enhanced merely by aeration of fish-ponds. By maintaining the oxygen above the critical level where oxygen deprivation actually limits metabolism, growth can be significantly improved. Elevation beyond the critical level may give further improvement owing to the effect of oxygen level on food consumption. The type of aerator used is important, however, as they vary widely in efficiency (Rappoport et al., 1976). A combination of efficient aeration with poly-culture may represent the most generally appropriate way of increasing yields over a wide variety of economic and environmental conditions.

REFERENCES

Adelman, I. R. (1977). Effects of bovine growth hormone on growth of carp (*Cyprinus carpio*) and the influences of temperature and photoperiod. *J. Fish. Res. Bd Can.* **34**: 509–515.

Adelman, I. R. & Smith, L. L. (1970). Effect of oxygen on growth and food conversion efficiency of northern pike. *Progve Fish Cult.* **32**: 93–96.

Adron, J. W., Blair, A., Cowey, C. B. & Shanks, A. M. (1976). Effects of dietary energy level and dietary energy source on growth, feed conversion and body composition of turbot (*Scophthalmus maximus*). *Aquaculture* **7**: 125–132.

Ball, J. N. (1969). Prolactin (fish prolactin or paralactin) and growth hormone. In *Fish physiology* **2**: 207–240. Hoar, W. S. & Randall, D. J. (eds). New York & London: Academic Press.

Barrington, E. J. W., Barron, N. & Piggins, D. J. (1961). The influence of thyroid powder and thyroxine upon growth of rainbow trout (*Salmo gairdneri*). *Gen. comp. Endocr.* **1**: 170–178.

Bashamohideen, M. & Parvatheswararao, V. (1976). Adaptations to osmotic stress in the freshwater euryhaline teleost *Tilapia mossambica* 10. Energetics. *Zool. Anz.* **197**: 47–56.

Basimi, R. A. (1973). *The tolerance limits of* Tilapia heudeloti (*Dumeril*). MS Fourah Bay College Library, University of Sierra Leone.

Beamish, F. W. H. (1972). Ration size and digestion in smallmouth bass, *Micropterus salmoides* Lacépède. *Can. J. Zool.* **50**: 153–165.

Brett, J. R. (1971). Satiation time, appetite and maximum food intake of sockeye salmon (*Oncorhynchus nerka*). *J. Fish Res. Bd Can.* **28**: 409–415.

Brett, J. R. & Shelbourn, J. E. (1975). Growth rate of sockeye salmon, *Oncorhynchus nerka*, in relation to fish size and ration level. *J. Fish. Res. Bd Can.* **32**: 2103–2110.

Brett, J. R., Shelbourn, J. E. & Shoop, C. T. (1969). Growth rate and body composition of fingerling sockeye salmon, *Oncorhynchus nerka*, in relation to temperature and ration size. *J. Fish. Res. Bd Can.* **26**: 2363–2394.

Brocksen, R. W. & Cole, R. E. (1972). Physiological response of three species of fishes to various salinities. *J. Fish. Res. Bd Can.* **29**: 399–405.

Brockway, D. R. (1950). Metabolic products and their effects. *Progve Fish Cult.* **12**: 127–129.

Brown, M. E. (1957). Experimental studies on growth. In *The physiology of fishes* 1: 361–400. Brown, M. E. (Ed.). New York and London: Academic Press.

Chaudhuri, H. (1976). Use of hormones in induced spawning of carps. *J. Fish. Res. Bd Can.* 33: 940–947.

Chaudhuri, H., Chakrabarty, R. B., Sen, P. R., Rao, N. G. S. & Jena, S. (1975). A new high in fish production in India with record yields by composite fish culture in freshwater ponds. *Aquaculture* 6: 343–356.

Chester Jones, I., Ball, J. N., Henderson, I. W., Sandor, T. & Baker, B. I. (1974). Endocrinology of fishes. In *Chemical zoology* 8: 523–593. Florkin, M. & Scheer, B. T. (eds). New York & London: Academic Press.

Chiang l'Kuei, Ching Chin-hsia & Ch'en Hsi-tao (1966). *Collected articles on the 7th Conference of the Committee of Fishery Research of the West Pacific Hydrobiology Institute*: 84–94. Peking: Chinese Academy of Science.

Clemens, H. P. & Inslee, T. (1968). The production of unisexual broods by *Tilapia mossambica* sex reversed with methyltestosterone. *Trans. Am. Fish. Soc.* 97: 18–21.

Cowey, C. B., Adron, J. W., Blair, A. & Shanks, A. M. (1974). Studies on the nutrition of marine flatfish. Utilization of various dietary proteins by plaice (*Pleuronectes platessa*). *Br. J. Nutr.* 31: 297–306.

Cowey, C. B., Adron, J. W., Brown, D. A. & Shanks, A. M. (1975). Studies on the nutrition of marine flatfish. The metabolism of glucose by plaice (*Pleuronectes platessa*) and the effect of dietary energy source on protein utilization in plaice. *Br. J. Nutr.* 33: 219–231.

Cowey, C. B., Pope, J. A., Adron, J. W. & Blair, A. (1971). Studies on the nutrition of marine flatfish. Growth of plaice, *Pleuronectes platessa*, on diets containing proteins derived from plants and other sources. *Mar. Biol.* 10: 145–153.

Cowey, C. B., Pope, J. A., Adron, J. W. & Blair, A. (1973). Studies on the nutrition of marine flatfish. The effect of oral administration of diethyl-stilboestrol and cyproheptadine on the growth of *Pleuronectes platessa*. *Mar. Biol.* 19: 1–6.

Cowey, C. B. & Sargent, J. R. (1972). Fish nutrition. *Adv. Mar. Biol.* 10: 383–492.

Dabrowska, H. & Wojno, T. (1977). Studies on the utilization by rainbow trout (*Salmo gairdneri*) of feed mixtures containing soya bean meal and an addition of amino acids. *Aquaculture* 10: 297–310.

Dadzie, S. (1975). A preliminary report on the use of methallibure in *Tilapia* culture. *Afr. J. Trop. Hydrobiol. Fish.* 4: 128–140.

Dahlberg, M. L., Shumway, D. L. & Doudoroff, P. (1968). Influence of dissolved oxygen and carbon dioxide on swimming performance of largemouth bass and coho salmon. *J. Fish. Res. Bd Can.* 25: 49–70.

Davis, G. E. & Warren, C. E. (1968). Estimation of food consumption rates. In *Methods for assessment of fish production in fresh waters*: 204–225. Ricker, W. E. (ed.). Oxford: Blackwell.

Dodd, J. M. & Matty, A. J. (1964). Comparative aspects of thyroid function. In *The thyroid gland*: 303–356. Pitt-Rivers, R. & Trotter, W. R. (eds). London: Butterworth.

Eales, J. G. (1974). Creation of chronic physiological elevation of plasma thyroxine in brook trout, *Salvelinus fontinalis*, and other teleosts. *Gen. comp. Endocr.* 22: 209–217.

Eales, J. G. & Sinclair, D. A. R. (1974). Enterohepatic cycling of thyroxine in starved and fed brook trout, *Salvelinus fontinalis* (Mitchill). *Comp. Biochem. Physiol.* 49A: 661–672.

Edwards, D. J., Austreng, E., Risa, S. & Gjedrem, T. (1977). Carbohydrate in rainbow trout diets. I. Growth of fish of different families fed diets containing different proportions of carbohydrate. *Aquaculture* **11**: 31–38.

Elliott, J. M. (1975a). The growth rate of brown trout (*Salmo trutta*) fed on reduced rations. *J. Anim. Ecol.* **44**: 823–842.

Elliott, J. M. (1975b). Number of meals in a day, maximum weight of food consumed in a day and maximum rate of feeding of brown trout, *Salmo trutta* L. *Freshwat. Biol.* **5**: 287–303.

Elliott, J. M. (1976). The energetics of feeding, metabolism and growth of brown trout (*Salmo trutta* L.) in relation to body weight, water temperature and ration size. *J. Anim. Ecol.* **45**: 923–948.

Fagerlund, U. H. M. & McBride, J. R. (1975). Growth increments and some flesh characteristics of juvenile coho salmon receiving diets supplemented with 17α-methyltestosterone. *J. Fish Biol.* **7**: 305–314.

Fischer, Z. (1972). The elements of energy balance in grass carp (*Ctenopharyngodon idella* Val.) III Assimilability of proteins, carbohydrates and lipids by fish fed plant and animal food. *Polski Archwm Hydrobiol.* **19**: 83–95.

Fontaine, M. (1976). Hormones and the control of reproduction in aquaculture. *J. Fish. Res. Bd Can.* **33**: 922–939.

Francis, A. A., Smith, F. & Pfuderer, P. (1974). A heart rate bioassay for the crowding factor in goldfish. *Progve Fish Cult.* **36**: 196–200.

Fry, F. E. J. (1971). The effect of environmental factors on the physiology of fish. In *Fish physiology* **6**: 1–98. Hoar, W. S. & Randall, D. J. (eds). New York & London: Academic Press.

Gerking, S. D. (1971). Influence of rate of feeding and body weight on protein metabolism of blue-gill sunfish. *Physiol. Zool.* **44**: 9–19.

Gorbman, A. (1969). Thyroid function and its control in fishes. In *Fish physiology* **2**: 241–274. Hoar, W. S. & Randall, D. J. (eds). New York & London: Academic Press.

Halver, J. E. (1972). *Fish nutrition.* New York & London: Academic Press.

Halver, J. E. (1976). Formulating practical diets for fish. *J. Fish. Res. Bd Can.* **33**: 1032–1039.

Hamada, A., Toshiomi, I., Tsda, T. & Kariya, T. (1975). Studies on the growth structure of fishes. I. Maximum growth of carp. *Bull. Jap. Soc. scient. Fish.* **41**: 147–154.

Hampson, B. L. (1976). Ammonia concentration in relation to ammonia toxicity during a rainbow trout rearing experiment in a closed freshwater-seawater system. *Aquaculture* **9**: 61–70.

Harvey, G. (1977). The anabolic revolution in agriculture. *New Scient.* **76**: 100–101.

Hepher, B., Chervinski, J. & Tagari, H. (1971). Studies on carp nutrition III. Experiments on the effect on fish yield of dietary protein source and concentration. *Bamidgeh* **23**: 11–37.

Hickling, C. F. (1966). On the feeding process of the white amur, *Ctenopharyngodon idella. Proc. zool. Soc. Lond.* **148**: 408–419.

Hickling, C. F. (1967). Fish hybridization. *FAO Fish. Rep.* **44** (4): 1–11.

Higgs, D. A., Donaldson, E. M., Dye, H. M. & McBride, J. R. (1975). A preliminary investigation of the effect of bovine growth hormone on growth and muscle composition of coho salmon (*Oncorhynchus kisutch*). *Gen. comp. Endocr.* **27**: 240–253.

Higgs, D. A., Donaldson, E. M., Dye, H. M. & McBride, J. R. (1976). Influence of bovine growth hormone and L-thyroxine on growth, muscle composition, and histological structure of gonads, thyroid, pancreas and pituitary of coho salmon *Oncorhynchus kisutch*, *J. Fish. Res. Bd Can.* **33**: 1585–1603.

Huisman, E. A. (1976). Food conversion efficiencies at maintenance and production levels for carp, *Cyprinus carpio* L., and rainbow trout, *Salmo gairdneri*, Richardson. *Aquaculture* **9**: 259–273.

Hyder, M. (1972). Endocrine regulation of reproduction in *Tilapia*. *Gen. comp. Endocr.* Suppl. **3**: 729–740.

Jalabert, B., Breton, B., Brzuska, E., Fostier, A. & Wieniawski, J. (1977). A new tool for induced spawning: the use of 17α hydroxy-20β-dihydroprogesterone to spawn carp. *Aquaculture* **10**: 353–364.

Job, S. V. (1969). The respiratory metabolism of *Tilapia mossambica* (Teleostei) II. The effect of size, temperature, salinity and partial pressure of oxygen. *Mar. Biol.* **3**: 222–226.

Kawamoto, N. Y. (1961). The influence of excretory substances of fishes on their growth. *Progve Fish Cult.* **23**: 70–75.

Kevern, N. R. (1966). Feeding rate of carp estimated by a radioisotopic method. *Trans. Am. Fish. Soc.* **95**: 363–371.

Kitamikado, M., Morishita, T. & Tachino, S. (1964). Digestibility of dietary protein in rainbow trout—I. Digestibility of several dietary proteins. *Bull. Jap. Soc. scient. Fish.* **30**: 46–49.

Knoeshe, R. (1976). Oxygen content in pellet intensive ponds and technical possibilities for improvement. *Z. Binnenfisch.* **23**: 48–56.

Koops, H., Tiews, H., Beck, H. & Gropp, J. (1976). Die Vertwertung von Sojaprotein durch die Regenbogenforelle (*Salmo gairdneri*). *Arch. Fischereiwiss.* **26**: 181–191.

Lee, D. J. & Putnam, G. B. (1973). The response of rainbow trout to varying protein/energy ratios on a test diet. *J. Nutr.* **103**: 916–922.

Mabaye, A. R. E. (1971). Observations on the growth of *Tilapia mossambica* fed on artificial diets. *Fish. Res. Bull. Zambia* **5**: 379–396.

McBride, J. R. & Fagerlund, U. H. M. (1973). The use of 17α-methyltestosterone for promoting weight increases in juvenile Pacific salmon. *J. Fish. Res. Bd Can.* **30**: 1099–1104.

MacLeod, M. G. (1977). Effects of salinity on food intake, absorption and conversion in the rainbow trout, *Salmo gairdneri*. *Mar. Biol.* **43**: 93–102.

Main, J. K., Allen, E., Chiszar, D. A. & Windell, J. T. (1976). Effects of a commercial appetite stimulant on feeding behavior in blue-gills. *Progve Fish Cult.* **38**: 211–212.

Mann, H. (1969). Difference in digestibility of plant and animal proteins by various kinds of fish. *EIFAC Tech. Pap.* **9**: 194–196.

Markert, J. R., Higgs, D., Dye, H. M. & MacQuarrie, D. W. (1977). Influence of bovine growth hormone on growth rate, appetite and food conversion of yearling coho salmon (*Oncorhynchus kisutch*) fed two diets of different composition. *Can. J. Zool.* **55**: 74–83.

Mazeaud, D. M. M., Mazeaud, F. & Donaldson, E. M. (1977). Primary and secondary effects of stress in fish: some new data with a general review. *Trans. Am. Fish. Soc.* **106**: 201–212.

Meske, V. & Pruss, H. D. (1977). Fish meal free fish food on the basis of algae powder. *Adv. Anim. Physiol. Anim. Nutrit.* **18**: 71–81.

Moav, R., Soller, M. & Hulata, G. (1976). Genetic aspects of the transition from traditional to modern fish farming. *Theoret. appl. Genet.* **47**: 285–290.

Moav, R. & Wohlfarth, G. (1976). Two-way selection for growth rate in the common carp (*Cyprinus carpio* L.). *Genetics* **82**: 83–101.

Moav, R., Wohlfarth, G., Schroeder, G. L., Hulata, G. & Barash, H. (1977). Intensive polyculture of fish in freshwater ponds. I. Substitution of expensive feeds by liquid cow manure. *Aquaculture* **10**: 25–43.

Moriarty, D. J. W. & Moriarty, C. M. (1973). The assimilation of carbon from phytoplankton by two herbivorous fishes: *Tilapia nilotica* and *Haplochromis nigripinnis*. *J. Zool., Lond.* **171**: 41–55.

Narayansingh, T. & Eales, J. G. (1975a). The influence of physiological doses of thyroxine on the lipid reserves of starved and fed brook trout, *Salvelinus fontinalis* (Mitchill). *Comp. Biochem. Physiol.* **52**B: 407–412.

Narayansingh, T. & Eales, J. G. (1975b). Effects of thyroid hormones on *in vivo* 1-^{14}C l-Leucine incorporation into plasma and tissue protein of brook trout (*Salvelinus fontinalis*) and rainbow trout (*Salmo gairdneri*). *Comp. Biochem. Physiol.* **52**B: 399–405.

Niimi, A. J. & Beamish, F. W. H. (1974). Bioenergetics and growth of largemouth bass (*Micropterus salmoides*) in relation to body weight and temperature. *Can. J. Zool.* **52**: 447–456.

Nomura, M. & Fuji, A. R. (1969). A review of recent knowledge of fish feed in Japan. *EIFAC Tech. Pap.* **9**: 169–193.

Nose, T. (1974a). Effects of amino acids supplemented to petroleum yeast on growth of rainbow trout fingerlings—I. A preliminary experiment. *Bull. Freshwat. Fish Res. Lab. Tokyo* **24**: 57–63.

Nose, T. (1974b). Effects of amino acids supplemented to petroleum yeasts on growth of rainbow trout fingerlings—II. Methionine and cystine. *Bull. Freshwat. Fish. Res. Lab. Tokyo* **24**: 101–109.

Ogino, C. & Chen, M. S. (1973a). Protein nutrition in fish—IV. Biological value of dietary proteins in carp. *Bull. Jap. Soc. scient. Fish.* **39**: 797–800.

Ogino, C. & Chen, M. S. (1973b). Protein nutrition in fish—III. Apparent and true digestibility of dietary proteins in carp. *Bull. Jap. Soc. scient. Fish* **39**: 649–651.

Otwell, W. S. & Merriner, J. V. (1975). Survival and growth of juvenile striped bass, *Morone saxatilis*, in a factorial experiment with temperature, salinity and age. *Trans. Am. Fish. Soc.* **104**: 560–566.

Paloheimo, J. E. & Dickie, L. M. (1966). Food and growth of fishes II. Effects of food and temperature on the relation between metabolism and weight. *J. Fish. Res. Bd Can.* **23**: 869–908.

Pandian, T. J. (1967). Intake, digestion, absorption and conversion of food in the fishes, *Megalops cyprinoides* and *Ophiocephalus striatus*. *Mar. Biol.* **1**: 16–32.

Payne, A. I. (1971). An experiment on the culture of *Tilapia esculenta* Graham and *Tilapia zillii* (Gervais) in fish ponds, *J. Fish Biol.* **3**: 325–340.

Payne, A. I. (1973). *A field and laboratory investigation into the feeding, bioenergetics and growth of* Barbus liberiensis *Steindachner (Pisces, Cyprinidae)*. Ph.D. Thesis: University of London.

Payne, A. I. (1975). The relative abundance of feeding habits of the grey mullet species occurring in an estuary in Sierra Leone, West Africa. *Mar. Biol.* **35**: 277–286.

Prugnin, Y., Shilo, S. & Mires, D. (1975). Grey mullet: a component in polyculture in Israel. *Aquaculture* **5**: 291–298.

Purdom, C. E. (1972). Induced polyploidy in plaice (*Pleuronectes platessa*) and its hybrid with the flounder (*Platichthys flesus*). *Heredity* **29**: 11–24.

Purdom, C. E. (1976). Genetic techniques in flatfish culture. *J. Fish. Res. Bd. Can.* **33**: 1088–1093.

Rappoport, U. & Sarig, S. (1975). The results of tests in intensive growth of fish at the Genosar (Israel) station ponds in 1974. *Bamidgeh* **27**: 75–82.

Rappoport, U., Sarig, S. & Marek, M. (1976). Results of tests of various aeration systems on the oxygen regime in the Genosar experimental ponds and growth of fish there in 1975. *Bamidgeh* **28**: 35–49.

Refstie, T., Vassvik, V. & Gjedrem, T. (1977). Introduction of polyploidy in salmonids by cytochalsin B. *Aquaculture* **10**: 65–74.

Reich, K. (1975). Multispecies fish culture (polyculture) in Israel. *Bamidgeh* **27**: 85–99.

Sarig, S. & Marek, M. (1974). Results of intensive and semi-intensive fish breeding techniques in Israel in 1971–1973. *Bamidgeh* **26**: 28–50.

Schroeder, G. L. (1975). Night time material balance for oxygen in fishponds receiving organic waste. *Bamidgeh* **27**: 65–74.

Shehadeh, Z. H., Madden, W. D. & Dohl, T. P. (1973). The effect of exogenous hormone treatment on spermiation and vitellogenesis in the grey mullet, *Mugil cephalus* L. *J. Fish Biol.* **5**: 479–488.

Simpson, T. H. (1975/76). Endocrine aspects of salmonid culture. *Proc. R. Soc. Edinb.* (B) **75**: 241–252.

Smith, R. J. F. (1976). Seasonal loss of alarm substance cells in North American cyprinoid fishes and its relation to abrasive spawning behavior. *Can. J. Zool.* **54**: 1172–1188.

Smith, R. R. (1971). A method for measuring digestibility and metabolizable energy of fish feeds. *Progve Fish Cult.* **33**: 132–134.

Solomon, D. J. (1977). A review of chemical communication in freshwater fish. *J. Fish Biol.* **11**: 363–377.

Solomon, D. J. & Brafield, A. E. (1972). The energetics of feeding metabolism and growth of perch (*Perca fluviatilis* L.) *J. Anim. Ecol.* **41**: 699–718.

Sundararaj, B. I. & Goswami, S. V. (1966). Effects of mammalian hypophysial hormones, placental gonadotropins, gonadal hormones and adrenal corticosteroids on ovulation and spawning in hypophysectomized catfish, *Heteropneustes fossilis* (Bloch). *J. exp. Zool.* **161**: 287–296.

Swingle, H. A. (1967). The future of pond fish culture. *FAO Fish Rep.* **44** (1): 7–10.

Tapiador, D. D., Henderson, H. F., Delmondo, M. N. & Tsusui, H. (1977). Freshwater fisheries and aquaculture in China. *FAO Fish. techn. pap.* No. **168**: 1–84.

Tiews, K., Gropp, J. & Koops, H. (1976). On the development of optimal rainbow trout pellet feeds. *Arch. Fischereiwiss.* **27**: 1–29.

Van Dyke, J. M. & Sutton, D. L. (1977). Digestion of duckweed (*Lemna* spp) by the grass carp (*Ctenopharyngodon idella*). *J. Fish Biol.* **11**: 273–278.

Warren, C. E. & Davis, G. E. (1967). Laboratory studies on the feeding, bioenergetics and growth of fish. In *The biological basis of freshwater fish production*: 175–214. Gerkin, S. D. (ed.). Oxford: Blackwell.

Whitworth, W. R. (1968). Effects of diurnal fluctuation of dissolved oxygen on the growth of brook trout. *J. Fish. Res. Bd Can.* **25**: 579–584.

Winberg, G. G. (1956). *Rate of metabolism and food requirements of fishes.* Belorussian State University, Minsk. (Translated from Russian by Fish. Res. Bd Can. Trans. Ser. No. 194, 1960).

Yamazaki, F. (1976). Application of hormones in fish culture. *J. Fish. Res. Bd Can.* **33**: 948–958.

Yashouv, A. (1956). Problems in carp nutrition. *Bamidgeh* **8**: 79–89.

Yashouv, A. (1957). The fish culture research station—Dor. *Bamidgeh* **9**: 32–43.

Yashouv, A. & Halevy, A. (1972). Experimental studies of polyculture in 1971. *Bamidgeh* **24**: 31–39.

Yone, Y., Sakomoto, S. & Furuichi, M. (1974). Studies on nutrition of Red Sea bream—IX. The basal diet for nutrition studies. *Rep. Fish. Res. Lab. Kyushu Univ.* **2**: 13–24.

Yu, M.-L. & Perlmutter, A. (1970). Growth inhibiting factors in the zebrafish, *Brachydanio rerio*, and the blue gourami, *Trichogaster trichopterus*. *Growth* **34**: 153–175.

Zeitoun, I. H., Ullrey, D. E. & Magee, W. T. (1976). Quantifying nutrient requirements of fish. *J. Fish. Res. Bd Can.* **33**: 167–172.

Author Index

From, J., 13, 27, 36, 37, 50, *60*, 66, 68, 69, 74, 75, 79, 81, *87*
Fromm, P. O., 14, *23*, 40, *56*, *59*
Frost, W. E., 115, *130*, 139, 144, 152, 153, *156*, 165, *176*
Fry, F. E. J., 6, *22*, 29, 42, 43, *56*, 403, 405, *411*
Fryer, G., 223, 224, 225, 226, 233, 234, 236, *238*, 269, 272, 284, 289, *299*
Fryer, J. N., 96, *99*
Fuji, A. R., 386, 387, *413*
Fuller, J. D., 108, 109, 117, 124, *130*, *131*
Furuichi, M., 399, *415*

G

Gadgil, M., 163, *175*, 285, *299*, 311, 313, *325*
Gadgill, M. D., 313, *325*
Garcia, L. E., 96, *99*
Garrod, D. J., 366, *381*
Gauld, J. A., 199, *202*
Gaut, V. C., 230, 236, *240*, 284, *302*
Geisler, R., 245, *259*
Geistdorfer, P., 345, *356*
George, R. Y., 344, *356*
Gerberich, J. B., 295, *299*
Gerking, S. D., 30, 32, 40, 52, *57*, 139, 152, *158*, 186, 194, *202*, 394, 396, *411*
Ghittino, P., 92, *99*
Gibson, J. R., 150, *156*
Gibson, M. B., 74, *86*
Gibson, R. N., 5, *22*, 272, 273, 282, 284, 286, *299*
Giddings, M. R., 93, *97*
Giesel, J. T., 375, *381*
Gilchrist, J. D. F., 342, 344, *356*
Gist, D. H., 93, *102*
Gjedrem, T., 209, *215*, 388, 403, *411*, *414*
Gjosaeter, J., 329, *356*
Glass, N. R., 43, *54*
Glenn, C. L., 139, *156*
Glut, C. F., 250, *259*
Godoy, M. P. de, 233, *238*
Goldman, B., 235, *238*, 272, *299*
Goldstein, L., 40, *56*
Golovinsakaya, K. A., 211, *216*

Gorbman, A., 91, *99*, 398, *411*
Gordon, J. D. M., 336, 338, 340, *356*, *358*
Gordon, M., 211, *216*
Goswami, S. V., 123, *131*, 399, 400, *414*
Gotting, K.-J., 12, *23*
Gould, S. J., 277, 288, *299*
Gourley, R. S., 7, 10, *27*, 311, 312, 313, *326*
Graham, M., 19, *23*
Gras, J., 93, *101*
Grassle, J. F., 329, *359*
Graumann, G. B., 195, 200, *202*
Gray, I. E., 80, *86*
Gray, J., 17, *23*
Grayton, B. D., 48, *57*
Grebe, J. J., 4, *23*
Green, J., 277, *299*
Greenwood, P. H., 223, 233, *238*, 267, *299*
Griffiths, W. E., 32, 33, *57*
Grigoryev, G. V., 345, *356*
Grimaldi, E., 194, *202*
Grimes, P., 4, *26*
Grimm, A. S., 5, *28*
Griswold, B. L., 193, *202*
Gropp, J., 386, 387, 388, *412*, *414*
Gross, W. L., 14, *23*
Groves, T. D. D., 48, *57*
Gudger, E. W., 295, *299*
Guerin-Ancey, O., 40, 41, *57*
Gulland, J. A., 19, *23*, 361, 378, 380, *381*
Gwahaba, J. S., 225, *238*

H

Haas, R., 244, 245, 251, 252, 253, 254, *259*
Hadley, N. F., 12, *27*
Haedrich, R. L., 150, *156*, 333, 334, 336, 340, 342, 343, 344, 345, *356*
Hafter, E., 187, *204*
Halevy, A., 389, 390, 393, 406, *415*
Hall, J. D., 32, *55*
Halliday, R. G., 329, *356*
Halver, J. E., 46, *55*, *57*, 91, *100*, 384, 387, 388, *411*
Hamada A., 396, *411*

Ihne, E., 1, *24*
Iles, T. D., 10, *24*, 148, 149, *156*, 193, 195, *203*, 223, 224, 225, 226, 234, *238*, 269, 284, 289, *299*
Imms, A. D., 274, *300*
Ince, B. W., 91/92, 94, *99*, *102*
Ingleton, P. M., 91, 97, *97*, *99*
Inslee, T., 211, *215*, 401, *410*
Irie, T., 6, *24*
Ishabashi, N., 67, *86*
Ishida, R., 111, *130*
Ishiwata, N., 37, *57*
Ivlev, V. S., 29, 31, 32, *57*, *58*
Iwamoto, T., 327, 330, 333, 335, 340, *356*
Iwata, K., 40, *57*

J

Jackson, P. B., 223, 224, 228, *238*
Jacobs, K., 264, 291, 295, *300*
Jalabert, B., 8, *24*, 211, *216*, 400, *412*
Jansons, R. A., 92, *101*
Jena, S., 391, 392, 406, 407, *410*
Jenkins, T. M., 45, *56*
Jennings, J. B., 13, *21*, 32, *57*
Jezierska, B., 48, *58*
Job, S. N., 74, *86*, 403, *412*
Johannes, R. E., 231, 233, *238*, 287, 291, *300*
Johansson-Sjobeck, M. L., 91, 93, *98*, *100*
Johnson, C. L., 91, *100*
Johnson, L., 200, *203*
John, T. M., 5, *24*, 91, 96, *100*, *101*
Johnston, C., 10, 12, 13, *24*, 64, 65, 66, 87, 277, *300*
Jones, A., 137, *156*
Jones, D. D., 19, *24*
Jones, D. W., 90, *98*
Jones, J. W., 90, *97*, 136, *159*, 320, 321, *325*
Jones, R., 10, 12, 13, *24*, 64, 65, 67, *87*, 277, *300*
Jones, S., 232, *239*
Joseph, M. M., 95, 96, *101*
Jubb, R. A., 245, *260*
June, F. C., 152, 153, *156*

K

Kajishima, T., 211, *217*
Kallman, K. D., 211, *216*
Kammacher, P., 211, *216*
Kamito, A., 281, *300*
Kaimler, E., 43, 48, *58*
Kändler, R., 194, *203*
Kaplan, R. S., 7, 10, *27*, 311, 312, 313, *326*
Kariya, T., 396, *411*
Karzinkin, G. S., 32, *58*
Kasahara, S., 208, *216*
Katz, Y., 92, *99*
Kaufman, G. A., 281, 289, *300*
Kavanav, J. Lee, 64, *87*
Kawamoto, N. Y., 402, 403, *412*
Kayes, T., 90, *99*
Kelso, D. O., 229, *240*
Kelso, J. R. M., 37, *58*
Kenmuir, D. H. S., 12, *24*
Kennedy, W. A., 182, *203*
Kerenyi, T., 186, 187/190, *202*
Kerkhoven, P. C., 150, *156*
Kerr, S. R., 52, *58*, 266, *300*
Kesteven, G. L., 116, *130*
Kevern, N. R., 32, *58*, 385, *412*
Kharkar, D. P., 329, *359*
Kimpe, P. de, 236, *239*
Kimura, M., 309, *325*
Kincaid, H. L., 209, *216*
King, P. E., 13, *26*, 140, *158*
Kinne, O. I., 40, *58*, 74, *87*, 256, *260*
Kipling, C., 139, 152, 153, *156*, 165, 166, *176*
Kirpichnikov, V. S., 209, *216*
Kirschfeld, K., 267, *300*
Kitamikado, M., 388, *412*
Kitchell, J. K., 33, *61*
Kittleman, L. R., 6, *25*
Kleerekoper, H., 40, *58*
Kleiber, M., 29, *58*
Kluge, K., 249, *260*
Kneib, R. T., 274, 277, *300*
Knight, J., 126, *132*
Knoeshe, R., 403, *412*
Knöppel, H.-A., 270, *300*
Koch, H., 331
Kohn, A. J., 274, *300*
Kohn, R. R., 179, 201, *203*

Subject Index

A

Abiotic factors, 235
Absolute fecundity, 162, 166
Adaptiveness, 263–297, 364, 375–376
Adenohypophysis, 125, 126
Adrenal gland   *see* Interrenal gland
Adrenaline, 93, 94
Adrenosterone, 92
Aestivation, 245
Age, in relation to,
  egg quality, 200
  egg size, 166, 168, 195, 200
  fecundity, 166, 168, 200
  reproductive capacity, 183
  reproductive cost, 195–199
  reproductive effort, 146, 147, 148,
    170
  river return differences, 320–323
  sexual maturity, 282, 315
  time of spawning, 169
Age determination, 5, 6, 179, 221–222,
  329–333
Ageing   *see* Age determination
Aging   *see* Senescence
Amino-acids, 152, 387, 388, 399
Ammonia, 40, 402–403
Anabolism, 1, 3, 4, 5, 6, 7, 8, 9, 12, 13,
  29
  anabolic achievement, 17
  anabolic cyclicity, 4, 5, 16, 18
  anabolic expenditure, 279, 280–281,
    287
  anabolic processes, 69
  anabolic scope, estimation of, 38
  gonad, 279
  secondary sexual characters, 11, 285
Anaerobic "burst" swimming, 274
Anatomical changes, 182–192
Anchovy, Pacific biomass, 17
"Annual" killifishes, 243–261
Annual rings, 329, 330, 332
Assimilated food, 66, 67
  mathematical formula for, 74–75
Assimilation efficiency, 384–385
Atresia, 108–109, 117, 123, 150, 151,
  152. 183, 186, 187

B

Bet-hedging, 162, 163, 164, 170, 174
Biomass, 17, 18, 19
Biorhythmicity, 5
Biosynthesis, 3, 9, 11
  biosynthetic activity, 6
Biotic pressures, 220, 221, 233, 236
Bottom feeding teleosts, 271–272
Breeding period   *see also* Spawning
  duration of, 232, 289, 294
Brood care   *see also* Brooding and
  Parental care, 294
Broods   *see also* Size
  number of, 280–281, 282, 293
Brooding   *see also* Parental care
  cessation, 228
  mouth, 224–225, 226, 227
  period of, 293, 294

C

Cannibalism, 154
Carbohydrates, 388
"Caring period", 226
Carp   *see also* Systematic Index
  diet, 387, 396
  hormone effect on growth, 398
  production and yields, 389–393
Catabolism, 3, 6, 7, 8, 29, 285
  catabolic changes, 5
  catabolic processes, 69, 73
  fasting, 66, 75, 79-80
  feeding, 66, 75
  reproductive behaviour, 11
Cholesterol, 94
Circadian cycles, 12
  growth cycle, 5
Circadian rhythms, 5, 6, 9, 125, 127
Circalunar cycles   *see* Lunar cycles
Circannual cycles, 5, 112, 115
Circannual rhythm, 9
Circatidal rhythm, 5
Climate, 2
Cod   *see also* Systematic Index
  Arctic, biomass, 17
  food conversion, 68

Systematic Index

Page numbers in *italics* refer to illustrations